Advances in Abstract Intelligence and Soft Computing

Yingxu Wang
University of Calgary, Canada

Information Science
REFERENCE

Managing Director:	Lindsay Johnston
Editorial Director:	Joel Gamon
Book Production Manager:	Jennifer Yoder
Publishing Systems Analyst:	Adrienne Freeland
Assistant Acquisitions Editor:	Kayla Wolfe
Typesetter:	Henry Ulrich
Cover Design:	Nick Newcomer

Published in the United States of America by
Information Science Reference (an imprint of IGI Global)
701 E. Chocolate Avenue
Hershey PA 17033
Tel: 717-533-8845
Fax: 717-533-8661
E-mail: cust@igi-global.com
Web site: http://www.igi-global.com

Library of Congress Cataloging-in-Publication Data

Advances in abstract intelligence and soft computing / Yingxu Wang, editor.

   pages cm

 Includes bibliographical references and index.

 Summary: "This book brings together the latest research in computer science, theoretical software engineering, cognitive science & informatics and highlights their influence on the processes of natural and machine intelligence"-- Provided by publisher.

 ISBN 978-1-4666-2651-5 (hardcover) -- ISBN 978-1-4666-2682-9 (ebook) -- ISBN 978-1-4666-2713-0 (print & perpetual access) 1. Soft computing. 2. Artificial intelligence. 3. Software engineering. I. Wang, Yingxu, editor of compilation.

 QA76.9.S63A386 2012

 005.1--dc23

                    2012029129

British Cataloguing in Publication Data
A Cataloguing in Publication record for this book is available from the British Library.

The views expressed in this book are those of the authors, but not necessarily of the publisher.

Table of Contents

Section 1
Computational Intelligence

Yousheng Tian, University of Calgary, Canada
Yingxu Wang, University of Calgary, Canada
Marina L. Gavrilova, University of Calgary, Canada
Guenther Ruhe, University of Calgary, Canada

Yuanyuan Zuo, Tsinghua University, China
Bo Zhang, Tsinghua University, China

Yuhong Chi, Tsinghua University, China
Fuchun Sun, Tsinghua University, China
Langfan Jiang, PLA, China
Chunyang Yu, Northeastern University, China
Chunli Chen, China University of Geosciences, China

Section 2
Cognitive Computing

Section 3
Software Science

Section 4
Applications of Computational Intelligence and
Cognitive Computing

Detailed Table of Contents

Section 1
Computational Intelligence

Chapter 1

Yousheng Tian, University of Calgary, Canada
Yingxu Wang, University of Calgary, Canada
Marina L. Gavrilova, University of Calgary, Canada
Guenther Ruhe, University of Calgary, Canada

It is recognized that the generic form of machine learning is a knowledge acquisition and manipulation process mimicking the brain. Therefore, knowledge representation as a dynamic concept network is centric in the design and implementation of the intelligent knowledge base of a Cognitive Learning Engine (CLE). This chapter presents a Formal Knowledge Representation System (FKRS) for autonomous concept formation and manipulation based on concept algebra. The Object-Attribute-Relation (OAR) model for knowledge representation is adopted in the design of FKRS. The conceptual model, architectural model, and behavioral models of the FKRS system is formally designed and specified in Real-Time Process Algebra (RTPA). The FKRS system is implemented in Java as a core component towards the development of the CLE and other knowledge-based systems in cognitive computing and computational intelligence.

Chapter 2

Yuanyuan Zuo, Tsinghua University, China
Bo Zhang, Tsinghua University, China

The sparse representation based classification algorithm has been used to solve the problem of human face recognition, but the image database is restricted to human frontal faces with only slight illumination and expression changes. This chapter applies the sparse representation based algorithm to the problem of generic image classification, with a certain degree of intra-class variations and background clutter. Experiments are conducted with the sparse representation based algorithm and Support Vector Machine

(SVM) classifiers on 25 object categories selected from the Caltech101 dataset. Experimental results show that without the time-consuming parameter optimization, the sparse representation based algorithm achieves comparable performance with SVM. The experiments also demonstrate that the algorithm is robust to a certain degree of background clutter and intra-class variations with the bag-of-visual-words representations. The sparse representation based algorithm can also be applied to generic image classification task when the appropriate image feature is used.

Chapter 3

    Yuhong Chi, Tsinghua University, China
    Fuchun Sun, Tsinghua University, China
    Langfan Jiang, PLA, China
    Chunyang Yu, Northeastern University, China
    Chunli Chen, China University of Geosciences, China

To control particles to fly inside the limited search space and deal with the problems of slow search speed and premature convergence of particle swarm optimization algorithm, this chapter applies the theory of topology, and proposed a quotient space-based boundary condition named QsaBC by using the properties of quotient space and homeomorphism. In QsaBC, Search space-zoomed factor and Attractor are introduced according to the dynamic behavior and stability of particles, which not only reduce the subjective interference and enforce the capability of global search, but also enhance the power of local search and escaping from an inferior local optimum. Four CEC'2008 benchmark functions are selected to evaluate the performance of QsaBC. Comparative experiments show that QsaBC can achieve the satisfactory optimization solution with fast convergence speed. Furthermore, QsaBC is more effective with errant particles, and has easier calculation and better robustness than other methods.

Chapter 4

    Ahmed Kharrat, University of Sfax, Tunisia
    Karim Gasmi, University of Sfax, Tunisia
    Mohamed Ben Messaoud, University of Sfax, Tunisia
    Nacéra Benamrane, USTO Oran, Algeria
    Mohamed Abid, University of Sfax, Tunisia

A new approach for automated diagnosis and classification of Magnetic Resonance (MR) human brain images is proposed. The proposed method uses Wavelets Transform (WT) as input module to Genetic Algorithm (GA) and Support Vector Machine (SVM). It segregates MR brain images into normal and abnormal. This contribution employs genetic algorithm for feature selection which requires much lighter computational burden in comparison with Sequential Floating Backward Selection (SFBS) and Sequential Floating Forward Selection (SFFS) methods. A percentage reduction rate of 88.63% is achieved. An excellent classification rate of 100% could be achieved using the support vector machine. The observed results are significantly better than the results reported in a previous research work employing Wavelet Transform and Support Vector Machine.

Chapter 5

Ling Zou, Changzhou University, China & State Key Laboratory of Robotics and System (HIT), China
Xinguang Wang, Changzhou University, China
Guodong Shi, Changzhou University, China
Zhenghua Ma, Changzhou University, China

Accurate classification of EEG left and right hand motor imagery is an important issue in brain-computer interface. Firstly, discrete wavelet transform method was used to decompose the average power of C3 electrode and C4 electrode in left-right hands imagery movement during some periods of time. The reconstructed signal of approximation coefficient A6 on the sixth level was selected to build up a feature signal. Secondly, the performances by Fisher Linear Discriminant Analysis with two different threshold calculation ways and Support Vector Machine methods were compared. The final classification results showed that false classification rate by Support Vector Machine was lower and gained an ideal classification results.

Chapter 6

Du Zhang, California State University, USA
Meiliu Lu, California State University, USA

One of the long-term research goals in machine learning is how to build never-ending learners. The state-of-the-practice in the field of machine learning thus far is still dominated by the one-time learner paradigm: some learning algorithm is utilized on data sets to produce certain model or target function, and then the learner is put away and the model or function is put to work. Such a learn-once-apply-next (or LOAN) approach may not be adequate in dealing with many real world problems and is in sharp contrast with the human's lifelong learning process. On the other hand, learning can often be brought on through overcoming some inconsistent circumstances. This paper proposes a framework for perpetual learning agents that are capable of continuously refining or augmenting their knowledge through overcoming inconsistencies encountered during their problem-solving episodes. The never-ending nature of a perpetual learning agent is embodied in the framework as the agent's continuous inconsistency-induced belief revision process. The framework hinges on the agents recognizing inconsistency in data, information, knowledge, or meta-knowledge, identifying the cause of inconsistency, revising or augmenting beliefs to explain, resolve, or accommodate inconsistency. The authors believe that inconsistency can serve as one of the important learning stimuli toward building perpetual learning agents that incrementally improve their performance over time.

Chapter 7

Tianyong Hao, Shanghai University of Electric Power, China
Feifei Xu, Shanghai University of Electric Power, China
Jingsheng Lei, Shanghai University of Electric Power, China
Liu Wenyin, City University of Hong Kong, China
Qing Li, City University of Hong Kong, China

A strategy of automatic answer retrieval for repeated or similar questions in user-interactive systems by employing semantic question patterns is proposed in this paper. The used semantic question pattern is a generalized representation of a group of questions with both similar structure and relevant semantics.

Specifically, it consists of semantic annotations (or constraints) for the variable components in the pattern and hence enhances the semantic representation and greatly reduces the ambiguity of a question instance when asked by a user using such pattern. The proposed method consists of four major steps: structure processing, similar pattern matching and filtering, automatic pattern generation, question similarity evaluation and answer retrieval. Preliminary experiments in a real question answering system show a precision of more than 90% of the method.

Section 2
Cognitive Computing

Human thought, perception, reasoning, and problem solving are highly dependent on causal inferences. This paper presents a set of cognitive models for causation analyses and causal inferences. The taxonomy and mathematical models of causations are created. The framework and properties of causal inferences are elaborated. Methodologies for uncertain causal inferences are discussed. The theoretical foundation of humor and jokes as false causality is revealed. The formalization of causal inference methodologies enables machines to mimic complex human reasoning mechanisms in cognitive informatics, cognitive computing, and computational intelligence.

Inconsistency is commonplace in the real world in long-term memory and knowledge based systems. Managing inconsistency is considered a hallmark of the plasticity of human intelligence. Belief revision is an important mental process that underpins human intelligence. To facilitate belief revision, it is necessary to know the localities and contexts of inconsistency and how different types of inconsistency are clustered. In this paper, the author provides a formal definition of locality of inconsistency and describes how to identify clusters of inconsistent circumstances in a knowledge base. The results pave the way for a disciplined approach to manage knowledge inconsistency.

Association mining aims to find valid correlations among data attributes, and has been widely applied to many areas of data analysis. This paper presents a semantic network-based association analysis model including three spreading activation methods. It applies this model to assess the quality of a dataset, and generate semantically valid new hypotheses for adaptive study design especially useful in medical studies. The approach is evaluated on a real public health dataset, the Heartfelt study, and the experiment shows promising results.

This paper explores applying qualitative reasoning to a driver's mental state in real driving situations so as to develop a working load for intelligent transportation systems. The authors identify the cognitive state that determines whether a driver will be ready to operate a device in car navigation. In order to identify the driver's cognitive state, the authors will measure eye movements during car-driving situations. Data can be acquired for the various actions of a car driver, in particular braking, acceleration, and steering angles from the experiment car. The authors constructed a driver cognitive mental load using the framework of qualitative reasoning. The response of the model was checked by qualitative simulation. The authors also verified the model using real data collected by driving an actual car. The results indicated that the model could represent the change in the cognitive mental load based on measurable data. This means that the framework of this paper will be useful for designing user interfaces for next-generation systems that actively employ user situations.

Chapter 12

Monitoring industrial machine health in real-time is not only in high demand, it is also complicated and difficult. Possible reasons for this include: (a) access to the machines on site is sometimes impracticable, and (b) the environment in which they operate is usually not human-friendly due to pollution, noise, hazardous wastes, etc. Despite theoretically sound findings on developing intelligent solutions for machine condition-based monitoring, few commercial tools exist in the market that can be readily used. This paper examines the development of an intelligent fault recognition and monitoring system (Melvin I), which detects and diagnoses rotating machine conditions according to changes in fault frequency indicators. The signals and data are remotely collected from designated sections of machines via data acquisition cards. They are processed by a signal processor to extract characteristic vibration signals of ten key performance indicators (KPIs). A 3-layer neural network is designed to recognize and classify faults based on a pre-determined set of KPIs. The system implemented in the laboratory and applied in the field can also incorporate new experiences into the knowledge base without overwriting previous training. Results show that Melvin I is a smart tool for both system vibration analysts and industrial machine operators.

Section 3
Software Science

Functional complexity is one of the most fundamental properties of software because almost all other software attributes and properties such as functional size, development effort, costs, quality, and project duration are highly dependent on it. The functional complexity of software is a macro-scope problem concerning the semantic properties of software and human cognitive complexity towards a given software system; while the computational complexity is a micro-scope problem concerning algorithmic analyses towards machine throughput and time/space efficiency. This paper presents an empirical study on the functional complexity of software known as cognitive complexity based on large-scale samples using a Software Cognitive Complexity Analysis Tool (SCCAT). Empirical data are obtained with SCCAT on 7,531 programs and five formally specified software systems. The theoretical foundation of software functional complexity is introduced and the metric of software cognitive complexity is formally modeled. The functional complexities of a large-scale software system and the air traffic control systems (ATCS) are rigorously analyzed. A novel approach to represent software functional complexities and their distributions in software systems is developed. The nature of functional complexity of software in software engineering is rigorously explained. The relationship between the symbolic and functional complexities of software is quantitatively analyzed.

Yingxu Wang, University of Calgary, Canada

Cyprian F. Ngolah, Sentinel Trending & Diagnostics Ltd., Canada

Xinming Tan, Wuhan University of Technology, China

Yousheng Tian, University of Calgary, Canada

Phillip C.-Y. Sheu, University of California, USA

Files are a typical abstract data type for data objects and software modeling, which provides a standard encapsulation and access interface for manipulating large-volume information and persistent data. File management systems are an indispensable component of operating systems and real-time systems for file manipulations. This paper develops a comprehensive design pattern of files and a File Management System (FMS). A rigorous denotational mathematics, Real-Time Process Algebra (RTPA), is adopted, which allows both architectural and behavioral models of files and FMS to be rigorously designed and implemented in a top-down approach. The conceptual model, architectural model, and the static/dynamic behavioral models of files and FMS are systematically presented. This work has been applied in the design and modeling of a real time operating system (RTOS+).

Yingxu Wang, University of Calgary, Canada

Cyprian F. Ngolah, Sentinel Trending & Diagnostics Ltd., Calgary, Canada

Xinming Tan, Wuhan University of Technology, China

Phillip C.-Y. Sheu, University of California, Irvine, USA

Abstract Data Types (ADTs) are a set of highly generic and rigorously modeled data structures in type theory. Lists as a finite sequence of elements are one of the most fundamental and widely used ADTs in system modeling, which provide a standard encapsulation and access interface for manipulating large-volume information and persistent data. This paper develops a comprehensive design pattern of formal lists using a doubly-linked-circular (DLC) list architecture. A rigorous denotational mathematics, Real-Time Process Algebra (RTPA), is adopted, which allows both architectural and behavioral models of lists to be rigorously designed and implemented in a top-down approach. The architectural models of DLC-Lists are created using RTPA architectural modeling methodologies known as the Unified Data

Models (UDMs). The behavioral models of DLC-Lists are specified and refined by a set of Unified Process Models (UPMs) in three categories namely the management operations, traversal operations, and node I/O operations. This work has been applied in a number of real-time and nonreal-time system designs such as a real-time operating system (RTOS+), a file management system (FMS), and the ADT library for an RTPA-based automatic code generation tool.

Chapter 16

Juan L. G. Guirao, Polytechnic University of Cartagena, Spain
Fernando L. Pelayo, University of Castilla - La Mancha, Spain

This paper provides an overview over the relationship between Petri Nets and Discrete Event Systems as they have been proved as key factors in the cognitive processes of perception and memorization. In this sense, different aspects of encoding Petri Nets as Discrete Dynamical Systems that try to advance not only in the problem of reachability but also in the one of describing the periodicity of markings and their similarity, are revised. It is also provided a metric for the case of Non-bounded Petri Nets.

Chapter 17

Yingxu Wang, University of Calgary, Canada
Jason Huang, University of Calgary, Canada
Jingsheng Lei, Shanghai University of Electrical Power, China

Arrays are one of the most fundamental and widely applied data structures, which are useful for modeling both logical designs and physical implementations of multi-dimensional data objects sharing the same type of homogeneous elements. However, there is a lack of a formal model of the universal array based on it any array instance can be derived. This paper studies the fundamental properties of *Universal Array* (UA) and presents a comprehensive design pattern. A denotational mathematics, *Real-Time Process Algebra* (RTPA), allows both architectural and behavioral models of UA to be rigorously designed and refined in a top-down approach. The conceptual model of UA is rigorously described by tuple- and matrix-based mathematical models. The architectural models of UA are created using RTPA architectural modeling methodologies known as the Unified Data Models (UDMs). The physical model of UA is implemented using linear list that is indexed by an offset pointer of elements. The behavioral models of UA are specified and refined by a set of Unified Process Models (UPMs). As a case study, the formal UA models are implemented in Java. This work has been applied in a number of real-time and nonreal-time systems such as compilers, a file management system, the real-time operating system (RTOS+), and the ADT library for an RTPA-based automatic code generation tool.

Chapter 18

Yingxu Wang, University of Calgary, Canada
Xinming Tan, Wuhan University of Technology, China

Trees are one of the most fundamental and widely used non-linear hierarchical structures of linked nodes. A binary tree (B-Tree) is a typical balanced tree where the fan-out of each node is at most two known as the left and right children. This paper develops a comprehensive design pattern of formal trees using the B-Tree architecture. A rigorous denotational mathematics, Real-Time Process Algebra (RTPA), is adopted, which allows both architectural and behavioral models of B-Trees to be rigorously designed and implemented in a top-down approach. The architectural models of B-Trees are created using RTPA architectural modeling methodologies known as the Unified Data Models (UDMs). The physical model of B-Trees is implemented using the left and right child nodes dynamically created in memory. The behavioral models of B-Trees are specified and refined by a set of Unified Process Models (UPMs) in three categories namely the management operations, traversal operations, and node I/O operations. This work has been applied in a number of real-time and nonreal-time system designs such as a real-time operating system (RTOS+), a general system organization model, and the ADT library for an RTPA-based automatic code generator.

Section 4
Applications of Computational Intelligence and Cognitive Computing

Chapter 19

Yuji Wang, Tsinghua University, China

Fuchun Sun, Tsinghua University, China

Huaping Liu, Tsinghua University, China

The four-channel architecture in teleoperation with force feedback has been studied in various existing literature. However, most of them focused on Lawrence architecture and did not research other cases. This paper proposes two other four-channel architectures: passive four-channel architecture and passive four-channel architecture with operator force. Furthermore, two types of multilateral shared control architecture based on passive four-channel architecture, which exists in space teleoperation, are put forward. One is dual-master multilateral shared control architecture, and the other is dual-slave multilateral shared control architecture. Simulations show that these four architectures can maintain stability in the presence of large time delay.

Chapter 20

Rosanne Vetro, University of Massachusetts Boston, USA

Dan A. Simovici, University of Massachusetts Boston, USA

Wei Ding, University of Massachusetts Boston, USA

This paper introduces entropy quad-trees, which are structures derived from quad-trees by allowing nodes to split only when those correspond to sufficiently complex sub-domains of a data domain. Complexity is evaluated using an information-theoretic measure based on the analysis of the entropy associated to sets of objects designated by nodes. An alternative measure related to the concept of box-counting dimension is also explored. Experimental results demonstrate the efficiency of entropy quad-trees to mine complex regions. As an application, the proposed technique is used in the initial stage of a crater detection algorithm using digital images taken from the surface of Mars. Additional experimental results are provided that demonstrate the crater detection performance and analyze the effectiveness of entropy quad-trees for high-complexity regions detection in the pixel space with significant presence of noise. This work focuses on 2-dimensional image domains, but can be generalized to higher dimensional data.

Chapter 21

Yusuke Manabe, Chiba Institute of Technology, Japan

Kenji Sugawara, Chiba Institute of Technology, Japan

Realization of human-computer symbiosis is an important idea in the context of ubiquitous computing. Symbiotic Computing is a concept that bridges the gap between situations in Real Space (RS) and data in Digital Space (DS). The main purpose is to develop an intelligent software application as well as establish the next generation information platform to develop the symbiotic system. In this paper, the authors argue that it is necessary to build 'Mutual Cognition' between human and system. Mutual cognition consists of two functions: 'RS Cognition' and 'DS Cognition'. This paper examines RS Cognition, which consists of many software functions for perceiving various situations like events or humans' activities in RS. The authors develop two perceptual functions, sitting posture recognition and human's location estimation for a person, as RS perception tasks. In the resulting experiments, developed functions are quite competent to recognize a human's activities.

Chapter 22

Generic cabling is a key component for multiplex cable wiring. It is one of the basic foundations of intelligent buildings. Using operation flow in generic cabling, the index constraints affecting generic cabling have been evolved in this paper. A mathematical model is built based on the ant colony algorithm with multiple constraints, and improvements were made on the original basis to extend the ant colony algorithm from the regular simple ant colony and structure to a multi-ant colony and structure. The equilibrium settlement of multiplex wiring is realized according to the introduction of the multi-ant colony model. The ant cycle model is combined to extend the optimization target from the local wiring path to the entire wiring path, and to solve the drawbacks existing in the regular ant colony algorithm and other search algorithms that take the local wiring path as the optimization target. The introduced retrospective algorithm make the ants avoid the path marked "invalid" in the subsequent search process and improves the search performance and convergence speed of the ant colony algorithm.

Chapter 23

The paper discusses the quadratic neural unit (QNU) and highlights its attractiveness for industrial applications such as for plant modeling, control, and time series prediction. Linear systems are still often preferred in industrial control applications for their solvable and single solution nature and for the clarity to the most application engineers. Artificial neural networks are powerful cognitive nonlinear tools, but their nonlinear strength is naturally repaid with the local minima problem, overfitting, and high demands for application-correct neural architecture and optimization technique that often require skilled users. The QNU is the important midpoint between linear systems and highly nonlinear neural networks because the QNU is relatively very strong in nonlinear approximation; however, its optimization and performance have fast and convex-like nature, and its mathematical structure and the derivation of the learning rules is very comprehensible and efficient for implementation. These advantages of QNU are demonstrated by using real and theoretical examples.

The fundamental objective in value-based software engineering is to integrate consistent stakeholder value propositions into the full extent of software engineering principles and practices so as to increase the value for software assets. In such a value-based setting, artifacts in software development such as requirement specifications, use cases, test cases, or defects, are not treated as equally important during the development process. Instead, they will be differentiated according to how much they are contributing, directly or indirectly, to the stakeholder value propositions. The higher the contributions, the more important the artifacts become. In turn, development activities involving more important artifacts should be given higher priorities and greater considerations in the development process. In this paper, a value-based framework is proposed for carrying out software evolutionary testing with a focus on test data generation through genetic algorithms. The proposed framework incorporates general principles in value-based software testing and makes it possible to prioritize testing decisions that are rooted in the stakeholder value propositions. It allows for a cost-effective way to fulfill most valuable testing objectives first and a graceful degradation when planned testing process has to be shortened.

Chapter 25

Understanding how the regulation of gene networks is orchestrated is an important challenge for characterizing complex biological processes. The DNA sequences that comprise promoters do not provide much direct information about regulation. A substantial part of the regulation results from the interaction of transcription factors (TFs) with specific cis regulatory DNA sequences. These regulatory sequences are organized in a modular fashion, with each module (enhancer) containing one or more binding sites for a specific combination of TFs. In the present work, the authors have proposed to investigate the inter motif distance between the important motifs in the promoter sequences of citrate synthase of different mammals. The authors have used a new distance measure to compare the promoter sequences. Results reveal that there exists more similarity between organisms in the same chromosome.

Preface

Software Science is a discipline that studies the theoretical framework of software as instructive and behavioral information, which can be embodied and executed by generic computers in order to create expected system behaviors and machine intelligence. *Intelligence science* is a discipline that studies the mechanisms and theories of abstract intelligence and its paradigms such as natural, artificial, machinable, and computational intelligence. The convergence of software and intelligent sciences forms the transdisciplinary field of *computational intelligence*, which provides a coherent set of fundamental theories, contemporary denotational mathematics, and engineering applications.

This book entitled *Advances in Abstract Intelligence and Soft Computing* is the third volume in the IGI Series of Advances in Software Science and Computational Intelligence. The book encompasses 25 chapters of expert contributions selected from the International Journal of Software Science and Computational Intelligence during 2011. The book is organized in four sections on:

1. Computational intelligence;
2. Cognitive computing;
3. Software science;
4. Applications in computational intelligence and cognitive computing.

Section 1. Computational Intelligence

Intelligence science studies theories and models of the brain, and the relationship between the concrete physiological brain and the abstract soft mind. Intelligence science is a new frontier with the fertilization of brain science, biology, psychology, neuroscience, cognitive science, cognitive informatics, philosophy, information science, computer science, anthropology, and linguistics. A fundamental view developed in software and intelligence sciences is known as abstract intelligence, which provides a unified foundation for the studies of all forms and paradigms of intelligence such as natural, artificial, machinable, and computational intelligence. *Abstract intelligence* (αI) is an enquiry of both natural and artificial intelligence at the neural, cognitive, functional, and logical levels from the bottom up. In the narrow sense, αI is a human or a system ability that transforms information into behaviors. However, in the broad sense, αI is any human or system ability that autonomously transfers the forms of abstract information between *data, information, knowledge,* and *behaviors* in the brain or intelligent systems.

Computational intelligence (CoI) is an embodying form of abstract intelligence (αI) that implements intelligent mechanisms and behaviors by computational methodologies and software systems, such as expert systems, fuzzy systems, cognitive computers, cognitive robots, software agent systems, genetic/

evolutionary systems, and autonomous learning systems. The theoretical foundations of computational intelligence root in cognitive informatics, software science, and denotational mathematics.

This section on computational intelligence encompasses the following seven chapters.

Chapter 1, *A Formal Knowledge Representation System (FKRS) for the Intelligent Knowledge Base of a Cognitive Learning Engine*, by Yousheng Tian, Yingxu Wang, Marina Gavrilova, and Guenther Ruhe, recognizes that the generic form of machine learning is a knowledge acquisition and manipulation process mimicking the brain. Therefore, knowledge representation as a dynamic concept network is centric in the design and implementation of the intelligent knowledge base of a Cognitive Learning Engine (CLE). This chapter presents a Formal Knowledge Representation System (FKRS) for autonomous concept formation and manipulation based on concept algebra. The Object-Attribute-Relation (OAR) model for knowledge representation is adopted in the design of FKRS. The conceptual model, architectural model, and behavioral models of the FKRS system is formally designed and specified in Real-Time Process Algebra (RTPA). The FKRS system is implemented in Java as a core component towards the development of the CLE and other knowledge-based systems in cognitive computing and computational intelligence.

Chapter 2, *Sparse Based Image Classification with Bag-of-Visual-Words Representations*, by Yuanyuan Zuo and Bo Zhang, presents a sparse representation based classification algorithm for human face recognition. The image database is restricted to human frontal faces with only slight illumination and expression changes. In this chapter, we apply the sparse representation based algorithm to the problem of generic image classification, with a certain degree of intra-class variations and background clutter. Experiments have been done with the sparse representation based algorithm and Support Vector Machine (SVM) classifiers on 25 object categories selected from the Caltech101 dataset. Experimental results show that without the time-consuming parameter optimization, the sparse representation based algorithm achieves comparable performance with SVM. The experiments also demonstrate that the algorithm is robust to a certain degree of background clutter and intra-class variations with the bag-of-visual-words representations. We argue that the sparse representation based algorithm can also be applied to generic image classification task when appropriate image feature is used.

Chapter 3, *Quotient Space-Based Boundary Condition for a Particle Swarm Optimization Algorithm*, by Yuhong Chi, Fuchun Sun, Langfan Jiang, Chunyang Yu, and Chunli Chen, proposes a novel quotient space-based boundary condition named QsaBC by using the properties of quotient space and homeomorphism for controling particles to fly inside the limited search space and dealing with the problems of slow search speed and premature convergence of particle swarm optimization algorithm. In QsaBC, Search space-zoomed factor and Attractor are introduced according to analyzing the dynamic behavior and stability of particles, which not only reduce the subjective interference and enforce the capability of global search, but also enhance the power of local search and escaping from an inferior local optimum. Four CEC'2008 benchmark functions were selected to evaluate the performance of QsaBC. Comparative experiments show that QsaBC can get the satisfactory optimization solution with fast convergence speed. Furthermore, QsaBC is more effective to do with errant particles, easier calculation, and better robustness than other experienced methods.

Chapter 4, *Medical Image Classification Using an Optimal Feature Extraction Algorithm and a Supervised Classifier Technique*, by Ahmed Kharrat, Karim Gasmi, Mohamed B. Messaoud, Nacéra Benamrane, and Mohamed Abid, presents a new approach for automated diagnosis and classification of Magnetic Resonance (MR) human brain images. The proposed method uses Wavelets Transform (WT) as input module to Genetic Algorithm (GA) and Support Vector Machine (SVM). It segregates MR brain images into normal and abnormal. Our contribution employs genetic algorithm for feature selection which requires much lighter computational burden in comparison with Sequential Floating Backward Selection (SFBS) and Sequential Floating Forward Selection (SFFS) methods. A percentage reduction rate of 88.63% is achieved. An excellent classification rate of 100% could be achieved using the support vector machine. The authors observe their results are significantly better than the results reported in a previous research work employing Wavelet Transform and Support Vector Machine.

Chapter 5, *EEG Feature Extraction and Pattern Classification based on Motor Imagery in Brain-Computer Interface*, by Ling Zou, Xinguan Wang, Guodong Shi, and Zhenghua Ma, identifies that accurate classification of EEG in left and right hand motor imagery is an important issue in brain-computer interface. Firstly, discrete wavelet transform method was used to decompose the average power of C3 electrode and C4 electrode in left-right hands imagery movement during some periods of time. The reconstructed signal of approximation coefficient A6 on the sixth level was selected to build up a feature signal. Secondly, the performances by Fisher Linear Discriminant Analysis with two different threshold calculation ways and Support Vector Machine methods were compared. The final classification results showed that false classification rate by Support Vector Machine was lower and gained an ideal classification results.

Chapter 6, *Inconsistency-Induced Learning for Perpetual Learners*, by Du Zhang and Meiliu Lu, identifies that one of the long-term research goals in machine learning is how to build never-ending learners. The state-of-the-practice in the field of machine learning thus far is still dominated by the one-time learner paradigm: some learning algorithm is utilized on data sets to produce certain model or target function, and then the learner is put away and the model or function is put to work. Such a learn-once-apply-next (or LOAN) approach may not be adequate in dealing with many real world problems and is in sharp contrast with the human's lifelong learning process. On the other hand, learning can often be brought on through overcoming some inconsistent circumstances. In this chapter, the authors propose a framework for perpetual learning agents that are capable of continuously refining or augmenting their knowledge through overcoming inconsistencies encountered during their problem-solving episodes. The never-ending nature of a perpetual learning agent is embodied in the framework as the agent's continuous inconsistency-induced belief revision process. The framework hinges on the agents recognizing inconsistency in data, information, knowledge, or meta-knowledge, identifying the cause of inconsistency, revising or augmenting beliefs to explain, resolve, or accommodate inconsistency. The authors believe that inconsistency can serve as one of the important learning stimuli toward building perpetual learning agents that incrementally improve their performance over time.

Chapter 7, *Toward Automatic Answers in an Interactive Question-Answer System*, by Tianyong Hao, Feifei Xu, Jingsheng Lei, and Wenyin Liu, proposes a strategy of automatic answer retrieval for repeated or similar questions in user-interactive systems by employing semantic question patterns. The used semantic question pattern is a generalized representation of a group of questions with both similar structure and relevant semantics. Specifically, it consists of semantic annotations (or constraints) for the variable components in the pattern and hence enhances the semantic representation and greatly reduces the ambiguity of a question instance when asked by a user using such pattern. The proposed method consists of four major steps: structure processing, similar pattern matching and filtering, automatic pattern generation, question similarity evaluation and answer retrieval. Preliminary experiments in a real question answering system show a precision of more than 90% of our method.

Section 2. Cognitive Computing

Computing systems and technologies can be classified into the categories of *imperative, autonomic,* and *cognitive* computing from the bottom up. The imperative computers are a passive system based on stored-program controlled mechanisms for data processing. The autonomic computers are goal-driven and self-decision-driven machines that do not rely on instructive and procedural information. Cognitive computers are more intelligent computers beyond the imperative and autonomic computers, which embody major natural intelligence behaviors of the brain such as thinking, inference, and learning. The increasing demand for non von Neumann computers for knowledge and intelligence processing in the high-tech industry and everyday lives require novel cognitive computers for providing autonomous computing power for various cognitive systems mimicking the natural intelligence of the brain.

Cognitive Computing (CC) is a novel paradigm of intelligent computing methodologies and systems based on *Cognitive Informatics* (CI), which implements computational intelligence by autonomous inferences and perceptions mimicking the mechanisms of the brain. CC is emerged and developed based on the transdisciplinary research in cognitive informatics, abstract intelligence, and *Denotational Mathematics* (DM). The latest advances in CI, CC, and DM enable a systematic solution for the future generation of intelligent computers known as *Cognitive Computers* (CogCs) that think, perceive, learn, and reason. A CogC is an intelligent computer for knowledge processing as that of a conventional von Neumann computer for data processing. CogCs are designed to embody *machinable intelligence* such as computational inferences, causal analyses, knowledge manipulations, machine learning, and autonomous problem solving.

This section on cognitive computing encompasses the following five chapters.

Chapter 8, *On Cognitive Models of Causal Inferences and Causation Networks*, by Yingxu Wang, reveals that human thought, perception, reasoning, and problem solving are highly dependent on causal inferences. The chapter presents a set of cognitive models for causation analyses and causal inferences. The taxonomy and mathematical models of causations are created. The framework and properties of causal inferences are elaborated. Methodologies for uncertain causal inferences are discussed. The theoretical foundation of humor and jokes as false causality is revealed. The formalization of causal inference methodologies enables machines to mimic complex human reasoning mechanisms in cognitive informatics, cognitive computing, and computational intelligence.

Chapter 9, *On Localities of Knowledge Inconsistency*, by Du Zhang, identifies that inconsistency is commonplace in the real world, in our long-term memory, and in knowledge based systems. Managing inconsistency is considered a hallmark of the plasticity of human intelligence. An important mental process that underpins human intelligence is belief revision. To facilitate belief revision, a necessary condition is that we need to know the localities and contexts of inconsistency, and how different types of inconsistency are clustered. In this chapter, we provide a formal definition of locality of inconsistency and describe how to use it to identify clusters of inconsistent circumstances in a knowledge base. The results in the chapter will help pave the way for a disciplined approach to managing knowledge inconsistency.

Chapter 10, *Adaptive Study Design through Semantic Association Rule Analysis*, by Ping Chen, Wei Ding, and Walter Garcia, aims to find valid correlations among data attributes which has been widely applied to many areas of data analysis. In this chapter we present a semantic network based association analysis model including three spreading activation methods, and apply this model to assess the quality of a dataset, and generate semantically valid new hypotheses for adaptive study design that is especially useful in medical studies. The authors evaluate their approach on a real public health dataset, the Heartfelt study, and the experiment shows promising results.

Chapter 11, *Qualitative Reasoning Approach to a Driver's Cognitive Mental Load*, by Shinichiro Sega, Hirotoshi Iwasaki, Hironori Hiraishi, and Fumio Mizoguchi, applies qualitative reasoning to a driver's mental state in real driving situations so as to develop a working load for intelligent transportation systems. The authors identify the cognitive state that determines whether a driver will be ready to operate a device in car navigation. In order to identify the driver's cognitive state, the authors measure eye movements during car-driving situations. The authors can acquire data for the various actions of a car driver, in particular braking, acceleration, and steering angles from our experiment car. They constructed a driver cognitive mental load using the framework of qualitative reasoning. They checked the response of our model by qualitative simulation. The authors also verified the model using real data collected by driving an actual car. The results indicated that our model could represent the change in the cognitive mental load based on measurable data. This means that the framework of this chapter will be useful for designing user interfaces for next-generation systems that actively employ user situations.

Chapter 12, *Intelligent Fault Recognition and Diagnosis for Rotating Machines using Neural Networks*, by Cyprian F. Ngolah, Ed Morden, and Yingxu Wang, examine the development of an intelligent fault recognition and monitoring system (Melvin I), which detects and diagnoses rotating machine conditions according to changes in fault frequency indicators. The signals and data are remotely collected from designated sections of machines via data acquisition cards. They are processed by a signal processor to extract characteristic vibration signals of ten key performance indicators (KPIs). A 3-layer neural network is designed to recognize and classify faults based on a pre-determined set of KPIs. The system implemented in the laboratory and applied in the field can also incorporate new experiences into the knowledge base without overwriting previous training. Results show that Melvin I is a smart tool for both system vibration analysts and industrial machine operators.

Section 3. Software Science

Software as instructive behavioral information has been recognized as an entire range of widely and frequently used objects and phenomena in human knowledge. Software science is a theoretical inquiry of software and its constraints on the basis of empirical studies on engineering methodologies and techniques for software development and software engineering organization. In the history of science and engineering, a matured discipline always gave birth to new disciplines. For instance, theoretical physics was emerged from general and applied physics, and theoretical computing was emerged from computer engineering. So does software science that emerges from and grows in the fields of software, computer, information, knowledge, and system engineering.

Software Science (SS) is a discipline of enquiries that studies the theoretical framework of software as instructive and behavioral information, which can be embodied and executed by generic computers in order to create expected system behaviors and machine intelligence. The discipline of software science studies the common objects in the abstract world such as software, information, data, concepts, knowledge, instructions, executable behaviors, and their processing by natural and artificial intelligence. From this view, software science is theoretical software engineering; while software engineering is applied software science in order to efficiently, economically, and reliably develop large-scale software systems. The phenomena that almost all the fundamental problems, which could not be solved in the last four decades in software engineering, simply stemmed from the lack of coherent theories in the form of software science. The vast cumulated empirical knowledge and industrial practice in software engineering have made this possible to enable the emergence of software science.

This section on software science encompasses the following six chapters.

Chapter 13, *Empirical Studies on the Functional Complexity of Software in Large-Scale Software Systems*, by Yingxu Wang and Vincent Chiew, recognizes that functional complexity is one of the most fundamental properties of software because almost all other software attributes and properties such as functional size, development effort, costs, quality, and project duration are highly dependent on it. The functional complexity of software is a macro-scope problem concerning the semantic properties of software and human cognitive complexity towards a given software system; while the computational complexity is a micro-scope problem concerning algorithmic analyses towards machine throughput and time/space efficiency. This chapter presents an empirical study on the functional complexity of software known as cognitive complexity based on large-scale samples using a Software Cognitive Complexity Analysis Tool (SCCAT). Empirical data are obtained with SCCAT on 7,531 programs and five formally specified software systems. The theoretical foundation of software functional complexity is introduced and the metric of software cognitive complexity is formally modeled. On the basis of cognitive complexity, the functional complexities of a large-scale software system, the air traffic control systems (ATCS), are rigorously analyzed. A novel approach to represent software functional complexities and their distributions in software systems is developed. The nature of functional complexity of software in software engineering is rigorously explained. The relationship between the symbolic and functional complexities of software is quantitatively analyzed.

Chapter 14, *The Formal Design Models of a File Management System (FMS)*, by Yingxu Wang, Cyprian F. Ngolah, Xinming Tan, Yousheng Tian, and Phillip C.-Y. Sheu, presents abstract files as a typical abstract data type for data objects and software modeling, which provides a standard encapsulation and access interface for manipulating large-volume information and persistent data. File management systems are an indispensable component of operating systems and real-time systems for file manipulations. This chapter develops a comprehensive design pattern of files and a File Management System (FMS). A rigorous denotational mathematics, Real-Time Process Algebra (RTPA), is adopted, which allows both architectural and behavioral models of files and FMS to be rigorously designed and implemented in a top-down approach. The conceptual model, architectural model, and the static/dynamic behavioral models of files and FMS are systematically presented. This work has been applied in the design and modeling of a real-time operating system (RTOS+).

Chapter 15, *The Formal Design Model of Doubly-Linked-Circular Lists (DLC-Lists)*, by Yingxu Wang, Cyprian F. Ngolah, Xinming Tan, and Phillip C.-Y. Sheu, formally models the Abstract Data Types (ADTs) as a set of highly generic and rigorously modeled data structures in type theory. Lists as a finite sequence of elements are one of the most fundamental and widely used ADTs in system modeling, which provide a standard encapsulation and access interface for manipulating large-volume information and persistent data. This chapter develops a comprehensive design pattern of formal lists using a doubly-linked-circular (DLC) list architecture. A rigorous denotational mathematics, Real-Time Process Algebra (RTPA), is adopted, which allows both architectural and behavioral models of lists to be rigorously designed and implemented in a top-down approach. The architectural models of DLC-Lists are created using RTPA architectural modeling methodologies known as the Unified Data Models (UDMs). The physical model of DLC-Lists is implemented using doubly linked nodes dynamically created in the memory. The behavioral models of DLC-Lists are specified and refined by a set of Unified Process Models (UPMs) in three categories namely the management operations, traversal operations, and node

I/O operations. This work has been applied in a number of real-time and nonreal-time system designs such as a real-time operating system (RTOS+), a file management system (FMS), and the ADT library for an RTPA-based automatic code generation tool.

Chapter 16, *Petri Nets and Discrete Event Systems*, by Juan L.G. Guirao and Fernando L. Pelayo, presents an overview over the relationship between Petri Nets and Discrete Event Systems as they have been proved as key factors in the cognitive processes of perception and memorization. In this sense, different aspects of encoding Petri Nets as Discrete Dynamical Systems that try to advance not only in the problem of reachability but also in the one of describing the periodicity of markings and their similarity, are revised. It is also provided a metric for the case of Non-bounded Petri Nets.

Chapter 17, *The Formal Design Models of the Universal Array (UA) and Its Implementation*, by Yingxu Wang, Jason Huang, and Jingsheng Lei, identifies that arrays are one of the most fundamental and widely applied data structures, which are useful for modeling both logical designs and physical implementations of multi-dimensional data objects sharing the same type of homogeneous elements. However, there is a lack of a formal model of the universal array based on it any array instance can be derived. This chapter studies the fundamental properties of Universal Array (UA) and presents a comprehensive design pattern of UA. A denotational mathematics, Real-Time Process Algebra (RTPA), is adopted, which allows both architectural and behavioral models of UA to be rigorously designed and refined in a top-down approach. The conceptual model of UA is rigorously described by tuple- and matrix-based mathematical models. The architectural models of UA are created using RTPA architectural modeling methodologies known as the Unified Data Models (UDMs). The physical model of UA is implemented using linear list that is indexed by an offset pointer of elements. The behavioral models of UA are specified and refined by a set of Unified Process Models (UPMs) for the creation, initialization, update, retrieve, and release operations of UA. As a case study, the formal UA models are implemented in Java, which demonstrate the seamless transformability from the formal specifications to code. This work has been applied in a number of real-time and nonreal-time systems such as compilers, a file management system, the real-time operating system (RTOS+), and the ADT library for an RTPA-based automatic code generation tool.

Chapter 18, *The Formal Design Models of Tree Architectures and Behaviors*, by Yingxu Wang and Xinming Tan, presents abstract trees as one of the most fundamental and widely used non-linear hierarchical structures of linked nodes. A binary tree (B-Tree) is a typical balanced tree where the fan-out of each node is at most two known as the left and right children. This chapter develops a comprehensive design pattern of formal trees using the B-Tree architecture. A rigorous denotational mathematics, Real-Time Process Algebra (RTPA), is adopted, which allows both architectural and behavioral models of B-Trees to be rigorously designed and implemented in a top-down approach. The architectural models of B-Trees are created using RTPA architectural modeling methodologies known as the Unified Data Models (UDMs). The physical model of B-Trees is implemented using the left and right child nodes dynamically created in memory. The behavioral models of B-Trees are specified and refined by a set of Unified Process Models (UPMs) in three categories namely the management operations, traversal operations, and node I/O operations. This work has been applied in a number of real-time and nonreal-time system designs such as a real-time operating system (RTOS+), a general system organization model, and the ADT library for an RTPA-based automatic code generator.

Section 4. Applications of Computational Intelligence and Cognitive Computing

A series of fundamental breakthroughs have been recognized and a wide range of applications has been developed in software science, abstract intelligence, cognitive computing, and computational intelligence in the last decade. Because software science and computational intelligence provide a common and general platform for the next generation of cognitive computing, some expected innovations in these fields will emerge such as cognitive computers, cognitive knowledge representation technologies, semantic searching engines, cognitive learning engines, cognitive Internet, cognitive robots, and autonomous inference machines for complex and long-series of inferences, problem solving, and decision making beyond traditional logic- and rule-based technologies.

This section on applications of computational intelligence and cognitive computing encompasses the following seven chapters.

Chapter 19, *Four-Channel Control Architectures for Bilateral and Multilateral Teleoperation*, by Yuji Wang, Fuchun Sun, and Huaping Liu, presets a four-channel architecture in teleoperation with force feedback in various existing literature. However, most of them focused on Lawrence architecture and did not research other cases. In this chapter we propose two other four-channel architectures: passive four-channel architecture and passive four-channel architecture with operator force. Furthermore, two types of multilateral shared control architecture based on passive four-channel architecture, which exists in space teleoperation are put forward, one is dual-master multilateral shared control architecture, and the other is dual-slave multilateral shared control architecture. Simulations show that these four architectures can maintain stability in the presence of large time delay.

Chapter 20, *Entropy Quad-Trees for High Complexity Regions Detection*, by Rosanne Vetro, Dan A. Simovici, and Wei Ding, introduces entropy quad-trees as structures derived from quad-trees by allowing nodes to split only when those correspond to sufficiently complex sub-domains of a data domain. Complexity is evaluated using an information-theoretic measure based on the analysis of the entropy associated to sets of objects designated by nodes. An alternative measure related to the concept of box-counting dimension is also explored. Experimental results demonstrate the efficiency of entropy quad-trees to mine complex regions. As an application, the authors used the proposed technique in the initial stage of a crater detection algorithm using digital images taken from Mars surface. Additional experimental results are provided that demonstrate the crater detection performance and analyze the effectiveness of entropy quad-trees for high-complexity regions detection in the pixel space with significant presence of noise. This work is focused on 2-dimensional image domains, but can be generalized to higher dimensional data.

Chapter 21, *Sitting Posture Recognition and Location Estimation for Human-Aware Environment*, by Yusuke Manabe and Kenji Sugawara, presents that the realization of human-computer symbiosis is a very important idea in the context of ubiquitous computing. Symbiotic Computing is a kind of concept to bridge the gap between situation in Real Space (RS) and data in Digital Space (DS). The purpose is mainly to develop an intelligent software application as well as to establish the next generation information platform in order to develop the symbiotic system. Therefore, the authors argue that it is necessary to build mutual cognition between human and system. Mutual cognition broadly consists of two functions: RS cognition and DS cognition. This chapter focuses on RS Cognition, which consists of many software functions for perceiving various situations such as events or human's activities in RS. In this study, the authors develop two perceptual functions, which are sitting posture recognition and human's location estimation for a person, as kinds of RS perception task. As the results of experiments, the authors found that their developed functions are quite competent to recognize a human's activities.

Chapter 22, *Generic Cabling of Intelligent Buildings Based on Ant Colony Algorithm*, by Yunlong Wang, and Guoming Luo, identifies that generic cabling is one of the basic foundations of intelligent buildings. Using operation flow in generic cabling, the index constraints affecting generic cabling have been evolved in this chapter. A mathematical model is built based on the ant colony algorithm with multiple constraints, and improvements were made on the original basis to extend the ant colony algorithm from the regular simple ant colony and structure to a multi-ant colony and structure. The equilibrium settlement of multiplex wiring is realized according to the introduction of the multi-ant colony model. The ant cycle model is combined to extend the optimization target from the local wiring path to the entire wiring path, and to solve the drawbacks existing in the regular ant colony algorithm and other search algorithms that take the local wiring path as the optimization target. The introduced retrospective algorithm make the ants avoid the path marked "invalid" in the subsequent search process and improves the search performance and convergence speed of the ant colony algorithm.

Chapter 23, *Potentials of Quadratic Neural Unit for Applications*, by Ricardo Rodriguez, Ivo Bukovsky, and Noriyasu Homma, discusses the quadratic neural unit (QNU) and highlights its attractiveness for industrial applications such as for plant modeling, control, and time series prediction. Linear systems are still often preferred in industrial control applications for their solvable and single solution nature and for the clarity to the most application engineers. Artificial neural networks are powerful cognitive nonlinear tools, but their nonlinear strength is naturally repaid with the local minima problem, overfitting, and high demands for application-correct neural architecture and optimization technique that often require skilled users. The QNU is the important midpoint between linear systems and highly nonlinear neural networks because the QNU is relatively very strong in nonlinear approximation; however, its optimization and performance have fast and convex-like nature, and its mathematical structure and the derivation of the learning rules is very comprehensible and efficient for implementation. These advantages of QNU are demonstrated by using real and theoretical examples.

Chapter 24, *A Value-Based Framework for Software Evolutionary Testing*, by Du Zhang, presents that the fundamental objective in value-based software engineering is to integrate consistent stakeholder value propositions into the full extent of software engineering principles and practices so as to increase the value for software assets. In such a value-based setting, artifacts in software development such as requirement specifications, use cases, test cases, or defects, are not treated as equally important during the development process. Instead, they will be differentiated according to how much they are contributing, directly or indirectly, to the stakeholder value propositions. The higher the contributions, the more important the artifacts become. In turn, development activities involving more important artifacts should be given higher priorities and greater considerations in the development process. In this chapter, the authors propose a value-based framework for carrying out software evolutionary testing with a focus on test data generation through genetic algorithms. The proposed framework incorporates general principles in value-based software testing and makes it possible to prioritize testing decisions that are rooted in the stakeholder value propositions. It allows for a cost-effective way to fulfill most valuable testing objectives first and a graceful degradation when planned testing process has to be shortened.

Chapter 25, *Comparison of Promoter Sequences Based on Inter Motif Distance*, by A. Meera and Lalitha Rangarajan, considers that understanding how the regulation of gene networks is orchestrated is an important challenge for characterizing complex biological processes. The DNA sequences that comprise promoters do not provide much direct information about regulation. A substantial part of the regulation results from the interaction of transcription factors (TFs) with specific CIS regulatory DNA sequences. These regulatory sequences are organized in a modular fashion, with each module (enhancer) containing one or more binding sites for a specific combination of TFs. In the present work, the authors propose to investigate the inter motif distance between the important motifs in the promoter sequences of citrate synthase of different mammals. Also they use a new distance measure to compare the promoter sequences. Results reveal that there exists more similarity between organisms in the same chromosome.

This book is intended to the readership of researchers, engineers, graduate students, senior-level undergraduate students, and instructors as an informative reference book in the emerging fields of software science, cognitive intelligence, and computational intelligence. The editor expects that readers of *Advances in Abstract Intelligence and Soft Computing* will benefit from the 25 selected chapters of this book, which represents the latest advances in research in software science and computational intelligence and their engineering applications.

Yingxu Wang
University of Calgary, Canada

Acknowledgment

Many persons have contributed their dedicated work to this book and related research. The editor would like to thank all authors, the associate editors of IJSSCI, the editorial board members, and invited reviewers for their great contributions to this book. I would also like to thank the IEEE Steering Committee and organizers of the series of IEEE International Conference on Cognitive Informatics and Cognitive Computing (ICCI*CC) in the last ten years, particularly Lotfi A. Zadeh, Witold Kinsner, Witold Pedrycz, Bo Zhang, Du Zhang, George Baciu, Phillip Sheu, Jean-Claude Latombe, James Anderson, Robert C. Berwick, and Dilip Patel. I would like to acknowledge the publisher of this book, IGI Global, USA. I would like to thank Dr. Mehdi Khosrow-Pour, Jan Travers, Kristin M. Klinger, Erika L. Carter, and Myla Merkel, for their professional editorship.

Section 1
Computational Intelligence

Chapter 1

A Formal Knowledge Representation System (FKRS) for the Intelligent Knowledge Base of a Cognitive Learning Engine

Yousheng Tian
University of Calgary, Canada

Marina L. Gavrilova
University of Calgary, Canada

Yingxu Wang
University of Calgary, Canada

Guenther Ruhe
University of Calgary, Canada

ABSTRACT

It is recognized that the generic form of machine learning is a knowledge acquisition and manipulation process mimicking the brain. Therefore, knowledge representation as a dynamic concept network is centric in the design and implementation of the intelligent knowledge base of a Cognitive Learning Engine (CLE). This paper presents a Formal Knowledge Representation System (FKRS) for autonomous concept formation and manipulation based on concept algebra. The Object-Attribute-Relation (OAR) model for knowledge representation is adopted in the design of FKRS. The conceptual model, architectural model, and behavioral models of the FKRS system is formally designed and specified in Real-Time Process Algebra (RTPA). The FKRS system is implemented in Java as a core component towards the development of the CLE and other knowledge-based systems in cognitive computing and computational intelligence.

1. INTRODUCTION

Knowledge representation is recognized as a central problem in machine learning. Traditional technologies for knowledge representation are relational knowledge bases, natural language

processing (NLP) technologies, and ontology (Crystal, 1987; Pullman, 1997; Brewster et al., 2004; Leone et al., 2010; Wang, 2009b; Tian et al., 2009). Knowledge base technologies represent knowledge by lexical and semantic relations (Debenham, 1989). WordNet and ConceptNet are typical lexical databases (Fellbaum, 1998;

DOI: 10.4018/978-1-4666-2651-5.ch001

Liu & Singh, 2004). Various rule-based systems are developed for knowledge representation using logical rules (Bender, 1996) and fuzzy rules (Zadeh, 1965, 2004; Surmann, 2000). NLP technologies are developed for text processing in natural languages (Liddy, 2001; Wilson & Keil, 2001). Although various methods were proposed in NLP, fundamental technologies of them can be classified into two categories such as the symbolic approach (Chomsky, 1957) and the computational linguistic approach (Pullman, 1997). The former treats language as character strings with syntactic relations such as formal grammars (Chomsky, 1957; Burton, 1976; Kaplan & Bresnan, 1982; Wang, 2009a) and text parsing (McDermid, 1991; Wang, 2010b). The latter studies computational processing of natural languages such as the translation theory (Weaver, 1949; Crystal, 1987) and information retrieval techniques (Chang et al., 2006; Zhao & Sui, 2008; Reisinger & Pasca, 2009; Hu et al., 2010). However, the NPL technologies lack detailed analytic power at the concept and attribute levels underpinning semantic analyses at the word-level (Burton, 1976; Wang, 2008b, 2010b). Ontology is the third approach to knowledge representation and modeling, which is a branch of metaphysics dealing with the nature of being, which treats a small-scale knowledge as a set of words and their semantic relations in a certain domain (Gruber, 1993; Cocchiarella, 1996; Brewster et al., 2004; Tiberino et al., 2005; Sanchez, 2010; Hao, 2010; Wang et al., 2011). However, ontology may only represent a set of static knowledge and is highly application specific. Therefore, ontology was not designed to enable machines to automatically generate and manipulate concept networks for knowledge representation as that of human beings.

In recent studies in cognitive informatics (Wang, 2007c) and cognitive computing (Wang, 2009c, 2010a), it is recognized that concepts are the basic unit of human thinking, reasoning, and communications (Pojman, 2003; Wang, 2008b). An internal knowledge representation theory known as the Object-Attribute-Relation (OAR) model is proposed by Wang (2007a), which reveals the logical foundation of concepts and their attributes based on physiological and biological observations (Wilson & Keil, 2001). The OAR model provides a logical view of the long-term memory of the brain, which is a triple (O, A, R), where O is a finite set of objects identified by unique symbolic names; A is a finite set of attributes for characterizing the objects; and R is a set of relations between an object and other objects or their attributes.

A denotational mathematical structure known as *concept algebra* was developed by Wang (2008b) for formal knowledge representation and manipulations, which is a novel mathematical means for the formal treatment of concepts and their algebraic relations, operations, and associative rules. In concept algebra, the generic mathematical model of concepts is elicited from both abstract and concrete concepts. A set of relational and compositional operators are modeled in concept algebra on the basis of the general concept model. The operational semantics of concept algebra is formally described in Wang et al. (2011). In concept algebra, attributes of concepts are identified as the meta-properties of a concept known as the intension (Wang, 2007a). New attributes are explored to refine a certain concept in order to make it more precise. For example, the entire organisms in biology can be modeled as a hierarchical structure known as kingdoms, phyla, classes, orders, families, genus, and species from the top down when more attributes are introduced into a certain level of concepts. Various studies have been conducted on attribute extraction in either manual approaches or semi-automatic approaches (Yan, 2006; Poesio & Almuhareb, 2008; Zhao & Sui, 2008; Sanchez, 2010).

This paper presents the design and implementation of a formal knowledge representation system (FKRS) based on the OAR model (Wang, 2007a) and concept algebra (Wang, 2008b). In order to rigorously design and implement FKRS, real-time process algebra (RTPA) (Wang, 2002, 2007b, 2008a, 2008c) is adopted to formally describe the architectural and behavioral models of FKRS. According to the RTPA methodology for system modeling and refinement, FKRS is modeled and refined using two fundamental techniques known as the *unified data models* (UDMs) and *unified process models* (UPMs) (Wang, 2007b). The remainder of this paper is organized as follows. The conceptual model of FKRS is described based on the theories of OAR and concept algebra in Section 2. The architectural model of FKRS in the form of a set of UDMs is rigorously described in Section 3. The functional design of FKRS by a set of behavioral models in the form of UPMs is elaborated in Section 4. Based on the architectural and behavioral models, the implementation of the FKRS system is presented in Section 5.

2. THE CONCEPTUAL MODEL OF THE FKRS SYSTEM

The Formal Knowledge Representation System (FKRS) is a subsystem of the Cognitive Learning Engine (CLE), which is designed for enabling machines to learn text-based knowledge in natural languages and symbolic notations. The conceptual model of FKRS can be described by the internal

knowledge representation subsystem and its interaction with the kernel of CLE as shown in Figure 1. The knowledge representation subsystem provides a coherent and rigorous system for knowledge representation and manipulation. The kernel of CLE is reported in Wang et al. (2011) that implemented concept algebra operations and fundamental processes of autonomous learning.

FKRS is designed as an integration of a functional subsystem and a support subsystem for rigorous knowledge representation. The functional subsystem of FKRS encompasses the components of concept formation, conceptual knowledge representation, and knowledge visualization. The concept formulation process generates structured concepts based on the OAR model and concept algebra. The relational and compositional knowledge manipulation processes implement concept and knowledge operations according to concept algebra, which form the key function for autonomous machine learning. The knowledge retrieval and visualization processes query and display learnt knowledge by structural concepts and their relations to the entire knowledge in OAR in a graphical form. The support subsystem of FKRS encompasses the components of file management and linguistic knowl-

Figure 1. The architecture of the FKRS system

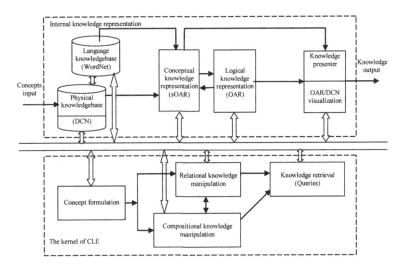

edge base. The file management process provides a unified interface for the system resources, the knowledge base with acquired knowledge, and the linguistic knowledge base. A set of standard functions such as file creation/release, open/close, read/write, as well as internal record access and update. WordNet (Fellbaum, 1998) is adopted as the general linguistic knowledge base for concept formation, attribute extraction, and knowledge modeling.

The knowledge representation models of the FKRS system are designed as shown in Figure 2. Between the structured (OAR-based) knowledge base with a dynamic concept network (DCN) and the unstructured linguistic knowledge base (linked-word-based), three knowledge representation models are introduced known as the formal model of concepts, the entire OAR, and the subject OAR (tOAR). Concept**UDM** is a Unified Data Model (UDM) of concepts that encompasses sets of attributes, objects, and internal and external relations where UDM is the RTPA type suffix. The OAR model, OAR**UDM**, provides a dynamic structure for the entire knowledge acquired by the system. The tOAR**UDM** model is a sub-OAR associated to a certain subject as the results of learning, which integrates a set of related concepts and their semantic associations presented. Each of the key models of FKRS will be further refined and formally described in Section 3.

3. THE ARCHITECTURAL MODEL OF THE FKRS SYSTEM

On the basis of the conceptual models of FKRS as described in Section 2, formal models of FKRS can be developed in a rigorous and systematical approach using RTPA (Wang, 2002, 2008a). According to the RTPA methodology for system modeling, specification, and refinement (Wang, 2007b), the top-level RTPA specification of FKRS§ is given in Equation 1, where its architecture, static behaviors, and dynamic behaviors are modeled in parallel. According to the RTPA notations (Wang, 2008a, 2008c), **§**, **ST**, **UDM**, **UPM**, and **PC** are type suffixes of a system, a system structure, a unified data model, a unified process model, and a process, respectively.

$$
\begin{aligned}
\text{FKRS\textbf{§}} \triangleq \ & \text{FKRS\textbf{§}.Architecture\textbf{UDM}} \\
& \| \ \text{FKRS\textbf{§}.StaticBehaviors\textbf{UPM}} \\
& \| \ \text{FKRS\textbf{§}.DynamicBehaviors\textbf{UPM}}
\end{aligned}
\tag{1}
$$

The architectural model of the FKRS system, FKRS**§**.Architecture**UDM**, can be refined as shown in Figure 3 by the five UDMs such as those of Concept**UDM**, OAR**UDM**, tOAR**UDM**, CKB**UDM**, and LKB**UDM**. In Figure 4, Concept**UDM** represents the structure of formal concepts where *n* in the squire brackets indicates the capacity of

Figure 2. Knowledge representation models of the FKRS system

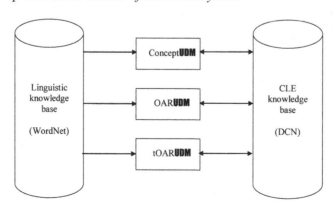

Figure 3. The top-level architecture of the FKRS system

```
FKRS§.Architecture𝗨𝗗𝗠 ≙
(   <Concept : ST | [n]>        // Models of Concepts
 || <OAR : ST | [1]>            // The logical knowledge representation
 || <tOAR : ST | [m]>           // The subject OARs
 || <CKB : File | [1]>          // The conceptual knowledge base
 || <LKB : ST | [1]>            // The linguistic knowledge base (WordNet)
)
```

concepts configured in the system. OAR**UDM** is a logical model of entire knowledge of the CLE machine as a dynamic concept network, which denotes the internal knowledge representation and physical knowledge schemes in the knowledge base. tOAR**UDM** is a sub-OAR that represents a subject of knowledge associated with a certain topic of an article. CKB**UDM** is the conceptual knowledge base implemented as a file in which each record is an item of OAR**UDM**. LKB**UDM** is a linguistic knowledge base that provides a logical representation of WordNet.

3.1. The General Concept Model

According to concept algebra, any concept can be uniquely modeled as a 6-tuple (Wang, 2008b). The UDM of Concept**UDM** is shown in Figure 4 with six fields where each of them is defined by a type and a certain constraint in RTPA. In Concept**UDM**, c**S** denotes the name of the concept as a string upto 255 characters; A**SET** a set of attributes of the concept; O**SET** a set of objects as instances of the concept; RC**SET** a set of internal relations between the objects and attributes; RI**SET**

and RO**SET** are the sets of input/output relations between the OAR and the concept or vice versa, respectively.

3.2. The OAR Model for Knowledge Representation

The formal model of knowledge, Knowledge**UDM**, can be rigorously represented by a set of concepts and their relations in the form of OAR**UDM** as shown in Figure 5. The core structure of the knowledge model with multiple interconnected items of OAR(i**N**)**UDM** is the 6-tuple as modeled in Concept**UDM** in Figure 4. The dynamic links OAR**UDM**.RI**SET** and OAR**UDM**.RO**SET** represent the input and output connection between the concept and other concepts in OAR**UDM**. Additional links, OAR**UDM**.RS**SET** and OAR**UDM**.RA**SET**, are adopted to implement the dynamic links to equivalent concepts known as the *synonym* and *antonym*. A time stamp, OAR**UDM**.TimeStamp**yyyy:MM:dd:hh:mm:ss**, is included for recording the time when a concept is initially created.

Figure 4. The UDM model of concepts

```
Concept𝗨𝗗𝗠 ≙ CST ::
{<c : S | 1 ≤ |cS| ≤ 255>,                          // ID of the concept
 <A : SET | ASET = {A₁ST, A₂ST, ..., AₙST}>,         // Attributes
 <O : SET | OSET = {O₁ST, O₂ST, ..., OₘST}>,         // Objects
 <RC : SET | RCSET = {(OSET × ASET)}SET>,            // Internal relations
 <RI : SET | RISET = {(C(iN)ST × C(iN)ST)}SET>,      // External input relations
 <RO : SET | ROSET = {(C(iN)ST × C(iN)ST)}SET>,      // External output relations
}
```

Figure 5. The UDM model of knowledge

$$\text{Knowledge}\textbf{UDM} \triangleq \mathop{R}_{i\textbf{N}=1}^{\#CurrentConcepts\textbf{N}} \text{OAR}(i\textbf{N})\textbf{UDM} ::$$

$\{<c: \textbf{S} \mid 1 \le \|c\textbf{S}\| \le 255>,$	// ID of the concept
$<A: \textbf{SET} \mid A\textbf{SET} = \{A_1\textbf{ST}, A_2\textbf{ST}, ..., A_n\textbf{ST}\}>,$	// Attributes
$<O: \textbf{SET} \mid O\textbf{SET} = \{O_1\textbf{ST}, O_2\textbf{ST}, ..., O_m\textbf{ST}\}>,$	// Objects
$<RC: \textbf{SET} \mid RC\textbf{SET} = \{(O\textbf{SET} \times A\textbf{SET})\}\textbf{SET}>,$	// Internal relations
$<RI: \textbf{SET} \mid RI\textbf{SET} = \{(C(i\text{'}\textbf{N})\textbf{ST} \times C(i\textbf{N})\textbf{ST})\}\textbf{SET}>,$	// Input relations
$<RO: \textbf{SET} \mid RO\textbf{SET} = \{(C(i\textbf{N})\textbf{ST} \times C(i\text{'}\textbf{N})\textbf{ST})\}\textbf{SET}>,$	// Output relations
$<RS: \textbf{SET} \mid \text{Equivalence}(C(i\textbf{N})\textbf{ST}, C(i\text{'}\textbf{N})\textbf{ST}) = 1>,$	// Synonym relations
$<RA: \textbf{SET} \mid \text{Equivalence}(C(i\textbf{N})\textbf{ST}, \overline{C}(i\text{'}\textbf{N})\textbf{ST}) = 1>,$	// Antonym relations
$<\text{TimeStamp}: \textbf{yyyy:MM:dd:hh:mm:ss} \mid 2000:01:01:00:00:00 \le$	
$\text{TimeStamp } \textbf{yyyy:MM:dd:hh:mm:ss} \le 2999:12:31:23:59:59>$	
$\}$	

Figure 6. The UDM model of the linguistic knowledge base

$$\text{LKB}\textbf{UDM} \triangleq \mathop{R}_{i\textbf{N}=1}^{SCB\textbf{N}.\#Words\textbf{N}} \text{Word}(i\textbf{N})\textbf{UDM} ::$$

$\{<\text{Word}: \textbf{S} \mid \text{Word}\textbf{S} \ne \varnothing>,$	
$<\text{Index}: \textbf{N} \mid \text{Index}\textbf{N} := i\textbf{N}>,$	
$<\text{Hyponym}: \textbf{SET} \mid \text{Hyponym}\textbf{SET} \ne \varnothing>,$	// Subconcepts
$<\text{Hypernym}: \textbf{SET} \mid \text{Hypernym}\textbf{SET} \ne \varnothing>,$	// Superconcepts
$<\text{Synonym}: \textbf{SET}>,$	// Equivalent concepts
$<\text{Antonym}: \textbf{SET}>$	// Opposite concepts
$\}$	

On the basis of the OAR**UDM** model, a *subject OAR* model, tOAR**UDM**, is an independent OAR on a certain topic stated in a paragraph or article, which is defined as an inheritance of OAR**UDM** according to concept algebra.

3.3. The UDM Model of the Linguistic Knowledge Base

The linguistic knowledge base of FKRS**§** adopts WordNet (Fellbaum, 1998). The logical structure of the linguistic knowledgebase, LKB**UDM**, is shown in Figure 6, which is composed by a set of Word(i**N**)**UDM**. Word**S** denotes the literature name of the word as a string of characters; Index**N** de-

notes the series number of the word in LKB**UDM**; Hyponym**SET** denotes a set of subconcepts related to the word; Hypernym**SET** denotes a set of superconcepts related to the word; and Synonym**SET** and Antonym**SET** are sets of equivalent or opposite concepts related to the word, respectively.

4. THE BEHAVIORAL MODELS OF THE FKRS SYSTEM

The functional behaviors of the FKRS**§** system can be modeled as a set of Unified Process Models (UPMs) according to RTPA (Wang, 2007b). FKRS**§**.StaticBehaviors**UPM** encompasses the

Figure 7. The UPMs of knowledge representation

```
KnowledeRepresentationUPM ≙
{  ConceptInitializationPC(<I:: oS,>; <O:: cST>; <UDM:: OARST,
                                       LKBST, SCBST >)
 | ConceptComparisonPC(<I::cST, c'ST,>; <O:: ¬R>;
                                       <UDM:: OARST, SCBST>)
 | AttributesExtractionPC(<I:: cST,>; <O:: ASET, OSET>;
                                       <UDM:: OARST, LKBST, SCBST>)
 | RelationalConceptAnalysisPC(<I:: cST,>; <O:: RISET, ROSET,
                                       RSSET, RASET>; <UDM:: OARST, SCBST>)
 | ConceptFormationPC(<I:: oS,>; <O:: cST>; <UDM:: OARST,
                                       LKBST, SCBST, FMSST, FilesST>)
}
```

Figure 8. The UPM model of concept initialization

```
ConceptInitializationPC(<I:: oS>; <O:: cUDM>;
                                   <UDM:: OARUDM, LKBUDM, SCBUDM>) ≙
{ → cUDM.cS := oS
  → cUDM.ASET := ∅
  → cUDM.OSET := ∅
  → cUDM.RCSET := ∅
  → cUDM.RISET := ∅
  → cUDM.ROSET := ∅
  → cUDM.RSSET := ∅
  → cUDM.RASET := ∅
}
```

processes of knowledge representation, knowledgebase manipulation, file management, and text file parser. Due to the limit of space, only the first UPM model, KnowledgeRepresentationUPM, is formally described in this section as outlined in Figure 7.

In the following subsections, KnowledgeRepresentation**UPM** will be further refined in a set of five behavioral processes known as those of concept initialization, concept comparison, attributes extraction, relational concept analysis, and concept formation.

4.1. Concept Initialization

The behavioral model of concept initialization, ConceptInitialization**PC**, is formally modeled as shown in Figure 8. ConceptInitialization**PC** cre-

ates a blank concept for holding information for a new piece of knowledge in the FKRS system. The input parameter of the process is an object name as a string. The output of the process is the structured concept initialized by dummy fields, where its identity, c**UDM**.c**S**, adopts the same object name oS as given in the input.

4.2. Concept Comparison

The behavioral model of concept comparison, ConceptComparison**PC**, is formally modeled as shown in Figure 9. ConceptComparison**PC** quantifies the equivalence of a pair of concepts, γ, in order to find their similarity in the normalized scope of [0, 1]. The input parameters of the process are two concepts. Its output is γ determined by the given formula basis on both sets of attributes

Figure 9. The UPM model of concept comparison

$$
\begin{aligned}
&\text{ConceptComparison}\textbf{PC}(<\text{I}::\ c\textbf{ST},\ c'\textbf{ST}>;\ <\text{O}::\ \gamma\textbf{R}>;\\
&\qquad\qquad\qquad\quad <\text{UDM}::\ \text{OAR}\textbf{UDM},\ \text{SCB}\textbf{UDM}>)\\
&\{\ //\ \text{Concept equivalence }(\gamma)\ \text{comparison}\\
&\quad\rightarrow\ g\textbf{R} := \frac{|\ c\textbf{UDM}.\text{A}\textbf{SET}\ |\ \cap\ |\ c'\textbf{UDM}.\text{A}\textbf{SET}\ |}{|\ c\textbf{UDM}.\text{A}\textbf{SET}\ \cup\ c'\textbf{UDM}.\text{A}\textbf{SET}\ |}\\
&\}
\end{aligned}
$$

of the concepts under processing. The usage of γ will be illustrated in Section 4.4 on relational concept analysis.

4.3. Attribute Extraction

The behavioral model of concept attribute extraction, AtributeExtraction**PC**, is formally modeled as shown in Figure 10. AtributeExtractionPC elicits related attributes and objects for a given concept from both the external linguistic knowledgebase LKB**UDM** (WordNet) and the internal knowledgebase Knowledge**UDM** as defined in Section 2. The input parameter of the process is a newly initialized concept. Its outputs are sets of related attributes and objects. The extraction of candidate attributes and objects starts by an external search in LKB**UDM** as a process of dictionary checking. In this step, AtributeExtraction**PC** iteratively searches all words in LKB**UDM** as follows: a) If an equivalent word is identified, the word is added into cUDM.OSET as a candidate object; b) The hyponyms of the word are disjoined into c**UDM**. A**SET** as candidate attributes; and c) Repeat steps (a) and (b) for each synonym of the equivalent word. As a result of the external search, the attributes and object semantically related to the given concept identified by c**UDM**.c**S**:= o**S** are elicited. Then, an internal search for existing knowledge in OAR**UDM** in term of related concepts is conducted in order to enhance the comprehension about the given concept under refining as follows: a) If an equivalent internal concept is identified, the object set of the equivalent concept is conjoined

to c**UDM**.O**SET** as a candidate object; and b) The attribute set of the concept are disjoined to c**UDM**. A**SET** as candidate attributes.

4.4. Relational Concept Analysis

The behavioral model of relational concept analysis, RelationalConceptAnalysis**PC**, is formally modeled as shown in Figure 11. The input parameter of the process is a newly established concept with defined sets of objects, attributes, and internal relations. Its outputs are four types of external relations with existing concepts in OAR**UDM**.

RelationalConceptAnalysis**PC** extends the sets of input, output, synonym, and antonym relations of a given concept associated to existing concepts in OAR**UDM**. It checks each internal concept c'**UDM** against the given concept c**UDM** in a loop for the following operations: a) It calls ConceptComparison**PC** to evaluate the equivalence between c'**UDM** and c**UDM**; b) If the analysis result indicates a synonym, the index number of c'**UDM** is added into c**UDM**.RS**SET**; c) If the analysis result indicates a related concept but not a synonym, the index number of c'**UDM** is added into both c**UDM**.RI**SET** and c**UDM**.RO**SET**; d) If the analysis result indicates no relation found, an antonym possibility is to be checked between the opposite attributes of the given concept and the current candidate concept. When the result is true, the index number of c'**UDM** is added into c**UDM**.RA**SET**; otherwise, it does nothing but exit.

Figure 10. The UPM model of attribute extraction

```
AttributeExtractionPC(<I:: cUDM>; <O:: ASET, OSET>; <UDM:: OARUDM, LKBUDM, SCBUDM>) ≙
{ → ASET := ∅
  → OSET := ∅
     LKBUDM.#WordsN
  →     R        (→ ◆ cUDM.cS = Word(iN)UDM.WordS                          // Extenal search
       iN=1
                   → OSET = OSET ∪ Word(iN)UDM.WordS

                     |Word(iN)UDM.HyponymSET|
                   →       R           ASET := ASET ∩ Word(iN)UDM.Hyponym(jN)SET.WordS
                          jN=1
                     |Word(iN)UDM.SynonymSET|
                   →       R           (→ OSET = OSET ∪ Word(iN)UDM.Synonym(jN)SET.IndexN
                          jN=1
                                        → ASET := ASET ∩ Word(iN)UDM.Hyponym(jN)SET.WordS
                                       )

                 )
     SCBUDM.#ConceptsN
  →     R        (→ ◆ cST.cS = OAR(iN)UDM.cS                                // Internal search
       iN=1
                   → OSET := OSET ∪ OAR(iN)UDM.OSET
                   → ASET := ASET ∩ OAR(iN)UDM.ASET
                 )
}
```

Figure 11. The UPM model of concept relational analysis

```
RelationalConceptAnalysisPC(<I:: cUDM>; <O:: RISET, ROSET, RSSET, RASET>; <UDM:: OARUDM, SCBUDM>) ≙
{ → RISET := ∅
  → ROSET := ∅
  → RSSET := ∅
  → RASET := ∅
     SCBUDM.#ConceptsN
  →     R        (→ c'UDM := OAR(iN)UDM
       iN=1
                   → ConceptComparisonPC(<I:: cUDM, c'UDM>; <O:: γR>; <UDM:: OARUDM, SCBUDM>)
                                                    // Concept equivalence (γ) comparison
                 → ( ◆ γR = 1.0                     // Synonyms
                       → RSSET := RSSET ∪ iN
                   | ◆ 0 < γR < 1.0                 // Relational concepts
                       → RISET := RISET ∪ iN
                       → ROSET := ROSET ∪ iN
                   | ◆ γR = 0
                       → ASET := cUDM.A̅SET           // Make antonyms of all attributes
                       → ( ◆ ASET = c'UDM.ASET
                             → RASET := RASET ∪ iN   // Antonyms
                         | ◆ ~                       // Independent concepts
                             → ⊗
                         )
                   )
                 )
}
```

Figure 12. The UPM model of concept formation

ConceptFormation**PC**(<**I**:: o**S**>; <**O**:: c**UDM**>; <**UDM**:: OAR**UDM**, LKB**UDM**, SCB**UDM**, FMS**UDM**, Files**UDM**>)

{ ↠ ConceptInitialization**PC**(<**I**:: o**S**>; <**O**:: c**UDM**>; <**UDM**:: OAR**UDM**, LKB**UDM**, SCB**UDM**>)   // Form new concept

↠ AttributeExtraction**PC**(<**I**:: c**UDM**>; <**O**:: A**SET**, O**SET**>; <**UDM**:: OAR**UDM**, LKB**UDM**, SCB**UDM**>)

→ c**UDM**.A**SET** := A**SET**

→ c**UDM**.O**SET** := O**SET**

→ c**UDM**.RC**SET** := O**SET** × A**SET**

↠ RelationalConceptAnalysis**PC**(<**I**:: c**UDM**>; <**O**:: RI**SET**, RO**SET**, RS**SET**, RA**SET**>; <**UDM**:: OAR**UDM**, SCB**UDM**>)

→ c**UDM**.RI**SET** := RI**SET**

→ c**UDM**.RO**SET** := RO**SET**

→ c**UDM**.RS**SET** := RS**SET**

→ c**UDM**.RA**SET** := RA**SET**

→ c**UDM**.TimeStamp**yyyy:MM:DD:hh:mm:ss** := SysClock**ST**.§t$_c$**YYYY:MM:dd:hh:mm:ss**

→ ↑(SCB**UDM**.#Concepts**N**)   // Update new concept

→ i**N** := SCB**UDM**.#Concepts**N**

→ OAR(i**N**)**UDM** := c**UDM**

→ ConceptMemorization**PC**(<**I**:: CKB**S**, OAR(i**N**)**UDM**>; <**O**:: CKB**UDM**>;
                              <**UDM**:: OAR**UDM**, CKB**UDM**, SCB**UDM**, FMS**UDM**, Files**UDM**>)   // Memorize new concept

$$\rightarrow \overset{|\text{c}\textbf{UDM}.\text{RI}\textbf{SET}|}{\underset{i\textbf{N}=1}{R}}$$ (→ CN**N** := c**UDM**.RI(i**N**)**SET**.CN**N**   // Update related concepts

→ OAR(CN**N**)**UDM**.RI**SET** := OAR(CN**N**)**UDM**.RI**SET** ∪ SCB**UDM**.#Concepts**N**

→ ConceptMemorization**PC**(<**I**:: CKB**S**, OAR(CN**N**)**UDM**>; <**O**:: CKB**UDM**>;
                              <**UDM**:: OAR**UDM**, CKB**UDM**, SCB**UDM**, FMS**UDM**, Files**UDM**>)
)

$$\rightarrow \overset{|\text{c}\textbf{UDM}.\text{RO}\textbf{SET}|}{\underset{i\textbf{N}=1}{R}}$$ (→ CN**N** := c**UDM**.RO(i**N**)**SET**.CN**N**

→ OAR(CN**N**)**UDM**.RO**SET** := OAR(CN**N**)**UDM**.RO**SET** ∪ SCB**UDM**.#Concepts**N**

→ ConceptMemorization**PC**(<**I**:: CKB**S**, OAR(CN**N**)**UDM**>; <**O**:: CKB**UDM**>;
                              <**UDM**:: OAR**UDM**, CKB**UDM**, SCB**UDM**, FMS**UDM**, Files**UDM**>)
)

$$\rightarrow \overset{|\text{c}\textbf{UDM}.\text{RS}\textbf{SET}|}{\underset{i\textbf{N}=1}{R}}$$ (→ CN**N** := c**UDM**.RS(i**N**)**SET**.CN**N**

→ OAR(CN**N**)**UDM**.RS**SET** := OAR(CN**N**)**UDM**.RS**SET** ∪ SCB**UDM**.#Concepts**N**

→ ConceptMemorization**PC**(<**I**:: CKB**S**, OAR(CN**N**)**UDM**>; <**O**:: CKB**UDM**>;
                              <**UDM**:: OAR**UDM**, CKB**UDM**, SCB**UDM**, FMS**UDM**, Files**UDM**>)
)

$$\rightarrow \overset{|\text{c}\textbf{UDM}.\text{RA}\textbf{SET}|}{\underset{i\textbf{N}=1}{R}}$$ (→ CN**N** := c**UDM**.RA(i**N**)**SET**.CN**N**

→ OAR(CN**N**)**UDM**.RA**SET** := OAR(CN**N**)**UDM**.RA**SET** ∪ SCB**UDM**.#Concepts**N**

→ ConceptMemorization**PC**(<**I**:: CKB**S**, OAR(CN**N**)**UDM**>; <**O**:: CKB**UDM**>;
                              <**UDM**:: OAR**UDM**, CKB**UDM**, SCB**UDM**, FMS**UDM**, Files**UDM**>)
)

}

4.5. Concept Formation

The behavioral model of concept formation, ConceptFormation**PC**, is formally modeled as shown in Figure 12. The input parameter of the process is a given identity of a new concept. Its output is the autonomously established concept linked with OAR**UDM**. ConceptFormation**PC** is a superprocess on the basis of the four previously modeled ones in this section, which establishes a new concept as follows: a) It calls ConceptInitialization**PC** to create a dummy concept with c**UDM**.cS:= oS; b) It calls AttributeExtraction**PC** to generate the internal parameters and relations such as c**UDM**.A**SET**, c**UDM**.O**SET**, and c**UDM**.RC-**SET**; c) It calls RelationalConceptAnalysis**PC** to establish external relations such as c**UDM**.RI**SET**, c**UDM**.RO**SET**, c**UDM**.RSSET, and c**UDM**.RA**SET**; d) If the analysis result indicates a synonym, the index number of c'**UDM** is added into c**UDM**.RS**SET**; c) If the analysis result indicates a related concept but not a synonym, the index number of c'**UDM** is added into both c**UDM**.RI**SET** and c**UDM**.RO**SET**; d) The newly established concept obtains a time stamp and series index number in OAR**UDM** after the total number of concepts in the system record is updated; e) It stores the established c**UDM** by

calling ConceptMemorization**PC**; and d) Each related concept in OAR**UDM** will have to be updated in the four loops for OAR(CN**N**) UDM. RI**SET**, OAR(CN**N**)**UDM**.RO**SET**, OAR(CN**N**)**UDM**. RS**SET**, and OAR(CN**N**)**UDM**.RA**SET**.

5. THE IMPLEMENTATION OF THE FKRS SYSTEM

A knowledge representation tool based on the formal models of FKRS**§** as presented in Sections 2 through 4 is developed in Java on the Windows platform. Concept representation and operations are implemented in a set of Java classes. Run-time tables are adopted to implement the internal data structures of concepts and OAR**UDM**, which can be fast accessed in order to increase learning and query speed.

The knowledge representation tool is part of the entire CLE system. An incremental approach was applied for developing FKRS (Ruhe et al., 2003, 2004; Wang, 2007b; Bhattacharya & Gavrilova, 2008). The current version of FKRS implements fundamental knowledge representation and manipulation functions such as object and relation analysis, concept formation, and attribute extrac-

Figure 13. The GUI of FKRS

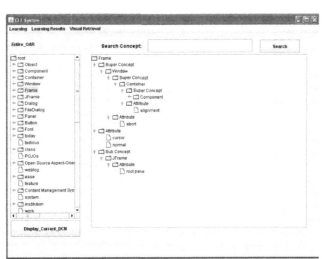

tion. Various text formats in pure text, structured text, html files, and PDF files have been tested to validate the robustness of this tool. The testing web contents include articles from wiki, open source forums, and journal papers.

The architecture and configuration of FKRS is shown in Figure 13 where knowledge is represented and stored in a novel knowledge base as a concept network. Because of the significant size of the knowledge base created and manipulated by the FKRS system, the knowledge visualization window may become extremely crowded during run-time. To solve this problem, only selected concepts and their relations are shown in the current window of machine knowledge. Therefore, a tree structure is introduced to represent a partial concept network with relations originally associated with the target concept as the root node in the concept network. On each root node representing a concept, eight forms of subtrees may be derived and visualized such as its objects, attributes, input relations, output relations, synonyms, antonyms, superconcepts, and subconcepts.

The FKRS system is designed for autonomously learning and inference of new concepts

according to concept algebra based on its knowledge base. For example, a superconcept, *DeskComputerSys$\mathbb{C}$*, can be derived by FKRS by concept *composition* ($\uplus$) defined in concept algebra using two given subconcepts, *DeskComputer$\mathbb{C}$* and *Printer$\mathbb{C}$*, as follows:

$$\text{DeskComputerSys}\mathbb{C} \triangleq C_5\mathbb{C}(A_5, O_5, R^c_5, R^i_5, R^o_5)$$
$$= (\text{Computer}\mathbb{C} \Rightarrow \text{DeskComputer}\mathbb{C}) \uplus \text{Printer}\mathbb{C}$$

$$= \begin{cases} A_5 = C'_3\mathbb{C}.A_3 \cup C_2\mathbb{C}.A_2 = C_3\mathbb{C}.\{a_1, a_2, a_3, a_4, a_5, a_6\} \\ \qquad\qquad\qquad \cup C_2\mathbb{C}.\{a_1, a_2, a_3, a_4, a_5, a_6\} \\ O_5 = C'_3\mathbb{C}.O_3 \cup C_2\mathbb{C}.O_2 = C_3\mathbb{C}.\{o_1, o_2, o_3\} \setminus o_1 \\ \qquad\qquad\qquad \cup C_2\mathbb{C}.\{o_1, o_2\} \\ R^c_5 = O_5 \times A_5 \\ R^i_5 = \mathfrak{K} \times C_5\mathbb{C} \\ R^o_5 = C_5\mathbb{C} \times \mathfrak{K} \end{cases}$$

A screenshot of the FKRS tool for concept manipulations powered by concept algebra is shown in Figure 14. In Figure 14, the operation of concept composition in concept algebra is autonomously carried out with two existing concepts in the machine. As a result, the superconcept,

Figure 14. A screenshot of concept composition in FKRS

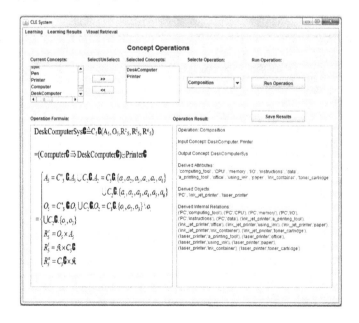

DeskComputerSys𝐂, is autonomously created. The above mechanisms of FKRS implement the fundamental capability for knowledge representation, learning, and reasoning in concept-algebra-based computational intelligence.

6. CONCLUSION

Towards the development of a cognitive learning engine (CLE), a formal knowledge representation system (FKRS) has been developed for autonomous concept formation and manipulation based on concept algebra. The object-attribute-relation (OAR) based knowledge model has established a solid foundation for knowledge representation. Concept algebra provides a powerful knowledge manipulation theory for concept formation and manipulation. The specifications of the FKRS system have been developed based on RTPA modeling technologies, which enables a formal approach towards the design and implementation of the highly abstract and complex FKRS system.

ACKNOWLEDGMENT

This paper is an extended and revised version of one of the best papers awarded in the 10ᵗʰ *IEEE International Conference on Cognitive Informatics and Cognitive Computing* (ICCI*CC 2011). The authors would like to acknowledge the Natural Science and Engineering Council of Canada (NSERC) for its partial support to this work. We would also acknowledge the graduate award of the Schulich foundation for this work. We would like to thank the anonymous reviewers for their valuable comments and suggestions.

REFERENCES

Bender, E. A. (1996). *Mathematical methods in artificial intelligence*. Los Alamitos, CA: IEEE Press.

Bhattacharya, P., & Gavrilova, M. L. (2008). Roadmap-based path planning - Using the Voronoi diagram for a clearance-based shortest path. *IEEE Robotics & Automation Magazine, 15*(2), 58–66. doi:10.1109/MRA.2008.921540

Brewster, C., O'Hara, K., Fuller, S., Wilks, Y., Franconi, E., & Musen, M. A. (2004). Knowledge representation with ontologies: The present and future. *IEEE Intelligent Systems, 19*(1), 72–81. doi:10.1109/MIS.2004.1265889

Burton, R. R. (1976). *Semantic grammar: A technique for efficient language understanding in limited domains* (Unpublished doctoral dissertation). University of California, Irvine, CA.

Chang, C.-H., Kayed, M., Girgis, M. R., & Shaalan, K. (2006). A survey of web information extraction system. *IEEE Transactions on Knowledge and Data Engineering, 18*(10), 1411–1428. doi:10.1109/TKDE.2006.152

Chomsky, N. (1957). *Syntactic structures*. The Hague, The Netherlands: Mouton.

Cocchiarella, N. (1996). Conceptual realism as a formal ontology. In Poli, R., & Simons, P. (Eds.), *Formal ontology* (pp. 27–60). London, UK: Kluwer Academic.

Crystal, D. (1987). *The Cambridge encyclopedia of language*. Cambridge, UK: Cambridge University Press.

Debenham, J. K. (1989). *Knowledge systems design*. Upper Saddle River, NJ: Prentice Hall.

Fellbaum, C. (1998). *WordNet: An electronic lexical database*. Cambridge, MA: MIT Press.

Gruber, T. (1993). A translation approach to portable ontology specifications. *Knowledge Acquisition, 5*(2), 199–220. doi:10.1006/knac.1993.1008

Hao, L. (2010). Ontology based automatic attributes extracting and queries translating for deep web. *Journal of Software, 5*, 713–720.

Hu, K., Wang, Y., & Tian, Y. (2010). A web knowledge discovery engine based on concept algebra. *International Journal of Cognitive Informatics and Natural Intelligence, 4*(1), 80–97. doi:10.4018/jcini.2010010105

Kaplan, R. M., & Bresnan, J. (1982). Lexical functional grammar: A formal system for grammatical representation. In Bresnan, J. (Ed.), *The mental representation of grammatical relations* (pp. 173–281). Cambridge, MA: MIT Press.

Leone, N., Pfeifer, G., Faber, W., Eiter, T., Gottlob, G., Perri, S., & Scarcello, F. (2006). The DLV system for knowledge representation and reasoning. *ACM Transactions on Computational Logic, 7*(3), 499–562. doi:10.1145/1149114.1149117

Liddy, E. D. (2001). Natural language processing. In Drake, M. (Ed.), *Encyclopedia of library and information science* (2nd ed.). New York, NY: Marcel Decker.

Liu, H., & Singh, P. (2004). ConceptNet - A practical commonsense reasoning toolkit. *BT Technology Journal, 22*(4), 211–225. doi:10.1023/B:BTTJ.0000047600.45421.6d

McDermid, J. (Ed.). (1991). *Software engineer's reference book.* Oxford, UK: Butterworth Heinemann.

Poesio, M., & Almuhareb, A. (2008). Extracting concept descriptions from the web: the importance of attributes and values. In *Proceedings of the Conference on Ontology Learning and Population: Bridging the Gap between Text and Knowledge* (pp. 29-44).

Pojman, L. P. (2003). *The theory of knowledge: Classical and contemporary readings.* Belmont, CA: Wadsworth/Thomson Learning.

Pullman, S. (1997). *Computational linguistics.* Cambridge, UK: Cambridge University Press.

Reisinger, J., & Pasca, M. (2009). Low-cost supervision for multiple-source attribute extraction. In *Proceedings of the 10th International Conference on Intelligent Text Processing and Computational Linguistics* (pp. 382-393).

Ruhe, G., Eberlein, A., & Pfahl, D. (2003). Trade-off analysis for requirements selection. *International Journal of Software Engineering and Knowledge Engineering, 13*, 345–366. doi:10.1142/S0218194003001378

Ruhe, G., & Ngo-The, A. (2004). Hybrid intelligence in software release planning. *International Journal of Hybrid Intelligent Systems, 1*, 99–110.

Sanchez, D. (2010). A methodology to learn ontological attributes from the web. *Data & Knowledge Engineering, 69*(6), 573–597. doi:10.1016/j.datak.2010.01.006

Surmann, H. (2000). Learning a fuzzy rule based knowledge representation. In *Proceedings of the ICSC Symposium on Neural Computation*, Berlin, Germany (pp. 349-355).

Tian, Y., Wang, Y., & Hu, K. (2009). A knowledge representation tool for autonomous machine learning based on concept algebra. *Transactions of Computational Science, 5*, 143–160.

Tiberino, A., Embley, D., Lonsdale, D., Ding, Y., & Nagy, G. (2005). Towards ontology generation from tables. *WWW: Internet and Information Systems, 8*(3), 261–285.

Wang, Y. (2002). The Real-Time Process Algebra (RTPA). *Annals of Software Engineering: An International Journal, 14*, 235–274. doi:10.1023/A:1020561826073

Wang, Y. (2007a). The OAR model of neural informatics for internal knowledge representation in the brain. *International Journal of Cognitive Informatics and Natural Intelligence, 1*(3), 66–77. doi:10.4018/jcini2007070105

Wang, Y. (2007b). *Software engineering foundations: A software science perspective.* Boca Raton, FL: Auerbach.

Wang, Y. (2007c). The theoretical framework of cognitive informatics. *International Journal of Cognitive Informatics and Natural Intelligence, 1*(1), 1–27. doi:10.4018/jcini.2007010101

Wang, Y. (2008a). RTPA: A denotational mathematics for manipulating intelligent and computational behaviors. *International Journal of Cognitive Informatics and Natural Intelligence, 2*(2), 44–62. doi:10.4018/jcini.2008040103

Wang, Y. (2008b). On concept algebra: A denotational mathematical structure for knowledge and software modeling. *International Journal of Cognitive Informatics and Natural Intelligence, 2*(2), 1–19. doi:10.4018/jcini.2008040101

Wang, Y. (2008c). Deductive semantics of RTPA. *International Journal of Cognitive Informatics and Natural Intelligence, 2*(2), 95–121. doi:10.4018/jcini.2008040106

Wang, Y. (2008d). On contemporary denotational mathematics for computational intelligence. *Transactions of Computational Science, 2,* 6–29. doi:10.1007/978-3-540-87563-5_2

Wang, Y. (2009a). A formal syntax of natural languages and the deductive grammar. *Fundamenta Informaticae, 90*(4), 353–368.

Wang, Y. (2009b). Toward a formal knowledge system theory and its cognitive informatics foundations. *Transactions of Computational Science, 5,* 1–19.

Wang, Y. (2009c). On cognitive computing. *International Journal of Software Science and Computational Intelligence, 1*(3), 1–15. doi:10.4018/jssci.2009070101

Wang, Y. (2010a). Cognitive robots: A reference model towards intelligent authentication. *IEEE Robotics and Automation, 17*(4), 54–62. doi:10.1109/MRA.2010.938842

Wang, Y. (2010b). On formal and cognitive semantics for semantic computing. *International Journal of Semantic Computing, 4*(2), 203–237. doi:10.1142/S1793351X10000833

Wang, Y., Tian, Y., & Hu, K. (2011). Semantic manipulations and formal ontology for machine learning based on concept algebra. *International Journal of Cognitive Informatics and Natural Intelligence, 5*(3), 1–29. doi:10.4018/IJCINI.2011070101

Weaver, W. (1949). Translation. In Locke, W. N., & Booth, A. D. (Eds.), *Machine translation of languages: Fourteen essays* (pp. 15–23). Cambridge, MA: MIT Press.

Wilson, R. A., & Keil, F. C. (2001). *The MIT encyclopedia of the cognitive sciences.* Cambridge, MA: MIT Press.

Yan, H. S. (2006). A new complicated-knowledge representation approach based on knowledge meshes. *IEEE Transactions on Knowledge and Data Engineering, 18*(1), 47–62. doi:10.1109/TKDE.2006.2

Zadeh, L. A. (1965). Fuzzy sets. *Information and Control, 8,* 338–353. doi:10.1016/S0019-9958(65)90241-X

Zadeh, L. A. (2004). Precisiated Natural Language (PNL). *AI Magazine, 25*(3), 74–91.

Zhao, Q., & Sui, Z. (2008). To extract ontology attribute value automatically based on WWW. In *Proceedings of the International Conference on Natural Language Processing and Knowledge Engineering* (pp. 1-7).

This work was previously published in the International Journal of Software Science and Computational Intelligence, Volume 3, Issue 4, edited by Yingxu Wang, pp. 1-17, copyright 2011 by IGI Publishing (an imprint of IGI Global).

Chapter 2
Sparse Based Image Classification With Bag-of-Visual-Words Representations

Yuanyuan Zuo
Tsinghua University, China

Bo Zhang
Tsinghua University, China

ABSTRACT

The sparse representation based classification algorithm has been used to solve the problem of human face recognition, but the image database is restricted to human frontal faces with only slight illumination and expression changes. This paper applies the sparse representation based algorithm to the problem of generic image classification, with a certain degree of intra-class variations and background clutter. Experiments are conducted with the sparse representation based algorithm and Support Vector Machine (SVM) classifiers on 25 object categories selected from the Caltech101 dataset. Experimental results show that without the time-consuming parameter optimization, the sparse representation based algorithm achieves comparable performance with SVM. The experiments also demonstrate that the algorithm is robust to a certain degree of background clutter and intra-class variations with the bag-of-visual-words representations. The sparse representation based algorithm can also be applied to generic image classification task when the appropriate image feature is used.

INTRODUCTION

The task of generic image classification involves two important issues. One is image representation, the other is classification algorithm.

Many image representation methods have been developed using various global features.

Region-based features have also been developed by segmenting an image into several locally uniform regions and extracting feature for each region. Recently, keypoint-based image features are getting more and more attention for computer vision area. Keypoints, also known as interest points or salient regions, refer to local image

DOI: 10.4018/978-1-4666-2651-5.ch002

patches which contain rich information, have some kind of saliency and can be stably detected under a certain degree of variations. The extraction of keypoint-based image feature usually includes two steps. First, keypoint detectors are used to automatically find the keypoints. Second, keypoint descriptors are used to represent the keypoint features. Performance has been evaluated among several different keypoint detectors and descriptors (Mikolajczyk et al., 2005; Mikolajczyk & Schmid, 2005).

Corresponding to the different kinds of image representation methods, many classification algorithms were studied (Csurka et al., 2004; Fergus, Perona, & Zisserman, 2003; Jing et al., 2004; Li & Perona, 2005; Sivic & Zisserman, 2003; Zhang et al., 2007). Image classification models can be divided into two classes. One class is generative models. The representative work is constellation model (Fergus, Perona, & Zisserman, 2003) which is a probabilistic model for object categories. The basic idea of this model is that an object is composed of several parts that are selected from the detected keypoints, with the appearance of the parts, scale, shape and occlusion modeled by probability density functions. A Bayesian hierarchical model was proposed (Li & Perona, 2005) for natural scene categories recognition, which learns the distribution of the visual words in each category.

The other class of image classification models is discriminative models, which have been proved to be effective for object classification (Csurka et al., 2004). A support vector machine (SVM) with the orderless bag of keypoints image representation was demonstrated to be effective for classification of texture and object images (Zhang et al., 2007). Zhang et al. (2006) proposed a hybrid of nearest neighbor classifiers and support vector machines to achieve good performance with reasonable computational complexity. Lazebnik et al. (2006) presented a multi-layer bag of keypoints feature with modified pyramid match kernels, which demonstrated that a well-designed

bag-of-features method can outperform more sophisticated approaches.

Recently, sparse coding has been used for the learning of visual vocabulary or codebook and image representation. Yang et al. (2009) adopted sparse coding instead of K-means cluster to quantize the image local features and proposed a linear spatial pyramid matching kernel using image representation based on sparse codes. Considering the mutual dependence among local features, Gao et al. (2010) proposed a Laplacian sparse coding method to learn the codebook and quantize local features more robustly.

In 2009, theory from sparse signal representation was applied to the problem of human faces recognition (Wright et al., 2009), in which a test face is represented as a sparse linear combination of the faces from the training set. A sparse representation based classification algorithm by computing l^1-minimization problem is proposed. The authors gave new insights into two important issues in face recognition: feature extraction and robustness to occlusion. Although good performance was obtained, the image database was strictly confined to human frontal faces with only slight illumination and expression changes. Detection, cropping and normalization of the faces were done beforehand.

Our work differs from Wright et al. (2009) mainly in the following three aspects.

1. **Application Domain:** We apply the sparse representation based classification algorithm to the problem of generic image classification with a certain degree of background clutter, scale, translation, and rotation variations within the same image class. No preprocessing needs to be done for each image.

2. **Image Feature Space:** Wright et al. (2009) studied on the low dimensional sub-space in the high dimensional pixel space, which required image pixels to be strictly aligned. The paper argued that even downsampled images and random projections can do as

well as conventional complex features, if the feature space dimension is sufficiently large and the sparse representation is computed correctly. In this paper, we mainly focus on the low dimensional sub-space in the high dimensional feature space. Bag-of-visual-words features are extracted to represent an image. No pixel alignment needs to be done in advance.

3. **Experimental Setup:** In the experiments, we achieve the experimental results by repeating for several times with randomly divided training sets and testing sets. As we know, performance can vary greatly with different images selected as the training samples. When experiments have been done on the AR-database which has more facial variation, 14 images with only illumination and expression changes were selected (Wright et al., 2009). The 7 images for training were designated as 4 neutral faces with illumination change, and 3 faces with only expression change.

This paper applies the sparse representation based algorithm to the problem of generic image classification. This work demonstrates that the sparse representation based algorithm can achieve comparable performance with SVM, with the bag-of-visual-words representations. In the remainder of this paper, the image feature extraction method is described, followed by a detailed description of the Sparse Representation based Classification

(SRC) algorithm. Then, the performances of the SRC algorithm are compared with SVM classifiers, and the experimental results are analyzed.

IMAGE FEATURE EXTRACTION

Keypoint-based features have been used in many image classification systems. The image feature extraction method includes the following four steps.

1. **Keypoint Detector:** The salient region detector (Kadir et al., 2004) and Scale Invariant Feature Transform (SIFT) (Lowe, 2004) interest points detector are two of the most popular keypoint detectors used in many image classification systems. Compared with the SIFT detector, the salient region detector can eliminate many keypoints located in cluttered backgrounds. As a result, we choose the salient region detector to find salient regions which exhibit unpredictability both in the local attributes space and the scale space. The unpredictability of image regions is measured by the Shannon entropy of the local image attributes, such as the pixel gray value. The number of regions detected in one image usually varies from dozens to hundreds. Figure 1 gives several examples of the salient region detector results for images from the Caltech 101 dataset.

Figure 1. Salient regions detected on some images from Caltech101

2. **Keypoint Descriptor:** Histograms of Oriented Gradients (HOG) descriptor (Dalal & Triggs, 2005), which is similar to SIFT descriptors, is used to describe each keypoint feature. This computes gradients for every pixel in the keypoint local patch. The gradient orientation (unsigned 0°-180°, or signed 0°-360°) is quantized into a certain number of bins. Local patches can be divided into different size blocks for computing the HOG features. Different block sizes and normalization schemes have been experimented (Dalal & Triggs, 2005). The results show that 2×2 blocks and the l^2-norm perform well.

3. **Visual Vocabulary Generation:** Part of the keypoint features are randomly selected from all the keypoint features extracted from every image in the database. These randomly chosen features are clustered using the k-means method to generate the visual vocabulary $\{w_1, w_2, \ldots, w_m\}$ of size m, with each visual word corresponding to a cluster center.

4. **\$:** The bag-of-visual-words model is used for the image feature representation, since this has been shown to be effective (Csurka et al., 2004; Lazebnik, Schmid, & Ponce, 2006; Zhang et al., 2007). For each keypoint local patch, compute the distance between the local patch feature and each visual word. The visual word w_i which has the minimum distance is assigned to the keypoint local patch. The frequency of each visual word in the vocabulary is counted to represent the image as a histogram of the visual words frequency. The problems related to the bag of visual words method, such as vocabulary size and weighting schemes, are discussed by Yang, Jiang, Hauptmann, and Ngo (2007).

IMAGE CLASSIFICATION BASED ON SPARSE REPRESENTATION

The sparse representation based classification algorithm has been used for human face recognition (Wright et al., 2009). Experiments showed that if the feature space dimension is sufficiently large, the SRC performance is comparable with the SVM. One advantage of the SRC is that the performance of various features converges as the feature space dimension increases. But with the SVM classifier, the performance of various features does not converge. That is, good performance of the SVM classifier depends on good feature extraction method.

Sparse representation based classification assumes that the training samples from a single class do lie on a subspace. As a result, a test sample y can be represented as a sparse linear combination of the training samples A, $y = Ax$. Instead of solving the NP-hard problem of finding x with the minimum l^0-norm, theory of sparse representation (Candes, Romberg, & Tao, 2006; Candes & Tao, 2006; Donoho, 2006) reveals that if the solution of x is sparse enough, the solution of finding the minimum l^0-norm is equal to the solution of finding the minimum l^1-norm, which can be solved in polynomial time by standard linear programming methods (Chen, Donoho, & Saunders, 2001).

The following gives a detailed description of the SRC algorithm.

1. **Dataset Preparation:** Randomly select a certain number of images per category as the training set, with the remaining images as the testing set.

2. **Computation of the Training Feature Matrix A:** For each training image from category i, extract the image feature $f \in R^m$, in which m is the image feature dimension. Image features belonging to the same category i form the sub-matrix A_i. Given a

training set with *k* categories, matrix *A* is composed of every sub-matrix A_i, $A = [A_1, A_2, ..., A_k]$; $A \in R^{m \times n}$, in which *n* is the total number of images in the training set.

3. **Solve the Optimization Problem:** For the given test image, extract the feature $y \in R^m$. Solve the l^1-minimization problem in (1) or (2). Equation (2) considers that the real data may have small noise.

$$\hat{x}_1 = \arg \min \|x\|_1 \quad \text{subject to} \quad Ax = y \tag{1}$$

$$\hat{x}_1 = \arg \min \|x\|_1 \quad \text{subject to} \quad \|Ax - y\|_2 \leq \varepsilon \tag{2}$$

4. **Compute the Residual Between *Y* and Its Estimate for Each Category:** Let $\delta_i(\hat{x}_1) \in R^n$ keep only nonzero entries in $\hat{x}_1$ that are associated with category *i*. We can approximate the testing image feature *y* as $\hat{y}_i = A\delta_i(\hat{x}_1)$, using only the coefficients of $\hat{x}_1$ which correspond to category *i*. For each category, compute the residuals $r_i = \|y - A\delta_i(\hat{x}_1)\|_2$, for *i*=1,2,...,*k*.

5. **Output the Test Image Label:** The test image is assigned to the category *i* that has the minimum residual between *y* and $\hat{y}_i$.

Steps 3 to 5 are repeated for each image in the testing set. The classification precision is then calculated for each category.

Figures 2 through 4 give an example of the SRC algorithm with the bag-of-visual-words representation. Figure 2 shows an example image with the histogram of visual word frequency feature. The horizontal axis indicates that the vocabulary includes 100 visual words. Figure 3 shows the values of *x*, which are the sparse representation coefficients of the test image by the training feature matrix *A*. The horizontal axis corresponds to the 15 training samples per category from 25 categories. This figure shows that the coefficients of only a few training samples from the first category have large values. Figure 4 shows the residuals r_i for each category. The test image is correctly assigned to the first category which has the minimum residual.

EXPERIMENTS

In this section, we present results of experiments on 25 object categories selected from the Caltech 101 dataset. Two image classification algorithms are compared, namely, SRC and SVM.

Experiment Dataset and Methods

Twenty five object categories were selected from the Caltech 101 dataset with each category containing 30 images. The images are not cropped or normalized in advance and have some background clutter. Since the keypoint-based features can only tolerate a certain degree of intra-class

Figure 2. Example image with the bag of visual words feature

 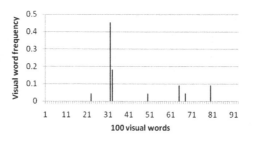

Figure 3. Coefficients of sparse representation

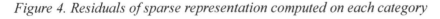

variations caused by scale, translation, rotation and background clutter, objects with rather large intra-class variations were not selected for the experiments. The task is to recognize objects on the 25 object categories dataset. The experiment procedure is as follows.

1. **Image Keypoint Detection and Description:** Color images are converted to grayscale images. Keypoint detector is used to find salient regions for each image. The gradients on each salient region are computed with the signed

orientation (0°-360°) quantized into 18 bins. Each region is divided into 2×2 blocks with the l^2-nomalized HOG feature computed for each block to give a 72-dimensional feature.

2. **Visual Vocabulary Generation:** Visual vocabulary is generated from randomly selected 10000 keypoint features. K-means method is used to cluster the selected features. In order to reduce the great difference of numbers of detected keypoints in different images, the number of keypoints per image is limited to 50. The vocabulary size is set to

Figure 4. Residuals of sparse representation computed on each category

100 and 150. A larger vocabulary size may be used when the number of images in the database increases.

3. **Image Feature Extraction:** Bag-of-visual-words feature is extracted for each image using the generated vocabulary. The histogram of visual words frequency is l^1-nomalized.

4. **Dataset Randomly Division:** For every object category, we randomly select designated number of images as the training set, with the remaining images as the testing set.

5. **SRC Classification:** Image features from the training set are used to compose the training feature matrix A for the SRC algorithm. For each test image, we solve the optimization problem (2) by SPGL1 (Berg & Friedlander, 2007) with the error tolerance $\varepsilon = 0.05$. Residuals between the test image feature and its estimates by the training samples from each category are computed. The category label with the minimum residual is assigned as the test image label.

6. **SVM Training and Testing:** Image features from the training set are used to train SVM models (Chang & Lin, 2001) with 5-fold cross validation. For each image in the testing set, SVM models are used to predict the test image label. The strategy of the multi-class SVM is to build a set of one-versus-one classifiers. That is, for k classes, $k(k-1)/2$ classifiers are trained with SVM, and the test image is assigned the class label that is selected by the most classifiers.

Five groups of experiments on SRC and SVM have been done with the following experimental setup: {100, 5}, {100, 10}, {100, 15}, {150, 10} and {150, 15}. The first entry refers to the vocabulary size, and the second entry refers to the number of training images per category.

With each experimental setup, steps 4) to 6) are repeated 5 times with different randomly selected training and testing images to average out the chances from the sampling of data. The final precision is reported as the mean of the results from the individual runs.

Comparison of Experiments on SRC and SVM

The SRC performance is compared with SVM on the 25 object categories, as shown in Figure 5, with the vocabulary size 100 and 15 training images per category. There is great variation of performance from around 30% to above 90% among different object classes. We will give an explanation why the classifiers perform well on some of the objects but not on the others.

Figure 5. Performance comparison between SRC and SVM, 15 training images per category, 100 visual words

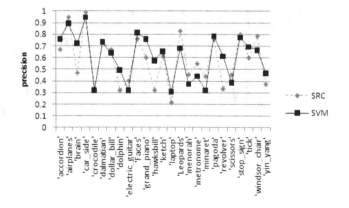

The object categories with good performance are listed in Table 1, under the experimental setup of 15 training images and the vocabulary size 100. A common property of the images from these categories is that similar patterns are repetitively detected as keypoints for many times. In the categories such as the airplane, pagoda, stop sign and Windsor chair, image patches composed of straight lines are detected around the contours of the objects, as shown in the left and middle images of Figure 1. The objects in the categories such as the Dalmatian and leopard have strong textures. As a result, many spots on the animal fur are detected, as shown in the right image of Figure 1. These image patches are not only distinctive, but also can be stably detected for many times. The features extracted from these patches lay the foundation of the good classification performance. In particular, when the detected keypoints are distinctive enough, the sparse representation based classifier can outperform SVM, as shown in Table 1 for the airplane, car side and leopard categories.

The classifiers do not perform well on the objects, such as the crocodile, dolphin, electric guitar, laptop and scissors. Examples of two images from the dolphin and electric guitar categories are shown in Figure 6. For the first two categories, the animals do not have obvious textures, unlike the Dalmatian and leopard; for the last three categories, the objects do not have distinct repetitive patterns. In other words, the HOG feature and bag-of-visual-words model cannot represent the shape of objects. It has its limitations in these cases.

Figure 6. Examples of images from classes with low performance

Table 1. Object categories with good performance

Object category	Precision (%)	
	SRC	SVM
airplane	94.7	89.3
car side	98.7	94.7
Dalmatian	73.3	73.3
face	76	81.3
leopard	82.7	68
pagoda	76	78.7
stop sign	80	77.3
Windsor chair	78.7	66.7

Figures 7 and 8 give the performance of SRC and SVM on the 25 object categories respectively, with the vocabulary size 100 and different number of training images. When using SRC classification algorithm, performances on the object categories with high precisions do not change much with the number of training images. Even with only 5 training images, we can still get satisfied results on these object categories. This is the same case on the object categories with low precisions, and the increase of number of training images does not lead to improved results. While on the object categories with middle precisions, more training images are helpful for getting better results. For example, performance of the dollar bill class increases from 43.2%, 55% to 66.7% as the number of training images per category increases from 5, 10 to 15.

When using SVM classifiers, for most classes, the performance changes significantly when the number of training images varies from 5 to 15 per class. For example, performance on the airplane category drops more than 10% as the number of training image reduced to 5 images per category.

Figures 9 and 10 give the performance of SRC and SVM, with the vocabulary size 150, 10 and 15 training images per category. These figures show a performance improvement as the

Figure 7. Performance of SRC on 25 object categories, with different number of training images, 100 visual words

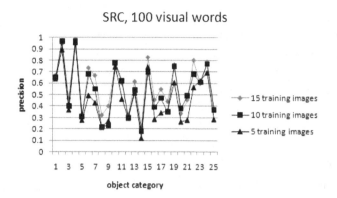

Figure 8. Performance of SVM on 25 object categories, with different number of training images, 100 visual words

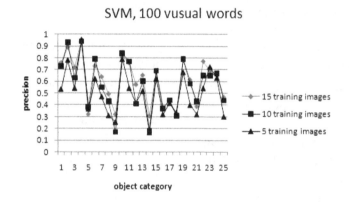

Figure 9. Performance of SRC on 25 object categories, with different number of training images, 150 visual words

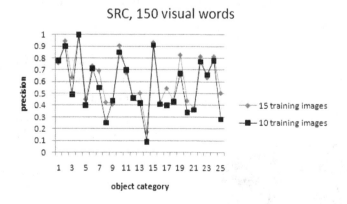

Figure 10. Performance of SVM on 25 object categories, with different number of training images, 150 visual words

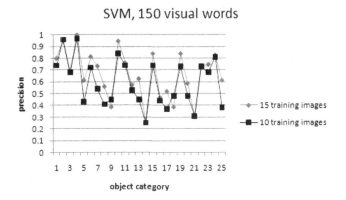

increase of the vocabulary size. The benefit from the increased vocabulary size is that the visual word features become more distinctive. However, using vocabulary of a larger size also means the increasing cost of clustering keypoints, bag-of-visual-words feature extraction, and running time of classification algorithms.

Figure 11 compares the average precision over the 25 object categories between SRC and SVM, under different number of training images per class, with the vocabulary size set to 100 visual words. When the number of training images per class is set to 5, 10, and 15, the average precisions of SRC algorithm are 47.1%, 53.4%, and 57.5% respectively; the average precisions of SVM classifiers are 50.4%, 57.5%, and 60.5% respectively.

If we set the vocabulary size to 150, performances of both of the algorithms are improved. The average precisions of SRC are 55.4% and 62.2%, compared to those of SVM 59.4% and 66.2%, when the number of training images per category is set to 10 and 15 respectively. With different vocabulary sizes and different number of training images, the performance of SRC is steadily slightly lower than SVM, around 3% to 4%.

The experiments demonstrate that performance of spare representation based classification algo-rithm is comparable to SVM classifiers, which are considered as powerful and effective learn-ing machines for many classification problems. One advantage of the sparse representation based algorithm is that it does not need any parameter optimization, and in some cases a few training examples can also give satisfied performance.

Analysis of Experimental Results

The basic assumption of the sparse based image classification is that the training samples from the same category lie on a sub-space. Therefore, we calculate the visual words distribution for each image class and try to find out if images from a single class can be represented by a few visual words for some categories.

Figure 12 shows the appearance of 100 visual words sorted in descending order according to the size of its membership. Figure 13 shows the visual words distributions of several image classes over which good performances have been obtained. The left panel shows some example images. The right panel shows the distribution of the visual words as well as the appearance of 10 most frequently occurred visual words for this image class. Figure 14 shows the visual words distributions of some image classes with low performances.

Figure 11. Average precision of SRC and SVM over 25 object categories, with different number of training images per class, 100 visual words

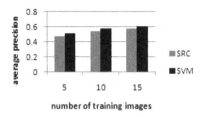

Figure 13 demonstrates that the image features from a single category, such as the airplane, car side, Dalmatian and leopard, have a rather sparse distribution over the 100 visual words. These image features from the same class can be represented by a few visual words. Relative to the high dimensional space spanned by all the visual words, the image features from the same class lie on a low dimensional sub-space. As a result, the assumption of the sparse based algorithm can be satisfied and good performances have been obtained.

We may further analyze the most frequently occurred visual words for these categories. Take the airplane category as an example. The frequently occurred visual words appear to be the horizontal or oblique line segments, which correspond to the edges located in the body or tail of an airplane. For images from the car side category, the most frequently occurred visual word corresponds to the round-shaped car wheels. These visual words can capture the common properties of images from the same category. Furthermore, the experiments demonstrate that the sparse based image classification with bag-of-visual-words representations is robust to a certain degree of background clutter and intra-class variations.

On the other hand, if the distribution of visual words is not sparse, the sparse based algorithm gives a low performance since no sub-space exists for the image features from the same category, such as the image classes shown in Figure 14. Therefore, the main factor affecting the performance is how to select proper features under appropriate granularity so that the image features from a single category lie on a low dimensional sub-space.

Figure 12. The appearance of 100 visual words sorted in descending order according to the size of its membership

Figure 13. The visual words distributions of image classes with good performance

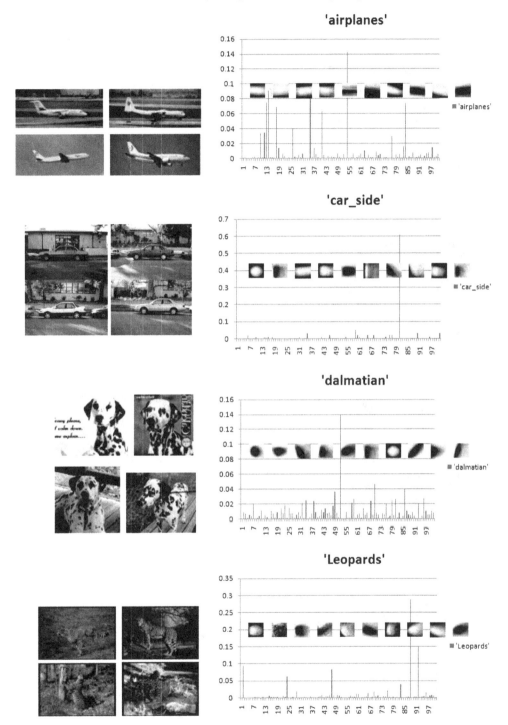

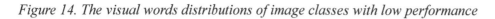

Figure 14. The visual words distributions of image classes with low performance

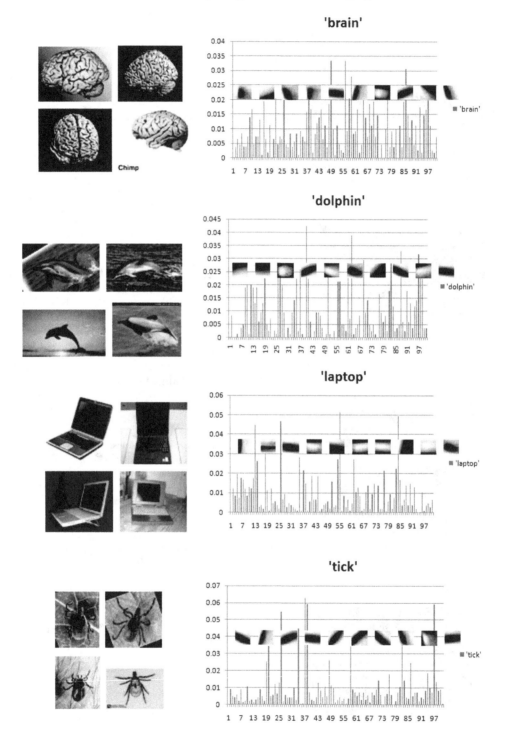

CONCLUSION

A sparse representation based classifier applied to generic image classification is presented in this paper. With image feature chosen to be histogram of visual words frequency, performances between the sparse representation based classifier and SVM are compared, under different visual vocabulary sizes and different number of training images per class. The experimental results show that without the time-consuming parameter optimization procedure, the sparse representation based classifier achieves comparable performance with SVM, only with a slightly decrease around 3% to 4% of average precision over the 25 object categories. The reason why the sparse representation algorithm works on generic image classes is that the keypoint-based features can overcome the problem of image alignment and background clutter. Therefore this method is robust to a certain degree of intra-class variations.

Furthermore, we give some analysis on the basic assumption required by the sparse based algorithm in the image feature space. If the image features from a single category have a sparse distribution over the visual vocabulary, the assumption is satisfied and good performance can be achieved. Otherwise, if there is no sub-space formed by the image features from the same class, the sparse based algorithm gives low performance. What is critical is how to choose appropriate image features so that a low dimensional sub-space exists for the images from a single category in the high dimensional feature space.

ACKNOWLEDGMENT

The work is supported by the National Natural Science Foundation of China under Grant No. 90820305 and the National Basic Research Program (973 Program) of China under Grant No. 2007CB311003.

REFERENCES

Berg, E., & Friedlander, M. (2007). *SPGL1: A solver for large-scale sparse reconstruction.* Retrieved from http://www.cs.ubc.ca/labs/scl/spgl1/

Candes, E., Romberg, J., & Tao, T. (2006). Stable signal recovery from incomplete and inaccurate measurements. *Communications on Pure and Applied Mathematics, 59*(8), 1207–1223. doi:10.1002/cpa.20124

Candes, E., & Tao, T. (2006). Near-optimal signal recovery from random projections: Universal encoding strategies? *IEEE Transactions on Information Theory, 52*(12), 5406–5425. doi:10.1109/TIT.2006.885507

Chang, C., & Lin, C. (2001). *LIBSVM: A library for support vector machines.* Retrieved from http://www.csie.ntu.edu.tw/~cjlin/libsvm/

Chen, S., Donoho, D., & Saunders, M. (2001). Atomic decomposition by basis pursuit. *Society for Industrial and Applied Mathematics Review, 43*(1), 129–159.

Csurka, G., Dance, C., Fan, L., Willamowski, J., & Bray, C. (2004). Visual categorization with bags of keypoints. In *Proceedings of the International Workshop on Statistical Learning of the European Conference on Computer Vision* (pp. 1-22).

Dalal, N., & Triggs, B. (2005). Histograms of oriented gradients for human detection. In. *Proceedings of the IEEE Conference on Computer Vision and Pattern Recognition, 1*, 886–893.

Donoho, D. (2006). For most large underdetermined systems of linear equations the minimal l_1-norm solution is also the sparest solution. *Communications on Pure and Applied Mathematics, 59*(6), 797–829. doi:10.1002/cpa.20132

Fergus, R., Perona, P., & Zisserman, A. (2003). Object class recognition by unsupervised scale-invariant learning. In *Proceedings of the IEEE Conference on Computer Vision and Pattern Recognition* (pp. 264-271).

Gao, S., Tsang, I., Chia, L., & Zhao, P. (2010). Local features are not lonely – Laplacian sparse coding for image classification. In *Proceedings of the IEEE Conference on Computer Vision and Pattern Recognition* (pp. 3555-3561).

Jing, F., Li, M., Zhang, H., & Zhang, B. (2004). An efficient and effective region-based image retrieval framework. *IEEE Transactions on Image Processing, 13*(5), 699–709. doi:10.1109/TIP.2004.826125

Kadir, T., Zisserman, A., & Brady, M. (2004). An affine invariant salient region detector. In T. Pajdla & J. Matas (Eds.), *Proceedings of the 8th European Conference on Computer Vision* (LNCS 3021, pp. 228-242).

Lazebnik, S., Schmid, C., & Ponce, J. (2006). Beyond bags of features: Spatial pyramid matching for recognizing natural scene categories. In *Proceedings of the IEEE Conference on Computer Vision and Pattern Recognition* (pp. 2169-2178).

Li, F., & Perona, P. (2005). A Bayesian hierarchical model for learning natural scene categories. In *Proceedings of the IEEE Conference on Computer Vision and Pattern Recognition* (pp. 524-531).

Lowe, D. (2004). Distinctive image features from scale-invariant keypoints. *International Journal of Computer Vision, 60*(2), 91–110. doi:10.1023/B:VISI.0000029664.99615.94

Mikolajczyk, K., & Schmid, C. (2005). A Performance evaluation of local descriptors. *IEEE Transactions on Pattern Analysis and Machine Intelligence, 27*(10), 1615–1630. doi:10.1109/TPAMI.2005.188

Mikolajczyk, K., Tuytelaars, T., Schmid, C., Zisserman, A., Matas, J., & Schaffalitzky, F. (2005). A comparison of affine region detectors. *International Journal of Computer Vision, 65*(1-2), 43–72. doi:10.1007/s11263-005-3848-x

Sivic, J., & Zisserman, A. (2003). Video Google: A text retrieval approach to object matching in videos. In *Proceedings of the IEEE International Conference on Computer Vision* (pp. 1470-1477).

Wright, J., Yang, A., Ganesh, A., Sastry, S., & Ma, Y. (2009). Robust face recognition via sparse representation. *IEEE Transactions on Pattern Analysis and Machine Intelligence, 31*(2), 210–227. doi:10.1109/TPAMI.2008.79

Yang, J., Jiang, Y., Hauptmann, A., & Ngo, C.-W. (2007). Evaluating bag-of-visual-words representations in scene classification. In *Proceedings of the International Workshop on Multimedia Information Retrieval* (pp. 197-206).

Yang, J., Yu, K., Gong, Y., & Huang, T. (2009). Linear spatial pyramid matching using sparse coding for image classification. In *Proceedings of the IEEE Conference on Computer Vision and Pattern Recognition* (pp. 1794-1801).

Zhang, H., Berg, A., Maire, M., & Malik, J. (2006). SVM-KNN: Discriminative nearest neighbor classification for visual category recognition. In *Proceedings of the IEEE Conference on Computer Vision and Pattern Recognition* (pp. 2126-2136).

Zhang, J., Marszalek, M., Lazebnik, S., & Schmid, C. (2007). Local features and kernels for classification of texture and object categories: A comprehensive study. *International Journal of Computer Vision, 73*(2), 213–238. doi:10.1007/s11263-006-9794-4

This work was previously published in the International Journal of Software Science and Computational Intelligence, Volume 3, Issue 1, edited by Yingxu Wang, pp. 1-15, copyright 2011 by IGI Publishing (an imprint of IGI Global).

Chapter 3
Quotient Space–Based Boundary Condition for Particle Swarm Optimization Algorithm

Yuhong Chi
Tsinghua University, China

Langfan Jiang
PLA, China

Fuchun Sun
Tsinghua University, China

Chunyang Yu
Northeastern University, China

Chunli Chen
China University of Geosciences, China

ABSTRACT

To control particles to fly inside the limited search space and deal with the problems of slow search speed and premature convergence of particle swarm optimization algorithm, this paper applies the theory of topology, and proposed a quotient space-based boundary condition named QsaBC by using the properties of quotient space and homeomorphism. In QsaBC, Search space-zoomed factor and Attractor are introduced according to the dynamic behavior and stability of particles, which not only reduce the subjective interference and enforce the capability of global search, but also enhance the power of local search and escaping from an inferior local optimum. Four CEC'2008 benchmark functions are selected to evaluate the performance of QsaBC. Comparative experiments show that QsaBC can achieve the satisfactory optimization solution with fast convergence speed. Furthermore, QsaBC is more effective with errant particles, and has easier calculation and better robustness than other methods.

INTRODUCTION

Particle swarm optimization (PSO) (Bratton & Kennedy, 2007) proposed by Kennedy and Eberhart (1995) is an evolutionary algorithm, based on social behaviors of organisms of fish schooling and bird flocking. In PSO, particles are free to fly inside the defined D-dimensional space dictated by optimization problems, where it is assumed that global optimum is inside, so that particles moving outside search space can't find global optimum. So that it is necessary to control

DOI: 10.4018/978-1-4666-2651-5.ch003

particles moving inside the limited search space by some way which is called boundary condition.

Though in the canonical PSO method is confessedly that nothing can prevent particles from going outside search space at anytime, and it is usually thought that it is just the behavior of few particles (Kennedy, 2005, 2008), Helwig and Wanka (2008) derived some surprised conclusions and proved that all particles leave search space in the first iteration with overwhelming probability when using uniform velocity initialization and if velocities are initialized to zero, all particles which have a better neighbor than themselves leave search space in the first iteration with overwhelming probability. More details can be found in Helwig and Wanka (2008). Various boundary conditions are proposed to enforce particles to move inside search space, among them, such as velocity-clipping and position-clipping (Eberhart & Shi, 2001) are simple and common boundary conditions widely used in PSO literatures, but velocity-clipping can't prevent particles from flying outside search space. To solve this problem, three kinds of boundary condition walls, namely, Absorbing, Reflecting, and Invisible, are imposed by Robinson and Yahya (2004), and Damping reported to provide robust performance by Huang and Mohan (2005) is a hybrid boundary condition that combines the characteristics offered by the Absorbing and Reflection. As cited in Xu and Yahya (2007), four kinds of walls are summarized and tested, among which the only difference is the way of treating errant particle's velocity. To address the invariant maximum velocity in above methods, the Random Velocity method is introduced by Li, Ren, and Wang (2007), where the upper and lower velocity boundaries keep on altering during the whole evolution. Different with other boundary conditions which keeping particles lying inside search space, the Periodic mode (Zhang, Xie, & Bi, 2004) provides an infinite search space for the flying of particles. Because all of boundary conditions strongly influence particle behavior, which means that they actually strongly influ-

ence the swarm performance, in a word, they are important for PSO, and significant performance differences when varying boundary conditions.

The purpose of this paper is to report an efficient and simple quotient space-based boundary condition for PSO, named QsaBC, by using the advantages of quotient space and homeomorphism, and where the swarm is not bounded by the end points. By analyzing the dynamic behavior and stability of particles, Search space-zoomed factor and Attractor are introduced in QsaBC which deal with the problem of errant particles, at the same time avoid premature convergence and improve search speed of convergence.

THEORY ANALYSIS FOR PSO

Dynamic Behavior of Particles

PSO algorithm can be defined as follows:

Suppose that a swarm consists of P particles moving around in the D-dimensional search space, and D is the number of parameters of the function being optimized. At the beginning process, each particle is randomly located and traverses search space with a random velocity. At each step, its velocity and new position of the ith particle will be updated according to the following two equations:

$$v_{id}(t+1) = \omega \times v_{id}(t) + c_1 \times r_1 \times (p_{id}(t) - x_{id}(t)) + c_2 \times r_2 \times (p_g(t) - x_{id}(t)). \quad (1)$$

$$x_{id}(t+1) = x_{id}(t) + v_{id}(t+1). \quad (2)$$

where $d \in [1, D]$, $i \in [1, P]$; t is current time step, r_1, $r_2 \in [0,1]$ are two separately generated uniformly distributed random number; c_1 and c_2 are acceleration coefficients; ω is inertia weight (Shi & Eberhart, 1998); $x_{id}(t)$ and $v_{id}(t)$ are the position and velocity of particle i at time step t, respectively; p_{id} is personal best position, i.e. the experience of particle i during its own wandering up to the *t*th time step; p_g is best position, if which was found by the entire swarm at time step *t*, it's called global best position, or else, it's called local best position. Each particle improves its cognitive ability step by step and achieves the optimal goal according to personal experience and social experience.

By substitution and collecting terms, Equations (1) and (2) can be collapsed into one:

$$x_{id}(t+1) =$$
$$x_{id}(t) + \omega \times (x_{id}(t) - x_{id}(t-1)) + \phi \times (\rho - x_{id}(t)). \tag{3}$$

where the relation

$v_{id}(t+1) = x_{id}(t+1) - x_{id}(t)$ is used, and let

$\phi = c_1 r_1 + c_2 r_2$, and $\rho = \dfrac{c_1 r_1 p_{id} + c_2 r_2 p_g}{c_1 r_1 + c_2 r_2}$.

From Equation (3), the next position of particle *i* is determined by three components in PSO:

1. **Current Position $x_{id}(t)$:** From which particle *i* moves to the next position $x_{id}(t+1)$. Current position is the memory ability of the movement trajectory of particle *i*, and manifests the dynamic characteristic of PSO algorithm.
2. **Habitual Movement $(x_{id}(t)-x_{id}(t-1))$:** Usually weighted by a value less than 1, which is the memory of particle *i* how it moved on each dimension in the previous step, i.e. the memory of its velocity magnitude and direction. Habitual movement can be thought of as a kind of momentum for the individual to persist doing in the direction it was already going. It is an idiosyncratic force, a tendency for particles to behave differently from their neighbors, to pursue their own goal and makes an important contribution to keep the variety of the swarm.
3. **Social Influence $(\rho-x_{id}(t))$:** It indicates the cognitive ability of particles, and gives the location of relatively best solution and the range of particle's investigation is scaled to

the variance of sources of influence based on the distance between particle and social influence.

It is worth noting that social influence and habitual movement usually contribute conflicting, or at least different for particles. The particle is attracted by social influence to move in the direction of the mean previous best position from its position, the adjustment for social influence, however, habitual movement hold a tendency of the particle to "keep doing it was going". Thus, the particle is not going directly toward its target, but circling around it.

STABILITY ANALYSIS

The method of one-particle and one-dimension was proposed by Ozcan and Mohan (1999) first for theoretical studies in PSO, and it is helpful in our study. And assumed personal best p_i and global best p_g kept constant, denoted by the symbols p and g, and rewriting (3) we can get:

$$x(t+1) = (1 + \omega - \phi) \times x(t) - \omega \times x(t-1) + \phi \times \rho. \tag{4}$$

Usually let $c_1 = c_2 = \lambda > 0$, r_1, $r_2 \sim U(0,1)$, and so the following results can be obtained:

$$E(r_1) = E(r_2) = \frac{1}{2}, \ E(\phi) = \frac{c_1 + c_2}{2} = \lambda, \text{ and}$$
$$E(\phi \times \rho) = \frac{\lambda}{2}(p+g) \text{ is denoted by the symbol } \tau.$$

We apply the expectation operator to both sides of Equation (4), thus, the iteration equation of sequence $\{E[x(t+1)]\}$ is:

$$E[x(t+1)] = \theta \times E[x(t)] - \omega \times E[x(t-1)] + \tau. \tag{5}$$

Figure 1. Examples of quotient construction

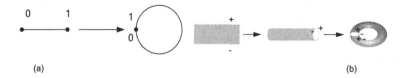

(a)   (b)

where $\theta = 1 + \omega - \lambda$, and it is easy to see Equation (5) has fixed point:

$$E[x]^* = \frac{\tau}{1 - \theta + \omega} = \frac{p + g}{2}. \qquad (6)$$

The corresponding characteristic polynomial of Equation (5) is:

$$P(z) = z^2 - \theta \times z + \omega = 0 \quad (n = 2). \qquad (7)$$

According to Jury Test (1964), the second order linear time invariant discrete system corresponds to Equation (5) is guaranteed to converge to E[x]*, if and only if the follow conditions of θ and ω are satisfied together:

$$\begin{cases} |\omega| < 1 \\ 1 - \theta + \omega > 0 \\ 1 + \theta + \omega > 0. \end{cases} \qquad (8)$$

By substituting $\theta = 1 + \omega - \lambda$ into Equation (8), we can get:

$$\begin{cases} |\omega| < 1 \\ 0 < \lambda < 2(1 + \omega). \end{cases} \qquad (9)$$

When PSO parameters are selected as Equation (9), and p and g are kept constant, they ensure each particle converges to the stable point (p+g)/2.

QUOTIENT SPACE-BASED BOUNDARY CONDITION FOR PSO

Quotient Space

It is well known that one can form a circle from a closed segment by bending the segment around and gluing the ends together, as shown in Figure 1(a), and form a cylindrical pipe from a rectangular by bending the rectangle around and welding two edges together, by further bending the cylinder around and welding the two circular rims together, one obtains a doughnut, or torus, as shown in Figure 1(b). Space obtained from a given space by welding or gluing subsets together are called quotients of the given space. Thus the torus is the quotient space of a rectangle, and the circle is the quotient space of a closed line.

For convenience, the relevant definitions of topology have been reproduced below.

Definition 1 (Quotient Space): Let X be a topological space and R an equivalence relation on X. a set $U \subset X / R$ is called open in the quotient topology if $\pi^{-1}(U)$ is open in X. X/R is called the quotient space of X by R. where $[x] \in X/R$ the equivalence class of $x \in X$, and $\pi: X \to X/R$ the natural mapping, so that $\pi(x) := [x]$.

Definition 2 (Homeomorphism): A bijective map $f: X \to Y$ is called a homeomorphism when both f and f^1 are continuous, that is when $U \subset X$ is open if and only if $f(U) \subset Y$ is. We often use the notation $X \cong Y$ for homeomorphic spaces.

Figure 2. QsaBC for PSO algorithm

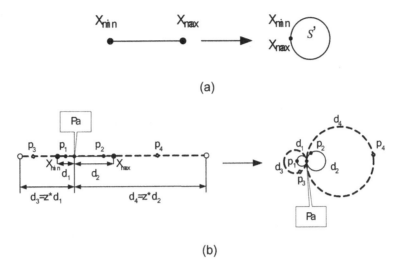

(a)

(b)

Theorem 1: $f : X \rightarrow Y$ is a quotient mapping if only if $f^* : X / R(f) \rightarrow Y$ is a homeomorphism, where $R(f) = \{(x, y) \in X \times X \mid f(x) = f(y)\}$ is an equivalence relation on X.

In PSO algorithm, each dimension of each particle is updated independently from others, and it's position on each dimension is limited by the bound value of the D-dimensional search space $[X_{min}, X_{max}]^D$, that means all particles move in the closed line $[X_{min}, X_{max}]$ on each dimension, and their movement is constrained by two end points X_{min} and X_{max}. If X_{min} and X_{max} are attached together like Figure 1(a), we can obtain a circle which has not the end point, so particles can move freely, as shown in Figure 2(a). This is an inspirer way to solve the problem of boundary condition in PSO.

By linear transformation and normalization, we can get Figure 2(a) from Figure 1(a).

As a simple application of Theorem 1, as shown in Figure 1(a), let $I = [0, 1]$ is a closed unit interval. S^1 is a circle obtained from the closed unit interval $[0, 1]$ by identifying 0 and 1. R is an equivalence relation on I, and $R = \{(x, y) \in I \times I = [0, 1] \times [0, 1] \mid x = y \quad or \quad \{x, y\} = \{0, 1\}\}$.

Consider the map: $f : I \rightarrow S^1$ defined by $t \mapsto f(t) = (\cos 2\pi t, \sin 2\pi t) \in S^1$.

Now since $f(0) = f(1)$; when $t \neq s$ and $\{t, s\} \neq \{0, 1\}$, $f(t) \neq f(s)$, hence $R(f) = \{(t, s) \in I \times I \mid f(t) = f(s)\} = R$.

Obviously, f is continuous surjective mapping, and we can prove that f is the quotient mapping, by Theorem 1, $f^* : I / R(f) \rightarrow S^1$ is a homeomorphism, that is $I / R \cong S^1$. More details can be found in Klaus (1984).

Hence, $[X_{min}, X_{max}]$ and S' are homeomorphic spaces, where $(r \times \cos 2\pi t', r \times \sin 2\pi t') \in S'$,

$$r = \frac{X_{max} - X_{min}}{2\pi},$$
$$t \in [X_{min}, X_{max}],$$
$$t' = \frac{t - X_{min}}{X_{max} - X_{min}},$$

and $f(t') \in S^1$. However the closed line $[X_{min}, X_{max}]$ and the circle S' looks so different, they have many same topological properties, and the optimum and its location are never changed.

QsaBC

Figure 2(b) illustrates operating principle of Qs-aBC for 1-D problem. In Figure 2(b), solid lines are original search space; dotted lines are zoomed space; solid points are particles inside original search space, and hollow points are particles flying outside original search space.

It appears from Figures 1 and 2 that each dimension is updated independently from others. So that QsaBC can be formulated as follows:

$$x'_{id}(t+1) = $$
$$\begin{cases} \mathrm{mod}(x_{id}(t+1) - P_a, (X_{\min} - P_a) \times z) / z + P_a, \\ \qquad\qquad\qquad\qquad x_{id}(t+1) < X_{\min} \\ \mathrm{mod}(x_{id}(t+1) - P_a, (X_{\max} - P_a) \times z) / z + P_a, \\ \qquad\qquad\qquad\qquad x_{id}(t+1) > X_{\max} \end{cases}$$
$$(10)$$

Where mod(x,y) is modulus function which is based on quotient space model and particularly designed to handle the boundary condition of PSO, and it is simple and easy to calculate. Furthermore, using topology invariants between the close line $[X_{\min}, X_{\max}]$ and the circle S, and analysis of the dynamic behavior and stability of particles, we introduce other important quantities in QsaBC, which are Search space-zoomed factor z and Attractor P_a, to improve the performance of PSO, more details are given as two following sections.

• **Search Space-Zoomed Factor:** As shown in Figure 2(b), if Search space-zoomed factor $z>1$, then original search space is magnified first and then reduced, else if $z<1$, original search space is reduce first and then magnified. When original search space is magnified, some particles going outside are included and become valid again, and then by reducing zoomed space and processing of quotient, all particles are controlled inside original search space. This process is benefit to keep the position

relation of the swarm and assure the global exploration where the algorithm searches widely around the space in order to identify optimal region.

Let Search space-zoomed factor $z=k\times\mathrm{rand}()$, where rand()$\in$ (0, 1) is a random number, k is a positive integer and selected by testing the optimized problem and the domain movement of the swarm.

• **Attractor:** Note that the centre of Search space-zoomed in QsaBC is not the geometric centre of original search space, but a new centre of social influence, called Attractor, which is a weighted average of personal best position and global best position. By the action of Attractor P_a, more particles are focused on the interesting region around the centre of social influence, thus which greatly improves convergence speed, and enforces local exploitation of PSO. In QsaBC the same Attractor for the swarm is employed, which can reduce random disturb.

In PSO, because personal best is equal to global best for the global-best particle, and from Equation (1), it is not affected by any else particles. This means that the global-best particle is stagnant and not benefit to improvement of the swarm. And the particle with personal best is equal to global best is also reduced search ability, hence, such a particle is always disturbed by Attractor P_a if it is flying outside original search space in QsaBC, and let $P_a=p_g-r\times b$, where $r=l\times(X_{\max}-X_{\min})/P$, $l>0$, b is a generated uniformly distributed random number, and P is population size. For other else particles, based on results of stability analysis, we set Attractor is a weighted average of personal best particle and global best particle. It's easy to see that Attractor not only improves the power of local search, but also keeps the diversity of the swarm.

Updating the position of the particle which flies outside original search space is the key step of QsaBC, which is controlled by Equation (10).

EXPERIMENTAL PROCEDURE

Experimental Setup

To evaluate the performance of the proposed QsaBC, some experiments have been performed on four CEC'2008 benchmark functions as cited in Tang et al. (2007). The formal definitions of the test functions are summarized in Table 1, where functions f_1 and f_4 are unimodal functions, and functions f_2 and f_3 are multimodal functions. For all considered functions z_i is given by $z=x-o$, where $x=[x_1,\ldots,x_D]$ is the candidate solution, and $o=[o_1,\ldots,o_D]$ is the shifted global optimum, in other words, the global optima of classical functions are shifted to a value $x^*=o$ different than zero and the function values of the global optima $f(x^*)$ are non-zero, so that the shifted global optimum may be located anyplace in search space, hence it is benefit to prevent exploitation of symmetry of search space and of the typical zero value associated with the global optimum. This shows that the CEC'2008 test functions are more universal and

difficult to be optimized than classical benchmark functions. The source codes for these functions are consulted from http://www.ntu.edu.sg/home/EPNSugan/ in this work. Functions are tested for two dimensions D=20 and D=100.

In this section, two comparison experiments have been used to test QsaBC. First, we compare QsaBC with four different boundary conditions on standard PSO. The other is to report the different performance between QsaBC and other boundary conditions used in three variant PSOs (Chen, Xin, & Peng, 2009; Jin, Joshua, & Lu, 2008; Liang, Qin, & Baskar, 2006), which were published on different international journals. For fair comparison, the following parameters are used in all cases: 1) population size is set to 15; 2) inertia weight is decreased linearly form 0.9 to 0.1; 3) $c_1=c_2=2$; 4) the acceptable error is set at 10^{-14}; 5) Search space-zoomed factor $z=100\times rand()$; 6) maximum number of generations is 10000; 7) Each version of each approach is run 50 times for each test function.

No. 1 On Standard PSO

The value $\log(f(x)-f(x^*))$ versus the number of iterations for D=20 and D=100 is plotted in Figure 3 and Figure 4, respectively, which illustrate the

Table 1. Four CEC'2008 benchmark functions employed in this study

Name	Function	Bounds	Global Optimum	
Shifted Sphere	$f_1(x) = \sum\limits_{i=1}^{D} z_i^2 + bias_1$	$[-100,100]^D$	$x^*=o$	$f_1(x^*) = bias_1 = -450$
Shifted Griewank	$f_2(x) = \dfrac{1}{4000}\sum\limits_{i=1}^{D} z_i^2 - \prod\limits_{i=1}^{D} \cos(\dfrac{z_i}{\sqrt{i}}) + 1 + bias_2$	$[-600,600]^D$	$x^*=o$	$f_2(x^*) = bias_2 = -180$
Shifted Rastrigin	$f_3(x) = \sum\limits_{i=1}^{D}(z_i^2 - 10\cos(2\pi z_i) + 10) + bias_3$	$[-5,5]^D$	$x^*=o$	$f_3(x^*) = bias_3 = -330$
Shifted Rosenbrock	$f_4(x) = \sum\limits_{i=1}^{D-1}(100(z_{i+1} - z_i^2)^2 + (z_i - 1)^2) + bias_4$	$[-100,100]^D$	$x^*=o$	$f_4(x^*) = bias_4 = 390$

comparison between QsaBC and four other boundary conditions on standard PSO, named Random Velocity, Damping, Invisible, and Periodic-mode, respectively. The statistical experimental results of 50 independent runs for $D=20$ and $D=100$ are summarized in Table 2 and Table 3, respectively.

From Figure 3 and Figure 4, it can be clearly observed that the results of QsaBC and four comparative boundary conditions are affected by increase of function dimension, i.e. the results obtained by these boundary conditions are deteriorated when function dimension increases, such as Damping and Invisible have competitive performance with QsaBC for $D=20$, but for test functions with $D=100$ their performance turn greatly worse than that of QsaBC, especially, Invisible is close to Random Velocity and Periodic-mode. Nevertheless, QsaBC has the fastest convergence and the best optima. This admirable performance is proved again in Tables 2 and 3.

It can be seen from Tables 2 and 3, QsaBc, Damping, and Invisible can obtain the similar performance for the simple unimodal function f_1 with low dimension, but for the same function f_1

with high dimension their performance are obviously different. QsaBC is the best, and Invisible is the worst. The interesting thing is for other three complex functions, whether $D=20$ or $D=100$, Damping is a little lower than QsaBC. Random Velocity and Periodic-mode are easy to trapped in local optimum, but they are not obviously worse than Invisible when function dimension increase.

To sum up the above arguments, the results of experiment Number 1 show that QsaBC has high convergence speed and good exploring capability to find the global minima. Moreover, QsaBC is more robust and consistent in all cases than other contrastive boundary conditions.

No. 2 on Variant PSOs

In this group, we choose three experienced variant PSOs, called DEPSO, LAPSO, and CLPSO, respectively. In DEPSO (Chen, Xin, & Peng, 2009), if certain components exceed search bound, set them to the bound and force corresponding velocity components to be zero; in LAPSO (Jin, Joshua, & Lu, 2008), some particles leaving search

Figure 3. Optimization Curves for Standard PSO with D=20

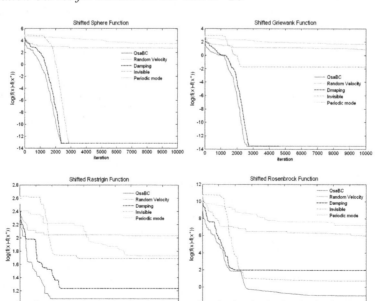

Figure 4. Optimization Curves for Standard PSO with D=100

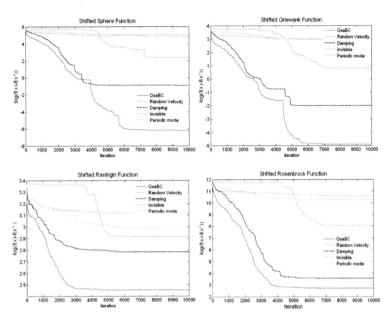

Table 2. Mean and SD Values of f(x)-f(x*) on Standard PSO with D=20

F		QsaBC	Damping	Invisible	Random	Periodic
f_1	Mean	2.28E-14	4.56E-14	3.42E-14	6.93E+2	1.70E+3
	Std	2.79E-14	3.42E-14	2.79E-14	2.17E+2	9.46E+2
f_2	Mean	0.018	0.021	0.024	9.549	16.39
	Std	1.42E-2	1.98E-2	2.05E-2	5.184	13.74
f_3	Mean	15.52	27.03	43.41	1.00E+2	75.14
	Std	1.24E-4	4.68E-2	2.76E+2	2.11E+4	1.68E+4
f_4	Mean	27.76	74.15	38.36	4.35E+4	2.11E+7
	Std	48.91	1.20E+2	65.48	3.09E+6	2.56E+7

Table 3. Mean and SD Values of f(x)-f(x*) on Standard PSO with D=100

F		QsaBC	Damping	Invisible	Random	Periodic
f_1	Mean	5.52E-05	0.016	2.28E+2	8.58E+4	9.82E+4
	Std	1.24E-4	4.68E-2	2.76E+2	2.11E+4	1.68E+4
f_2	Mean	3.37E-2	1.70E-1	4.131	6.98E+2	8.92E+2
	Std	5.64E-2	2.77E-1	4.572	1.10E+2	91.94
f_3	Mean	2.90E+2	4.43E+2	9.70E+2	1.33E+3	8.38E+2
	Std	64.03	63.80	94.78	69.45	1.45E+2
f_4	Mean	4.51E+2	9.21E+2	2.11E+8	3.67E+10	1.56E+10
	Std	3.22E+2	6.03E+2	3.85E+8	9.57E+9	3.06E+9

Figure 5. Optimization curves for variant psos with D=30

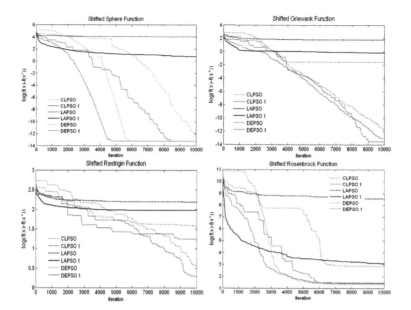

space are limited to random place between X_{min} and X_{max}, not the exactly boundary; and in CLPSO (Liang, Qin, & Baskar, 2006), Invisible boundary condition is employed.

To test the performance of QsaBC on the above different variant PSOs, we replaced their original boundary conditions by QsaBC, and named DEPSO 1, LAPSO 1 and, CLPSO 1, respectively. The value $\log(f(x)-f(x^*))$ versus the number of iterations for $D=30$ is plotted in Figure 5, which illustrates the different performance between QsaBC and other boundary conditions on variant

PSOs. The mean and SD values of 50 independent runs for $D=30$ are summarized in Table 4.

From Figure 5 and Table 4, we can see the comparative algorithms with QsaBC converge obviously faster, and achieve better performance than the corresponding original algorithms. Especially, for DEPSO and LAPSO, the improvement of performance is significant, because the performance difference between the original algorithm and the comparative one is over 10^5 for several cases.

Table 4. Mean and SD Values of f(x)-f(x) on Variant PSOs with D=30*

F		CLPSO	CLPSO 1	LAPSO	LAPSO 1	DEPSO	DEPSO 1
f_1	Mean	5.7E-14	5.7E-14	1.24E+4	5.241	39.69	5.7E-14
	Std	1.26E-29	1.26E-29	2.79E+3	5.423	1.19E+2	1.26E-29
f_2	Mean	6.51E-11	1.78E-11	93.30	0.951	6.77E-2	4.67E-3
	Std	1.69E-10	5.10E-11	40.09	1.38E-1	1.83E-1	7.50E-3
f_3	Mean	4.116	1.687	1.47E+2	72.38	35.94	25.65
	Std	1.779	0.829	17.53	10.68	10.20	7.111
f_4	Mean	37.89	24.93	4.70E+8	1.07E+3	1.13E+6	70.62
	Std	19.08	2.634	4.399E+8	1.10E+3	3.40E+6	38.71

In conclusion, whether standard PSO or variant PSOs, all of boundary conditions strongly influence the swarm behavior, and actually strongly influence the algorithm performance, hence they are important and have significant performance differences. The results obtained in this study proved that QsaBc significantly surpasses the other comparative methods on all selected test functions with different dimensions for convergence and stability.

CONCLUSION

We propose a novel quotient space-based boundary condition for PSO, which is relatively simple and easy to implement. Four CEC'2008 benchmark functions were employed to evaluate the performance of QsaBC, and the results show that QsaBC is a useful method to deal with boundary condition, and explores solution space more effectively. The solution stability and quality of QsaBC for PSO are better than other comparative methods. Moreover, QsaBC converges to the global minima with faster speed. As for the future work along this line, the authors will strive to focus on the theory of PSO.

ACKNOWLEDGMENT

This work was supported by the National Science Fund for Distinguished Young Scholars (Grant No: 60625304), the National Key Project for Basic Research of China (Grant No: G2009CB724002, G2007CB311003), and the Tsinghua National Laboratory for Information Science and Technology (TNList) Cross-discipline Foundation. The authors are very grateful to Prof. Chen Jie and Dr. Xin Bin for the source code of their DEPSO.

REFERENCES

Bratton, D., & Kennedy, J. (2007). Defining a standard for particle swarm optimization. In *Proceedings of the IEEE Swarm Intelligence Symposium* (pp. 120-127). Washington, DC: IEEE Computer Society.

Chen, J., Xin, B., & Peng, Z. (2009). Statistical learning makes the hybridization of particle swarm and differential evolution more efficient--a novel hybrid optimizer. *Science in China Series F: Information Sciences, 52*(7), 1278–1282. doi:10.1007/s11432-009-0119-4

Eberhart, R. C., & Shi, Y. H. (2001). Particle swarm optimization: Developments, applications, and resources. In *Proceedings of the IEEE International Conference on Evolutionary Computation 1*, (Vol. 1, pp. 81-86). Washington, DC: IEEE Computer Society.

Helwig, S., & Wanka, R. (2008). Theoretical analysis of initial particle swarm behavior. In G. Rudolph, T. Jansen, S. Lucas, C. Poloni, & N. Beume (Eds.), *Proceedings of the 10th International Conference on Parallel Problem Solving from Nature* (LNCS 5199, pp. 889-898).

Huang, T., & Mohan, A. S. (2005). A hybrid boundary condition for robust particle swarm optimization. *IEEE Antennas and Wireless Propagation Letters, 4*, 112–117. doi:10.1109/LAWP.2005.846166

Jin, Y., Joshua, K., & Lu, H. (2008). The landscape adaptive particle swarm optimizer. *Application Soft Computing, 8*(1), 295–304. doi:10.1016/j.asoc.2007.01.009

Jury, E. I. (1964). *Theory and application of the z-transform method.* New York, NY: John Wiley & Sons.

Kennedy, J. (2005). Why does it need velocity? In *Proceedings of the IEEE Swarm Intelligence Symposium* (pp. 38-44). Washington, DC: IEEE Computer Society.

Kennedy, J. (2008). How it works: Collaborative trial and error. *International Journal of Computational Intelligence Research, 4*(2), 71–78. doi:10.5019/j.ijcir.2008.127

Kennedy, J., & Eberhart, R. C. (1995). Particle swarm optimization. In []. Washington, DC: IEEE Computer Society.]. *Proceedings of the IEEE International Conference on Neural Networks, 4*, 1942–1948. doi:10.1109/ICNN.1995.488968

Klaus, J. (1984). *Topology*. New York, NY: Springer.

Li, J., Ren, B., & Wang, C. (2007). A random velocity boundary condition for robust particle swarm optimization. In K. Li, G. W. Irwin, M. Fei, & S. Ma (Eds.), *Proceedings of the Life System Modeling and Simulation International Conference on Bio-Inspired Computational Intelligence and Applications* (LNCS 4688, pp. 92-99).

Liang, J., Qin, A., & Baskar, S. (2006). Comprehensive learning Particle swarm optimizer for global optimization of multimodal functions. *IEEE Transactions on Evolutionary Computation, 10*(3), 81–295. doi:10.1109/TEVC.2005.857610

Ozcan, E., & Mohan, C. (1999). Particle swarm optimization: Surfing the waves. In *Proceedings of the IEEE International Congress on Evolutionary Computation* (pp. 1939-1944). Washington, DC: IEEE Computer Society.

Robinson, J., & Yahya, R. (2004). Particle swarm optimization in electromagnetic. *IEEE Transactions on Antennas and Propagation, 52*(2), 397–407. doi:10.1109/TAP.2004.823969

Shi, Y. H., & Eberhart, R. C. (1998). A modified particle swarm optimizer. In *Proceedings of the IEEE International Congress on Evolutionary Computation* (pp. 69-73). Washington, DC: IEEE Computer Society.

Tang, K., Yao, X., Suganthan, P. N., MacNish, C., Chen, Y. P., Chen, C. M., et al. (2007). *Benchmark functions for the CEC'2008 special session and competition on large scale global optimization* (Tech. Rep. No. NCL-TR-2007012). Hefei, China: University of Science and Technology of China.

Xu, S., & Yahya, R. (2007). Boundary conditions in particle swarm optimization revisited. *IEEE Transactions on Antennas and Propagation, 55*(3), 760–765. doi:10.1109/TAP.2007.891562

Zhang, W. J., Xie, X. F., & Bi, D. C. (2004). Handling boundary constraints for numerical optimization by particle swarm flying in periodic search space. In []. Washington, DC: IEEE Computer Society.]. *Proceedings of the IEEE International Congress on Evolutionary Computation, 2*, 2307–2311.

This work was previously published in the International Journal of Software Science and Computational Intelligence, Volume 3, Issue 1, edited by Yingxu Wang, pp. 78-89, copyright 2011 by IGI Publishing (an imprint of IGI Global).

Chapter 4
Medical Image Classification Using an Optimal Feature Extraction Algorithm and a Supervised Classifier Technique

Ahmed Kharrat
University of Sfax, Tunisia

Mohamed Ben Messaoud
University of Sfax, Tunisia

Karim Gasmi
University of Sfax, Tunisia

Nacéra Benamrane
USTO Oran, Algeria

Mohamed Abid
University of Sfax, Tunisia

ABSTRACT

A new approach for automated diagnosis and classification of Magnetic Resonance (MR) human brain images is proposed. The proposed method uses Wavelets Transform (WT) as input module to Genetic Algorithm (GA) and Support Vector Machine (SVM). It segregates MR brain images into normal and abnormal. This contribution employs genetic algorithm for feature selection which requires much lighter computational burden in comparison with Sequential Floating Backward Selection (SFBS) and Sequential Floating Forward Selection (SFFS) methods. A percentage reduction rate of 88.63% is achieved. An excellent classification rate of 100% could be achieved using the support vector machine. The observed results are significantly better than the results reported in a previous research work employing Wavelet Transform and Support Vector Machine.

1. INTRODUCTION

Magnetic resonance (MR) imaging is currently an indispensable diagnostic imaging technique in the study of the human brain (Neeraj et al., 2010). It's a non-invasive technique that provides fairly good contrast resolution for different tissues and generates an extensive information pool about the condition of the brain. Such information has dramatically improved the quality of brain pathology diagnosis and treatment. However this big amount of data makes manual interpretation impossible

DOI: 10.4018/978-1-4666-2651-5.ch004

and necessitates the development of automated image analysis tools. Computing technologies and systems may be classifed into the categories of imperative, autonomic, and cognitive from the bottom up according to theories of cognitive informatics (Wang, 2009).

There is a variety of automated diagnostic tools that are developed by applying sophisticated signal/image processing techniques utilizing transforms and, may be, subsequently applying some computational intelligent techniques. In one possible methodology, the process of automatic segregation of normal/abnormal subjects, based on brain MRIs, is illustrated as a three-step process: feature extraction, feature selection and nonlinear classification.

To extract features from the MR brain images several image analysis methods are used: e.g. Gabor filters, Independent Component Analysis (ICA) (Moritz et al., 2000), techniques employing statistical feature extraction (like mean, median, mode, quartiles, standard deviation, kurtosis, skewness, etc.) (Begg et al., 2005), Fourier Transform (FT) based techniques (Bracewell, 1999), Wavelet Transform (WT) based techniques (Mallat, 89; Kharrat et al., 2009), etc. while Fourier Transform provides only frequency analysis of signals, Wavelet Transforms provide time-frequency analysis, which makes it a useful tool for time-space-frequency analysis and particularly for pattern recognition.

We use Genetic Algorithm (GA) to find minimum features subset giving optimum discrimination between extracted features. GA proves to be the most efficient compared with classical algorithms (Siedlecki et al., 1989) including sequential forward selection (SFS), sequential backward selection (SBS), sequential floating forward selection (SFFS) and sequential floating backward selection (SFBS).

We apply machine learning algorithms to obtain the classification of images under two categories, either normal or abnormal (Chaplot et al., 2006; El-Dahsan et al., 2009; Zacharaki et al., 2009). Support Vector Machines (SVMs) are widely used for classification tasks due to their appealing generalization properties and their computational efficiency.

The rest of the paper is organised as follows. Section 2 presents the Wavelet transform for feature extraction. Section 3 is devoted for feature selection employed for Genetic Algorithm. Image Classification is presented in Section 4. The performance evaluation, the feasibility and superiority of the proposed approach is conducted in Section 5. Finally, the section 6 presents our conclusions.

2. FEATURE EXTRACTION USING WAVELET TRANSFORM

For the feature extraction there is a wide variety of multi-resolution approaches mainly Fourier transform (FT) and wavelet transform (WT). Wavelets are mathematical tools for analysis of complex datasets. These mathematical functions decompose data into different frequency components and then study each component with a resolution matched to its scale. Compared with Fourier transform, wavelet transform seems as an efficient tool in many ways. The Fourier Transform suffers from the limitation that the provided image representation is based only on its frequency content and is not localized in time. Another problem is that the Fourier Transform cannot provide time evolving effects of frequencies in non stationary signals whereas wavelet transform functions provides a hierarchy of scales ranging from the coarsest scale in stationary or in non-stationary signals. Hence wavelet transform has received much attention as a promising tool for feature extraction from images because it can represent an image at various resolutions and because there is a wide range of choices for the wavelet functions.

The mother wavelet is the basis of a wavelet transform. As the pixel intensity values vary smoothly, we choose Daubechies-2 (Mallat, 1989; Kharrat et al., 2009) for efficient representation of smoothly changing signals. Although Daubechies-2 is expensive to compute, it is better than Haar wavelet and can render excellent classification accuracy. Daubechies-2 level 1 wavelet approximation coefficient of the MR brain images are extracted and used as feature vector for optimisation.

The extraction of a variety of 44 features is performed by wavelet transform due to its multi-resolution representation. In frequency and spatial domains, both mean and range of each measure over the four offset angles are used as features:

- **Frequency Domain Includes:** Angular second moment, Contrast, inverse difference moment, sum average, sum entropy, Entropy, Difference entropy, Cluster Prominence, Cluster Shade, Dissimilarity, Energy, Homogeneity and Inverse difference normalized (Haralick et al., 1973; Michael, 1994; Dhawale et al., 2007).
- **Spatial Domain Includes:** Correlation, Variance, sum variance, Difference variance, information measure of correlation I, information measure of correlation II, maximal correlation coefficient, Correlation mat and Maximum probability (Haralick et al., 1973; Kalpalatha et al., 2009).

3. FEATURE SELECTION ALGORITHMS

3.1. Selection Problem

Feature selection refers to algorithms that output a subset of the input feature set. Y represents the original set of features and X represents the selected subset that is $X \subseteq Y$. Feature selection criterion are of crucial importance. They divide feature selection methods into two categories: the filter method and the wrapper one (Kohavi et al., 1997). Whereas the wrapper method uses classification accuracy as feature selection criteria; the filter method employs various measurements as shown in Figure 1.

Despite the rapidity of the filter approach, it does not improve the performance of the classification stage. In our paper we use the wrapper method.

3.2. Overview of Feature Selection Algorithms

Feature selection algorithms are divided into two main categories: artificial neural networks (ANN), and statistical pattern recognition (SPR) techniques giving the optimal solution or suboptimal feature set. In the suboptimal methods, one can maintain a population of subsets or store a single "current" feature subset and make modifications to it. Also algorithms may be deterministic, producing the same subset on a given problem, or stochastic having a random element to produce different subsets on every run. The Figure 2 shows the tree of some representative feature selection algorithms.

3.2.1. Suboptimal Method

These methods are not guaranteed to produce the optimal result as they don't examine all possible subsets. They include deterministic, Single-Solution Methods and deterministic, stochastic Multiple-Solution Methods.

3.2.1.1. Deterministic, Single-Solution Methods

They are the most commonly used methods for performing selection. Being referred to as sequential method, deterministic single solution method start with a single solution and iteratively add or

Figure 1. Feature selection methods (a) Filter approach for feature selection (b) Wrapper approach for feature selection

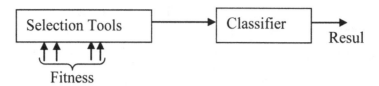

(a) Filter approach for feature selection

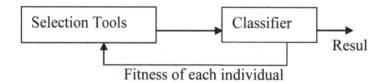

(b) Wrapper approach for feature selection

remove features until some termination criterion is met. They are split into those that start with the full set and delete features. Kittler (1978) compares these algorithms with the optimal branch-and-bound algorithm by applying a synthetic two-class Gaussian data set. Pudil et al. (1994) modify Kittler's comparative study by introducing sequential floating forward selection (SFFS) and sequential floating backward selection (SFBS).

3.2.1.2. Deterministic, Multiple-Solution Methods

They are referred to as "feature selection lattice" since they treat the space of subsets as a graph. Siedlecki and Sklansky (1989) have discussed the performance of "beam search" and a best-first search in the space of feature subsets and induced that both methods maintain a queue of possible solutions.

Figure 2. Categories of feature selection algorithms

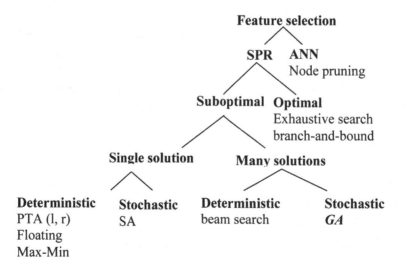

3.2.1.3. Stochastic, Multiple-Solution Methods

Among Stochastic, Multiple-Solution Methods, we can use the genetic algorithm. GA is an evolutionary method inspired by the natural process of evolutional. It allows a randomised search guided by a certain fitness measure. A feature subset is identified by a particular binary string of length n, with a zero or one in position i denoting the absence or presence of feature i in the set. In each iteration of the algorithm (generation), a fixed number (population) of possible solutions (chromosomes) is generated by means of applying certain "genetic" operators in a stochastic process guided by a fitness measure. Each chromosome is evaluated to determine its "fitness". New chromosomes are created from old chromosomes by the processes of recombination, crossover and mutation which represent the most important genetic operators. Siedlecki and Sklansky (1989) introduced the use of genetic algorithms (GA) for feature selection.

3.2.2. Optimal Methods

Among optimal method brand-and-bound (BB) feature selection algorithm. Narendra and Fukunaga (1977) introduced this algorithm to find the optimal subset of features much more quickly than exhaustive search. Yu and Yuan (1993) modified Narendra and Fukunaga's branch and bound algorithm and introduced BAB+. They showed that BAB+ outperforms the original algorithm both analytically and experimentally. Their modification essentially recognizes all "string-structure subtrees".

3.3. Feature Selection Via Genetic Algorithm

Genetic algorithms are stochastic global adaptive search techniques based on the mechanisms of natural selection. GAs comprises a subset of Darwinian evolution-based optimisation techniques focusing on the application of selection, mutation, and recombination to a population of competing problem solutions. Recently, GAs have been recognized as parallel, iterative optimizers and efficient techniques to solve optimization problems (Huang et al., 2006), including many pattern recognition and classification tasks. Compared with other optimization techniques, GAs start with a random initial population containing a number of chromosomes where each one represents a solution of the problem which performance is evaluated by a fitness function (1). They operate in cycles called generations; the population undergoes reproduction in a number of iterations.

$$fitness = W_A \times Accuracy + W_{nb} \times \frac{1}{N} \qquad (1)$$

where W_A is the weight of accuracy and W_{nb} is the weight of N feature participated in classification where $N \neq 0$.

The GA maintains a population of competing feature transformation matrices. To evaluate each matrix in this population, the input patterns are multiplied by the matrix, producing a set of transformed patterns which are then sent to a classifier. The classifier typically divides the patterns into a training set, used to train the classifier, and a testing set, used to evaluate classification accuracy. The accuracy obtained is then returned to the GA as a measure of the quality of the transformation matrix used to obtain the set of transformed patterns. Using this information, the GA searches for a transformation that minimizes the dimensionality of the transformed patterns, while maximizing classification accuracy.

Basically, GA consists of three main stages: Selection, Crossover and Mutation. At each step, the Genetic algorithm selects individuals from the current population to be parents and uses them to produce the children for the next generation. The parents who are subject to genetic operators produce offspring. The offspring which may be better than their parents are inserted into the population. Candidate solutions are usually represented as strings of fixed length, called chromosomes. A fitness or objective function is used to reflect the goodness of each member of the population and to measure the fitness of a chromosome. Chromosomes of low fitness are eliminated and the ones of high fitness are kept and moved to the next generation. The application of these three basic operations is repeated for many generations and finally stops when reaching individuals that represent the optimum solution to the problem.

GA can be applied to the tuning of brain MRIs in clinical medicines to ensure the selection of optimal feature set. The block diagram for the entire system is given in Figure 3.

The goal of GA System is to find a subset of size r among d variables ($r<<d$), which optimizes the performance of the classifier.

4. SUPPORT VECTOR MACHINE FOR CLASSIFICATION

4.1. Review of Support Vector Machine Learning

A support vector machine, introduced by Vapnik, is a supervised, multivariate classification method that takes as input labeled data from two classes and outputs a model file for classifying new unlabeled/labeled data into one of two classes. The method has previously been applied to neuroimaging data (Chaplot et al., 2006; El-Dahshan et al., 2009; Zacharaki et al., 2009; Fan et al., 2005). It yields successful classification results mainly making binary classification and solving linear and non linear classification problems. The image data doesn't need to satisfy the assumptions of random Gaussian field theory so that image smoothing is unnecessary. The use of SVM, involves two basic steps namely training and testing. Training an SVM involves feeding known data to the SVM, to form a finite training set. The training set allows SVM to get its intelligence to classify unknown data. SVMs are related to other multivariate methods such as canonical variate analysis, a method successfully applied to fatty acid images of patients with Alzheimer's disease (Magnin et al., 2009). SVM is based on the structural risk minimization principle from the statistical learning theory. It is applied basically for the binary classification and then extended to the multiclass case (Yan, 2007). Suppose we have a training set composed of N samples $X = \{X_i\}_{i \leq N}$, $X_i \in \Re^n$. Let scalar y denote its class label that is, $y = \pm 1$. Let $\{(x_i, y_i), i = 1, 2, ..., l\}$ denote a given set of l training samples.

4.1.1. Linear Separation

It is the simplest case where the input patterns are linearly separated by a hyper-plane defined in (2),

$$F(x) = WT\ x + b = 0 \tag{2}$$

where W is an adjustable weight vector, and b is the bias term. For each training example x_i the $f(x) \geq 0$ for $y_i = +1$ and $f(x) \leq 0$ for $y_i = -1$. If y is "1", it means that the input example is normal. If y is "-1", the input example is abnormal. In Figure 2, the margin between two hyper-planes H_1:

Figure 3. Block diagram of the entire system

$W^T x_1 + b = 1$ and H_2: $W^T x_1 + b = -1$ is $\dfrac{2}{\|w\|}$, and the hyper-plane that maximizes the margin is the optimal separating hyper-plane. Thus, the optimization is now a convex quadratic programming problem.

4.1.2. Non Linear Separation

It is the case in which the linear hyper-plane could not be found to separate data even with the use of relaxation variable. It uses a non-linear operator $\Phi(.)$ to map the input pattern x into higher-dimensional space. The non-linear classifier so obtained is defined as in (3),

$$F(x) = WT\ \Phi(x) + b \qquad (3)$$

Which is linear in terms of the transformed data $\Phi(x)$ but non linear in terms of the original data x. Following non-linear transformation, the parameters of the decision function *f(x)* are determined by the following minimization criteria,

$$MinJ(W, \xi) = \frac{1}{2}\|W\|^2 + C\sum \xi_I \qquad (4)$$

Subject to

$$y_i(W^T \Phi(x_i) + b) \geq 1 - \xi_i, \qquad (5)$$

4.2. Support Vector Machine Kernel Functions

The kernel function in an SVM has an important role that consists in implicitly mapping the input vector (through an inner product) onto a high-dimensional feature space. It aims at controlling the empirical risk and classification capacity in order to maximize the margin between the classes and to minimize the true costs. When choosing a kernel function, it is necessary to check whether the set is linearly or non-linearly separable. When the set is linearly separable, $K(Xi,X)$ is kernel function and means inner product $\langle X_i, X \rangle$. When the set is non-linearly separable, $K\ (Xi,\ X)$ is kernel function, and it must satisfy the Mercer condition. Mercer's theorem states that a non-linear mapping underlies a kernel $K(Xi,X)$ provided that $K(Xi,X)$ is a positive integral operator (Scholkopf, 1999); that is, for every square integrable function *g(.)* defined on the kernel $K(Xi,X)$, the kernel satisfies the following condition,

$$\iint K(x,y)g(x)g(y)dxdy \geq 0 \qquad (6)$$

There are several types of kernel learning methods that satisfy Mercer's condition such as polynomial and RBF. These are among the most commonly used kernels in SVM research.

4.2.1. Polynomial Learning Machine

The polynomial kernel is defined as follows,

$$K(x,\ y)\ = (x^T y + 1)^P \qquad (7)$$

Where p, the order of a kernel, is a positive constant.

To construct polynomial decision rules of degree 'd', one can use the following function for convolution of the inner product,

$$K(x, x_i) = [(x \times x_i) + 1]^d \qquad (8)$$

The decision function becomes,

$$F(x) = sign(\sum_{Support} y_i \alpha_i [(x_i \times x) + 1]^d - b) \qquad (9)$$

Which is a factorization of the d-dimensional polynomials in n-dimensional input space.

Figure 4. Separating hyper-plane between two classes

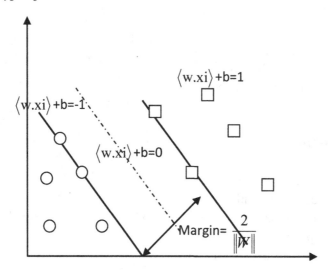

4.2.2. Radial Basis Function Machines

Classical radial basis function machine uses the following set of decision rules,

$$F(x) = sign(\sum_{i=1}^{N} \alpha_i y_i K_y (|x - x_i| - b) \qquad (10)$$

where N is the number of support vectors, γ the width parameter of the kernel function, $K_\gamma (|x - x_i|)$ depends on the distance $|x - x_i|$ between two vectors.

5. PERFORMANCE EVALUATION

5.1. Data

The images used in this work, are some of the benchmark images downloaded from the Harvard Medical School webpage, freely available in public domain (Keith et al., 1999). The images belong to the whole brain atlas, where the brain image datasets are acquired using several imaging technologies. We have tested our classification algorithm for several MR images, some of which belong to normal brain and others belong to pathological brain Figure 5. All these normal and pathological benchmark axial images are three weighted ones (enhanced T1, proton density (PD) and T2). These images are acquired at several positions of the transaxial planes as 256×256 sizes. By convention, for all images, the subject's left is at the right of the image. For each image available, the location of the image in the whole brain dataset is shown in the side view, i.e. in the sagittal image. For our case study, we have considered a total of 83 transaxial images (29 belonging to normal brain and 54 belonging to pathological brain, suffering from a low grade glioma, Meningioma, bronchogenic carcinoma, Glioblastoma multiforme, Sarcoma and Grade IV tumors) in several brain locations. For these pathological brains, suffering from tumors, we have included images acquired at different time instants. The main objective of our algorithm is to segregate normal brain MR images from pathological brain MR images. We have considered that all images belonging to seven persons (four men and three women). Their ages vary between 22 and 81 years.

Figure 5. A sample MR image (a) normal brain, (b) abnormal brain, (c) Alzheimer's disease

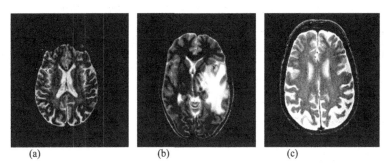

(a)   (b)   (c)

5.2. Experimental Results

The proposed methodology of classifying MR images of human brain is shown in Figure 6. The method uses the steps of feature extraction, feature selection and classification.

For each image, we implement Wavelet transform and we extract five features from these outputs. As described before we applied the genetic algorithm parameters to reduce the number of extracted features. The Genetic algorithm parameters chosen as described in Table 1 prove to be more useful and accurate as they give better selection results.

We perform various feature selection algorithms to evaluate their performances. Table 2 summarized the classification results.

In the case of classification of normal and pathological brain, the Sequential Floating Backward Selection (SFBS) method achieves a classification result of 100% with 11 of the available 44 features. This accuracy is similar to that obtained by only 7 features for the Sequential Floating Forward Selection (SFFS) method. Using GA, the selected feature set contains only 5 features

to achieve the same classification accuracy of 100%. The feature size is reduced by 88.63%. The classifier accuracies for different feature set sizes for the feature selection methods are illustrated in Table 2. This theoretical result is due to the perfect separation between data in the selected base.

Table 3 presents the best chromosomes found by the algorithm during the execution. The classification performance of 100% is obtained with 5 of the whole available features. Therefore it is possible to classify the normal brain and pathological brain with minimum number of features. Thus the cost of classifier can be reduced.

The feature vectors and output labels, for all images form a complete dataset are divided into two subsets: a training dataset and a testing dataset. We use 12 normal brain images and 20 abnormal images in the training phase; whereas in the testing phase, we use 29 normal brain images and 54 abnormal images. The SVM classifier is trained utilizing the training dataset. Then the SVM is implemented in testing phase. In testing phase, each feature vector, corresponding to a test image, is individually input to the SVM classi-

Figure 6. MR images classification

Table 1. Parameters of GA

GA property	Value/Method
Size of generation	100
Initial population size	30
Performance index/ fitness function	fitness Equation (1)
Selection method	Tournoi
Probability of selection	0.05
Crossover method	Arithmetic crossover
Crossover Probability	0.9
Number of crossover points	1
Mutation method	Uniform mutation
Mutation Probability	0.01

fier, which produces a continuous output. If the continuous output is positive, then this continuous output is assigned to the output class $k_{class} =+1$ (belonging to normal brain). Conversely, if the continuous output is negative, then it is assigned to the output class $k_{class} =-1$ (belonging to abnormal brain). To determine whether the test image is correctly classified or not we compare the output class with the corresponding k_i (which is already known before hand for the test image). This process is repeated for each exemplar in testing dataset, i.e. each test image. Finally, the testing classification accuracy of the algorithm is

Table 2. Results of feature selection by sequential search algorithms (forward and backward) and genetic algorithm (Kharrat et al., 2010)

Feature selection	Number of features	Classifier accuracy by normal and pathological brain	Percentage reduction
SFBS	11	100%	75%
SFFS	7	100%	84.09%
GA	7	100%	84.09%
	6	100%	86.36%
	5	100%	88.63%

Table 3. Results of feature selection performed by GA for wavelet features

Feature selection	Feature set	Classifier accuracy
GA	Mean of Correlation, mean of Maximum probability, mean of Difference variance, mean of Information measure of correlation I, mean of Inverse difference moment normalized, range of Contrast, range of Homogeneity	100%
	Mean of contrast, mean of Information measure of correlation I, mean of homogeneity, mean of Inverse difference moment normalized, mean of homogeneity, range of autocorrelation	100%
	Mean of contrast, mean of homogeneity, mean of sum average, mean of sum variance, range of autocorrelation	100%

reported on the basis of the classification performance for the entire testing dataset.

Two major parameters applied in SVM, C and γ, must be set appropriately. Parameter C represents the cost of the penalty and parameter γ is the width of the kernel function. The choice of C value influences the classification outcome and γ value affects the partitioning outcome in the feature space (Scholkopf, 2001). Hence, the values of $C =8$ and $\gamma =2$, as the best optimised parameters to apply in our implementation. To guarantee valid results for making predictions regarding new data, the dataset is further randomly partitioned into training sets and independent test sets via a k-fold cross validation. Each of the k subsets acted as an independent holdout test set for the model trained with the remaining k-1 subsets. The advantages of cross validation are that all of the test sets were independent and the reliability of the results could be improved. The data set is divided into k subsets for cross validation. A typical experiment uses $k=5$. Other values may be used according to the data set size. For a small data set, it may be better to set larger *k*, because this leaves more examples in the training set. This study used *k*=5, meaning that all of the data will be divided into 5 parts, each of which will take turns at being the testing data set. The other four data parts serve as the training data set for adjusting the model prediction parameters.

The linear kernel, the RBF and polynomial functions are used for SVM training and testing. The accuracy of classification is high in RBF kernel (100%) in comparison with the linear and polynomial kernels.

Table 4 presents the performance comparison of our proposed method, compared to recently reported brain MR classification results in Chaplot's manuscript (Chaplot et al., 2006). In this reference, the same image data base is analysed. They proposed two methods (self-organizing maps and support vector machine) for this classification and they achieved classification accuracy of the order of 94 and 98%, respectively. To achieve these accuracies, they were compelled to utilize huge sizes of feature vectors. They utilized 4761 features extracted from DWT. In comparison with these methods, our system requires only 5 features extracted from WT to be input to the GA for feature optimisation and then for classification. The feature size is reduced by 88.63%. The implementation of our contribution requires much lighter computational burden, which is an important factor while implementing these tools in real time. Hence our proposed system could satisfy two competing requirements simultaneously. They could achieve higher classification accuracy and this could be achieved with a very small size of feature vector. In this context, we would also like to mention that the results in Chaplot's manuscript (Chaplot et al., 2006) were reported considering a total of 52 image slices (including 6 of normal brain and 46 of abnormal brain). On the other hand, our results are presented considering a total of 83 images (including 29 of normal brain and 54 of abnormal brain).

All experiments were carried out using an Intel core 2 duo machine, with 4GO RAM and a processor speed of 2GHz, run under Windows XP environment. The average CPU time consumed for extracting features, for each image, was approximately 0.07s. For all images the average is 5.249s. In the implementation phase, the classifier consumed an average time of 4.469 ms. In comparison with our method Multilayer Preceptron (MLP) requires 89×10^3 ms.

5.3. Discussion

The classification accuracy of 100% is achieved by using only five features: *mean of contrast*, *mean of homogeneity*, *mean of sum average*, *mean of sum variance* and *range of autocorrelation*. Actually, the features selected by the genetic algorithm, are very related with the appearance of images of the tumors database. By examining the images of abnormal brain we can see that the area of the tumor is characterized by a high degree of brightness. Furthermore, its color distribution is

Table 4. Classification performance comparison for brain MR images

Algorithm	No. of features extracted	Classification accuracy
DWT-SOM (Chaplot et al., 2006)	4761	94%
DWT-SVM with linear kernel (Chaplot et al., 2006)	4761	96.15%
DWT-SVM with polynomial kernel (Chaplot et al., 2006)	4761	98%
DWT-SVM with radial basis function based kernel (Chaplot et al., 2006)	4761	98%
Our proposed WT-GA-SVM based classifier	5	100%

regular. This explains the main reason of selection of the contrast and the auto-correlation features as descriptive characteristics of the tumor. In fact, a contrast is a distinctive characteristic of light distribution of an image or between two image points. The auto-correlation can detect regularity and repeated profiles in a signal. In addition, a tumor is an area where the distribution of colors is regular. So that the values are fairly close. Therefore, these aspects also explain the choice of the variance, the homogeneity and the average features as descriptive characteristics of the tumor. In particular, the homogeneity has an opposite behavior of the contrast. In fact, the homogeneity characteristic is related with the texture homogeneous regions. The variance characterizes the distribution of gray levels around the mean value.

The classification accuracy of our method is more efficient then the Chaplot's method. These results prove that global features are more discriminative than block or pixel ones in our context. This is easily interpreted in dataset images.

In this work, we developed a classification technology to facilitate the information management capacity which constitutes a discipline of Cognitive Informatics.

6. CONCLUSION

In this paper a new approach for automatic classification of normal or abnormal MR Images using WT, GA and SVM classifier is proposed. This algorithm reduces the number of features, saves execution time and preserves data complexity. The performance of our contribution in terms of classification accuracy is interpreted. The results show that the proposed method gives better results in comparison with the methods presented in the literature. The classification accuracy of our method is more efficient then the Chaplot's method. It suggests that our three-step algorithm is promising for image classification in a medical imaging application. This automated analysis system, which requires much lighter computational time, could be further used for classification of image with different pathological condition, types and disease status.

ACKNOWLEDGMENT

The authors would like to thank Dr. Khalil Chtourou, Biophysics and Nuclear Medicine from the CHU Habib Bourguiba, Department of Nuclear Medicine, Tunisia-Sfax, is acknowledged for providing several clarifications on the medical aspects of the datasets. They are also grateful to Mrs. Ines Kallel for her helpful review of the manuscript.

REFERENCES

Begg, R. K., Palaniswami, & Owen, M., B. (2005). Support vector machines for automated gait classification. *IEEE Transactions on Bio-Medical Engineering, 52*(5), 828–838. doi:10.1109/TBME.2005.845241

Bracewell, R. N. (1999). *The Fourier transform and its applications*. New York, NY: McGraw-Hill.

Chaplot, S., Patnaik, L. M., & Jagannathan, N. R. (2006). Classification of magnetic resonance brain images using wavelets as input to support vector machine and neural network. *Journal of Biomedical Signal Processing, 1*(2), 86–92. doi:10.1016/j.bspc.2006.05.002

Dhawale, C. A., & Sanjeev, J. (2007). Comparison of statistical methods for texture analysis. In *Proceedings of the International Conference Advances in Computer Vision and Information Technology* (pp. 686-698).

El-Dahshan, E. A., Salem, A. B. M., & Younis, T. H. (2009). A hybrid technique for automatic MRI brain images classification. *Informatica, 54*(1), 55–67.

Fan, Y., Shen, D., & Davatzikos, C. (2005). Classification of structural images via high-dimensional image warping, robust feature extraction, and SVM. In J. S. Duncan & G. Gerig (Eds.), *Proceedings of the 8th International Conference on Medical Image Computing and Computer Assisted Intervention* (LNCS 3749, pp. 1-8).

Guermeur, Y. (2007). *SVM multiclass: Théorie et applications*. Retrieved from http://www.loria.fr/~guermeur/HDR_YG.pdf

Haralick, R., Shanmugam, K., & Dinstein, I. (1973). Textural features for image classification. *IEEE Transactions on Systems, Man, and Cybernetics*, 610–621. doi:10.1109/TSMC.1973.4309314

Huang, C. L., & Wang, C. J. (2006). A GA-based feature selection and parameters optimization for support vector machine. *Journal of Expert Systems with Application*, 31(2), 231–240. doi:10.1016/j.eswa.2005.09.024

Kalpalatha, R. T., & Kumaravel, N. (2009). Texture analysis of bone CT images for classification and characterization of bone quality. *International Journal of Soft Computing*, 4(5), 223–228.

Keith, A. J., & Alex, J. B. (1999). *The whole brain atlas*. Boston, MA· Harvard Medical School.

Kharrat, A., BenMessaoud, M., Benamrane, N., & Abid, M. (2009). Detection of brain tumor in medical images. In *Proceedings of the 3rd IEEE International Conference on Signals, Circuits & Systems*, Tunisia (pp. 1-6).

Kharrat, A., BenMessaoud, M., Benamrane, N., & Abid, M. (2010). Genetic algorithm for feature selection of MR brain images using wavelet co-occurrence. In *Proceedings of the IEEE International Conference on Signals and Information Processing, Changsha, China* (pp. 606-610).

Kittler, J. (1978). Feature set search algorithms. *Pattern Recognition and Signal Processing*, 41-60.

Kohavi, R., & George, H. J. (1997). Wrappers for feature subset selection. *Artificial Intelligence*, 1(2), 273–324. doi:10.1016/S0004-3702(97)00043-X

Magnin, B., Mesrob, L., Kinkingnéhun, S., Pélégrini, I. M., Colliot, O., & Sarazin, M. (2009). Support-vector-machine based classification of Alzheimer's disease from whole brain anatomical MRI. *Journal of Neuroradiology*, 51(2), 73–83. doi:10.1007/s00234-008-0463-x

Mallat, S. G. (1989). A theory of multiresolution signal decomposition: The wavelet representation. *IEEE Transactions on Pattern Analysis and Machine Intelligence*, 674–693. doi:10.1109/34.192463

Michael, J. C. (1994). *The effect of variation in illuminant direction on texture classification*. Unpublished doctoral dissertation Heriot-Watt University. Edinburgh, Scotland.

Moritz, C. H., Haughton, V. M., Cordes, D., Quigley, M., & Meyerand, M. E. (2000). Whole-brain functional MR imaging activation from finger tapping task examined with independent component analysis. *AJNR. American Journal of Neuroradiology*, 21(9), 1629–1635.

Narendra, P. M., & Fukunaga, K. (1977). A branch and bound algorithm for feature subset selection. *IEEE Transactions on Computers*, 26(9), 917–922. doi:10.1109/TC.1977.1674939

Neeraj, S., & Lalit, M. A. (2010). Automated medical image segmentation techniques. *Journal of Medical Physics*, 35(1), 3–14. doi:10.4103/0971-6203.58777

Pudil, P., Novovicova, J., & Kittler, J. (1994). Floating search methods in feature selection. *Pattern Recognition Letters*, 15(11), 1119–1125. doi:10.1016/0167-8655(94)90127-9

Scholkopf, B. (1999). *Advances in kernel methods: Support vector learning*. Cambridge, MA: MIT Press.

Scholkopf, B., & Smola, A. J. (2001). *Learning with kernels support vector machines, regularization, optimization and beyond*. Cambridge, MA: MIT Press.

Siedlecki, W., & Sklanky, J. (1989). A note on genetic algorithms for large-scale feature selection. *Journal of Pattern Recognition Letters*, *10*(5), 335–347. doi:10.1016/0167-8655(89)90037-8

Wang, Y. (2009). On cognitive computing. *International Journal of Software Science and Computational Intelligence*, *1*(3), 1–15. doi:10.4018/jssci.2009070101

Yu, B., & Yuan, B. (1993). A more efficient branch and bound algorithm for feature selection. *Pattern Recognition*, *26*(6), 883–889. doi:10.1016/0031-3203(93)90054-Z

Zacharaki, E., Wang, S., Chawla, S., Soo, Y. D., Wolf, R., Melhem, E., & Davatzikos, C. (2009). Classification of brain tumor type and grade using MRI texture and shape in a machine learning scheme. *Magnetic Resonance in Medicine*, *62*(6), 1609–1618. doi:10.1002/mrm.22147

This work was previously published in the International Journal of Software Science and Computational Intelligence, Volume 3, Issue 2, edited by Yingxu Wang, pp. 19-33, copyright 2011 by IGI Publishing (an imprint of IGI Global).

Chapter 5

EEG Feature Extraction and Pattern Classification Based on Motor Imagery in Brain–Computer Interface

Ling Zou
Changzhou University, China & State Key Laboratory of Robotics & System (HIT), China

Guodong Shi
Changzhou University, China

Xinguang Wang
Changzhou University, China

Zhenghua Ma
Changzhou University, China

ABSTRACT

Accurate classification of EEG left and right hand motor imagery is an important issue in brain-computer interface. Firstly, discrete wavelet transform method was used to decompose the average power of C3 electrode and C4 electrode in left-right hands imagery movement during some periods of time. The reconstructed signal of approximation coefficient A6 on the sixth level was selected to build up a feature signal. Secondly, the performances by Fisher Linear Discriminant Analysis with two different threshold calculation ways and Support Vector Machine methods were compared. The final classification results showed that false classification rate by Support Vector Machine was lower and gained an ideal classification results.

INTRODUCTION

Brain-computer interface (BCI) is a communication system by which a person can send messages without any use of peripheral nerves and muscles (Wolpaw et al., 2002; Vuckovic, 2009; Schalk et al., 2008; Waldert et al., 2009). The technology holds great promise for people who can't use their arms or hands normally because they have had the damaged region, such as amyotrophic lateral sclerosis (ALS) (Sellers et al., 2006; Iversen et al., 2008), spinal cord injury (Müller-Putz et al., 2005), brainstem stroke (Sitaram et al., 2007), or

DOI: 10.4018/978-1-4666-2651-5.ch005

quadriplegic patients (Hoffmann et al.08). BCI system, by extracting signals directly from the brain, might help to restore abilities to patients who have lost sensory or motor function because of their disabilities (Blankertz et al., 2010; Guger et al., 2009). In fact, BCI is used as a surrogate for the people who are disabled, in the case of a neuromotor prosthesis, acts to interpret brain signals and drive the appropriate effectors (e.g., muscles or a robotic arm) (Hoffmann et al., 2008; Lee et al., 2009). So, it has great social value and application prospect. As an interdisciplinary technology, BCI has become a research hotspot of brain cognition research, rehabilitation engineering, biomedical engineering, automatic human-machine control, and so on.

A number of groups around the world are developing BCI systems, in which surface electroencephalography (EEG) is used because it is noninvasive and mobile (Li et al., 2010; Yamawaki et al., 2006). The cognitive task most commonly used in BCI studies is motor imagery, as it produces changes in EEG that occur naturally in movement planning and are relatively straightforward to detect. Motor imagery, defined as mental simulation of a kinesthetic movement (Jeannerod et al., 1999), has been well established that the imagination of each left and right hand movement results in event-related desynchronization (ERD) of mu-band power in the contralateral sensorimotor areas, which is also the case for physical hand movements (Pfurtscheller et al., 2001). Brain activities modulated by motor imagery of either the left or right hand are regarded as good features for BCIs, because such activities are readily reproducible and show consistent EEG patterns on the sensorimotor cortical areas (Hollinger et al., 1999). Moreover, thanks to the contralateral localization of the oscillatory activity, the activities evoked from left and right hand motor imagery are, comparatively, readily discriminated (Ince et al., 2006; Kamousi et al., 2007). The signals generated in the motor cortex can be recorded from electrodes over central head regions and

the research has produced encouraging results (Ramsey et al., 2006; Pfurtschelle et al., 2010; Hwang et al., 2009). The aim is to train subjects to control the cursor automatically by using the operant conditioning approach (Li et al., 2010).

Many methods have been proposed to BCI in the past few years (Sitaram et al., 2007; Hoffmann et al., 2008; Blankertz et al., 2010; Li et al., 2010; Yamawaki et al., 2006; Pfurtscheller et al., 2010; Hwang et al., 2009; Ince et al., 2006). As a classifier, linear discriminant analysis (LDA), support vector machine (SVM) and neural network were used (Garrett et al., 2003; Gysels et al., 2005; Kayikcioglu et al., 2010). Recursive least squares and LDA algorithms were used to aim at classify left- or right- hand movement (Garrett et al., 2001). During mental imagination of specific movements, the adaptive multiple regressions where the result EEG recorded from the sensorimotor cortex were classified on-line and were used for cursor control (McFarland et al., 2005). Due to the high-dimensional and artificial noise (e.g., eyes blinks) of the EEG signals, the nonlinear classification methods are better than the linear ones (Garrett et al., 2003). Therefore, we will use the nonlinear methods to classify the high-dimensional and artificial noisy EEG signals.

EEG Feature extraction and pattern classification is always a difficult problem during the BCI study. In this paper, we propose a method to classify the EEG of mental tasks for left-hand movement imagination and right-hand movement imagination. The goal of this study was to prove the viability of a movement imagery prediction brain-computer interface (BCI), and to expect that the two mental tasks can be classified with higher classification rate. Firstly, a rational time window was set by calculating the average power of C3 electrode and C4 electrode in left-right hands imagery movement. The time window's average power was then decomposed by discrete wavelet transform (DWT). The reconstructed signal of approximation coefficient A6 on the sixth level was selected to build up a feature signal. Secondly,

Fisher Linear Discriminant Analysis (FLDA) was used with two different threshold calculation ways and obtained good misclassification rate. We also used Support Vector Machine (SVM) to compare the performance with Fisher Linear Discriminant Analysis. The final classification results showed that false classification rate by Support Vector Machine was lower and gained an ideal classification results.

1. METHOD

In this paper, we used data collected during online BCI experiments, and analyzed them offline as described later in this section.

1.1. Data Set Description

Data set was provided by Department of Medical Informatics, Institute for Biomedical Engineering, University of Technology Graz (Pfurtscheller, 2002).

This dataset was recorded from a normal subject (female, 25y) during a feedback session. The subject sat in a relaxing chair with armrests. The task was to control a feedback bar by means of imagery left or right hand movements. The order of left and right cues was random. The experiment consists of 7 runs with 40 trials each. All runs were conducted on the same day with several minutes break in between. Given are 280 trials of 9s length. The first 2s was quite, at t=2s an acoustic stimulus indicates the beginning of the trial, the trigger channel (#4) went from low to high, and a cross "+" was displayed for 1s; then at t=3s, an arrow (left or right) was displayed as cue. At the same time the subject was asked to move a bar into the direction of the cue. The recording was made using a G.tec amplifier and an Ag/AgCl electrodes. Three bipolar EEG channels (anterior '+', posterior '-') were measured over C3, Cz and C4. The EEG was sampled with 128Hz; it was filtered between 0.5 and 30Hz.

1.2. Feature Extraction

Because the channel Cz showed its independence of the motor imagery, only channel C3 and C4 were used for feature extraction. The duration of each experiment was 9 seconds, but the part which played a role for the task of classification may be just one period. In order to find a suitable time window, the average power of different imagine tasks of C3 and C4 channel was computed firstly, so as to provide effective reference of the next step.

The formula for calculating average power is:

$$P_{(j)} = \frac{1}{N} \sum_{i=1}^{N} x^2_{f(i,j)} \tag{1}$$

$x^2_{f(i,j)}$ is the jth EEG data of the ith time experiment, $P_{(j)}$ is the average power of the jth EEG data corresponding to the N time experiments.

We could calculate the average power of C3 and C4 when one imagined left-hand movement corresponding to 0~9 seconds, which were named as LPC3 and LPC4 shown in Figure 1. The average power of C3 and C4 when one imagined right-hand movement corresponding to 0~9 seconds were named as RPC3 and RPC4 shown in Figure 2.

From Figure 1 and Figure 2, there were significant differences between the energy of left hand imagery movement and right hand imagery movement for the time window period (3.5 – 8 seconds). The average power obtained by C3-channel was greater than C4-channel when imagined left hand movement; the average power obtained by C3-channel was less than C4-channel when imagined right hand movement. It was in line with ERD/ERS features of motor imagery. Event-related desynchronization potentials generated in contralateral and event-related synchronization potentials generated in ipsilateral of the brain when one has unilateral limb movement or imaged movement. Thus, we could take the aver-

Figure 1. The relationship between the time and the average power of the C3 electrode and C4 electrode for left-hand imagery movement

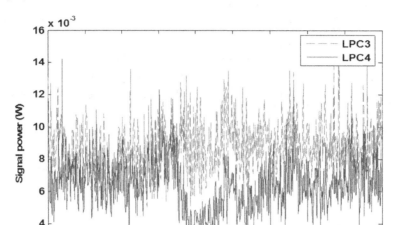

age power at time window (3.5~8 seconds) as the source signal to be further analyzed.

In this study, we chose the Daubechies wavelets as the basic wavelet functions for their simplicity and general purpose applicability in a variety of time-frequency representation problems (Polikar et al., 2007). According to the sampling frequency of 128 Hz, a 6 level decomposition to the average power at time window (3.5- 8 seconds) was used, thus having 6 scales of details (d1-d6) and a final approximation (a6). The decomposition results were shown in Figures 3 and 4.

Here, the final approximation signals of C3 and C4 when imagined left-hand movement were

Figure 2. The relationship between the time and the average power of the C3 electrode and C4 electrode for right-hand imagery movement

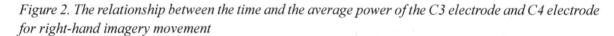

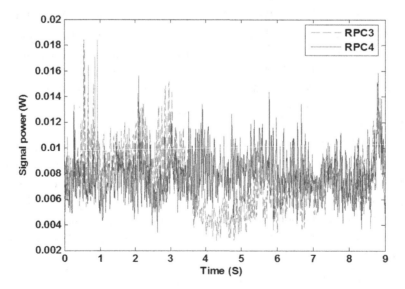

Figure 3. The wavelet decomposition of the C3 electrode and C4 electrode for left-hand imagery movement

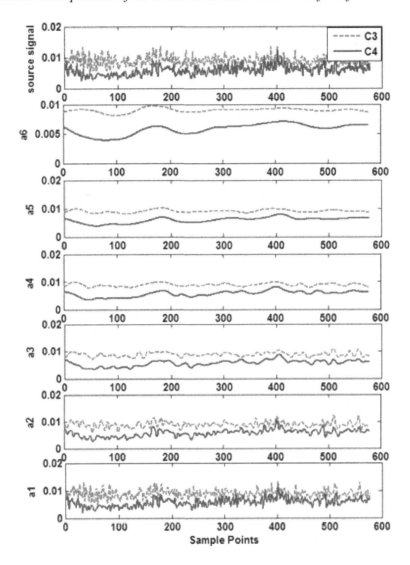

indicated as LC3A6 and LC4A6, respectively, while the final approximation signals of C3 and C4 when imagined right-hand movement were indicated as RC3A6 and RC4A6, respectively. The results showed that there was significant difference between left-hand and right-hand imagery movement concerning the signal of approximation coefficient A6 on the sixth level. The value of LC3A6 was bigger than LC4A6 when imagined left-hand movement, while the value of RC3A6 was smaller than RC4A6 when imagined

right-hand movement. Supposing LA6 and RA6 were the difference of the signal of approximation coefficient A6 on the sixth level of C3 and C4, respectively, they are defined as the following equations:

$$LA6 = L3A6 - L4A6 \qquad (2)$$

$$RA6 = R3A6 - R4A6 \qquad (3)$$

Figure 4. The wavelet decomposition of the C3 electrode and C4 electrode for right-hand imagery movement

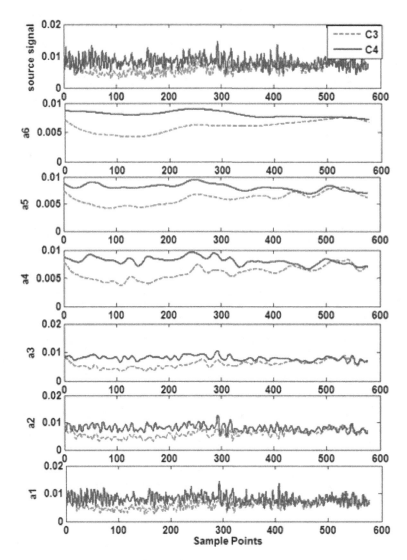

The curve of LA6 and RA6 was shown in Figure 5. Obviously, LA6 and RA6 can be selected as the features for distinguish the left-right hands imagery movement.

1.3. Classification

In order to demonstrate the effectiveness of the proposed features in BCI application, the FLDA classification method and SVM method were used in this paper. For the sake of self-containment, this section briefly introduced the FLDA and SVM.

1.3.1. FLDA Classifier

The goal in Fisher's linear discriminant analysis (FLDA) was to compute a discriminate vector that separates two or more classes as well as possible. Here we considered the two-class case. We were given a set of input vectors $x_i \in R^D$, $i \in \{1...N\}$ and the corresponding class-labels $y_i = \{-1,1\}$. Denoting by N_1 the number of training examples for which $y_i = 1$, by C_1 the set of indices i for which $y_i = 1$, and using analogous

Figure 5. The feature signals of the left-right hands imagery movement

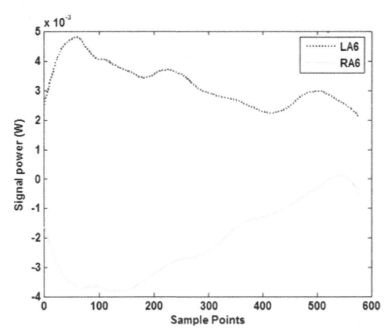

definitions for N_2, C_2, the objective function for computing a discriminate vector $w \in R^D$ is

$$J(w) = \frac{(\mu_1 - \mu_2)^2}{\sigma_1^2 + \sigma_2^2} \qquad (4)$$

Where

$$\mu_k = \frac{1}{N_k} \sum_{i \in C_k} w^T x_i, \qquad (5)$$

$$\sigma_k^2 = \sum_{i \in C_k} (w^T x_i - \mu_k)^2 \qquad (6)$$

This means that one was searching for discriminate vectors that result in a large distance between the projected means and small variance around the projected means (small within-class variance) .To compute directly the optimal discriminate vector for a training data set, matrix equations for the quantities $(\mu_1 - \mu_2)^2$ and

$\sigma_1^2 + \sigma_2^2$ can be used. We first define the class means m_k :

$$m_k = \frac{1}{N_k} \sum_{i \in C_k} x_i \qquad (7)$$

Now we can define the between-class scatter matrix S_B and the within-class scatter matrix S_W.

$$S_B = (m_1 - m_2)(m_1 - m_2)^T \qquad (8)$$

$$S_W = \sum_{k=1}^{2} \sum_{i \in C_k} (x_i - m_k)(x_i - m_k)^T \qquad (9)$$

With the help of these two matrices, the objective function for FLDA can be written as a Rayleigh quotient

$$J(w) = \frac{w^T S_B w}{w^T S_W w} \qquad (10)$$

By computing the derivative of J and setting it to zero, one can show that the optimal solution for w satisfies the following equation:

$$w \propto S_W^{-1}(m_1 - m_2) \tag{11}$$

The classification was conducted as follows:

$$x \in \begin{cases} class & 1 \ , & if & y > 0 \\ class & 2 \ , & if & y < 0 \end{cases} \tag{12}$$

1.3.2. SVM Classifier

SVM was a classification algorithm based on statistical learning theory. The invention of SVM was driven by underlying statistical learning theory, i.e., following the principle of structural risk minimization that was rooted in VC dimension theory, which makes its derivation even more profound (Lin et al., 2009). The SVM has been a topic of extensive research with wide applications in machine learning and engineering. The output of a binary SVM classifier can be computed by the following expression:

$$f(x) = \text{sgn}(\sum_{i=1}^{n} \alpha_i^* y_i K(x_i, x) + b^*) \tag{13}$$

where $\left\{x_i, y_i\right\}_{i=1}^{N}$ were training samples with input vector $x_i = R^d$; class labels $y_i \in \left\{-1, 1\right\}, \alpha_i \geq 0$ were Lagrangian multipliers obtained by solving a quadratic optimization problem; b was the bias, and $k\left\{x_i, x_j\right\}$ was called kernel function in SVM. There were two typical kernel functions: linear kernel and RBF kernel:

$$K(x_i, x_j) \begin{cases} x^T x_i \\ \exp(-\frac{1}{2\sigma^2} \| x - x_i \|^2) \end{cases} \tag{14}$$

where σ was the kernel parameter. It was fair to note that the parameters C and σ should be tuned properly for accurate prediction of unseen amples. In this study, they were selected using LIBSVM by 5-fold cross-validation over the following grid of (C, σ): $(2^{-7} \dots 2^7) \times (2^{-10} \dots 2^3)$.

The protruding characteristics of SVM lies in its elegant mechanism of handling nonlinear function classes, i.e., nonlinear information processing is carried out by means of linear techniques in an implicit high-dimensional feature space mapped by a nonlinear transformation $\phi(x_i)$ from original input space. Although the analytical expressions of $\phi(x_i)$ is unknown, only the inner product operations $\phi(x_i)^T \phi(x_j)$ are involved, the kernel functions can be used to substitute the inner product operations according to the Mercer theorem. Vapnik's theory showed that the SVM solution was found by minimizing both the error on the training set (empirical risk) and the complexity of the hypothesis space, expressed in terms of VC dimension. In this sense, the decision function found by SVM is a tradeoff between learning error and model complexity.

2. RESULTS

Taking into account the different number of samples of experiments may have an impact on classification results, the raw data were carried out on grouping at the beginning of the experiment. The first group consisted of 70 training samples and 70 test samples, recorded as Data 1. The second group consisted of 140 training samples and 70 test samples, denoted by Data 2.

Misdiscriminant rate (MR) was the main criteria for measure of classifier performance.

$$MR = \frac{classsified \quad incorrectly \quad samples}{sample \quad population} \times 100\% \tag{15}$$

Figure 6. The classification result based on FLDA method and using Data 1

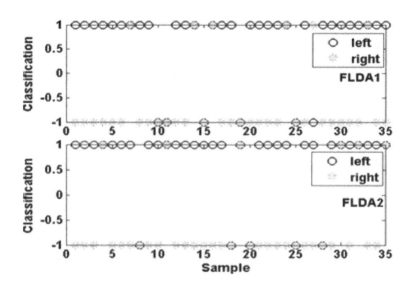

In this paper, two different methods of threshold calculating were used in achieving Fisher linear discriminant analysis algorithm. One threshold value was the mid-point of class center projection of two types. The other threshold was the weighted average based on the class frequency of two class centers. So as to facilitate the discussion, here denoted FLDA1 and FLDA2 respectively.

Classification results were shown in Figures 6 and 7. Here, ○ denote imagined left hand movement (category marked was 1), ✳ denote imagined right hand movement (category marked was -1).

The parameter selections of SVM kernel function have experiencing method, trying method, as well as through a number of optimization methods, where the methods described above

Figure 7. The classification result based on FLDA method and using Data 2

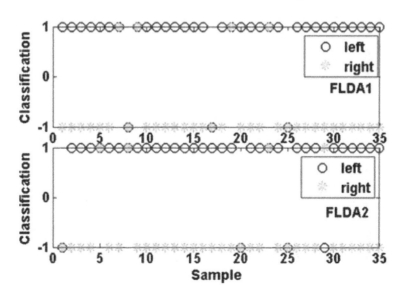

Figure 8. The classification result based on SVM method and using Data 1

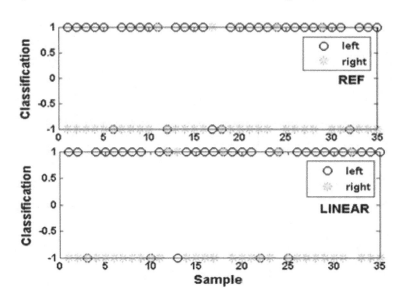

were used. After determining these parameters, we can identify unknown samples by the classification algorithm. Ref and Linear kernel function were used in SVM. Classification results were shown in Figures 8 and 9. Experimental results were shown in Table 1.

3. DISCUSSION

It can be seen from the Figure 6 that in FLDA1 classification, at the 10th point, ○ was assigned to the class -1, while the ○ belonged to category 1 originally; at the 7th point, ✳ was

Figure 9. The classification result based on SVM method and using Data 2

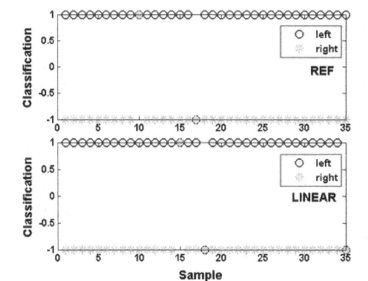

Table 1. Classification of different methods

Discriminate Criterion		FLDA		SVM	
		FLDA1	FLDA2	RBF	LINEAR
MR %	Data1	17.65	16.18	14.58	14.65
	Data2	10.29	11.24	3.94	4.28

assigned to the class 1, while ✳ belonged to category -1 originally. Therefore, there have been misclassified. Likewise, it is same for the subsequent figures.

From Table 1, we could see that in the case of using Data 1 (or Data 2) data set, when we used Fisher linear discriminant analysis method with different threshold calculated, the results obtained were almost the same, this is because the number of left-right hand motor imagery of raw EEG data was quite close, when we used SVM with different kernel function method for classification, the two classification results were quite close, which indicated support vector machine is not very sensitive for the choice of kernel function. The results obtained from Data 2 were superior to the results obtained from data1 for both algorithms. It is indicated that recognition rate increased with the training set increased, which is more evident for SVM classifier.

4. CONCLUSION

The above experimental results showed that both the LDA classifier and SVM classifier are effective based on DWT feature extraction when identifying the different mental tasks from EEG signals; the SVM classifier is more effective.

The experimental results indicated the rational of feature extraction and classification algorithm, which also accumulated experience and laid the foundation for the following study of online brain-computer interface system.

We could also see that the classification method is offline, and the subject is normal. In the future,

we would make further study on online BCI for the people with movement disorder, which would promote BCI application in rehabilitation project.

ACKNOWLEDGMENT

This work was supported by the open project of the State Key Laboratory of Robotics and System (HIT),the open project of the State Key Laboratory of Cognitive Neuroscience and Learning and the Natural science fund for colleges and universities in Jiangsu Province (10KJB510003).

REFERENCES

Blankertz, B., Sannelli, C., Halder, S., Hammer, E. M., Kübler, A., & Müller, K. R. (2010). Neurophysiological predictor of SMR-based BCI performances. *NeuroImage, 51*(4), 3–9. doi:10.1016/j.neuroimage.2010.03.022

Garrett, D., David, A. P., Anderson, C. W., & Thaut, M. H. (2003). Comparison of linear, nonlinear, and feature selection methods for EEG signal classification. *IEEE Transactions on Neural Systems and Rehabilitation Engineering, 11*(2), 141–144. doi:10.1109/TNSRE.2003.814441

Guger, C., Daban, S., Sellers, E., Holzner, C., Krausz, G., & Carabalona, R. (2009). How many people are able to control a P300-based brain-computer interface (BCI)? *Neuroscience Letters, 462*(1), 94–98. doi:10.1016/j.neulet.2009.06.045

Guger, C., Schlögl, A., Neuper, C., Walterspacher, D., Strein, T., & Pfurtscheller, G. (2001). Rapid prototyping of an EEG-based brain-computer interface (BCI). *IEEE Transactions on Neural Systems and Rehabilitation Engineering, 9*(1), 49–58. doi:10.1109/7333.918276

Gysels, E., Renevey, P., & Celka, P. (2005). SVM-based recursive feature elimination to compare phase synchronization computed from broadband and narrowband EEG signals in brain-computer interfaces. *Signal Processing, 85*(11), 2178–2189. doi:10.1016/j.sigpro.2005.07.008

Hoffmann, U., Vesin, J. M., Ebrahimi, T., & Diserens, K. (2008). An efficient P300-based brain-computer interface for disabled subjects. *Journal of Neuroscience Methods, 167*(1), 15–25. doi:10.1016/j.jneumeth.2007.03.005

Höllinger, P., Beisteiner, R., Lang, W., Lindinger, G., & Berthoz, A. (1999). Mental representations of movements. Brain potentials associated with imagination of eye movements. *Clinical Neurophysiology, 110*(5), 790–805. doi:10.1016/S1388-2457(98)00042-X

Hwang, H. J., Kwon, K., & Im, C. H. (2009). Neurofeedback-based motor imagery training for brain-computer interface (BCI). *Journal of Neuroscience Methods, 179*(1), 50–56. doi:10.1016/j.jneumeth.2009.01.015

Ince, N. F., Arica, S., & Tewfik, A. (2006). Classification of single trial motor imagery EEG recordings with subject adapted non-dyadic arbitrary time-frequency tilings. *Journal of Neural Engineering, 3*(3), 235–244. doi:10.1088/1741-2560/3/3/006

Iversen, I. H., Ghanayim, N., Kübler, A., Neumann, N., Birbaumer, N., & Kaiser, J. (2008). A brain-computer interface tool to assess cognitive functions in completely paralyzed patients with amyotrophic lateral sclerosis. *Clinical Neurophysiology, 119*(10), 14–23. doi:10.1016/j.clinph.2008.07.001

Jeannerod, M., & Frak, V. (1999). Mental imaging of motor activity in humans. *Current Opinion in Neurobiology, 9*(6), 35–39. doi:10.1016/S0959-4388(99)00038-0

Kamousi, B., Amini, A. N., & He, B. (2007). Classification of motro imagery by means of cortical current density estimation and Von Neumann entropy. *Journal of Neural Engineering, 4*, 17–25. doi:10.1088/1741-2560/4/2/002

Kayikcioglu, T., & Aydemir, O. (2010). A polynomial fitting and k-NN based approach for improving classification of motor imagery BCI data. *Pattern Recognition Letters, 31*(11), 1207–1215. doi:10.1016/j.patrec.2010.04.009

Lee, J. H., Ryu, J., Jolesz, F. A., Cho, Z. H., & Yoo, S. S. (2009). Brain-machine interface via real-time fMRI: Preliminary study on thought-controlled robotic arm. *Neuroscience Letters, 450*(1), 1–6. doi:10.1016/j.neulet.2008.11.024

Li, Y. Q., Long, J. Y., Yu, T. Y., Yu, Z. L., Wang, C. C., Zhang, H. H., & Guan, C. T. (2010). An EEG based BCI system for 2-D cursor control by combining Mu/Beta rhythm and P300 potential. *IEEE Transactions on Bio-Medical Engineering, 57*(10), 495–505.

Lin, H. J., & Yeh, J. P. (2009). Optimal reduction of solutions for support vector machines. *Applied Mathematics and Computation, 214*(2), 329–335. doi:10.1016/j.amc.2009.04.010

McFarland, D. J., & Wolpaw, J. R. (2005). Sensorimotor rhythm-based brain-computer interface (BCI): feature selection by regression improves performance. *IEEE Transactions on Neural Systems and Rehabilitation, 13*(3), 372–379. doi:10.1109/TNSRE.2005.848627

Müller-Putz, G. R., Scherer, R., Pfurtscheller, G., & Rupp, R. (2005). EEG-based neuroprosthesis control: A step towards clinical practice. *Neuroscience Letters, 382*(1-2), 69–74.

Pfurtscheller, G., & Neuper, C. (2001). Motor imagery and direct brain-computer communication. *Proceedings of the IEEE, 89*, 23–34. doi:10.1109/5.939829

Pfurtscheller, G., Solis-Escalante, T., Ortner, R., Linortner, P., & Muller-Putz, G. R. (2010). Self-paced operation of an SSVEP-based orthosis with and without an imagery-based "brain switch:" A feasibility study towards a hybrid BCI. *IEEE Transactions on Neural Systems and Rehabilitation Engineering, 18*(4), 9–14. doi:10.1109/TNSRE.2010.2040837

Pfurtscheller, H., & Schlögl, A. (2002). *BCI competition II: Data set III (motor imagery)*. Retrieved May 18, 2009, from http://www.bbci.de/competition/ii/

Polikar, R., Topalis, A., Green, D., Kounios, J., & Clark, C. M. (2007). Comparative multiresolution wavelet analysis of ERP spectral bands using an ensemble of classifiers approach for early diagnosis of Alzheimer's disease. *Computers in Biology and Medicine, 37*, 542–556. doi:10.1016/j.compbiomed.2006.08.012

Ramsey, N. F., van de Heuvel, M. P., Kho, K. H., & Leijten, F. S. S. (2006). Towards human BCI applications based on cognitive brain systems: an investigation of neural signals recorder from the dorsolateral prefrontal cortex. *IEEE Transactions on Neural Systems and Rehabilitation, 14*(2), 14–17.

Schalk, G., Bruuner, P., Gerhardt, L. A., Bischof, H., & Wolpaw, J. R. (2008). Brain-computer interfaces (BCIs): Detection instead of classification. *Journal of Neuroscience Methods, 167*(1), 51–62. doi:10.1016/j.jneumeth.2007.08.010

Sellers, E. W., & Donchin, E. (2006). A P300-based brain-computer interface: initial tests by ALS patients. *Clinical Neurophysiology, 117*(3), 38–48. doi:10.1016/j.clinph.2005.06.027

Sitaram, R., Zhang, H. H., Guan, C. T., Thulasidas, M., Hoshi, Y., & Ishikawa, A. (2007). Temporal classification of multichannel near-infrared spectroscopy signals of motor imagery for developing a brain-computer interface. *NeuroImage, 34*(4), 16–27. doi:10.1016/j.neuroimage.2006.11.005

Vuckovic, A. (2009). Non-invasive BCI: how far can we get with motor imagination? *Clinical Neurophysiology, 120*(8), 22–23. doi:10.1016/j.clinph.2009.06.007

Waldert, S., Pistohl, T., Braun, C., Ball, T., Aertsen, A., & Mehring, C. (2009). A review on directional in neural signals for brain-machine interfaces. *The Journal of Physiology, 103*(3-5), 44–54.

Wolpaw, J. R., Birbaumer, N., McFarland, D. J., Pfurtscheller, G., & Vaughan, T. M. (2002). Brain-computer interfaces for communication and control. *Clinical Neurophysiology, 113*(6), 67–91. doi:10.1016/S1388-2457(02)00057-3

Yamawaki, N., Wilke, C., Liu, Z. M., & He, B. (2006). An enhanced time-frequency-spatial approach for motor imagery classification. *IEEE Transactions on Neural Systems and Rehabilitation Engineering, 14*(2), 50–54. doi:10.1109/TNSRE.2006.875567

This work was previously published in the International Journal of Software Science and Computational Intelligence, Volume 3, Issue 3, edited by Yingxu Wang, pp. 43-56, copyright 2011 by IGI Publishing (an imprint of IGI Global).

Chapter 6
Inconsistency-Induced Learning for Perpetual Learners

Du Zhang
California State University, USA

Meiliu Lu
California State University, USA

ABSTRACT

One of the long-term research goals in machine learning is how to build never-ending learners. The state-of-the-practice in the field of machine learning thus far is still dominated by the one-time learner paradigm: some learning algorithm is utilized on data sets to produce certain model or target function, and then the learner is put away and the model or function is put to work. Such a learn-once-apply-next (or LOAN) approach may not be adequate in dealing with many real world problems and is in sharp contrast with the human's lifelong learning process. On the other hand, learning can often be brought on through overcoming some inconsistent circumstances. This paper proposes a framework for perpetual learning agents that are capable of continuously refining or augmenting their knowledge through overcoming inconsistencies encountered during their problem-solving episodes. The never-ending nature of a perpetual learning agent is embodied in the framework as the agent's continuous inconsistency-induced belief revision process. The framework hinges on the agents recognizing inconsistency in data, information, knowledge, or meta-knowledge, identifying the cause of inconsistency, revising or augmenting beliefs to explain, resolve, or accommodate inconsistency. The authors believe that inconsistency can serve as one of the important learning stimuli toward building perpetual learning agents that incrementally improve their performance over time.

1. INTRODUCTION

An important question in the long-term objective of machine learning research is how to build lifelong or never-ending learners (Mitchell, 2006; Thrun & Mitchell, 1995; Thrun, 1995, 1998). The state-of-

the-practice in the field of machine learning thus far is largely dominated by the one-time learner paradigm: some learning algorithms are utilized on data sets to produce certain results such as a model or a target function, and then the learner is put away and the results are put to work (Mitchell,

DOI: 10.4018/978-1-4666-2651-5.ch006

2006). Such a learn-once-apply-next (or LOAN) approach is not adequate for an intelligent agent to deal with many real world problems and is in sharp contrast with human's lifelong learning process. On the other hand, learning is often brought on through some stimulus. What triggers an agent to be a perpetual learner, always ready to be engaged in the next round of learning to incrementally improve its performance, is another dimension of the desirable lifelong learning behavior for perpetual learning agents.

Inconsistency is ubiquitous in the real world, in human behaviors, and in the computing systems we build (Brachman & Levesque, 2004; Gotesky, 1968; Zhang, 2009a, 2009b, 2010a, 2010b, 2011a, 2011b; Zhang & Grégoire, 2011). Inconsistency manifests itself in a plethora of phenomena at different levels in the depth of knowledge, ranging from data, information, knowledge, meta-knowledge, to expertise. Each time when an inconsistency or a conflicting circumstance arises during its problem solving episode, an agent recognizes the nature of such inconsistency, and overcomes the inconsistency through refining or augmenting its knowledge. Such an agent can be engaged in a continuous and alternating sequence of problem-solving episodes and inconsistency-induced-learning episodes, with each such iteration resulting in an incremental performance improvement for the agent. This inconsistency-induced learning capability can play a pivotal role in developing perpetual learning agents.

In this paper, our focus is on utilizing such inconsistency-induced learning to build perpetual learning agents that incrementally improve their performance over time. We describe a framework for perpetual learning agents that are capable of continuously revising or augmenting their knowledge through overcoming inconsistencies encountered during their problem-solving episodes. In the framework, inconsistencies an agent confronts during its problem-solving episodes serve as the learning stimuli, and the perpetual learning process is embodied in the continuous inconsistency-induced belief revisions. The main contributions of our work include: (1) some fundamental concepts for perpetual learning agents; (2) the role of inconsistency in learning; (3) inconsistency-induced learning that proves to be a viable and useful approach toward building perpetual learning agents; and (4) the generality and flexibility of the proposed framework in accommodating different types of inconsistencies.

The rest of the paper is organized as follows. Section 2 offers a brief review on related work. Section 3 describes the proposed framework for perpetual learning agents. Section 4 provides a summary of various types of inconsistencies that can serve for the purpose of learning stimuli. In Section 5, we discuss the inconsistency-induced learning for a particular type of inconsistency and use an example to illustrate how such a framework accomplishes the continuous learning process. Finally, Section 6 concludes the paper with remarks on future work.

2. RELATED WORK

How to build lifelong learners for intelligent agent systems has been an important agenda item in the field (Mitchell, 2006; Thrun & Mitchell, 1995; Thrun, 1995, 1998). Reports of some initial research results toward this long-term objective have emerged recently.

The work reported in Carlson, Betteridge, Kisiel, Settles, Hruschka, and Mitchell (2010) discussed results in developing a never-end language learner called NELL. NELL relies on semi-supervised learning methods and a collection of knowledge extraction methods to learn noun phrases from specified semantic categories and with specified semantic relations. With an initial seed ontology of 123 categories and 55 relations, NELL was able to learn 242,453 new facts from the web with an estimated precision of 74% during a period of 67 days. NELL has four component learners: a pattern learner, a semi-structured extractor, a morphological classifier, and a rule learner. Candidate facts produced by component learners have to pass the muster of the knowledge integrator in order to be promoted to the status of beliefs in the knowledge base. NELL also accommodates human interaction to approve or reject inference rules learned by the rule learner component.

An agent system called ALICE was described in Banko and Etzioni (2007) that conducts life-long learning to build a set of concepts, facts and generalizations with regard to a particular topic directly from a large volume of Web text. Starting from a domain-specific corpus of texts, some background knowledge, and a control strategy, ALICE learns to update and refine a theory of the domain. Different strategies have been used by ALICE to generate and prioritize different tasks of theory-learning.

Continual learning is defined in Ring (1997) as a continual process where learning occurs over time, and time is monotonic: An agent with continual learning capability possesses sequential and incremental knowledge. What experience it acquires at one point in time when dealing with one task is retained and can be reused later to solve a different task. A continual learner has the following properties (Ring, 1997): (1) It is autonomous. (2) Learning is embodied in problem solving. (3) Nature of learning is incremental. There is no fixed training set. (4) Learning occurs at multiple time steps. (5) Learning is hierarchical. Knowledge an agent acquires now can be built upon and modified later.

An agent system called CHILD was described in Ring (1997). CHILD, capable of Continual, Hierarchical, Incremental Learning and Development, combines reinforcement learning (Q-learning) with the temporal transition hierarchies

learning algorithm and learns in a highly restricted subset of possible environments.

YAGO is a large and extendable ontology capable of unifying facts automatically extracted from Wikipedia Web documents to concepts in WordNet (Suchanek, Kasneci, & Weikum, 2007). YAGO exhibits its continuous learning capability by allowing new facts to be incrementally added to an existing knowledge base. Knowledge gleaned by YAGO is of high quality in terms of coverage and accuracy.

There are a number of important differences between the aforementioned work and the focuses of research in this paper.

1. We emphasize the dimension of the stimulus for learning, i.e., what can be the causes for initiating a learning process? This is not necessarily the focus in related work. In general, there can be many possible learning stimuli. We consider inconsistency induced causes for initiating learning episodes in this work.

2. Our reported results have a problem-solving slant, i.e., learning to incrementally improve performance for solving problems at hand, whereas the related work is primarily geared toward the general task of knowledge-acquisition, or building an ontology or a domain theory.

3. The timing in learning process also differs: our proposed framework adopts discrete learning episodes (as triggered by conflicting phenomena), whereas the learning process in related work is largely continuous, not necessarily triggered by any events.

4. We utilize inconsistency related heuristics for perpetual learning.

5. Most of the related work (with the exception of CHILD) is web-centric in the sense that learning is carried out with regard to web texts. Our proposed framework is not necessarily web-centric.

3. PROPOSED FRAMEWORK

Before describing the proposed framework for inconsistency induced learning, we need to define several necessary concepts.

Definition 1: A perpetual learning agent (PeLA) is one that engages in a continuous and alternating sequence of problem-solving episodes and learning episodes. In such an alternating sequence, we use *learning burst* (LB(i), the ith learning burst) and *applying burst* (AB(i), the ith applying burst) to represent reoccurring learning episodes and knowledge application (problem solving) episodes. Two transitions exist for such perpetual learning agent: from learning to applying (LAT(i), the ith learning to applying transition) after the agent's knowledge is refined or augmented; and from applying to learning (ALT(i), the ith applying to learning transition) when the agent needs to be engaged in refining or augmenting its knowledge.

Schematically, we use a horizontal line to separate the learning phases from applying phases. Each bell shape above the line indicates an LB(i), and each reverse bell shape below the line describes an AB(i) (Figure 1). The transition points are where an LB and an AB meet at the line. Let LB(i)$\searrow$AB(i) denote the meet point where LB(i) immediately precedes AB(i) in time; and AB(i)$\nearrow$LB(i+1) denote the meet point where AB(i) immediately precedes LB(i+1). Then

$$LAT(i) = LB(i)\searrow AB(i) \qquad (1)$$

$$ALT(i) = AB(i)\nearrow LB(i+1) \qquad (2)$$

Let $\hat{S}$ (i) be a finite sequence of events with index i and $[\hat{S}$ (i)$]^+$ denote that $\hat{S}$ (i) occurs at least once (i=1,2,…).

$$[\hat{S}\ (i)]^+ ::= [\hat{S}\ (i)] \mid [\hat{S}\ (1) \rightarrow \hat{S}\ (2)] \mid [\hat{S}\ (1) \rightarrow \hat{S}\ (2) \rightarrow \hat{S}\ ] \mid \ldots\ldots (3) \qquad (3)$$

The behavior of a perpetual learning agent h(PeLA) can then be defined as follows:

Figure 1. Perpetual learning

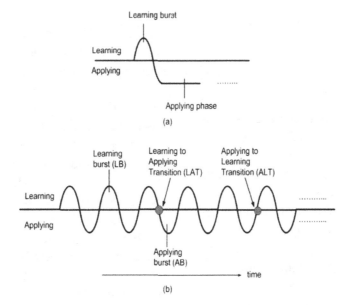

$$h(\text{PeLA}) = [\text{LB}(i) \rightarrow \text{LAT}(i) \rightarrow \text{AB}(i) \rightarrow \text{ALT}(i)]^+$$
$$i=1, 2, 3, \ldots \tag{4}$$

An LB bell shape denotes a single learning session and an AB bell shape represents one or more problem solving session(s).

Figure 1 depicts the difference between the learn-once-apply-next paradigm (Figure 1 (a)) and the perpetual learning paradigm (Figure 1 (b)). The behavior of a LOAN agent, denoted as $h(\text{PeLA})_{\text{LOAN}}$, is a special case of (4) where the second transition point ALT(i) is indefinitely postponed:

$$h(\text{PeLA})_{\text{LOAN}} = [\text{LB}(1) \rightarrow \text{LAT}(1) \rightarrow \text{AB}(1)] \tag{5}$$

Our focus in this paper is on utilizing the inconsistent circumstances encountered during problem solving episodes as triggers for ALT(i), and as heuristics for LB(i+1). We use $\text{LB}(i)_I$ to indicate the inconsistency-induced learning episode, and the following denotation to emphasize inconsistency-triggered transition:

$$\text{ALT}(i)_I = \text{AB}(i) \nearrow_I \text{LB}(i+1) \tag{6}$$

As a result, the framework is proposed to support the following behaviors of a PeLA:

$$h(\text{PeLA})_I = [\text{LB}(i)_I \rightarrow \text{LAT}(i) \rightarrow \text{AB}(i) \rightarrow \text{ALT}(i)_I]^+ \tag{7}$$

Definition 2: A perpetual learning agent has (a) a knowledge base (KB) for persistent knowledge and beliefs, and domain or ontological constraints, assumptions and defaults; (b) a meta knowledge base (mKB) for the agent's meta-knowledge (knowledge on how to apply domain knowledge in KB during problem solving); (c) a working memory (WM) where reasoning takes place with activated beliefs from KB and problem specific facts; (d) a component called CAL (Coordinator

for Applying burst and Learning burst) that recognizes inconsistency and initiates learning bursts, and (e) a learning module that is triggered by some inconsistent circumstance during problem solving process and carries out inconsistency induced learning that leads to KB, mKB, or WM (or any combination of the three) refinement or augmentation.

Now we are in a position to describe the proposed framework for perpetual learners. As shown in Figure 2, there is an initial bootstrap of the agent's KB. After that, the agent is able to be participating in the problem solving process.

The next AB will last as long as the agent is capable of competently solving problems based on its KB, mKB and WM. When a conflicting situation arises in WM during the problem solving process, CAL detects it, suspends the current problem solving session, passes the specific inconsistent circumstance to the learning module, and waits for the result from the learning module. Thus, CAL initiates the next learning burst. The learning module in turn carries out the learning process by recognizing the type of inconsistency in the conflicting circumstance, selecting the appropriate learning method or heuristics to explain, resolve, or accommodate the identified inconsistency. Some human interaction may be required at this stage. The outcome of the learning process could be: either KB or mKB being refined or augmented, or WM being revised, or some or all of them being updated, or none of them being changed (in the case that human expert's discernment indicates otherwise). Afterward, the learning module notifies CAL of the result, and passes any WM revisions to CAL, and CAL in turn refreshes WM with any changes from the learning module and restarts the problem solving session that was suspended as a result of encountering the conflicting circumstance. This signifies the end of the current LB and the agent is ready to enter the next AB to pick up where it left off during its previous AB. The agent will continue engaged in

Figure 2. Proposed framework of i²Learning for perpetual learners

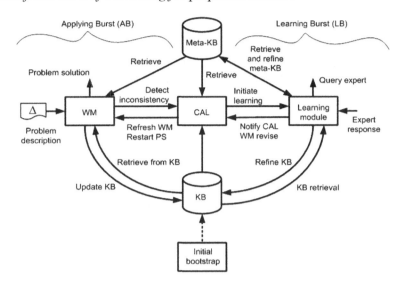

problem solving until it detects the next inconsistent scenario. Each such iteration results in an incremental performance improvement for the agent. We call such an inconsistency-induced learning as *i²Learning*.

The logic of the learning module is captured in Figure 3. The types of learning that help improve the agent's performance are essentially embodied in the types of inconsistency handling. There have been various manifestations of inconsistent data, information, knowledge, and meta-knowledge in different domains (Zhang, 2009a, 2009b, 2010a, 2010b, 2011a, 2011b; Zhang & Grégoire, 2011). A list of categories and inconsistent morphologies within each category is given in the next section.

The proposed framework is an overarching structure that accommodates growth and expansion in various inconsistency specific learning. Depending on which types of inconsistency the learning module can recognize and what corresponding algorithms or heuristics it comes equipped with in handling the inconsistency at hand, its inconsistency-induced learning capacities can change dynamically. The inconsistent scenarios a PeLA encounters at different points in time may be different for various ALT(i) and the learning strategies it adopts in the subsequent

LB(i+1) can vary accordingly. The box in heavy dotted line in Figure 3 can embody a rich set of inconsistency-specific learning algorithms.

Depending on how inconsistencies are generated in WM, there can be different paces or rates for learning. When inconsistencies are encountered in WM during problem solving sessions, then the rate of learning is driven by how frequent conflicting decisions or actions arise during knowledge application. On the other hand, inconsistencies can be intentionally injected into WM to induce learning bursts during the time when an agent is not engaged in problem solving. We regard this latter case as inconsistency-induced *speedup learning*. The primary objective of the agents is problem solving, and learning is just the means for agents to get progressively better at what they do.

Let iCateg be a set of inconsistency categories, and iMorph$_c$ be a set of inconsistent morphologies in a given inconsistency category c∈iCateg. We can regard i²Learning as a framework that accommodates a set of learning algorithms for specific inconsistency category-morphology pairs:

i²Learning = {i²Learning(c, m) | (c∈iCateg) ∧ (m∈iMorph$_c$)}

Figure 3. The learning module

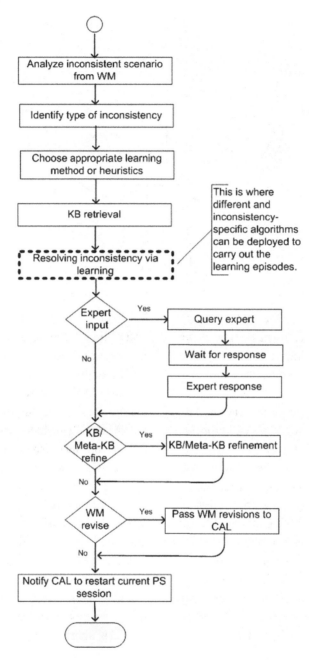

For each category c and an inconsistent morphology m in c, <c, m>, there is a <c, m> specific learning algorithm i²Learning(c, m) that underpins the process of overcoming this particular inconsistency (Figure 4). This allows for the perpetual learning agent to incrementally augment its inconsistency-induced learning capabilities as additional types of inconsistency are identified and their respective learning algorithms developed.

Figure 4. Inconsistency-specific learning algorithms

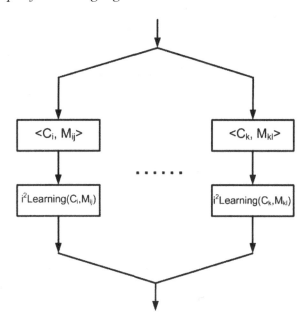

4. INCONSISTENCY CATEGORIES AND MORPHOLOGIES

At each stratification in the depth-of-knowledge hierarchy, knowledge can be represented in different formalisms and operationalized in various circumstances. Across the hierarchy of knowledge stratifications, inconsistent phenomena can arise in different categories and manifest themselves in different morphologies. Table 1 captures a list of some possible categories of inconsistency and some specific inconsistent morphologies within each category.

When cast in the light of a declarative formalism (classic logic, defeasible logic, description logic, or default logic), inconsistency can take on the following morphologies Zhang (2010b): (1) complementary: an atom and its negation; (2) mutually exclusive: mutually exclusive predicates that are syntactically different and semantically opposite of each other; (3) incompatible: an atom and the negation of its syntactically different but logically equivalent relation; (4) anti-subsumption: the antagonistic situation where a subtype is no longer subsumed by its supertype; (5) anti-

supertype: the converse of the anti-subsumption where the negation of the supertype and one of its subtypes hold at the same time; (6) asymmetric: a symmetric relation and its negation both hold; (7) anti-inverse: a relation and the negation of its inverse relation exist; (8) mismatching: a concept and the negation of one of its conjunctive and substantiating sub-concepts hold; (9) disagreeing: propositions having reified but disagreeing quantities for the same attribute; (10) contradictory: relations containing attribute values that violate type restrictions or integrity constraints; (11) precedence: opposite precedence relationships being asserted for the same set of entities; and (12) inconsistent probability value (iProbVal): if $\Delta \vDash L$, the probability value for L is outside the region specified by the extreme values of probabilities for Δ (Genesereth & Nilsson, 1987).

When the concept of time is incorporated into the formalism that is used to develop a system, depending on the interval relationships antagonistic propositions have, there are partial temporal inconsistency, and complete temporal inconsistency (Zhang, 2009a).

Table 1. Categories and morphologies of inconsistency

Category	Morphology
Declarative (DEC)	*Complementary inconsistency* (cpm)
	Mutually exclusive inconsistency (mex)
	Incompatible inconsistency (inc)
	Anti-subsumption inconsistency (ats)
	Anti-supertype inconsistency (atu)
	Asymmetric inconsistency (asm)
	Anti-inverse inconsistency (ati)
	Mismatching inconsistency (mim)
	Disagreeing inconsistency (dsa)
	Contradictory inconsistency (cot)
	Precedence inconsistency (pcd)
	iProbVal inconsistency (prb)
Temporal (TEM)	*Partial temporal inconsistency* (pti)
	Complete temporal inconsistency (cti)
Spatial (SPA)	*Topological inconsistency* (top)
	Location/attribute inconsistency (lai)
	Structural/semantic constraint violations (ssc)
Ontological (ONT)	*Conflicting concept subsumptions* (ccs)
	Contradicting membership relations (cmr)
Epistemic (EPI)	*Locally inconsistency* (loc)
	P2P inconsistency (p2p)
Argumentation (ARG)	*Rebutting arguments* (rba)
	Undercutting arguments (uca)
	Counterarguments (cta)
Contextual (CTX)	*Properties inconsistent with contexts* (pic)
	Properties inconsistent to expectations (pie)
Anomaly (ANO)	*Point anomalies* (pta)
	Contextual anomalies (cta)
	Collective anomalies (cla)
Learning (LEA)	*Complete and inconsistent hypothesis* (cih)
	Incomplete and inconsistent hypothesis (iih)
	Inconsistent classification/regression (icr)
Polymorphism (POL)	*Identity inconsistency* (idi)
	Metric inconsistency (mti)
Granularity (GRA)	*Attribute-oriented generalization induced inconsistency* (agi)
	Inter-stratification inconsistency (isi)
Integrity (ITG)	*Single dependence inconsistency* (sdi)
	Multi-dependence inconsistency (mdi)

continued on following page

Table 1. Continued

Category	Morphology
Inheritance (IHT)	*Property inheritance induced inconsistency* (pii)
	Exception induced inconsistency (eii)
Uncertainty (UNC)	*Closed-world assumption induced inconsistency* (cwa)
	Crowdsource induced inconsistency (csi)
Modeling (MOD)	*Class inconsistency* (cli)
	Sequence inconsistency (sqi)
	Statechart inconsistency (sci)

In the context of geospatial knowledge, the inconsistent morphologies include: topological inconsistency (violations of geometrical properties and spatial relations); location/attribute inconsistency (spatial objects having conflicting geometric locations); and structural/semantic constraint violations (Rodriguez, 2004).

An ontology contains meta-knowledge that provides a formal and explicit specification of a shared conceptualization for things in a problem domain. In the ontological category, inconsistency can result from circumstances such as conflicting concept subsumptions and from contradicting membership relations (Huang, van Harmelen, & ten Teije, 2005).

In a multi-agent system, autonomous agents have their own local knowledge and data about the world they are in. When agents exchange data or fuse knowledge during collaboration, inconsistency can arise due to their epistemic differences. Two types of epistemic inconsistency are defined for a data integration setting among autonomous agents in Calvanese, De Giacomo, Lembo, Lenzerini, and Rosati (2008). Local inconsistency refers to a situation where an agent's local data are inconsistent. P2P inconsistency describes a circumstance in which an agent A_i's local data (either A_i's native data, or data previously from another agent A_j but currently in A_i) conflict with data coming from the agent A_k.

From the perspective of argumentation systems, inconsistency manifests itself in terms of a rebutting argument which has a claim that is the negation of another argument's claim, an undercutting argument which has a claim that contradicts some of the assumptions of another argument, and a counterargument which is either a rebutting or an undercutting argument with regard to another argument (Besnard & Hunter, 2008).

Contextual inconsistency stems from contextual related circumstances where responses to events are inconsistent either with the context or with regard to expectations. Inconsistent deception technique epitomizes such contextual inconsistency as defensive measures for information assurance and security (Neagoe & Bishop, 2006).

Anomaly is a term being used to describe entities that are not consistent with expected patterns or behaviors (Chandola, Banerjee, & Kumar, 2009). Other terms such as outliers, exceptions, or peculiarities have also been utilized in the same context as anomalies in different domains. A point anomaly is an entity that is inconsistent with the rest of the entities; a contextual anomaly is an entity that is inconsistent either in pattern or in behavior with the rest of entities in a specific context; and collective anomalies refer to a set of entities that is inconsistent with respect to the entire entity set (Chandola, Banerjee, & Kumar, 2009).

Inductive logic programming (ILP) is one of the learning approaches. In ILP, a learned hypothesis h is represented as a set of first-order clauses. Let FP and FN denote the sets of false positive and false negative instances when h is used to predict unseen cases. h is inconsistent but complete if FP $\neq \varnothing$ and FN $= \varnothing$. h is inconsistent and incomplete if FP $\neq \varnothing$ and FN $\neq \varnothing$ (Lavrač & Džeroski, 1994). In disagreement based semi-supervised learning, the learner takes advantage of the inconsistent classifications or regressions, and improves the learning performance through ironing out the disagreement (Zhou & Li, 2010).

Polymorphism is another category where inconsistency stems from multiple ways of handling things (e.g., multiple ways of assigning identities, or measuring properties). The setuid inconsistency (when a process' ruid $\neq$ euid) in Unix flavored operating systems (Zhang, 2011b), epitomizes the identity inconsistency that creates potential security vulnerability due to a user process gaining elevated privileges). Another salient case pertains to metric inconsistency as witnessed in the 1999 NASA Mars Climate Orbiter failure where the inconsistency between the English unit and the metric unit of the navigation information by two separate teams ultimately contributed to the demise of the mission (Lloyd, 1999).

When generalizing a concept to promote it to a higher level of abstraction by suppressing its details at the current level (stratification), or specializing it from a higher stratification to a lower one, or dealing with concepts at different stratifications, the granularity at which concepts are defined and utilized may become an issue that will give rise to inconsistency. Results in Tsumoto and Hirano (2011) and Zhu and Shan (2006) illustrate cases of attribute-oriented generalization inconsistency, and inter-stratification inconsistency.

Integrity constraints play a pivotal role in guaranteeing the correctness of databases. Central to the integrity constraints are functional dependencies that specify that when certain attribute values are identical, certain other attribute values must be identical accordingly. When such dependencies are violated, it results in inconsistency (Martinez, Pugliese, Simari, Subrahmanian, & Prade, 2007). There are single functional dependence

inconsistency and multi functional dependencies inconsistency (Martinez, Pugliese, Simari, Subrahmanian, & Prade, 2007) and conditional functional dependencies (Fan, Geerts, Lakshmanan, & Xiong, 2009; Yeh & Puri, 2010).

Inheritance offers an effective type of logical reasoning for abstraction, classification and generalization in hierarchies of concepts or objects (Brachman & Levesque, 2004). Defeasible inheritance allows for inherited properties to be defeated or revised, thus creating situations where different paths in a given hierarchical structure of concepts end up sanctioning inconsistent concepts (Horty, 1994; Touretzky, Horty, & Thomason, 1987). Chief among the possible conflicting cases are property inheritance induced inconsistency and exception induced inconsistency.

Inconsistency can be generated as a result of uncertainty, ambiguity, imprecision vagueness, or imperfection (Dubois, Lang, & Prade, 1994). There are crowdsource-induced inconsistency and closed-world assumption induced inconsistency, among other things.

As an integral part of a formal design model, there are conditions that evaluate portions or aspects of the model to a truth value True or False. In the context of software design models, these conditions are referred to as consistency rules (Egyed, 2011). Inconsistency arises in such a model when there is a violation of some consistency rule. For UML-based models, there are class inconsistency, sequence inconsistency and statechart inconsistency (Egyed, 2011).

In order to facilitate the discussions that follow, we use uppercase letters and lowercase letters to represent the categories and morphologies in categories (as given in Table 1), respectively. Hence we have the following:

iCateg = {DEC, TEM, SPA, ONT, EPI, ARG, CTX, ANO, LEA, POL, GRA, ITG, IHT, UNC, MOD} iMorph$_{DEC}$ = {cpm, mex, inc, ats, atu, asm, ati, mim, dsa, cot, pcd, prb}

iMorph$_{TEM}$ = {pti, cti}

iMorph$_{SPA}$ = {top, lai, ssc}

iMorph$_{ONT}$ = {ccs, cmr}

iMorph$_{EPI}$ = {loc, p2p}

iMorph$_{ARG}$ = {rba, uca, cta}

iMorph$_{CTX}$ = {pic, pie}

iMorph$_{ANO}$ = {pta, cta, cla}

iMorph$_{LEA}$ = {cih, iih, icr}

iMorph$_{POL}$ = {idi, mti}

iMorph$_{GRA}$ = {agi, isi}

iMorph$_{ITG}$ = {sdi, mdi}

iMorph$_{IHT}$ = {pii, eii}

iMorph$_{UNC}$ = {cwa, csi}

iMorph$_{MOD}$ = {cli, sqi, sci}

5. INCONSISTENCY INDUCED LEARNING

In order for a perpetual learning agent to be operational, an adequate number of i²Learning algorithms need to be in place for various inconsistent morphologies as shown in Table 1. In this section, we use an i²Learning algorithm for a particular type of inconsistency, i²Learning(DEC, cpm), as an example to illustrate how the learning process is carried out in the proposed framework.

Complementary inconsistency refers to the derivation of an atom and its negation such as P(x) and ¬P(x). Let L_i and L_k be literals: L_i, L_k ∈{P(x), ¬P(x)} ∧ (L_i = ¬L_k). We use $L_i \neq L_k$ to denote complementary inconsistency, which can stem from a number of causes such as epistemic conflicts, conflicting defaults, belief revisions, lack of complete information, or defeasible inheritance (Zhang & Grégoire, 2011).

Definition 3: Four sets are defined as follows:
- Let I be a set containing conflicting circumstances or contradicting pieces of evidence expressed as pairs of complementary literals.
- Let ℵ denote the set of heads (conclusions) of the rules that explain the inconsistency.
- Let ℘ contain the set of predicates that appear in WM and that will be utilized during the learning bursts.
- Let R be the set of refined rules produced at the end of a learning burst. □

Once KB∪WM yields some conflicting literals, CAL detects the inconsistency and places complementary literals in I. It then generates ℘ based on the content of WM and produces ℵ through dependence analysis with regard to predicate(s) in I. Afterwards, CAL passes I, ℘, ℵ to the algorithm below as input. The algorithm, adopted from Mitchell (1997) and Quinlan and Cameron-Jones (1993), uses *Foil_Gain* as the heuristics in refining rule(s) that have their heads in ℵ. The set R of revised rule(s) will be the output of the algorithm (Box 1).

Once the algorithm produces R in a learning burst, refining KB amounts to:

$$KB = KB - R_{old} \cup R \qquad (9)$$

In the remainder of this section, we use an illustrative example to demonstrate how the aforementioned algorithm works in the proposed

Box 1.

```
Algorithm for i²Learning(DEC, cpm)
Input:        I, ℘, ℵ
Output:       R
R = ∅
E₊: set of ground literals for which p∈ℵ is positive
E₋: set of ground literals for which p∈ℵ is negative
while (E₊ ≠ ∅) do {
    r: p(..)←, where p∈ℵ ∧ precond(r) = ∅
    E_p- = E_-
    while  (E_p- ≠ ∅) do {
L_B = argmax{Foil_Gain(L, r)}
          L∈℘
add L_B to precond(r): p(..)← ...∧ L_B
E_p- = E' where E'= {e | (e ∈ E_p-) ∧ (precond(r) ⊢ e)}
    }
    R = R∪{r}
    E₊ = E₊ - {e | (e ∈ E₊) ∧ (r ⊢ e)}
}
return(R);
```

Let R_old be the following set before a learning burst:

$$R_{old} = \{r \mid r \in KB \wedge head(r) \in \aleph\} \qquad (8)$$

framework. The example below is abstracted from a real story on human perpetual learning behavior. Dave was on sabbatical visiting in Hong Kong, and stayed in a furnished apartment building. Before he had the internet connection set up in his room, he had to rely on the wireless connection available to residents in the lobby area. At the time when he checked in, he was told that any residents can enjoy the free wireless connection in the lobby area. When he can't connect with his laptop, but another resident John was able to, Dave approached the front desk, was subsequently given an authentication code, and was told that a resident having an authentication code can get connected in the lobby area. After finishing checking his emails, Dave kept the authentication code and went up to his room. The next day, when Dave came down to the lobby with the authentication code he kept from the day

before, he found out that the code did not work this time. Again after approaching the front desk, he was told that a fresh authentication code was only valid for three hours after its being utilized. It was not until after the third time that Dave learned, through an incremental and piecemeal manner, the complete knowledge on how to take advantage of the free wireless connection service in the lobby area. Dave knew full well that this complete knowledge he just acquired may or may not apply to another hotel or apartment and that when the same circumstance arises in the future, the learning process can be expedited by asking for not only the authenticate code necessary, but also its valid period at the same time.

The learning process in this real story indicates the following. (1) Contradictory circumstances in problem solving often serve to trigger an agent's next learning episode. (2) Knowledge is often acquired in an incremental and piecemeal fashion. An agent may iterate the learning process multiple times to gain full knowledge about some task. (3) The outcome of a learning process usually results in the agent's KB being refined or augmented. (4) Meta-knowledge can also be garnered (knowledge about how to learn domain knowledge better and faster next time).

What we have below is to encode Dave's perpetual learning patterns and knowledge refinement process into an agent using rules and the algorithm i^2Learning(DEC, cpm). The predicates we use below are self-explanatory. timestamp(x,y) indicates that x has a timestamp limit of y. ¬timestamp(x,y) indicates that x is not in the timestamp limit of y.

As the result of initial bootstrapping, KB_0 contains the following knowledge:

$$
\begin{array}{l}
\text{hasConnection(x)} \leftarrow \text{resident(x)} \\
\text{connected(x)} \leftarrow \text{hasConnection(x)} \\
\neg\text{connected(x)} \leftarrow \neg\text{hasConnection(x)} \\
\text{resident(john)} \\
\text{resident(dave)} \qquad\qquad\qquad\qquad KB_0
\end{array}
$$

At the time when the agent "Dave" failed to connect, WM_0, on the other hand, has the following facts:

$$
\begin{array}{l}
\text{hasConnection(john)} \\
\neg\text{hasConnection(dave)} \\
\text{hasAuthenCode(john, c)} \qquad\qquad WB_0
\end{array}
$$

CAL detects that there exists the following complementary inconsistency in $KB_0 \cup WM_0$ (the symbol "⊢" represents the derivation of the right-hand-side from the left-hand-side via some inference rule).

$KB_0 \cup WM_0 \vdash \{$connected(dave), ¬connected(dave)$\}$

The aforementioned complementary inconsistency would cause CAL to initiate an episode of learning to resolve the contradiction. The input passed to the learning module from CAL consists of the following:

I = {connected(dave), ¬connected(dave)}

$\wp$ = {resident, hasAuthenCode}

$\aleph$ = {hasConnection}

The algorithm i^2Learning(DEC, cpm) will use Foil_Gain to select a predicate in $\wp$ to be added to the condition part of the rule with "hasConnection" ($\in \aleph$) as its head so as to further refine the rule by excluding negative cases it covers. The learning burst LB_1 will refine the "hasConnection" rule into the following:

R = {hasConnection(x)←
resident(x)∧hasAuthenCode(x, y)}

Hence KB_1 now contains the following:

$$
\begin{array}{l}
\text{hasConnection(x)} \leftarrow \text{resident(x)} \wedge \text{hasAuthenCode(x, y)} \\
\text{connected(x)} \leftarrow \text{hasConnection(x)} \\
\neg\text{connected(x)} \leftarrow \neg\text{hasConnection(x)} \\
\text{resident(john)} \\
\text{resident(dave)} \qquad\qquad\qquad\qquad KB_1
\end{array}
$$

This refined KB_1 would capture the knowledge that allows an agent (being a resident and having an authentication code) to have the connection to the wireless system. When an agent tries to connect again using an authentication code that is beyond its 3-hour timestamp limit, WM now has the following state WM_1 (assuming that another agent for John has acquired complete knowledge already):

$$
\begin{array}{l}
\text{hasConnection(john)} \\
\neg\text{hasConnection(dave)} \\
\text{hasAuthenCode(john, } c_1) \\
\text{hasAuthenCode(dave, } c_2) \\
\text{timeStamp(} c_1, 3) \\
\neg\text{timeStamp(} c_2, 3) \qquad\qquad WB_1
\end{array}
$$

This would result in the following complementary inconsistency being detected. Though the same inconsistent circumstance occurs multiple times, each has a different cause.

$KB_1 \cup WM_1 \vdash \{connected(dave), \neg connected(dave)\}$

This time, CAL initiates the learning burst LB_{i+1} to resolve the contradiction with the following input passed to the learning module:

$I = \{ connected(dave), \neg connected(dave)\}$

$\wp = \{resident, hasAuthenCode, timeStamp\}$

$\aleph = \{hasConnection\}$

The learning burst LB_{i+1} will result in the following refined rule:

$R=\{hasConnection(x) \leftarrow resident(x) \wedge hasAuthen\\Code(x, y) \wedge timeStamp(y, 3)\}$

Therefore, KB_2 now contains the following:

hasConnection(x) ← resident(x)∧hasAuthenCode(x, y) ∧ timeStamp(y, 3)
connected(x) ← hasConnection(x)
¬connected(x) ← ¬hasConnection(x)
resident(john)
resident(dave) KB_2

KB_2 is now complete with regard to the knowledge for proper connection to the wireless network in the lobby area.

6. CONCLUSION

In this paper, we discussed the general issue of building an agent system that can be engaged in the so-called never-ending or perpetual learning during its lifetime, and examined how inconsistency can serve as an important stimulus in such a perpetual learner. We described a framework for developing perpetual i²Learning agent systems, and gave a certain level of design details on how the learning module in the framework would carry out the learning-through-overcoming-inconsistency paradigm. An algorithm was given for handling a specific case, the complementary inconsistency. Using an illustrative example, we explained how i²Learning(DEC, cpm) can be solidified within the framework. Our ultimate goal is to see to it that this proposed framework allows an agent to pursue a continuous and alternating sequence of learning and problem solving, with each learning burst resulting in an incremental performance improvement.

The main contributions of this research work can be summarized as follows. (1) We introduce some basic concepts regarding perpetual learning agents. (2) We shed light on the role of inconsistency in learning process. (3) i²Learning proves to be another viable and useful tool for building perpetual learning agents. (4) Our proposed framework is general and flexible in accommodating different types of inconsistencies as learning stimuli. As quoted in Gotesky (1968), Henri Poincare once said that contradiction is the prime stimulus for scientific research. Indeed, inconsistency can be very good learning stimulus for perpetual learning agents as well.

Future work can be pursued in the following directions. Empirical studies are needed to substantiate the viability and utility of the framework. Details of the i²Learning algorithms for frequently encountered inconsistencies still need to be fleshed out. How the framework can accommodate meta-knowledge learning is another issue worth exploring.

ACKNOWLEDGMENT

The authors would like to express their sincere appreciations to the anonymous reviewers for their comments that help improve the content and the presentation of this paper.

REFERENCES

Banko, M., & Etzioni, O. (2007, October). Strategies for lifelong knowledge extraction from the web. In *Proceedings of the Fourth International Conference on Knowledge Capture*, Whistler, BC, Canada (pp. 95-102).

Besnard, P., & Hunter, A. (2008). *Elements of argumentation*. Cambridge, MA: MIT Press.

Brachman, R. J., & Levesque, H. J. (2004). *Knowledge representation and reasoning*. San Francisco, CA: Morgan Kaufmann.

Calvanese, D., De Giacomo, G., Lembo, D., Lenzerini, M., & Rosati, R. (2008). Inconsistency tolerance in P2P data integration: An epistemic logic approach. *Information Sciences, 33*, 360–384.

Carlson, A., Betteridge, J., Kisiel, B., Settles, B., Hruschka, E. R., Jr., & Mitchell, T. M. (2010, July). Toward an architecture for never-ending language learning. In *Proceedings of the AAAI Conference on Artificial Intelligence*, Atlanta, GA.

Chandola, V., Banerjee, A., & Kumar, V. (2009). Anomaly detection: A survey. *ACM Computing Surveys, 41*(3). doi:10.1145/1541880.1541882

Dubois, D., Lang, J., & Prade, H. (1994). Possibilistic logic. In Hogger, C., Gabbay, D., & Robinson, J. (Eds.), *Handbook of logic in artificial intelligence and logic programming* (*Vol. 3*, pp. 439–513). Oxford, UK: Oxford University Press.

Egyed, A. (2011). Automatically detecting and tracking inconsistencies in software design models. *IEEE Transactions on Software Engineering, 37*(2), 188–204. doi:10.1109/TSE.2010.38

Fan, W., Geerts, F., Lakshmanan, L., & Xiong, M. (2009). Discovering conditional functional dependencies. In *Proceedings of the International Conference on Data Engineering* (pp. 1231-1234).

Genesereth, M. R., & Nilsson, N. J. (1987). *Logical foundations of artificial intelligence*. San Francisco, CA: Morgan Kaufmann.

Gotesky, R. (1968). The uses of inconsistency. *Philosophy and Phenomenological Research, 28*(4), 471–500. doi:10.2307/2105687

Horty, J. (1994). Some direct theories of nonmonotonic inheritance. In D. Gabbay, C. Hogger, & J. Robinson (Eds.), *Handbook of logic in artificial intelligence and logic programming. Volume 3: Nonmonotonic reasoning and uncertain reasoning* (pp. 111-187). Oxford, UK: Oxford University Press.

Huang, Z., van Harmelen, F., & ten Teije, A. (2005). Reasoning with inconsistent ontologies. In *Proceedings of the 19th International Joint Conference on Artificial Intelligence*, Edinburgh, Scotland (pp. 454-459).

Lavrač, N., & Džeroski, S. (1994). *Inductive logic programming: Techniques and applications*. New York, NY: Ellis Horwood.

Lloyd, R. (1999). *Metric mishap caused loss of NASA orbiter*. Retrieved from http://www.cnn.com/TECH/space/9909/30/mars.metric.02/

Martinez, M. V., Pugliese, A., Simari, G. I., Subrahmanian, V. S., & Prade, H. (2007). How dirty is your relational database? An axiomatic approach. In K. Mellouli (Ed.), *Proceedings of the 9th European Conference on Symbolic and Quantitative Approaches to Reasoning with Uncertainty*, Hammamet, Tunisia (LNCS 4724, pp. 103-114).

Mitchell, T. (1997). *Machine learning*. New York, NY: McGraw-Hill.

Mitchell, T. (2006). *The discipline of machine learning* (Tech. Rep. No. CMU-ML-06-108). Pittsburgh, PA: Carnegie Mellon University.

Neagoe, V., & Bishop, M. (2006, September 19-22). Inconsistency in deception for defense. In *Proceedings of the Workshop on New Security Paradigms*, Schloss Dagstuhl, Germany (pp. 31-38).

Quinlan, J. R., & Cameron-Jones, R. M. (1993, April 5-7). FOIL: A midterm report. In *Proceedings of the European Conference on Machine Learning*, Vienna, Austria (Vol. 667, pp. 3-20).

Ring, M. B. (1997). CHILD: A first step towards continual learning. *Machine Learning, 28*, 77–105. doi:10.1023/A:1007331723572

Rodriguez, A. (2004). Inconsistency issues in spatial databases. In L. Bertossi, A. Hunter, & T. Schaub (Eds.), *Inconsistency Tolerance* (LNCS 3300, pp. 237-269).

Suchanek, F. M., Kasneci, G., & Weikum, G. (2007). YAGO: A core of semantic knowledge unifying WordNet and Wikipedia. In *Proceedings of the International World Wide Web Conference* (pp. 697-706).

Thrun, S. (1995). *Lifelong learning: A case study* (Tech. Rep. No. CMU-CS-95-208). Pittsburgh, PA: Carnegie Mellon University.

Thrun, S. (1998). Lifelong learning algorithms. In Thrun, S., & Pratt, L. (Eds.), *Learning to learn*. Boston, MA: Kluwer Academic. doi:10.1007/978-1-4615-5529-2_8

Thrun, S., & Mitchell, T. (1995). Lifelong robot learning. *Robotics and Autonomous Systems, 15*, 25–46. doi:10.1016/0921-8890(95)00004-Y

Touretzky, D., Horty, J., & Thomason, R. (1987). A clash of intuitions: the current state of monmonotonic multiple inheritance systems. In *Proceedings of the Tenth International Joint Conference on Artificial Intelligence* (pp. 476-482).

Tsumoto, S., & Hirano, S. (2011, August). Fuzziness from attribute generalization in information table. In *Proceedings of the 7th IEEE International Conference on Cognitive Informatics*, Stanford, CA (pp. 455-461).

Yeh, P., & Puri, C. (2010, October). An efficient and robust approach for discovering data quality rules. In *Proceedings of the 22nd IEEE International Conference on Tools with Artificial Intelligence*, Arras, France (pp. 248-255).

Zhang, D. (2009a). On temporal properties of knowledge base inconsistency. In M. L. Gavrilova, C. J. K. Tan, Y. Wang, & K. C. C. Chan (Eds.), *Transactions on Computational Science V* (LNCS 5540, pp. 20-37).

Zhang, D. (2009b, July). Taming inconsistency in value-based software development. In *Proceedings of the Twenty First International Conference on Software Engineering and Knowledge Engineering*, Boston, MA (pp. 450-455).

Zhang, D. (2010a). Inconsistency: The good, the bad, and the ugly. *International Transactions on Systems Science and Applications, 6*(2-3), 131–145.

Zhang, D. (2010b). Toward a classification of antagonistic manifestations of knowledge. In *Proceedings of the Twenty Second International Conference on Tools with Artificial Intelligence*, Arras, France (pp. 375-382).

Zhang, D. (2011a). On localities of knowledge inconsistency. *International Journal of Software Science and Computational Intelligence, 3*(1), 61–77. doi:10.4018/jssci.2011010105

Zhang, D. (2011b). The utility of inconsistencies in information security and digital forensics. In Özyer, T., Kianmehr, K., & Tan, M. (Eds.), *Recent trends in information reuse and integration* (pp. 381–397). Berlin, Germany: Springer-Verlag. doi:10.1007/978-3-7091-0738-6_19

Zhang, D., & Grégoire, É. (2011). The landscape of inconsistency, a perspective. *International Journal of Semantic Computing, 5*(3), 1–22. doi:10.1142/S1793351X11001237

Zhou, Z. H., & Li, M. (2010). Semi-supervised learning by disagreement. *Knowledge and Information Systems, 24*(3), 415–439. doi:10.1007/s10115-009-0209-z

Zhu, H., & Shan, L. (2006). Well-formedness, consistency and completeness of graphic models. In *Proceedings of the 9th International Conference on Computer Modeling and Simulation* (pp. 47-53).

This work was previously published in the International Journal of Software Science and Computational Intelligence, Volume 3, Issue 4, edited by Yingxu Wang, pp. 33-51, copyright 2011 by IGI Publishing (an imprint of IGI Global).

Chapter 7
Toward Automatic Answers in User–Interactive Question Answering Systems

Tianyong Hao
Shanghai University of Electric Power, China

Jingsheng Lei
Shanghai University of Electric Power, China

Feifei Xu
Shanghai University of Electric Power, China

Liu Wenyin
City University of Hong Kong, China

Qing Li
City University of Hong Kong, China

ABSTRACT

A strategy of automatic answer retrieval for repeated or similar questions in user-interactive systems by employing semantic question patterns is proposed in this paper. The used semantic question pattern is a generalized representation of a group of questions with both similar structure and relevant semantics. Specifically, it consists of semantic annotations (or constraints) for the variable components in the pattern and hence enhances the semantic representation and greatly reduces the ambiguity of a question instance when asked by a user using such pattern. The proposed method consists of four major steps: structure processing, similar pattern matching and filtering, automatic pattern generation, question similarity evaluation and answer retrieval. Preliminary experiments in a real question answering system show a precision of more than 90% of the method.

1. INTRODUCTION

Though just emerged a couple of years ago, User-Interactive Question Answering (UIQA) (Liu et al., 2009; Buy Answers Consultation Ltd, 2011), *aka*, Collaborative (or Community) Question Answering (CQA) systems, e.g., Yahoo! Answers, Baidu Knows, and Naver, are becoming popular online information services now. Compared with a search engine, which can automatically return a long list of ranked, possibly relevant but usually long documents, and hence requires a user's manual, and sometimes, very tedious filtration to find the exact answer, a question answering

DOI: 10.4018/978-1-4666-2651-5.ch007

system just returns direct and exact answers, and thus, is more preferable. Moreover, only about 80% of desired information can be found by search engines, and even if the user is lucky, it still takes time for the user to manually filter and find the exact answer from the returned long list of documents. With the collaborative efforts from the huge number of users with various knowledge backgrounds, the user may obtain his/her desired information from UIQA/CQA systems with little effort. Hence, we are anticipating a new wave of hot Web information services based on such UIQA/CQA systems since they are natural complements to the automatic search engines; or alternatively, they can be used as manual search engines to meet the ever-increasing information need of users.

Given their Web 2.0 nature, UIQA/CQA systems have accumulated more and more questions and answers with ratings, which in turn become good sources of automatic search engines. For example, Yahoo! Answers alone has acquired an archive of more than 40 million questions and 500 million answers, according to 2008 estimates. However, unaware of previous questions and answers accumulated, or being unwilling to spend time in searching for them, people often ask repeated or very similar questions. As a result, repeated answers need to be provided again and again and cause a huge waste of resources. Hence, it is a new challenge to develop a suitable method that can make reuse of these accumulated questions and answers effectively.

In this paper, we propose a new scheme in our UIQA system (Buy Answers Consultation Ltd, 2011) which can accumulate the questions and answers in a more structured, and even a more semantic-oriented way. We wish such scheme can make it possible to automatically and accurately answer repeated or similar questions based on previously accumulated question-answer pairs (QA pairs). The proposed scheme involves so called semantic question patterns, each of which is designed to generalize a class of questions with the same sentence structure and relevant semantics (Hao et al., 2007). A question pattern is

a generalized question with one or several blank slots, each of which is referred to as a variable component in this paper. Each variable component in a particular pattern is annotated by a semantic label, which is used not only to remind users to fill in correct words when using it, but also let machines know the semantics (from the label) of the filled-in words. Hence, it is called a semantic question pattern.

An initial set of frequently used semantic question patterns are extracted using an automatic question pattern generation method (Hao et al., 2008). These extracted patterns are further revised by human experts and stored in the pattern database in our system (Buy Answers Consultation Ltd, 2011). The system encourages users to ask questions with question patterns. When a user asks a new question in free-text, the system first tries to match it with a suitable pattern in the pattern database. If there is no pattern matched well, the system automatically creates a new pattern and lets the user confirm. Once the user confirms, the created pattern is added into the pattern database which is subject to validation by administrators (or experts). Whether a well-matched pattern is found or a new pattern is created, the question is converted into a pattern-based question, which consists of the pattern ID and the filled-in words for the variable component(s). Such pattern-based questions are accumulated in the question database with certain structures and semantics. Based on such organization, finding similar questions becomes much easier by just checking whether they have the same pattern ID and matching the filled-in words in the variable component(s). Once a similar question is found, its correct answer(s) can be used to reply the new question. Hence, higher efficiency and accuracy are expected than simply matching all text in the questions.

Using semantic question patterns, our automatic approach to answering repeated or similar questions consists of four main steps: (1) structure processing, (2) pattern matching and filtering, (3) automatic pattern generation, (4) question similarity evaluation and answer retrieval. Step

1 obtains the main structure and key nouns of a new question. Step 2 first finds the patterns from the pattern database which have similar structures to the main structure of the new question. These patterns are then filtered by the semantic labels of the key nouns of the new question to obtain the best matched pattern. The semantic labels here are automatically extracted from the label list in our Tagger Ontology (Hao et al., 2007), which is mapped to WordNet (Princeton University, 2007). If there is no pattern matching the new question, the system automatically generates a new semantic question pattern in Step3. Finally in Step 4, the most similar questions are retrieved by evaluating the similarity between the key nouns of the new question and their counterparts in the previously accumulated questions with the best matched pattern. The answers associated to those similar questions are then retrieved to answer the new question.

We implemented the proposed method in our UIQA system, BuyAns (Buy Answers Consultation Ltd, 2011). To evaluate the performance of the method, we randomly selected 400 questions from the system with their semantic patterns as ground truth. After parameter training, preliminary experimental results show that the precision of acquisition of the best answer to a new question can reach 90.8% on our testing dataset.

The rest of this paper is organized as follows: Section 2 introduces the related work including frequently asked question retrieval and the semantic patterns. Section 3 presents the proposed method in detail. Preliminary experiments with result analysis are shown in Section 4. Section 5 summarizes this paper and discusses the future work.

2. RELATED WORK

Question answering (QA) is an emerging new information service following the popularization of search engines. Automatic QA systems were designed to find the most relevant parts (usually in short paragraphs or just one or two sentences) in long documents with respect to user queries. The QA track in the Text REtrieval Conference (TREC) (Voorhees, 1999) enables researchers to share their experiences and provides a global metric for assessing QA system performance. After a decade of constant efforts of research, automatic QA has become a new well-known sub-area of information retrieval.

The user scenario of UIQA/CQA is different, in the sense that the answers are provided by other users manually. Compared with those returned by automatic QA systems, the manual answers in UIQA/CQA systems are more relevant and accurate. Automatically answering repeated or similar questions in UIQA/CQA systems is more like the process of answering or retrieving frequently asked questions (FAQ). In general, FAQ retrieval is a task of retrieving information from a set of free-text documents or semi-structured text documents. It retrieves the existing QA pairs from the frequently-asked question files (or databases) (Burke et al., 1997) rather than generates the desired answers in automatic QA systems. FAQ systems include the following two characteristics: (1) They are designed for retrieval of very frequent, popular, and highly reusable QA pairs; (2) QA pairs are generally provided, verified, and periodically maintained by domain experts.

FAQ retrieval has been an important research area in the past few years (Wu et al., 2005). Auto-FAQ (Whitehead, 1995) relied on a shallow, surface-level analysis for similar question retrieval. FAQ-Finder (Hammond et al., 1995) adopted two major aspects, i.e., concept expansion using the hypernyms defined in WordNet and the TF-IDF weighted score in retrieval process. In FAQ-Finder, certain question types may not be detected correctly, for examples, interrogative words like "what" and "how" are just the substrings of interrogative phrases "for what" and "how large", respectively. This misdetection may degrade system performance. To eliminate the above problem in FAQ-Finder, Tomuro combined lexicon with semantic features to automatically extract the interrogative words from a corpus of questions (Tomuro, 2002). Besides WordNet, FALLQ (Lenz et al., 1998) retrieved FAQs via case-based reasoning (CBR). Sneiders used question templates with entity slots that were replaced by data instances from the underlying database to interpret the structure of queries and questions (Sneiders, 2002). Berger et al. (2000) proposed a statistical lexicon correlation method for FAQ retrieval. Jeon et al. (2005) extended this method by introducing a translation model, which can estimate word translation probabilities, to find similar questions in CQA archives. Their report showed their method's significant improvements over previous methods. However, without the support of the semantics explicitly represented in the free-text question database, this method is far from mature for application in real CQA systems, because its precision among top 10 retrieved questions is still less than 0.5.

A structural question pattern is a generalization of a group of questions which have similar structures. It has been demonstrated that patterns can facilitate machine understanding and information retrieval as well. Among 65 participating systems in the TREC-10 QA competition, the winning system only used one resource to analyze the question: a fairly extensive list of surface patterns, which is a kind of structural pattern (Deepak et al., 2002). Many CQA systems use patterns to tackle user's questions and extract answers. Ion gives three different linguistic patterns to extract relevant information (Ion, 1999). However, all of these patterns do not include semantic information and are therefore called "poor-knowledge approaches" (Maximiliano et al., 2001). Without semantically analyzing questions and answers, they can hardly be used to extract precise answers or relevant information.

To overcome these shortcomings, we propose a new kind of semantic pattern which is based on structural pattern, but is also enriched with semantic labels (Hao et al., 2007). These semantic labels are actually semantic annotations, which can reduce the ambiguity of the questions and enhance semantic representation of the question when a user uses them to ask questions. Meanwhile, this pattern allows UIQA/CQA systems to locate answers based on its semantic type and filter out irrelevant answers by matching the semantic components of question patterns. Our semantic pattern is defined based on structural pattern, in which a semantic label is added to constrain the semantic type of the filled-in content in each corresponding variable component. A semantic pattern is mainly composed of five components: Question_Target, Question_Type, Concept, Event, and Constraint. Among these five parts, Question_Target, Question_Type, and Concept are essential components, while Event and Constraint are optional and can be added if necessary. For example, given a question "Who is the mayor of Calgary?", the question target is <Target: Human/Individual>, the question type is "<Q>Who</Q>" and two variable components are the two key concepts annotated as "[Human\Title]" and "[Location\City]", respectively. The question and the corresponding semantic question pattern are shown in Figure 1.

These labels are important semantic annotations for machine understanding. Therefore, it is important to define and manage these labels. A Tagger Ontology is designed in two levels to maintenance these labels, in which IS_A relationship is used to represent the basic relationship between two items in one semantic label (Hao et al., 2009). The semantic labels in the Tagger Ontology are defined as [*Concept 1*] \ [*Concept 2*], where *Concept 1* and *Concept 2* have the relationship of *Subcategory*(*Concept1, Concept2*). The Tagger Ontology consists of 7 first level concepts and 63 second level concepts in total. It is organized in a certain concept hierarchy and can be mapped to WordNet by a predefined mapping table.

Figure 1. An example question and its semantic question pattern

Question: *"Who is the mayor of Calgary?"*

Semantic Pattern: *<Target: Human\individual>*
<Q>Who</Q> is [Human\Title] of [Location\City]?

3. THE METHOD

Our proposed method for automatically answering repeated or similar questions relies on the semantic question patterns which we encourage users to use. We assume all questions we accumulated in our QA system were asked previously by our users using semantic question patterns, which contain explicit structures and semantics. Even if a user has no knowledge of patterns and just asks a new question in free-text, our QA system first tries to match it with a suitable pattern in the pattern database. If there is no pattern matched well, the system automatically creates one or more new patterns using a pattern generation method (Hao et al., 2008) and let the user select or confirm. Hence, in our method, we exploit both structural matching and semantic matching between the new questions and accumulated questions. Given a new question, we first obtain its main structure and key nouns and then find the patterns from the pattern database which have similar structure to the main structure. These patterns are then filtered by the semantic labels of the key nouns of the new question to obtain the best matched pattern. The semantic labels of the key nouns are automatically found from the label list in our Tagger Ontology (Hao et al., 2007), which is mapped to WordNet. Finally, the most similar questions are found by evaluating the similarity between the key nouns of the new question and its counterparts in the accumulated questions previously asked with the matched pattern. The answers of those similar questions are retrieved as the answers for the new question. Figure 2 shows the entire flowchart of the propose method for automatically answering

repeated or similar questions. There are mainly three modules (labeled by dashed rectangles), namely, (1) structure processing, (2) pattern matching and filtering, (3) automatic pattern generation, (4) question similarity evaluation and answer retrieval. The steps in each of these modules are presented in more details in the following subsections.

3.1. Structure Processing

Even though we assume all questions are asked using patterns, we still accept free-text questions if the user finds no suitable patterns or simply wants to ask using free-text. In this case, given a new free-text question without a semantic pattern, the step of structure processing is necessary, which is to extract the question's main structure and key nouns. Otherwise, if the question is asked with a semantic pattern and its main structure and key nouns (and other pattern information) can be retrieved very easily based on theirs pattern relation.

The main structure is a simplified representation of the original question. It can be regarded as a template question with key nouns replaced by slots. The question type is firstly found by a simple matching with a list of keywords for known question types. All nouns are then extracted based on Part-of-Speech. Name Entity Recognition (NER) is used to identify certain atomic elements of information in text, including person names, company/organization names, locations, dates/times, percentages and monetary amounts. We mainly focus on recognizing people names and location names in this paper. No more than three key nouns are finally selected from these nouns

Figure 2. Flowchart of the propose method

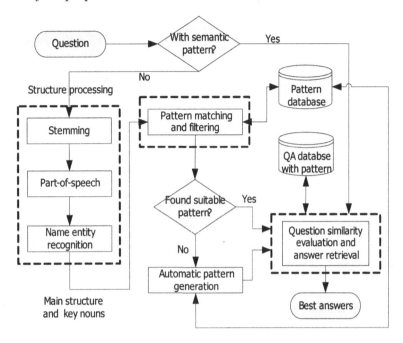

and name entities. The key nouns in a question are those nouns which can be selected for generalization and semantically labeling if a semantic pattern is automatically generated for this question. An entropy-based evaluation method is used to evaluate which nouns from all nouns are more suitable to be generalized. The detailed methods of finding key nouns can be found in our previous paper on automatic generation of semantic patterns (Hao et al., 2007).

Next, we use an example to illustrate how to obtain the main structure of a question. For example, given a question "Who is the mayor of Calgary?" we first acquire the question type "Who" by checking our question type list ("What", "Who", "When", "Where", "How", "How much" etc.) and label it as "<Q>Who</Q>". Based on Part-of-Speech, "mayor" is a noun, and according to NER, "Calgary" is extracted as a name entity of location. Both are key nouns according to entropy calculation and finally we obtain the main structure as "<Q>Who</Q> is [key noun] of [key noun]?"

3.2. Pattern Matching and Filtering

After obtaining the main structure (MS) of a question, the pattern matching procedure is used to find the question patterns which best match with the main structure. The procedure includes the following three steps.

Step 1: Retrieve an Initial Pattern Set (IPS) from the pattern database

This step is to match and retrieve all patterns which are relevant to the main structure (MS) of question q obtained in previous subsection from the pattern database. The resulting patterns are referred to as the Initial Pattern Set (IPS). The matching method is described in more detail as follows.

The MS is firstly split into a set of words and these words are then used to match with all patterns in the pattern database. The matching is done simply by counting matched words. The structure matching score for a pattern p_i is calculated by the Equation (1), where MS_q and MS_{pi} are the set of words in the main structure of question q and that of pattern p_i, respectively.

$$Score_{structure}(p_i) = \frac{2 \times \left| MS_q \cap MS_{p_i} \right|}{\left| MS_q \right| + \left| MS_{p_i} \right|} \qquad (1)$$

Step 2: Assign best semantic label for each key noun

For each key noun in the question, we calculate its similarity to all semantic labels in the label list in our Tagger Ontology using WordNet. The most important role of the Tagger Ontology is to tag nouns in the main structure with suitable semantic labels. For better understanding and easy usage by common users, it contains only two-level concepts, such as "Location\City". The similarity calculation method is as follows.

For a key noun kn and a label list $LL(sl_1, sl_2, ..., sl_i ..., sl_m)$, the similarity between kn and a semantic label ll_i is calculated by Equation (2) to take into account of both the relative depth of the nouns/labels and their distance in WordNet. Distance is usually used in the tree-based similarity calculation (Simpson et al., 2011) in WordNet. However, two concept pairs with the same distance may have different intuitional similarities perceived by our human beings. For example, the distance-based calculation method may generate the same similarity between "car" and "truck" and between "instrumentality" and "article" since the two groups of concepts have the same distance value. However, the first two concepts are more similar intuitively since they are more concrete concepts compared with the latter two. Lewis (2001) proposes a measurement of local density to solve this problem. Nonetheless, the space is divided over which density are calculated into two or more regions for each calculation thus the computation is very time-consuming. Based on this perception, we introduce the depth factor

into similarity calculation and propose a simple but efficient depth-based calculation, which is shown in the first part of Equation (2), with the distance-based calculation shown in the last part of the equation.

$$Sim(kn, sl_i) = \frac{Depth(kn) + Depth(sl_i)}{2 Max_{depth}} \times \frac{1}{\left(-\log \dfrac{1}{Distance(kn, sl_i)} + 1\right)} \qquad (2)$$

where $Depth(kn)$ is the number of levels of term kn from the root node "Entity" in WordNet; Max_{depth} is the maximum number of the levels in the taxonomy of WordNet; $Distance(kn, sl_i)$ is the minimum length of any ancestral path between these two terms in WordNet.

By this similarity formula, the best sl with the maximum similarity value can be selected and assigned as the best semantic label for this key noun.

Step 3: Acquire Matched Pattern Set (MPS) by semantic label filtering

In Step 1, we mainly consider structure matching when obtaining IPS. With the best semantic labels of question q obtained from Step 2, this step is to further compare the semantic labels of q with that of each candidate pattern p_i in IPS to get final Matched Pattern Set (MPS). Define SL_q as the semantic label set of q and SL_{pi} as that of a candidate pattern p_i. The semantic label-based matching score $Score_{sl}(p_i)$ of pattern p_i can be calculated using Equitation (3), where the matching strategy is similar to the structure-based matching in Step 1.

$$Score_{sl}(p_i) = \frac{2 \times \left| SL_q \cap SL_{p_i} \right|}{\left| SL_q \right| + \left| SL_{p_i} \right|} \qquad (3)$$

$$Score_{final}(p_i) = \sqrt{Score_{structure}(p_i) \times Score_{sl}(p_i)}$$
$$(4)$$

Therefore, the final matching score can be calculated using both the structure-based and semantic label-based matching scores. The detailed method is shown in Equation (4). The patterns which have higher final matching score than a threshold λ, which is trained in our experiments, are the final matched patterns.

3.3. Automatic Pattern Generation

If there is no pattern matched, the system will help the user to create a new pattern automatically. We propose a method for automatic generation of semantic patterns based on the definition of semantic patterns. It can analyze a free-text question to form its main structure. WordNet and the Tagger Ontology are then used to tag suitable nouns and verbs to obtain corresponding semantic labels. The main structure combined with labeled semantic information forms a new semantic question pattern. It consists of three main modules: (1) Structure processing and name entity recognition, (2) Entropy based selection of suitable nouns/verbs for generalization, (3) Semantic mapping and tagging. The method is described in more detail as follows.

Given a free-text question, we first analyze the sentence by structure processing and name entity recognition (NER) to obtain the main structure of the question. NER is used to identify certain atomic elements of information in text, including person names, company/organization names, locations, dates & times, percentages and monetary amounts. We mainly focus on recognizing people names and location names in this paper. Since NER affects the result of part of speech (POS) and the obtained main structure, we design a kind of tagger for name entity recognition, which can identify the common entity names based on our entity

dictionaries. The main structure can be seen as a simplified representation of the original question. It includes all the important parts of the question, such as question types, nouns and verbs, which are most useful in pattern generation. In addition, with the main structure we can ignore some useless information (such as the stop words and some meaningless words) for pattern generation. This procedure is similar to the structure processing step presented in Section 3.2.

All nouns and verbs in the main structure are candidates for generalization to form new patterns. However, some of them are more suitable to be generalized such that the generated patterns can cover more questions and are easily understood by users. We developed a method based on the entropy model to evaluate the sensitivity/suitability of a certain term in the question for generalization.

Before we describe our evaluation strategy, we would like to give some definitions first. Let Q refer to a question, term T_i (noun or verb) is the *i-th* nouns or verbs in Q, the upper concept of T_i is SC_j, and among all terms which have the same upper concept SC_j, the probability of T_i to occur is $p(T_i)$. The entropy value of upper concept SC_j can be calculated by Equation (5).

$$H(SC_j) = - \sum_{(T_i \in SC_j)} p(T_i) \log p(T_i) \qquad (5)$$

A higher entropy value $H(SC_j)$ means a bigger variety of words to replace T_i under the same concept and the more suitability of T_i for generalization and tagging. When it exceeds a threshold δ, we can select it as a candidate for semantic tagging. For better usage for common users in our system, we use γ to limit the number of selected nouns/verbs in the same question or the number of blanks in the pattern to be generalized. That is, if the number of selected nouns/verbs is more than γ, we only select top γ terms whose upper concepts have top entropy values.

95

After the main structure is obtained, the selected nouns/verbs are sent to the semantic tagging module to choose suitable semantic labels. This module includes two key steps: (1) Query from WordNet, and (2) Matching from the tagger ontology. The purpose of using WordNet is to label the nouns and verbs by their upper concepts. In the main structure, each noun and verb is searched in WordNet to get all of their upper concepts. The upper concepts obtained in the first step are mapped to the labels in the tagger ontology in the second step. The most important role of the tagger ontology is to tag nouns and verbs in the main structure with suitable semantic keywords. These tagged keywords contain semantic description and hierarchical relationship of concepts in the ontology and can therefore be understood by machines easily. It is also useful for manual questioning or answering. Users can understand the required content in the blanks of the patterns by their semantic labels when filling the blanks.

3.4. Question Similarity Evaluation and Answer Retrieval

Again, we assume all accumulated questions were posted with semantic patterns. Hence we referred to the accumulated question database as QA database with pattern. Since each question is assigned a unique pattern ID in our pattern database, we can acquire related questions and answers easily by querying their pattern IDs in the QA database with pattern.

For a new question q, now that we have already obtained its MPS in the previous step in Section 3.2 we can acquire a candidate question set QC (qc_1, qc_2 ... qc_n) from the QA database with pattern. Each question qc_i is a question with a pattern in MPS. For each qc we can obtain its key nouns KNC (knc_1, knc_2, knc_m) ($1 < m \leq 3$) easily since it is associated with a certain pattern. The similarity $Sim(kn_i, knc_i)$ between each key noun kn_i in q

and its counterpart knc_i in candidate qc can be calculated using the same method in Step 2 in Section III.B. The final similarity between kn_i and knc_i can be calculated by the Equation (6), where $Sim(kn_i, ll_i)$ is the similarity between kn_i and its label sl_i obtained from Equation (2), and $\pm$ is a weighting coefficient.

$$Sim_{final}(kn_i, knc_i) = \\ \pm \times Sim(kn_i, knc_i) + (1 - \pm) \times Sim(kn_i, sl_i) \quad (1 < i \leq \mathrm{m})$$

(6)

Finally, for the new question q, we calculate the similarity between q and each question candidate qc in QC, as mentioned before, using Equation (7), where $Score_{final}(p)$ is the matching score of p obtained from Equation (4). The question candidate with the highest similarity value is selected as the best matched question.

$$Sim(q, qc) = Score_{final}(p) \times \frac{\sum_{i=1}^{m} Sim_{final}(kn_i, knc_i)}{m}$$

(7)

With this best matched question, we can retrieve best answer for the question from QA database. In a typical UIQA system, askers usually make decision on which answer is the best answer based on their judgment. If the askers fail to select, the system usually help decide the best answer based on answer rating, answer quality evaluation, and time factor. Therefore, we can suppose all questions in our QA database in our system already have the associated best answers. Therefore, the correct answers associated with the best matched question can be returned to answer the new question q. It is worth noting that the time-relative questions can be asked either by complementing time in question directly or by adding time constraint if a specific pattern is used to ask.

4. EXPERIMENTS AND EVALUATION

We implemented our proposed method for answering repeated or similar question into our UIQA system. When a user posts a question in free text, the system analyzes its structure and suggests him/her with a short list of matched patterns (also filled in corresponding content automatically) from our pattern database. If the user would like to use a pattern, he/she can select and use a relevant pattern to ask the question. A hovering tip which contains a semantic label also appears when the user moves her mouse on a textbox (corresponding to a blank in the pattern). The user interface for this purpose is shown in Figure 3. If there is no matched pattern, the system generates a few semantic question patterns automatically for the user to select. However, the user may still choose to use the original free-text to ask. Currently, there are more than 480 semantic patterns accumulated in our system.

Even though the user does not use semantic pattern to ask, that is, the asking procedure is similar to the normal UIQA procedure, our system can also automatically answer this question by using our proposed method if there are similar questions answered before. The scenario is as follow: When the user submits a free-text question, this system automatically applies our proposed method described in Section 3. It firstly analyzes the question to obtain its main structure and key nouns. The main structure is then matched with the semantic patterns at the structure level and the key nouns are compared with semantic labels in Tagger Ontology to calculate their semantic similarity. The obtained best labels are further used to match with semantic patterns. Finally, the most similar questions are found by evaluating the similarity between the key nouns of the new question and its counterparts in the accumulated questions previously asked with the matched pattern. The answers of those similar questions are retrieved as the answers for the new question. Figure 4 shows an example of question with "auto answer", which is obtained based on the previous strategy.

To evaluate our method's accuracy, we randomly selected a set of 400 questions from our

Figure 3. User interface for user to select and confirm automatically matched semantic patterns

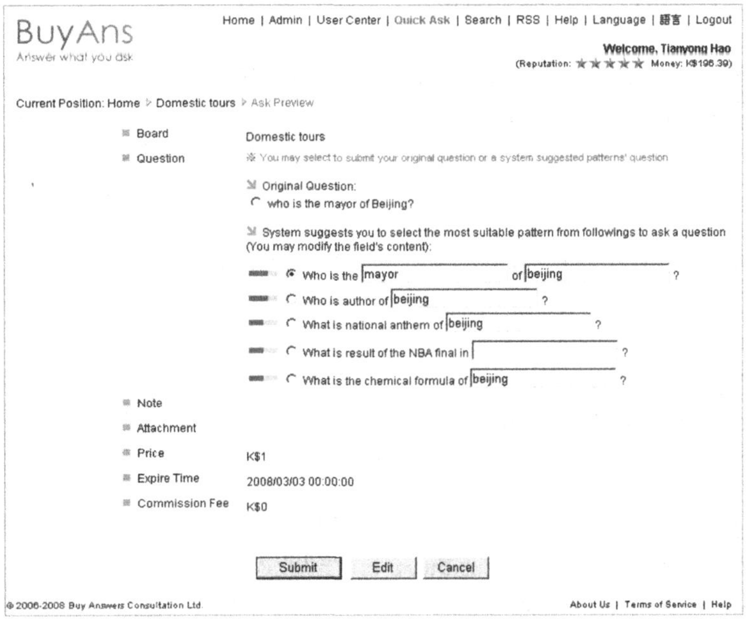

Figure 4. User interface of automatic question answering based on the propose method

accumulated question database (QA Database with Pattern in our BuyAns system) (http://www. BuyAns.com/ or http://www.cs.cityu.edu.hk/QA) as our ground truth dataset. We developed a program to modify each question in the ground truth dataset by changing words or adding words randomly and use these changed questions as queries. Those changed questions with only one changed word in each question form the testing dataset defined as C_1. Those changed questions with two changed words in each question form the testing dataset defined as C_2. The ground truth dataset and the testing datasets are available in our experiment website (http://www.BuyAns.com/experiments/auto-answer/ and http://144.214.120.174/QA/experiments/auto-answer/). The implemented model can also be accessed and tested online at the demo website (http://www.BuyAns.com/experiments/auto-answer/experiment_auto_answer.aspx and http://144.214.120.174/QA/experiment_auto_answer.aspx).

We evaluate our method's precision of answer retrieval using the formula defined in Equation (8), where "|*Correctly retrieved answers*|" is the number of all the correct answers retrieved from

the ground truth dataset for all the queries, and "|*Total retrieved answers*|" is the number of the total answers retrieved from the ground truth dataset for all the queries.

$$Precision = \frac{\left| Correctly\ retrieved\ answers \right|}{\left| Total\ retrieved\ answers \right|} \times 100\%$$

(8)

We first train the value of parameter λ, which is the threshold of pattern matching described in Section 3.2. The training dataset contains 50 questions selected from the ground truth dataset. The corresponding 50 randomly changed questions in C_1 and C_2, as mentioned before, are used as queries for matching with the questions in our QA database. The average precision, calculated by (6), varies when we use different λ. Finally, we found when λ is about 0.2, we can obtain the best average precisions, which is over 0.9. Hence, we select $\lambda = 0.2$ in the rest of our experiments.

With this best value (0.2) of parameter λ, we further run the experiments of structure matching on the rest 350 testing questions in our ground truth dataset, which are divided into 35 groups (since it is difficult to show the precision distribution of all 350 questions in a single figure), in C_1 and C_2, respectively. Our system analyzes each testing question in C_1 and C_2 to obtain its main structure and tries matching it with its ground truth pattern. The results show the precision distribution over 35 groups of questions, as shown in the Figure 5.

We can see that most of matching scores, which are defined in Equation (4), for the testing questions in both C_1 and C_2, exceed the threshold (λ =0.2). Hence, if the matching score between the retrieved pattern and the pattern in ground truth is larger than this threshold (λ =0.2), we regard the matching as correct matching. In this sense, all C_1 testing questions can be correctly matched to their ground truths and the average ratio of correct matching for C_2 is also as high as 94.3%. Therefore, we are confident that this method can indeed retrieve relevant question patterns thus find similar questions.

Next, with the same threshold λ =0.2, we test our method with all procedures (including pattern matching, question similarity evaluation and answer retrieval) on the 350 testing questions in C_1 and C_2 similarly. The precision of our proposed method is 94.4% and 90.8% on C_1 and C_2, respectively. The precision on C_1 is much higher than that for C_2 due to the features of our dataset that

C_2 has more modified words than C_1. Though precision on C_2 is lower, it is more reliable since the repeated or similar questions usually have more than one different word. Admittedly, more experiments on the testing datasets with more modified words are required to further prove the performance of our proposed method.

5. CONCLUSION AND FUTURE WORK

This paper presents an approach to automatically answering repeated or similar questions by using semantic patterns. By encouraging users to ask questions with patterns, the accumulated questions are well-structured and semantically labeled for more accurate matching with new questions. The approach consists of three major steps, namely, structure processing, pattern matching and filtering, and question similarity evaluation and answer retrieval. Preliminary experiments show the precision of our proposed automatic question answering method is over 90% on our testing dataset. Therefore, we believe that the question matching based on semantic patterns can be more accurate and efficient, and thus provide more accurate answer to repeated or similar questions. However, due to time limit, the current experiment scale in

Figure 5. Experimental result for structure matching

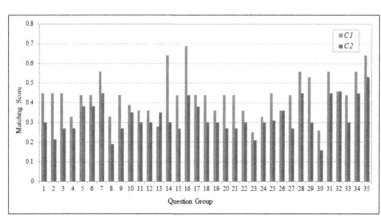

this version is not very large. We are continuing to prepare larger datasets for more comprehensive experiments. Further experimental results will also be shown in our experiment website later (http://www.BuyAns.com/experiments/auto-answer/ and http://144.214.120.174/QA/experiments/auto-answer/).

ACKNOWLEDGMENT

The work described in this paper was fully supported by the Natural Science Foundation of China (under grant no. 60863001, No.61073038, No.61073189, 91024012), the Innovation Program of Shanghai Municipal Education Commission (No.10ZZ115), and a grant from City University of Hong Kong (Project No. 7008043).

REFERENCES

Berger, A., Caruana, R., Cohn, D., Freitag, D., & Mittal, V. (2000). Bridging the lexical chasm: Statistical approaches to answer-finding. In *Proceedings of the 23rd Annual International ACM SIGIR Conference on Research and Development in Information Retrieval* (pp. 192-199).

Burke, R. D., Hammond, K., Kulyukin, V., Lytinen, S. L., Tomuro, N., & Schoenberg, S. (1997). *Question answering from frequently-asked-question files: experiences with the FAQ finder system* (Tech. Rep. No. TR-97-05). Chicago, IL: University of Chicago.

Buy Answers Consultation Ltd. (2008). *BuyAns*. Retrieved from http://www.BuyAns.com/

Deepak, R., & Eduard, H. (2002). Learning surface text patterns for a question answering system. In *Proceedings of the 40th Annual Meeting on Association for Computational Linguistics*, Philadelphia, PA.

Hammond, K., Bruke, R., Martin, C., & Lytinen, S. (1995). Faq-Finder: a case based approach to knowledge navigation. In *Proceedings of the Working Notes of the AAAI Spring Symposium on Information Gathering from Heterogeneous Distributed Environments*.

Hao, T. Y., Hu, D. W., Liu, W. Y., & Zeng, Q. T. (2007). Semantic patterns for user-interactive question answering. *Journal of Concurrency and Computation-practice & Experience, 20*, 1–17.

Hao, T. Y., Ni, X. L., Quan, X. J., & Liu, W. Y. (2009). Automatic construction of semantic dictionary for question categorization. *Journal of Systemics. Cybernetics and Informatics, 7*(6), 86–90.

Hao, T. Y., Song, W. P., & Liu, W. Y. (2008, January 16-18). Automatic generation of semantic patterns for user-interactive question answering. In *Proceedings of the Asia Information Retrieval Symposium*, Harbin, China.

Ion, M. (1999). Extraction patterns for information extraction tasks: a survey. In *Proceedings of the Workshop on Machine Learning for Information Extraction*, Orlando, FL.

Jeon, J., Croft, W. B., & Lee, J. H. (2005). Finding similar questions in large question and answer archives. In *Proceedings of the 14th ACM International Conference on Information and Knowledge Management*, Bremen, Germany.

Lenz, M., Hbner, A., & Kunze, M. (1998). Question answering with textual CBR. In *Proceedings of the International Conference on Flexible Query Answering Systems*, Denmark (pp. 236-247).

Lewis, W. D. (2001). Measuring conceptual distance using WordNet: The design of a metric for measuring semantic similarity. *Coyote Papers, 12*, 9–16.

Liu, W., Hao, T., Chen, W., & Feng, M. (2009). A Web-based platform for user-interactive question-answering. *World Wide Web: Internet and Web Information Systems, 12*(2), 107–124.

Maximiliano, S. N., Armando, S., & Manuel, P. (2001). Semantic pattern learning through maximum entropy-based wsd technique. In *Proceedings of the 5th Workshop on Computational Language Learning*, Toulouse, France.

Princeton University. (2007). *WordNet: A lexical database for English*. Retrieved from http://wordnet.princeton.edu/

Simpson, T., & Dao, T. (2011). *WordNet-based semantic similarity measurement*. Retrieved from http://www.codeproject.com/KB/string/semantic-similaritywordnet.aspx

Sneiders, E. (2002). Automated question answering using question templates that cover the conceptual model of the database, natural language processing and information systems. In *Proceedings of the 6th International Conference on Applications of Natural Language to Information Systems-Revised Papers*, Sweden.

Tomuro, N. (2002). Question terminology and representation for question type classification. In *Proceedings of the 2nd International Workshop on Computational Terminology*, Taipei, Taiwan.

Voorhees, E. (1999). The TREC-8 question answering track report. In *Proceedings of the Eighth National Institute of Standards and Technology Text REtrieval Conference* (pp. 743-751).

Whitehead, S. D. (1995). Auto-FAQ: An experiment in cyberspace leveraging. *Journal of Computer Networks and ISDN Systems*, 28, 137–146. doi:10.1016/0169-7552(95)00101-2

Wu, C. H., Yeh, J. F., & Chen, M. J. (2005). Domain-specific FAQ retrieval using independent aspects. *ACM Transactions on Asian Language Information Processing*, 4(1), 1–17. doi:10.1145/1066078.1066079

This work was previously published in the International Journal of Software Science and Computational Intelligence, Volume 3, Issue 4, edited by Yingxu Wang, pp. 52-66, copyright 2011 by IGI Publishing (an imprint of IGI Global).

Section 2
Cognitive Computing

Chapter 8
On Cognitive Models of Causal Inferences and Causation Networks

Yingxu Wang
University of Calgary, Canada

ABSTRACT

Human thought, perception, reasoning, and problem solving are highly dependent on causal inferences. This paper presents a set of cognitive models for causation analyses and causal inferences. The taxonomy and mathematical models of causations are created. The framework and properties of causal inferences are elaborated. Methodologies for uncertain causal inferences are discussed. The theoretical foundation of humor and jokes as false causality is revealed. The formalization of causal inference methodologies enables machines to mimic complex human reasoning mechanisms in cognitive informatics, cognitive computing, and computational intelligence.

1. INTRODUCTION

Causal inference is one of the central capabilities of human brains that play a crucial role in thinking, perception, reasoning, and problem solving (Zadeh, 1975; Payne & Wenger, 1998; Smith, 2001; Sternberg, 1998; Wang, 2003, 2007b, 2009b; Wang et al., 2009). Inferences are a cognitive process that reasons a possible causality from given premises between a pair of cause and effect. A causal inference can be conducted based on empirical observations, formal inferences, and/or statistical norms (Bender, 1996; Wang, 2007a, 2007b, 2008; Wilson & Keil, 2001).

DOI: 10.4018/978-1-4666-2651-5.ch008

Definition 1: A *causation* is a relationship between a sole or multiple causes and a single or multiple effects.

A causation is usually a pair of (*cause, effect*). The causal relations may be 1-1, 1-*n*, *n*-1, and *n*-*m*, where *n* and *m* are integers greater than 1 that represent multiple relations. The *cause* in a causation is a premise state such as an event, phenomenon, action, behavior, or existence; while the *effect* is a consequent or conclusive state such as an event, phenomenon, action, behavior, or existence.

Definition 2: An *inference* is a cognitive process that deduces a conclusion, particularly a causation, based on evidences and reasoning.

Formal logic inferences may be classified as deductive, inductive, abductive, and analogical inferences (Hurley, 1997; Ross, 1995; Schoning, 1989; Smith, 2001; Sternberg, 1998; Tomassi, 1999; van Heijenoort, 1997; Wang, 2007b, 2007c; Wang et al., 2009; Wilson & Keil, 2001). *Deduction* is a cognitive process by which a specific conclusion necessarily follows from a set of general premises. *Induction* is a cognitive process by which a general conclusion is drawn from a set of specific premises based on a set of samples in reasoning or experimental evidences. *Abduction* is a cognitive process by which an inference to the best explanation or most likely reason of an observation or event. *Analogy* is a cognitive process by which an inference about the similarity of the same relations holds between different domains or systems, and/or examines that if two things agree in certain respects then they probably agree in others.

Although logic inferences may be carried out on the basis of abstraction and symbolic reasoning with crisp sets and Boolean logic, more human inference mechanisms and rules such as those of intuitive, empirical, heuristic, and perceptive inferences, are fuzzy and uncertain, which are yet to be studied by fuzzy inferences on the basis of fuzzy sets and fuzzy logic (Zadeh, 1965, 1975, 2006; Wang, 2008).

This paper presents a theory of causation network toward machine-enabled inference and reasoning in cognitive informatics and computational intelligence. In the remainder of this paper, the taxonomy and mathematic models of causations are explored in Section 2 based on the causation network. The framework and properties of causal inferences are described in Section 3. Methodologies for uncertain causal inferences are elaborated in Section 4, followed by the analysis of humor and jokes as false causality.

2. THE TAXONOMY AND NETWORKS OF CAUSATIONS

Causality is a universal phenomenon because any rational state, event, action, or behavior has a cause. Further, any sequence of states, events, actions, or behaviors may be identified as a series of causal relations. It is recognized that the most general form of causations is that of many-to-many, i.e., a network relationship among the causes and effects. Therefore, this section puts emphases of causality modeling on the framework of causal inferences and the formal causal representation technology known as causation networks.

2.1 The Taxonomy of Causations

This section explores the taxonomy of causations and their generic properties. The simplest causation known as the binary or pairwise causation is analyzed below.

Definition 3: A *binary causation* κ_b is a binary relation that links a pair of events or states as the cause P and effect Q, i.e.:

$$\kappa_b \mathbf{BL} \triangleq (P\mathbf{BL} \vdash Q\mathbf{BL})\mathbf{BL} \tag{1}$$

where ⊢ denotes yield and the cause, effect, and propositions are in type Boolean as denoted by the type suffix BL. Hence, $\kappa_b BL = T$ called a *valid* causation, otherwise it is a *fallacy*, i.e., $\kappa_b BL = F$.

Equation 1 can also be denoted in a vertical structure as follows:

$$\kappa_b \mathbf{BL} \triangleq \left| \frac{Premises\mathbf{BL}}{Conclusion\mathbf{BL}} \right| = \left| \frac{P\mathbf{BL}}{Q\mathbf{BL}} \right| \qquad (2)$$

The binary causation as given in Equations 1 and 2 can be extended to complex ones such as *n*-nary, chain, reflective, and loop causalities as follows.

Definition 4: An *n-nary causation* κ_n is a composite form of binary causation where multiple causes $P_1\mathbf{BL}, P_2\mathbf{BL}, ..., P_n\mathbf{BL}$, mutually result in an effect, i.e.:

$$\kappa_n \mathbf{BL} \triangleq ((P_1\mathbf{BL} \wedge P_2\mathbf{BL} \wedge ... \wedge P_n\mathbf{BL}) \vdash Q\mathbf{BL})\mathbf{BL}$$
$$= (\bigwedge_{i=1}^{n} P_i\mathbf{BL} \vdash Q\mathbf{BL})\mathbf{BL} \qquad (3)$$

Definition 5: A *chain causation* κ_c is a series of *n* causations where each state Q_i, $1 \le i \le n$, as an effect of a preceding cause, is the cause of a succeeding effect Q_{i+1}, i.e.:

$$\kappa_c \mathbf{BL} \triangleq (P\mathbf{BL} \vdash Q_1\mathbf{BL} \vdash Q_2\mathbf{BL} \vdash ... \vdash Q_n\mathbf{BL})\mathbf{BL}$$
$$= (P\mathbf{BL} \overset{n}{\underset{i=1}{\vdash}} Q_i\mathbf{BL})\mathbf{BL} \qquad (4)$$

There are also reflective causations in which two or more events, states, or propositions are mutually cause and effect directly or indirectly.

Definition 6: A *reflective causation* κ_r is a bi-directional causation where two states P

and Q are mutually cause and effect with each other, i.e.:

$$\kappa_r \mathbf{BL} \triangleq (P\mathbf{BL} \vdash Q\mathbf{BL})\mathbf{BL} \wedge (Q\mathbf{BL} \vdash P\mathbf{BL})\mathbf{BL} \qquad (5)$$

Definition 7: A *loop causation* κ_l is an indirect reflective causation where an indirect effect Q_n becomes a cause of the cause P in the loop, i.e.:

$$\kappa_l \mathbf{BL} \triangleq (P\mathbf{BL} \vdash (Q_1\mathbf{BL} \vdash Q_2\mathbf{BL} \vdash ... \vdash Q_n\mathbf{BL}) \vdash P\mathbf{BL})\mathbf{BL}$$
$$= (P\mathbf{BL} \overset{n}{\underset{i=1}{\vdash}} Q_i\mathbf{BL} \vdash P\mathbf{BL})\mathbf{BL} \qquad (6)$$

A framework of causations can be described by the set of definitions and properties of the five-type causations as given in Equations 1 through 6. Examples of the binary, *n*-nary, chain, reflective, and loop causations will be elaborated in Section 3.

2.2 The Causation Network

In formal causal analyses, either a cause or an effect may also be a composite entity that represents a chain of causality as shown in Definition 5. Therefore, the concept of a causality network can be introduced as follows.

Definition 8: A *causation network* (*CN*) is a digraph $(N, \vec{R})$ where each node in N represents a cause $c \in C_i$, $1 \le i \le n$, and/or an effect $e \in E_j$, $1 \le j \le m$, and each directed relation (edge) →, κ_{CN}, $\kappa_{CN} \in \vec{R}$, is a binary causation, i.e.:

$$CN \triangleq (N, \vec{R})$$
$$= {}^o{}_{CN} : \underset{i=1}{\overset{n}{X}} C_i \rightarrow \underset{i=j}{\overset{m}{X}} E_j, \ \bigcup_{i=1}^{n} C_i \cap \bigcup_{i=j}^{m} E_j \ne \varnothing \qquad (7)$$

Figure 1. A sample causation network

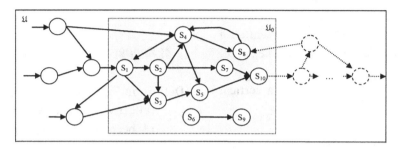

where × denotes a Cartesian product, $N = \bigcup\limits_{i=1}^{n} C_i \cup \bigcup\limits_{i=j}^{m} E_j$, and $\vec{R} = N \times N$.

According to Definition 8, in a CN as modeled in Equation 7, the reflective and loop causations are indicated by $\bigcup\limits_{i=1}^{n} C_i \cap \bigcup\limits_{i=j}^{m} E_j \neq \varnothing$. Otherwise, a *restricted* CN with $\bigcup\limits_{i=1}^{n} C_i \cap \bigcup\limits_{i=j}^{m} E_j = \varnothing$ is called a regular CN, CN_r, in which no reflective and loop causality is allowed.

A generic CN model can be illustrated in Figure 1 where the entire causation network U denotes the complete causal discourse. Figure 1 demonstrates that a certain set of specific causations on the partial causal discourse U_0, $U'_0 \sqsubseteq U$, is only a sub-network of causalities as a current window on U. However, all future or unknown causations on U are denoted by the dotted circles, which are always unpredictable before a true causality on U_0 is discovered.

All forms of the binary, n-nary, chain, reflective, and loop causations as modeled in Definitions 3 through 7, as well as their combinations, can be found in the CN as given in Figure 1, which can be illustrated in the following examples.

Example 1: The five forms of causations can be identified in the CN as given in Figure 1 as follows:
- A binary causation: $S_6 \vdash S_9$
- An *n*-nary causation: $(S_5 \wedge S_7) \vdash S_{10}$
- A chain causation: $S_1 \vdash S_2 \vdash S_7 \vdash S_{10}$
- A reflective causation: $S_4 \vdash S_8 \vdash S_4$
- A loop causation: $S_1 \vdash S_2 \vdash S_4 \vdash S_1$

It is noteworthy that, in conventional logical causality analyses, the unchanged and/or indirect causations are usually omitted in the space $U \backslash U_0$. However, many unknown and complex causations may only be found in the entire context on U according to the holistic view on CNs.

3. THE FRAMEWORK AND PROPERTIES OF CAUSAL INFERENCES

On the basis of CNs, causations can be classified as static and dynamic ones where the former is a causal relation between invariant states; and the latter is a causal relation between transitions of causes and effects as a result of changes of states on U.

Definition 9: A *static causation* κ_s is a stable relation between a set of causes C and a set of effects E, i.e.:

$$\kappa_s : C \vdash E, \quad C, E \sqsubseteq \mathfrak{U} \tag{8}$$

The time property of causations is that a causal relation is often dynamic rather than static.

Definition 10: A *dynamic causation* $\Delta\kappa$ is a transitional relation κ_d between changes of causes in C, $\Delta C \subseteq C$, and/or changes of effects in E, $\Delta E \subseteq E$, i.e.:

$$\Delta\kappa = \frac{d}{dt}(\kappa_d : C \vdash E)$$
$$= \kappa_d : \frac{dC}{dt} \vdash \frac{dE}{dt} \qquad (9)$$
$$= \kappa_d : \Delta C \vdash \Delta E$$

It is recognized that human attentions are sensitive on recognizing dynamic changes in the foreground of a given CN. As a result, the static and constant causes that form the context discourse of a particular causation may often be omitted. Therefore, the CN model and static/dynamic causal analysis methodologies provide a theoretical foundation for the widely used empirical technique of experiments. For instance, when a series of experiments are conducted in the same laboratory under the same conditions, observations in causal analyses will eliminate the unchanged things as meaningful causes. However, ignoring the invariant causes may lead to a serious fallacy in causal analyses and formal inferences. That is, philosophically, the following theorem must be recognized.

Theorem 1: The *universal causal discourse* U is the constant cause of any effect observed on it, without it nothing may happen and may be inferred.

In causal analyses based on CN, a static or dynamic causation should be determined on the basis of at least two separate observations as snapshots of the causal context U_0, $U'_0 \sqsubseteq U$. Then, anything changed during the sample period is a dynamic cause and/or effect. This leads to a rigorous model of dynamic CNs.

Definition 11: The *dynamic* CN, ΔCN, is a differential of a static CN on U'_0, which elicits

the changed causalities during a given observation period, i.e.:

$$\Delta CN \triangleq \frac{d}{dt} CN$$
$$= \frac{d}{dt}(^o{}_{CN} : \mathbf{X}_{i=1}^{n} C_i \to \mathbf{X}_{i=j}^{m} E_j) \qquad (10)$$
$$= {}^{o\prime}{}_{CN} : \mathbf{X}_{i=1}^{n} \frac{d}{dt} C_i \to \mathbf{X}_{i=j}^{m} \frac{d}{dt} E_j$$

It is noteworthy that the sample period for causality observations must be precisely determined otherwise some fast changing causes or effects would be missed. The sample interval for causal analyses obeys Nyquist's law (Tucker Jr., 1997) as follows.

Theorem 2 *(Nyquist's law of sampling)*: The sampling frequency f_s must be greater than twice the maximum frequency f_{max} of the changes of states on U, i.e.:

$$f_s > 2f_{max} \qquad (11)$$

Theorem 2 indicates that the sampling rate in causal analyses should be two times higher than that of the highest change frequency of events and states in a given CN. Otherwise, important causations of fast changing states may be overlooked.

Lemma 1: In a causal inference, a cause $c \in C$ always happens before an effect $e \in E$, except in a loop and reflective causality, i.e.:

$$\forall\kappa : c \vdash e \sqsubseteq \mathfrak{U} \wedge c \neq e, \ t_c < t_e \qquad (12)$$

However, the timing behavior of common sense causations may be totally different in reflective and loop causations as given in Corollary 1.

Corollary 1: In a reflective or loop causation, the cause may happen at the same time as that of the effect, even later than it, i.e.:

$$\exists \kappa : c \vdash e \sqsubseteq \mathfrak{U} \wedge \kappa' : e \vdash c \sqsubseteq \mathfrak{U}, \ t_c \geq t_e \tag{13}$$

Both Lemma 1 and Corollary 1 can be directly proven by the structure of CNs as given in Definition 8 and Figure 1.

A framework of causal inferences can be classified into four categories known as the *intuitive, empirical, heuristic,* and *rational* causations as shown in Table 1. Although the rational causations have been intensively studied in logic, operational theories, and computational intelligence, the intuitive, empirical, and heuristic causalities are still lack of rigorous models and rules in formal causal analyses. Because all categories of causal inferences play important roles in both human and machine reasoning, their complex and uncertain rules are yet to be explored in the following sections.

4. UNCERTAIN CAUSAL INFERENCES

The nature of uncertainty stems from the constraints of human cognitive ability and the general principle of information scarcity. This section analyzes a special category of causations in uncertain context, which are caused by imperfect data, insufficient information, and/or unknown mechanisms or causal relations.

Definition 12: *Uncertainty* is a factor, thing, or state that is undependable, unknown, or indefinite.

In formal inferences, uncertainty can be categorized into the types of "to be" and "to do" uncertainties.

Definition 13: The *to be* uncertainty is an indeterminable truth, while the *to do* uncertainty is an indeterminable behavior.

From the view point of time, both types of uncertainties may be classified into three categories known as the past, current, future uncertainty. The reasons how they remain as uncertainty and potential approaches to dealing with them would be different as summarized in Table 2.

In the category of future uncertainties in Table 2, if the three steps can be completed, the "to be" and "to do" uncertainty would be removed. However, the complexity for exhaustive searching in a large state space is always too high to be cognitively maintainable. For example, a recent finding in formal game theory (Wang, 2007a), reveals that the complexity of games is $O(nk^{n-1})$. That is, when the number of independent parties (variables) n and alternative strategies k of the parties are greater than $(n, k) = (5, 5)$, the complexity of the game will become almost unmanageable with more than 78,125 matches. This explains why most examples of games mainly study binary ones ($n=2$), because of the purpose to restrict any behavioral uncertainty.

The uncertain causal inference is a complex reasoning process usually involving huge amount of searching and analyses. Typical predicative methodologies for uncertain inferences are Bayesian conditional probability (Wilson & Keil, 2001) and fuzzy inferences (Zadeh, 1965). It is recognized that although probability theory is a powerful mathematical means in causal analyses, it does not work very well in the contexts of natural and computational intelligence where the nature of problems is always with uncertainty, unknown probability, uneven probability distributions,

Table 1. The framework of causal inferences

No.	Category	Causation	Approach
1	**Intuitive**		
1.1		Arbitrary	Based on the easiest or most familiar choice
1.2		Preference	Based on propensity, hobby, tendency, expectation
1.3		Common sense	Based on axioms and judgment
2	**Empirical**		
2.1		Trial and error	Based on exhaustive trials
2.2		Experiment	Based on experiment results
2.3		Experience	Based on existing knowledge
2.4		Consultant	Based on professional consultation
2.5		Estimation	Based on rough evaluation
3	**Heuristic**		
3.1		Principles	Based on scientific theories
3.2		Ethics	Based on philosophical judgment and belief
3.3		Representative	Based on common rules of thumb
3.4		Availability	Based on limited information or local maximum
3.5		Anchoring	Based on presumption or bias and their justification
4	**Rational**		
4.1	Static		
4.1.1		Minimum cost	Based on minimizing energy, time, money
4.1.2		Maximum benefit	Based on maximizing gain of usability, functionality, reliability, quality, dependability
4.1.3		Maximum utility	Based on cost-benefit ratio
4.2	Dynamic		
4.2.1		Interactive events	Based on automata
4.2.2		Games	Based on competition mechanisms

non-monotonic probability trends, and intricate probability dependencies. Therefore, fuzzy inference technologies are needed for provide a more powerful means.

A fuzzy inference is an advanced form of formal inferences that enables qualitative and/or quantitative evaluation of the degree of confidential level for a given causation on the basis of fuzzy expressions.

Definition 14: A *fuzzy binary causation* $\widetilde{\kappa_b}$ is a binary relation that links a pair of events or states as a fuzzy cause $\widetilde{P}$ and a fuzzy effect $\widetilde{Q}$, i.e.:

$$\widetilde{\kappa_b}\mathbf{FZ} \triangleq (\widetilde{P}\mathbf{FZ} \vdash \widetilde{Q}\mathbf{FZ})\mathbf{FZ} \qquad (14)$$

where **FZ** denote a type suffix of fuzzy inferences.

A set of fuzzy causal analyses, such as fuzzy deduction, fuzzy induction, fuzzy abduction, and fuzzy analogy, can be derived based on Definitions 14. Then, a framework of fuzzy inferences and reasoning can be systematically established as described in Wang (2009a): "Fuzzy Inferences

Table 2. Analysis of uncertain causations

No.	Category of uncertainty	Reasons to be uncertainty	Approach to dealing with
1	Current	scarcity of information, and/or cognitive limit on underpinning theories and causality	(i) To obtain (provide) enough information; (ii) to find rational causalities in the entire CN.
2	Past	scarcity of information, and/or cognitive limit on underpinning theories and causality	(i) To obtain (provide) enough information; (ii) to find rational causalities in the entire CN.
3	Future	unpredictable future occurrences, and/or cognitive limit on underpinning theories and causality	(i) To seek the whole state space; (ii) to find entire relations among the variables in the state space; (iii) to establish rational causalities among the variables and relations.

Methodologies for Cognitive Informatics and Computational Intelligence," and related work (Wang, 2010b, 2011).

5. FALSE CAUSALITY: A RATIONAL EXPLANATION OF HUMOR AND JOKES

Humor is the way in which people see that some things are amusing or the ability to be amused by things. A joke is a story or trick that is said or done in order to make people laugh. Humor and jokes are an interesting phenomenon in human causal reasoning based on false causality that lead to an amusing surprise.

Definition 15: A *humorous statement*, or a *joke*, is a false causality on the basis of semantic ambiguities that causes an amusing surprise.

There are three essential factors constituting of humor in a joke as described in Definition 15, which are: (i) The *reason*: a semantic ambiguity; (ii) The *process*: a false causality; and (iii) The *effect* (result): the revealing of an amusing surprise. Therefore, humor or a joke can be formally defined as follows.

Definition 16: The *formal model* of a *humorous statement* or a *joke, h*, is a false causal inference process, $\tilde{c} \vdash_F e'$, resulted in by the semantic ambiguity of a cause $\tilde{c}$, that reveals an amusement or pleasant surprise, (:, when the true causality $\tilde{c} \vdash_T e$ is realized, i.e.:

$$h \triangleq \exists \tilde{c}, \ \tilde{c} \left\langle \begin{matrix} \vdash_F e' \rightarrow \\ \vdash_T e \rightarrow \end{matrix} \right\rangle \otimes \rightarrow (: \tag{15}$$

where $\vdash_T$ and $\vdash_F$ denote a true or false causal inference, respectively.

Assuming the three basic categories of reasoning are denoted, respectively, as: *to be* $|=,$, *to have* $|\subset$, and *to do* $|>$ (Wang, 2007a, 2008), typical jokes in natural languages may be rigorously expressed using Equation 15 as follows.

Example 2: In a logical reasoning, a kid states that it is general that all dogs have 4 legs. A cat has also 4 legs, therefore the cat is a dog.

According to Definition 16, joke h_1 can be formally described as a false causality as follows.

$$h_1 \triangleq \forall dogs \ |\subset (\#leg = 4) \land \exists a\_cat \ |\subset (\#leg = 4)$$
$$\rightarrow \left\langle \begin{matrix} \vdash_F the\_cat \ |= a\_dog \rightarrow \\ \vdash_T \#leg(the\_cat) \ |= \#leg(any\_dog) \rightarrow \end{matrix} \right\rangle \otimes \rightarrow (:$$

Example 3: Two friends, *A* and *B*, are sleeping in a tent during the night in the field. Suddenly, *A* was wakened up and asked: "I am worrying why there are so many stars in the sky?". *B* answered: "Because the sky is clear." "No," *A* yelled: "I meant our tent had disappeared!"

According to Definition 16, joke h_2 can be formally described as a false causality as follows in Box 1.

Example 4: A man *A* called his friend *B* for an emergent help. He said on the phone that he got lost and needs a pick up. "Where are you?" *B* asked. *A* answered: "I am standing opposite the street of my house." *B* realized that *A* was drunk.

According to Definition 16, joke h_3 can be formally described as a false causality as follows in Box 2.

Example 5: A boy in an elementary school did an experiment on a rare insect with 4 legs. He found that he could not stop the insect by simply commanding "don't move" in cases when he tied its two or three legs. Therefore, he reported that the insect may only listen to human instructions when all of its 4 legs are tied.

Box 1.

$$h_2 \triangleq \exists A \wedge B \text{ in a tent @night,}$$
$$QueryA \text{ (I am worrying why there are so many stars in the sky?)}$$
$$\rightarrow \left\langle \begin{array}{l} \vdash_F AnswerB \text{ (The sky} \models \text{clear)} \qquad\qquad \rightarrow \\ \vdash_T AnswerA\_expected \text{ (Their tent} \vert > \text{dispered)} \rightarrow \end{array} \right\rangle \otimes \rightarrow (:$$

Box 2.

$$h_3 \triangleq \exists A \vert > \text{lost, } A \vert > (B \vert > \text{pickup}(A)),$$
$$QueryB \text{ (Where are you ?)} \rightarrow AnswerA \text{ (Opposite the street of A's house.)}$$
$$\rightarrow \left\langle \begin{array}{l} \vdash_F A \vert > \text{lost} \quad \rightarrow \\ \vdash_T A \vert > \text{drunk} \rightarrow \end{array} \right\rangle \otimes \rightarrow (:$$

Box 3.

$$h_1 \triangleq \exists \text{ An insect } \vert \subset (\# leg = 4),$$
$$\rightarrow Tie(2 \text{ legs}) \wedge Command(\text{don't move!}) \vert > \text{no effect;}$$
$$\rightarrow Tie(3 \text{ legs}) \wedge Command(\text{don't move!}) \vert > \text{no effect;}$$
$$\rightarrow Tie(4 \text{ legs}) \wedge Command(\text{don't move!}) \vert > \text{succeed.}$$
$$\rightarrow \left\langle \begin{array}{l} \vdash_F \text{ It listens when 4 legs are tied.} \qquad\qquad\qquad\qquad\qquad \rightarrow \\ \vdash_T \text{ Nothing to do with its listening ability; It cannot move any more.} \rightarrow \end{array} \right\rangle \otimes \rightarrow (:$$

According to Definition 16, joke h_4 can be formally described as a false causality as follows in Box 3.

The formal model of humour and jokes, as given in Definition 16, not only explains the nature and essences of human humor, but also enables machines to understand homer in natural languages in a rigorous approach (Wang, 2010a). The theories and models can be applied in conveying human amusing false causality into machines and systems of computational intelligence in order to allow the implied false causality in a joke to be understood or revealed by artificial intelligence and cognitive computing systems.

6. CONCLUSION

This paper has investigated into two gifted privileges of human intelligence known as causality and inferences. The taxonomy and cognitive models of causations and causal analyses have been formally modeled in this work. The causation network has been introduced to facilitate causal analyses. A set of formal properties and methodologies of causal inferences have been developed. Interesting findings of this work have demonstrated that highly complex inference mechanisms and rules of the natural intelligence may be rigorously treated and modeled by formal causal analyses on the basis of causation networks. Therefore, it is possible to enable machines and computational intelligent systems to mimic the formally described causal analysis and inference rules and mechanisms on the basis of cognitive and denotational mathematical models.

ACKNOWLEDGMENT

A number of notions in this work have been inspired by Prof. Lotfi A. Zadeh during my sabbatical leave at BISC, UC Berkeley as a visiting professor. I am grateful to Prof. Zadeh for his vision, insight, and kind support. The author acknowledges the Natural Science and Engineering Council of Canada (NSERC) for its partial support to this work. The author would like to thank the anonymous reviewers for their valuable comments and suggestions.

REFERENCES

Bender, E. A. (1996). *Mathematical methods in artificial intelligence*. Palo Alto, CA: IEEE Computer Society Press.

Hurley, P. J. (1997). *A concise introduction to logic* (6th ed.). Belmont, CA: Wadsworth Publishing.

Payne, D. G., & Wenger, M. J. (1998). *Cognitive psychology*. Geneva, IL: Houghton Mifflin.

Ross, T. J. (1995). *Fuzzy logic with engineering applications*. New York, NY: McGraw-Hill.

Schoning, U. (1989). *Logic for computer scientists*. New York, NY: Birkhauser Boston.

Smith, K. J. (2001). *The nature of mathematics* (9th ed.). Belmont, CA: Brooks Cole Publishing.

Sperschneider, V., & Antoniou, G. (1991). *Logic: A foundation for computer science*. Reading, MA: Addison-Wesley.

Sternberg, R. J. (1998). *In search of the human mind* (2nd ed.). New York, NY: Harcourt Brace.

Tomassi, P. (1999). *Logic*. London, UK: Routledge. doi:10.4324/9780203197035

Tucker, A. B. Jr. (1997). *The computer science and engineering handbook*. Boca Raton, FL: CRC Press.

van Heijenoort, J. (1997). *From Frege to Godel, a source book in mathematical logic 1879-1931*. Cambridge, MA: Harvard University Press.

Wang, Y. (2003). On cognitive informatics. *Brain and Mind: A Transdisciplinary Journal of Neuroscience and Neurophilosophy, 4*(2), 151-167.

Wang, Y. (2007a). *Software engineering foundations: A software science perspective.* Boca Raton, FL: Auerbach Publications.

Wang, Y. (2007b). The cognitive processes of formal inferences. *International Journal of Cognitive Informatics and Natural Intelligence, 1*(4), 75–86. doi:10.4018/jcini.2007100106

Wang, Y. (2007c). Towards theoretical foundations of autonomic computing. *International Journal of Cognitive Informatics and Natural Intelligence, 1*(3), 1–21. doi:10.4018/jcini.2007070101

Wang, Y. (2008). On contemporary denotational mathematics for computational intelligence. In M. L. Gavrilova et al. (Eds.), *Transactions on Computational Science 2* (LNCS 5150, pp. 6-29).

Wang, Y. (2009a). Fuzzy inferences methodologies for cognitive informatics and computational intelligence. In *Proceedings of the IEEE 8th International Conference on Cognitive Informatics* (pp. 241-248). Washington, DC: IEEE Computer Society.

Wang, Y. (2009b). On abstract intelligence: Toward a unified theory of natural, artificial, machinable, and computational intelligence. *International Journal of Software Science and Computational Intelligence, 1*(1), 1–17. doi:10.4018/jssci.2009010101

Wang, Y. (2010a). Cognitive robots: A reference model towards intelligent authentication. *IEEE Transactions on Robotics and Automation, 17*(4), 54–62. doi:10.1109/MRA.2010.938842

Wang, Y. (2010b). On formal and cognitive semantics for semantic computing. *International Journal of Semantic Computing, 4*(2), 203–237. doi:10.1142/S1793351X10000833

Wang, Y. (2011). On concept algebra for computing with words (CWW). *International Journal of Semantic Computing, 4*(3), 331–356. doi:10.1142/S1793351X10001061

Wang, Y., Kinsner, W., Anderson, J., Zhang, D., Yao, Y., & Sheu, P. (2009). A doctrine of cognitive informatics. *Fundamenta Informaticae-Cognitive Informatics, Cognitive Computing, and Their Denotational Mathematical Foundations, 90*(3), 203–228.

Wilson, R. A., & Keil, F. C. (2001). *The MIT encyclopedia of the cognitive sciences.* Cambridge, MA: MIT Press.

Zadeh, L. A. (1965). Fuzzy sets. *Information and Control, 8,* 338–353. doi:10.1016/S0019-9958(65)90241-X

Zadeh, L. A. (1975). Fuzzy logic and approximate reasoning. *Syntheses, 30,* 407–428. doi:10.1007/BF00485052

Zadeh, L. A. (2006). Generalized theory of uncertainty (GTU) – principal concepts and ideas. *Computational Statistics & Data Analysis, 51,* 15–46. doi:10.1016/j.csda.2006.04.029

This work was previously published in the International Journal of Software Science and Computational Intelligence, Volume 3, Issue 1, edited by Yingxu Wang, pp.50-60, copyright 2011 by IGI Publishing (an imprint of IGI Global).

Chapter 9
On Localities of Knowledge Inconsistency

Du Zhang
California State University, USA

ABSTRACT

Inconsistency is commonplace in the real world in long-term memory and knowledge based systems. Managing inconsistency is considered a hallmark of the plasticity of human intelligence. Belief revision is an important mental process that underpins human intelligence. To facilitate belief revision, it is necessary to know the localities and contexts of inconsistency and how different types of inconsistency are clustered. In this paper, the author provides a formal definition of locality of inconsistency and describes how to identify clusters of inconsistent circumstances in a knowledge base. The results pave the way for a disciplined approach to manage knowledge inconsistency.

1. INTRODUCTION

Inconsistency is ubiquitous in the real world, in our long-term memory, and in knowledge based systems. Inconsistency manifests itself in a plethora of phenomena ranging from expertise, meta-knowledge, knowledge, information, to data. Managing inconsistency is considered an accepted part of life (Gotesky, 1968). As observed in (Shastri & Grannes, 1996), "we often hold inconsistent

beliefs in our long-term memory without being explicitly aware of such inconsistencies. But at the same time, we often recognize contradictions in our beliefs when we try to bring inconsistent knowledge to bear on a particular task." From human psychological perspective, when confronted with an inconsistent circumstance, an individual attempts to reason from inconsistency to consistency (Johnson-Laird et al., 2004). The model theory of reasoning to consistency suggests that

DOI: 10.4018/978-1-4666-2651-5.ch009

the mental processes consist of three components: inconsistency detection, belief revision, and inconsistency resolution through explanation (Johnson-Laird et al., 2004).

Managing inconsistency is a hallmark of the *plasticity* of human intelligence. Central to this is the concept of *cognitive penetrability* introduced by Zenon Pylyshsyn (1989): the pattern of behavior can be altered in a rational way by changing subjects' beliefs about the task. The plasticity of human intelligence lies in the fact that many mental processes dealing with sensation, cognition, perception, emotion, action, and interaction are cognitively penetrable: the knowledge, beliefs, goals and expectations a person possesses could influence the experience, behaviors and consequent judgments the person has in those mental processes.

If a system is cognitively penetrable then the function it computes is sensitive, in a semantically coherent way, to the organism's goals, beliefs and expectations, in other words, the function can be altered in a way that bears some logical relation to what the system knows (Pylyshyn, 1999). As exhibited in the natural cognitive systems, human beings can revise their goals, beliefs, expectations, and plans in the face of fresh evidence or as a result of inferences which update previously held beliefs.

When an individual is forced to revise beliefs in the presence of an inconsistency, a long-standing hypothesis is that a minimal change should be made to the previously held beliefs so as to accommodate the fresh evidence (Johnson-Laird et al., 2004). To do so, a necessary condition is that we need to know the localities and contexts of inconsistency, and how different types of inconsistency are clustered.

This paper is an extension to our early results (Zhang, 2010a). Our focus is on a formal definition of locality of inconsistency at knowledge level and on how to utilize this definition to identify clusters of inconsistent circumstances in a knowledge base system. We use locality of inconsistency as a tool

to separate relevant and contributing cognitions from irrelevant ones with regard to a particular inconsistent circumstance, and to provide support for chunking inconsistent knowledge into refined and manageable sizes.

The rest of the paper is organized as follows. We briefly review in Section 2 different types of knowledge inconsistency. Section 3 provides a brief recap of the fixpoint semantics for knowledge bases, which we rely on later when dealing with the issue of capturing localities of inconsistency. In Section 4, we offer a formal definition of locality of inconsistency in terms of a concept called antagonistic cognitive distance. We describe four algorithms in Section 5 on how to identify localities for four different types of inconsistency. Finally we conclude the paper in Section 6 with remark on future work.

2. KNOWLEDGE INCONSISTENCY TYPES

Since the process of identifying locality of inconsistency will be affected by various types of inconsistency to be encountered, it is necessary to know how many types of knowledge inconsistency we need to deal with. In our previous work, we have identified the following twelve types of inconsistency (Zhang, 2008, 2009, 2010b) which are briefly summarized as follows.

1. Complementary inconsistency refers to an atom and its negation.
2. Mutually exclusive inconsistency stems from mutually exclusive predicates that are syntactically different and semantically opposite of each other (see an example later in Sections 4 and 5).
3. Incompatible inconsistency is caused by having an atom and the negation of its syntactically different but logically equivalent relation (synonymous predicate).

4. Anti-subtype inconsistency captures the antagonistic situation where a subtype is no longer subsumed by its supertype.

5. Anti-supertype inconsistency is the converse of the anti-subtype inconsistency where the negation of the supertype and one of its subtypes hold at the same time.

6. Asymmetric inconsistency deals with the circumstance in which a symmetric relation and its negation both hold.

7. Anti-inverse inconsistency describes the conflicting situation where a relation and the negation of its inverse relation exist.

8. Mismatching inconsistency occurs when a concept and the negation of one of its conjunctive and substantiating sub-concepts hold.

9. Disagreeing inconsistency pertains to propositions having reified but disagreeing quantities for the same attribute.

10. Contradictory inconsistency happens when relations contain attribute values that violate type restrictions or integrity constraints.

11. Precedence inconsistency involves opposite precedence relationships being asserted for the same set of entities (e.g., *Precedence*(x, y) and *Precedence*(y, x).

12. Inconsistent probability value type has to do with the fact that if $\Delta \vDash L$, the probability value for L is outside the region specified by the extreme values of probabilities for Δ.

Table 1 summarizes the notations we adopt for the aforementioned inconsistency types.

Let p_i and p_j denote the predicates in L_i and L_j, respectively. When there is no confusion, we may apply the aforementioned notation in Table 1 to the underlying predicates instead. For instance, we may use $p_1 \not\simeq p_2$ to indicate that p_1 and p_2 are mutually exclusive predicates causing $L_1 \not\simeq L_2$, the mutually exclusive type of inconsistency.

3. A FIXPOINT CHARACTERIZATION

There are a number of fixpoint semantics for a logical theory (Fitting, 1991, 2002): classical two-valued, two-valued with stratification, three-valued for handling negation, four-valued for dealing with inconsistency and incompleteness, and the truth value space of [0, 1].

In our previous results (Zhang, 2005, 2007), we adopted the four-valued logic *FOUR* as defined in (Belnap, 1977; Ginsberg, 1988). *FOUR* has the truth value set of {*true*, *false*, $\perp$, $\top$} where *true* and *false* have their canonical meanings in the classical two-valued logic, $\perp$ indicates *undefined* or *don't know*, and $\top$ is *overdefined* or *contradiction*.

The four-valued logic *FOUR* is the smallest nontrivial bilattice, a member in a family of similar structures called bilattices (Ginsberg, 1988). Bilattices offer a general framework for reasoning with multi-valued logics and have many theoretical and practical benefits (Ginsberg, 1988).

According to Belnap (1977), there are two natural partial orders in *FOUR*: *knowledge* ordering $\leq_k$ and *truth* ordering $\leq_t$ such that:

$$\perp \leq_k false \leq_k \top, \perp \leq_k true \leq_k \top \text{ and}$$

Table 1. Types of knowledge inconsistency

Name	Notation	Type
Complementary	$L_i \neq L_k$	$I_{\neq}$
Mutually exclusive	$L_i \not\simeq L_k$	$I_{\not\simeq}$
Incompatible	$L_i \not\cong L_k$	$I_{\not\cong}$
Anti-subtype	$L_i \sqsubseteq L_k$	$I_{\not\sqsubseteq}$
Anti-supertype	$L \Leftrightarrow (\sqcup L_i)$	$I_{\Leftrightarrow}$
Asymmetric	$L_i \not\Downarrow L_k$	$I_{\Downarrow}$
Anti-inverse	$L_i \not\simeq L_k$	$I_{\neq}$
Mismatching	$L \not\equiv (\sqcap L_i)$	$I_{\not\equiv}$
Disagreeing	$L_i \gneqq L_k$	$I_{\gneqq}$
Contradictory	$L_i \approx L_k$	$I_{\approx}$
Precedence	$L_i \not\succ L_k$	$I_{\not\succ}$
iProbVal	$Prob(L) \notin Prob(\Delta)$	I_{iP}

$false \leq_i \top \leq_i true, false \leq_i \perp \leq_i true.$

Both partial orders offer a complete lattice. The meet and join for $\leq_k$, denoted as $\otimes$ and $\oplus$, respectively, yield: $false \otimes true = \perp$ and $false \oplus true = \top$. The meet and join for $\leq_i$, denoted as $\wedge$ and $\vee$, respectively, result in: $\top \wedge \perp = false$ and $\top \vee \perp = true$.

The knowledge negation reverses the $\leq_k$ ordering while preserving the $\leq_i$ ordering. The truth negation reverses $\leq_i$ ordering while preserving $\leq_k$ ordering.

For a knowledge base Ω, we define a transformation T_Ω, which is a "revision operator" (Fitting, 2002) that revises our beliefs based on the general knowledge and specific facts in Ω. It can be shown that T_Ω is monotonic and has a least fixpoint $lfp(T_\Omega)$ with regard to $\leq_k$ (Fitting, 1991; Fitting, 2002).

$lfp(T_\Omega)$ contains all the derivable conclusions from the KB through some inference method. Let Γ_Ω be the set of domain (ontological) constraints for a given KB Ω, We define an augmented fixpoint $lfp^+(T_\Omega)$ for Ω as follows:

$$lfp^+(T_\Omega) = lfp(T_\Omega) \cup \Gamma_\Omega$$

Thus, the semantics of a KB Ω can be defined in terms of $lfp^+(T_\Omega)$. With $lfp^+(T_\Omega)$ in place, we can deal with the following situations: (1) conflicting facts in $lfp(T_\Omega)$; (2) antagonistic constraints in Γ_Ω; and (3) facts in $lfp(T_\Omega)$ that are contradicting with domain or ontological constraints in Γ_Ω.

4. LOCALITY OF KNOWLEDGE INCONSISTENCY

In physics, the principle of locality refers to the fact that an object is directly influenced only by its immediate surroundings and that distant objects cannot have direct influence on one another. In computer systems, locality of reference characterizes certain predictable (temporal and spatial) patterns of accessing memory locations (Denning, 2006). In database area, the term of locality of inconsistency was used to describe the circumstance where consistency violations irrelevant to a given query are ignored to obtain query centric consistent answers from inconsistent databases (Bertossi & Chomicki, 2003).

In the context of knowledge management, the locality principle can be utilized to establish where antagonistic cognitions occur in the knowledge landscape and how different types of inconsistency are clustered. Through the use of a cognitive distance measure, we define the concept of locality of inconsistency. This definition has several benefits for managing knowledge inconsistency.

1. First, such a locality of inconsistency concept can be used to separate relevant and contributing cognitions from irrelevant ones with regard to a particular inconsistent circumstance. It provides support for chunking inconsistent knowledge or cognitions into refined and manageable sizes.
2. Second, the locality of inconsistency lends itself to helping infer the context and impact of a given inconsistent circumstance.
3. Patterns of locality of inconsistency can be established for various inconsistent circumstances ahead of time so that managing inconsistency does not have to be just reactive. We can predict or preempt circumstances that are detrimental to the reasoning process.

In the remainder of this section, we first introduce some additional notations to be used in the discussion, then offer a definition on antagonistic cognitive distance, and finally give a definition on locality of inconsistency.

Definition 1: Given two literals L_i and L_k, let p_i and p_k denote the predicates in L_i and L_k, and let τ_i and τ_k be vectors of terms for L_i and L_k, respectively.

$\tau_i = \tau_k$ if $|\tau_i| = |\tau_k|$ and τ_i and τ_k have the same terms at corresponding positions.

$\tau_i \neq \tau_k$ if $\neg(\tau_i = \tau_k)$.

Let $\tau_i=(t_{i1}, t_{i2})$ and $\tau_k=(t_{k1}, t_{k2})$, $\tau_i \leftrightarrow \tau_k$ if

$(t_{i1} \neq t_{k1} \wedge t_{i2} \neq t_{k2} \wedge t_{i1} \neq t_{k2} \wedge t_{i2} \neq t_{k1})$.

Let $\tau_i=(t_{i1}, t_{i2})$ and $\tau_k=(t_{k1}, t_{k2})$, $\tau_i \bowtie \tau_k$ if

$(t_{i1} = t_{k2} \wedge t_{i2} = t_{k1})$. $L_i = L_j$ if $(p_i = p_j \wedge \tau_i = \tau_j)$.

If p_i and p_k satisfy the condition for any of the twelve inconsistency types in Table 1, we use $p_i \gtrless p_k$ as a shorthand to denote that. Otherwise, we use $p_i \gtrdot p_k$, to indicate that there does not exist any inconsistency between L_i and L_k.

The concept of antagonistic cognitive distance we define below describes the propensity of two distinct cognitions becoming conflicting.

Definition 2: Given two literals L_i and L_k, let p_i and p_k denote the predicates in L_i and L_k, and let τ_i and τ_k be vectors of terms for L_i and L_k, respectively, the *antagonistic cognitive distance* between the two literals L_i and L_k, denoted as $acd(L_i, L_k)$, is defined below:

$acd(L_i, L_k) = 0$, when $L_i = L_k$;

$acd(L_i, L_k) = 0.1$, when

$[(L_i \neq L_k) \vee (L_i \not\approx L_k) \vee (L_i \cong L_k) \vee (L_i \not\sqsubseteq L_k)]$

$\wedge (\tau_i = \tau_k)$; or

$[(L_i \not\vdash L_k) \vee (L_i \not\approx L_k)] \wedge [(L_i = \neg L_k)$

$\wedge (\tau_i \bowtie \tau_k)]$; or

$[(L_i \gtrneqq L_k) \wedge (\tau_i = (t_s, t_m)) \wedge (\tau_k = (t_s, t_n))$

$\wedge (t_m \gtrneqq t_n)]$; or

$[(L_i \approx L_k) \wedge (\tau_i = (t_s, t_m)) \wedge (\tau_k = (t_s, t_n))$

$\wedge (t_m \approx t_n)]$; or

$[(L_i > L_k) \wedge (\tau_i \bowtie \tau_k)]$.

$acd(L_i, \mathbf{L}_{di}) = 0.1$, when

$(L_i \Leftrightarrow \uplus L_j) \wedge (\mathbf{L}_{di} = \uplus L_j') \wedge (\uplus L_j' \neq \uplus L_j)$.

$acd(L_i, \mathbf{L}_{co}) = 0.1$, when

$(L_i \equiv \sqcap L_j) \wedge (\mathbf{L}_{co} = \sqcap L_j') \wedge (\sqcap L_j' \not\equiv \sqcap L_j)$.

$acd(L_i, \mathbf{L}_\Delta) = 0.1$, when

$(\mathbf{L}_\Delta \vDash L_i) \wedge (Prob(L_i) \notin Prob(\mathbf{L}_\Delta))$.

$acd(L_i, L_k) = 0.3$, when $(p_i = p_k \wedge L_i = \neg L_k \wedge \tau_i \neq \tau_k)$;

$acd(L_i, L_k) = 0.5$, when $(p_i \gtrless p_k \wedge (\tau_i \neq \tau_k \vee \tau_i \leftrightarrow \tau_k))$

$acd(L_i, L_k) = 1$, when $p_i \gtrdot p_k$.

The distance function *acd* has the following properties.

1. $acd(L_i, L_i) = 0$;
2. $acd(L_i, L_k) \geq 0$, when L_i and L_k are different;
3. $acd(L_i, L_k) = acd(L_k, L_i)$; and
4. $acd(L_i, L_k) \leq acd(L_i, L_j) + acd(L_j, L_k)$.

Table 2 gives some example sets of literals, and their antagonistic cognitive distances.

To facilitate the definition of the locality of inconsistency, we use R and $\wp$ to denote a concept group and a set of anchoring predicates ($\wp \subseteq R$) for a particular antagonistic circumstance, respectively, for a given inconsistency type. For instance, Chinese zodiac is a group of twelve concepts that relate each year to an animal and its salient attributes based on a 12-year cycle. If we choose

Table 2. Examples of acd values

Set of Literals	acd()
S_1={*Father(John, Mike), ¬Dad(John, Mike)*}	0.1
S_2={*Surgeon(John), ¬Doctor(John)*}	0.1
S_3={*MarriedTo(John,Jane), ¬MarriedTo(Jane,John)*}	0.1
S_4={*ParentOf(John, Mike), ¬ChildOf(Mike, John)*}	0.1
S_5={*Memory(a_1, 2GB), Memory(a_1, 1500MB)*}	0.1
S_6={*Created(a_1,Nov01-07), Deployed(a_1,Oct01-07)*}	0.1
S_7={*Precedence(a_5, a_2), Precedence(a_2, a_5)*}	0.1
S_8={*Animalia(SeaHorse), ¬Animalia(SeaWeed)*}	0.3
S_9={*Animalia(Dog), Plantae(SeaWeed)*}	0.5
S_{10}={*BrokerAgent(a_1), MsgReceived(a_1, m_1)*}	1.0

to use a predicate for each of the twelve animals, we have the following set of predicates:

R = {*Rat, Ox, Tiger, Rabbit, Dragon, Snake, Horse,*

Sheep, Monkey, Rooster, Dog, Boar}

The aforementioned twelve predicates form a mutually exclusive and jointly exhaustive group of concepts. If John was born on 1987, then *Rabbit* (John, 1987) is true in a given knowledge base according to the zodiac. To have another fact *Horse* (John, 1987) in the knowledge base would create a particular type of antagonistic circumstance: mutually exclusive inconsistency. In this case, the set of predicates that anchors the inconsistency is: ℘ = {*Rabbit, Horse*}.

Definition 3: For a given inconsistency type I, a *locality of inconsistency* with regard to I refers to a set of inconsistent literals that is denoted as $LOI_I(R, ℘)$. $LOI_I(R, ℘)$ satisfies the following condition where p_i and p_k denote the predicates in L_i and L_k, respectively:

$$\forall L_i \in LOI_I(R, ℘). \exists L_k \in LOI_I(R, ℘).$$

$$[(L_i \in R) \wedge (L_k \in R) \wedge (p_i \in ℘) \wedge (p_k \in ℘)$$

$$\wedge (acd(L_i, L_k) = 0.1)].$$

Definition 3 allows a particular cluster of inconsistent cases to be specified with regard to the tuple: <I, R, ℘>. Adjusting the size of ℘ would result in different sized localities belonging to the same concept group and of the same type of inconsistency to be identified.

Given a knowledge base which may contain some or multiple types of inconsistency, we can now identify clusters of inconsistency at three levels of granularity: *inter-inconsistency-type* localities, *intra-inconsistency-type* localities, and *intra-concept-group* localities.

Definition 4: Three levels of granularity for localities of inconsistency can be defined as follows.
   ○ Two localities or clusters of inconsistency belonging to two distinct inconsistency types are referred to as inter-inconsistency-type localities.
   ○ Distinct localities of inconsistency within the same inconsistency type but stemming from different concept groups denote intra-inconsistency-type localities.
   ○ For a particular concept group, there may be different sets of predicates in the group that anchor different conflicting circumstances, thus resulting in intra-concept-group localities.

Table 3. Levels of inconsistency localities

Granularity	Circumstances	
	Inconsistency Type	**Concept Group**
Inter-Inconsistency	Different	Different or same
Intra-Inconsistency	Same	Different
Intra-Concept Group	Same	Same

Table 3 summarizes the circumstances for the occurrences of the three levels of localities of inconsistency.

Figure 1 depicts the landscape of where different localities of inconsistency reside. Twelve areas in the landscape are annotated by the respective symbols of inconsistency types and are not arranged in any particular order. There is no attached significance to the sizes of the areas, or to the adjacency between or among different areas.

In Figure 1, inter-inconsistency-type localities are localities of inconsistency appearing in distinct areas. For instance, the locality pertaining to the "kingdoms-of-living-things" (see Example 1 in Section 5) and the locality in the "ancestry" concept group (see Example 2 in Section 5) are inter-inconsistency-type appearing in "mutually exclusive" and "incompatible" areas, respectively. Within an area for a particular inconsistency type, there can be localities of inconsistency stemming from different concept groups that denote intra-inconsistency-type localities. For example, one locality in "kingdoms-of-living-things" and another in "Chinese zodiac", though belonging to distinct concept groups,

both are clusters of mutually exclusive inconsistency. For a particular concept group in an area, there may be different sets of predicates in the group that anchor different conflicting circumstances, thus corresponding to intra-concept-group localities (see examples in Section 5). Finally, for a particular concept group R, predicates in R may be involved in localities of inconsistency in different areas in the landscape. For example, {Animalia, Plantae} are predicates in the "kingdoms-of-living-things" concept group (see Example 1 in Section 5), the locality of inconsistency {Animalia(SeaCucumber), Plantae(SeaCucumber)} appears in the "≇" area, whereas the locality of inconsistency {Animalia(SeaCucumber), ¬Animalia(SeaCucumber)} would appear in the "≠" area."

5. ALGORITHMS TO CAPTURE LOI

Given $lfp^+(T_\Omega)$ for a knowledge base Ω, an inconsistency type I, a concept group R, and a set of anchoring predicates $\wp$ for a particular antagonistic circumstance (of type I), we can define an

Figure 1. Inconsistency landscape

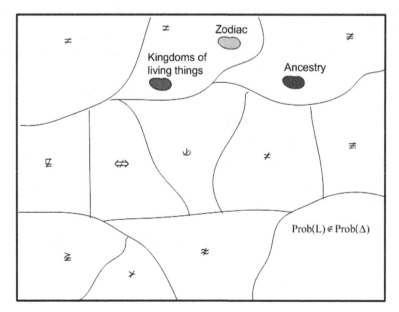

algorithm to capture and identify $LOI_i(R, \wp)$. In this section, we will describe four algorithms for the following types of inconsistency: mutually exclusive, incompatible, contradictory, and anti-inverse.

5.1. Algorithm for LOI of mutually exclusive type

Mutually exclusive inconsistency usually takes place with a group of concepts or predicates that are mutually exclusive and jointly exhaustive. The Algorithm 1 assumes that such mutually exclusive concept group is provided as an input.

Example 1: Suppose we have a knowledge base for classifying all the living things on earth. There are at least five kingdoms of living things: *Animalia* (the animals), *Plantae* (the plants), *Fungi* (fungus and related organisms), *Protista* (the single-celled eukaryotes), and *Monera*[1] (the prokaryotes), which are mutually exclusive, but jointly exhaustive for all the living things. If a living thing is an animal, it cannot be a member of the plants family or any other kingdom. Otherwise, there is an instance of the mutually exclusive inconsistency. In general, there can be many different concept groups where concepts within a group are mutually exclusive and

Algorithm 1.

Input:
 lfp⁺(T_Ω) for a knowledge base Ω,
 R: a concept group of mutually exclusive
   Predicates (p∈R ∧ q∈R ∧ p≇q), and
 ℘ ⊆ R;
Output:
 LOI≇ (R, ℘);
£℘ = {L_i | L_i ∈ lfp⁺(T_Ω) ∧ p_i∈℘}
LOI≇ (R, ℘) = ∅;
𝒦 = ∅;

*Let **C** be a set of 2-combinations for ℘:* $\binom{|\cdot|}{2}$ *if |℘|>1.*

while *|C| ≠ 0* **do** {
   if *{p, q}∈ **C*** **then** {
      while *[(p(τ_i)∈£℘) ∧ (q(τ_j)∈£℘) ∧ (τ_i = τ_j)*
         *∧ {p(τ_i), q(τ_j)}⊄ **K***]
      do {
         K = **K** ∪ *{p(τi), q(τj)}*;
      }
      C = C -{p, q};
   }
}
*LOI≇(R, ℘) = **K**;*
*return(**LOI**≇(R, ℘));*

---

jointly exhaustive. The kingdoms-of-living-things is just one such a concept group. We use R to denote this.

R = {*Animalia, Plantae, Fungi, Protista, Monera*}

If the KB also contains for instance knowledge about the Chinese zodiac, then another group of twelve mutually-exclusive-and-jointly-exhaustive concepts can be defined (e.g., R'={*Rat, Ox, Tiger, ..., Pig*}).

Given the following set of assertions in the knowledge base Ω about living things (Box 1):

If $\wp_a$ = {*Animalia, Plantae*}, then we can use Algorithm 1 to obtain LOI≇(R, $\wp_a$) as follows.

LOI≇(R, $\wp_a$) = {*Animalia(SeaCucumber)*,

Plantae(SeaCucumber),

Animala(SeaWeed), Plantae(SeaWeed)}

If $\wp_b$ = {*Plantae, Fungi*}, then we can obtain LOI≇(R, $\wp_b$) as follows.

LOI≇(R, $\wp_b$) = {*Fungi(SeaCucumber)*,

Plantae(SeaCucumber), Fungi(SeaWeed),

Plantae(SeaWeed)} If $\wp_c$ = {*Animala, Fungi*}, then we can obtain LOI≇(R, $\wp_c$) as follows.

LOI≇(R, $\wp_c$) = {*Fungi(SeaCucumber)*,

Animala(SeaCucumber), Fungi(SeaWeed),

Animalia(SeaWeed)}

Figure 2 indicates the localities of mutually exclusive inconsistency for $\wp_a$, $\wp_b$, and $\wp_c$, respectively. LOI≇(R, $\wp_a$), LOI≇(R, $\wp_b$), and LOI≇(R, $\wp_c$) are intra-concept-group localities.

If $\wp_d$ = $\wp_a \cup \wp_b \cup \wp_c$ = {*Animalia, Plantae, Fungi*}, then LOI≇(R, $\wp_d$) can be obtained as follows.

LOI≇(R, $\wp_d$) = LOI≇(R, $\wp_a$) ∪ LOI≇(R, $\wp_b$)

∪ LOI≇(R, $\wp_c$)

= {*Animala(SeaCucumber)*,

Animala(SeaWeed), Plantae(SeaCucumber),

Plantae(SeaWeed), Fungi(SeaCucumber),

Fungi(SeaCucumber)}

Figure 3 depicts the locality of inconsistency for $\wp_d$.

5.2. Algorithm for LOI of Incompatible Type

Incompatible inconsistency occurs when a knowledge base contains a set of synonymous concepts or predicates and a predicate and the negation of its synonymous concept hold at the same time. Algorithm 2 assumes that such synonymous concepts or predicates are given as input.

Example 2: Given R and *lfp*⁺(T_Ω) for a knowledge base Ω below:

R = {*Father, Dad, MaleParent, Papa*}

lfp⁺(T_Ω) = {..., *Father(John, Mike)*,

¬*Dad(John, Mike), MaleParent(John, Mike)*,

Box 1.

> *lfp*⁺(T_Ω) = {..., *Animalia(SeaCucumber)*,
> *Animalia(SeaWeed), Animalia(SeaHorse)*,
> *Plantae(SeaCucumber), Plantae(SeaWeed)*,
> *Fungi(SeaCucumber), Fungi(SeaWeed)*,
> Protista(Algae), Monera(*Streptococcus*),...}

Figure 2. LOI≇ for ℘ₐ, ℘ᵦ, and ℘꜀

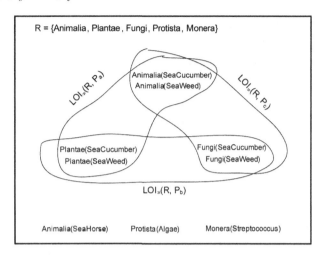

¬*Father(Pete, Jane), MaleParent(Pete, Jane),*

Dad(Pete, Jane), Papa(Bill, Dick), …}

If ℘ₐ = {*Father, Dad*}, then we can apply Algorithm 2 to obtain LOI≅(R, ℘ₐ) as follows.

LOI≅(R, ℘ₐ) = { *Father(John, Mike),*

¬*Dad(John, Mike),* ¬*Father(Pete, Jane),*

Dad(Pete, Jane)}

If ℘ᵦ = {*Dad, MaleParent*}, then we can obtain LOI≅(R, ℘ᵦ) as follows.

LOI ≅(R, ℘ᵦ) = {¬*Dad(John, Mike),*

MaleParent(John, Mike)}

If ℘꜀ = {*Father, MaleParent*}, then we can obtain LOI≅(R, ℘꜀) as follows.

LOI≅(R, ℘꜀) = {¬*Father(Pete, Jane),*

Figure 3. LOI≇ for ℘_d

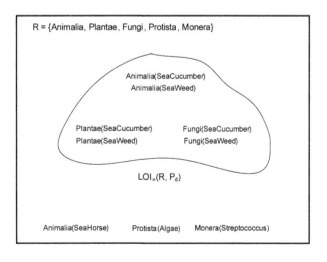

Algorithm 2. Identifying $LOI_{\ncong}(R, \wp)$

```
Input:
  lfp⁺(T_Ω) for a knowledge base Ω,
  R: a concept group of synonymous predicates
(p∈R ∧ q∈R ∧ p≅q), and
  ℘⊆R;
Output:
  LOI_≇(R, ℘);
Ł_℘ = {L_i | L_i∈ lfp⁺(T_Ω) ∧ p_i∈℘}
LOI_≇(R, ℘) = ∅;
K = ∅;

Let C be a set of 2-combinations for ℘: ( |℘| )   if |℘|>1.
                                        (  2  )

while |C| ≠ 0 do {
    if {p, q}∈ C then {
        while [(p(τ_i)∈Ł_℘) ∧ (¬q(τ_j)∈Ł_℘) ∧ (τ_i = τ_j)
            ∧ {p(τ_i), ¬q(τ_j)}⊈ K]
        do {
            K= K ∪ {p(τi), ¬q(τj)};
        }
        while [(¬p(τi)∈_L℘) ∧ (q(τj)∈_L℘) ∧ (τi = τj)
            ∧ {¬p(τi), q(τj)}⊈ K]
        do {
            K= K ∪ {¬p(τi), q(j)};
        }
        C = C -{p, q};
    }
}
LOI≇(R, ℘_j) = K;
return(LOI≇(R, ℘)_j);
```

MaleParent(Pete, Jane)}

Figure 4 indicates the localities of incompatible inconsistency for $\wp_a$, $\wp_b$, and $\wp_c$, respectively. $LOI_{\ncong}(R, \wp_a)$, $LOI_{\ncong}(R, \wp_b)$, and $LOI_{\ncong}(R, \wp_c)$ are intra-concept-group localities.

If $\wp_d = \wp_a \cup \wp_b \cup \wp_c = \{Father, Dad, MaleParent\}$, then $LOI_{\ncong}(R, \wp_d)$ can be obtained as follows.

$LOI_{\ncong}(R, \wp_d) = LOI_{\ncong}(R, \wp_a) \cup LOI_{\ncong}(R, \wp_b)$

$\cup LOI_{\ncong}(R, \wp_c)$

$= \{ Father(John, Mike), \neg Dad(John, Mike),$

MaleParent(John, Mike), ¬Father(Pete, Jane),

MaleParent(Pete, Jane), Dad(Pete, Jane)}

Figure 5 shows the locality of incompatible inconsistency for $\wp_d$.

Figure 4. LOI$_{\neq}$ for $\wp_a$, $\wp_b$, and $\wp_c$

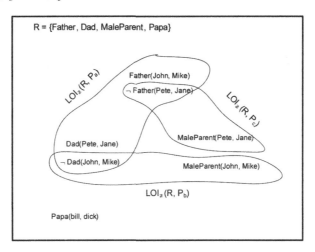

5.3. Algorithm for LOI of Contradictory Type

Contradictory inconsistency arises when concepts or predicates in a knowledge base violate some domain or ontological constraints. Algorithm 3 assumes that such domain or ontological constraints are known.

Example 3: Given R and *lfp*$^+$(T$_\Omega$) for a knowledge base Ω below, and some ontological constraints stating that agent systems must be created before they can be deployed or in service and that an agent system's deployment must precede its service becoming available:

R = {*Created, Deployed, InService*}

lfp$^+$(T$_\Omega$) = {…, *Created*(a_1, *Nov01-09*),

Created(a_3, *Jan15-10*), *Deployed*(a_3, *Feb12-08*),

Figure 5. LOI$_{\neq}$ for $\wp_d$

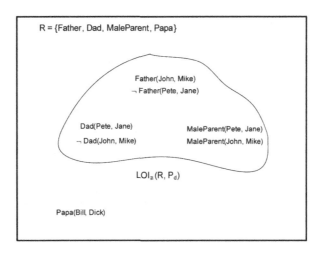

Algorithm 3. Identifying $LOI_{\not\approx}(R, \wp)$

Input:

  $lfp^+(T_\Omega)$ for a knowledge base Ω,

  R: a concept group of predicates constrained by some domain or ontological condition(s) in Γ^I.

  $\wp \subseteq R$;

Output:

  $LOI_{\not\approx}(R, \wp)$;

$Ł_{\wp} = \{L_i \mid L_i \in lfp^+(T_\Omega) \wedge p_i \in \wp\}$

$LOI_{\not\approx}(R, \wp) = \varnothing$;

$K = \varnothing$;

Let C be a set of 2-combinations for $\wp$: $\begin{pmatrix} \mid\wp\mid \\ 2 \end{pmatrix}$ *if $\mid\wp\mid > 1$.*

while *$\mid C \mid \neq 0$* **do** {

  if *$\{p, q\} \in C$* **then** {

    while *$[(p(t_i, t_j) \in Ł_{\wp}) \wedge (q(t_i, t_k) \in Ł_{\wp}) \wedge (t_j \not\approx_i t_k)$*

      *$\wedge \{p(t_i, t_j), q(t_i, t_k)\} \not\subseteq$ **K**]*

    do {

      $K = K \cup \{p(ti, j), q(ti, k)\}$;

    }

    $C = C - \{p, q\}$;

  }

}

*$LOI_{\not\approx}(R, \wp) =$ **K**;*

*return(**$LOI_{\not\approx}(R, \wp)$**);*

InService$(a_1,$ Oct20-09), InService$(a_3,$ Jan02-08),...}

If $\wp_a = \{Created, Deployed\}$, then we can apply Algorithm 3 to obtain $LOI_{\not\approx}(R, \wp_a)$ as follows.

$LOI_{\not\approx}(R, \wp_a) = \{Created(a_3, Jan15\text{-}10),$

Deployed$(a_3,$ Feb12-08)}

If $\wp_b = \{Created, InService\}$, then we can obtain $LOI_{\not\approx}(R, \wp_b)$ as follows.

$LOI_{\not\approx}(R, \wp_b) = \{Created(a_1, Nov01\text{-}09),$

Created$(a_3,$ Jan15-10), InService$(a_1,$ Oct20-09),

InService$(a_3,$ Jan02-08)}

If $\wp_c = \{Deployed, InService\}$, then we can obtain $LOI_{\not\approx}(R, \wp_c)$ as follows.

$LOI_{\not\approx}(R, \wp_c) = \{ Deployed(a_3, Feb12\text{-}08),$

InService$(a_3,$ Jan02-08)}

Figure 6 indicates the localities of contradictory inconsistency for $\wp_a$, $\wp_b$, and $\wp_c$, respectively. $LOI_{\not\approx}(R, \wp_a)$, $LOI_{\not\approx}(R, \wp_b)$, and $LOI_{\not\approx}(R, \wp_c)$ are intra-concept-group localities.

If $\wp_d = \wp_a \cup \wp_b \cup \wp_c = \{Created, Deployed, InService\}$, then $LOI_{\not\approx}(R, \wp_d)$ can be obtained as follows.

Figure 6. $LOI_{\not\approx}$ for $\wp_a$, $\wp_b$, and $\wp_c$

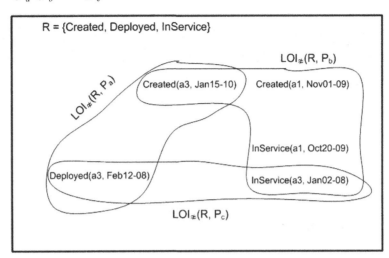

$LOI_{\not\approx}(R, \wp_d) = LOI_{\not\approx}(R, \wp_a) \cup LOI_{\not\approx}(R, \wp_b)$

$\cup \, LOI_{\not\approx}(R, \wp_c)$

$= \{Created(a_1, Nov01\text{-}09),$

$Created(a_3, Jan15\text{-}10), Deployed(a_3, Feb12\text{-}08),$

$InService(a_1, Oct20\text{-}09), InService(a_3, Jan02\text{-}08)\}$

Figure 6 illustrates the locality of contradictory inconsistency for $\wp_d$.

5.4. Algorithm for LOI of Anti-Inverse Type

Predicates p and q are *inverse* of each other, denoted as p⋈q, if ∀x.∀y. [p(x, y) ⊃ q(y, x)] (e.g., *ParentOf*(x, y) and *ChildOf*(y, x)). Anti-inverse inconsistency happens when a concept and the negation of its inverse hold at the same time. Algorithm 4 for Figure 7 relies on having a set of inverse predicates as its input.

Example 4: Given R and $lfp^+(T_\Omega)$ for a knowledge base Ω below:

$R = \{SendTo, ReceiveFrom\}$

$lfp^+(T_\Omega) = \{..., SendTo(a_2, a_4), \,^\neg SendTo(a_6, a_9),$

$^\neg ReceiveFrom(a_4, a_2), ReceiveFrom(a_9, a_6), ...\}$

If $\wp = \{SendTo, ReceiveFrom\}$, then we can apply Algorithm 4 to obtain $LOI_{\not\cong}(R, \wp)$ as follows.

$LOI_{\not\cong}(R, \wp) = \{SendTo(a_2, a_4), \,^\neg SendTo(a_6, a_9),$

$^\neg ReceiveFrom(a_4, a_2), ReceiveFrom(a_9, a_6)\}$

Figure 8 indicates the locality of anti-inverse inconsistency for $\wp$.

5.5. LOI Involving Multiple Types of Inconsistency

$LOI_{\not\approx}(R, \wp_d)$, $LOI_{\not\cong}(R, \wp_d)$, $LOI_{\not\times}(R, \wp_d)$, and $LOI_{\not\perp}(R, \wp)$ are inter-inconsistency-type localities residing in different areas in the inconsistency landscape (Figure 1). We can also use LOI to characterize the quality of query results returned from a knowledge base. For instance, if the result of a query **q** to a knowledge base contains several different types of inconsistency, say complementary, mutually exclusive, and incompatible, then the localities of inconsistency as contained in the

Algorithm 4. Identifying LOI$_{\neq}$(R, ℘)

```
Input:
  lfp⁺(T_Ω) for a knowledge base Ω,
  R: a concept group of inverse predicates
      (p∈R ∧ q∈R ∧ p≭q), and
  ℘⊆R;
Output:
  LOI_≭(R, ℘);
Ł_℘ = {L_i | L_i∈ lfp⁺(T_Ω) ∧ p_i∈℘}
LOI_≭(R, ℘) = ∅;
K = ∅;

Let C be a set of 2-combinations for ℘:  ( |℘| )   if |℘|>1.
                                          (  2  )

while |C| ≠ 0 do {
    if {p, q}∈ C then {
        while [(p(τ_j)∈Ł_℘) ∧ (¬q(τ_k)∈Ł_℘) ∧ (p≭q)
        ∧ (τ_i⋈τ_k) ∧ {p(τ_j), ¬q(τ_k)}⊈ K]
        do {
            K= K ∪ {p(τi), ¬q(τk)}.
        }
        while [(¬p(τi)∈_Ł℘) ∧ (q(τk)∈_Ł℘) ∧ (p≭q)
            ∧ (τi⋈τ_k) ∧ {¬p(τi), q(τk)}⊈ K]
        do {
            K= K ∪ {¬p(τi), q(_rk)};
        }
        C = C -{p, q};
    }
}
LOI≭(R, ℘) = K;
return(LOI≭(R, ℘));
```

results of **q**, denoted as LOI[**q**], can be expressed as follows

$$LOI[\mathbf{q}] = LOI≭() ∪ LOI≠() ∪ LOI≢().$$

If on the other hand the result of **q** includes several different (intra-inconsistency-type) localities of a particular inconsistency type (e.g., (Ri, ℘x), (Rj, ℘y), (Rk, ℘z) in, say mutually exclusive inconsistency, where Ri, Rj, and Rk are different concept groups, and ℘x, ℘y, and ℘z are different sets of anchoring predicates in Ri, Rj, and Rk, respectively), then the localities of inconsistency as contained in the results of **q** can be expressed as follows

$$LOI[\mathbf{q}] = LOI≭(Ri, ℘_x) ∪ LOI≭(Rj, ℘_y)$$

$$∪ LOI≭(Rk, ℘z).$$

When LOI[**q**] = ∅, then we know that the query result is free of any inconsistency.

Figure 7. LOI$_{\neq}$ for $\mathcal{P}_d$

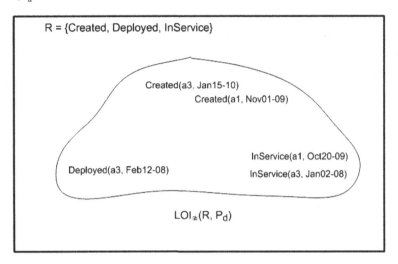

CONCLUSION

Managing knowledge inconsistency is a hallmark of the plasticity of human intelligence. Many human mental processes are cognitively penetrable. When confronted with inconsistency, we revise our beliefs and adjust patterns of behaviors in a rational way so that they become consistent with fresh evidence. During the belief revision process, a principle of minimalism is followed. Toward that end, we need to be able to identify the localities and contexts of inconsistency.

In this paper, we introduced the concept of antagonistic cognitive distance between the two literals. Based on this concept, a formal definition of locality of inconsistency was described. We demonstrated how to use locality of inconsistency to identify clusters of varying sizes of inconsistent circumstances in a knowledge base. Our contribution lies in the fact that locality of inconsistency can be utilized as an effective tool

Figure 8. LOI$_{\neq}$ for $\mathcal{P}$

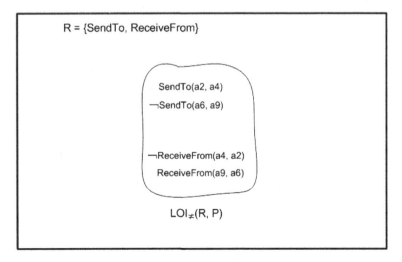

to separate relevant and contributing cognitions from irrelevant ones with regard to a particular inconsistent circumstance, and to provide support for chunking inconsistent knowledge into refined and manageable sizes, which in turn, lends itself to the principle of minimalism in the belief revision process.

Future work can be pursued in the following directions. (1) Locality of inconsistency based approaches to help infer the context, intent, and impact of a given inconsistent circumstance. (2) Locality of inconsistency based patterns to be used in predicting or preempting some detrimental inconsistent circumstances in knowledge management.

ACKNOWLEDGMENT

The author would like to express sincere appreciation to the anonymous reviewers whose comments helped improve both the technical contents and the presentation of this paper.

REFERENCES

Belnap, N. D. (1977). A useful four-valued logic. In Epstein, G., & Dunn, J. (Eds.), *Modern uses of multiple-valued logic* (pp. 8–37). Dordrecht, The Netherlands: D. Reidel. doi:10.1007/978-94-010-1161-7_2

Bertossi, L., & Chomicki, J. (2003). Query answering in inconsistent databases. In Chomicki, J., Meyden, R., & Saake, G. (Eds.), *Logics for emerging applications of databases* (pp. 43–83). Berlin, Germany: Springer-Verlag.

Denning, P. J. (2006). The locality principle. In Barria, J. (Ed.), *Communication Networks and Computer Systems* (pp. 43–67). London, UK: Imperial College Press.

Fitting, M. (1991). Bilattices and the semantics of logic programming. *The Journal of Logic Programming*, *11*, 91–116. doi:10.1016/0743-1066(91)90014-G

Fitting, M. (2002). Fixpoint semantics for logic programming: A survey. *Theoretical Computer Science*, *278*(1-2), 25–51. doi:10.1016/S0304-3975(00)00330-3

Ginsberg, M. L. (1988). Multivalued logics: A uniform approach to inference in artificial intelligence. *Computational Intelligence*, *4*(3), 265–316. doi:10.1111/j.1467-8640.1988.tb00280.x

Gotesky, R. (1968). The uses of inconsistency. *Philosophy and Phenomenological Research*, *28*(4), 471–500. doi:10.2307/2105687

Johnson-Laird, P. N., Legrenzi, P., & Girotto, V. (2004). Reasoning from inconsistency to consistency. *Psychological Review*, *111*(3), 640–661. doi:10.1037/0033-295X.111.3.640

Pylyshyn, Z. (1989). Computing in cognitive science. In Posner, M. I. (Ed.), *Foundations of cognitive science* (pp. 49–92). Cambridge, MA: MIT Press.

Pylyshyn, Z. (1999). Is vision continuous with cognition? The case for cognitive impenetrability of visual perception. *The Behavioral and Brain Sciences*, *22*, 341–423. doi:10.1017/S0140525X99002022

Shastri, L., & Grannes, D. J. (1996). A connectionist treatment of negation and inconsistency. In *Proceedings of the 18th Conference of the Cognitive Science Society*, San Diego, CA (pp. 142-147).

Zhang, D. (2005). Fixpoint semantics for rule base anomalies. In *Proceedings of the 4th IEEE International Conference on Cognitive Informatics*, Irvine, CA (pp. 10-17). Washington, DC: IEEE Computer Society.

Zhang, D. (2007). Fixpoint semantics for rule base anomalies. *International Journal of Cognitive Informatics and Natural Intelligence, 1*(4), 4–25. doi:10.4018/jcini.2007100102

Zhang, D. (2008). Quantifying knowledge base inconsistency via fixpoint semantics. *Transactions on Computational Science 2. LNCS, 5150,* 145–160.

Zhang, D. (2009). Taming inconsistency in value-based software development. In *Proceedings of the 21ˢᵗ International Conference on Software Engineering and Knowledge Engineering,* Boston, MA (pp. 450-455).

Zhang, D. (2010a). Harnessing locality for knowledge inconsistency management. In *Proceedings of the 9ᵗʰ IEEE International Conference on Cognitive Informatics,* Beijing, China (pp. 325-332).

Zhang, D. (2010b). Toward A classification of antagonistic manifestations of knowledge. In *Proceedings of the 22ᵗʰ IEEE International Conference on Tools with Artificial Intelligence,* Arras, France (pp. 375-382).

ENDNOTES

[1] In the six-kingdom of living things classification, *Monera* is further divided into *Eubacteria* and *Archaebacteria*.

[2] If $p(t_i, t_j) \in R$ and $q(t_i, t_k) \in R$, we use $t_j \approx_\Gamma t_k$ to denote that t_j and t_k violate the domain or ontological constraint.

This work was previously published in the International Journal of Software Science and Computational Intelligence, Volume 3, Issue 1, edited by Yingxu Wang, pp. 61-77, copyright 2011 by IGI Publishing (an imprint of IGI Global).

Chapter 10
Adaptive Study Design Through Semantic Association Rule Analysis

Ping Chen
University of Houston-Downtown, USA

Wei Ding
University of Massachusetts-Boston, USA

Walter Garcia
University of Houston-Downtown, USA

ABSTRACT

Association mining aims to find valid correlations among data attributes, and has been widely applied to many areas of data analysis. This paper presents a semantic network-based association analysis model including three spreading activation methods. It applies this model to assess the quality of a dataset, and generate semantically valid new hypotheses for adaptive study design especially useful in medical studies. The approach is evaluated on a real public health dataset, the Heartfelt study, and the experiment shows promising results.

1. INTRODUCTION

Association rule mining has been widely applied to numerous domains, such as analysis of market-basket datasets, text mining, and disease diagnosis (Agrawal et al., 1996). Association rules whose support and confidence are above user-specified thresholds are considered statistically significant and presented to end-users. While these objective measures are effective to reduce rule redundancy, incorporation of subjective and domain-specific knowledge is still a critical challenge for association analysis, and this knowledge should be represented in a more structured way to maximize its usage. Hence, we choose semantic network to represent knowledge for association analysis. Semantic network has been implemented in many knowledge bases. Concepts and ideas in the human

DOI: 10.4018/978-1-4666-2651-5.ch010

brain have been shown to be semantically linked, which motivates the modern research of semantic network (Quillian, 1998). On recent development on human memory study was described in Widrow et al., 2010), and a general cognitive knowledge representation model was described in Ramirez 2010. Numerous knowledge representation models for more specific areas are also proposed recently to tailor and model interesting aspects of knowledge (Chen et al., 2009).

A semantic network represents knowledge as a directed graph, where vertices represent concepts and edges represent semantic relations between the concepts. Figure 1 shows a sample semantic network whose vertices represent concepts and edges are labeled with names of relations. This semantic network was created in the case study (Section 8) when we examined the Heartfelt adolescent health study. Concepts are organized into a hierarchical structure by is-a edges, and other edges show causal relations, e.g., observable entity diagnose disease or syndrome, stressed is a mental process, diseases can be result of mental process. Comparing with other knowledge representation models, a semantic network has the following advantages:

1. **Easy to Use:** A user needs little training or computer background to build semantic networks. Semantic networks are easy to understand and its explanation is usually straightforward.

2. **Flexible, Incremental, and Easy To Update:** Building a semantic network does not require a user to have a complete or perfect understanding at the beginning. Instead, the building processing can be incremental, and knowledge can be updated locally as a user gets more familiar with a domain.

3. **Generative:** A semantic network is not a merely static structure; instead it has a vertex-firing mechanism called spreading activation. Firing or activation of a vertex sends activation to its semantically connected neighbor vertices. Spreading activation only accesses local neighbor vertices, so its time complexity does not grow with the size of the network.

In this paper we will discuss a semantic network-based association analysis model. With this model we will provide the following analysis techniques:

Figure 1. A fragment of semantic network used in our case study

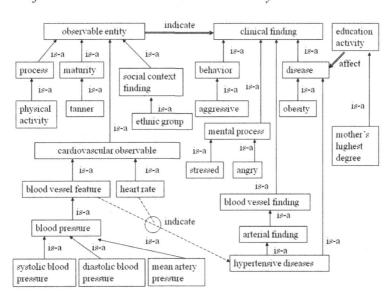

1. **Hypothesis Generation:** New hypotheses are generated through generalization and inference from the association rule set, and give end-users directions for further investigation.

2. **Data Quality Assessment:** A dataset is just an imperfect and incomplete reflection of a real-world object or scenario. By analyzing association rules we can assess the quality of original dataset.

Our work is closely related to cognitive informatics, which is a transdisciplinary field emerging from Cognitive Science, Computational Intelligence, Artificial Intelligence, Formal Semantics, and Human-Computer Interaction. A set of cognitive models for causation analyses and causal inferences was proposed in Wang 2011, which formalized causal inference methodologies to simulate subtle aspects of human reasoning.

This paper is organized as follows. In Section 2, we provide some background knowledge on related technologies including ontology, concept algebra, semantic computing, and computing with words (CWW). In Section 3 we discuss a knowledge model to represent domain and user knowledge. We present three spreading activation methods in Section 4. In Section 5 we discuss how to model semantic analysis on association rules. In Sections 6 and 7 we discuss how to assess data quality and generate hypothesis based on association mining. We evaluate our method in Section 8 using a real-world public health dataset. Related work is discussed in Section 9. We conclude in Section 10.

2. BACKGROUND

Semantic network has been applied to many fields since its introduction in Artificial Intelligence in 1960's. Many techniques in the general field of symbolic computing have been studies recently. Here we provide a brief review of several critical fields.

Ontology study focuses on formally representing knowledge as a set of concepts and relations among these concepts (Ganter et al., 2005). The goal of an ontology is to provide a shared and interchangeable vocabulary for the modeling of a domain. Hundred of ontology systems have been created for numerous domains, such as Basic Formal Ontology for scientific research, BioPAX for Biology, Customer Complaint Ontology for e-Business, Cell Cycle Ontology for medicine.

Formal concept analysis aims to building an ontology from a domain of object and entities automatically along with their relations and properties. The theoretical foundation of this filed include applied lattice and order theory (Gruber, 1993).

Semantic computing focuses on understanding of meaning/semantics in a general computing environment. It studies the following critical problems (Mendel, 1999):

1. User intention analysis and automatic processing;
2. Data semantics analysis and processing;
3. User goal understanding.

Computing with words (CWW) was proposed by Zadeh in 1996 using his Fuzzy Logic theory to activate and convert words into a mathematical representation (Zadeh, 1996). Fuzzy set is adopted as the machinery to transform input words to output words, and then back to users. Much work has been done since then, please refer to (Lawry, 2001, 2003; Mendel, 2001, 2002, 2003, 2007) for more details. CWW has many potential applications, e.g., Internet search engines, summarization, information extraction.

3. ASSOCIATION MODELING WITH A SEMANTIC NETWORK

We define a semantic network SN for association rule analysis as an extended directed graph, SN = (V, A, H, S, T) (Chen, 2008),

- V is a set of vertices that denote the attributes in the dataset and relevant concepts from its domain, $V = \{v_1, v_2, \cdots, v_k\}$;
- A is a set of association edges connecting multiple vertices, $A = \{(v_1, v_2, \cdots, v_n, \rightarrow u) \mid v_i, u \in V, (i = 1, \cdots, n)\}$. An association edge $v_1, v_2, \cdots, v_n \rightarrow u$ denotes an association among attributes, with $v_1, v_2, \cdots, v_n$ as the antecedent part of an association (also called the body), and u as the consequent part (also called the head).

For example, the association blood vessel feature, heart rate $\rightarrow$ hypertensive diseases is shown in Figure 1, which involves three vertices. Semantically an association edge means associated-with. In practice an edge often can be labeled with more specific relations, such as result-of, indicate, etc. If we know what values of these attributes take, an association edge can represent one or multiple association rules, $v_1 = a_1, v_2 = a_2, \cdots, v_n = a_n \rightarrow u = a$;

- H is a set of is-a edges connecting two vertices, $H = \{(v, u) \mid v, u \in V\}$. An edge v is-a u denotes a subclass-superclass relation, with v as the child, and u as the parent;
- S is a label set, $S = \{KNOWN, BASIC\}$. An association edge can be labeled with KNOWN, BASIC, or both. KNOWN labels are specified by end-users. A KNOWN association edge means that this association is already known by the user.

An experienced user knows a lot about his/her domain, and may label many KNOWN tags. So relatively less UNKNOWN knowledge will be extracted. A novice user may label only a few KNOWN tags, and a large amount of knowledge will be classified as UNKNOWN, and this is exactly what this user needs to learn.

The goal of our method is not to always incorporate all existing knowledge about a domain and make genuine discoveries, instead we aim to generating unknown knowledge customized for a specific user and improve his/her understanding about the domain. Whether this unknown knowledge is unknown to the whole domain is left to users for further analysis. Probably some new knowledge can be discovered. A BASIC edge can be obtained from a user or other knowledge sources. BASIC association edges represent highly confident principles about a domain, e.g., observable entity indicates clinical finding. There are two ways to specify BASIC labels, closed scheme and open scheme. In closed scheme, BASIC association edges exhaustively list all valid associations among vertices, and by default, any other associations are not allowed. In open scheme, a BASIC association edge means that an association among connected vertices is not allowed, and by default, all other associations are allowed, although they may or may not hold in practice. Basically whether to choose open or closed scheme is determined by the development of a domain. For a well-established domain, such as cardiovascular research, there exists very comprehensive correlation knowledge at least among basic concepts (high level entities in UMLS (U. S. National Library of Medicine, 2007) Semantic Network). In this case, a closed scheme can be adopted. The open scheme will be more suitable for an emerging field. BASIC edges are used to identify semantically invalid association rules. For example, the rule Gender = Male $\rightarrow$ Mother's Highest Degree = Master is generated in our case study, but it is not a valid rule since there is no association between Gender and Mother's Highest Degree. In the rest of our paper, the closed knowledge assumption is adopted. In the case of open assumption, the invalid rules can be further processed to identify contradictions to the given knowledge and shown to the user in order to identify interesting and useful exceptions. For a well-explored domain, our method is still useful. Knowledge generated from our technique can be used to verify and validate existing knowledge obtained with other types of techniques, especially knowledge based on personal direct or indirect experience. This is why in our semantic network we have BASIC and KNOWN labels. If a BASIC or KNOWN labeled edge is violated many times, its validity should be further examined.

- T is a set of attribute-value pairs, and T = $\{v_i = a_i \mid v_i \in V\}$.

These pairs are provided by users as not interesting or trivial instances. For example, in public health domain, Obesity = No is usually not interesting, but Hypertension = Yes is interesting.

Creation of such a semantic network can be highly automated if there exist electronic domain knowledge sources. Figure 1 shows a fragment of semantic network built for our case study. The vertices are medical concepts from a dataset. These concepts are connected with associated-with and causal relations shown as $\Rightarrow$ and is-a shown as $\rightarrow$ (dashed line if its label is KNOWN, solid line if its label is BASIC).

4. SPREADING ACTIVATION METHODS

To create a high-quality semantic network, often we have to acquire many association edges and their labels from end-users and other knowledge sources. However, the hierarchical design of our semantic network can greatly lighten the burden of knowledge acquisition, and many associations can be generated by spreading activation, and a user does not have to specify every association explicitly as in other existing methods. Here are the three spreading activation methods:

1. $v_1 \rightarrow u_1 \wedge u_1 \rightarrow u_2 \models v_1 \rightarrow u_2$

Generally associations are transitive.

2. v_1 is-a $v_2 \wedge v_2 \rightarrow u \models v_1 \rightarrow u$

The antecedent part of a rule can be specialized, which is called deduction in logic. For example, Tweety is-a bird $\wedge$ bird $\rightarrow$ fly $\models$ Tweety $\rightarrow$ fly.

With this method, all the associations between v_2's children and u can be replaced by a single association $v_2 \rightarrow u$. For example, we do not have to specify, heart rate $\rightarrow$ clinical finding, mean artery pressure $\rightarrow$ clinical finding, $\cdots$, instead, one association observable entity $\rightarrow$ clinical finding will be sufficient.

3. u_1 is-a $u_2 \wedge v \rightarrow u_1 \models v \rightarrow u_2$

The consequent part of a rule can be generalized, e.g., fly is-a move $\wedge$ bird $\rightarrow$ fly $\models$ bird $\rightarrow$ move. With this method, all the associations between v and u1's parents can be replaced by a single association $v \rightarrow u_1$. For example, we do not have to specify, observable entity $\rightarrow$ blood vessel finding, observable entity $\rightarrow$ arterial finding, $\cdots$, instead, one association observable entity $\rightarrow$ hypertensive diseases will be sufficient.

5. SEMANTIC ASSOCIATION RULE ANALYSIS

Association rules are statistically supported by data, but not matter how massive the data is, it is just a sampling of bits and pieces at discrete times about an object or scenario, and often contains noise and erroneous information. Inevitably, rules generated from such data can be simply coincidence or even wrong. With semantic analysis, we are able to detect trivial or known association rules, weed out invalid association rules that conflict with common sense or domain knowledge, and generate a semantically validated association rule set. During this process, the basic operation is to match an association rule with the association edges in the semantic network, which will be discussed first.

Suppose we have an association rule:

$$R: v_1 = a_1, \cdots, v_n = a_n \rightarrow u = a$$

where v_i and u are attributes of a dataset, and the a_i and a are their values.

Definition 1: A rule R is known to a semantic network SN iff $\forall i$

$v_i \rightarrow u \in A$ and labeled with KNOWN, or $v_i \rightarrow u$ can be generated by applying the three spreading activation methods on KNOWN association edges in A.

Otherwise, a rule R is unknown to SN.

Definition 2: An association rule is semantically correct iff $\forall i$

$v_i \rightarrow u \in A$ and labeled with BASIC, or $v_i \rightarrow u$ can be generated by applying the three spreading activation methods on BASIC association edges in A. otherwise, it is semantically incorrect.

Suppose we have the following rule:

R1: blood pressure = high $\rightarrow$ hypertensive diseases = yes

In the semantic network shown in Figure 1, there does not exist a BASIC association edge between blood pressure and hypertensive diseases. But according to the spreading activation method 2: the antecedent part of a rule can be specialized, we can specialize blood vessel feature in the association blood vessel feature $\rightarrow$ hypertensive diseases and generate R1. Hence, R1 is semantically correct.

Let's look at another example,

R2: heart rate = high $\rightarrow$ Mother's degree = Bachelor

R2 is simply a coincidence, and cannot be validated by the semantic network and is semantically incorrect.

Definition 3: A rule R is non-trivial to a semantic network SN if $\exists v_i = a_i \in T$ (i = 1, 2, $\cdots$, n) or u = a$\in$ T; otherwise, R is trivial.

If all attribute-value pairs in a rule are uninteresting, this rule is classified as trivial. This definition proposes a new semantic interestingness measure. A trivial rule may be correct or incorrect, but a user has little interest in it. For example, here is a rule from our case study,

OBESITY=0 STRESS1=0 ACCOM1=0 BORED1=0 RUSH1=0 $\rightarrow$ TAXHYN=0 conf: (0.96)

This rule means, if a person is not obese, does not feel stressed, accomplished, bored, or rushed, then with 96% confidence he/she does not have hypertensive diseases. Such a rule may be correct since it does not violate any common sense or domain knowledge, but it is not interesting to physicians. In practice, there may be many such trivial rules, and it is important that they are separated from interesting rules. Note that a rule is interesting provided there is at least one attribute-value pair that is not in the set T. This means that a rule like OBESITY = 0, DISEASE = YES will be considered interesting even if OBESITY = 0 is in T provided that DISEASE – YES is not in T. Also note that we do not propose to delete any transactions from the database based on T, we only use T to classify the generated rules.

As shown in Figure 2, using the semantic network described in the previous section, we group association rules into 5 semantic categories: *trivial, known and correct, known and incorrect, unknown and incorrect, and unknown and correct*. This group process is straightforward by matching association rules with labeled edges (trivial, BASIC, KNOWN) in our semantic network. Generally a user will be interested in the last category: unknown and correct. Some users may also be interested in the known and incor-

Figure 2. Semantic association rule analysis system

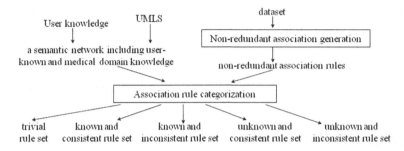

rect category, which indicates the contradictory knowledge from users and other domain sources.

Closed scheme requires a complete list of all valid associations (labeled as BASIC), which may look unrealistic in practice. However, in an established field, usually we have exhaustive knowledge about properties and relations of at least high-level concepts. For example, UMLS list totally 6864 associations among 189 high-level concepts (called Semantic Types), and it is unlikely that there still exist any unknown relations among them. Spreading activation methods can be used to generate associations among more specific concepts.

The quality of semantic network plays an important role in the grouping process. The more domain knowledge is incorporated and the better understanding a user has of the dataset, the unknown and correct categories will be more concise and precise. Then objective measure based methods can be applied to this group and filter out redundant association rules. By integrating objective methods with our approach, we can successfully identify non-trivial, non-redundant, semantically correct, and user-specific rules.

6. HYPOTHESIS GENERATION

Generating high-quality new hypotheses is very important for knowledge discovery in scientific study. With concepts semantically organized and correlated in a semantic network, the intuition for generating hypotheses is that if two concepts are associated, maybe their semantically connected neighbors (children and siblings) are also associated. We have the following hypothesis generation methods (Chen et al., 2010),

Hypothesis Generation Method 1:

$$\{v\text{'s child}\} \rightarrow u \models v \rightarrow u$$

This is called induction in logic. If v's child is associated with u, likely v is also associate with u. Induction is useful when the direct observation of v is difficult or impossible when v is an abstract concept.

Hypothesis Generation Method 2:

$$\{v\text{'s sibling}\} \rightarrow u \models v \rightarrow u$$

Analogy is another technique used by human beings to generate hypotheses.

If these generated hypotheses already exist in the rule set, they will be discarded, and only new hypotheses are kept. Hypotheses are not necessarily facts, but they are more likely to be true than random guess, and they provide directions for further investigation. Additional constraints can reduce the number of hypotheses and keep only highly plausible ones, e.g., using only immediate children and siblings.

7. DATA QUALITY ASSESSMENT

A dataset is just a sampling of a real-world object or scenario at different spatial and temporal points or intervals. Naturally we want to assess the quality of a dataset, that is, how precisely they reflect reality. Data quality is a multi-dimensional concept including completeness, appropriate amount, amount of errors/missing values, objectivity, believability (Padmanabhan & Tuzhilin, 1998, 2000). Among these properties, what directly affect the quality of association rules are:

1. Whether the amount of collected data is appropriate.

    If the collected data is not enough to approximate the true scenario precisely, we will get many wrong or coincident rules (false negative).

2. Whether the set of data attributes is semantically coherent.

An association rule is valid only if the attributes in the rule are semantically relevant. Rules generated by semantically isolated attributes will likely be coincident instead of valid. A poorly designed experiment with many isolated attributes will miss many useful and interesting rules (false positive).

Let N_x denote the number of rules of type x. To measure these two factors, we propose the following metrics,

Data Quality Metric 1:

$$Q_{size} = \frac{N_{KnownCorrect} + N_{UnknownCorrect}}{N_{nontrivial\ rules}}$$

We calculate the ratio of the number of semantically valid rules to the number of nontrivial rules. The intuition is that the larger a dataset is, the more closely it should reflect the basic domain

principles, and the less semantically incorrect rules will be generated.

Data Quality Metric 2:

$$Q_{attribute} = \frac{N_{NewHypotheses}}{N_{UnknownCorrect} + N_{NewHypotheses}}$$

Since the hypotheses are generated by replacing original attributes with semantically similar attributes (children, siblings) in the unknown and correct rules, the more new hypotheses we get, the more semantically incomplete the original attribute set is.

3. A CASE STUDY

Public health monitoring and analysis is very important to national policy makers and general public. Public health data is generally of large volume, noisy, and high-dimensional, which is an ideal test bed for data mining techniques. Therefore we chose a public health data set collected in the Heartfelt study as our case study. All experiments were performed on a Pentium 4 3.0GHz PC running Windows XP. We used the Apriori algorithm implemented in Weka 3.4 (Witten, 2005) to generate association rules.

8.1. The Heartfelt Study

In 1999, the Heartfelt study was conducted to collect data on adolescent health. The target population for this study was African, European, and Hispanic American adolescents, aged 11-16 years, residing in a large metropolitan city in southeast Texas with an ethnically diverse population. 383 adolescents were recruited, and the collected data included totally 105 attributes and 16912 records. The attributes include age, gender, ethnic/racial group, physical maturity, resting blood pressure and heart rate, ambulatory blood pressure, heart rate and moods reported at 30-minute intervals, body mass index, fat free mass, psychological characteristics such as anger and hostility. Numerous findings have been reported based on bio-statistical analysis of the Heartfelt study, such as stress-induced alterations of blood pressure (Meininger, 1999), association of obesity and poor sleep quality (Gupta et al., 2002), ethnic group differences in moods and ambulatory blood pressure (Meininger, 2001), relationship of ambulatory blood pressure to physical activity (Eissa et al., 2001), etc. Here are a few findings that have been reported in medical literature:

1. Sleep quality *associated-with* obesity
2. Ethnicity, age, body mass index, height, maturity *associated-with* systolic blood pressure
3. Fat mass, percent body fat *associated-with* heart rate
4. Mood, ethnicity, maturity, gender *associated-with* systolic blood pressure, diastolic blood pressure

These associations were found with bio-statistical techniques, and are different from association rules generated by Apriori algorithm. Some transformations are necessary for evaluation, for example, association 4 can be mapped to the following association rules:

- Ethnicity = African American, Maturity = high, mood = neutral, gender = boy → systolic blood pressure = high
- Maturity = low, mood = rushed → diastolic blood pressure = high
- Ethnicity = Hispanic American, Maturity = high, mood = neutral, gender = girl → diastolic blood pressure = high

8.2. Building a Semantic Network from UMLS to Analyze the Heartfelt Study

Unified Medical Language System (UMLS) is designed to help an information system understand the meanings of concepts and terms and their relationships in biomedical and health domain (U. S. National Library of Medicine, 2007). The UMLS Knowledge Sources are multi-purpose, and can be used to create, process, retrieve, integrate, and aggregate biomedical and health information. UMLS divides medical ontology knowledge into three sources: the SPECIALIST lexicon, the Metathesaurus, and the Semantic Network. The SPECIALIST lexicon is designed to provide lexical information for the SPECIALIST Natural Language Processing System. The Metathesaurus is a multi-lingual vocabulary database that contains definitions of biomedical terms, their various names (such as synonyms and abbreviations), and the relationships among them. The Semantic Network categorizes all concepts in the Metathesaurus into semantic types, such as clinical finding, organisms, physical activity, etc. The Semantic Network also defines a set of relationships between biomedical concepts. These relationships provide the structure for the Semantic Network. The primary relationship is the is-a link, which establishes the hierarchy within the Semantic Network. Besides, there are also a set of non-hierarchical relationships, e.g., associated-with, affect, functionally related to. Here are a few examples,

- C0002871|CHD|C0002891|is-a|MSH

Neonatal (encoded by C0002891) has is-a relations to Anemia (C0002871)

- C0002871|RO|C0002886|clinically associated with |

CCPSS Megaloblastic anemia due to folate deficiency has clinically associated with relationship to Anemia (C0002871)

Using UMLS we created a semantic network for the Heartfelt dataset as follows (a fragment of the semantic network is shown in Figure 1):

1. Analyze the attributes in the Heartfelt dataset, assign the attributes that are semantically similar to the same vertex, e.g., age of subject in years and age of subject in months are assigned to one vertex, and totally we obtain 39 vertices;

2. Extract parent and child concepts (totally 162) of the original attributes from UMLS, and add these new concepts and their is-a relations into the semantic network. As shown in Figure 1, majority of concepts are organized into the observable entity tree and clinical finding tree;

3. Find the semantic type of each attribute using UMLS. Different concepts can have the same semantic type, and we found totally 9 semantic types. UMLS provides 49 relations among these semantic types, and they were added into the network as associated-with or more specific edges, e.g., affect and indicate, and labeled with BASIC ;

4. Ask a user to add additional associated-with edges labeled with KNOWN and specify trivial attribute-value pairs. In our experiment, we add associated-with edges that should be known by general public, such as body mass index is associated with obesity, age is associated with sexual maturity, etc. Trivial attribute-value pairs are generally not interesting to medical personnel, such as obesity = no, blood pressure = normal, etc.

It took us about two hours to set up this semantic network. Although actual time can vary from one dataset to another and from one user to another user, once the semantic network is set up, it can be reused by other users and revised to analyze similar datasets.

8.3. Experiment Results and Discussion

We applied our hypothesis generation method to the association rules generated from Heartfelt dataset, and totally we generated 1920 new hypotheses for further investigation. These hypotheses point out new attributes that a user may collect in future experiments. These hypotheses introduced new attributes (siblings and children of original attributes, excluded if they already exist), we do not have any real values for these attributes. Instead, these hypotheses describe possible correlations among semantically relevant attributes. For example,

ZBMI is associated with Maternal obesity syndrome.

ZBMI is the z-score of body mass index that measures obesity, and it is reasonable that ZBMI relates to maternal obesity syndrome. These hypotheses should be of high quality since they are based on the rules generated from real data and validated by the basic biomedical principles specified in our semantic network.

We calculated Qsize and Qattribute according to two metrics proposed in Section 6,

Qsize =0.36

Qattribute =0.07

The value of Qsize is low and indicates that the dataset is small, which is common in biomedical field due to the prohibitive data collecting cost. A small Qattribute shows that the attributes in the dataset are semantically self-closed since not many hypothesis can be generated, which indicates that the Heartfelt study was very carefully designed.

4. RELATED WORK

Association rule mining aims to detect relationships or associations between specific values of categorical variables in large data sets. Association rule mining has been proved to be very useful in many applications. Various techniques have been adopted. For example, one feature-based technique was proposed using rough set theory (Liu, 2010). One major obstacle in practice is how to identify correct, interesting, user-specific rules from a huge number of redundant, wrong, or trivial rules. Recently association rule post-processing has become a very active research area. Based on whether external knowledge sources are used, we can divide the existing methods into objective measure based methods and knowledge based methods.

Objective measure based methods do not require any domain information besides the rule set itself, and can be used by both domain experts and novice users. However, lack of domain knowledge makes it impossible to detect wrong rules that are just coincidence and do not make sense, and lack of user input results in presenting many rules already known by users. Based on the analysis tasks this type of methods can be further divided into:

1. **Metric-Based Rule Evaluation:** This type of approaches uses metrics to evaluate the significance or interestingness of an association rule, such as lift, statistical hypothesis tests. Uninteresting rules will be discarded. However, as shown in (Wang et al., 2003), each metric has different properties and may be useful only for some specific domains and applications and choosing the right metric is often difficult.

2. **Rule Summarization and Generalization:** To reduce the number of rules that need manual analysis, rules are analyzed with their context (Liu et al., 2006). These methods investigate relations among rules in order to present users a concise rule set.

3. **Rule Ranking:** Han et al. (2002) and Xin et al. (2006) discussed how to extract top-k significant rules with low redundancy.

5. CONCLUSION

In this paper, we discussed how to model domain knowledge with a semantic network and apply it to association rule analysis. Our semantic association rule analysis can generate semantically valid hypothesis, and assess data quality. We successfully applied our method to a public health dataset and obtained promising results.

ACKNOWLEDGMENT

This work is funded by United States National Science Foundation grant CNS 0851984 and United States Department of Homeland Security grant 2009-ST-061-C10001.

REFERENCES

Agrawal, R., Mannila, H., Srikant, R., Toivonen, H., & Verkamo, A. I. (1996). Fast discovery of association rules. In Fayyad, U. M., Piatetsky-Shapiro, G., Smyth, P., & Uthurusamy, R. (Eds.), *Advances in knowledge discovery and data mining*. Menlo Park, CA: AAAI Press.

Chen, P., & Garcia, W. (2010, July 7-9). Hypothesis generation and data quality assessment through association mining. In *Proceedings of the 9th IEEE International Conference on Cognitive Informatics*, Beijing, China.

Chen, P., Verma, R., Meininger, J. C., & Chan, W. (2008). Semantic analysis of association rules. In *Proceedings of the International FLAIRS Conference* (pp. 270-275).

Eissa, M., Meininger, J. C., Nguyen, T., & Chan, W. (2001). The relationship of ambulatory blood pressure to physical activity in a tri-ethnic population of obese and nonobese adolescents. *American Journal of Hypertension*, *20*(2), 140–147. doi:10.1016/j.amjhyper.2006.07.008

Ganter, B., Stumme, G., & Wille, R. (Eds.). (2005). *Formal concept analysis: Foundations and applications (LNAI 3626)*. Berlin, Germany: Springer-Verlag.

Gruber, T. R. (1993). A translation approach to portable ontology specifications. *Knowledge Acquisition*, *5*(2), 199–220. doi:10.1006/knac.1993.1008

Gupta, N. K., Mueller, W. H., Chan, W., & Meininger, J. C. (2002). Is obesity associated with poor sleep quality in adolescents? *American Journal of Human Biology: The Official Journal of the Human Biology Council*, *14*(6).

Han, J., Wang, J., Lu, Y., & Tzvetkov, P. (2002). Mining top-k frequent closed patterns without minimum support. In *Proceedings of the IEEE International Conference on Data Mining* (pp. 211-218).

Lawry, J. (2001). An alternative to computing with words. *International Journal of Uncertainty, Fuzziness and Knowledge-Based Systems*, *9*, 3–16. doi:10.1142/S0218488501000958

Lawry, J., Shanahan, J., & Ralescu, A. (Eds.). (2003). *Modeling with words (LNAI 2873)*. New York, NY: Springer.

Liu, B., Zhao, K., Benkler, J., & Xiao, W. (2006). Rule interestingness analysis using OLAP operations. In *Proceedings of the 12th ACM SIGKDD International Conference on Knowledge Discovery and Data Mining*, Philadelphia, PA (pp. 297-306).

Liu, Y., Jiao, L., Bai, G., & Feng, B. (2010). Feature based rule learner in noisy environment using neighbourhood rough set model. *International Journal of Software Science and Computational Intelligence*, *2*(2), 66–85. doi:10.4018/jssci.2010040104

Meininger, J. C., Liehr, P., Chan, W., Smith, G., & Mueller, W. H. (2001). Developmental, gender, and ethnic group differences in moods and ambulatory blood pressure in adolescents. *Annals of Behavioral Medicine: A Publication of the Society of Behavioral Medicine*, *28*(1), 10-19.

Meininger, J. C., Liehr, P., Mueller, W. H., Chan, W., Smith, G. L., & Portman, R. J. (1999). Stress-induced alterations of blood pressure and 24h ambulatory blood pressure in adolescents. *Blood Pressure Monitoring*, *4*(3-4).

Mendel, J. M. (1999, June). Computing with words, when words can mean different things to different people. In *Proceedings of the Third International ICSC Symposium on Fuzzy Logic and Applications*, Rochester, NY.

Mendel, J. M. (2001). *Uncertain rule-based fuzzy logic systems: Introduction and new directions*. Upper Saddle River, NJ: Prentice Hall.

Mendel, J. M. (2002). An architecture for making judgments using computing with words. *International Journal of Applied Mathematics and Computer Science*, *12*(3), 325–335.

Mendel, J. M. (2003). Fuzzy sets for words: A new beginning. In *Proceedings of the 12th IEEE International Conference on Fuzzy Systems*, St. Louis, MO (pp. 37-42).

Mendel, J. M. (2007). Computing with words and its relationships with fuzzistics. *Information Sciences*, *177*, 988–1006. doi:10.1016/j.ins.2006.06.008

Mendel, J. M., & John, R. I. (2002, July). Footprint of uncertainty and its importance to type-2 fuzzy sets. In *Proceedings of the 6th IASTED International Conference on Artificial Intelligence and Soft Computing*, Banff, AB, Canada (pp. 587-592).

Padmanabhan, B., & Tuzhilin, A. (1998). A belief-driven method for discovering unexpected patterns. In *Proceedings of the 4th ACM SIGKDD International Conference on Knowledge Discovery and Data Mining*.

Padmanabhan, B., & Tuzhilin, A. (2000). Small is beautiful: Discovering the minimal set of unexpected patterns. In *Proceedings of the 6th ACM SIGKDD International Conference on Knowledge Discovery and Data Mining*, Boston, MA (pp. 54-63).

Pipino, L., Lee, Y., & Wang, R. (2002). Data quality assessment. *Communications of the ACM, 45*(4). doi:10.1145/505248.506010

Quillian, M. R. (1998). Semantic memory. In Minsky, M. (Ed.), *Semantic information processing*. Cambridge, MA: MIT Press.

Ramirez, C., & Valdes, B. (2010). A general knowledge representation model for the acquisition of skills and concepts. *International Journal of Software Science and Computational Intelligence, 2*(3), 1–20. doi:10.4018/jssci.2010070101

Sahar, S. (2002). On incorporating subjective interestingness into the mining process. In *Proceedings of the IEEE International Conference on Data Mining* (p. 681).

Sheu, P., Yu, H., Ramamoorthy, C. V., Joshi, A., & Zadeh, L. A. (2010). *Semantic computing*. New York, NY: John Wiley & Sons.

Tan, P. N., Kumar, V., & Srivastava, J. (2002, July). Selecting the right interestingness measure for association patterns. In *Proceedings of the 8th ACM SIGKDD International Conference on Knowledge Discovery and Data Mining* (pp. 32-41).

U. S. National Library of Medicine. (2007). *Unified medical language system*. Retrieved from http://www.nlm.nih.gov/research/umls/

Wang, K., Jiang, Y., & Lakshmanan, L. V. S. (2003, August). Mining unexpected rules by pushing user dynamics. In *Proceedings of the 9th ACM SIGKDD International Conference on Knowledge Discovery and Data Mining*, Washington, DC (pp. 246-255).

Wang, Y. (2011). On cognitive models of causal inferences and causation networks. *International Journal of Software Science and Computational Intelligence, 3*(1), 50–60.

Webb, G. I. (2006). Discovering significant rules. In *Proceedings of the 12th ACM SIGKDD International Conference on Knowledge Discovery and Data Mining*, Philadelphia, PA (pp. 434-443).

Widrow, B. C., & Aragon, J. (2010). Cognitive memory: Human like memory. *International Journal of Software Science and Computational Intelligence, 2*(4), 1–15. doi:10.4018/jssci.2010100101

Witten, I. H., & Frank, E. (2005). *Data mining: Practical machine learning tools and techniques* (2nd ed.). San Francisco, CA: Morgan Kaufmann.

Xin, D., Cheng, H., Yan, X., & Han, J. (2006). Extracting redundancy-aware top-k patterns. In *Proceedings of the 12th ACM SIGKDD International Conference on Knowledge Discovery and Data Mining*, Philadelphia, PA (pp. 444-453).

Zadeh, L. A. (1996). Fuzzy logic = computing with words. *IEEE Transactions on Fuzzy Systems, 4*, 103–111. doi:10.1109/91.493904

This work was previously published in the International Journal of Software Science and Computational Intelligence, Volume 3, Issue 2, edited by Yingxu Wang, pp. 34-48, copyright 2011 by IGI Publishing (an imprint of IGI Global).

Chapter 11
Qualitative Reasoning Approach to a Driver's Cognitive Mental Load

Shinichiro Sega
Denso IT Laboratory, Inc., Japan

Hironori Hiraishi
Akita National College of Technology, Japan

Hirotoshi Iwasaki
Denso IT Laboratory, Inc., Japan

Fumio Mizoguchi
Tokyo University of Science, Japan

ABSTRACT

This paper explores applying qualitative reasoning to a driver's mental state in real driving situations so as to develop a working load for intelligent transportation systems. The authors identify the cognitive state that determines whether a driver will be ready to operate a device in car navigation. In order to identify the driver's cognitive state, the authors will measure eye movements during car-driving situations. Data can be acquired for the various actions of a car driver, in particular braking, acceleration, and steering angles from the experiment car. The authors constructed a driver cognitive mental load using the framework of qualitative reasoning. The response of the model was checked by qualitative simulation. The authors also verified the model using real data collected by driving an actual car. The results indicated that the model could represent the change in the cognitive mental load based on measurable data. This means that the framework of this paper will be useful for designing user interfaces for next-generation systems that actively employ user situations.

1. INTRODUCTION

This paper proposes a new design methodology for a man-machine system by applying qualitative reasoning to the mental load in an interactive environment. We identify the cognitive state that determines whether the driver will be ready to operate a device in car navigation. From this cognitive-state identification, we develop a minimum mental load methodology to achieve comfortable machine operation. In addition, we

DOI: 10.4018/978-1-4666-2651-5.ch011

empirically measure and verify the heavy loads experienced by a series of car drivers.

Although the research into *qualitative reasoning* has been vigorously developed, including various naïve physical understandings (De Kleer & Brown, 1984), the modeling of electronic circuits (Dague, Raiman, & Devès, 1987), the diagnosis of an airplane engine (Abbot, 1988) medical diagnosis (Ohwada & Mizoguchi, 1988), application of environmental learning (Forbus & Whalley, 1994), modeling of car parts (Šuc, Vladusic, & Bratko, 2004), and dynamics systems, no previous qualitative-reasoning studies considered the cognitive state and mental load. Of course, in order to identify the cognitive state, it is necessary to measure data relating to this state. In this paper, we will measure the driver eye movements while driving.

We would like to observe that, although there are many studies about the relationship between eye movement and cognitive processes, no research has measured eye data in a real man-machine environment in car navigation. We define "eye movement data measurement" as measuring the eye movement of automobile drivers on a public road. We can acquire data for the various actions of a car driver, in particular braking, acceleration, and steering angles, from our experiment car. Since we can naturally recognize the relationship between the driver's cognition status and the associated mental load and eye movements from our acquired data, it is the most realistic approach that data measurement using this method can apply to qualitative reasoning.

As background for these studies, we should point out several things. First, next-generation systems not only raise the issue of upgrading the functions but must also respond to just-in-time function choices and service provision. Second, next-generation systems will recognize the user's status, such as the heavy load of aging drivers, and then will make it possible for users to operate the machines. In addition, a machine response that modifies the user's status is also necessary when the system judges the user's mental status. These background studies are thus based on the fact that providing information to the driver when he has a low cognitive load is preferable to providing excess information to a driver when he is overly stressed.

To achieve these next-generation services, we use bio-information such as heart rate and blood pressure, and then infer the status of the user. Although there are some mathematical analyses in the fields of biomedical engineering and brain science, including engineering control models that are applied to bio-information, they still remain at the model analysis stage. Still, there are very important insights in these developed models (Findlay & Gilchrist, 2003). An objective of these studies is to understand human reactions, so we introduce these important insights as the basis of our model development. In particular, our modeling in this paper is based on the "*Data Limited and Resource Limited*" model from Norman and Bobrow (1975) (hereafter referred to as the N&B model) since the N&B model is able to give us a very effective observation of human and resource allocations.

Although there are both individual differences in the cognition process and fuzziness in unconscious reflection, there are common characteristics of cognition in the nature of eye movement, specifically in the generation of saccade and the relationship between the cognition of close observation and heavy loads. The eye movement data differs from other physiological data with regard to the possibility of observing the cognition status.

The remainder of this paper is organized as follows. In the next section, we discuss how to capture the driver's heavy cognition loads and then how to analyze them from the observable eye movements and the driver's actions. The third section explains the driver cognitive mental load model from the viewpoint of qualitative reasoning. We establish a qualitative model that focuses on the relationships among variables, such as the proportional variables and their differentials. The fourth section verifies our qualitative model using qualitative simulation and checks how well our model can explain real data. In particular, we employ qualitative reasoning in Cognitive Qualitative Simulation (COGSIM), a modified QSIM (Kuipers, 1994) for our analyses. The final section contains our conclusions and discusses the effectiveness of our overall approach.

2. DRIVING MODEL AND FEATURES OF EYE MOVEMENT

This section describes the target data we can actually measure and explains the model and theory developed in our research. It then discusses how the driver's cognitive mental load can be determined.

2.1. Eye Movement and Driving Data

We used the eye movement measuring device in Figure 1. The device[1] can measure horizontal and vertical viewing angles in degrees. We can obtain 60 data points per second.

The Controller Area Network[2] (CAN) is an in-vehicle LAN used to gather the driving data. We can obtain the accelerator depression (0% to 100%), braking signal (0 or 1), steering signal (-450 to 450 degrees), a signal representing the gear (0 to 4), the front separation (in meters), and so on. To measure these, we modified a Toyota Crown, and we can now obtain 10 data points per second.

Figure 1. Eye movement and driving data in our COGSIM

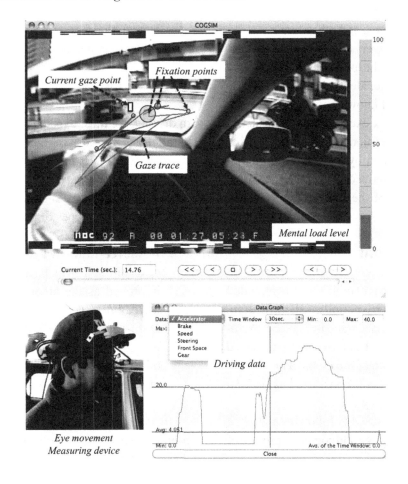

These data can be measured while driving. Figure 1 presents the data displayed in our COGSIM. The current gaze point, the trace of the gaze, and the fixation points[3] are displayed within an image of the driver's view. The driving data is displayed as a time series graph. In addition, COGSIM gives us the mental load based on a qualitative cognitive mental load model to be described.

2.2. Driving Model

Perception-cognition-action is the general model of decision-making. It is also related to robot design and agent negotiation (Mizoguchi, Nishiyama, Ohwada, & Hiraishi, 1999) and became the concept underlying our driving model.

- **Perception:** Drivers perceive changes in speed, the front separation, the road situation, and so on. They also observe road signs, pedestrians, and other cars.
- **Cognition:** Drivers determine the next action based on the perceived changes and objects. This includes predictions based on experience and knowledge.
- **Action:** Drivers execute the action determined by cognition. Reflex actions that are not generated by decision and prediction are also defined. This corresponds to the operation of the risk hedge in sudden braking.

2.3. Eye Movement

Eye movement consists of rapid movement, called saccade, and stationary periods, called fixation, as we can see in the gaze trace in Figure 1. Actually, saccade is defined as movement at a speed of 100 degrees/second or more, and a movement of three degrees or less is considered as fixation (Findlay & Gilchrist, 2003).

Since saccade is caused by following a target, it is related to the perception and cognition process of observers. The Findlay and Walker model (Findlay & Gilchrist, 2003) explains the mechanism of saccade generation. Saccade is related to perception and is generated by spatial selection and searching of the eye. A fixed eyeball enables us to recognize a target. The cognitive process thus generates the fixation. The perception of a specific temporal change such as a warning signal or a sign that the target will appear is also indicated.

Thus, we can regard the features of eye movement in driving as follows.

- **Saccade:** Saccade is caused by a change in the road situation, or the appearance of pedestrians or cars. It is considered as a factor in perception in the driving model.
- **Fixation:** Fixation is regarded as a factor of cognition in which the drivers determine the next action by recognizing changes in the environment and objects. It is also related to the perception of temporal changes such as signal changes and road signs.

2.4. N&B Model

In driving, we must execute several processes in parallel, such as driving and environment recognition. The N&B model (Norman & Bobrow, 1975) indicates the performance level when some processes are executed simultaneously. It defines the following two types of processes.

- **Resource-Limited Process:** This is a process through which the performance is improved as the amount of a resource is increased.
- **Data-Limited Process:** This is a process in which the performance is independent of the amount of resource. The performance depends only on the given data.

In particular, resource-limited processes compete when they require the same resource.

In this case, a resource-limited process changes to a data-limited process. Most processes are resource-limited until a certain point beyond which the performance is not improved even if more resources are consumed.

Here, we can regard the cognitive mental load as the resource. For example, the operation of the accelerator makes a vehicle speed up, and the mental load for environment recognition increases while accelerating. We can therefore consider that the processes of driving and environment recognition are competitive with the same resource allocated to them (i.e., the resource is allocated to accelerator operation and environment recognition at the same time). Therefore, we can assume that the resource adjusts the speed so the vehicle does not go too fast.

Thus, we can identify the amount of resource as the driver cognitive mental load, with the resource allocated to several processes during driving. We can also understand that the total amount of the resource is the permissible amount of the driver's mental load, representing the different levels of an individual's experience and skill.

3. QUALITATIVE MODEL OF THE DRIVER COGNITIVE MENTAL LOAD

Figure 2 illustrates the driver cognitive mental load model we constructed based on the discussion in the previous section. It consists of perception, cognition, action, and eye movement. The details are discussed in the following paragraphs.

3.1. Cognition Model

The cognition model has a resource that represents the cognitive mental load. It is the part of the model in which the next action is decided based on the amount of available resource.

The *resource* is defined as the total amount of resource and is basically a fixed amount.

The *resource* is the sum of *rest* (the remainder) and *used* (the amount used). The *used* amount is the sum of *used_a*, which is related to an internal change in perception, and *used_p*, which is related to environmental change. These are described in detail in the next section.

3.2. Perception Model

The perception model consists of internal change and environmental change, which includes external change and temporal change.

Internal change is related to the action model. Change is caused by the execution of an action. This is influenced by the driver's intentional operation and is a predictable change for us. For example, when we operate the accelerator, we can estimate the change of speed then we grip the steering wheel and re-settle ourselves.

In contrast, environmental change is passive and is not related to intention. The change of a signal, the movement of pedestrians and other cars, and the appearance of obstacles are environmental changes.

Thus, the features of each change are different, so we separate each factor of the cognitive mental load and associate them with the above *used_a* and *used_p*. Environmental change is divided into external change and temporal change in order to relate to the eye-movement model.

3.3. Eye-Movement Model

The eye-movement model has saccade and fixation according to the saccade generation model (Findlay & Gilchrist, 2003). Saccade is related to the internal and external changes in the perception model. Fixation is related to the temporal change in perception and to the decision represented as a factor of recognition and decision-making in the cognition model.

Figure 2. Driver cognitive mental load model

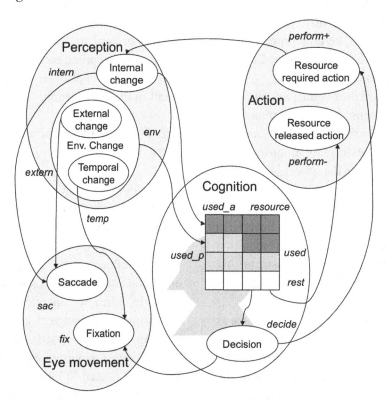

3.4. Action Model

The following two actions are defined in the action model.

- **Resource-Required Action:** This is an action that consumes a resource, corresponding to a resource-limited process. In driving, this corresponds to operations performed to drive the vehicle forward, including operating the accelerator and the steering wheel as needed to follow the road.
- **Resource-Free Action:** This is a data-limited process and does not require a resource. If anything, this is an action that releases a used resource. It additionally includes reflex actions. In driving, this corresponds to operations performed to slow the vehicle. Examples of these actions include braking and the steering-wheel control needed to avoid obstacles.

The action model is the mechanism used to coordinate the resource consumption through the repeated execution of these actions. For example, the accelerator makes the vehicle speed up and the used resource increases. If too much of the resource is used, a resource-free action like braking is invoked. If an obstacle appears in the road, the used resource increases rapidly; sudden braking and abrupt steering are invoked as reflex actions.

A resource-required action is related to the decision in the cognition model since it is caused by decision-making. The resource-free action is also related to *rest* because it increases the remaining resource.

3.5. Constraint Relations and Parameters

Figure 3 depicts the constraint relations between the parameters of each factor in Figure 2. Table 1 lists the range and landmark value of each parameter, with reference to the description found in Kuipers (1994).

The cognition model has relations such as *resource = used + rest* and *used = used_a + used_p*. A maximum amount *full* is assigned to each parameter. Here, *used* and *used_a* have a threshold *th*. For *used*, *th* indicates the threshold of the reflex action. For *used_a*, *th* is the threshold where the resource-limited process changes to a data-limited process in the N&B model. Therefore, the performance is not improved even if a resource amount greater than *th* is spent. The *decide* parameter represents the decisiveness. If the used resource increases (the mental load increases), then the decisiveness decreases. Parameters *decision* and *used* are related to monotonically decreasing *M-*.

The action model has the *perform+* parameter, which is the performance of a resource-required action, and the *perform-* parameter, which is the performance of a resource-free action. A maximum performance *max* is assigned to each parameter. A resource-required action consumes *decide* in the cognition model. The *perform+* and *decide* parameters are related to *M-*. A resource-free action increases the remainder. Parameters *perform-* and *rest* are associated with monotonically increasing *M+*. The *th* of *perform-* is the threshold that indicates whether or not the resource-free action is a reflex action. Here, when the performance is between 0 and *th*, the action is a reflex action; if the performance exceeds *th*, the action is not a reflex action.[4]

Figure 3. Constraint relations of our qualitative model

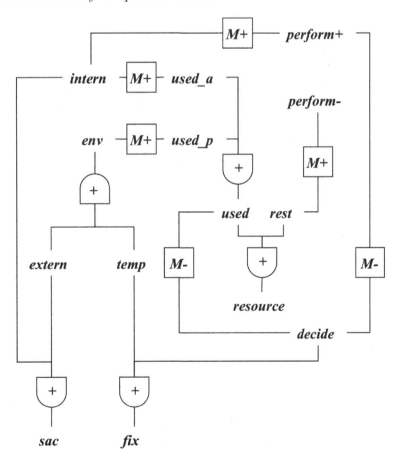

Table 1. Range of parameters

Model	Parameter	Range
Cognition	*resource*	*0 full*
	used	*0 th full*
	used_a	*0 th full*
	used_p	*0 full*
	decide	*0 max*
Action	*perform+*	*0 max*
	perform-	*0 th max*
Perception	*intern*	*0 max*
	env	*0 inf*
	extern	*0 inf*
	temp	*0 inf*
Eye movement	*sac*	*0 inf*
	fix	*0 inf*

The perception model has the parameter *intern*, which represents the amount of internal change. Since internal change is caused by the execution of a resource-required action, *intern* and *perform+* are associated with $M+$. Parameters *env*, which indicates the amount of environmental change; *extern*, which indicates the amount of external change; and *temp*, which indicates the amount of temporal change, are also defined. These parameters are related by *env = extern + temp*. Parameters *intern* and *used_a* are associated with $M+$, and parameters *env* and *used_p* are associated with $M+$.

Eye movement includes *sac* representing saccade and *fix* representing fixation. These have the following relations: *sac = extern + intern* and *fix = temp + decide*.

4. VERIFICATION OF OUR QUALITATIVE MODEL

In order to verify our qualitative model of the driver cognitive mental load, we checked the behavior of our model using qualitative simulation

and determined how well our model can explain real data.

We used COGSIM with QSIM (Kuipers, 1994) embedded. COGSIM has functions involving verification from the model and the interpretation of real data. Qualitative simulation by QSIM, visualization of driving and eye movement data as in Figure 1, and translation to qualitative data are thus possible.

4.1. Qualitative Simulation

To check the resource consumption, which represents the cognitive mental load, we qualitatively simulated cases with and without environmental change. The environmental change includes external change and temporal change.

Figure 4 presents the simulation result for the case with no environmental change. Three states were generated. The graphs plot the change of *used_a*, which indicates the resource consumption associated with the execution of the resource-required action. State 1 (upper left) represents the most suitable consumption of the resource for maximum performance. The used resource reaches *th* at *T1*, then consumption becomes constant. State 2 (upper right) represents the situation in which few resources are consumed. The amount becomes constant at *UA1*, before *th* is reached. In State 3 (lower left), the resource is consumed even if *th* is reached. This therefore represents a situation in which too much resource is consumed. This happens when *decide* also decreases, although *used_a* reached *th* at *T1* (lower right). However, the performance of the resource-required action never exceeds *max*. This indicates a situation in which resources are wasted. In these three states, the total resource *used* did not increase over *th*, indicating that the reflex action was not invoked because there was no environmental change and no unexpected factor.

Figure 5 plots the simulation result for the case with environmental change. Two states (States 1 and 2) where total resource *used* did not exceed

Figure 4. Simulation result without environmental changes

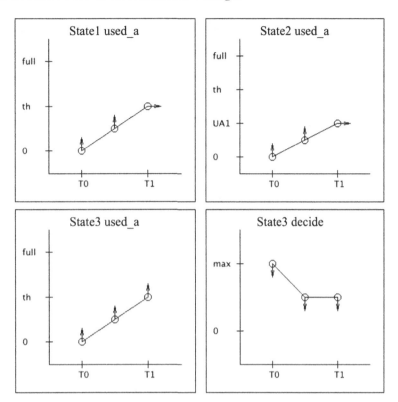

th and three states (States 3, 4 and 5) where *used* exceeded *th* are generated. The two states that did not exceed *th* were situations in which the consumption became constant after the resource reached *th* and before the resource reached *th*. Because the internal changes are small even though there are some environmental changes, the sum of *used_p* and *used_a* does not exceed *th*, so these two states do not invoke a reflex action. The three states that exceeded *th* correspond to the three states of *used_a* without any environmental change. We found that *perform-* exceeded *th* in all three states and that a reflex action was invoked (Figure 5, lower right).

Thus, qualitative simulation showed us the behavior of the N&B model and the change in resource consumption with environmental change, so that we could determine whether a reflex action was invoked. Thus, we verified that our model functions accurately without contradiction.

4.2. Interpretation of Real Data

We measured driving and eye-movement data of two subjects, an inexperienced driver (Subject A) and a skilled driver (Subject B). We experimented for about 60 minutes on three types of roads: a road with little traffic (Road 1, 10min), an urban road with much traffic (Road 2, 30min), and a road with moderate traffic (Road 3, 20min).

Our COGSIM translates the real data into qualitative data. The time-series data are divided at a constant interval, and the data for each interval is averaged. Each type of data, such as rate of the accelerator, is divided into several stages. Each stage change is thus judged as increasing or decreasing. In our experiment, we set the interval at five seconds and established three stages for each data set.[5]

Table 2 describes the relationship between the parameters and the acquired data. The steering

Figure 5. Simulation result with environmental changes

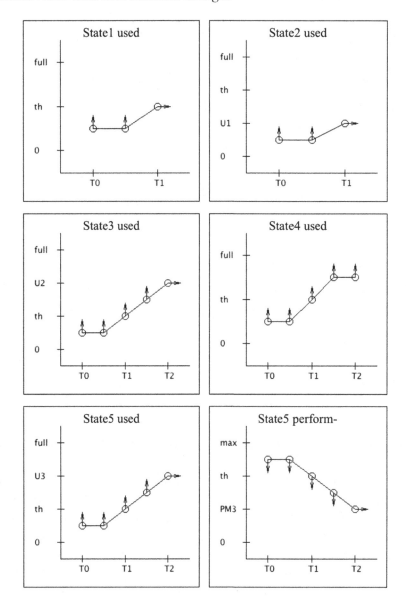

signal depends on the situation, so it is basically interpreted as a resource-required action, but if it contradicts the accelerator, it is interpreted as a resource-free action.

Parameters other than those in Table 2 are not interpreted from real data but can be determined by using our model as in the following equations.

$$\text{extern} = \text{sac} - \text{intern} \tag{1}$$

$$\text{decide} = -(\text{perform}+) \tag{2}$$

$$\text{temp} = \text{fix} - \text{decide} = \text{fix} + \text{perform}+ \tag{3}$$

$$\begin{aligned}\text{env} &= \text{extern} + \text{temp} = \text{sac} - \text{intern} \\ &+ \text{fix} + \text{perform}+ = \text{sac} + \text{fix}\end{aligned} \tag{4}$$

$$\text{rest} = \text{perform}- \tag{5}$$

$$\text{used} = -\text{rest} = -(\text{perform}-) \tag{6}$$

Table 2. Relationship between the parameters and the acquired data

Parameter	Acquired data
sac	Frequency of saccade (times/sec)
fix	Continuous time of fixation (sec)
perform+	Press rate of the accelerator Steering signal
perform-	Braking signal Steering signal
intern	Speed (km/h)

$$used\_a = intern = perform+ \tag{7}$$

$$used\_p = used - used\_a = -(perform- + perform+) \tag{8}$$

Since *sac* is the sum of *intern* and *extern*, there is also the relation of Equation 1. The change in *extern* can thus be derived from parameters *sac* and *intern* in Table 2, which are interpreted from real data. Parameter *decide* changes in the opposite direction from parameter *perform+* (see Equation 2), and *fix* is the sum of *temp* and *decide*. There is thus the relation of Equation 3. Parameter *env* is the sum of *extern* and *temp*. Since there is the relation of *intern* = *perform+*, parameter *env* is formulated as Equation 4. We can thus determine the environmental change *env* from measurable changes in eye movement such as saccade and fixation.

We can also determine parameter *used_p* related to the environmental change from the measurable change of the driving data. Since *perform-* and *rest* change in the same direction in our model, *perform-* is opposite to *used* (see Equations 5 and 6). Parameter *used_a* exhibits the same change as *intern*, and also *intern* and *perform+* change in the same direction (see Equation 7). Therefore, parameter *used_p* can thus be interpreted from measurable parameters such as *perform-* and *perform+* (see Equation 8).

Here, *env* and *used_p* change in the same direction in our model. Comparing *env* and *used_p* reveals the effectiveness of our model. The change in *env* is calculated from the eye movement, and the change in *used_p* is calculated from the driving data. If the changes correspond, our model can represent the real data without contradiction.

Each parameter represents only the direction of change. The sum of two parameters of the same direction becomes the same direction. When one parameter is constant, the sum becomes the same direction as the other parameter. However, the direction cannot be calculated if the two parameters have different direction. Nonetheless, we can determine the direction from the direction of a neighboring parameter. We nevertheless treat the case we cannot determine as unknown.

Table 3 presents the result of comparing the change of *env* and *used_p*, and indicates the percent of real data that our model can interpret. "Correspond" in Table 3 is the rate of correspondence between the change of *env* and *used_p*. "Constant" is the percent of the case in which one side is constant. "Opposite" is the percent of the opposite direction. Unknown is the percent of unknown mentioned above. First, the rate of completely opposite is only 11%, and the rate of perfect correspondence is 54%. Because each stage change is judged as increasing or decreasing, real data actually changes even if qualitatively judged as constant. We can understand such slow change from the direction of the other parameter when one parameter is constant. If we include the case of constant parameters, our model can interpret more than 80% of the data.

This means that our model can represent the cognitive mental load from unconscious changes in driving actions as well as biological reactions such as eye movement. We did not find any differences due to the subject or road situations because the qualitative analysis does not consider the absolute value of each factor. Eliminating the influences of the noise and the individual variations etc. enables interpreting the essential cognitive mental load.

Table 3. Interpretation rate of real data (%)

		Correspond	Constant	Opposite	Unknown
Road1	SubA	53	28	14	5
	SubB	51	30	11	8
Road2	SubA	53	40	5	2
	SubB	53	32	10	5
Road3	SubA	56	23	12	9
	SubB	55	28	13	4
Avg.		54	30	11	5

The external change and temporal change related to the environmental change can also be extracted objectively from the movie data of the driver's view. For example, we can observe the changes of signals and the presence of oncoming cars and pedestrians. However, the perception of environmental change differs with driving experience and the situation. A change that imposes a load on one driver may not present a load for other drivers. This is a characteristic of situated cognition (Clancey, 1997) where human cognition changes according to the situation. We have extracted environmental change factors from the eye movement. As a result, our model could cope with situated cognition, and a high rate of interpretation was achieved.

The high interpretation rate between the change in *env* from eye movement and the cognitive load *used_p* from the driving data means that we can determine the driver's cognitive mental load from just the driving data and our qualitative model. Eye movement is a factor in objectively determining the perception and cognition of drivers in our research, and it enables us to construct a qualitative model with high accuracy by associating it with driving data gathered in real time. In fact, a real application does not require the measurement of eye movement, and we can use the mental load based on just the driving data from the CAN and our model, like COGSIM in Figure 1. The driving data is divided into several stages. The mental load level changes when the data changes stages.

5. CONCLUSION

This paper has described how to analyze and use the cognitive mental load derived from measurable biological data and user actions such as driving tasks and eye movements. We constructed a driver cognitive mental load using the framework of qualitative reasoning. We applied past research results such as saccade generation (Findlay & Gilchrist, 2003) and resource-allocation (Norman & Bobrow, 1975). We checked the response of our model by qualitative simulation and verified the model using real data collected by driving an actual car. The results indicated that our model could represent the change in the cognitive mental load based on measurable data. This means that the framework of qualitative reasoning will be effective for designing user interfaces for next-generation systems that actively employ user situations.

Since the cognitive mental load depends on subjective evaluations, it is difficult to obtain evaluations while executing tasks. It is also difficult to embed the response to the mental load in systems. However, the qualitative model enables a system to obtain the user's cognitive mental load from measurable biological data and user actions. It reacts according to the user situation.

We will be able to use a variety of biological information following the future development of equipment and sensors. Also, we can consider that the features of the biological data will be clarified further as progress continues in research into biomedical engineering and brain science. The framework of this paper thus enables us to use biological information positively. For further study, we will consider the attention processes related the auditory system in addition to the visual system in the framework of parallel distributed cognitive processing.

REFERENCES

Abbott, K. W. (1988). Robust operative diagnosis as problem solving in a hypothesis space. In *Proceedings of the AAAI Conference on Artificial Intelligence* (pp. 369-374).

Clancey, W. J. (1997). *Situated cognition: On human knowledge and computer representations*. Cambridge, UK: Cambridge University Press.

Dague, P., Raiman, O., & Devès, P. (1987). Troubleshooting: When modeling is the trouble. In *Proceedings of the AAAI Conference on Artificial Intelligence* (pp. 590-595).

De Kleer, J., & Brown, J. S. (1984). A qualitative physics based on confluences. *Artificial Intelligence*, *24*(1-3), 7–83. doi:10.1016/0004-3702(84)90037-7

Findlay, J. M., & Gilchrist, I. D. (2003). *Active vision*. Oxford, UK: Oxford University Press. doi:10.1093/acprof:oso/9780198524793.001.0001

Forbus, K. D., & Whalley, P. B. (1994). Using qualitative physics to build articulate software for thermodynamics education. In *Proceedings of the AAAI Conference on Artificial Intelligence* (pp. 1175-1182).

Kuipers, B. (1994). *Qualitative reasoning*. Cambridge, MA: MIT Press.

Mizoguchi, F., Nishiyama, H., Ohwada, H., & Hiraishi, H. (1999). Smart office robot collaboration based on multi-agent programming. *Artificial Intelligence*, *114*(1-2), 57–94. doi:10.1016/S0004-3702(99)00068-5

Norman, D. A., & Bobrow, D. G. (1975). On data-limited and resource-limited processes. *Cognitive Psychology*, *7*, 44–64. doi:10.1016/0010-0285(75)90004-3

Ohwada, H., & Mizoguchi, F. (1988). An examination for applicability of FGHC: The experience of designing qualitative reasoning system. In *Proceedings of the International Conference on Fifth Generation Computer Systems* (pp. 1193-1200).

Šuc, D., Vladusic, D., & Bratko, I. (2004). Qualitatively faithful quantitative prediction. *Artificial Intelligence*, *158*(2), 189–214. doi:10.1016/j.artint.2004.05.002

ENDNOTES

[1]   EMR-8 is produced by NAC Image Tech., Inc. (http://www.eyemark.jp)

[2]   This is a standard used for the data transfer between in-vehicle equipment. The International Organization for Standardization is standardizing it as ISO 11898 and ISO 11519.

[3]   The size of the circle indicates the length of stopping time.

[4]   The performance of a resource-free action increases from 0 to max. We can consider the beginning of the execution as the reflex action.

[5]   This yielded the least contradiction in our experiment.

This work was previously published in the International Journal of Software Science and Computational Intelligence, Volume 3, Issue 4, edited by Yingxu Wang, pp. 18-32, copyright 2011 by IGI Publishing (an imprint of IGI Global).

Chapter 12
Intelligent Fault Recognition and Diagnosis for Rotating Machines using Neural Networks

Cyprian F. Ngolah
Sentinel Trending & Diagnostics Ltd., Canada

Ed Morden
Sentinel Trending & Diagnostics Ltd., Canada

Yingxu Wang
University of Calgary, Canada

ABSTRACT

Monitoring industrial machine health in real-time is not only in high demand, it is also complicated and difficult. Possible reasons for this include: (a) access to the machines on site is sometimes impracticable, and (b) the environment in which they operate is usually not human-friendly due to pollution, noise, hazardous wastes, etc. Despite theoretically sound findings on developing intelligent solutions for machine condition-based monitoring, few commercial tools exist in the market that can be readily used. This paper examines the development of an intelligent fault recognition and monitoring system (Melvin I), which detects and diagnoses rotating machine conditions according to changes in fault frequency indicators. The signals and data are remotely collected from designated sections of machines via data acquisition cards. They are processed by a signal processor to extract characteristic vibration signals of ten key performance indicators (KPIs). A 3-layer neural network is designed to recognize and classify faults based on a pre-determined set of KPIs. The system implemented in the laboratory and applied in the field can also incorporate new experiences into the knowledge base without overwriting previous training. Results show that Melvin I is a smart tool for both system vibration analysts and industrial machine operators.

DOI: 10.4018/978-1-4666-2651-5.ch012

1. INTRODUCTION

Various studies have been done on the application of neural networks to provide intelligent solutions for machine condition monitoring and fault diagnosis (Samhouri et al., 2009; Peng, 2004; Srinivasan, 2003; McCormick & Nandi, 1996; Umesh & Srinivasan, 2005; Gerlad et al., 2000; Aravindh et al., 2010; Yangwen, 2009; Tetsuro & Wang, 2008; Balakrishnan & Honavar, 1995; Saxena & Saad, 2004; Shiroishi et al., 1997). For example, Srinivasan (2003) described a neural network to identify the approximate location of damage due to cracks through the analysis of changes in the neural frequencies. McCormick and Nandi (1996) described neural network methods for automatically classifying machine conditions from the vibration time series. Umesh and Srinivasan (2005) carried out studies on experimental data simulation of faults such as parallel misalignment, angular misalignment, unbalance, crack, light and heavy rubs, looseness and bearing clearance. Saxena and Saad (2004) carried out research on fault diagnosis in rotating mechanical systems using Self-Organizing Maps.

Despite these theoretically sound findings on developing intelligent solutions based on neural networks for machine condition based monitoring, there are virtually no commercial tools in the market that can be readily used. This paper reports the design and implementation of a tool that uses neural network technology for deriving intelligent fault recognition based on observation of changes in various fault frequency indicators.

An Artificial Neural Network (ANN) is an intelligent information processing paradigm that imitates the biological nervous systems. In the brain, electrochemical signals pass between neurons through the synapses. In neural network analysis, the signal between neurons is simulated by interlinked circuits and software, which apply weights to the input nodes and use an activation function to scale the neuron's output to an acceptable range. Thus, the basic element in an ANN is the artificial neuron node, which receives and combines signals from many other neurons through input paths in the same way as the biological neuron receives and processes signals via axons. The output of a neural network is therefore a linear combination of inputs, determined by weights that simulate synapses in the biological neural system. The weights are usually selected such that when the element is presented with input data, the output is as close to the desired output as possible. A typical neuron in an ANN has two modes of operation - the training mode and the using mode. In the training mode, the neuron can be trained to fire (or not) for particular input patterns, while in the using mode, when a taught input pattern is detected at the input, its associated output becomes the current output of the ANN. If the input pattern is not yet present in the trained set of the input patterns, a predetermined firing rule is used to determine whether to fire or not. Neural networks make use of two types of values – weights and thresholds. Weights define the interaction between the neurons, while thresholds define what it takes to get a neuron to fire.

In condition based monitoring systems, data is acquired from various types of machines via sensors. By analyzing the collected vibration data, possible faults such as unbalance, bent shaft, shaft crack, bearing clearance, rotor rub, misalignment, and looseness can be identified. Because a lot of industrial machines operate in remote areas, they are often inaccessible at certain periods of the year. A system that remotely collects vibration data in real-time, processes it, detects possible faults and makes recommendations on predictive maintenance will certainly reduce downtime and associated consequences.

This paper is an extended version of Ngolah et al. (2011) and presents the development of a mechanism for fault recognition and classification based on fault frequency indicators using the neural network technology. In this paper, Section 2 gives an overview of the set of tools that have been developed to provide intelligence on online machine condition based monitoring. Section 3 describes the design and implementation of a neural network for recognizing machine faults. Section 4 presents experimental results of the system and Section 5 draws a set of conclusions and presents future directions.

2. THE OVERALL STRUCTURE OF THE MELVIN I SYSTEM

The intelligent fault recognizer known as Melvin I is a component of a large system (Melvin) developed to offer an open and expandable online machine condition monitoring system for rotating machinery. The overall system is divided into four subsystems, which perform data acquisition, signal conditioning and processing, fault recognition and prediction, and fault reporting. Figure 1 presents the top level view of the four subsystems of Melvin. The next two sub-sections present a detailed discussion on the data acquisition and signal conditioning/processing mechanisms used in this work. A detailed discussion on the design and implementation of the fault recognition component is presented is Section 3.

2.1. Data Acquisition for Melvin

The work reported in this paper has been carried out on reciprocating compressors used for processing natural gas. A reciprocating compressor uses pistons to compress gas. On each compressor, there is a central crankshaft that can drive up to six pistons inside cylinders. The crankshaft is generally driven by an external motor. As the pistons draw backwards, gas is injected from an intake valve in the compressor. This gas is in turn injected into the cylinders of the pistons, and is then compressed by the reciprocating action of the pistons. The compressed gas is discharged either to be used immediately by a pneumatic machine, or stored in compressed air tanks. To monitor the health of these machines, data must be collected from suitable locations on it for processing. Figure 2 shows a typical reciprocating compressor, where each of the possible data collection points (C4A, C4V, C2V, 1VC, etc.) is indicated. Common bearing locations include drive end horizontal, drive end vertical, drive end axial, outboard horizontal, outboard vertical, and outboard axial. Depending on the types of machines and faults being monitored, data may be collected from all or only a subset of these points.

Figure 1. System overview of Melvin

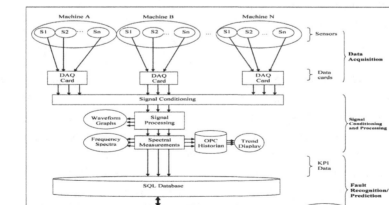

Figure 2. Data collection points on a reciprocating compressor

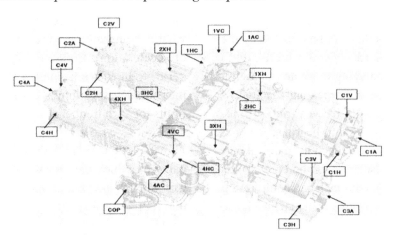

Vibration signals are collected using piezo-electric transducers attached to locations on a rotating machine based on the VDI 2056 standard guidelines (Kumaraswamy et al., 2002). In reciprocating machinery, many mechanical characteristics change with the machine's speed. As the rotational speed changes, the frequency bandwidth of each individual harmonic gets wider and some frequency components can overlap. Thus, a simple Fast Fourier Transform power spectrum analysis may not be adequate to identify characteristic vibration components. To take care of this situation, a tachometer is mounted close to the rotating machine and used to measure the number of pulses per revolution. The measured value is then used to calculate the speed of the machine in real-time as the machine rotates.

2.2. Signal Processing and Conditioning for Melvin

Raw time waveform data is collected in the time domain through the piezo-electric accelerometers. This has to be converted into the frequency domain so as to isolate the various frequencies of interest. To be able to acquire data, suitable data acquisition parameters such as sampling rate (f_s) and the number of samples (N) in a given window must be determined. The faster the sampling rate, the more accurate the data acquired. However, a higher sampling rate entails intensive processing time of the processor. The sampling rate used in this work is 12,800 samples per second, but different sampling rates can be used depending on the problems being monitored.

Ten key performance frequency indicators (KPIs) were calculated based on the nature and type of faults being monitored by our system. One of the most common analysis methods to analyze noise and vibration signals is the fast Fourier Transform (FFT) analysis (Loan, 1992). This method identifies and quantifies the frequency components of noise and vibration signals in a time domain signal. However, in reciprocating machinery, many mechanical characteristics change with speed. As such, machinery noise and vibration tests also require a run-up or coast-down test to be conducted as well. When the rotational speed changes, the frequency bandwidth of each individual harmonic also gets wider, thus causing some frequency components to overlap. This can cause the resulting FFT power spectrum to become blurred. In such a situation, the FFT power spectrum approach will no longer help in identifying characteristic vibration components.

In this paper, the order analysis technique has been used to calculate some characteristics frequency indicators that can be affected by the machine's speed. Order analysis (Gade et al, 1995) is a technique for analyzing noise and vibration signals in rotating or reciprocating machinery. Such machinery typically has a variety of mechanical parts such as a shaft, bearing, gearbox, fan blade, belt, etc., where each mechanical part generates unique noise and vibration patterns as the machine operates, with each part contributing a unique component to the overall machine noise and vibration.

In this work, depending on the type of faults, the key performance frequencies are calculated either in frequencies or orders. The first order is usually the machine's rotational speed and order n is defined as n times the rotational speed of the machine. Table 1 shows the different KPIs used in this experiment and their associated types. Certain frequency components (shown in column 1 of Table 1) such as the overall vibration (OVR), 120 Hz, and the high frequency component (1-5KHz) are measured in frequency while others such as SubHarm, 1X, 2X, 3-5X, 5-10X, 10-20X, and 20-50X are in orders. Table 1 shows the different parameters used in deriving information about each key performance indicator. Column 1 is the name of the KPI, Column 2 is a description of what is being measured (displacement, velocity or acceleration), Column 3 shows the type (order or frequency), Column 4 shows the units of measurements, Columns 5 and 6 show the band limits for each frequency component, Columns 7 and 8 show respectively the alert and alarm limits for each KPI, Column 9 shows the database field name on which data for that KPI is stored, and Column 10 shows possible faults associated to that KPI when it is either in alert or alarm.

The collected data is stored in a control server called the Object Linking and Embedded (OLE) for Process Control (OPC) to display real-time trends, and also on an SQL server for fault diagnosis and prediction by Melvin. OPC (http://www.opcfoundation.org/) is a software interface standard that permits Windows programs to communicate with industrial hardware devices. This paper only reports the development of the fault recognition component (Melvin I), which recognizes and classifies faults based on fault frequency indicators.

Table 1. KPI Setup for Melvin I

Definition						Alarms Set-points		General	
KPI	Description	Types	Units	Start	End	Alert	Alarm	Example Tag_Name	Possible Faults
OVR	Acceleration	Hz	G's RMS	0.0	5000	1.0	2.0	FA_429U1_S0_K0	General Machine Failure
SubHarm	Displacement	Order		0.3	0.8	1.0	2.0	FA_429U1_S0_K1	Bent shaft, Bearing- typical Fundamental Train Frequency – "Cage Failure
1X	Displacement	Order		0.8	1.5	4.0	6.0	FA_429U1_S0_K2	Unbalance, looseness, rotor bar problem
2X	Velocity	Order	In/sec Pk	1.5	2.5	0.15	0.25	FA_429U1_S0_K3	Misalignment, bent shaft,
120 Hz	Acceleration	Hz		119	121	0.05	0.1	FA_429U1_S0_K4	Rotor/stator air gap issue, distorted case, deflected casing
3-5X	Velocity	Order	In/sec Pk	3.5	5.5	0.15	0.25	FA_429U1_S0_K5	Excessive load, bent shaft
5-10X	Velocity	Order	In/sec Pk	5.5	10.5	0.07	0.15	FA_429U1_S0_K6	Twisting deflections, Bent shaft
10-20X	Velocity	Order	In/sec Pk	10.5	20.5	0.10	0.18	FA_429U1_S0_K7	Twisting deflections
20-50X	Velocity	Order	In/sec Pk	20.5	50.5	0.07	0.15	FA_429U1_S0_K8	Twisting deflections
1-5KHz	Acceleration	Hz	G's RMS	1000	5000	0.1	0.18	FA_429U1_S0_K9	Bearing failure, lubrication

3. THE NEURAL NETWORK FOR FAULT RECOGNITION IN MELVIN I

On each reciprocating compressor (Figure 2), there may be many data collection points. Each data collection point requires a sensor. As described in Section 2, each sensor collects ten data points which are stored in a database and subsequently used to diagnose possible faults. Thus, if there were 1000 machines with data being collected on ten different points for each compressor, then there will be a total of 10x10x1000 (100,000) numerical values collected simultaneously. The number gets bigger if the number of machines to monitor increases. With this large number of numerical vales being collected, it becomes very difficult to track changes on individual values in real-time. There is therefore, a need for a solution that simultaneously tracks changes in patterns rather than individual numerical values.

The approach adopted in this paper is the use of the neural network technology to implement a pattern recognition algorithm which receives KPI data from all the sensors and processes it to give accurate diagnosis of possible faults. The next sections present the design of a neural network mechanism developed for fault diagnosis and prediction in Melvin.

3.1. Design of Melvin I

The kernel architecture of Melvin I is designed as a multilayer perceptron with feedforward neural network using the Backpropagation training algorithm (Rumelhat et al., 1995; Heaton, 2008). The neural network has three layers: the input, hidden and output layers. The input layer contains ten neurons that receive inputs corresponding to ten KPI values as described in Table 1. The hidden layer has five neurons, while the output layer has a single neuron. Figure 3 shows the layout of neurons for a single sensor. Input neurons receive KPI values from an SQL database. The activity of each hidden neuron is determined by

the activities of the input neurons and the weights on the connections between the input and hidden neurons. In Figure 3, W_{ijk} represents weight k for neuron j in layer i.

In this architectural design, the following factors were taken into consideration:

1. **Rapid and Stable Training:** The system is designed to be capable of incorporating new experiences with minimal training time, and without overwriting previous training experiences.
2. **Hypothesis Generation Capability:** The system is designed to be capable of suggesting additional fault possibilities in order to fully identify a fault. This is realized by having an interactive component of the system where experts/users can provide further input in situations when the system is unable to diagnose a certain fault. The knowledge obtained from such interaction is incorporated into the knowledge base for future reference.

3.2. Implementation of Melvin I

Melvin I performs three major tasks: data acquisition, feature extraction, and fault identification. Data acquisition involves the collection of data that indicates the health conditions of machines. The data acquisition mechanism has been described in Section 2. Feature extraction and the techniques for implementing Melvin I are described in the following subsections.

1. **Feature Extraction:** Feature extraction is the process of detecting features hidden in the acquired data using signal transformation technologies. According to empirical data, machine faults are associated with certain frequencies based on each machine's rotating speed. With frequency domain signals, it is necessary to extract the amplitudes corresponding to these frequencies. By observing

Figure 3. Network layers in Melvin for a single sensor

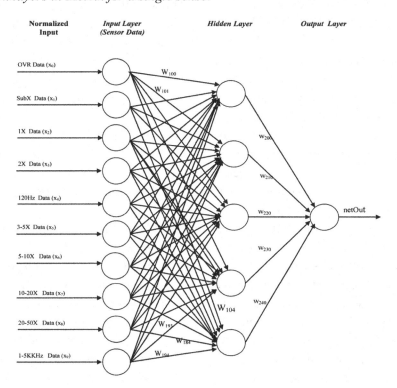

the changes in amplitudes, conclusions can be drawn on possible machine faults. The extraction of the different features of interest was discussed in Section 2. The next section describes how the extracted features can be used in the development of Melvin I.

2. **Training of Melvin I:** The training of a neural network requires a suitable training set and a training algorithm. The training algorithm used in the implementation of Melvin is based on the Backpropagation algorithm (Rumelhat et al., 1995; Heaton, 2008) and is fully described below. Three training sets are employed in the training of Melvin as described below.

   a. **Data Normalization:** In this implementation, we have used the alert values in Table 1 to normalize the input values into each neuron, which is set to 1 if the value is above the alert threshold and 0 otherwise. Thus, an input pattern of {1,0,0,0,0,0,0,0,0,0} indicates that the value of the first KPI (OVR) is above the alert threshold, a pattern such as {0,1,1,0,0,0,0,0,0,0} shows that the values for the SubHarm and 1X key performance indicators are above the alert thresholds, and a pattern such as {0,0,0,1,0,0,0,1,1,1] shows that the values of 2X,10-20X,20-50X and 1-5KHz are above the alert limits.

   b. **The Training Set:** The training data are represented by three arrays:

      i. **The Pattern_Input Set:** This is a 2-D array, initially holding input patterns with single fault indicators for each of the ten KPIs. Each row of this array holds a separate pattern corresponding to the ten input neurons, while each column holds respectively KPI values for OVR, SubHarm, 1X, 2X, 120Hz,

3-5X, 5-10X, 10-20X, 20-50X and 1-5KHz in that order. This set initially contains 11 patterns with the first pattern representing no fault, and the remaining ten patterns corresponding to single faults for the ten KPIs. However, more training patterns will be added dynamically to the training set as a new fault is identified during the network's operation. These patterns will be used to provide initial training for the neural network to recognize the indicated faults.

ii. **The Fault_Code Set:** This is a 2-D array that holds 11 different codes corresponding to the 11 input patterns in (1) above. This array grows dynamically. As new faults are recognized and further trainings performed, new fault codes can also be added into this set.

iii. **The Fault_Set:** This is a 1-D array that holds corresponding fault types as shown on the last column of Table 1 for the 11 fault codes as described in (2) above. This array also grows dynamically, which is used to report a given fault once its corresponding fault code is identified.

c. **The Training Algorithm:** As each pattern of training data from the *Pattern_Input Set* is presented to the neural network, an error is calculated between the actual output of the neural network and the expected output specified in the training *Fault_Code Set*. The Backpropagation algorithm can be modeled by a set of equations to accomplish its task as follows:

$$Y_i = A(\sum_{i=0}^{9} x_i w_i) \tag{1}$$

$$NetOut_j = A(\sum_{j=0}^{4} Y_i w_j) \tag{2}$$

Equation (1) is used to calculate each neuron's output (Y_i) in the second layer, where x_i is the input value into a neuron i and w_i the weight assigned to the connection into neuron i Equation (2) is used to calculate the entire neural network's output (NetOut) for a given pattern, where Y_i is the input value from neuron i in the second layer into neuron j in the third layer, w_j the weight assigned to the connection into neuron j, and A the sigmoid activation function used to scale the neural network's output.

The training of the ANN is accomplished in two phases: In the first phase, the inputs and the initial weights are propagated forward through the different layers using Equations (1) and (2) to calculate the network's output (*NetOut_i*) for each training pattern i. This is used to calculate the error (*err_i*) between the expected output (*ExpectedOutput_i*) and the actual output using Equation (3). The Initial weights for training Melvin I were randomly assigned using a random number generator function in C-sharp.

$$err_i = ExpectedOutput_i - netOut_i \tag{3}$$

In the second phase, the error (*err_i*) is propagated backwards through the network in order to adjust the initial weights for the next iteration using the delta rule (Rumelhat et al., 1995) in Equation (4), where μ is the learning rate, and Δw_{ij} the change in weights between neurons i and j. This change is added to the weight used in the previous iteration to get the new weight that will be used in the next iteration.

$$\Delta w_{ij} = 2\mu x_i (err_k)_j \tag{4}$$

To get an overall network error after each iteration (epoch), the average network error (*netError*) is obtained by calculating the mean square root of all errors in the training set using Equation (5), where n is the number of patterns in the training set. The *NetError* acts as the global rate of error for the entire network and is used to advance to the next iteration if the target error level has not been reached.

$$NetError = \sqrt{\frac{1}{n} \sum_{i=0}^{n-1} (err_i)^2} \qquad (5)$$

d.   **Coding Melvin I:** The programming language used in implementing Melvin I is C-Sharp. It is selected because of its flexibility in handling matrix mathematics in order to program the functions as defined in Equations 1 through 5. C# is also found useful in implementing the feedforward neural network architecture and the Backpropagation algorithms. Two important parameters used in the implementation of a feedforward neural network using Backpropagation algorithm are the learning rate as shown in Equation (4) and the momentum rate. The former specifies the degree to which the weights are modified in each iteration, while the latter specifies the degree to which the previous training iteration influences the current one. The learning rate and momentum rates used in the implementation of Melvin I are 0.7 and 0.9, respectively. The desired error tolerance is 1%.

4. RESULTS

4.1. Experimental Setup

To evaluate the performance of Melvin I, a Pro-point 6" Bench Grinder was used to simulate a rotating machine. Five sensors were connected to different locations of the grinder. These were then connected to the TCP/IP data acquisition card (Melvin DAQ). The sampling rate (f_s) was set as 12,800 samples per second and the window size (number of samples) was 4,096 samples. The Pro-point 6" Bench Grinder had a machine speed of 3,599 rpm. Using a data acquisition and signal processing software developed in our Lab, data was extracted from the raw vibration signals for each of the ten KPIs per sensor and stored in an SQL database every second.

4.2. System Evaluation

There are two operation modes of Melvin I known as the "train" and "use" modes.

1.   The "Train" Mode

The "Train" mode is a one-time operation used during initial training of the network. Melvin I is trained according to the algorithms, training data sets, and the learning parameters as described in Section 3.2. Figure 4 is a screenshot of the training results for one of the sensors (MIH). Training begins with the specification of the server on which the acquired data are stored. Based on the selected server, databases for all machines processed by the server are automatically generated as shown on the top left window of Figure 4. The trained neural network can be duplicated for machines with similar characteristics. However, for machines with dissimilar characteristics, the training parameters must be individually adjusted to reflect the special features of the machine. For example, alarm and alert limits are machine and fault dependent. The training sets for each machine must therefore take this into consideration. Also, depending on the type of machines, the number of measurement points may vary. As can be seen on the bottom left window of Figure 4, the Edson machine had five sensors namely CIA, CIA2, MIA, MIH and MOH. The training results shown in Figure 4 are for the MIH sensor. The same faults were being monitored in all five sensors. Consequently, the

Figure 4. The training mode of Melvin I

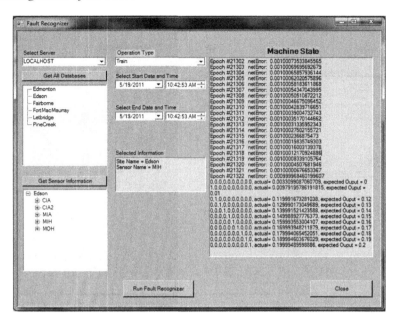

training for the MIH sensor was used to recognize faults in all of the sensors.

The total network training took 14 minutes on an Intel Core Duo processor of 2.53 GHz running Windows 7 operating system. The upper part of the machine state window in Figure 4 shows the last few iterations (epochs) during the training. It can be seen that the target error of 1% was attained after 21,332 iterations (epochs). The bottom part of the Machine State window in Figure 4 shows the actual and expected outputs for each of the training sets. After the initial training, the state of the trained network and the corresponding training data sets are saved for future applications and Melvin I is ready for the "Use" mode. The next section shows test results obtained during the "Use" mode for different faults and their combinations.

2. The "Use" Mode

In the "Use" mode, users select from a database the machine from which to diagnose possible faults. Once a machine is selected, the user specifies which sensors to use in diagnosing faults by clicking on an appropriate sensor from the sensor information window as shown in Figure 5. The user interface of Melvin I provides a flexibility for navigating between sensors and machines modeled in the configuration database. Once in the "use" mode, the saved state of the trained network and the training sets are loaded for Melvin I to run. To enable the network to build on the existing knowledge base, the "use" mode has facilities for adding new fault information to the existing trained set. Figure 5 shows a fault reporting user interface for Melvin I. In this experiment, the server used for holding acquired data was located on the local machine (localhost). KPI data from the data acquisition card for five sensors CIA, CIA2, MIA, MIH, and MOH was processed using the signal processing/conditioning mechanisms described in Section 2. This data was stored in database tables corresponding to the sensors. The KPI data can be accessed using the tree structure on the bottom left window of the user interface. The results reported in this paper were carried out on the Edson database. To check for faults on a given machine, the user first selects the "use" mode as shown in Figure 5. The user then selects

Figure 5. Results with no faults

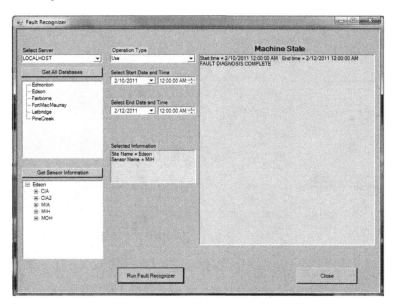

the machine, the sensor, and the period on which to check for faults. The fault recognizer is then run against the set of parameters. If a known fault is recognized, Melvin I displays the fault type, time of occurrence and information about the fault in the machine state window. If no fault is found, a message is displayed indicating that the fault diagnosis operation completed without any fault. Figure 5 shows the diagnosis results with no faults. If an unknown fault is encountered, an interactive window is presented, which allows the user to add new information about the fault. This is then added automatically to the existing trained set for future use.

To evaluate the system, Melvin I was used to test for faults between the times 2/10/2011 12:00:00 and 2/12/2011 12:00:00. As can be seen on the machine state window in Figure 5, the system reports that the diagnosis has completed and no fault is reported. This is because no known fault was found within the specified period. Such a situation occurs when the machine is in good health within the specified period.

Applying the acquired data from the Bench Grinder saved in the SQL database, a number of single faults were seeded by introducing faults at the KPIs *OVR*, *1X* and *120Hz* at times 2/10/2011 14:22:07, 2/10/2011 19:36:26 and 2/10/2011 19:36:40 respectively. The tool was run with the same parameters as in Figure 5. Figure 6 shows the results of this operation. The newly introduced faults are recognized and reported at the indicated times corresponding to the seeded faults.

To test for a fault or multiple faults that have not yet been presented in the trained set, combined faults were introduced at the KPIs *2X*, *3-5X* and *20-50X* at time 2/10/2011 14:22:35. The tool was run against the same set of parameters as in Figure 6. Figure 7 shows the results after this operation. A dialog box is presented to the user to describe the new fault. In order to facilitate training, Melvin I also gives an indication on the severity of changes on different KPIs. This is done through the calculation of a KPI dominant factor that determines which KPI deviates most from its expected threshold. For example, for the newly introduced set of faults, Melvin I shows that the change in the amplitude corresponding to the fourth KPI (2X) is greater than for all the other KPIs. During initial training, this provides useful

Figure 6. Recognition of single faults

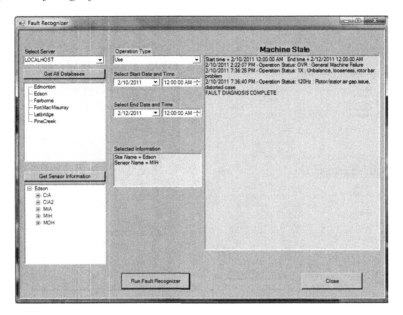

information that can be used by the knowledge experts to give more accurate information on faults corresponding to a given pattern.

To test for the newly-acquired knowledge, Melvin I was run against the same data set as in Figure 7. Figure 8 shows results of Melvin I against the same input data at a different time with the newly added faults. It is seen that the faults that

were introduced in Figure 7 are now recognized and reported without any further training. This shows that the knowledge acquired during the training in Figure 7 has been added to the knowledge base without overriding any previous training.

Figure 7. Dialog for newly encountered fault

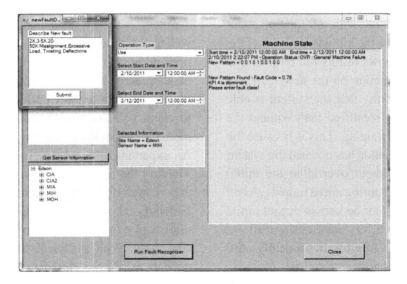

Figure 8. Recognition of new faults after training

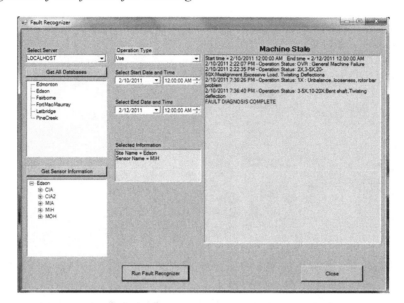

4.3. Discussion

In Figures 5 through 8, a set of screenshots of
the Melvin I user interface is demonstrated. Figure 5 shows the results when there was no fault
within the given period (2/10/2011 12:00:00am
to 2/12/2011 12:00:00am). In Figure 6, the simulated faults (OVR, 1X and 120Hz) are recognized
and reported. Figure 7 shows the case when a
new fault that is not present in the trained set is
encountered. The system interacts with the user
to add more information about the new fault.
This new fault, together with information about
it, is in turn added to the knowledge base of the
system. Figure 8 shows results run on the same
data set after information on the new fault was
added. It is noteworthy that the system is able
to report the newly identified fault without the
need for additional training. This is because the
newly added information has updated the system
knowledge base without overriding the initial
knowledge acquired during initial training. As all
the fault classes cannot be known during initial
training, this option is very important as it allows
the knowledge base to grow dynamically until
enough knowledge has been acquired.

5. CONCLUSION

Despite theoretically sound findings on developing
intelligent solutions for machine condition-based
monitoring, it is hard to find commercial tools in
the market that can be readily used. This paper
reports research work done on the development
of a component of an intelligent system (Melvin
I) that remotely diagnoses an industrial machine's
health based on the observation of changes in
vibration fault frequency indicators. The paper
first presents an overview on the architecture
adopted on the implementation of Melvin I as
well as a detailed discussion on the data acquisition and signal processing mechanisms used. The
development of a 3-layer neural network, which
uses input from ten key performance indicators
to classify faults is also reported. Melvin I is
trained using an initial training set of 11 patterns.
An expandable knowledge base is designed for
Melvin I that is capable of accommodating new
experiences during the system's operation. As a
fault not yet known to the system is detected, new
information on this fault is updated to its knowledge base. With sufficient training, the neural
network is able to classify faults not yet in its

knowledge base. Experimental results demonstrate that Melvin I is a powerful tool for both vibration analysts and industrial machine operators. Melvin I has been tested on data remotely collected from industrial machines on site. The results so far are encouraging. Further work on Melvin I will be to improve the fault recognition success rate. Another future direction area will be to develop Melvin II, which extends the system's functionality from fault diagnosis to fault prediction and prevention.

ACKNOWLEDGMENT

The authors would like to acknowledge the Alberta Government through Alberta Innovates Technology Futures for sponsoring this project. They would also like to acknowledge the International Institute for Cognitive Informatics and Cognitive Computing (IICICC), University of Calgary, for the industrial collaboration towards the realization of this project. They would like to thank the anonymous reviewers for their valuable comments on this work.

REFERENCES

Aravindh, K. B., Saranya, G., Selvakumar, R., Swetha, S. R., Saranya, M., & Sumesh, E. P. (2010). Fault detection in induction motor using WPT and multiple SVM. *International Journal of Control and Automation, 3*(2).

Balakrishnan, K., & Honavar, V. (1995). *Evolutionary design of neural architecture – A preliminary taxonomy and guide to literature* (Tech. Rep. No. 95-01). Ames, IA: Artificial Intelligence Research Group, Iowa State University.

Bracewell, R. N. (1986). *The Fourier transform and its applications* (2nd rev. ed.). New York, NY: McGraw-Hill.

Gade, S., Herlufsen, H., Konstantin-Hensen, H., & Wismer, N. J. (1995). *Order tracking analysis (Tech. Review Note No. 2)*. Naerum, Denmark: Bruel & Kjaer.

Gerald, M., & Javadpour, K. R. (2000). An ARTMAP neural network-based machine condition monitoring system. *Journal of Quality in Maintenance Engineering, 6*(2), 86–105. doi:10.1108/13552510010328095

Heaton, J. (2008). *Introduction to neural networks in C* (2nd ed.). Chesterfield, MO: Heaton Research.

Kumaraswamy, S., Rakesh, J., & Nalavade, A. K. (2002). Standardization of absolute vibration level and damage factors for machinery health monitoring. In *Proceedings of the Second International Conference on Vibration Engineering and Technology of Machinery* (pp. 16-18).

McCormick, A. C., & Nandi, A. K. (1996). A comparison of artificial neural networks and other statistical methods for rotating machine condition classification. In *Proceedings of the IEEE Colloquium on Modeling and Signal Processing for Fault Diagnosis*, Leicester, UK (pp. 2/1-2/6).

Ngolah, C. F., Morden, E., & Wang, Y. (2011). An intelligent fault recognizer for rotating machinery via remote characteristic vibration signal detection. In *Proceedings of the 10th IEEE International Conference on Cognitive Informatics & Cognitive Computing* (pp. 135-143).

Peng, Y. (2004). Intelligent condition monitoring using fuzzy inductive learning. *Journal of Intelligent Manufacturing, 15*, 373–380. doi:10.1023/B:JIMS.0000026574.95637.36

Rumelhat, D. E., Durbin, R., Golden, R., & Chauvin, Y. (1995). *Backpropagation: Theory, architectures, and applications* (pp. 1–33). Mahwah, NJ: Lawrence Erlbaum.

Samhouri, M., Al-Ghandoor, A., Ali, S. A., Hinti, I., & Massad, W. (2009). An intelligent machine condition monitoring system using time-based analysis: Neuro-fuzzy versus neural network. *Jordan Journal of Mechanical and Industrial Engineering, 3*(4), 294–305.

Saxena, A., & Saad, A. (2004). Fault diagnosis in rotating mechanical systems using self-organizing maps. In *Proceedings of the Conference on Artificial Neural Networks in Engineering*, St. Louis, MO.

Shiroishi, J., Li, Y., Liang, S., Kurfess, T., & Danyluk, S. (1997). Bearing condition diagnostics via vibration & acoustic emission measurements. *Mechanical Systems and Signal Processing, 11*(5), 693–705. doi:10.1006/mssp.1997.0113

Srinivasan, K. S. (2003). *Fault diagnosis in rotating machines using vibration monitoring and artificial neural network* (Unpublished doctoral dissertation). Indian Institute of Technology, Delhi, India.

Tetsuro, M. H., & Wang, P. C. (2008). Fault diagnosis and condition surveillance for plant rotating machinery using partially-linearized neural network. *Computers & Industrial Engineering, 55*(4), 783–794. doi:10.1016/j.cie.2008.03.002

Umesh, K. N., & Srinivasan, K. S. (2005). Study of effects of misalignment on vibration signatures of rotating machinery. In *Proceedings of the National Conference Mechanical Engineering*, Mangalore, India.

This work was previously published in the International Journal of Software Science and Computational Intelligence, Volume 3, Issue 4, edited by Yingxu Wang, pp. 67-83, copyright 2011 by IGI Publishing (an imprint of IGI Global).

Section 3
Software Science

Chapter 13
Empirical Studies on the Functional Complexity of Software in Large-Scale Software Systems

Yingxu Wang
University of Calgary, Canada

Vincent Chiew
University of Calgary, Canada

ABSTRACT

Functional complexity is one of the most fundamental properties of software because almost all other software attributes and properties such as functional size, development effort, costs, quality, and project duration are highly dependent on it. The functional complexity of software is a macro-scope problem concerning the semantic properties of software and human cognitive complexity towards a given software system; while the computational complexity is a micro-scope problem concerning algorithmic analyses towards machine throughput and time/space efficiency. This paper presents an empirical study on the functional complexity of software known as cognitive complexity based on large-scale samples using a Software Cognitive Complexity Analysis Tool (SCCAT). Empirical data are obtained with SCCAT on 7,531 programs and five formally specified software systems. The theoretical foundation of software functional complexity is introduced and the metric of software cognitive complexity is formally modeled. The functional complexities of a large-scale software system and the air traffic control systems (ATCS) are rigorously analyzed. A novel approach to represent software functional complexities and their distributions in software systems is developed. The nature of functional complexity of software in software engineering is rigorously explained. The relationship between the symbolic and functional complexities of software is quantitatively analyzed.

DOI: 10.4018/978-1-4666-2651-5.ch013

1. INTRODUCTION

Although computational complexity of algorithms and programs have been well studied in computer science (Hartmanis & Stearns, 1965; Hartmanis, 1994; Zuse, 1997; Wang, 2009), the functional complexity of software in software engineering (McDermid, 1991; Wang, 2009a) is yet to be rigorously explored from both theoretical and empirical aspects. If it is perceived that the computational complexity is a micro-scope problem concerning algorithmic analyses towards machine's throughput and efficiency, the functional complexity of software is a macro-scope problem concerning the semantic space of software and human cognitive complexity towards a given software system (Wang, 2003a, 2007b; Wang & Chiew, 2010; Wang et al., 2006). Conventional computational complexity theories are mainly focused on time and space properties of a given problem, which is usually a function of the input size $O(f(n))$ in the domains of real number ($\mathbb{R}$). However, software functional complexity is a two dimensional hyper-structure ($\mathbb{HS}$) between the interactions of the architectural data objects and the behavioral operations (Shao & Wang, 2003; Wang, 2009). Therefore, there is a practical need to study the functional properties of software and how they fundamentally affect human cognration, design, and manipulation in software engineering.

It is recognized that functional complexity is one of the most fundamental properties of software, because almost all other software properties and attributes such as functional size, development effort, costs, quality, and project duration, are highly dependent on it. The quantification and measurement of software functional complexity have been a persistent fundamental problem in software engineering (Hartmanis & Stearns, 1965; Basili, 1980; Kearney et al., 1986; Melton, 1996; Fenton & Pfleeger, 1998; Lewis & Papadimitriou, 1998; Wang, 2003b, 2007a). The taxonomy of the complexity and size measures of software can be classified into the categories of *computational*

complexity (time and space) (Hartmanis, 1994; McDermid, 1991), *symbolic* complexity (Lines of Code (LOC)) (Halstead, 1977; Albrecht & Gaffney, 1983; McDermid, 1991), *structural* complexity (control flow, cyclomatic) (McCabe, 1976; Zuse, 1977), *functional* complexity (function points, cognitive complexity) (Albrecht, 1979; Wang, 2007a, 2009; Shao & Wang, 2003). The most simple and intuitive measure of software complexity is the symbolic complexity, which is conventionally adopted as a measure in term of Lines of Code (LOC) (Halstead, 1977; Albrecht & Gaffney, 1983; McDermid, 1991). However, the functional complexity of software is so intricate and non-linear, which is too hard to be measured or even estimated in LOC. In order to improve the accuracy and measurability, McCabe proposed the cyclomatic complexity measure (McCabe, 1976) based on Euler's theorem (Lipschutz & Lipson, 1997) in the category of structural complexity. However, it only considered the internal loop architectures of software systems without taking into account of the throughput of the system in terms of data objects and other important internal architectures such as the sequential, branch, and embedded constructs. Because the linear blocks of code are oversimplified as one unit as in graph theory, the cyclomatic complexity is not sensitive to linear structures and external data complexity as well as their impact on the basic structures. Albrecht (1979) introduced the concept of *function point* of software (Albrecht, 1979), which is a weighted product of a set of functional characteristics of software systems. However, the physical meaning of a unit function point is not rigorously defined instead of various empirical studies.

In order to improve the understanding of the nature of software functional complexity, the semantic properties of software have to be systematically studied (Wang, 2006, 2009, 2001). The two-dimensional semantic space of software indicates that the cognitive complexity of software is a measure for the functional complexity for both software design and comprehension, which is a product of the architectural and operational complexities of software. Cognitive complexity provides a profound approach to explain and measure the functional complexity of software as well as the associated effort in software engineering. The cognitive complexity metrics consider the effect of both internal structures of software and the I/O data objects under processing (Wang, 2009), which is a formal measurement for cross-platform analysis of complexities, sizes, as well as development efforts and costs of software systems in the phases of design, implementation, and maintenance in software engineering.

This paper presents an empirical study on the functional complexity of software known as cognitive complexity based on large-scale samples and the development of a Software Cognitive Complexity Analysis Tool (SCCAT). Empirical data are obtained with SCCAT on 7,531 shareware programs in late phase processes of software engineering and 5 formally specified software systems in early phase of software engineering. In the remainder of this paper, Section 2 presents the theoretical foundations of the functional complexity of software, which introduces the mathematical model and the metrics of software cognitive complexity. Section 3 analyzes the functional and cognitive complexities of a large-scale software system, the air traffic control systems (ATCS), based on the functional, architectural, and behavioral complexities and their distributions in the software system. On the basis of the formal models of software functional complexities and the empirical data of the ATCS system, the nature of functional complexity of software and empirical observations in software engineering are explained in Section 4. The relationship between the symbolic and functional complexities of software is rigorously revealed. The large-scale real world data provide solid evidences for the effectiveness of the functional complexity measurement of software systems and the practical applications of the cognitive complexity metrics in software engineering.

2. THEORETICAL FOUNDATIONS OF SOFTWARE FUNCTIONAL COMPLEXITY

It has been empirically observed that programmers do feel fundamentally different from that of machines on the functional complexity of software in software engineering. Further, the functional complexity is exponentially unpredictable when the symbolic size [LOC] is above a certain threshold of 100-200 [LOC] (Shao & Wang, 2003). The curiosity to explain the nature of software complexity leads to the study on the functional complexity of software in general and the cognitive complexity of software in particular.

2.1. The Mathematical Models of Functional Complexity of Software

It is observed that the nature of software functional complexity is underpinned by the structure of the semantic space of software (Wang, 2006, 2007a, 2008e). The characteristics of the semantic space can be formally described by the semantic function of programs.

Definition 1: The *semantic function* of a program $\wp$, $f_\theta(\wp)$, is a finite set of values V determined by a Cartesian product on a finite set of variables S and a finite set of executing steps T, i.e.:

$$f_\theta(\wp) = f : T \times S \to V$$

$$= \begin{pmatrix} & s_1 & s_2 & \cdots & s_m \\ t_0 & \bot & \bot & \cdots & \bot \\ t_1 & v_{11} & v_{12} & & v_{1m} \\ \vdots & \vdots & \vdots & \ddots & \vdots \\ t_n & v_{n1} & v_{n1} & \cdots & v_{nm} \end{pmatrix} \quad (1)$$

where $T = \{t_0, t_1, ..., t_n\}$, $S = \{s_1, s_2, ..., s_m\}$, and V is a set of values dynamically determined by $v(t_i, s_j)$, $0 \le i \le n$, and $1 \le j \le m$.

According to Definition 1, the semantic space of a program can be represented by a two-dimensional plane as shown in Figure 1. The semantic space of software indicates that software functional complexity is not a simple linear entity. Instead, it is complex hyper-structure that is proportional not only to the number of operations (operational complexity), but also to the number of data objects under operation (architectural complexity). That is, the functional complexities of software are a product of its operational and architectural complexities.

Theorem 1: The *functional complexity* of software is proportional to the size of the Cartesian plain of the *semantic space* of software, which is a product of the operational complexity and the object architectural complexity.

Proof 1: Theorem 1 can be directly proven on the basis of Definition 1.

Theorem 1 indicates that the functional complexity of software is not a one-dimensional linear structure as that of the symbolic complexity [LOC] suggests. In other words, the symbolic complexity in the unit of [LOC] may not be suitable and rigor for predicting and measuring software complexity.

2.2. The Metrics of Functional Complexity of Software

Definition 1 and Theorem 1 indicate that software functional complexity needs to be rigorously measured with a two-dimensional metric that considers both the operational and structural complexities as a product. With this notion, the measurement of cognitive complexity of software is derived in the following subsections.

It is recognized that there are commonly ten basic control structures (BCS's) in software modeling as shown in Table 1 (Wang, 2005, 2007a) according to Real-Time Process Algebra (RTPA) (Wang, 2002, 2008a, 2008b, 2008c, 2008d, 2008e). The cognitive weights of the set of BCS's have been quantitatively determined based on a series of empirical experiments (Shao & Wang, 2003) on their relative cognitive coefficients as given in Table 1. It is noteworthy that, although the *absolute* cognitive weight towards a BCS may be variously different from individual to individual in program design and comprehension, the *relative* cognitive weights between the ratio $w'(BCS_i) / w(BCS_1)$, $2 \leq i \leq 10$, remain stable. In other words, the relative ratio normalized onto the most basic sequential BCS helps to eliminate the subjectivity among individuals in determining the objective cognitive weights of the ten BCS's.

There are two structural patterns of BCS's in a given software system S: the *sequential* and the *embedded* BCS's. In the former, all BCS's are related in a linear layout in S, therefore the operational complexity of S is a sum of the cognitive weights of all linear BCS's. However, in the latter, some BCS's are embedded in others, hence the operational complexity of S is a sum of the sums of the cognitive weights of inner BCS's. In general, both types of BCS configurations in S may be combined in various ways. Therefore, a general method for calculating the operational complexity of software can be derived as follows.

Figure 1. The semantic space of software systems

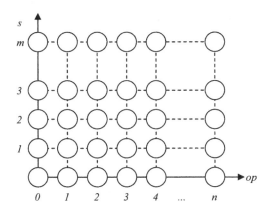

Table 1. BCS's of software and calibrated cognitive weights

BCS (i)	RTPA Notation	Description	Calibrated Cognitive Weight (w_i)
1	$\rightarrow$	Sequence	1
2	|	Branch	2
3	|... |...	Switch	3
4	R^i	For-loop	7
5	R^+	Repeat-loop	7
6	R^*	While-loop	8
7	$\circ$	Function call	7
8	$\dot{O}$	Recursion	11
9	|| or $\oint$	Parallel	15
10	$\not{z}$	Interrupt	22

Definition 2: The *operational complexity* of a software system S, $C_{op}(S)$, is determined by the sum of the cognitive weights of its n linear blocks composed by individual BCS's, $w(BCS)$, i.e.:

$$C_{op}(S) = \sum_{k=1}^{n_c} C_{op}(C_k)$$
$$= \sum_{k=1}^{n_c} \sum_{i=1}^{m_k} w(k, i) \quad [F] \qquad (2)$$

The cognitive weights, $w(k, BCS)$, in Eq. 2 can be formally modeled and empirically studied as shown in Table 1.

Definition 3: The *relative cognitive weight* of a BCS, $w(BCS_i)$, is determined by a relative ratio between the tested comprehension effort $w'(BCS_i)$ and the reference comprehension effort of the sequential BCS_1, $w'(BCS_1)$ = 1, i.e.:

$$w\left(BCS_i\right) = \frac{w'\left(BCS_i \mid 2 \le i \le 10\right)}{w'\left(BCS_1 \mid w'(BCS_1) = w'(SEQ) \equiv 1\right)} \qquad (3)$$

Definition 4: The *unit of operational complexity* of a software system S is a single sequential operation called a unit function F, i.e.:

$$C_{op}(S) = 1 \; [F] \Leftrightarrow \#(SeqOP(S)) = 1 \qquad (4)$$

With the cognitive weight of the sequential operator defined as a unit function for the operational complexity, general process relations in software structures can be quantitatively measured using Eq. 2. It is obvious that for a fully sequential software system where only w(sequence) = 1 [F] is involved, its operational complexity is reduced to the symbolic complexity equivalent to LOC. However, in more generic cases, the actual operational complexity of software is much greater than that of the symbolic complexity in LOC.

According to Theorem 1, the second dimension that determines the functional complexity of software is the architectural complexity of a given software system. The architectural complexity is proportional to the number of its global and local data objects, such as inputs, outputs, data structures, and internal variables modeled in the program.

Definition 5: The *architectural complexity* of a software system S, $C_a(S)$, is determined by the number of data objects at system and component levels, i.e.:

$$C_a(S) = OBJ(S)$$
$$= \sum_{j=1}^{n_{UDM}} OBJ(UDM_j) + \sum_{k=1}^{n_C} OBJ(C_k) \; [O] \qquad (5)$$

where *OBJ* is a function that counts the number of data objects in a given data structure. The first item in Equation 5 measures the number of global variables known as the unified data model (UDM). The second item is equivalent to the sum of the number of local variables in all n_c components.

Definition 6: The *unit of architectural complexity* of software is a single data object, modeled either globally or locally, called an object *O*, i.e.:

$$C_a(S) = 1\ [O] \Leftrightarrow \#(\mathrm{OBJ}(S)) = 1 \qquad (6)$$

On the basis of the elaborations of software architectural and operational complexities, the cognitive complexity of software systems is introduced as follows as a fundamental measure of the functional complexity and sizes of software systems.

Theorem 2: The *cognitive complexity* $C_c(S)$ of a software system *S* is a product of the operational complexity $C_{op}(S)$ and the architectural complexity $C_a(S)$, i.e.:

$$
\begin{aligned}
C_c(S) &= C_{op}(S) \bullet C_a(S) \\
&= \{\sum_{k=1}^{n_C} \sum_{i=1}^{\#(C_s(C_k))} w(k,i)\} \bullet \\
&\quad \{\sum_{j=1}^{n_{UDM}} \mathrm{OBJ}(UDM_j) + \sum_{k=1}^{n_C} \mathrm{OBJ}(C_k)\} \quad [\mathrm{FO}]
\end{aligned}
$$
$$(7)$$

Proof 2: Theorem 1 can be formally proven on the basis of Theorem 1 where the operational and architectural complexities are orthogonally modeled.

Theorem 2 indicates that the functional complexity, in term of the cognitive complexity, is a chain of embedded computational operations onto a set of data objects modeled in the software. Because the cognitive complexity of a software system is proportional to both its operational and architectural complexities, the more the architec-

tural data objects and the higher the operational complicity onto these data objects, the higher the functional complexity of the given system.

Definition 7: The *unit of cognitive complexity* of software is a single sequential operation onto a single data object called a *function-object FO*, i.e.:

$$
\begin{aligned}
C_f &= C_{op} \bullet C_a \\
&= 1\ [\mathrm{F}] \bullet 1\ [\mathrm{O}] \qquad (8) \\
&= 1\ [\mathrm{FO}]
\end{aligned}
$$

According to Definition 7, the physical meaning of functional complexity is how many equivalent function-objects [FOs] modeled in a given software system. The cognitive complexity as a formal measure of software size and functionality enables the quantitative determination of software functional complexity and design efforts in software engineering. It will be demonstrated in the next section that the cognitive complexity is the most distinguishable and more accurate measure for the inherent functional complexity of software systems.

Corollary 1: Software *functional size* is orthogonal, which is proportional to both its *operational* and *architectural* complexities. The more the architectural data objects and the higher the operational complicity onto these objects, the larger the functional size of the system.

3. ANALYSES OF THE FUNCTIONAL COMPLEXITY OF THE AIR TRAFFIC CONTROL SYSTEM (ATCS)

An Air Traffic Control System (ATCS) is among the most demanding software systems and the most challenging software design technologies (Ross, 1986; Bass, Clements, & Kazman, 1998; Smith, 1993; Gibbs, 1994; Perry, 1997; Nolan, 1999; Peter & Pedrycz, 2000; de Neufville & Odoni, 2003; Ball et al., 2007; Braun & Gianoplus, 2009; Hansman & Odoni, 2009; Kontogiannis & Malakis, 2009; Debelack et al., 2010). In a case study, Len Bass et al. reported that the ATCS is hard real-time, safety-critical, and highly distributed. It is a hard real-time system because timing demands must be met absolutely. It is a safety-critical system because human lives may be lost for any system malfunction. It is highly distributed because it requires a large group of controllers to work co-operatively to guide aircrafts through the airway system (Bass, Clements, & Kazman, 1998; Sha et al., 1990; Tanenbaum, 1994; Wang, Zeng et al., 2010; Wang, Ngolah et al., 2010).

It is recognized that over 2/3 large-scale software projects have been failed (McDermid, 1991; Bass, Clements, & Kazman, 1998; Wang, 2007a). A major reason of the failures was because of the highly complex software systems created by a team may eventually not be able to understand by any individual in the project. The complexity may easily grow out of the intellectual manageability of an individual in the team at any level when the system is integrated in the final phase. Not only at the system architect's and managers' level who may lose their cognitive ability for pinpointing and tracing the details of system behaviors, but also at the programmers' level who may lose their cognitive ability for comprehending the intricate connections and relationship of a certain component with the remainder of the entire system. In addition, the highly dependent interpersonal coordination requirement may result in an extremely high rework rate when the system design is not rigorously specified in a formal and precise model. These dilemmas are identified as the key causes of the failures in complex software development such as the ATCS, the real-time operating system, the digital telephone switching system, and the distributed banking system (Wang, 2007a).

The following subsections present the applications of the metrics of functional complexity, particularly the cognitive complexity, in the

quantitative analyses and modeling of the ATCS system.

3.1. The Functional Architecture of the ATCS Software System

The ATCS controls aircrafts (flights) passing through the air space within an administrative zone or across multiple zones. There are multiple entities in ATCS such as the airport, flights, aircrafts, tower controller, approach controller, en route controller, runways, gates, radars, communication networks, ground services, and passengers. The conceptual model of ATCS can be abstracted by a number of interconnected air traffic administration zones as shown in Figure 2. Each administration zone is divided into three control areas known as the terminal, approach, and en route areas. Corresponding to them, the controllers in the areas are known as the tower (airport) controller, approach controller, and en route controller. In the air space, an aircraft's heading direction is modeled in 360° clockwise starting from East as 0°. That is, East, South, West, and North are defined as 0° (3 O'clock), 90° (6 O'clock), 180° (9 O'clock), and 270° (12 O'clock) in ATCS, respectively. ATCS dispatching functions are carried out by wireless communications in which verbal instructions are sent to the pilots and acknowledged verbally by the pilots.

The functional architectural model of the ATCS software is shown in Figure 3, which encompasses five subsystems known as those of system management, airport control, en route control, approach control, and system dynamic behaviors. Each software subsystem of ATCS is refined by a number of components at the third level of the system model. There are two components in the system management subsystem such as system initialization and system clock. The airport control subsystem consists of three components known as the terminal control, landing control, and take-off control. Within each component in the airport control subsystem, there are sets of three, five,

Figure 2. The conceptual model of ATCS

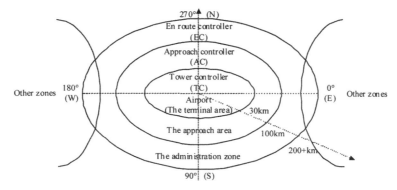

and five subcomponents, respectively. The subsystem of en route control involves the components of en route flight detection, incoming en route registration, incoming en route monitor, and outgoing en route monitor. The approach control subsystem encompasses components of approach flight detection, incoming approach monitor, and outgoing approach monitor. In the last subsystem of dynamic behaviors, five components are modeled known as the process deployment, landing dispatching, takeoff dispatching, en route dispatching, and approach dispatching.

In Figure 3, the distributions of both the symbolic sizes C_s [LOC] and functional complexities in term of the cognitive complexity C_c [FO] are identified for each subsystems and components, respectively, in the brackets of each component, which will be derived in the following subsections.

3.2. The Architectural Attributes of ATCS

The architecture of the ATCS software system can be rigorously modeled by a set of unified data models (Wang, 2007a) with a coherent set of data objects and attributes.

Definition 8: A *Unified Data Model* (UDM) is a generic architectural model for a software system as well as its internal control structures, and its interfaces with hardware

components, which can be rigorously modeled and refined as an *n*-tuple, i.e.:

$$UDM \triangleq \mathop{R}_{i=1}^{n}(S_i \mid \forall e \in S_i, p_i(e)) \qquad (9)$$

where $\mathop{R}\limits_{i=1}^{n}$ is the big-R notation of RTPA that denotes a repetitive structure or operation; S_i, $1 \leq i \leq n$, is a set that is equivalent to a type in computing for elements e, in which all e share the property $p_i(e)$.

According to Definitions 5 and 6, the architectural complexity of the ATCS system can be rigorously analyzed. As a result, the configurations of UDMs and attributes of ATCS is shown in Table 2 where the unit of architectural complexity is objects (O). The architectural model of the ATCS system as shown in Table 2 encompasses 14 UDMs, which can be categorized into five subsystems known as those of the system, the airport control structures, landing control, takeoff control, and system control structures. Each UDM encapsulates a set of architectural attributes identified by the number of objects that is equivalent to the number of fields modeled in the UDMs. Further details may be referred to the complete models of ATCS in RTPA (Wang, 2002, 2008e, 2008c). Based on the 14 UDMs with 197 objects, the average architectural complexity of the ATCS software system is 12 [O] ranged from minimum

Figure 3. The architecture and functional distribution of ATCS

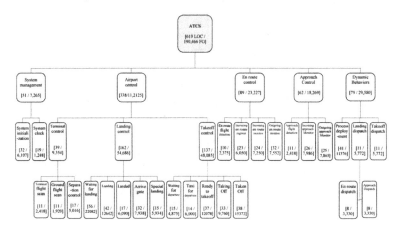

3 [O] to maximum 40 [O]. It is noteworthy that although the entire ATCS system may be highly complicated, its architectural and data objects are relatively limited with 12 objects in average.

3.3. The Behavioral Attributes of ATCS

The behavioural functions of the ATCS software system can be rigorously modeled by a set of unified process models (Wang, 2007a) that operate onto the architectural UDMs of ATCS.

Definition 9: The *Unified Process Model* (UPM) of a program $\wp$ is a composition of a finite set of m processes according to the event-based process dispatching rules, $@e_k\mathbf{S} \mapsto P_k\mathbf{PC}$, i.e.:

$$UPM \triangleq \wp$$
$$= \mathop{R}_{k=1}^{m}(@e_k\mathbf{S} \mapsto P_k\mathbf{PC})$$
$$= \mathop{R}_{k=1}^{m}[@e_k\mathbf{S} \mapsto \mathop{R}_{i=1}^{n-1}(s_i(k)\ r_{ij}(k)\ s_j(k))], j = i+1$$
(10)

where s_i and s_j are one of the 17 RTPA meta-processes, r_{ij} is one of the 17 RTPA algebraic process operators, and e_k is an event.

The functional model of the ATCS system encompasses seven functional subsystems known as those of system management, airport (terminal) control, en route control, approach control, landing control, takeoff control, and system dynamic behaviors as shown in Table 3. The 27 behavioral UPMs in each of the seven subsystems are listed in the second column in Table 3. The behavioral attributes of each UPM are comparatively analyzed by the conventional symbolic complexity C_s [LOC] and cognitive complexity C_c [FO]. The latter is a product of the operational complexity C_{op} [F] and the architectural complexity C_a [O]. According to Definition 2, the statistics of distributions of behavioral attributes in the 27 UPMs of the seven subsystems is shown in Table 3. Further details may be referred to the complete models of ATCS in RTPA (Wang, 2008a, 2008c).

According to the empirical and derived data obtained in Table 3, the average symbolic complexity of the ATCS system is only 23 [LOC] per component. However, the corresponding average cognitive complexity of ATCS is 7,058 [FO] per UPM. The equivalency between the symbolic complexity and cognitive complexity in ATCS is as follows:

$$\begin{cases} 1.000\ [LOC] & = & 307.845\ [FO] \\ 1.000\ [FO] & = & 0.003\ [LOC] \end{cases}$$
(11)

Table 2. Architectural attributes of the ATCS system

No.	ID of UDM	Description	Objects (UDMs) C_A [O]
1	§(ATCS)	**System**	7
2	AirportControlSys**ST**	**Airport Control Structures**	5
2.1	Runways**ST**	The Runways	20
2.2	Gates**ST**	The Gates	3
2.3	TC**ST**	The Tower Controller	8
2.4	AC**ST**	The Approach Controller	8
2.5	EC**ST**	The En Route Controller	10
3	LandingControlSys**ST**	**Landing Control**	13
4	TakeoffControlSys**ST**	**Takeoff Control**	13
5	SystemControl**ST**	**System Control Structures**	6
5.1	SysClock**ST**	The System Clock	5
5.2	SCB**ST**	The System Control Block	40
5.3	FCB**ST**	The Flight Control Block	40
5.4	TCB**ST**	The Tower Control Block	7
5.5	ACB**ST**	The Approach Control Block	6
5.6	ECB**ST**	The En Route Control Block	6
# of components (UDMs)			16
Total objects [O]			197
Average objects [O]			12
Maximum objects [O]			40
Minimum objects [O]			3

Equation 11 and Table 3 indicate that because of the higher the complexity of a given system, the higher the ratio of FO/LOC, the symbolic complexity of software may result in a significant under-estimation of the functional complexity of software. This explains the reasons of why a typical large-scale and real-time software system such as ATCS is highly complicated, because it represents a tremendous cognitive functional complexity of a software system to the architects, programs, quality engineers, managers, and users. This observation also provides evidence to J.V. Guttag's assertion that "large software system are among the most complex systems engineered by man (Guttag, 2002)."

3.4. Analysis of the Distributions of Functions and Complexities in the ATCS System

On the basis of the quantitative analyses of the architectural and functional attributes of ATCS using SCCAT, a rich set of empirical data are obtained for illustrating the function and complexity distributions in the ATCS system. The data provide a novel view to visually represent the architectural and functional complexities and sizes of any software system.

A perspective on the architectural configuration of ATCS is shown in Figure 4 based on the data obtained in Table 2. In Figure 4, the numbers of

Table 3. Behavioral attributes of the ATCS system

No.	Description	Symbolic Complexity C_s [LOC]	Functional Complexity C_f (FO) = C_c (FO)		
			Architectural Complexity C_a [O]	Operational Complexity C_{op} [F]	Cognitive Complexity C_c [FO]
1	**System Management**				
1.1	System Initialization	32	197	31	6,107
1.2	System Clock	19	48	26	1,248
2	**Airport Control (Terminal Control)**				
2.1	Terminal Flight Scan	11	93	26	2,418
2.2	Ground Flight Scan	11	96	20	1,920
2.3	Separation Control	17	88	57	5,016
3	**En Route Control**				
3.1	En route Flight Detection	10	95	25	2,375
3.2	Incoming En Route Registration	23	110	55	6,050
3.3	Incoming En Route Monitor	24	125	58	7,250
3.4	Outgoing En Route Monitor	32	118	64	7,552
4	**Approach Control**				
4.1	Approach Flight Detection	11	93	26	2,418
4.2	Incoming Approach Monitor	26	121	66	7,986
4.3	Outgoing Approach Monitor	25	121	65	7,865
5	**Landing Control**				
5.1	Waiting for Landing	56	122	181	22,082
5.2	Landing	42	129	98	12,642
5.3	Landed	17	105	58	6,090
5.4	Arriving Gate	32	126	63	7,938
5.5	Special Landing Processes	15	129	46	5,934
6	**Takeoff Control**				
6.1	Waiting for Departure	15	125	39	4,875
6.2	Taxi for Departure	14	125	48	6,000
6.3	Ready to Takeoff	37	122	99	12,078
6.4	Takingoff	33	122	8 0	9,760
6.5	Takenoff	38	122	126	15,372
7	**System Dynamic Behaviors**				
7.1	Process Deployment	41	48	237	11,376
7.2	Landing Dispatching	11	111	52	5,772
7.3	Takeoff Dispatching	11	111	52	5,772
7.4	En Route Dispatching	8	111	30	3,330
7.5	Approach Dispatching	8	111	30	3,330
# of components [UPMs]		27	27	27	27
Total functions		619 [LOC]	3,024 [O]	1,758 [F]	190,466 [FO]

continued on following page

Table 3. Continued

No.	Description	Symbolic Complexity C_s [LOC]	Functional Complexity C_f (FO) = C_c (FO)		
			Architectural Complexity C_a [O]	Operational Complexity C_{op} [F]	Cognitive Complexity C_c [FO]
Average function		23 [LOC]	112 [O]	65 [F]	7,058 [FO]
Minimum function		8 [LOC]	48 [O]	20 [F]	1,248 [FO]
Maximum function		56 [LOC]	197 [O]	237 [F]	22,082 [FO]

data objects in the seven subsystems of ATCS, such as the high-level structures of the system, airport control, landing control, takeoff control, and system control are illustrated in the three-dimensional distributions. It is obvious that the system control and airport control are the two largest architectural subsystems in ATCS. In particular, components 5.2 (the system control block) and 5.2 (the flight control block), and 2.2 (the runways) are the three most complex structural components in ATCS.

The perspective on the functional configuration of ATCS can be represented by the distributions of its symbolic and cognitive complexities, respectively. The functional distribution of ATCS measured by the symbolic complexity C_s [LOC] is illustrated in Figure 5, which shows the numbers of lines of code distributed in the seven subsystems

such as system management, airport (terminal) control, en route control, approach control, landing control, takeoff control, and system dynamic behaviors.

The functional distribution of ATCS measured by the functional complexity C_c [FO] is illustrated in Figure 6. Figure 6 shows the distributions of cognitive complexity in term of function-objects in the seven subsystems of ATCS. The cognitive complexity distribution in a system provides a new approach to represent a more accurate software functional complexity and their partitions in a software system. It also provides an intuitive indicator for showing where the main workload and costs are located in a software development project in software engineering.

Figure 4. The structural configuration of ATCS in architectural complexity (C_a [O])

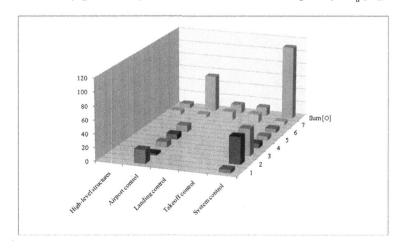

Figure 5. The functional distribution of ATCS in symbolic size (C_s [LOC])

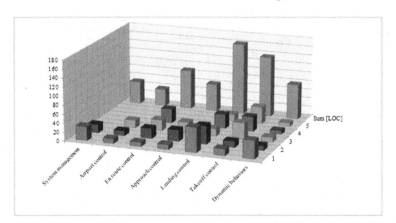

Contrasting Figures 5 and 6, a number of interesting observations about the nature of software complexity distributions may be obtained. For example, the conventional symbolic complexity distribution in Figure 5 may suggest that the size/effort distribution in ATCS is in a descending pattern across subsystems (5, 6, 3, 7, 4, 1, 2). However, the functional measures in Figure 6 reveal a different view as that of (5, 6, 7, 3, 4, 2, 1). In other words, the real functional complexity, as well as effort and costs of ATCS, is distributed not only differently, but also at a much higher magnitude up to 190,466 [FO].

4. FUNDAMENTAL FINDINGS ON SOFTWARE FUNCTIONAL COMPLEXITY

On the basis of the formal models of software functional complexities in Section 2 and the empirical studies on a number of large-scale software systems using the SCCAT tool in Section 3, the nature of the functional complexity can be better explained in software engineering. New perspectives on the relationship between the symbolic and functional complexities of software can also be rigorously analyzed.

Figure 6. The functional distribution of ATCS in cognitive size (C_c [FO])

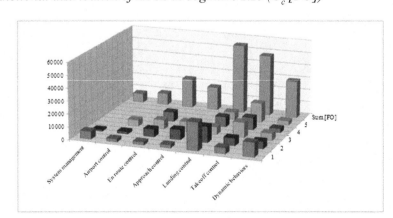

4.1. The Nature of Functional Complexity of Software

The orthogonality of software functional complexity is formally explained in Theorem 1 and Corollary 1, which provides the theoretical foundation of software functional complexity. The orthogonal property of functional complexity shows that the more the architectural data objects and the higher the operational complicity onto these data objects, the higher the functional complexity of a given software system. In case any or both of the orthogonal dimensions is/are zero, there is no functional complexity in the given system.

Corollary 2: Software functionality is embodied by an orthogonal interaction (operation) between the data objects modeled in the architectures (UDMs) and the behavioral operations modeled by the computational processes (UPMs).

Corollary 3: The *basic unit* of software functional complexity is a *function-object* (FO) determined by two independent attributes known as the architectural complexity C_a [O] and operational complexity C_o [F].

Corollary 4: The symbolic complexity $C_s(S)$ is a special case of the operational complexity $C_{op}(S)$, where the cognitive weights of all kinds of BCS's, w_i(BCS), are simplified as a constant one, i.e.:

$$
\begin{aligned}
C_{op}(S) &= \sum_{k=1}^{n_C} \sum_{i=1}^{m_k} w(k,i) \\
&= C_s(S), w(k,i) \equiv 1 \\
&= C_s(S) \quad [\text{LOC}]
\end{aligned}
\tag{12}
$$

Corollary 4 presents an important property of the relationship between conventional symbolic complexity and the operational complexity of software. It reveals that the measure of symbolic complexity in LOC is oversimplified on software functional complexity. As a result, it cannot actually represent the real functional complexities and sizes of software systems. Further, real-world case studies show that programs with similar symbolic complexities may possess widely different functional complexities in terms of the cognitive complexities. According to Corollary 4, the actual complexity and size of software systems were significantly underestimated when the conventional symbolic measurement in [LOC] is adopted. Therefore, a more accurate and rational complexity measurement, the cognitive complexity, needs to be established in software engineering.

4.2. Empirical Findings on Software Functional Complexity

It is a profound finding that functional complexity of software in software engineering is fundamentally different from that of the time and space complexity of algorithms traditionally modeled in computer science. Further, the cognitive complexity of software is significantly different from the points of view of human beings and machines in software engineering. Based on the empirical data obtained from the ATCS system and the SCCAT tool, the following observations and findings are identified on software functional complexities:

1. Although a software system would be extremely large, the average size of its components is usually quite small. For example, since there are 27 UPMs with 619 [LOC] in the ATCS system, the average symbolic complexity of ATCS is only 23 [LOC] per components corresponding to an average cognitive complexity of 7,058 [FO]. These empirical evidences provide solid support for the well known principles of modularization and component-based development in software engineering, which could not be explained using the symbolic complexity measure.

2. The symbolic complexity may dramatically under estimate the real complexity of software systems. For example, as shown in Table 3, with the same symbolic complexities $C_s(2.1) = C_s(2.2) = 11$ [LOC] for the UPMs of terminal flight scan and ground flight scan, their cognitive complexities would be largely different, i.e., $C_c(2.1) = 2,418$ [FO], while $C_c(2.2) = 1,920$ [FO].

3. The symbolic complexity is not sensitive to represent the functional complexities of software. For example, as shown in Table 3, although the difference $\Delta C_s = C_s(6.1) - C_s(6.2) = 15 - 14 = 1$ [LOC] for the UPMs of waiting for departure and taxi for departure, the real difference of their functional complexities would be as great as $\Delta C_c = C_c(6.1) - C_c(6.2) = 4,875 - 6000 = -1,125$ [FO].

4. Following observations (b) and (c), the effort (E) or workload of a software project may not be accurately estimated on the basis of the symbolic complexity C_s [LOC], because there is a lack of linear or predicative correlation between C_s and E. This finding helps to explain why so many software engineering projects, particularly large ones, were failed due to budget deficits, unacceptable delays, and/or quality sacrifices.

5. The configuration of complex software systems may be better expressed by the 3-D distributions of system functional complexity among all components in different subsystems as shown in Figures 3 and 6.

6. The optimal symbolic size (C_s) of a software component is constrained by a threshold of 100-200 [LOC] (Shao & Wang, 2003; Chew & Wang, 2006). No well structured component would be greater than the threshold. Otherwise, the cognitive complexity (C_c) and development effort (E) will be largely unpredictable.

The findings demonstrate that the cognitive complexity is highly distinguishable for modeling and measuring software functional complexities, sizes, and efforts of software projects in software engineering. Therefore, the functional complexity measure in term of the cognitive complexity is more accurate than that of the symbolic complexity in lines of code.

5. CONCLUSION

This paper has presented an empirical study on the functional complexity of software known as cognitive complexity based on a large set of large-scale samples. In order to demonstrate that programmers do perceive software functional complexities differently from that of computers, and to rationally model the functional sizes and complexities of software systems, the semantic space of software and its cognitive foundation have been studied. According to the cognitive complexity theory, it is found that the traditional time, cyclomatic, and symbolic complexities do not work very well to actually reflect the real complexity of software systems in design, representation, cognition, and/or comprehension in software engineering. The cognitive complexity of software systems has been formally and rigorously elaborated with comparative case studies. The Software Cognitive Complexity Analysis Tool (SCCAT) has been developed to automatically analyze a comprehensive set of real-world programs and large-scale software systems.

This paper has revealed that the functional complexity of software is a product of its architectural and operational complexities on the basis of software semantic space theories. It has been found that programmers and computers are sensitive to different forms of software complexities, where the former focus on the functional complexity in software engineering based on the semantics of software; while the latte put emphases on the computational complexity based on time and space consumptions. A number of interesting characteristics on software functional complexities have been identified such as: a) Programs with similar symbolic complexities C_s [LOC] can possess greatly different cognitive complexities C_c [FO]; b) The symbolic complexity C_s [LOC] does not represent the throughput or the input size of problems, which may be captured by the architectural complexity measure C_a [O]; and c) Cognitive complexity C_c [FO] provides a more accurate measurement for the real semantic complexity of software systems by coherently integrating both the operational and architectural complexities, which provide insights into human cognition in software engineering.

ACKNOWLEDGMENT

The authors would like to acknowledge the Natural Science and Engineering Council of Canada (NSERC) for its partial support to this work. The author would like to thank the anonymous reviewers for their valuable suggestions and comments on this work.

REFERENCES

Albrecht, A. J. (1979, October). Measuring application development productivity. In *Proceedings of the IBM Applications Development Joint SHARE/GUIDE Symposium* (pp. 83-92).

Albrecht, A. J., & Gaffney, J. E. (1983). Software function, source lines of code, and development effort prediction: A software science validation. *IEEE Transactions on Software Engineering, 9*(6), 639–648. doi:10.1109/TSE.1983.235271

Ball, M. O., Barnhart, C., Nemhauser, G., & Odoni, A. (2007). Air transportation: Irregular operations and control. In Barnhart, C., & Laporte, G. (Eds.), *Handbook in operations research and management science* (*Vol. 14*, pp. 1–73). Oxford, UK: Elsevier.

Basili, V. R. (1980). *Qualitative software complexity models: A summary in tutorial on models and methods for software management and engineering*. Los Alamitos, CA: IEEE Press.

Bass, L., Clements, P., & Kazman, R. (1998). *Software architecture in practice*. Reading, MA: Addison-Wesley.

Braun, E. L., & Gianoplus, A. S. (2009). A digital computer system for terminal-area air traffic control. *IRE Transactions on Space Electronics and Telemetry, 5*(2), 66–72.

Chiew, V., & Wang, Y. (2006, May 8-10). Design of a cognitive complexities measurement and analysis tool (CCMAT). In *Proceedings of the 19th Canadian Conference on Electrical and Computer Engineering*, Ottawa, ON, Canada.

de Neufville, R., & Odoni, A. (2003). *Airport systems: Planning, design and management*. New York, NY: McGraw-Hill.

Debelack, A. S., Dehn, J. D., Muchinsky, L. L., & Smith, D. M. (2010). Next generation air traffic control automation. *IBM Systems Journal, 34*(1), 63–77. doi:10.1147/sj.341.0063

Fenton, N. E., & Pfleeger, S. L. (1997). *Software metrics: A rigorous & practical approach*. Boston, MA: PWS.

Fenton, N. E., & Pfleeger, S. L. (1998). *Software metrics: A rigorous and practical approach* (2nd ed.). Pacific Grove, CA: Brooks/Cole Wadsworth.

Gibbs, W. (1994). Software's chronic crisis. *Scientific American*, 86–95. doi:10.1038/scientificamerican0994-86

Guttag, J. V. (2002). Abstract data types, then and now. In Broy, M., & Denert, E. (Eds.), *Software pioneers* (pp. 443–452). Berlin, Germany: Springer-Verlag. doi:10.1007/978-3-642-59412-0_28

Halstead, M. H. (1977). *Elements of software science*. New York, NY: Elsevier North-Holland.

Hansman, R. J., & Odoni, A. (2009). Air traffic control. In Belobaba, P., Odoni, A., & Barnhart, C. (Eds.), *The global airline industry*. New York, NY: John Wiley & Sons. doi:10.1002/9780470744734.ch13

Hartmanis, J. (1994). On computational complexity and the nature of computer science, 1994 Turing award lecture. *Communications of the ACM, 37*(10), 37–43. doi:10.1145/194313.214781

Hartmanis, J., & Stearns, R. E. (1965). On the computational complexity of algorithms. *Transactions of the AMS, 117*, 258–306. doi:10.1090/S0002-9947-1965-0170805-7

Kearney, J. K., Sedlmeyer, R. L., Thompson, W. B., Gray, M. A., & Adler, M. A. (1986). Software complexity measurement. *Communications of the ACM, 29*(11), 1044–1050. doi:10.1145/7538.7540

Kontogiannis, T., & Malakis, S. (2009). A proactive approach to human error detection and identification in aviation and air traffic control. *Safety Science, 47*(5), 693–706. doi:10.1016/j.ssci.2008.09.007

Lewis, H. R., & Papadimitriou, C. H. (1998). *Elements of the theory of computation* (2nd ed.). Upper Saddle River, NJ: Prentice Hall.

Lipschutz, S., & Lipson, M. (1997). *Schaum's outline of theories and problems of discrete mathematics* (2nd ed.). New York, NY: McGraw-Hill.

McCabe, T. H. (1976). A complexity measure. *IEEE Transactions on Software Engineering, 2*(6), 308–320. doi:10.1109/TSE.1976.233837

McDaniel, E., & Lawrence, C. (1990). *Levels of cognitive complexity: An approach to the measurement of thinking* (pp. 1–49). New York, NY: Springer. doi:10.1007/978-1-4612-3420-3_1

McDermid, J. A. (Ed.). (1991). *Software engineer's reference book*. Oxford, UK: Butterworth-Heinemann.

Melton, A. (Ed.). (1996). *Software measurement*. International Thomson Computer Press.

Nolan, M. (1999). *Fundamentals of air traffic control* (3rd ed.). Pacific Grove, CA: Brooks/Cole Wadsworth.

Perry, T. S. (1997). In search of the future of air traffic control. *IEEE Spectrum, 34*(8), 18–35. doi:10.1109/6.609472

Peters, J. F., & Pedrycz, W. (2000). *Software engineering: An engineering approach*. New York, NY: John Wiley & Sons.

Ross, N. (1986). Air traffic control systems. In Bonsall, P., & Bell, M. (Eds.), *Information technology applications in transport* (pp. 165–189). Leiden, The Netherlands: VNU Science.

Sha, L., Rajkumar, R., & Lehoczky, J. P. (1990). Priority inheritance protocols: An approach to real-time synchronization. *IEEE Transactions on Computers, 1175*. doi:doi:10.1109/12.57058

Shao, J., & Wang, Y. (2003). A new measure of software complexity based on cognitive weights. *IEEE Canadian Journal of Electrical and Computer Engineering, 28*(2), 69–74. doi:10.1109/CJECE.2003.1532511

Smith, R. E. (1993). *Psychology*. Eagan, MN: West.

Tanenbaum, A. S. (1994). *Distributed operating systems*. Upper Saddle River, NJ: Prentice Hall.

Wang, Y. (2002a). The real-time process algebra (RTPA). *Annals of Software Engineering: An International Journal, 14*, 235–274. doi:10.1023/A:1020561826073

Wang, Y. (2002b, August). Keynote: On cognitive informatics. In *Proceedings of the First IEEE International Conference on Cognitive Informatics*, Calgary, AB, Canada (pp. 34-42). Washington, DC: IEEE Computer Society.

Wang, Y. (2003a). On cognitive informatics. *Brain and Mind: A Transdisciplinary Journal of Neuroscience and Neurophilosophy, 4*(2), 151-167.

Wang, Y. (2003b, May). The measurement theory for software engineering. In *Proceedings of the Canadian Conference on Electrical and Computer Engineering*, Montreal, QC, Canada (pp. 1321-1324). Washington, DC: IEEE Computer Society.

Wang, Y. (2005, August). Keynote: Psychological experiments on the cognitive complexities of fundamental control structures of software systems. In *Proceedings of the 4th IEEE International Conference on Cognitive Informatics* (pp. 4-5). Washington, DC: IEEE Computer Society.

Wang, Y. (2006). On the informatics laws and deductive semantics of software. *IEEE Transactions on Systems, Man and Cybernetics. Part C, Applications and Reviews, 36*(2), 161–171. doi:10.1109/TSMCC.2006.871138

Wang, Y. (2007a). *Software engineering foundations: A transdisciplinary and rigorous perspective* (CRC Book Series in Software Engineering, Vol. II). New York, NY: Auerbach.

Wang, Y. (2007b). The theoretical framework of cognitive informatics. *International Journal of Cognitive Informatics and Natural Intelligence, 1*(1), 1–27. doi:10.4018/jcini2007010101

Wang, Y. (2008a). On contemporary denotational mathematics for computational intelligence. *Transactions of Computational Science, 2*, 6–29. doi:10.1007/978-3-540-87563-5_2

Wang, Y. (2008b). On the Big-R notation for describing iterative and recursive behaviors. *International Journal of Cognitive Informatics and Natural Intelligence, 2*(1), 17–28. doi:10.4018/jcini.2008010102

Wang, Y. (2008c). RTPA: A denotational mathematics for manipulating intelligent and computational behaviors. *International Journal of Cognitive Informatics and Natural Intelligence, 2*(2), 44–62. doi:10.4018/jcini.2008040103

Wang, Y. (2008d). Mathematical laws of software. *Transactions of Computational Science, 2*, 46–83. doi:10.1007/978-3-540-87563-5_4

Wang, Y. (2008e). Deductive semantics of RTPA. *International Journal of Cognitive Informatics and Natural Intelligence, 2*(2), 95–121. doi:10.4018/jcini.2008040106

Wang, Y. (2009). On the cognitive complexity of software and its quantification and formal measurement. *International Journal of Software Science and Computational Intelligence, 1*(2), 31–53. doi:10.4018/jssci.2009040103

Wang, Y. (2010). On formal and cognitive semantics for semantic computing. *International Journal of Semantic Computing, 4*(2), 203–237. doi:10.1142/S1793351X10000833

Wang, Y., & Chiew, V. (2010). On the cognitive process of human problem solving. *Cognitive Systems Research, 11*(1), 81–92. doi:10.1016/j.cogsys.2008.08.003

Wang, Y., Ngolah, C. F., Zeng, G., Sheu, P. C.-Y., Choy, C. P., & Tian, Y. (2010). The formal design models of a real-time operating system (RTOS+): Conceptual and architectural frameworks. *International Journal of Software Science and Computational Intelligence, 2*(2), 105–122. doi:10.4018/jssci.2010040106

Wang, Y., Wang, Y., Patel, S., & Patel, D. (2006). A layered reference model of the brain (LRMB). [C]. *IEEE Transactions on Systems, Man, and Cybernetics, 36*(2), 124–133. doi:10.1109/TSMCC.2006.871126

Wang, Y., Zeng, G., Ngolah, C. F., Sheu, P. C.-Y., Choy, C. P., & Tian, Y. (2010). The formal design models of a real-time operating system (RTOS+): Static and dynamic behavior models. *International Journal of Software Science and Computational Intelligence, 2*(3), 79–105. doi:10.4018/jssci.2010070106

Zuse, H. (1997). *A framework of software measurement*. Berlin, Germany: Walter de Gruyter.

Chapter 14
The Formal Design Model of a File Management System (FMS)

Yingxu Wang
University of Calgary, Canada

Xinming Tan
Wuhan University of Technology, China

Cyprian F. Ngolah
Sentinel Trending & Diagnostics Ltd., Canada

Yousheng Tian
University of Calgary, Canada

Phillip C.-Y. Sheu
University of California, USA

ABSTRACT

Files are a typical abstract data type for data objects and software modeling, which provides a standard encapsulation and access interface for manipulating large-volume information and persistent data. File management systems are an indispensable component of operating systems and real-time systems for file manipulations. This paper develops a comprehensive design pattern of files and a File Management System (FMS). A rigorous denotational mathematics, Real-Time Process Algebra (RTPA), is adopted, which allows both architectural and behavioral models of files and FMS to be rigorously designed and implemented in a top-down approach. The conceptual model, architectural model, and the static/ dynamic behavioral models of files and FMS are systematically presented. This work has been applied in the design and modeling of a real-time operating system (RTOS+).

1. INTRODUCTION

A file is an encapsulation of structured data and information in both a logical form and a physical implementation (Hsiao & Harary, 1970; Roberts, 1972; Wang, Ngolah, Tan, et al., 2010). Files can be classified as *sequential* and *random* files. The former are files that organize information

as a list of ordered records; while the latter are files with sorted records by bi-directional links that can be directly accessed by the key of the record (McDermid, 1991; Wang, Zeng, Ngolah, et al., 2010; Wang, Ngolah, Zeng, et al., 2010). A file can be formally modeled by an abstract data type (Guttag, 1977; Broy et al., 1984; Cardelli & Wegner, 1985; Stubbs & Webre, 1985), which is

DOI: 10.4018/978-1-4666-2651-5.ch014

a logical model of a complex and/or user defined data structure with a set of predefined operations.

Definition 1: An *Abstract Data Type* (ADT) is an abstract model of data objects with a formal encapsulation of its logical architecture and predefined operations of the data object.

A number of ADTs have been identified in computing and system modeling such as *stack, queue, sequence, record, array, list, tree, file,* and *graph* (Broy et al., 1984; Wang, 2007; Wang, Ngolah, Tan, et al., 2010). ADTs possess the following properties: (i) An extension of type constructions by integrating both data structures and functional behaviors; (ii) A hybrid data object modeling technique that *encapsulates* both user defined data structures (types) and allowable operations on them; (iii) The interface and implementation of an ADT are separated. Detailed implementation of the ADT is hidden to applications that invoke the ADT and its predefined operations. Files are a typical ADT in data objects and software modeling, which provides a means for manipulating large volume and persistent information.

A *File Management System* (FMS) is an indispensable component of operating systems and real-time systems for file manipulation and maintenance. In this paper, the record-level behaviors of files will be modeled by a file ADT; while the system-level behaviors of files will be modeled by the FMS.

In order to rigorously model the file ADT and FMS, the denotational mathematics known as Real-Time Process Algebra (RTPA) (Wang, 2002, 2007, 2008a, 2008b, 2008c, 2008d, 2009a; Wang, Tan, & Ngolah, 2010) is adopted. According to the RTPA methodology for system modeling and refinement, a universal file and the FMS can be formally modeled using two fundamental techniques known as the unified data models and unified process models (Wang, 2007).

Definition 2: A *Unified Data Model* (UDM) is a *generic architectural* model of a software system, its internal control structures, and its interfaces with hardware components, which can be rigorously modeled and refined in denotational mathematics as a tuple, i.e.:

$$UDM \triangleq (\mathbf{R}_{i\mathbf{N}=1}^{n\mathbf{N}} < S_i \mid \forall e_i \in S_i, p(e_i) >) \tag{1}$$

Definition 3: The *Unified Process Model (UPM)* of a *program* $\wp$ is a composition of a finite set of *m* processes according to the time-, event-, and interrupt-based process dispatching rules (Box 1).

This paper develops a comprehensive design pattern of the file ADT and FMS. RTPA is adopted to rigorously design and implement both architectural and behavioral models of files and manipulations in a top-down approach. In the remainder of this paper, the conceptual model of the file ADT and FMS are described as the initial requirements for the system. The architectural

Box 1.

$$
\begin{aligned}
UPM &\triangleq \wp \\
&= \mathbf{R}_{k=1}^{m}(@e_k\mathbf{s} \hookmapsto P_k) \\
&= \mathbf{R}_{k=1}^{m}[@e_k\mathbf{s} \hookmapsto \mathbf{R}_{i=1}^{n-1}(s_i(k)\ r_{ij}(k)\ s_j(k))], j = i+1
\end{aligned} \tag{2}
$$

model of the file ADT and FMS are created as a set of UDMs based on the conceptual models using the RTPA architectural modeling methodologies. Then, the static behaviors of the file ADT and FMS are modeled and refined by a set of UPMs. The dynamic behaviors of the file ADT and FMS are formally specified and refined by process scheduling and system dispatching models with UPMs.

2. THE CONCEPTUAL MODELS OF FILES AND FMS

Various file structures have been empirically studied for information storage and retrieval (Hsiao & Harary, 1970; Roberts, 1972; Bollella, 2002; Silberschatz et al., 2003; Wang, Ngolah, Tan, et al., 2010). However, there is a lack of rigorous file model as an ADT with a set of formally specified behaviors. Further, the formal model of a file management system (FMS) and the set of administrative operations on files as a whole were not rigorously studied. This section describes the conceptual model of files and FMS. On the basis of the conceptual models as the design requirements, a set of formal models of files and FMS will be derived.

2.1 The Conceptual Model of the File ADT

Files are a typical ADT for manipulating large-volume information and persistent data with a standard encapsulation and access interface. Files are characterized by the separation of its logical interface and physical implementation in design and implementations.

Definition 4: A *file* is an abstract model of a large set of data records that can be permanently stored in memory and accessed sequentially or directly.

The basic unit of a file is a record, which is a structure with a certain type of data and a unique key. Records in a file may be arranged in a sequential or sorted format. A file with these internal structures is called a sequential or a random file, respectively. A sequential file may be accessed by sequential read and appended write. A random file is accessed by indexed read and order-reserving write (insert).

Figure 1 shows an indexed-record architectural model of the file ADT, where the file is represented by two components known as the index table and the records. This conceptual architecture of files enables information to be accessed by the mechanism of two-stage mappings, i.e.:

$$Index\mathbf{N} \rightarrow Key\mathbf{N} \rightarrow Record\mathbf{RT} \qquad (3)$$

The advantage of the File ADT architecture as modeled in Figure 1 using a set of indexed records, rather than a linked list, is that it allows a record to be inserted, deleted, and/or appended without changing the logical and physical order of any existing record. Instead, it just requires a change of the mapping pointer from the index table to the records. Therefore, the novel conceptual model supports both sequential and random access to files. Using the key of a record, the target record can be randomly accessed; while using the entry index via the index table, the target record can be sequentially accessed according to its order of creation. Another advantage of this approach is that the index table is small and can be held in main memory while physical records are stored in the secondary memory. This is an important feature for a file management system in real-time operating systems where memory is limited.

2.2 The Conceptual Model of the FMS

Definition 5: A *File Management System* (FMS) is a subsystem of an operating system that manages a set of files as well as their status, resources, and access paths.

Figure 1. The conceptual architecture of files using indexed-records

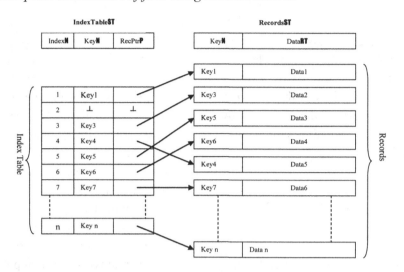

The major function of an FMS is to map logical files onto physical storage devices such as internal memory or external disks. Most file systems organize files by a tree-structured directory. A file in the file system can be identified by its name and detailed attributes provided by the file directory. The most frequently used method for directory management is a *hash table*. A physical file system can be implemented by contiguous, linked, and indexed allocation. Contiguous allocation may suffer from external fragmentation. Direct-access is inefficient with linked allocation. Indexed allocation may require substantial overheads for its index block.

On the basis of the conceptual models of files and FMS, formal design models for Files**ST** and FMS**ST** can be developed in a rigorous and systematical approach using RTPA (Wang, 2002, 2008c, 2008d). According to the RTPA methodology for system modeling, specification, and refinement (Wang, 2007, 2008d), the top-level RTPA specification of Files**ST** and FMS**ST** are given in Figures 2 and 3, respectively, where || indicates that the three subsystems are related in parallel, and **§**, **ST**, and **PC** are type suffixes of *system, system structure,* and *process,* respectively (Wang, 2007).

The following sections create and refine the UDM models of Files**ST** and FMS**ST** according the top-level specification given in Figures 2 and 3. Then, the static and dynamic behavioural models, FilesST.StaticBehaviorsPC, FilesST.DynamicBehaviorsPC, FMSST.StaticBehaviorsPC, and FMSST.DynamicBehaviorsPC, will be developed and refined in Sections 5 and 6.

3. THE ARCHITECTURAL MODELS OF THE FILE ADT AND FMS

According to Definition 2, a UDM is a generic architectural model of a software system as well as its hardware components, interfaces, and internal control structures. This section develops formal architectural models of the file ADT and FMS using UDM modeling technologies.

Figure 2. The UDM of the top-level architecture of file ADTs

§(Files) ≜ Files**§**.Architecture**ST**
    || Files**§**.StaticBehaviors**PC**
    || Files**§**.DynamicBehaviors**PC**

Figure 3. The UDM of the top-level architecture of the FMS

$(FMS) ≜ FMS§.Architecture**ST**
|| FMS§.StaticBehaviors**PC**
|| FMS§.DynamicBehaviors**PC**

3.1 The UDM of the File ADT

Based on the conceptual model of files informally described in Section 2.1, the UDM of the file architecture can be formally specified. The UDM of file ADT, Files**ST**, is modeled using a pair of two components known as the index table, IndexTable**ST**, and a set of records, Records**ST**, both modeled as an array as shown in Figure 4. The IndexTable**ST**

is a system structure (**ST**) that uses index**N** to find the key, Key**N**, in the index table, which points to a certain record in Records**ST**. The Records**ST** is another system structure for files with a set of records that holds the information Data**RT** indexed by Key**N**, where **RT** denotes the data in a flexible type determinable at run-time. It is noteworthy that the relations among all records in Records**ST**, or the sequential or structural relations of the data in a file, are defined by the IndexTable**ST**. That is, the IndexTable**ST** is a sequential structure relating to the creation time of a record; while Records**ST** is a sorted series of records determined by the keys. This flexible two-stage structure of Files**ST** supports both sequential and random access to the file. Using the key of a record, Key**N**, the target

Figure 4. The UDM architecture of the file ADT

```
Files ST ≜ FileID ST ::
              (<#Records N | 0 ≤ #Records N ≤ MaxRecords N>;
                    #Records N
              <    R    (<IndexTable(Index N) ST: Array ST>, <Records(Key N) ST: Array ST>;
                  Index N=0
              <Created BL | Created BL = {(T, Yes), (F, No)}>;
              <Opened BL | Opened BL = {(T, Yes), (F, No)}>;
              <Closed BL | Closed BL = {(T, Yes), (F, No)}>;
              <Saved BL | Saved BL = {(T, Yes), (F, No)}>;
              <Full BL | Full BL = {(T, Yes), (F, No)}>;
              <Empty BL | Empty BL = {(T, Yes), (F, No)}>;
              <Renamed BL | Renamed BL = {(T, Yes), (F, No)}>;
              <Copied BL | Copied BL = {(T, Yes), (F, No)}>;
              <Cleared BL | Cleared BL = {(T, Yes), (F, No)}>;
              <Saved BL | Saved BL = {(T, Yes), (F, No)}>;
              )
                                                         #Records N
FileID ST.IndexTable(Index N) ST ≜     R    (< Index : N | 0 ≤ Index N ≤ #Records N>;
                                          Index N=0
                                                    <Key : N>
                                                    )

FileID ST.Records(Key N) ST ≜
       #Records N
       R    (<Key : N | 0 ≤ Key N ≤ #Records N>;
      Key N=0
              <Data : RT>;
              <Inserted BL | Inserted BL = {(T, Yes), (F, No)}>;
              <Retrieved BL | Retrieved BL = {(T, Yes), (F, No)}>;
              <Updated BL | Updated BL = {(T, Yes), (F, No)}>;
              <Appended BL | Appended BL = {(T, Yes), (F, No)}>;
              <Deleted BL | Deleted BL = {(T, Yes), (F, No)}>;
              )
```

record can be randomly (directly) accessed; while the entries in IndexTable**N** can be sequentially accessed to locate a particular record through its index generated over time when a record is created.

A number of control variables are specified in Files**ST**. FileID**ST** represents the name of a specific file modeled by Files**ST**. #Record**N** is the maximum number of records controlled by the capacity of the file. In addition, a set of operation status as Boolean variables is specified in Records**ST** denoting the results of record operations such as inserted, retrieved, updated, appended, and deleted. Similarly, a set of operation status is specified in FileID**ST** denoting the results of file-level operations such as created, opened, closed, saved, empty, full, renamed, copied, cleared, and deleted.

3.2 The UDM of FMS

FMS provides administrative and resource management for a large set of individual files modeled as an ADT in the previous subsection. The FMS is a typical structure of computing systems and an important part of abstract resources as well as their handling in operating systems (Silberschatz et al., 2003; Wang, Zeng, Ngolah, et al., 2010; Wang, Ngolah, Zeng, et al., 2010). FMS is often a part of an operating system or a system with databases and permanent records of information.

Based on the conceptual model of the FMS architecture informally described in Section 2.2, the UDM of the FMS architecture can be formally specified as shown in Figure 5.

FMS**ST** models a set of files up to the system capacity specified by #Files**N**. Each file in FMS-

ST is a pair of components with the logical file and its physical implementation. The logical files are in the type of Files**ST**, while the corresponding physical files are modeled by a memory block, MEM**ST**, in internal memory or external storage of a computing system.

4. THE BEHAVIORAL PROCESS MODELS OF THE FILE ADT

The behaviors and operations of files can be categorized at two levels: the entire file and its internal records. The former is modeled by the FMS for file and memory resource administration; while the latter is modeled by the file ADT for record-level manipulations under the support of FMS. This section describes the static behaviors of the file ADT using UPM models. The UPMs of FMS will be developed in next section.

A static behavior is an encapsulated function of a given system that can be determined before run-time (Wang, 2007). The static behaviors of the file ADT, Files**§**.StaticBehaviors**PC**, can be described via operations on its architectural models (UDMs), i.e., Files**§**.Architecture**PC**.

4.1 The Top Level UPM of the File ADT

On the basis of the UDM models of Files**ST** developed in the preceding subsection, the behaviors of the file ADT can be modeled as a set of UPMs operating on the UDMs of Files**ST** and related input variables. The high-level behavioral model of the file ADT is specified by Files**§**.StaticBe-

Figure 5. The UDM architecture of the FMS

$$
\begin{aligned}
\mathbf{FMSST} \triangleq (\ &<\#Files : \mathbf{N}\ |\ 0 \le \#Files\mathbf{N} \le MaxFiles\mathbf{N}\text{-}1>; \\
&< \overset{\#Files\mathbf{N}}{\underset{i\mathbf{N}=1}{R}} (<LogicalFile(i\mathbf{N})\mathbf{ST}: Files\mathbf{ST}>, <PhysicalFile(i\mathbf{N})\mathbf{ST}: MEM\mathbf{ST}>)>; \\
&)
\end{aligned}
$$

haviors**PC** as shown in Figure 6. The schemas of the UPMs in Figure 6 model the input data objects (<**I**:: (…)>), output data objects (<**O**:: (…)>), and operated UDMs (<**UDM**:: (…)>) for each specific process of Files**ST**. The UDMs play an important role in system architectural design as global and permanent I/O structures, which usually have a longer life-span than those of the process(es) that created and/or invoked them, particularly in a real-time system.

4.2 UPMs of the Behavioral Processes of the File ADT

In the following subsections, each of the static behaviors of the file ADT, Files**§**.StaticBehaviors**PC**, as given in Figure 6 will be further refined by a set of UPMs using the denotational mathematical notations and methodologies of RTPA.

a) The UPM of the Insert Record Process

The *insert record* process of Files**§**, InsertRec**PC**, is formally modeled as shown in Figure 7, which writes a new record into the file based on the value of its key in the sorted list of all records. The input arguments of the process are the target file ID, the key and data of the record. Its outputs are the status of the insert operation and the sequential index assigned to the inserted record in the index table. InsertRec**PC** is a write operation on to a physically existing and logically opened file. When the file is not full, the process generates a sequential index, Index**N**, based on the current number of records in the file, FileID**ST**.#Record**N**, before it is updated by one. Index**N** is then used to find the assigned

location of the new record in the index table. The key of the record is registered in IndexTable**ST** determined by the index, and the data of the record is written into Records**ST** indexed by the key. When the key of the given record is out of range or the file is full, InsertRec**PC** generates a specific error message FileID**ST**.Records**ST**.Inserted**BL**:=**F**.

b) The UPM of the Retrieve Record Process

The *retrieve record* process of Files**ST**, RetrieveRec**PC**, is formally modeled as shown in Figure 8, which reads the contents of a specific record in the given file. The input arguments of the process are the target file ID and the key of the given record. Its outputs are the contents of the record and the status of the retrieve operation. RetrieveRec**PC** is a read-only operation to report the data contents of the target record in Files**ST**. RetrieveRec**PC** checks if the file has been opened and if the given key, Key**N**, is valid in the current scope of records in the file. If so, it allocates the matched record in Records**ST** by Key**N**, and outputs data**RT** from the record. Then, the operation status is set as FileID**ST**.Records**ST**.Retrieved**BL**:= **T**. When the file is not opened or the key is out of scope, RetrieveRec**PC** generates a specific error message FileID**ST**.Records**ST**.Retrieved**BL**:= **F**.

c) The UPM of the Update Record Process

The *update record* process of Files**ST**, UpdateRec**PC**, is formally modeled as shown in Figure 9, which changes the data of a specific record in the file. The input arguments of the process are

Figure 6. The high-level behavioral model of the file ADT

```
Files §.StaticBehaviors PC ≙
{   InsertRec PC(<I:: FileID S, Key N, Data RT>; <O:: FileID ST.Records ST.Inserted BL, Index N>; <UDM:: FileID ST>)
 | RetrieveRec PC(<I:: FileID S, Key N>; <O:: Data RT, FileID ST.Records ST.Retrieved BL>; <UDM:: FileID ST>)
 | UpdateRec PC(<I:: FileID S, Key N, Data RT>; <O:: FileID ST.Records ST.Updated BL>; <UDM:: FileID ST>)
 | AppendRec PC(<I:: FileID S, Key N, Data RT>; <O:: FileID ST.Records ST.Appended BL>; <UDM:: FileID ST>)
 | DeleteRec PC(<I:: FileID S, Key N>; <O:: FileID ST.Records ST.Deleted BL>; <UDM:: FileID ST>)
}
```

Figure 7. The UPM model of the insert record process

```
InsertRecPC(<I:: FileID S, Key N, DataRT>; <O:: FileID ST.RecordsST.InsertedBL, IndexN>;
            <UDM:: FileID ST>) ≙
{
  → ( ◆ FileIDST.OpenedBL = T
        → ( ◆ 0 ≤ #RecordN < MaxRecordN
              → IndexN := FileIDST.#RecordN
              → ↑(FileIDST.#RecordN)
              → FileID ST.IndexTable(IndexN)ST.Key N := Key N
              → FileID ST.Records(Key N)ST.DataRT := DataRT
                 → FileIDST.RecordsST.InsertedBL := T
            | ◆~
                 → FileIDST.RecordsST.InsertedBL := F
                 → ! ("Record index is out of range or File is full.")
          )
      | ◆~
          → FileIDST.RecordsST.InsertedBL := F
          → ! (" 'FileIDST' has not been opened. ")
    )
}
```

the target file ID, the key of the specific record, and the data to be updated. Its output is the status of the update operation. Before the operation is carried out, UpdateRecPC checks if the file has been opened and if the given key, KeyN, is valid in the current scope of records in the file. If so, it allocates the matched record in RecordsST by KeyN, and writes new data into the record. Then, the operation status is set as FileIDST.RecordsST.UpdatedBL:= T. When the file is not opened or the key is out of scope, UpdateRecPC generates

a specific error message FileIDST.RecordsST.UpdatedBL:= F.

d) The UPM of the Append Record Process

The *append record* process of FilesST, AppendRecPC, is formally modeled as shown in Figure 10, which adds a new record at the tail of the file. The input arguments of the process are the target file ID, and the new record in the pair (KeyN,

Figure 8. The UPM model of the retrieve record process

```
RetrieveRecPC(<I:: FileID S, Key N>; <O:: Data RT, FileID ST.RecordsST.RetrievedBL>;
              <UDM:: FileID ST>) ≙
{
  → ( ◆ FileIDST.OpenedBL = T
        → ( ◆ 0 ≤ KeyN ≤ #RecordN
              → DataRT := FileID ST.Records(Key N)ST.DataRT
              → FileIDST.RecordsST.RetrievedBL := T
            | ◆~
              → FileIDST.RecordsST.RetrievedBL := F
              → ! ("Record index is out of range.")
          )
      | ◆~
          → FileIDST.RecordsST.RetrievedBL := F
          → ! (" 'FileIDST' has not been opened. ")
    )
}
```

Figure 9. The UPM model of the update record process

```
UpdateRecPC(<I:: FileID S, Key N, DataRT>; <O:: FileID ST.RecordsST.UpdatedBL>;
              <UDM:: FileID ST>) ≜
{
  → ( ◆ FileIDST.OpenedBL = T
          → ( ◆ 0 ≤ KeyN ≤ #RecordN
                  → FileID ST.Records(Key N)ST.DataRT := DataRT
                    → FileIDST.RecordsST.UpdatedBL := T
              | ◆~
                    → FileIDST.RecordsST.UpdatedBL := F
                    → ! ("Record key is out of range.")
            )
      | ◆~
            → FileIDST.RecordsST.UpdatedBL := F
            → ! (" 'FileIDST' has not been opened. ")
      )
}
```

Data$N$). Its output is the status of the append operation. AppendRec**PC** checks if the file has been opened and if it is not full. If so, it increases the number of records, #Records$N$, in the file by one, and generates the index address, Index$N$, for the new record in the index table. Then, the new record for appending, (Key$N$, Data$N$), is added to the end of Files**ST** and the last Files**ST** element in the index table is updated to point to the appended record. As a result, the operation status is set as FileID**ST**.Records**ST**.Appended**BL**:= **T**. When the file is not opened or full, AppendRec**PC** generates a specific error message FileID**ST**.Records**ST**.Appended**BL**:= **F**.

e) The UPM of the Delete Record Process

The *delete record* process of Files**§**, DeleteRec**PC**, is formally modeled as shown in Figure 11, which logically removes a record from the file based on a given key. The input arguments

Figure 10. The UPM model of the append record process

```
AppendRecPC(<I:: FileID S, Key N, DataRT>; <O:: FileID ST.RecordsST.AppendedBL>;
              <UDM:: FileID ST>) ≜
{
  → ( ◆ FileIDST.OpenedBL = T
          → ( ◆ 0 ≤ #RecordN < MaxRecordN
                  → ↑(FileIDST.#RecordN)
                  → IndexN := FileIDST.#RecordN
                  → FileID ST.IndexTable(IndexN)ST.Key N := Key N
                  → FileID ST.Records(Key N)ST.DataRT := DataRT
                  → FileIDST.RecordsST.AppendedBL := T
              | ◆~
                    → FileIDST.RecordsST.AppendedBL := F
                    → ! (" 'FileIDST' is full.")
            )
      | ◆~
            → FileIDST.RecordsST.AppendedBL := F
            → ! (" 'FileIDST' has not been opened. ")
      )
}
```

of the process are the target file ID and the key of the record. Its outputs are the status of the delete operation. When the file is open and not empty, DeleteRec**PC** checks if the given key, Key**N**, is valid in the current scope of records in the file. If so, it allocates the matched record Index**N** in IndexTable**ST** by Key**N**. The information (Key**N**, Data**N**) corresponding to the specific record are reset to undefined (⊥). After the logical deletion of the record, the IndexTable**ST** will be rearranged where the remaining index (Index**N**, Key**N**) following the deleted record in the index table will be shifted one element to the front. Then, the number of records in the file, #Record**N**, is reduced by one and the operation status is set as FileID**ST**.Records**ST**.Deleted**BL**:= **T**. When the key of the given record is out of range or the file is empty, DeleteRec**PC** generates a specific error message FileID**ST**.Records**ST**.Deleted**BL**:= **F**.

It is noteworthy that if the file architecture adopts the traditional bi-directionally linked record chain, a delete record operation may result in a need to rearrange the double pointers of all remaining records following the deleted record in the chain. Therefore, the cost and complexity would be quite high. However, the two-level indexed record structure for files as designed in the architecture, Files**ST**, only requires the updating of the simple IndexTable**ST**, which may be maintained in the internal memory.

Figsures 7 through 11 describe a set of five UPMs of the file ADT in a coherent design and using a unified formal notation. With the RTPA specification and refinement methodology, the mechanisms, architectures, and behaviors of Files**ST** at the record-level are rigorously and precisely modeled. The next section describes file manipulations at the system level.

5. THE BEHAVIORAL PROCESS MODELS OF FMS

The record-level manipulation behaviors of Files**§**.StaticBehaviors**PC** have been modeled in the preceding section. The system-level behaviors of the file management system, FMS**§**.StaticBehaviors**PC**, will be developed in this section that manipulate files as a whole based on the architectural models (UDMs) FMS**§**.Architecture**ST**.

5.1 The Top Level UPM of the File ADT

The UPMs of behaviors of the file management system, FMS**§**.StaticBehaviors**PC**, can be modeled by a set of 10 behavioral processes for file system administrations and file manipulations as shown in Figure 12.

5.2 UPMs of the Behavioral Processes of FMS

The following subsections describe how each of the 10 behavioral processes of FMS**§**.StaticBehaviors**PC** as specified in Figure 12 is modeled and refined using the denotational mathematical notations and methodologies of RTPA.

a) The UPM of the Create File Process

The *create file* process of FMS**§**, CreateFile**PC**, is formally modeled as shown in Figure 13, which establishes a new file in system memory or disk and links it to a specified logical ID of file. The input arguments of the process are the given name of the file as well as its size and the type of data in records. The output result of the process is the status of file creation operation. CreateFile**PC** calls a system support process, AllocateObject**PC**, to set up a physical file and links it to the logical name of FileID**ST**. If a memory block is successfully allocated, CreateFile**PC** sets the initial value of each status of file manipulations as modeled in FSM**ST**; otherwise, it reports an error FMS**§**.Created**BL**:= **F**. In case the given FileID**ST** has already existed, CreateFile**PC** results in a specific error message FMS**§**.Created**BL**:= **F**.

In Figure 14, the support processes, AllocateObject**PC**, is designed for dynamic memory

Figure 11. The UPM model of the delete record process

```
DeleteRecPC(<I:: FileIDS, KeyN>; <O:: FileIDST.RecordsST.DeletedBL>; <UDM:: FileIDST>) ≙
{
  → ( ◆ FileIDST.OpenedBL = T
        → ( ◆ 0 ≤ KeyN ≤ #RecordN
                      #RecordN
              →     R    ( ◆ FileIDST.IndexTable(iN)ST.KeyN = KeyN
                    iN=0
                              → FileIDST.Records(KeyN)ST.DataRT := ⊥
                              → FileIDST.Records(KeyN)ST.KeyN := ⊥
                                            #RecordN-1
                              →          R          (FileIDST.IndexTable(jN)ST.KeyN := FileIDST.Index(jN+1)ST.KeyN)
                                         jN=iN
                              → ↓(FileIDST.#RecordN)
                              → FileIDST.RecordsST.DeletedBL := T
                              → ∅
                    )
              | ◆~
                    → FileIDST.RecordsST.DeletedBL := F
                    → ! ("Key is out of range.")
            )
      | ◆~
            → FileIDST.RecordsST.DeletedBL := F
            → ! (" 'FileIDST' has not been opened. ")
    )
}
```

allocation and management for file creation. The AllocateObjectPC process as shown in Figure 14 finds out a suitable block of available memory for the requiring ObjectST, whose size, ObjectST. SizeB, is determined by:

$$ObjectST.SizeB = \#ElementsN \times Byte(ElementTypeRT)N \quad (4)$$

AllocateObjectPC repetitively requests a unit of suitable bytes for each element of ObjectST. Then, it links the logical ID of the object to the allocated memory block denoted by the RTPA memory allocation operator ObjectIDS ⇐ MEM(ObjectIDS)ST. If memory allocation is failed, AllocateObjectPC feeds back an error message ObjectIDST.ExistedBL = F.

b) The UPM of the Open File Process

The *open file* process of FMS§, OpenPC, is formally modeled as shown in Figure 15, which logically opens a given file in order to give access to a certain user and, at the same time, to prevent any other users to open it concurrently. The input argument of the process is the given file ID. Its output is the status of the open operation. OpenPC checks if the specific file has been created and is not currently open by any other process. If so, it seizes the FileIDST by setting it as being opened, i.e., FileIDST.OpenedBL:= T and

Figure 12. The high-level behavioral model of FMS

```
FMS§.StaticBehaviorsPC ≙
  (  CreateFilePC (<I:: FileID S, SizeN, ElementRT>; <O:: FileID ST.CreatedBL>; <UDM:: FMS ST, Files ST>)
   | OpenPC (<I:: FileIDS>; <O:: FileIDST.OpenedBL>; <UDM:: FMSST, FilesST>)
   | ClosePC (<I:: FileIDS>; <O:: FileIDST.ClosedBL>; <UDM:: FMSST, FilesST>)
   | SavePC (<I:: FileIDS>; <O:: FileIDST.SavedBL>; <UDM:: FMSST, FilesST>)
   | EmptyTestPC (<I:: FileIDS>; <O:: FileIDST.EmptyBL>; <UDM:: FMSST, FilesST>)
   | FullTestPC (<I:: FileIDS>; <O:: FileIDST.FullBL>; <UDM:: FMSST, FilesST>)
   | ReNamePC (<I:: FileIDS, NewFileNameS>; <O:: FileIDST.RenamedBL>; <UDM:: FMSST, FilesST>)
   | CopyPC (<I:: FileIDS, NewFileNameS>; <O:: FileIDST.CopiedBL>; <UDM:: FMSST, FilesST>)
   | ClearPC (<I:: FileIDS>; <O:: FileIDST.ClearedBL>; <UDM:: FMSST, FilesST>)
   | DeleteFilePC (<I:: FileIDS>; <O:: FileIDST.DeletedBL>; <UDM:: FMSST, FilesST>)
  )
```

Figure 13. The UPM model of the file creation process

```
CreateFilePC(<I:: FileID S, SizeN, DataTypeRT>;
              <O:: FileID ST.CreatedBL>; <UDM:: FMS ST, Files ST>) ≙
{
  → ( ◆ FileIDST.CreatedBL = F
        → ObjectIDS := FileIDS
        → #ElementsN := FileIDST.SizeN
        → ElementTypeRT := DataTypeRT
        ↣ AllocateObjectPC(<I:: ObjectIDS, #ElementsN, ElementTypeRT)>;
                          <O:: ObjectAllocatedBL>; <UDM:: MEMST>)
              → ( ◆ ObjectAllocatedBL = T
                    → FileIDS ⇐ MEM(ObjectIDS)ST
                    → FileIDST.SizeN := SizeN
                    → FileIDST.#RecordN := 0
                    → IndexTableST(0N).KeyRT := ⊥
                    → RecordsST(0N).DataRT := ⊥
                    → FileIDST.CreatedBL := T
                    → FileIDST.OpenedBL := F
                    → FileIDST.ClosedBL := T
                    → FileIDST.SavedBL := T
                    → FileIDST.EmptyBL := T
                    → FileIDST.FullBL := F
                    → FileIDST.RenamedBL := F
                    → FileIDST.CopiedlBL := F
                    → FileIDST.ClearedBL := F
                    → FileIDST.ReleasedBL := F
                 | ◆~
                    → FileIDST.CreatedBL := F
                    → ! (" 'FileIDST' creation is failed.")
                 )
     | ◆~
        → FileIDST.CreatedBL := F
        → ! (" 'StackIDST' has already been existed.")
     )
}
```

Figure 14. The UPM model of the allocate object process

```
AllocateObjectPC(<I:: ObjectIDS, #ElementsN, ElementTypeRT >;
                 <O:: ObjectIDST.ExistedBL>, <UDM:: ObjectIDST, MemoryST>) ≙
{
  nN := #ElementsN
       nN
  → R    New (ObjectID(iN)ST : ElementTypeRT)
     iN=1
  → ( ◆ ObjectAllocatedBL = T
        → ObjectIDS ⇐ MEM(ObjectIDS)ST
        → ObjectIDST.ExistedBL := T
     | ◆ ~
        → ObjectIDST.ExistedBL := F
     )
}
```

Figure 15. The UPM model of the open file process

```
OpenPC(<I:: File ID S>; <O:: FileID ST.OpenedBL>; <UDM:: FMS ST, Files ST>) ≜
{
  → ( ◆ FileIDST.CreatedBL = T ∧ FileIDST.OpenedBL = F
          → FileIDST.OpenedBL := T
          → FileIDST.ClosedBL := F

      | ◆~
          → FileIDST.OpenedBL := F
          → ! (" 'FileIDST' has not been created or is being used.")
      )
}
```

FileIDST.ClosedBL:= F. Otherwise, it reports an error FileIDST.OpenedBL:= F.

c) The UPM of the Close File Process

The *close file* process of FMS§, ClosePC, is formally modeled as shown in Figure 16, which logically closes a given file in order to maintain its data safety and allow new access by any other user. The input argument of the process is the given file ID. Its output is the status of the close operation. ClosePC checks if the specific file has been created and is currently open. If so, it closes the FileIDST by setting FileIDST.ClosedBL:= T and FileIDST.OpenedBL:= F. Otherwise, it reports an error FileIDST.ClosedBL:= F.

d) The UPM of the Save File Process

The *save file* process of FMS§, SavePC, is formally modeled as shown in Figure 17, which saves all

current records of the file into permanent storage device such as a disk. The input argument of the process is the given file ID. Its output is the status of the save operation. SavePC checks if the specific file has been created and is opened. If so, it repetitively saves each record of the file into the disk modeled by MEMST(BaseAddressP + OffsetP)RT. The BaseAddressP of the file is determined by the addressing mechanism of RTPA, i.e., BaseAddressP ⇒ MEM(FileIDS)ST. The OffsetP of the file is determined by the sequential index number iN in the IndexTableST. After all records have been saved in a disk, SavePC sets FileIDST.SavedBL:= T. Otherwise, it reports an error FileIDST.SavedBL:= F.

e) The UPM of the File Empty Test Process

The *empty test* process of FMS§, EmptyTestPC, is formally modeled as shown in Figure 18, which

Figure 16. The UPM model of the close file process

```
ClosePC(<I:: File ID S>; <O:: FileID ST.ClosedBL>; <UDM:: FMS ST, Files ST>) ≜
{
  → ( ◆ FileIDST.CreatedBL = T ∧ FileIDST.OpenedBL = T
          → FileIDST.ClosedBL := T
          → FileIDST.OpenedBL := F
      | ◆~
          → FileIDST.ClosedBL := F
          → ! (" 'FileIDST' has not been created or was not opened.")
      )
}
```

Figure 17. The UPM model of the save file process

$$
\begin{aligned}
&\text{Save}\textbf{PC}(<\textbf{I}:: \text{FileID}\textbf{S}>; <\textbf{O}:: \text{FileID}\textbf{ST}.\text{Saved}\textbf{BL}>; <\textbf{UDM}:: \text{FMS}\textbf{ST}, \text{Files}\textbf{ST}>) \triangleq \\
&\{ \\
&\quad \rightarrow (\ \blacklozenge\ \text{FileID}\textbf{ST}.\text{Created}\textbf{BL} = \textbf{T} \wedge \text{FileID}\textbf{ST}.\text{Opened}\textbf{BL} = \textbf{T} \\
&\qquad\qquad \rightarrow \text{Offset}\textbf{P} := 0 \\
&\qquad\qquad \rightarrow \text{BaseAddress}\textbf{P} \Rightarrow \text{MEM}(\text{FileID}\textbf{S})\textbf{ST} \\
&\qquad\qquad\qquad\quad^{\#\text{Records}\textbf{N}} \\
&\qquad\qquad \rightarrow \underset{i\textbf{N}=1}{R} \quad (\ \rightarrow \text{Key}\textbf{N} := \text{FileID}\textbf{ST}.\text{IndexTable}(i\textbf{N})\textbf{ST}.\text{Key}\textbf{N} \\
&\qquad\qquad\qquad\qquad\qquad \rightarrow \text{MEM}\textbf{ST}(\text{BaseAddress}\textbf{P} + \text{Offset}\textbf{P})\textbf{RT} := \text{FileID}\textbf{ST}.\text{Records}(\text{Key}\textbf{N})\textbf{ST}.\text{Data}\textbf{RT} \\
&\qquad\qquad\qquad\qquad\qquad \rightarrow \uparrow(\text{Offset}\textbf{P}) \\
&\qquad\qquad\qquad\qquad\qquad) \\
&\qquad\qquad \rightarrow \text{FileID}\textbf{ST}.\text{Saved}\textbf{BL} := \textbf{T} \\
&\qquad | \blacklozenge\sim \\
&\qquad\qquad \rightarrow \text{FileID}\textbf{ST}.\text{Saved}\textbf{BL} := \textbf{F} \\
&\qquad\qquad \rightarrow !\ (\text{`` `FileID}\textbf{ST'} \text{ does not exist and/or didn't open."}) \\
&\quad) \\
&\}
\end{aligned}
$$

detects whether a given file is empty. The input argument of the process is the target file ID. Its output is the status of the file as being empty. The status of an empty file is characterized by FileID$\textbf{ST}$.#Records$\textbf{N}$ = 0. Therefore, EmptyTest$\textbf{PC}$ verifies if the number of records in the file is zero in order to determine whether the file is empty or not. When the given file does not exist or has not been opened, EmptyTest$\textbf{PC}$ generates a specific error message FileID$\textbf{ST}$.Empty$\textbf{BL}$:= $\textbf{F}$.

f) The UPM of the File Full Test Process

The *full test* process of the FMS$\textbf{§}$, FullTest$\textbf{PC}$, is formally modeled as shown in Figure 19, which detects whether a given file is full. The input argument of the process is the target file ID. Its output

is the status of the file as being full. The status of a full file is characterized by FileID$\textbf{ST}$.#Records$\textbf{N}$ = FileID$\textbf{ST}$.Size$\textbf{N}$. Therefore, FullTest$\textbf{PC}$ verifies if the file size has reached the maximum byte of allocated memory in order to determine whether the file is full or not. When the given file does not exist or has no been opened, FullTest$\textbf{PC}$ generates a specific error message FileID$\textbf{ST}$.Full$\textbf{BL}$:= $\textbf{F}$.

g) The UPM of the File Rename Process

The *file rename* process of FMS$\textbf{§}$, ReName$\textbf{PC}$, is formally modeled as shown in Figure 20, which replace the ID of a file by a new name. The input arguments of the process are the given file ID and the new name of the file. Its output is the status

Figure 18. The UPM model of the empty file test process

$$
\begin{aligned}
&\text{EmptyTest}\textbf{PC}(<\textbf{I}:: \text{File ID }\textbf{S}>; <\textbf{O}:: \text{File ID }\textbf{ST}.\text{Empty}\textbf{BL}>; <\textbf{UDM}:: \text{FMS }\textbf{ST}, \text{Files}\textbf{ST}>) \triangleq \\
&\{ \\
&\quad \rightarrow (\ \blacklozenge\ \text{FileID}\textbf{ST}.\text{Created}\textbf{BL} = \textbf{T} \wedge \text{FileID}\textbf{ST}.\text{Opened}\textbf{BL} = \textbf{T} \\
&\qquad\quad \rightarrow (\ \blacklozenge\ \text{FileID}\textbf{ST}.\text{\#Records}\textbf{N} = 0 \\
&\qquad\qquad\qquad \rightarrow \text{FileID}\textbf{ST}.\text{Empty}\textbf{BL} := \textbf{T} \\
&\qquad\qquad\qquad \rightarrow \text{FileID}\textbf{ST}.\text{Full}\textbf{BL} := \textbf{F} \\
&\qquad\qquad | \blacklozenge\sim \\
&\qquad\qquad\qquad \rightarrow \text{FileID}\textbf{ST}.\text{Empty}\textbf{BL} := \textbf{F} \\
&\qquad\quad) \\
&\quad | \blacklozenge\sim \\
&\qquad \rightarrow \text{FileID}\textbf{ST}.\text{Empty}\textbf{BL} := \textbf{F} \\
&\qquad \rightarrow !\ (\text{`` `FileID}\textbf{ST'} \text{ does not exist."}) \\
&\quad) \\
&\}
\end{aligned}
$$

Figure 19. The UPM model of the full file test process

```
FullTestPC(<I:: File ID S>; <O:: FileID ST.Full BL>; <UDM:: FMS ST, Files ST>) ≙
{
  → ( ◆ FileIDST.CreatedBL = T ∧ FileIDST.OpenedBL = T
          → ( ◆ FileIDST. #RecordsN = FileIDST.SizeN
                  → FileIDST.FullBL := T
                  → FileIDST.EmptyBL := F
              | ◆~
                  → FileIDST.FullBL := F
              )
    | ◆~
          → FileIDST.FullBL := F
          → ! (" 'FileIDST' does not exist.")
      )
}
```

of the rename operation. ReNamePC checks if the specific file has been created and is currently closed. If so, it re-allocates the memory block identified by the current FileIDS to the new file ID, i.e., NewFileNameS. Then, the old file ID is replaced by NewFileNameS and the process sets FileIDST.ReNamedBL:= T. Otherwise, it reports an error FileIDST.ReNamedBL:= F.

h) The UPM of the Copy File Process

The *copy file* process of FMS§, CopyPC, is formally modeled as shown in Figure 21, which reproduces a given file physically in the memory and logically in FMS§. The input arguments of the process are the existing file ID and the name of its copy. Its output is the status of the copy operation. CopyPC checks if the target file has been created and is currently open. If so, it calls

the process of CreatePC as modeled in Figure 13 to physically establish a new file with the same size and record type of FileIDST. The contents of FileIDST are physically copies into NewFileNameST in memory. The memory block identified by NewFileNameS is linked to its logical name, and the process sets FileIDST.CopiedBL:= T. Otherwise, it reports an error FileIDST.CopiedBL:= F.

i) The UPM of the Clear File Process

The *clear file* process of FMS§, ClearPC, is formally modeled as shown in Figure 22, which logically sets the given file as empty. The input argument of the process is the given file ID. Its output is the status of the clear operation. It is noteworthy that ClearPC only logically sets the file size controller FileIDST.#RecordsN = 0 in order to denote the file has been cleaned, rather than

Figure 20. The UPM model of the file rename process

```
ReNamePC(<I:: File ID S, NewFileNameS>; <O:: FileID ST.RenamedBL>; <UDM:: FMS ST, Files ST>) ≙
{
  → ( ◆ FileIDST.CreatedBL = T ∧ FileIDST.ClosedBL = T
          → NewFileNameS ⇐ MEM(FileIDS)ST
          → FileIDS := NewFileNameS
          → FileIDST.RenamedBL := T
    | ◆~
          → FileIDST.RenamedBL := F
          → ! (" 'FileIDST' does not exist.")
      )
}
```

Figure 21. The UPM model of the copy file process

```
CopyPC(<I:: File ID S, NewFileNameS>; <O:: FileID ST.CopiedBL>; <UDM:: FMS ST, Files ST>) ≜
{
  → ( ◆ FileIDST.CreatedBL = T ∧ FileIDST.OpenedBL = T
      ↦ CreateFilePC(<I:: NewFileNameS, FileID ST.SizeN, FileID ST.ElementRT>;
                       <O:: NewFileNameST.CreatedBL>; <UDM:: FMSST>)
      → ( ◆ NewFileNameST.CreatedBL = T
          → MEM(NewFileNameS)ST := MEM(FileIDS)ST
          → NewFileNameS ⇐ MEM(NewFileNameS)ST
          → FileIDST.CopiedBL := T
        | ◆~
          → FileIDST.CopiedBL := F
          → ! (" 'NewFileNameST'' has not created.")
        )
    | ◆~
      → FileIDST.CopiedBL := F
      → ! (" 'FileIDST' and/or 'NewFileNameST'' do not exist.")
    )
}
```

removes all data elements of the file physically. Therefore, ClearPC is different from the process DeletePC, which physically removes the target file as well as its contents from the memory. When successful, ClearPC sets FileIDST.ClearedBL = T and declares the file as empty, closed, and not opened at the same time. In case the given file does not exist, ClearPC generates a specific error message FileIDST.ClearedBL = F.

j) The UPM of the Delete File Process

The *delete file* process of FMS§, DeletePC, is formally modeled as shown in Figure 23, which physically removes a given file and releases its related memory. The input argument of the pro-

cess is the given file ID. Its output is the status of the delete operation. DeleteFilePC releases and returns the memory space of the physical file to the system by calling a system support process, ReleaseObjectPC, for dynamic memory manipulation as illustrated in Figure 23. It then disconnects the physical file in memory and its logical name administrated by FMS§. If the given file has not been created or is not opened, DeleteFilePC produces a specific error message FileIDST.DeletedBL = F.

In Figure 23, the ReleaseObjectPC process is a support process as shown in Figure 24, which is invoked by the delete file process. The ReleaseObjectPC process identifies an associate memory block of a given ObjectIDS and discon-

Figure 22. The UPM model of the clear file process

```
ClearPC(<I:: File ID S>; <O:: FileID ST.ClearedBL>; <UDM:: FMS ST, Files ST>) ≜
{
  → ( ◆ FileIDST.CreatedBL = T ∧ FileIDST.OpenedBL = T
      → FileIDST.#RecordsN := 0
      → FileIDST.ClearedBL := T
      → FileIDST.EmptyBL := T
      → FileIDST.ClosedBL := T
      → FileIDST.OpenedBL := F
    | ◆~
      → FileIDST.ClearedBL := F
      → ! (" 'FileIDST' does not exist.")
    )
}
```

Figure 23. The UPM model of the delete file process

```
DeleteFilePC(<I:: FileIDS>; <O:: FileIDST.DeletedBL>; <UDM:: FMSST, FilesST>) ≜
{
 → ( ◆ FileIDST.CreatedBL = T ∧ FileIDST.ClosedBL = T
      → FileIDS := FileIDS
      ↣ ReleaseObjectPC(<I:: ObjectIDS>; <O:: ObjectReleasedBL>; <UDM:: MEMST>)
      → ( ◆ ObjectReleasedBL = T
           → FileIDS ⇍ MEM(PhysicalFileST)
           → FileIDST.DeletedBL := T
         | ◆~
           → FileIDST.DeletedBL := F
           → ! (Target memory for 'FileIDST' has not been found.)
         )
    | ◆~
      → FileIDST.DeletedBL := F
      → ! ('FileIDST' does not existed.)
    )
}
```

nects the object from the memory. After the release operation, the object is set to be undefined, i.e., ObjectID**S**:= ⊥. If memory release is failed, ReleaseObject**PC** feeds back an error message ObjectID**ST**.Released**BL**:= **F**.

6. THE DYNAMIC BEHAVIORAL MODELS OF THE FILE ADT AND FMS

Dynamic behaviors of a system are run-time process deployment and dispatching mechanisms based on the static behaviors modeled in UPMs. The dynamic behaviors of Files**ST** and FMS**ST** integrate and dispatch the static behavioral processes of them as modeled in Files**§**.StaticBehaviors**PC** and FSM**§**.StaticBehaviors**PC**. Based on the UPMs developed in the preceding sections, this section models the dynamic behaviors of the file ADT and FMS at run-time via the dynamic processes of system dispatching elaborated by the event-driven mechanisms of the system.

6.1 The Dynamic Behavior Model of the File ADT

The dynamic behaviors of the File ADT, Files**§**. DynamicBehaviors**PC**, are shown in Figure 25, which serve as an interface of the system to external users who can invoke any pre-defined process in the file ADT. The dynamic behaviors of Files**§** at run-time can be formally specified using the RTPA process dispatching methodology. Files**§**.DynamicBehaviors**PC** as given in Figure 25 establishes a set of top-level run-time relations

Figure 24. The UPM model of the release object process

```
ReleaseObjectPC(<I:: ObjectIDS>; <O:: ObjectIDST.ReleasedBL>; <UDM:: ObjectIDST, MemoryST>) ≜
{
 → ObjectIDS ⇍ MEM(ObjectST)ST
 → ReleasePC(<I:: MEM(ObjectST)>; <O:: ⓢMemoryReleasedBL>; <UDM:: MemoryST>)
 → ObjectIDS := ⊥
 → ( ◆ MemoryReleasedBL = T
      → ObjectIDST.ReleasedBL := T
   | ◆ ~
      → ObjectIDST.ReleasedBL := F
   )
}
```

of the five system events such as @InsertRecord**S**, @RetrieveRecord**S**, @UpdateRecord**S**, @AppendRecord**S**, and @DeleteRecord**S** with the five predefined UPMs such as InsertRec**PC**, RetrieveRec**PC**, UpdateRec**PC**, AppendRec**PC**, and DeleteRec**PC** in corresponding pairs. Any exceptional event that is not specified as a valid one in the system will be ignored by the skip operator (→ ∅). The event-driven dispatching mechanism also puts Files**§** into the context of a specific application.

6.2 The Dynamic Behavior Model of the FMS

The dynamic behaviors of FMS, FMS**§**.DynamicBehaviors**PC**, are shown in Figure 26, which serve as an interface of the system to external users who can invoke any pre-defined process in FMS. On the basis of FMS**§**.StaticBehaviors**PC**

developed in the preceding sections as a set of UDMs, the dynamic behaviors of FMS**§** at run-time can be formally specified using the RTPA process dispatching methodology. FMS**§**.DynamicBehaviors**PC** given in Figure 26 establish a set of top-level run-time relations between the 10 pairs of events and processes such as (@CreateFile**S** ↪ CreateFile**PC**), (@OpenFile**S** ↪ Open**PC**), (@ CloseFile**S** ↪ Close**PC**), (@SaveFile**S** ↪ Save**PC**), (@EmptyTest**S** ↪ EmptyTest**PC**), (@FullTest**S** ↪FullTest**PC**), (@ReName**S** ↪ReName**PC**), (@ Copy**S** ↪Copy**PC**), (@Clear**S** ↪Clear**PC**), and (@DeleteFile**S** ↪DeleteFile**PC**). Any exceptional event that is not specified as a valid one in the system will be ignored by the skip operator (→ ∅).

The practical formal engineering methodology of RTPA for system modeling and specification provides a coherent notation system and systematical approach for large-scale software and hybrid system design and implementation. A

Figure 25. The dynamic behavioral model of the file ADT

```
FilesST.DynamicBehaviorsPC ≜
{ § →
 ( @ InsertRecordS      ↪ InsertRecPC(<I:: FileID S, Key N, DataRT>;
                                  <O:: FileID ST.RecordsST.InsertedBL, IndexN>; <UDM:: Files ST>)
 | @RetrieveRecordS  ↪ RetrieveRecPC(<I:: FileIDS, KeyN>;
                                  <O:: DataRT, FileIDST.RecordsST.RetrievedBL>; <UDM:: FilesST>)
 | @UpdateRecordS    ↪ UpdateRecPC(<I:: FileIDS, KeyN, DataRT>;
                                  <O:: FileIDST.RecordsST.UpdatedBL>; <UDM:: FilesST>)
 | @AppendRecordS    ↪ AppendRecPC(<I:: FileIDS, KeyN, DataRT>;
                                  <O:: FileIDST.RecordsST.AppendedBL>; <UDM:: FilesST>)
 | @DeleteRecordS     ↪ DeleteRecPC(<I:: FileIDS, KeyN>; <O:: FileIDST.RecordsST.RecDeletedBL>;
                                  <UDM:: FilesST>)
 | → ∅
 ) → §
}
```

Figure 26. Dynamic Behaviors of the file management system

```
FMSST.DynamicBehaviorsPC ≜
{ § →
 (  @CreateFileS  ↪  CreateFilePC (<I:: FileIDS, SizeN, ElementRT>; <O:: FileIDST.CreatedBL>; <UDM:: FMSST, FilesST>)
 | @OpenFileS   ↪  OpenPC (<I:: FileIDS>; <O:: FileIDST.OpenedBL>; <UDM:: FMSST, FilesST>)
 | @CloseFileS  ↪  ClosePC (<I:: FileIDS>; <O:: FileIDST.ClosedBL>; <UDM:: FMSST, FilesST>)
 | @SaveFileS   ↪  SavePC (<I:: FileIDS>; <O:: FileIDST.SavedBL>; <UDM:: FMSST, FilesST>)
 | @EmptyTestS ↪  EmptyTestPC (<I:: FileIDS>; <O:: FileIDST.EmptyBL>; <UDM:: FMSST, FilesST>)
 | @FullTestS   ↪  FullTestPC (<I:: FileIDS>; <O:: FileIDST.FullBL>; <UDM:: FMSST, FilesST>)
 | @ReNameS    ↪  ReNamePC (<I:: FileIDS, NewFileNameS>; <O:: FileIDST.RenamedBL>; <UDM:: FMSST, FilesST>)
 | @CopyS      ↪  CopyPC (<I:: FileIDS, NewFileNameS>; <O:: FileIDST.CopiedBL>; <UDM:: FMSST, FilesST>)
 | @ClearS     ↪  ClearPC (<I:: FileIDS>; <O:: FileIDST.ClearedBL>; <UDM:: FMSST, FilesST>)
 | @DeleteFileS ↪  DeleteFilePC (<I:: FileIDS>; <O:: FileIDST.DeletedBL>; <UDM:: FMSST, FilesST>)
 | → ∅
 ) → §
}
```

series of formal design models of real-world and real-time applications in RTPA have been developed using RTPA notations and methodologies (Wang, 2002, 2007, 2008a, 2008b, 2008c, 2008d, 2009a; Wang & Huang, 2008; Wang, Tan, & Ngolah, 2010) in the formal design engineering approach, such as the telephone switching system (TSS) (Wang, 2009b), the lift dispatching system (LDS) (Wang et al., 2009), the automated teller machine (ATM) (Wang, Zeng, Ngolah, et al., 2010), the real-time operating system (RTOS+) (Wang, Zeng, Ngolah, et al., 2010; Wang, Ngolah, Zeng, et al., 2010), the autonomic code generator (RTPA-CG) (Wang, Tan, & Ngolah, 2010), the ADTs (Wang, Ngolah, Tan, et al., 2010), and the air traffic control system (to be reported). Further studies have demonstrated that RTPA is not only useful as a generic notation and methodology for software engineering, but also good at modeling human cognitive processes in cognitive informatics and computational intelligence as reported in (Wang, 2008d, 2009a, 2010a, 2010b, 2010c; Wang & Ruhe, 2007; Wang & Chiew, 2010).

CONCLUSION

Files provide a powerful means for manipulating large-volume information and persistent data in computing. Files and file management system play a primordial role in software system modeling and development, particularly in operating systems, database systems, and the Internet-based systems. This paper has developed a comprehensive design pattern of the file ADT and FMS. The conceptual model, architectural model, and the static/dynamic behavioral models of the files and FMS have been systematically presented. A novel architecture of files using two-stage indexed records has been developed, which allows both sequential and random files to be modeled and implemented on a unified structure, and suitable for real-time applications gained from the small index table manipulations of files. RTPA has been

adopted to rigorously design and implement both architectural and behavioral models of files and manipulations in a top-down approach. A wide range of applications of the formal patterns of the file ADT and the FMS system have been identified and reviewed.

ACKNOWLEDGMENT

The authors would like to acknowledge the Natural Science and Engineering Council of Canada (NSERC) for its partial support to this work. We would like to thank the anonymous reviewers for their valuable comments and suggestions.

REFERENCES

Bollella, G. (2002). *The real-time specification for java.* Reading, MA: Addison-Wesley.

Broy, M., Pair, C., & Wirsing, M. (1984). A systematic study of models of abstract data types. *Theoretical Computer Science, 33,* 139–1274. doi:10.1016/0304-3975(84)90086-0

Cardelli, L., & Wegner, P. (1985). On understanding types, data abstraction and polymorphism. *ACM Computing Surveys, 17*(4), 471–522. doi:10.1145/6041.6042

Guttag, J. V. (1977). Abstract data types and the development of data structures. *Communications of the ACM, 20*(6), 396–404. doi:10.1145/359605.359618

Hsiao, D., & Harary, F. (1970). A formal system for information retrieval from files. *Communications of the ACM, 13,* 67–73. doi:10.1145/362007.362015

McDermid, J. (1991). *Software engineer's reference book.* Boca Raton, FL: CRC Press.

Mitchell, J. C. (1990). Type systems for programming languages. In van Leeuwen, J. (Ed.), *Handbook of Theoretical Computer Science* (pp. 365–458). Cambridge, MA: MIT Press.

Roberts, D. C. (1972). File organization techniques. *Advances in Computers, 12,* 115–174. doi:10.1016/S0065-2458(08)60509-4

Silberschatz, A., Galvin, P., & Gagne, G. (2003). *Applied operating system concepts* (1st ed.). New York, NY: John Wiley & Sons.

Stubbs, D. F., & Webre, N. W. (1985). *Data structures with abstract data types and pascal.* Belmont, CA: Brooks Cole Publishing.

Wang, Y. (2002). The real-time process algebra (RTPA). *Annals of Software Engineering: An International Journal, 14,* 235–274. doi:10.1023/A:1020561826073

Wang, Y. (2004). Operating systems. In Dorf, R. (Ed.), *The engineering handbook* (2nd ed.). Boca Raton, FL: CRC Press.

Wang, Y. (2007). *Software engineering foundations: A software science perspective.* Boca Raton, FL: Auerbach Publications.

Wang, Y. (2008a). RTPA: A Denotational Mathematics for Manipulating Intelligent and Computational Behaviors. *International Journal of Cognitive Informatics and Natural Intelligence, 2*(2), 44–62. doi:10.4018/jcini.2008040103

Wang, Y. (2008b). Mathematical Laws of Software. *Transactions on Computational Science, 2,* 46–83. doi:10.1007/978-3-540-87563-5_4

Wang, Y. (2008c). Deductive Semantics of RTPA. *International Journal of Cognitive Informatics and Natural Intelligence, 2*(2), 95–121. doi:10.4018/jcini.2008040106

Wang, Y. (2008d). On Contemporary Denotational Mathematics for Computational Intelligence. *Transactions on Computational Science, 2,* 6–29. doi:10.1007/978-3-540-87563-5_2

Wang, Y. (2009a). Paradigms of Denotational Mathematics for Cognitive Informatics and Cognitive Computing. *Fundamenta Informaticae, 90*(3), 282–303.

Wang, Y. (2009b). The Formal Design Model of a Telephone Switching System (TSS). *International Journal of Software Science and Computational Intelligence, 1*(3), 92–116. doi:10.4018/jssci.2009070107

Wang, Y. (2010a). Cognitive Robots: A Reference Model towards Intelligent Authentication. *IEEE Robotics and Automation, 17*(4), 54–62. doi:10.1109/MRA.2010.938842

Wang, Y. (2010b). On Formal and Cognitive Semantics for Semantic Computing. *International Journal of Semantic Computing, 4*(2), 203–237. doi:10.1142/S1793351X10000833

Wang, Y. (2010c). On Concept Algebra for Computing with Words (CWW). *International Journal of Semantic Computing, 4*(3), 331–356. doi:10.1142/S1793351X10001061

Wang, Y., & Chiew, V. (2010). On the Cognitive Process of Human Problem Solving. *Cognitive Systems Research: An International Journal, 11*(1), 81–92. doi:10.1016/j.cogsys.2008.08.003

Wang, Y., & Huang, J. (2008). Formal Modeling and Specification of Design Patterns Using RTPA. *International Journal of Cognitive Informatics and Natural Intelligence, 2*(1), 100–111. doi:10.4018/jcini.2008010108

Wang, Y., Ngolah, C. F., Ahmadi, H., Sheu, P. C. Y., & Ying, S. (2009). The Formal Design Model of a Lift Dispatching System (LDS). *International Journal of Software Science and Computational Intelligence, 1*(4), 98–122. doi:10.4018/jssci.2009062506

Wang, Y., Ngolah, C. F., Tan, X., Tian, Y., & Sheu, P. C.-Y. (2010). The Formal Design Models of a Set of Abstract Data Models (ADTs). *International Journal of Software Science and Computational Intelligence*, *2*(4), 72–104. doi:10.4018/jssci.2010100106

Wang, Y., Ngolah, C. F., Zeng, G., Sheu, P. C.-Y., Choy, C. P., & Tian, Y. (2010). The Formal Design Models of a Real-Time Operating System (RTOS+): Conceptual and Architectural Frameworks. *International Journal of Software Science and Computational Intelligence*, *2*(2), 105–122. doi:10.4018/jssci.2010040106

Wang, Y., & Ruhe, G. (2007). The Cognitive Process of Decision Making. *International Journal of Cognitive Informatics and Natural Intelligence*, *1*(2), 73–85. doi:10.4018/jcini.2007040105

Wang, Y., Tan, X., & Ngolah, C. F. (2010). Design and Implementation of an Autonomic Code Generator based on RTPA (RTPA-CG). *International Journal of Software Science and Computational Intelligence*, *2*(2), 44–67. doi:10.4018/jssci.2010040103

Wang, Y., Zeng, G., Ngolah, C. F., Sheu, P. C.-Y., Choy, C. P., & Tian, Y. (2010). The Formal Design Model of a Real-Time Operating System (RTOS+): Static and Dynamic Behavior Models. *International Journal of Software Science and Computational Intelligence*, *2*(3), 79–105. doi:10.4018/jssci.2010070106

Wang, Y., Zhang, Y., Sheu, P., Li, X., & Guo, H. (2010). The Formal Design Models of an Automatic Teller Machine (ATM). *International Journal of Software Science and Computational Intelligence*, *2*(1), 102–131. doi:10.4018/jssci.2010101907

Chapter 15
The Formal Design Model of Doubly–Linked–Circular Lists (DLC–Lists)

Yingxu Wang
University of Calgary, Canada

Xinming Tan
Wuhan University of Technology, China

Cyprian F. Ngolah
Sentinel Trending & Diagnostics Ltd., Calgary, Canada

Phillip C.-Y. Sheu
University of California, Irvine, USA

ABSTRACT

Abstract Data Types (ADTs) are a set of highly generic and rigorously modeled data structures in type theory. Lists as a finite sequence of elements are one of the most fundamental and widely used ADTs in system modeling, which provide a standard encapsulation and access interface for manipulating large-volume information and persistent data. This paper develops a comprehensive design pattern of formal lists using a doubly-linked-circular (DLC) list architecture. A rigorous denotational mathematics, Real-Time Process Algebra (RTPA), is adopted, which allows both architectural and behavioral models of lists to be rigorously designed and implemented in a top-down approach. The architectural models of DLC-Lists are created using RTPA architectural modeling methodologies known as the Unified Data Models (UDMs). The behavioral models of DLC-Lists are specified and refined by a set of Unified Process Models (UPMs) in three categories namely the management operations, traversal operations, and node I/O operations. This work has been applied in a number of real-time and nonreal-time system designs such as a real-time operating system (RTOS+), a file management system (FMS), and the ADT library for an RTPA-based automatic code generation tool.

1. INTRODUCTION

Data object modeling is a process to creatively extract and abstractly represent a real-world problem by data models. A list is a finite sequence of elements where the order information of its elements is preserved beyond that of sets (Stubbs & Webre, 1985; McDermid, 1991; Bollella et al., 2002). Many important data objects can be modeled and implemented by lists such as a set of data with keys, a sentence for natural language parsing, a sequential file, a tree, and a graph (Wiener and Pinson, 2000).

DOI: 10.4018/978-1-4666-2651-5.ch015

A list can be formally modeled by an Abstract Data Type (ADT) (Guttag, 1977; Broy et al., 1984; Cardelli & Wegner, 1985; Stubbs & Webre, 1985), which is an abstract logical model of a complex and/or user defined data structure with a set of predefined operations. Using types to model real-world entities can be traced back to the mathematical thought of Bertrand Russell in1900s (Russell, 1903) and Georg Cantor in 1932 (Lipschutz & Lipson, 1997). A number of ADTs have been identified in computing and system modeling such as *stack, queue, sequence, record, array, list, tree, file,* and *graph* (Broy et al., 1984; Mitchell, 1990; McDermid, 1991; Wang, 2007; Wang, Ngolah, Tan, Tian, & Sheu, 2010). ADTs possess the following properties: (1) An extension of type constructions by integrating both data structures and functional behaviors; (2) A hybrid data object modeling technique that *encapsulates* both user defined data structures and allowable operations on them; (3) The interface and implementation of an ADT are separated where detailed implementation of the ADT is hidden to applications that invoke the ADT and its predefined operations.

In order to formally model the list ADT, an expressive denotational mathematics, Real-Time Process Algebra (RTPA) (Wang, 2002, 2007, 2008a, 2008b, 2008c, 2008d; Wang, Tan, & Ngolah, 2010), is adopted, which allows both architectural and behavioral models of lists to be rigorously designed and implemented in a top-down approach. According to the RTPA methodology for system modeling and refinement, a formal list can be rigorously modeled using two fundamental techniques known as the unified data models and the unified process models (Wang, 2007).

Definition 1: A *Unified Data Model* (UDM) is a generic architectural model for a software system, its internal control structures, and its interfaces with hardware components, which can be rigorously modeled and refined as an *n*-tuple, i.e.:

$$UDM \triangleq \mathop{R}_{i=1}^{n} (S_i \mid \forall e \in S_i, p_i(e) >) \qquad (1)$$

where S_i, $1 \leq i \leq n$, is a set and also a type of elements e that share the property p_i.

Definition 2: The *Unified Process Model (UPM)* of a *program* ℘ is a composition of a finite set of *m* processes according to the time-, event-, and interrupt-based process dispatching rules, $@e_k S \hookrightarrow P_k$, i.e.:

$$
\begin{aligned}
UPM &\triangleq \wp \\
&= \mathop{R}_{k=1}^{m} (@e_k S \hookrightarrow P_k) \\
&= \mathop{R}_{k=1}^{m} [@e_k S \hookrightarrow \mathop{R}_{i=1}^{n-1} (s_i(k) r_{ij}(k) s_j(k))], j = i+1
\end{aligned}
$$
$$(2)$$

where s_i and s_j are one of the 17 RTPA meta-processes, r_{ij} is one of the 17 RTPA algebraic process operations, and e_k is a general, timing, or interrupt event.

This paper develops a comprehensive design pattern of formal lists using a doubly-linked-circular (DLC) model. In the remainder of this paper, the conceptual models of lists are described as the initial requirements for describing the list ADT. The architectural model of lists is created as a set of UDMs based on doubly linked and circular nodes dynamically created in the memory. The static behaviors of lists are modeled and refined by a set of UPMs in three categories namely the management operations, traversal operations, and node I/O operations. The dynamic behaviors of lists are formally specified and refined by process scheduling and system dispatching models with UPMs.

2. THE CONCEPTUAL MODEL OF DLC-LISTS

A list is a typical ADT for manipulating large-volume information and dynamic data with a standard encapsulation and access interface. Lists are characterized by the separation of its logical interface and physical implementation in design and implementations. Lists as a finite sequence of elements are one of the most fundamental and widely used ADTs in system modeling. This section describes the conceptual model of lists. On the basis of the conceptual models as design requirements, a set of formal models of lists will be rigorously developed.

Definition 3: A *list l* is a finite sequence with n elements $e_1, e_2, \ldots, e_n$ where all elements share a common data type such as a string (**S**), natural number (**N**), real number (**R**), record (the structural type, **ST**), or array (**Array**), i.e.:

$$l \, A <e_1, e_2, \ldots, e_n> \tag{3}$$

where e_i**RT** $\in$ {**S, N, R, ST, Array,** ...} as defined in RTPA.

Many important data objects and ADTs can be modeled and implemented by lists such as a set of data with keys, a sentence for natural language parsing, and a sequential file. Lists are also the fundamental data model for complex nonlinear structures such as trees and graphs. A sequential program can also be perceived as a finite list of statements (operations).

Various lists may be design and implemented in different forms using an array, a record, a set of doubly-linked records, and a set of doubly-linked-circular records. This paper puts emphases on the doubly-linked-circular record model of lists, because other simple forms of lists may be derived or tailored based on it.

Definition 4: A *doubly linked circular list* (DLC-List) is a list represented and implemented by a sequence of dynamically allocated nodes with a pair of links toward the prior and next nodes where the head and tail nodes are circularly linked.

It is noteworthy that there are two different but interactive facets in the models of DLC-Lists known as its architectures and behaviors. The conceptual model of the DLC-List is shown in Figure 1. In the DLC model of lists, two global pointers, Head**P** and CurrentPtr**P**, are provided in the pointer type (**P**) that point to the designated first and current node, respectively. The nodes are represented as a set of bidirectionally linked records. Each of which consists of a set of attributes such as the key**N** in type of natural number, the data**RT** in run-time type for implementation

Figure 1. The conceptual model of the architecture of DLC-Lists

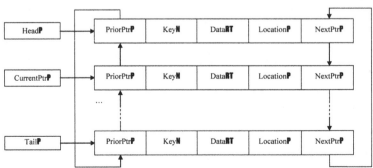

Figure 2. The conceptual model of the behaviors of DLC-Lists

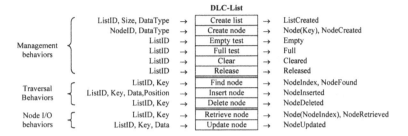

flexibility, as well as structural pointers PriorPtr**P**, NextPtr**P**, and Location**P**. The pointer, Location**P**, links a node of the DLC-List to its physical address assigned by dynamic memory allocation techniques such as Location**P**:= *new*(NodeID**S**) during node creation (Figure 2).

Based on the architectural model, the behavioral models of DLC-Lists can be designed. The typical functional behaviors of DLC-Lists are identified such as create list, create node, empty test, full test, clear, and release; find node, insert node, and delete node; as well as retrieve node and update node. Both the architectural and behavioral models of DLC-Lists will be refined in the following sections.

3. THE ARCHITECTURAL MODELS OF DLC-LISTS

On the basis of the conceptual models developed in the preceding section, the top-level ADT model of the DLC-List, List**S**, can be specified in RTPA as shown in Figure 3. The architectural model specifies that the DLC-List encompasses three parallel subsystems known as its architecture, static behaviors, and dynamic behaviors. According to the RTPA methodology for system modeling, specification, and refinement (Wang, 2007, 2008a), the following subsections will refine the top level framework of List**S** into detailed architectural models (UDMs). Then, the static and dynamic behavioural models, List**S**.StaticBehaviors**PC** and

List**S**.DynamicBehaviors**PC**, will be developed and refined in Sections 4 and 5.

The UDM model of DLC-Lists, List**S**.Architecture**ST**, as shown in Figure 4 provides a generic architectural model for any concrete list in applications with three categories of design attributes known as follows: a) The *architectural* attributes determine the configuration of the list such as its logical size (Size**N**), physical size (MemSize**N**), current number of nodes (#Nodes**N**), the head pointer (Head**P**), the current pointer (CurentPtr**P**), the tail pointer (Tail**P**), the index number of a node (NodeIndex**N**), and the position for node insertion (Position**N**) such as a position at the current pointer and the prior or next of a given node identified by a key; b) The *node* attributes model a sorted sequence of *n* nodes constrained by #Nodes**N** indexed by i**N** equivalent to its Key**N**. There are five fields for each node in the list: Key**N**, Data**RT**, PriorPtr**P**, NextPtr**P**, and Location**P** (the physical location of the node); and c) The *status* attributes are a set of indicators of operational results in Boolean type with a status prefix & such as &ListCreated**BL**, &NodeCreated**BL**, &NodeFound**BL**, &NodeRetrieved**BL**, &NodeUpdated**BL**, &NodeInserted**BL**, &NodeDe-

Figure 3. The top-level architecture of the DLC-List

List**S** ≜ List**S**.Architecture**ST**
 || List**S**.StaticBehaviors**PC**
 || List**S**.DynamicBehaviors**PC**

Figure 4. The UDM model of DLC-Lists

$$
\begin{aligned}
&\text{List} \S.\text{Architecture} \mathbf{ST} \triangleq \text{List } \mathbf{ST} :: \\
&(<\text{ListID} : \mathbf{S} \mid 1 \leq \text{ListID } \mathbf{S} \leq 255>, \\
&\ <\text{Size} : \mathbf{N} \mid 0 \leq \text{Size} \mathbf{N} \leq \text{MaxSize } \mathbf{N}>, \\
&\ <\#\text{Nodes}: \mathbf{N} \mid 0 \leq \#\text{Nodes} \mathbf{N} \leq \text{Size} \mathbf{N}>, \\
&\ <\text{MemSize} : \mathbf{H} \mid 0 \leq \text{MemSize} \mathbf{H} \leq \text{MaxMem} \mathbf{H}>, \\
&\ < \overset{\#Nodes\mathbf{N}}{\underset{i\mathbf{N}=0}{R}} \ \text{Node}(i\,\mathbf{N})\,\mathbf{ST} :: (<\text{Key} : \mathbf{N} \mid 0 \leq \text{Key } \mathbf{N} \leq \text{Size} \mathbf{N}>, \\
&\hspace{6cm} <\text{Data} : \mathbf{RT} \mid \text{Data} \mathbf{RT} \in \{\mathbf{S}, \mathbf{N}, \mathbf{R}, \mathbf{ST}, ...\}>, \\
&\hspace{6cm} <\text{PriorPtr} : \mathbf{P} \mid 0 \leq \text{PriorPtr} \mathbf{P} \leq \text{MemSize} \mathbf{H}>, \\
&\hspace{6cm} <\text{NextPtr} : \mathbf{P} \mid 0 \leq \text{NextPtr} \mathbf{P} \leq \text{MemSize} \mathbf{H}> \\
&\hspace{6cm} <\text{Location} : \mathbf{P} \mid 0 \leq \text{Location} \mathbf{P} \leq \text{MemSize} \mathbf{H}> \\
&\hspace{6cm}) \\
&\ <\text{Head} : \mathbf{P} \mid 0 \leq \text{Head} \mathbf{P} \leq \text{MemSize} \mathbf{H}>, \\
&\ <\text{CurrentPtr} : \mathbf{P} \mid 0 \leq \text{CurrentPtr} \mathbf{P} \leq \text{MemSize} \mathbf{H}>, \\
&\ <\text{Tail} : \mathbf{P} \mid 0 \leq \text{Tail } \mathbf{P} \leq \text{MemSize} \mathbf{H}>, \\
&\ <\text{NodeIndex} : \mathbf{N} \mid 0 \leq \text{NodeIndex} \mathbf{N} \leq \text{Size} \mathbf{N}>, \\
&\ <\text{Position} : \mathbf{N} \mid \text{Position} \mathbf{N} = \{(1, \text{CurrentPtr}), (2, \text{AfterKey}), (3, \text{BeforeKey})\}>, \\
&\ <\textcircled{S}\text{ListCreated} : \mathbf{BL} \mid \textcircled{S}\text{ListCreated} \mathbf{BL} = \{(\mathbf{T}, \text{Yes}), (\mathbf{F}, \text{No})\}>, \\
&\ <\textcircled{S}\text{NodeCreated} : \mathbf{BL} \mid \textcircled{S}\text{NodeCreated} \mathbf{BL} = \{(\mathbf{T}, \text{Yes}), (\mathbf{F}, \text{No})\}>, \\
&\ <\textcircled{S}\text{NodeFound} : \mathbf{BL} \mid \textcircled{S}\text{NodeFound} \mathbf{BL} = \{(\mathbf{T}, \text{Yes}), (\mathbf{F}, \text{No})\}>, \\
&\ <\textcircled{S}\text{NodeRetrieved} : \mathbf{BL} \mid \textcircled{S}\text{NodeRetrieved} \mathbf{BL} = \{(\mathbf{T}, \text{Yes}), (\mathbf{F}, \text{No})\}>, \\
&\ <\textcircled{S}\text{NodeUpdated} : \mathbf{BL} \mid \textcircled{S}\text{NodeUpdated} \mathbf{BL} = \{(\mathbf{T}, \text{Yes}), (\mathbf{F}, \text{No})\}>, \\
&\ <\textcircled{S}\text{NodeInserted} : \mathbf{BL} \mid \textcircled{S}\text{NodeInserted} \mathbf{BL} = \{(\mathbf{T}, \text{Yes}), (\mathbf{F}, \text{No})\}>, \\
&\ <\textcircled{S}\text{NodeDeleted} : \mathbf{BL} \mid \textcircled{S}\text{NodeDeleted} \mathbf{BL} = \{(\mathbf{T}, \text{Yes}), (\mathbf{F}, \text{No})\}>, \\
&\ <\textcircled{S}\text{Empty} : \mathbf{BL} \mid \textcircled{S}\text{Empty} \mathbf{BL} = \{(\mathbf{T}, \text{Yes}), (\mathbf{F}, \text{No})\}>, \\
&\ <\textcircled{S}\text{Full} : \mathbf{BL} \mid \textcircled{S}\text{Full} \mathbf{BL} = \{(\mathbf{T}, \text{Yes}), (\mathbf{F}, \text{No})\}>, \\
&\ <\textcircled{S}\text{Cleared} : \mathbf{BL} \mid \textcircled{S}\text{Cleared} \mathbf{BL} = \{(\mathbf{T}, \text{Yes}), (\mathbf{F}, \text{No})\}>, \\
&\ <\textcircled{S}\text{Released} : \mathbf{BL} \mid \textcircled{S}\text{Released} \mathbf{BL} = \{(\mathbf{T}, \text{Yes}), (\mathbf{F}, \text{No})\}> \\
&)
\end{aligned}
$$

leted$\mathbf{BL}$, &Empty$\mathbf{BL}$, &Full$\mathbf{BL}$, &Cleared$\mathbf{BL}$, and &Released$\mathbf{BL}$. Each field of attributes in the UDM of lists is modeled by a primitive type of RTPA (Wang, 2007) and constrained by a certain scope or initial value given in the right-hand side of the vertical bar. It is noteworthy that the type of the data elements in a node is specified in the run-time type $\mathbf{RT}$, i.e., $\mathbf{RT} \in \{\mathbf{S}, \mathbf{N}, \mathbf{R}, \mathbf{ST}, ...\}$, for design flexibility. However, the data elements of concrete nodes must be instantiated once it is chosen at run-time for a specific implementation of the generic abstract list.

The architectural model, List$\mathbf{ST}$, can be accessed or invoked in two ways as expressed in Equation 4.1 and 4.2. The random access in Equatiopn. 4.1 allows a node of the list to be located by its pointer NodePtr$\mathbf{P}$; While the sequen-

tial access in Equation 4.2 provides an additional approach to enable a node of the list to be located by its index number NodeIndex$\mathbf{N}$ or the key.

$$\text{TargetNode}\mathbf{P} := \text{List}\mathbf{ID}(\text{NodePtr}\mathbf{P})\mathbf{ST}.\text{Location}\mathbf{P} \tag{4.1}$$

$$\text{TargetNode}\mathbf{P} := \text{ListID}\mathbf{ST}.\text{Node}(\text{NodeIndex}\mathbf{N})\ \mathbf{ST}.\text{Location}\mathbf{P} \tag{4.2}$$

4. THE BEHAVIORAL PROCESS MODELS OF DLC-LISTS

The static behaviors of the DLC-Lists, List$\mathbf{S}$. StaticBehaviors$\mathbf{PC}$, can be specified by a set of functional operations on its architectural model

(UDM), i.e., List**§**.Architecture**PC**. On the basis of the UDM models of List**ST** developed in the preceding subsection, the behaviors of the list ADT can be modeled as a set of UPMs operating on the UDMs of List**ST** and related input variables. The high-level behavioral model of DLC-Lists is specified by List**§**.StaticBehaviorsPC as shown in Figure 5. The schemas of the UPMs in Figure 5 model the input data objects <**I**:: (…)>, output data objects <**O**:: (…)>, and operated UDMs <**UDM**:: (…)> for each specific process of List**§**. The UDMs play an important role in system architectural design as global and permanent I/O structures, which usually have a longer life-span than those of the process(es) that created and/or invoked them, particularly in real-time and embedded systems.

As informally modeled in Figure 2, the behavioral models of DLC-Lists are specified by a set of 11 UPMs in three categories known as the management operations (such as CreateList**PC**, CreateNode**PC**, EmptyTest**PC**, FullTest**PC**, Clear**PC**, and Release**PC**), traversal operations (such as FindNode**PC**, InsertNode**PC**, and DeleteNode**PC**), and node I/O operations (such as RetrieveNode**PC** and UpdateNode**PC**). In the following subsections, each of the static behaviors of DLC-Lists, List**§**.StaticBehaviors**PC**, as given in Figure 5 will be further refined by a set of UPMs using the denotational mathematical notations and methodologies of RTPA.

4.1. The Behavioral Model of the List Creation Process

The *list creation* process, CreateList**PC**, is formally modeled as shown in Figure 6, which establishes a new list in system memory or on a disk and links it to a specified logical ID of the list, ListID**S**. The input arguments of the process are the given name of the list as well as its size (or maximum capacity of nodes) and the type of data in each node. The output result of the process is the status of the list creation operation @ListCreated**BL**. The UDM operated by this process is List**ST**.

CreateList**PC** calls a system support process, AllocateObject**PC** (Wang, Ngolah, Tan, Tian, & Sheu, 2010), to physically set up the head node of the list using dynamic memory allocation technology. If a memory block is successfully obtained for the head node of the list, CreateList**PC** initializes the ListID**ST** by the following operations: a) *List initialization* connects the head pointer and the current pointer to the memory block, and assigns its expected size; b) *Head node initialization* sets the values of key and location of the head node, and leaves the data and both pointers undefined until the node insertion process; and c) *Status initialization* sets the initial values of statuses of the list as modeled in List**ST**. Otherwise, it reports an error ListID**ST**.&Created**BL**:= **F** with an exception warning of memory allocation failed. In case the given ListID**ST** has already

Figure 5. The high-level UPM model of DLC-List behaviors

```
List§.StaticBehaviorsPC ≜
 ( CreateListPC(<I:: ListIDS, SizeN, DataRT>; <O:: ⓢListCreatedBL>; <UDM:: ListST>)
 | CreateNodePC(<I:: NodeIDS, DataRT>; <O:: Node(KeyN)ST, ⓢNodeCreatedBL>; <UDM:: ListST>)
 | FindNodePC(<I:: ListIDST, KeyN>; <O:: NodeIndexN, ⓢNodeFoundBL>; <UDM:: ListST>)
 | RetrieveNodePC(<I:: ListIDST, KeyN>; <O:: ListIDST.Node(NodeIndexN)ST, ⓢNodeRetrievedBL>; <UDM:: ListST>)
 | UpdateNodePC(<I:: ListIDST, KeyN, DataRT>; <O:: ⓢNodeUpdatedBL>; <UDM:: ListST>)
 | InsertNodePC(<I:: ListIDST, KeyN, DataST, PositionN>; <O:: ⓢNodeInsertedBL>; <UDM:: ListST>)
 | DeleteNodePC(<I:: ListIDST, KeyN>; <O:: ⓢNodeDeletedBL>; <UDM:: ListST>)
 | EmptyTestPC(<I:: ListIDS>; <O:: ⓢEmptyBL>; <UDM:: ListST>)
 | FullTestPC(<I:: ListIDS>; <O:: ⓢFullBL>; <UDM:: ListST>)
 | ClearPC(<I:: ListIDS>; <O:: ⓢClearedBL>; <UDM:: ListST>)
 | ReleasePC(<I:: ListIDS>; <O:: ⓢReleasedBL>; <UDM:: ListST>)
 )
```

Figure 6. The UPM model of the list creation process

```
CreateListPC(<I:: ListID S, SizeN, DataRT>; <O:: ⓢListCreatedBL>; <UDM:: List ST>) ≙
{
  → ( ◆ ListIDST.ⓢListCreatedBL = F
        → ObjectIDS := ListIDS
        → #ElementsN := 1
        → ElementTypeRT := DataRT
        ↦ AllocateObjectPC(<I:: ObjectIDS, #ElementsN, ElementTypeRT>;
                        <O:: ⓢObjectAllocatedBL>; <UDM:: MEMST>)
        → ( ◆ ⓢObjectAllocatedBL = T
              → ListIDST.HeadP ⇐ MEM(ObjectIDS)ST        // List initialization
              → ListIDST.CurrentPtrP := ListIDST.HeadP
              → ListIDST.TailP := ListIDST.CurrentPtrP
              → ListIDST.SizeN := SizeN
              → ListIDST.#NodesN := 1
              → ListIDST.Nodes(0)ST.KeyN := 0              // Head node initialization
              → ListIDST.Nodes(0)ST.DataRT := ⊥
              → ListIDST.Nodes(0)ST.PriorPtrP := ListIDST.TailP
              → ListIDST.Nodes(0)ST.NextPtrP := ListIDST.TailP
              → ListIDST.Nodes(0)ST.LocationP ⇐ MEM(ObjectIDS)ST
              → ListIDST.ⓢEmptyBL := T                     // Status initialization
              → ListIDST.ⓢFullBL := F
              → ListIDST.ⓢListCreatedBL := T
            | ◆ ~
              → ListIDST.ⓢListCreatedBL := F
              → ! ('ListST memory allocation was failed.')
          )
    | ◆ ~
        → BTreeIDST.ⓢTreeCreatedBL := F
        → ! ('ListIDST has already been existed.')
    )
}
```

existed, CreateList**PC** results in a specific error message ListID**ST**.&Created**BL**:= **F**.

4.2. The Behavioral Model of the Node Creation Process

The *node creation* process, CreateNode**PC**, is formally modeled as shown in Figure 7, which establishes a new node in system memory or on a disk and links it to a specified logical node, NodeID**S**. The input arguments of the process are the given name of the node and the type of data for dynamic memory allocation. The output results of the process are the node as identified by its key and the status of the node creation operation. CreateNode**PC** calls the system support process, AllocateObject**PC**, to physical set up the node in memory. If a memory block is successfully

obtained for the node of the list, CreateNode**PC** links the node to the allocated memory block and initializes the node's physical location, while leaving the data, key, and both pointers undefined until the node insertion process; Otherwise, it reports an error ListID**ST**.&NodeCreated**BL**:= **F** with an exception warning of memory allocation failed.

4.3. The Behavioral Model of the Node Finding Process

The *node finding* process, FindNode**PC**, is formally modeled as shown in Figure 8, which searches for a specific node based on its given key. The input arguments of the process are the given name of the list and the key as sequential number of the node. The output results of the process are the index of the node and the status of the node searching

Figure 7. The UPM model of the node creation process

```
CreateNodePC(<I:: NodeIDS, DataRT>; <O:: Node(KeyN)ST, ⓢNodeCreatedBL>; <UDM:: ListST>) ≙
{
  → <ObjectIDS, NofElementsN, ElementTypeRT> := <NodeIDS, 1, DataRT>
  ↣ AllocateObjectPC(<I:: ObjectIDS, #ElementsN, ElementTypeRT)>; <O:: ⓢObjectAllocatedBL>;
                    <UDM:: MEMST>)
  → ( ◆ ⓢObjectAllocatedBL = T
        → ListS := ListIDS
        → ListIDST.Node(iN)ST.KeyN := ⊥
        → ListIDST.Node(iN)ST.DataRT := ⊥
        → ListIDST.Node(iN)ST.PriorPtrP := ⊥
        → ListIDST.Node(iN)ST.NextPtrP := ⊥
        → ListIDST.Node(iN)ST.LocationP ⇐ MEM(ObjectIDS)ST
        → ListIDST.ⓢNodeCreatedBL := T
     | ◆ ~
        → ListIDST.ⓢNodeCreatedBL := F
        → ! ('Node memory allocation was failed.')
    )
}
```

operation. FindNode**PC** initializes the search result as false before checking if the size of the list is empty. If not, FindNode**PC** iteratively compares the key of each node and the given key in order to find the target node. If it is found, FindNode**PC** returns the NodeIndex**N**, sets the search result as true, and exits the loop. Otherwise, the search result remains false. The result of FindNode**PC** will be used by other list operation processes such as RetrieveNode**PC**, UpdateNode**PC**, and DeleteNode**PC** for identifying the target node.

4.4. The Behavioral Model of the Node Retrieval Process

The *node retrieval* process, RetrieveNode**PC**, is formally modeled as shown in Figure 9, which reads and shows the contents of a target node in a list identified by the key. The input arguments of the process are the given name of the list and the key of the target node. The output results of the process are the node as identified by its key and the status of the node retrieval operation. RetrieveNode**PC** checks if the target list exists and is not empty before the following operations: a) Search the target node with Key**N** by calling FindNode**PC**; b) If the target node is found, display each field of the target node on the standard monitor, CRT**ST**, of the system supported by the process ShowNode**PC**, and set ListID**ST**.&NodeRetrieved**BL**:= **T**; c) Otherwise, report an error ListID**ST**.&NodeRetrieved**BL**:= **F** with an exception warning of "node was not found." In case the given ListID**ST** did not exist or

Figure 8. The UPM model of the node finding process

```
FindNodePC(<I:: ListIDST, KeyN>; <O:: NodeIndexN, ⓢNodeFoundBL>; <UDM:: ListST>) ≙
{
  → ListIDST.ⓢNodeFoundBL := F
  → ( ◆ ListIDST.#NodesN ≠ 0

          ListST.#NodesN
     →         R            ◆ ListIDST.Node(iN)ST.KeyN = KeyN
              iN=0
                               → NodeIndexN := iN
                               → ListIDST.ⓢNodeFoundBL := T
                               → ∅
    )
}
```

Figure 9. The UPM model of the node retrieval process

was empty, RetrieveNode**PC** results in a specific error message ListID**ST**.&Retrieved**BL**:= **F**.

4.5. The Behavioral Model of the Node Update Process

The *node update* process, UpdateNode**PC**, is formally modeled as shown in Figure 10, which writes new data into the target node in a list identified by the key. The input arguments of the process are the given name of the list, the key of the target node, and the data for updating. The output result of the process is the status of the node update operation. UpdateNode**PC** checks if the target list exists and is not empty before the following operations: a) Search the target node with Key**N** by calling Find-Node**PC**; b) If the target node is found, replace the data field of the target node with given Data**RT**, and set ListID**ST**.&NodeUpdated**BL**:= **T**; c) Otherwise, report an error ListID**ST**.&NodeUpdated**BL**:= **F** with an exception warning of "node was not found." In case the given ListID**ST** did not exist or was empty, UpdateNode**PC** results in a specific error message ListID**ST**.&NodeUpdated**BL**:= **F**.

4.6. The Behavioral Model of the Node Insertion Process

The *node insertion* process, InsertNode**PC**, is formally modeled as shown in Figure 11, which inserts a newly created node at the current pointer position or a specific position before or after a given node in the list. The input arguments of the process are the list ID, the key of target node, the data, and the position for node insertion. Its output is the status of the insert operation. InsertNode**PC** checks if the target list exists and is not full before the following operations: a) Create the new node to be inserted by calling CreateNode**PC**; b) Depending on the given insertion position, do the following: (1) If the insertion position is at the current pointer (Position**N** = 1), append the new node into the list at the current position, update the links of both nodes, increase the counter ListID**ST**.#Nodes**N** by one, assign the key of the new node to be equal to the current number of nodes, and set ListID**ST**.&NodeInserted**BL**:= **T**; (2) If the insert position is after the target node identified by Key**N** (Position**N** = 2), find the target node, insert the new node into the list after the target node, update the links of the new node, the target node, and the

Figure 10. The UPM model of the node update process

```
UpdateNodePC(<I:: ListID ST, Key N, DataRT>; <O:: §NodeUpdatedBL>; <UDM:: List ST>) ≙
{
    → ( ◆ ListIDST.§ListCreatedBL = T ∧ ListIDST.§EmptyBL ≠ T
            → FindNodePC(<I:: ListIDST, KeyN>; <O:: NodeIndexN, §NodeFoundBL>; <UDM:: ListST>)
            → ( ◆ ListIDST.§NodeFoundBL = T
                    → ListIDST.Node(NodeIndexN)ST.DataRT := DataRT
                    → ListIDST.§NodeUpdatedBL:= T
                | ◆ ~
                    → ListIDST.§NodeUpdatedBL:= F
                    → ! ('The node was nor found in ListIDST,')
                )
        | ◆ ~
            → ListIDST.§NodeUpdatedBL:= F
            → ! ('ListIDST did not exist or was empty.')
        )
}
```

original node following the target node, increase the counter ListIDST.#NodesN by one, assign the key of the new node equal to NodeIndexN + 1, and set ListIDST.&NodeInsertedBL:= T; (3) If the insert position is before the target node identified by KeyN (PositionN = 3), find the target node, insert the new node into the list in front of the target node, update the links of the new node, the target node, the original node prior to the target node, increase the counter ListIDST.#NodesN by one, assign the key of the new node equal to NodeIndexN - 1, and set ListIDST.&NodeInsertedBL:= T; c) After the insertion operation, the sequence of affected nodes following the newly inserted node must be updated. This is implemented by increasing the keys of all affected nodes by one. Then, the full status of the list is checked; and d) In cases the target node could not be found, the given node could not be created, or the list did not exist or was full, an exception condition will be set by ListIDST.&NodeInsertedBL:= F.

4.7. The Behavioral Model of the Node Deletion Process

The *node deletion* process, DeleteNodePC, is formally modeled as shown in Figure 12, which removes a specific node at a given position in the list. The input arguments of the process are the list ID and the key of the target node. Its output is the status of the deletion operation. DeleteNodePC checks if the target list exists and is not empty

before the following operations: a) Find the target node to be deleted by calling FindNodePC; b) If the target node is allocated with the return of its NodeIndexN, do the following: (1) Determine the pointer of the target node, save both of its prior and next pointers, delete the target node by calling the support process ReleaseObjectPC, and disconnect the memory block from the target node; (2) Maintain the list by updating the node immediately before and after the deleted node, decrease ListIDST.#NodesN by one, and set ListIDST.&NodeInsertedBL:= T; (3) After the delete operation, the sequence of affected nodes following the deleted node must be updated. This is implemented by decreasing the keys of all affected nodes by one. Then, the empty status of the list is checked; and d) In cases the given node could not be found as well as the list did not exist or was empty, an exception condition will be set by ListIDST.&NodeDeletedBL:= F.

4.8. The Behavioral Model of the List Empty Test Process

The *empty test* process, EmptyTestPC, is formally modeled as shown in Figure 13, which detects whether a given list is empty. The input argument of the process is the target list ID. Its output is the status of the list as being empty or not. The status of an empty list is characterized by ListIDST.#NodesN = 1 where only the head node exists. Therefore, EmptyTestPC verifies if

Figure 11. The UPM model of the node insertion process

```
InsertNodePC(<I:: ListIDST, KeyN, DataST, PositionN>; <O:: ⓢNodeInsertedBL>; <UDM:: ListST>) ≙
{ → ( ◆ ListIDST.ⓢCreatedBL = T ∧ ListIDST.ⓢFullBL ≠ T
        ↣ CreateNodePC(<I:: NodeIDS, KeyN, DataRT>; <O:: NodeST, ⓢNodeCreatedBL>; <UDM:: ListST>)
        → ( ◆ ListIDST.NodeCreatedBL = T
             → ( ◆ PositionN = 1                                  // Insert a node at current position
                    → NodeST.PriorPtrP := ListIDST.CurrentPtrP
                    → NodeST.NextPtrP := ⊥
                    → ListID(CurrentPtrP)ST.NextP := NodeST.LocationP
                    → ListIDST.CurrentPtrP := NodeST.LocationP
                    → ↑ (ListIDST.#NodesN)
                    → iN := ListIDST.#NodesN
                    → NodeST.KeyN := iN
                    → ListIDST.ⓢNodeInsertedBL := T
                | ◆ PositionN = 2                                 // Insert a node after a given node
                    ↣ FindNodePC(<I:: ListIDST, KeyN>; <O:: NodeIndexN, ⓢNodeFoundBL>; <UDM:: ListST>)
                    → ( ◆ ListIDST.ⓢNodeFoundBL = T
                          → TargetNodeP := ListIDST.Node(NodeIndexN)ST.LocationP
                          → NodeST.PriorPtrP := TargetNodeP
                          → NodeST.NextPtrP := ListID(TargetNodeP)ST.NextPtrP
                          → TargetNodeST.NextPtrP := NodeST.LocationP
                          → iN := NodeIndexN + 1
                          → NodeST.KeyN := iN
                          → ↑ (ListIDST.#NodesN)
                          → ListIDST.ⓢNodeInsertedBL := T
                       | ◆ ~
                          → ListIDST.ⓢNodeInsertedBL := F
                          → ! ('The target node was not found in ListIDST.')
                       )
                | ◆ PositionN = 3                                 // Insert a node before a given node
ListIDST.#RecordN   ↣ FindNodePC(<I:: ListIDST, KeyN>; <O:: NodeIndexN, ⓢNodeFoundBL>; <UDM:: ListST>)
      R             → ( ◆ ListIDST.ⓢNodeFoundBL = T
   jN=iN                  → TargetNodeP := ListIDST.Node(NodeIndexN)ST.LocationP
                          → NodeST.PriorPtrP := ListID(TargetNodeP)ST.PriorPtrP
                          → NodeST.NextPtrP := TargetNodeP
                          → TargetNodeST.PriorPtrP := NodeST.LocationP
                          → iN := NodeIndexN
                          → NodeST.KeyN := iN -1
                          → ↑ (ListIDST.#NodesN)
                          → iN := NodeIndexN
                          → ListIDST.ⓢNodeInsertedBL := T
                       | ◆ ~
                          → ListIDST.ⓢNodeInsertedBL := F
                          → ! ('The target node was not found in ListIDST.')
                       )
                | ◆ ~
                    → ∅
               )
             →              ↑(ListIDST.Node(jN)ST.KeyN)     // Update keys of nodes following the inserted n ode

             → ◆ ListIDST.#NodesN = ListIDST.SizeN
                 → ListIDST.ⓢFullBL := T
          | ◆ ~
             → ListIDST.ⓢNodeInsertedBL := F
             → ! ('The given node was not created due to memory limitation.')
          )
     | ◆ ~
        → ListIDST.ⓢNodeInsertedBL := F
        → ! ('ListIDST was full or not existed.')
    )
}
```

Figure 12. The UPM model of the node deletion process

```
DeleteNodePC(<I:: ListID ST, Key N>; <O:: ⓈNodeDeletedBL>; <UDM:: List ST>) ≜
{
  → ( ◆ ListIDST.ⓈCreatedBL = T ∧ ◆ ListIDST.EmptyBL ≠ T
        → FindNodePC(<I:: ListIDST, KeyN>; <O:: NodeIndexN, ⓈNodeFoundBL>; <UDM:: ListST>)
        → ( ◆ ⓈNodeFoundBL = T
              → TargetNodeP := ListIDST.Node(NodeIndexN)ST.LocationP
              → TempPriorP := ListID(TargetNodeP)ST.PriorPtrP
              → TempNextP := ListID(TargetNodeP)ST.NextPtrP
              → ObjectIDP := TargetNodeP
              ↣ ReleaseObjectPC(<I:: ObjectIDP>; <O:: ⓈObjectReleasedBL>; <UDM:: MEMST>)
              → TargetNodeP ⇍ MEM(ObjectIDP)ST
              → ListID(TempPriorP)ST.NextPtrP := TempNextP
              → ListID(TempNextP)ST.PriorPtrP := TempPriorP
              → ListIDST.ⓈNodeDeletedBL := T
              → ↓ (ListIDST.#NodesN)
              → iN := NodeIndexN + 1

              →              ↓ (ListIDST.Node(jN)ST.KeyN)  // Update keys of nodes following the deleted node

              → ◆ ListIDST.#NodesN = 1
                   → ListIDST.ⓈEmptyBL := T
           | ◆ ~
              → ListIDST.ⓈNodeDeletedBL := F
              → ! ('The target node was not found.')
           )
     | ◆ ~
        → ListIDST.ⓈNodeDeletedBL := F
        → ! ('The list did not exist or was empty.')
  )
}
```

the number of nodes in the list is one in order to determine whether it is empty. When the given list did not exist, EmptyTest**PC** generates a specific error message ListID**ST**.&Empty**BL**:= **F**.

4.9. The Behavioral Model of the List Full Test Process

The *full test* process, FullTest**PC**, is formally modeled as shown in Figure 14, which detects whether a given list is full. The input argument of the process is the target list ID. Its output is the status of the list as being full or not. The status of a full list is characterized by ListID**ST**.#Nodes**N** = ListID**ST**.

Figure 13. The UPM model of the list empty test process

```
EmptyTestPC(<I:: ListID S>; <O:: ⓈEmptyBL>; <UDM:: List ST>) ≜
{
  → ( ◆ ListIDST.ⓈCreatedBL = T
        → ( ◆ ListIDST.#NodesN = 1
              → ListIDST.ⓈEmptyBL := T
              → ListIDST.ⓈFullBL := F
           | ◆ ~
              → ListIDST.ⓈEmptyBL := F
          )
     | ◆ ~
        → ! ('ListIDST did not exist.")
  )
}
```

Figure 14. The UPM model of the list full test process

```
FullTestPC(<I:: ListID S>; <O:: ⓢFull BL>; <UDM:: List ST>) ≙
{
  → ( ◆ ListIDST.ⓢCreatedBL = T
        → ( ◆ ListIDST.#NodesN = ListIDST.SizeN
              → ListIDST.ⓢFullBL := T
              → ListIDST.ⓢEmptyBL := F
          | ◆ ~
              → ListIDST.ⓢFullBL := F
          )
    | ◆ ~
        → ! ('ListIDST did not exist.')
    )
}
```

SizeN. Therefore, FullTestPC verifies if the number of nodes has reached the defined capacity of the list in order to determine whether it is full. When the given list did not exist, FullTestPC generates a specific error message ListIDST.&FullBL:= F.

4.10. The Behavioral Model of the List Clear Process

The *list clear* process, ClearPC, is formally modeled as shown in Figure 15, which not only logically sets the given list as empty, but also physically releases all existing nodes in memory. The input argument of the process is the given list ID. Its output is the status of the clear operation. ClearPC is equivalent to the sequential operations to first release the given list and then to re-create it by calling ReleaseListPC and CreateListPC, respectively. In case the given list did not exist, ClearPC generates a specific error message ListIDST.&ClearedBL = F.

4.11. The Behavioral Model of the List Release Process

The *list release* process, ReleasePC, is formally modeled as shown in Figure 16, which physically removes a given list and releases the memory

Figure 15. The UPM model of the list clear process

```
ClearPC(<I:: ListID S>; <O:: ⓢClearedBL>; <UDM:: List ST>) ≙
{
  → ( ◆ ListIDST.ⓢCreatedBL = T
        → SizeN := ListIDST.SizeN
        → DataRT := ListIDST.Node(0)RT.DataRT
        ↣ ReleasePC(<I:: ListIDS>; <O:: ⓢReleasedBL>; <UDM:: ListST>)
        ↣ CreateListPC(<I:: ListIDS, SizeN, DataRT>; <O:: ⓢListCreatedBL>; <UDM:: ListST>)
        → ListIDST.ⓢClearedBL := T
        → ListIDST.ⓢEmptyBL := T
    | ◆ ~
        → ListIDST.ⓢClearedBL := F
        → ! ('ListIDST did not exist.')
    )
}
```

Figure 16. The UPM model of the list release process

```
ReleasePC(<I:: ListIDS>; <O:: ⓢReleasedBL>; <UDM:: ListST>) ≙
{
  → ( ◆ ListIDST.ⓢCreatedBL = T
          ListIDST.#NodesN
     →         R              ( → ObjectIDP := ListIDST.Node(iN)ST.LocationP
              iN=0
                                ↣ ReleaseObjectPC(<I:: ObjectIDP>; <O:: ⓢObjectReleasedBL>; <UDM:: MEMST>)
                                → ListIDST.Node(iN)ST.LocationP ⇍ MEM(ObjectIDP)ST
                              )
       → ListIDS ⇍ MEM(ListIDP)ST
       → ListIDST.ⓢReleasedBL := T
       → ListIDST.ⓢCreatedBL := F
    | ◆ ~
       → ListIDST.ⓢ ReleasedBL := F
       → ! ('ListIDST did not exist.')
    )
}
```

occupied. The input argument of the process is the given list ID. Its output is the status of the release operation. ReleasePC frees and returns the memory block of each node to the system by calling a system support process, ReleaseObjectPC (Wang, Ngolah, Tan, Tian, & Sheu, 2010) for dynamic memory manipulation. It then disconnects the logical name of the list and its physical entity in memory. If the given list has not been created, ReleasePC produces a specific error message ListIDST.&ReleasedBL = F.

5. THE DYNAMIC BEHAVIORAL MODEL OF DLC-LISTS

According to the RTPA methodology, dynamic behaviors of a system are run-time process deployment and dispatching mechanisms based on the static behaviors modeled in UPMs, which is particularly useful when the List§ is a component or embedded part of a large software system. The dynamic behaviors of List§ integrate and dispatch the static behavioral processes of lists as modeled in List§.StaticBehaviorsPC. Based on the UPMs developed in the preceding sections, this section models the dynamic behaviors of the DLC-List at run-time via the dynamic processes of system dispatching elaborated by the event-driven mechanisms of the system.

The dynamic behaviors of DLC-Lists, List§.DynamicBehaviorsPC, are shown in Figure 17, which serve as an interface of the system to external users who can invoke any pre-defined process in the list ADT. The dynamic behaviors of List§ at run-time can be formally specified using the RTPA process dispatching methodology. List§.DynamicBehaviorsPC as given in Figure 17 establishes a set of top-level run-time relations between the 11 pairs of events and processes such as (@CreateListS ↳ CreateListPC), (@CreateNodeS ↳ CreateNodePC), (@FindNodeS ↳ FindNodePC), (@RetrieveNodeS ↳ RetrieveNodePC), (@UpdateNodeS ↳ UpdateNodePC), (@InsertNodeS ↳ InsertNodePC), (@DeleteNodeS ↳ DeleteNodePC), (@ClearS ↳ClearPC), (@EmptyTestS ↳ EmptyTestPC), (@FullTestS ↳FullTestPC), and (@ReleaseS ↳ReleasePC). Any exceptional event

Figure 17. The UPM model of the dynamic behaviors of the DLC-List

```
List§.DynamicBehaviorsPC ≙
{ § →
  ( @CreateListS     ↳ CreateListPC(<I:: ListIDS, SizeN, DataRT>; <O:: ⓢListCreatedBL>; <UDM:: ListST>)
  | @CreateNodeS     ↳ CreateNodePC(<I:: NodeIDS, DataRT>; <O:: Node(KeyN)ST, ⓢNodeCreatedBL>; <UDM:: ListST>)
  | @FindNodeS       ↳ FindNodePC(<I:: ListIDST, KeyN>; <O:: NodeIndexN, ⓢNodeFoundBL>; <UDM:: ListST>)
  | @RetrieveNodeS   ↳ RetrieveNodePC(<I:: ListIDST, KeyN>; <O:: ListIDST.Node(NodeIndexN)ST, ⓢNodeRetrievedBL>;
                                       <UDM:: ListST>)
  | @UpdateNodeS     ↳ UpdateNodePC(<I:: ListIDST, KeyN, DataRT>; <O:: ⓢNodeUpdatedBL>; <UDM:: ListST>)
  | @InsertNodeS     ↳ InsertNodePC(<I:: ListIDST, KeyN, DataST, PositionN>; <O:: ⓢNodeInsertedBL>; <UDM:: ListST>)
  | @DeleteNodeS     ↳ DeleteNodePC(<I:: ListIDST, KeyN>; <O:: ⓢNodeDeletedBL>; <UDM:: ListST>)
  | @EmptyTestS      ↳ EmptyTestPC(<I:: ListIDS>; <O:: ⓢEmptyBL>; <UDM:: ListST>)
  | @FullTestS       ↳ FullTestPC(<I:: ListIDS>; <O:: ⓢFullBL>; <UDM:: ListST>)
  | @ClearS          ↳ ClearPC(<I:: ListIDS>; <O:: ⓢClearedBL>; <UDM:: ListST>)
  | @ReleaseS        ↳ ReleasePC(<I:: ListIDS>; <O:: ⓢReleasedBL>; <UDM:: ListST>)
  | ~                → ∅
  ) → §
}
```

that is not specified as a valid one in the system will be ignored by the skip operator (→ ∅). The event-driven dispatching mechanism also puts List§ into the context of a specific application.

The practical formal engineering methodology of RTPA for system modeling and specification provides a coherent notation system and a systematical approach for large-scale software and hybrid system design and implementation. A series of formal design models and frameworks of real-world and real-time applications in RTPA have been developed using RTPA notations and methodologies (Wang, 2002, 2007, 2008a; Wang & Huang, 2008; Wang, Tan, & Ngolah, 2010) in the formal design engineering approach, such as the telephone switching system (TSS) (Wang, 2009b), the lift dispatching system (LDS) (Wang et al., 2009), the automated teller machine (ATM) (Wang, Zhang, Sheu, Li, & Guo, 2010), the real-time operating system (RTOS+) (Wang et al., 2010a, 2010b), the autonomic code generator (RTPA-CG) (Wang, Tan, & Ngolah, 2010), the ADTs (Wang, Ngolah, Tan, Tian, & Sheu, 2010), the file management system (FMS) (Wang et al., 2011), and the air traffic control system (to be reported). Further studies have demonstrated that RTPA is not only elegant and practically useful as a generic notation and hierarchical methodology for software engineering, but also good at modeling human cognitive processes in cognitive informatics and computational intelligence as reported in (Wang, 2008d, 2009a, 2010a, 2010b, 2010c; Wang & Ruhe, 2007; Wang & Chiew, 2010).

6. CONCLUSION

Lists are one of the most fundamental and widely used ADTs in system modeling. However, there was a lack of a formal and complete model for lists. This paper has developed a comprehensive design pattern of formal lists using a doubly-linked-circular (DLC) model of lists. The conceptual model, architectural model, and static/dynamic behavioral models of lists have been systematically presented. The generic UDM and the 12 UPMs of lists have provided a set of rigorous architectural and behavioral models of formal lists based on them any concrete lists can be derived and implemented. An expressive and elegant denotational mathematics, Real-Time Process Algebra (RTPA), has been adopted to rigorously design and refine both architectural and behavioral models of lists and their manipulations in a top-down approach. This work has been applied in a number of real-time and nonreal-time system designs such as a real-time operating system (RTOS+), a file management system (FMS), and the ADT library for an RTPA-based automatic code generation tool.

ACKNOWLEDGMENT

The authors would like to acknowledge the Natural Science and Engineering Council of Canada (NSERC) for its partial support to this work. We would like to thank the anonymous reviewers for their valuable comments and suggestions.

REFERENCES

Bollella, G., Brosgol, B., Furr, S., Hardin, D., Dibble, P., Gosling, J., & Turnbull, M. (2002). *The real-time specification for java*. Reading, MA: Addison-Wesley.

Broy, M., Pair, C., & Wirsing, M. (1984). A systematic study of models of abstract data types. *Theoretical Computer Science, 33*, 139–1274. doi:10.1016/0304-3975(84)90086-0

Cardelli, L., & Wegner, P. (1985). On understanding types, data abstraction and polymorphism. *ACM Computing Surveys, 17*(4), 471–522. doi:10.1145/6041.6042

Guttag, J. V. (1977). Abstract data types and the development of data structures. *Communications of the ACM, 20*(6), 396–404. doi:10.1145/359605.359618

Lipschutz, S., & Lipson, M. (1997). *Schaum's outline of theories and problems of discrete mathematics* (2nd ed.). New York, NY: McGraw-Hill.

McDermid, J. (Ed.). (1991). *Software engineer's reference book*. Oxford, UK: Butterworth Heinemann.

Mitchell, J. C. (1990). Type systems for programming languages . In van Leeuwen, J. (Ed.), *Handbook of theoretical computer science* (pp. 365–458). Amsterdam, The Netherlands: North Holland.

Russel, B. (1903). *The principles of mathematics*. London, UK: George Allen & Unwin.

Stubbs, D. F., & Webre, N. W. (1985). *Data structures with abstract data types and Pascal*. Monterey, CA: Brooks/Cole Publishing.

Wang, Y. (2002). The real-time process algebra (RTPA). *Annals of Software Engineering: An International Journal, 14*, 235–274. doi:10.1023/A:1020561826073

Wang, Y. (2007). *Software engineering foundations: A software science perspective* (*Vol. 2*). Boca Raton, FL: Auerbach Publications.

Wang, Y. (2008a). RTPA: A denotational mathematics for manipulating intelligent and computational behaviors. *International Journal of Cognitive Informatics and Natural Intelligence, 2*(2), 44–62. doi:10.4018/jcini.2008040103

Wang, Y. (2008b). Mathematical laws of software. *Transactions of Computational Science, 2*, 46–83. doi:10.1007/978-3-540-87563-5_4

Wang, Y. (2008c). Deductive semantics of RTPA. *International Journal of Cognitive Informatics and Natural Intelligence, 2*(2), 95–121. doi:10.4018/jcini.2008040106

Wang, Y. (2008d). On contemporary denotational mathematics for computational intelligence. *Transactions of Computational Science, 2*, 6–29. doi:10.1007/978-3-540-87563-5_2

Wang, Y. (2009a). Paradigms of denotational mathematics for cognitive informatics and cognitive computing. *Fundamenta Informaticae, 90*(3), 282–303.

Wang, Y. (2009b). The formal design model of a telephone switching system (TSS). *International Journal of Software Science and Computational Intelligence, 1*(3), 92–116. doi:10.4018/jssci.2009070107

Wang, Y. (2010a). Cognitive robots: A reference model towards intelligent authentication. *IEEE Robotics and Automation, 17*(4), 54–62. doi:10.1109/MRA.2010.938842

Wang, Y. (2010b). On formal and cognitive semantics for semantic computing. *International Journal of Semantic Computing, 4*(2), 203–237. doi:10.1142/S1793351X10000833

Wang, Y. (2010c). On concept algebra for computing with words (CWW). *International Journal of Semantic Computing, 4*(3), 331–356. doi:10.1142/S1793351X10001061

Wang, Y., & Chiew, V. (2010). On the cognitive process of human problem solving. *Cognitive Systems Research: An International Journal, 11*(1), 81–92. doi:10.1016/j.cogsys.2008.08.003

Wang, Y., & Huang, J. (2008). Formal modeling and specification of design patterns using RTPA. *International Journal of Cognitive Informatics and Natural Intelligence, 2*(1), 100–111. doi:10.4018/jcini.2008010108

Wang, Y., Ngolah, C. F., Ahmadi, H., Sheu, P. C. Y., & Ying, S. (2009). The formal design model of a lift dispatching system (LDS). *International Journal of Software Science and Computational Intelligence, 1*(4), 98–122. doi:10.4018/jssci.2009062506

Wang, Y., Ngolah, C. F., Tan, X., Tian, Y., & Sheu, P. C. Y. (2010). The formal design models of a set of abstract data models (ADTs). *International Journal of Software Science and Computational Intelligence, 2*(4), 72–104. doi:10.4018/jssci.2010100106

Wang, Y., Ngolah, C. F., Tan, X., Tian, Y., & Sheu, P. C. Y. (2011). The formal design models of a file management systems (FMS). *International Journal of Software Science and Computational Intelligence, 3*(1), 90–113.

Wang, Y., Ngolah, C. F., Zeng, G., Sheu, P. C. Y., Choy, C. P., & Tian, Y. (2010a). The formal design models of a real-time operating system (RTOS+): Conceptual and architectural frameworks. *International Journal of Software Science and Computational Intelligence, 2*(2), 105–122. doi:10.4018/jssci.2010040106

Wang, Y., Ngolah, C. F., Zeng, G., Sheu, P. C. Y., Choy, C. P., & Tian, Y. (2010b). The formal design models of a real-time operating System (RTOS+): Static and dynamic behavior models. *International Journal of Software Science and Computational Intelligence, 2*(3), 79–105. doi:10.4018/jssci.2010070106

Wang, Y., & Ruhe, G. (2007). The cognitive process of decision making. *International Journal of Cognitive Informatics and Natural Intelligence, 1*(2), 73–85. doi:10.4018/jcini.2007040105

Wang, Y., Tan, X., & Ngolah, C. F. (2010). Design and implementation of an autonomic code generator based on RTPA (RTPA-CG). *International Journal of Software Science and Computational Intelligence, 2*(2), 44–67. doi:10.4018/jssci.2010040103

Wang, Y., Zhang, Y., Sheu, P. C. Y., Li, X., & Guo, H. (2010). The formal design models of an automatic teller machine (ATM). *International Journal of Software Science and Computational Intelligence, 2*(1), 102–131. doi:10.4018/jssci.2010101907

Wiener, R., & Pinson, L. J. (2000). *Fundamentals of OOP and data structures in java*. Cambridge, UK: Cambridge University Press.

This work was previously published in the International Journal of Software Science and Computational Intelligence, Volume 3, Issue 2, edited by Yingxu Wang, pp. 83-102, copyright 2011 by IGI Publishing (an imprint of IGI Global).

Chapter 16
Petri Nets and Discrete Events Systems

Juan L. G. Guirao
Polytechnic University of Cartagena, Spain

Fernando L. Pelayo
University of Castilla - La Mancha, Spain

ABSTRACT

This paper provides an overview over the relationship between Petri Nets and Discrete Event Systems as they have been proved as key factors in the cognitive processes of perception and memorization. In this sense, different aspects of encoding Petri Nets as Discrete Dynamical Systems that try to advance not only in the problem of reachability but also in the one of describing the periodicity of markings and their similarity, are revised. It is also provided a metric for the case of Non-bounded Petri Nets.

INTRODUCTION

The interaction between perception and/or memorization with information exposing time are consistent with a theory which relates processing time to perceived duration, see Thomas (1975). It is mainly due because such temporal information is obtained from both a sort of timer processing and a visual information processing, so attention effectiveness is a function of these two processings, in which the range of durations become so important that it has been proved that there is a minimum quantum of time (discrete measurements) below which neither work. These facts also open the field of considering timed formalisms (Pelayo, 2005) for properly describing and analyzing these issues.

In Wang (2002), a seed study of the Cognitive Models of the brain can be found. Among others, a description of the memorizing process is there shown, moreover Wang has given an implementation of this cognitive process in RTPA, which has been taken by the authors of this paper as reference in Barquilla (2008) to formally describe this cognitive process

DOI: 10.4018/978-1-4666-2651-5.ch016

Petri Nets (Petri, 1966) and Dynamical Systems (Arrowsmith, 1990) have increased their popularity during the last decades. Both mathematical tools have many analysis methods available and have become classical for modeling discrete-event processes.

In fact, many papers (David, 1991, 1994; Silva, 1990) show how discrete-event processes can be modeled by Petri Nets. There are also papers that present how to model these processes by discrete-event dynamical systems (Foursov, 2006).

Thus, it motivates to analyze if there exists any relation between these tools and what advantages are taking each one. Mainly, we wonder if a given Petri net corresponds directly to dynamical systems and the Petri Net properties have counterparts in the corresponding dynamical system.

In Foursov (2006), the authors make a partial attempt to do that, i.e., based on formal power series, they obtain an algorithm that allows checking whether a given weighted Petri net corresponds to a continuous polynomial dynamical system. But in this context, different initial states of the Petri net (different initial markings) could correspond to different dynamical systems.

Therefore, the work of giving a correspondence between Petri nets and dynamical systems was incomplete and we proposed (Guirao, 2011) different ways that try to solve not only the problem of reachability, but also the one of describing the periodicity of markings and their similarity.

The structure of the paper is as follows: We show how Petri nets can be used to model discrete-event processes. It is explained how to define the state space and the evolution operator in order to encode Petri nets as discrete dynamical systems. The next section is dedicated to introduce a metric for the states space; it is based on the Bayre metric, usually employed when modeling computer processes. We deal with giving a proper metric for non-bounded Petri nets. Finally, some conclusions and further research directions are presented.

PETRI NETS MODELING DISCRETE-EVENTS PROCESSES

A Petri Net is a bipartite graph constituted by two kinds of nodes, namely, places and transitions that alternate on a path made up of consecutive arcs. Places are usually represented by circles and transitions by boxes or rectangles. The number of places is finite and not zero and the same occurs for the number of transitions (David, 1994). More rigorously:

Definition 1: A Petri Net (PN) is a triple $N = (P, T, F)$ consisting of two finite sets P and T, and a relation F defined over $P \cup T$, such that:

1. $P \cap T = \varnothing$
2. $F \subseteq (P \times T) \cup (T \times P)$
3. $dom\,(F) \cup cod\,(F) = P \cup T$

P is said to be the *set of places*, T is called the *set of transitions* and F is named the *flow relation*.

A Petri Net is a very useful tool in order to model a concurrent system due to not only their graphical nature, but also because of being able to simulate concurrent execution of actions in a system, in this sense, Petri Nets are marked. That is, the state of a system described by a PN is captured by means of the so called *Markings*.

Definition 2: Let $N = (P, T, F)$ be a Petri Net. A function $M : P \to \mathbb{N}$ is a Marking of N. Thus, (P, T, F, M) is a Marked Petri Net, MPN.

Markings of Petri Nets are graphically represented by including in the places as many points as tokens.

Given a MPN (P, T, F, M) with $P = \left\{ p_1, ..., p_n \right\}$, a marking M of it is codified as the n-tuple containing in position i the number of tokens in place p_i, i.e., it is codified as $(M(p_1),...,M(p_n))$.

The evolution of a MPN is captured both by the following firing rule which establishes when a transition can be fired and the marking obtained after firing.

Definition 3: Let $N = (P, T, F, M)$ be a MPN. A transition $t \in T$ is enabled at a marking M, denoted by $M[t\rangle$, if $\forall\, p \in P\, /\, (p, t) \in F$, we have $M(p) > 0$ ($M(p) = 1$, for safe PNs).

An enabled transition $t \in T$ can be fired, thus producing a new marking, M':

$$M'(p) = M(p) - W_f(p, t) + W_f(p, t) \quad \forall\, p \in P$$

$$\text{where } W_f(x) = \begin{cases} 1 & if \quad x \in F \\ 0 & if \quad x \notin F \end{cases}$$

$$\forall\, x \in (P \times T) \cup (T \times P)$$

It is denoted by $M[t\rangle M'$.

In order to facilitate the understanding of the evolution of a PN, it could be adequate to consider that the firing of a transition has zero duration and that every enabled transitions are fired at the same time.

In the next example, extracted from David (1994), the concepts presented above will be illustrated and our purposes will be motivated.

Example 1: The discrete-event system we want to model is constituted by two billiard balls, A and B, which move along the same straight line, parallel to one of the bands.

A can move to the right or to the left and the same occurs for B. If in the initial state of the system, A moves to the right while B moves to the left with the same speed, in a certain moment, they will hit and then the balls set off again in the opposite direction (it can be assumed with the

same speed). When a ball strikes a band, sets off in the other direction again (we also assume with the same speed).

This discrete-event system is modeled by the PN of Figure 1.

The event hitting is associated to the initial state of the system, which can be formalized by the marking $M_0 = (1, 1, 0, 0)$, and the transition T_1. It is not known when this event will occur, but it is sure that it will occur because this transition is enabled.

After firing T_1, the initial state of the system evolves to a new state that can be formalized by the marking $M_1 = (0, 0, 1, 1)$, what makes the transitions T_2 and T_3 to be enabled. At this point, both transitions could be fired at the same time (or not). If it happens, the system evolves to the initial state so arising a periodic state of the system of period 2. On the contrary, if T_2 is fired before T_3, an intermediate state appears $M_2 = (1, 0, 0, 1)$, but after that the system evolves to the initial state, also providing a periodic state, but of period 3 in this case.

Similarly, a periodic state of period 3 is obtained if T_3 is fired before T_2.

From the point of view of the dynamics, describing the orbital structure of a system and analyzing whether or not this structure remains when the system is perturbed is the most interesting issue (Arrowsmith, 1990; Wiggins, 1990). So, it motivates our attempt for modeling PNs as discrete dynamical systems.

PETRI NETS AS DISCRETE DYNAMICAL SYSTEMS

It is worth our while to remark that, since a place can belongs to the precondition set of more than one different transition, a token in it could potentially enable more than one transition. Thus, after firing different transitions, more than one marking can be reached. This fact has lead us to consider as

Figure 1. Billiard balls

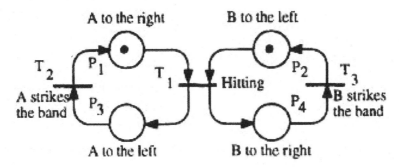

phase space not the set of binary n-tuples but the set of all its subsets, in order to properly capture these cases.

Our first approach to encode PNs as DDSs associates the MOPN of Figure 2 the state vector (1,1,1,0,0),in the direct way that, the number of tokens in place p_i appears as the i component of the n-binary state vector which encodes the net. Of course the model of DDS needs to be enough descriptive of its PN (both static and dynamic properties), therefore all the possible

evolutions of the PN must be captured and it is clear that the MOPN of Figure 2 can evolve to any of the nets of Figure 3, in consequence the state space of our DDSs must be $P\left(\mathrm{N}^n\right)$ ($P\left(\{0,1\}^n\right)$ for 1-safe Petri Nets).

DEFINITION OF THE DDS

Given a MOPN $N=(P,T,F,M)$, we define its associated DDS as the triple (X,τ,Φ), where:

Figure 2. MOPN whose state vector is (1,1,1,0,0)

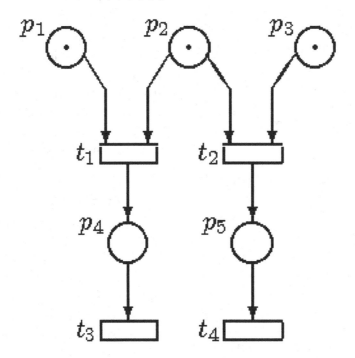

Figure 3. MOPNs whose state vectors are (0,0,1,1,0) and (1,0,0,0,1)

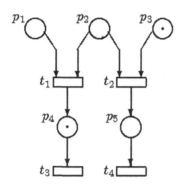 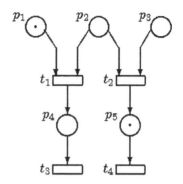

- $X = P(\mathrm{N}^n)$ is the set of all subsets of N^n, being n the number of places of the MOPN

- τ is the monoid $\mathrm{N} \cup \{0\}$

- $\Phi : \tau \, x \, X \to X$ is the evolution operator Φ verifying:

  ○ $\Phi(0,A) = A \; \forall \, A \in X$,   i.e., $\Phi_0 = Id_X$

  ○ $\Phi(1,A) = B \; A,B \in X$, where:

    ▪ $A = \{x_1,...,x_k\}$ where $x_i \in \mathrm{N}^n$ encodes Markings of the MOPN N

    ▪ $B = \bigcup_{i=1}^{k} B_i$

    ▪ $B_i = \bigcup_{j=1}^{t} \{y_i^j\}$,   i.e., the union of all (t) possible reachable markings from x_i, defined by $x_i [R_i \rangle y_i^j$ being R_i the set of transitions of the net enabled at marking x_i

  ○ $\Phi(t,\Phi(s,A)) = \Phi(t+s,A)$ $\forall \, t,s \in \tau, \; \forall \, A \in X$

A METRIC FOR THE DDS ASSOCIATED TO A 1-SAFE PETRI NET

In this case $X = P(\{0,1\}^n)$. The following distance determines a topology T on this set, such that the pair $(P(\{0,1\}^n), \mathrm{T})$ is a complete or compact topological (state) space.

In order to do that, following some of the ideas in Rodriguez-Lopez (2008), we begin by defining on $\{0,1\}^n$ a metric, induced from the Bayre metric (Baker, 1996), given by

$$d(x,y) = \frac{1}{2^{l(x \Pi y)}} - \frac{1}{2^n} \quad x,y \in \{0,1\}^n$$

where $l(x \Pi y)$ is the length of the longest common initial part of the vectors x and y.

Theorem 1: The function d is a metric on $\{0,1\}^n$.
Proof 1: See Guirao (2011).

From d, the distance, dd, between a vector $x \in \{0,1\}^n$ and a set of vectors $B \in P(\{0,1\}^n)$ is defined as:

$$dd(x,B) = \min\{d(x,y) : y \in B\}$$
$$x \in \{0,1\}^n \text{ and } B \in P(\{0,1\}^n)$$

this allows to define the distance between two elements A, $B \in P(\{0,1\}^n)$ as ddd

$$ddd(A,B) =$$
$$\max\{d(x,B), d(A,y): x \in A, y \in B\}$$
$$A, B \in P(\{0,1\}^n)$$

Theorem 2: The function ddd defined over $P(\{0,1\}^n)$ is a metric.

Proof 2: See Guirao (2011).

Theorem 3: $(P(\{0,1\}^n), ddd)$ is a complete metric space.

Proof 3: From the definition of d it is clear that the minimum distance between two elements of $\{0,1\}^n$ is $\dfrac{1}{2^n}$ then every Cauchy's succession converges.

METRICS FOR NON-BOUNDED PETRI NETS

In this case $X = P(\mathbb{N}^n)$, and this new kind of state vector does not coexists coherently with the distance d defined for the case of 1-safe Petri Nets. This is mainly because for the {\it binary} scenario a difference in the marking of a place means that every transition which has this place as precondition could potentially be enabled in one case and necessarily disabled in the other, meanwhile for this case in which the number of tokens in a place belongs to $\mathbb{N}$, this is not true in general therefore as the firing of transitions is the basis for the dynamics of PNs, this becomes a key factor for properly defining the dynamics of PNs and should be so considered.

Let's see it by means of the following example where Figures 4, 5 and 6 show three markings of the same OPN whose codifications are $(0,1,0,5,1,0)$, $(0,1,1,4,1,0)$ and $(0,1,2,3,1,0)$ respectively. If we compute the distance between the second (Figure

5) and the first (Figure 4), and the distance between the second (Figure 5) and the third (Figure 6) the same value is obtained, since the first difference in the codification of the markings appears in the third place in both cases, but meanwhile both the MOPN of Figure 5 and that of Figure 6 are able to fire the transition t2, on the contrary, the MOPN of Figure 3 is not able to fire this transition.

For the sake of solving this, we have chosen the *transition vector* as reference for the new metric, this transition vector can be naturally defined as the ordered binary tuple with as many elements as transitions on the PN, where 1 in position i means that transition t_i is enabled, and 0 means the contrary. We denote as $tv(x)$ the transition vector of the marking encoded by x.

Now we redefine the distance between markings:

$$D(x,y) = \frac{1}{2^{l(tv(x) \, \Pi \, tv(y))}} - \frac{1}{2^m} \quad x, y \in \mathbb{N}^n$$

where $l(tv(x) \Pi tv(y))$ is the length of the longest common initial part of the transition vectors of x and y, and $m \in \mathbb{N}$ is the number of transitions of the PN.

Although the function D properly solves the stated problem between the enabling or not of the transition $t2$ of the examples, once the first difference of two transition vectors appears, the function D is blind over what happens in the following transitions. To make this problem clear, let us consider the new marking of this PN whose codification is $(0,1,1,4,0,1)$, see Figure 7, its associated transition vector is $(0,1,0,1)$. The distance between the nets of Figure 4 and Figure 5 according to D equals the distance of the pair of nets of Figure 4 and Figure 7 by D, but again this is blind to the very different behaviour of the pair of nets of Figure 4 and Figure 7, and the not so different behaviour of the pair of Figure 4 and

Figure 4. Marking (0,1,0,5,1,0) of the PN. Transition vector (0,0,1,0).

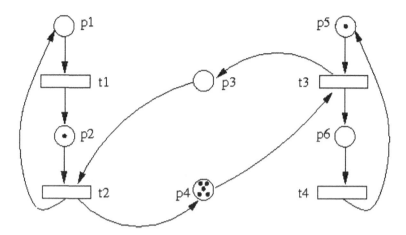

Figure 5, in terms of the transitions they are able to fire.

We finally decided to define the distance of two elements as:

$$distance\,(\,x\,,\,y\,) = \frac{1}{2^{\,match\quad(tv(x)\,=\,tv(y))}} - \frac{1}{2^{\,m}}$$

$$x\,,\,y \in \mathrm{N}^{\,n}$$

where $match\quad(\,tv\,(\,x\,) = tv\,(\,y\,)\,)$ is the number of coincides on the transition vectors of

$x\,,\,y \in \mathrm{N}^{\,n}$ and $m \in \mathrm{N}$ is the number of transitions of the PN.

From this pseudometric $dis\tan ce$, we define the $Dis\tan ce$ between a vector $x \in \mathrm{N}^{\,n}$ and a set B of vectors $\mathrm{N}^{\,n}$, i.e., an element in $P\,(\,\mathrm{N}^{\,n}\,)$, in this manner:

$$Distance\,(\,x\,,\,B\,) = \min\,\{\,dis\tan ce\,(\,x\,,\,y\,) : y \in B\,\}$$

$x \in \mathrm{N}^{\,n}$ and $B \in P\,(\,\mathrm{N}^{\,n}\,)$

Figure 5. Marking (0,1,1,4,1,0) of the PN. Transition vector (0,1,1,0).

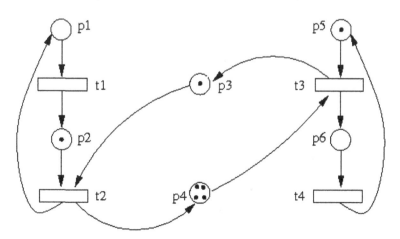

Figure 6. {Marking (0,1,2,3,1,0) of the PN. Transition vector (0,1,1,0).

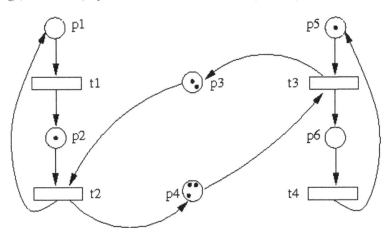

and, consequently, we establish the $DISTANCE$ between $A, B \in P\left(\mathrm{N}^n\right)$

$$DISTANCE\ (A,B) = \max\{Distance(x,B), Distance(A,y) : x \in A, y \in B\}$$

$$A, B \in P\left(\mathrm{N}^n\right)$$

The distance $DISTANCE$ so defined determines a quasi-pseudometric on $P\left(\mathrm{N}^n\right)$.

CONCLUSIONS AND FURTHER RESEARCH DIRECTIONS

Given the 1-safe MOPN $N = (P, T, F, M)$ its associated DDS (X, τ, Φ) has been defined as well as the distance ddd which makes $\left(P\left(\{0,1\}^n\right), ddd\right)$ a complete metric space. Since in this case of discrete dynamical system, we have a finite state space $P\left(\{0,1\}^n\right)$ with $2^{\left(2^n\right)}$ elements, it is immediate that every orbit must be either periodic or eventually periodic, thus every orbit is an invariant set of the system. However, it is interesting to study the different

Figure 7. Marking (0,1,1,4,0,1) of the PN. Transition vector (0,1,0,1).

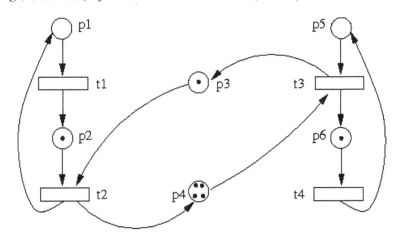

coexistent periods of its orbits and the existence (or not) of fixed points and their basin of attraction (Baker, 1998; Romaguera, 2003).

Over Non-bounded Petri Nets, it has been presented a metric for the set of markings of every Non-bounded Ordinary Petri Net. This metric is different to the one of the case of 1-safe Petri Nets, in fact it is based on the (enabled) transition vector associated to each Marking and it gives very valuable information over the behaviour of the corresponding PN.

In this last case the phase space is infinite but again the way of defining the evolution operator is quite far for the optimum. We plan to study this case specially related with the analytic power of the Incidence Matrix associated to a Petri Net.

The authors are interested in studying the correspondence of the reachability problem and bisimulation equivalence on the PN model, and the dynamics of the associated DDS.

On the other hand, the study of periodicity of Markings in a PN has not been properly studied so far. The authors plan also to study this subject as the example of the billiard balls has shown as very interesting.

ACKNOWLEDGMENT

This work has been partially supported by project TIN2009-14312-C02-02.

REFERENCES

Arrowsmith, D. K., & Place, C. M. (1990). *An introduction to dynamical systems*. Cambridge, UK: Cambridge University Press.

Baker, J. W., & Vink, E. P. (1996). A metric approach to control flow semantics. *Annals of the New York Academy of Sciences*, *806*, 11–27. doi:10.1111/j.1749-6632.1996.tb49156.x

Baker, J. W., & Vink, E. P. (1998). Denotational models for programming languages: Applications of Banach's fixed point theorem. *Topology Applications*, *85*, 35–52. doi:10.1016/S0166-8641(97)00140-5

Barquilla, N. L., Nuñez, M., & Pelayo, F. L. (2008). A comparative study of STOPA and RTPA. *Transactions on Computational Science*, *2*, 224–245.

David, R. (1991). Modeling of dynamics systems by Petri Nets. In *Proceedings of the 1ˢᵗ European Control Conference* (pp. 136-147).

David, R., & Alla, H. (1994). Petri nets for modeling of dynamics systems. *Automatica*, *30*, 136–147. doi:10.1016/0005-1098(94)90024-8

Foursov, M. V., & Hespel, C. (2006). Weighted petri nets and polynomial dynamical systems. In *Proceedings of the 17ᵗʰ International Symposium on Mathematical Theory of Networks and Systems* (pp. 1539-1546).

Guirao, J. L. G., Pelayo, F. L., & Valverde, J. C. (2011). Modelling dynamics of concurrent computing systems. *Computers & Mathematics with Applications (Oxford, England)*, *61*, 1402–1406. doi:10.1016/j.camwa.2011.01.008

Pelayo, F. L., Cuartero, F., Valero, V., Pelayo, M. L., & Merayo, M. G. (2005). How does memory work? By timed-arc petri nets. In *Proceedings of the 4ᵗʰ IEEE International Conference on Cognitive Informatics* (pp. 128-135).

Petri, C. A. (1966). *Communications with automata* (Tech. Rep. No. RADC-TR-65-377). New York, NY: New York University Press.

Rodriguez-Lopez, J., Romaguera, S., & Valero, O. (2008). Denotational semantics for programming languages, balanced quasi-metrics and fixed points. *International Journal of Computer Mathematics*, *85*(3), 623–630. doi:10.1080/00207160701210653

Romaguera, S., & Sanchis, M. (2003). Applications of utility functions defined on quasi-metric spaces. *Journal of Mathematical Analysis and Applications, 283,* 219–235. doi:10.1016/S0022-247X(03)00285-3

Silva, M., & Valette, R. (1990). *Petri nets and flexible manufacturing.* Retrieved from http://homepages.laas.fr/robert/papers.pri/design.pri/maphiro89.pdf

Thomas, E. A. C., & Weavery, W. B. (1975). Cognitive processing and time perception. *Perception & Psychophysics, 17*(4), 363–367. doi:10.3758/BF03199347

Wang, Y. (2002). Cognitive models of the brain. In *Proceedings of the 1ˢᵗ IEEE International Conference on Cognitive Informatics* (pp. 259-269).

This work was previously published in the International Journal of Software Science and Computational Intelligence, Volume 3, Issue 3, edited by Yingxu Wang, pp. 13-22, copyright 2011 by IGI Publishing (an imprint of IGI Global).

Chapter 17
The Formal Design Models of a Universal Array (UA) and its Implementation

Yingxu Wang
University of Calgary, Canada

Jason Huang
University of Calgary, Canada

Jingsheng Lei
Shanghai University of Electrical Power, China

ABSTRACT

Arrays are one of the most fundamental and widely applied data structures, which are useful for modeling both logical designs and physical implementations of multi-dimensional data objects sharing the same type of homogeneous elements. However, there is a lack of a formal model of the universal array based on it any array instance can be derived. This paper studies the fundamental properties of Universal Array (UA) and presents a comprehensive design pattern. A denotational mathematics, Real-Time Process Algebra (RTPA), allows both architectural and behavioral models of UA to be rigorously designed and refined in a top-down approach. The conceptual model of UA is rigorously described by tuple- and matrix-based mathematical models. The architectural models of UA are created using RTPA architectural modeling methodologies known as the Unified Data Models (UDMs). The physical model of UA is implemented using linear list that is indexed by an offset pointer of elements. The behavioral models of UA are specified and refined by a set of Unified Process Models (UPMs). As a case study, the formal UA models are implemented in Java. This work has been applied in a number of real-time and nonreal-time systems such as compilers, a file management system, the real-time operating system (RTOS+), and the ADT library for an RTPA-based automatic code generation tool.

DOI: 10.4018/978-1-4666-2651-5.ch017

1. INTRODUCTION

Although it is difficult to image higher dimensional structures in data and architectural modeling when the number of dimensions is greater than three, there are fundamental needs in science and engineering to model a wide range of natural entities and abstract artifacts in higher dimensions. For example, in physics, despite the natural world is conveniently perceived as three dimensional, the abstract world is modeled by 11 dimensions (11-D) or even higher ones according to the string theories (Becker, 2007). In cognitive informatics, the human behavioral space is a 4-dimensional structure known as object, action, space, and time (Wang, 2007). In computational linguistics, a sentence, its syntactic structure, and semantic space are recognized by 1-D, 2-D, and 5-D models, respectively (Wang, 2009c). In computer science, there are numerals entities and abstract data models that are multi-dimensional arrays or matrices such as in numerical methods, computational intelligence, and weather predication (Chapra & Ganale, 2002; Stubbs & Webre, 1985).

An array is a linear data structure with homogeneous elements accessible by random or sequential addressing. The mathematical model of arrays is a vector (1-D array) or a tuple of matrices (n-D arrays) (Stubbs & Webre, 1985; Matlab, 2010). Arrays are the most fundamental and widely used data structures to model both logical designs and physical implementations of multi-dimensional data objects that share the same type of elements. Arrays are the most fundamental and widely used data structures in computing and everyday life. Various important data objects can be modeled and implemented by arrays such as a set of numbers, a list of names, a relational database, and a dictionary of words in a language (McDermid, 1991; Wiener & Pinson, 2000). Arrays play a central role in Matlab where the fundamental data models are vectors and matrices that can be implemented by 1-D and *n*-D arrays in computing, respectively (Matlab, 2010).

Data object modeling is a process to creatively extract and abstractly represent a real-world problem by data models based on the constraints of given computing resources (Wang, 2008b). An arbitrary array can be formally modeled by an Abstract Data Type (ADT) (Guttag, 1977; Broy et al., 1984; Cardelli & Wegner, 1985; Stubbs & Webre, 1985), which is a logical model of a complex and/or user defined data structure with a set of predefined operations. Using types to model real-world entities can be traced back to the mathematical thought of Bertrand Russell in 1900s (Russell, 1903) and George Cantor in 1932 (Lipschutz & Lipson, 1997). A number of ADTs have been identified in computing and system modeling such as *stack, queue, sequence, record, array, list, tree, file,* and *graph* (Broy et al., 1984; Mitchell, 1990; McDermid, 1991; Wang, 2007; Wang, Ngolah, Tan, Tian, & Sheu, 2010). ADTs possess the following properties: (i) An extension of type constructions by integrating both data structures and functional behaviors; (ii) A hybrid data object modeling technique that *encapsulates* both user defined data structures and allowable operations on them; (iii) The interface and implementation of an ADT are separated where detailed implementation of the ADT is hidden to applications that invoke the ADT and its predefined operations.

In order to formally model the universal array as an ADT, an expressive denotational mathematics, Real-Time Process Algebra (RTPA) (Wang, 2002, 2007, 2008a, 2008b, 2008c, 2008d, 2009a; Wang, Tan, & Ngolah, 2010), is adopted, which allows both architectural and behavioral models of universal array to be rigorously designed and implemented in a top-down approach. According to the RTPA methodology for system modeling and refinement, a universal array can be rigorously modeled using two fundamental techniques known as the unified data models and the unified process models (Wang, 2007).

Definition 1: A *Unified Data Model* (UDM) is a generic architectural model for a software system as well as its internal control structures and its interfaces with hardware components, which can be rigorously modeled and refined as an *n*-tuple, i.e.:

$$\text{UDM} \triangleq \mathop{R}\limits_{i=1}^{n}(s_i \mid \forall e \in S_i, p_i(e)) \tag{1}$$

where $\mathop{R}\limits_{i=1}^{n}$ is the big-R notation of RTPA that denotes a repetitive or recursive structure or operation; S_i, $1 \le i \le n$, is a set that is equivalent to a type in computing for elements *e*, in which all *e* share the property $p_i(e)$.

Definition 2: The *Unified Process Model* (UPM) of a *program* ℘ is a composition of a finite set of *m* processes according to the event-based process dispatching rules, $@e_k \mathbf{S} \hookrightarrow P_k \mathbf{PC}$, i.e.:

$$\begin{aligned} UPM \triangleq \; & ℘ \\ = \; & \mathop{R}\limits_{k=1}^{m}(@e_k\mathbf{S} \hookrightarrow P_k\mathbf{PC}) \\ = \; & \mathop{R}\limits_{k=1}^{m}[@e_k\mathbf{S} \hookrightarrow \mathop{R}\limits_{i=1}^{n-1}(s_i(k)\ r_{ij}(k)\ s_j(k))], j = i+1 \end{aligned} \tag{2}$$

where s_i and s_j are one of the 17 RTPA meta-processes, r_{ij} is one of the 17 RTPA algebraic process operators, and e_k is an event.

This paper develops a comprehensive design pattern of UA and studies its fundamental properties. In the remainder of this paper, the conceptual model of universal array is rigorously described by matrix-based mathematical models in Section 2. The architectural models of universal array are created using RTPA architectural modeling methodologies known as UDMs in Section 3, where the physical model of universal array is implemented using a linear list that is indexed by the offset of elements. The behavioral models of universal array are specified and refined in Section 4 by a set of UPMs for the creation, initialization, update, retrieve, and release operations on the universal array. The formal universal array models are implemented in Java in Section 5 in order to demonstrate the seamless transformability from the formal specifications to code.

2. THE CONCEPTUAL AND MATHEMATICAL MODELS OF UA

An array is an ADT with homogeneous elements accessible by random or sequential addressing. In order to create a universal array that can be used to derive any array as its instance in compiler designs and applications, the basic properties and formal models of the universal arrays are analyzed in this section.

Theorem 1: The *universal array* (UA) is a 4-tuple configured by the number of dimensions, the sizes of each dimension, the type of data elements, and the type of indexes, i.e. (Box 1).

where the element type **RT** denote a run-time type that is application specific, and the type of index is usually in the type of natural number **N**.

Box 1.

$$\text{UA}\mathbf{ST} \triangleq (\# Dimensions\mathbf{N}, \mathop{R}\limits_{i\mathbf{N}=0}^{\#Dimensions\mathbf{N}-1} SizeOfDimension(i\mathbf{N})\mathbf{N}, ElementType\mathbf{RT}, IndexType\mathbf{N}) \tag{3}$$

Proof 1: (a) The 4 parameters are necessary because the UA cannot be uniquely determined without any of them; and (b) The 4 parameters are sufficient because all parameters required for determining the unique UA are provided.

Definition 3: The *logical model* of UA is a general *n*-D array in which any element is allocated by a set of indexes for each of the dimensions, i.e.:

$$Element\textbf{RT} = \text{UA}(\overset{\text{\#Dimensions}\textbf{N}-1}{\underset{i\textbf{N}=0}{R}} Index(i\textbf{N})\textbf{P})\textbf{ST}$$

(4)

$$Size\textbf{N} = \overset{\text{\#Dimensions}\textbf{N}-1}{\underset{i\textbf{N}=0}{\prod}} SizeOfDimension(i\textbf{N})\textbf{N}$$

(5)

The UA is not only useful for rigorously explaining the theoretical foundation of arrays and the essential attributes that determine the architecture and behaviors of any array, but also practical for explicitly modeling complex physical entities in the natural world and abstract artifacts in the perceived worlds.

Definition 4: The *mathematical model* of UA is an *n*-D matrix *M* as follows:

$$UA \triangleq \overset{m_{n-1}}{\underset{i_{n-1}=1}{R}} \overset{m_{n-2}}{\underset{i_{n-2}=1}{R}} \cdots \overset{m_0}{\underset{i_0=1}{R}} M(i_0, i_1, \ldots, i_{n-2}, i_{n-1})$$

(6)

where m_i, $0 \le i < n-1$, is the size of the *i*th dimension of *M*.

Example 1: According to Definition 4, when *n* = 2, the instance of UA is a $k \times p$ matrix M_2 with the sizes of each dimension as *k* and *p*, respectively, i.e.:

$$UA\Big|_{n=2} = M_2 = \begin{bmatrix} e_{11} & e_{12} & \cdots & e_{1j} & \cdots & e_{1p} \\ e_{21} & e_{22} & \cdots & e_{2j} & \cdots & e_{2p} \\ \cdots & & \cdots & & \cdots & \\ e_{k1} & e_{k2} & \cdots & e_{kj} & \cdots & e_{kp} \end{bmatrix}$$

(7)

An important concept of UA is its offset that is a pointer for determining the logical address or physical location of a data element in the array.

Definition 5. The *offset* of an array, Offset**N**, is a pointer for determining the logical or physical address of an arbitrary element in the array, which can be recursively calculated as follows in Box 2 where an *n*-D array is mapped into an equivalent 1-D linear list structure and Offset(0)**N**.

Definition 6: The *physical model* of UA is a 1-D linear array of memory in which any element is indexed and located by the offset as a relative address in the domain [0 .. SizeN – 1], i.e.:

$$Element\textbf{RT} = \text{UA}\textbf{ST}(Offset\textbf{N})$$

(9)

Corollary 1: The *uniqueness of UA* states that any concrete array in any application is an instance of UA.

Proof 2: Corollary 1 can be directly proven based on Theorem 1.

Corollary 2: The necessary and sufficient condition for *uniquely access* an element of UA

Box 2.

$$Offset\textbf{N} \triangleq \overset{\text{\#Dimensions}\textbf{N}-1}{\underset{i\textbf{N}=0}{R}} Offset(i\textbf{N})\textbf{N} \bullet SizeOfDimension(i\textbf{N})\textbf{N} + Index(i\textbf{N})\textbf{P}$$

(8)

244

is to specify a set of n indexes for each of the dimensions, i.e.:

$$Element\mathbf{RT} \triangleq \mathrm{UA}(\mathop{R}_{i\mathbf{N}=0}^{\#\mathrm{Dimensions}\mathbf{N}-1} Index(i\mathbf{N})\mathbf{P}))\mathbf{ST}.Element\mathbf{RT}$$
(10)

or to specify the *offset* derived from the n indexes when the UA is perceived as an equivalent 1-D structure, i.e.:

$$Element\mathbf{RT} \triangleq \mathrm{UA}(Offset\mathbf{N})\mathbf{ST}.Element\mathbf{RT}$$
(11)

Proof 3: Equation 10 as given in Corollary 2 can be proven by the settings of the logical and mathematical models of UA as given in Definitions 3 and 4; while Equation 11 in Corollary 2 can be proven by the definition of the offset in Equation 8.

The conceptual, logical, mathematical, and physical models of UA may be illustrated by n-D data structures. A set of Matlab simulations of complex 3-D arrays is shown in Figure 1. When $n > 3$, the UA may be decomposed as a $(3k + n')$D array, $n' = mod\ (3)$, where k is a positive integer. That is, an embedded 3-D array of $(n-3)$D arrays where its elements are low dimensional arrays. This decomposition process can be extended to multiple layers in order to represent any high dimensional array. For example, a 5-D array can be perceived as a 3-D array with its elements as 2-D arrays. Similarly, a 10-D array can be reduced to a 3-D array of 3-D arrays of 3-D arrays of 1-D arrays.

A more convenient approach to represent UA when $n > 3$ is to use an n-column table as explained in Example 2.

Example 2: A 5-D, $2 \times 2 \times 2 \times 2 \times 2$, array is illustrated in Table 1 where the number of elements of data in natural number type $E\mathbf{N}$ is determined according to Equation 5, i.e.:

$$Size\mathbf{N} = \prod_{i\mathbf{N}=0}^{\#\mathrm{Dimensions}\mathbf{N}-1} SizeOfDimension(i\mathbf{N})\mathbf{N} = \prod_{i\mathbf{N}=0}^{4} 2 = 2^5 = 32$$

Any concrete array as an instance of UA, particularly when the dimension is greater than 3, can be conveniently denoted in the table form as shown in the above example. As indicated by Equation 5 and Table 1, the number of elements in a higher dimensional array is extremely large and grows exponentially.

Based on the architectural model, the behavioral models of UA can be designed as shown in Figure 2. The typical functional behaviors of UA are identified such as create array, initialize array, update element, retrieve element, and release. Both the architectural and behavioral models of UA will be refined in the following sections using RTPA.

Figure 1. Illustration of the architectures of UA by 3-D arrays simulated by Matlab

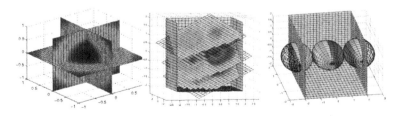

Table 1. A 5-D array represented by a table

Offset [0 .. 31]	Indexes					Element EN [1 .. 32]
	I_0 [0 .. 1]	I_1 [0 .. 1]	I_2 [0 .. 1]	I_3 [0 .. 1]	I_4 [0 .. 1]	
0	0	0	0	0	0	1
1	0	0	0	0	1	2
2	0	0	0	1	0	3
3	0	0	0	1	1	4
4	0	0	1	0	0	5
5	0	0	1	0	1	6
6	0	0	1	1	0	7
7	0	0	1	1	1	8
8	0	1	0	0	0	9
9	0	1	0	0	1	10
10	0	1	0	1	0	11
11	0	1	0	1	1	12
12	0	1	1	0	0	13
13	0	1	1	0	1	14
14	0	1	1	1	0	15
15	0	1	1	1	1	16
16	1	0	0	0	0	17
17	1	0	0	0	1	18
18	1	0	0	1	0	19
19	1	0	0	1	1	20
20	1	0	1	0	0	21
21	1	0	1	0	1	22
22	1	0	1	1	0	23
23	1	0	1	1	1	24
24	1	1	0	0	0	25
25	1	1	0	0	1	26
26	1	1	0	1	0	27
27	1	1	0	1	1	28
28	1	1	1	0	0	29
29	1	1	1	0	1	30
30	1	1	1	1	0	31
31	1	1	1	1	1	32

3. THE ARCHITECTURAL MODEL OF UA

The top-level architectural model of UA, UArray§, as a system (§) encompassing its architecture, static behaviors, and dynamic behaviors, can be specified in RTPA as shown in Equation 12. According to the RTPA methodology for system modeling, specification, and refinement (Wang, 2007, 2008a), the following subsections will refine the top level framework of UArray§ into detailed UDMs and UPMs.

Figure 2. The conceptual model of UA behaviors

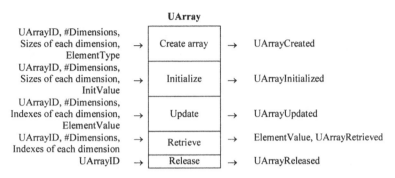

UArray § $\triangleq$ UArray §.ArchitectureST
 ||UArray §.StaticBehaviorsPC
 || UArray §.DynamicBehaviorsPC

(12)

The architecture of UArray**§** can be rigorously modeled using the UDM technology of RTPA, which is a predefined class of system hardware or internal control models that can be inherited or implemented by corresponding UDM objects as specific instances in the succeeding architectural refinement for the system. The UDM model of UA, UArray**§**.Architecture**ST**, as shown in Figure 3 provides a generic architectural model for any concrete array in applications with four key fields, i.e., #Dimensions**N**, $\displaystyle\mathop{R}_{i\mathbf{N}=0}^{\text{\#Dimensions}\mathbf{N}-1}$ SizeOfDimension(i**N**)**N**, Offset**N**, and Element**RT**,

where the constraints for each field are given in the right-hand side of the vertical bar. Supplement to the key architectural attributes, there is a set of status fields in the UDM, which models the current operational status of the UArrayID**ST** in Boolean type such as Created**BL**, Initialized**BL**, Updated**BL**, Retrieved**BL**, and Released**BL**. It is noteworthy that the type of data elements in the UA model is specified in the run-time type **RT**, i.e., **RT** $\in$ {**S**, **N**, **R**, **ST**, …}, for design flexibility. However, the data elements in a concrete UA must be in the same type once it is chosen at run-time for a specific implementation of an instance of the generic UA.

According to Corollary 2, the architectural model UArrayID**ST** can be accessed in two ways. The *random* access as expressed in Equation 10 allows an element of the UA to be located by the

Figure 3. The UDM model of the universal array

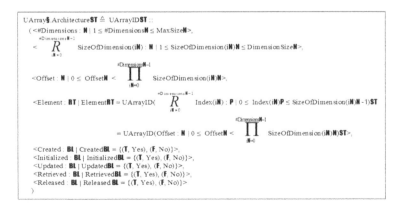

n indexes Index(i**N**)**P**, $0 \leq i\mathbf{N} < n\mathbf{N}$; While the *sequential* access as described in Equation 11 provides an additional approach to enable a node of the UA to be located by its offset Offset**N**.

Example 3: The UA model, UArrayID**ST**, as a general abstract array can be easily tailored to describe a low-dimensional concrete array such as a 2-D or 5-D array. For instance, assuming #Dimensions**N** = 2, an instance of a 2-D array can be derived from UA as follows in Box 3.

Similarly, a 5-D array instance can be derived as follows in Box 4.

4. THE STATIC BEHAVIORAL MODEL OF UA

The static behaviors of UA as an ADT, UArray**§**. StaticBehaviors**PC**, are described via operations on its architectural models (UDMs), i.e., UArray**§**. Architecture**PC**. On the basis of the UDM models of UA developed in the preceding subsection, the behaviors of UArray**ST** can be modeled as a set of UPMs operating on the UDMs of UArray**ST** as given in Figure 3.

The high-level behavioral model of UA is specified by UArray**§**.StaticBehaviors**PC** as shown in

Figure 4, which encompasses a set of five UPMs known as UA creation (Create**PC**), initialization (Initialization**PC**), element update (Update**PC**), element retrieve (Retrieve**PC**), and release (Release PC). The schemas of the UPMs in Figure 4 model the input data objects <**I**:: (…)>, output data objects <**O**:: (…)>, and operated UDMs <**UDM**:: (…)> for each specific process of UArray**ST**. The UDMs play an important role in system architectural design as global and permanent I/O structures, which usually have a longer life-span than those of the process(es) that created and/ or invoked them, particularly in real-time and embedded systems.

The following subsections describe how each of the five behavioral processes of UArray**§**. StaticBehaviors**PC** as specified in Figure 4 are modeled and refined using the denotational mathematical notations and methodologies of RTPA.

4.1. The Behavioral Model of the UA Creation Process

The *UA creation* process, Create**PC**, is formally modeled as shown in Figure 5, which establishes a new array in system memory, or on a disk, and links it to a specified logical ID of the UA, UArray**S**. The input arguments of the process are the given name of the UA, as well as the three control attributes of UA such as its number of dimensions,

Box 3.

$$\text{UArrayID}(\overset{1}{\underset{i\mathbf{N}=0}{R}} \text{Index}(i\mathbf{N})\mathbf{P})\mathbf{ST} = \text{UArrayID}(\text{Index}_0\mathbf{P}, \text{Index}_1\mathbf{P},)\mathbf{ST}$$

Box 4.

$$\text{UArrayID}(\overset{4}{\underset{i\mathbf{N}=0}{R}} \text{Index}(i\mathbf{N})\mathbf{P})\mathbf{ST} = \text{UArrayID}(\text{Index}_0\mathbf{P}, \text{Index}_1\mathbf{P}, \text{Index}_2\mathbf{P}, \text{Index}_3\mathbf{P}, \text{Index}_{\P4}\mathbf{P})\mathbf{ST}$$

Figure 4. The high-level UPM model of the UA behaviors

$$
\begin{aligned}
&\text{UArray} \S.\text{StaticBehaviors}\mathbf{PC} \triangleq \\
&\quad (\ \text{Create}\mathbf{PC} (\langle\mathbf{I}:: \text{UArrayID}\mathbf{S}, \#\text{Dimensions}\mathbf{N}, \overset{\#Dimensions\mathbf{N}-1}{\underset{i\mathbf{N}=0}{R}} \text{SizeOfDimension}(i\mathbf{N})\mathbf{N}, \text{ElementType}\mathbf{RT}\rangle; \\
&\qquad\qquad \langle\mathbf{O}:: \text{UArrayID}\mathbf{ST}.\text{\textcircled{s}Created}\mathbf{BL}\rangle; \langle\mathbf{UDM}:: \text{UArray}\mathbf{ST}\rangle) \\
&\quad | \text{Initialize}\mathbf{PC} (\langle\mathbf{I}:: \text{UArrayID}\mathbf{S}, \#\text{Dimensions}\mathbf{N}, \overset{\#Dimensions\mathbf{N}-1}{\underset{i\mathbf{N}=0}{R}} \text{SizeOfDimension}(i\mathbf{N})\mathbf{N}, \text{InitValue}\mathbf{RT}\rangle; \\
&\qquad\qquad \langle\mathbf{O}:: \text{UArrayID}\mathbf{ST}.\text{\textcircled{s}Initialized}\mathbf{BL}\rangle; \langle\mathbf{UDM}:: \text{UArray}\mathbf{ST}\rangle) \\
&\quad | \text{Update}\mathbf{PC} (\langle\mathbf{I}:: \text{UArrayID}\mathbf{S}, \#\text{Dimensions}\mathbf{N}, \overset{\#Dimensions\mathbf{N}-1}{\underset{i\mathbf{N}=0}{R}} \text{Index}(i\mathbf{N})\mathbf{P}, \text{ElementValue}\mathbf{RT}\rangle; \\
&\qquad\qquad \langle\mathbf{O}:: \text{UArrayID}\mathbf{ST}.\text{\textcircled{s}Updated}\mathbf{BL}\rangle; \langle\mathbf{UDM}:: \text{UArray}\mathbf{ST}\rangle) \\
&\quad | \text{Retrieve}\mathbf{PC} (\langle\mathbf{I}:: \text{UArrayID}\mathbf{S}, \#\text{Dimensions}\mathbf{N}, \overset{\#Dimensions\mathbf{N}-1}{\underset{i\mathbf{N}=0}{R}} \text{Index}(i\mathbf{N})\mathbf{P}\rangle; \\
&\qquad\qquad \langle\mathbf{O}:: \text{UArrayID}\mathbf{ST}.\text{\textcircled{s}Retrieved}\mathbf{BL}, \text{ElementValue}\mathbf{RT}\rangle; \langle\mathbf{UDM}:: \text{UArray}\mathbf{ST}\rangle) \\
&\quad | \text{Release}\mathbf{PC} (\langle\mathbf{I}:: \text{UArrayID}\mathbf{S}\rangle; \langle\mathbf{O}:: \text{UArrayID}\mathbf{ST}.\text{\textcircled{s}Released}\mathbf{BL}\rangle; \langle\mathbf{UDM}:: \text{UArray}\mathbf{ST}\rangle) \\
&\quad)
\end{aligned}
$$

sizes of each dimensions, and the type of all elements. The output result of the process is the status of the array creation operation. The UDM operated by this process is UArray**ST**.

Create**PC** calls a system support process, AllocateObject**PC** (Wang, 2007), to physically set up the whole space of the UA using dynamic memory allocation technology. The total space of the UA is determined by #Elements**N** × Byte(ElementType**RT**)**N**. If a memory block is successfully obtained for the array, Create**PC** connects the logical name UArray**S** to the memory block, and sets UArrayID**ST**.&Created**BL**:= **T**; Otherwise, it reports an error UArrayID**ST**.&Created**BL**:= **F** with an exceptional warning of memory allocation failed. In case the given UArrayID**S** has already existed, Create**PC** results in a specific error message UArrayID**ST**.&Created**BL**:= **F**.

Figure 5. The UPM model of the UA creation process

$$
\begin{aligned}
&\text{Create}\mathbf{PC} (\langle\mathbf{I}:: \text{UArrayID}\mathbf{S}, \#\text{Dimensions}\mathbf{N}, \overset{\#Dimensions\mathbf{N}-1}{\underset{i\mathbf{N}=0}{R}} \text{SizeOfDimension}(i\mathbf{N})\mathbf{N}, \text{ElementType}\mathbf{RT}\rangle; \\
&\qquad \langle\mathbf{O}:: \text{UArrayID}\mathbf{ST}.\text{\textcircled{s}Created}\mathbf{BL}\rangle; \langle\mathbf{UDM}:: \text{UArray}\mathbf{ST}\rangle) \triangleq \\
&\{ \\
&\quad \rightarrow (\ \blacklozenge\ \text{UArrayID}\mathbf{ST}.\text{\textcircled{s}Created}\mathbf{BL} = \mathbf{F} \\
&\qquad \rightarrow \text{ObjectID}\mathbf{S} := \text{UArrayID}\mathbf{S} \\
&\qquad \rightarrow \#\text{Elements}\mathbf{N} := \overset{\#Dimensions\mathbf{N}-1}{\underset{i\mathbf{N}=0}{\prod}} \text{SizeOfDimension}(i\mathbf{N})\mathbf{N} \\
&\qquad \rightarrow \text{ElementType}\mathbf{RT} := \text{ElementType}\mathbf{RT} \\
&\qquad \rightarrow \text{AllocateObject}\mathbf{PC}(\langle\mathbf{I}:: \text{ObjectID}\mathbf{S}, \#\text{Elements}\mathbf{N}, \text{ElementType}\mathbf{RT})\rangle; \\
&\qquad\qquad \langle\mathbf{O}:: \text{\textcircled{s}ObjectAllocated}\mathbf{BL}\rangle; \langle\mathbf{UDM}:: \text{MEM}\mathbf{ST}\rangle) \\
&\qquad \rightarrow (\ \blacklozenge\ \text{\textcircled{s}ObjectAllocated}\mathbf{BL} = \mathbf{T} \\
&\qquad\qquad \rightarrow \text{UArrayID}\mathbf{ST}.\text{\textcircled{s}Created}\mathbf{BL} := \mathbf{T} \\
&\qquad\quad | \blacklozenge \sim \\
&\qquad\qquad \rightarrow \text{UArrayID}\mathbf{ST}.\text{\textcircled{s}Created}\mathbf{BL} := \mathbf{F} \\
&\qquad\qquad \rightarrow !\ (\text{'Memory allocation failed.'}) \\
&\qquad\quad) \\
&\quad | \blacklozenge \sim \\
&\qquad \rightarrow \text{UArrayID}\mathbf{ST}.\text{\textcircled{s}Created}\mathbf{BL} := \mathbf{F} \\
&\qquad \rightarrow !\ (\text{'UArrayID}\mathbf{ST}\text{ has already been existed.'}) \\
&\quad) \\
&\}
\end{aligned}
$$

4.2. The Behavioral Model of the UA Initialization Process

The *UA initialization* process, Initialize**PC**, is formally modeled as shown in Figure 6, which sets each element of the array with the same initial value given by InitValue**RT**. The input arguments of the process are the target array ID, number of dimensions, the sizes of each dimensions, and the given initial value. Its output is the status of the initialization operation. Initialize**PC** checks the existence of the target array, calculates the total elements in the array, and puts the initial value into each element of the array indexed by the offset. Then the status of the operation is set UArrayID**ST**.Initialized**BL**:= **T**. When the target array does not exist, Initialize**PC** generates a specific error message and sets UArrayID**ST**.Initialized**BL**:= **F**.

According to Corollary 2, the initialization operations for each individual element as described in Figure 6 can be carried out in two approaches, as presented in Box 5.

However, the first approach via the offset access as adopted in the UPM of Figure 6 is more efficient for high dimensional array operations without providing the individual indexes and processing their updating in each step of operations for all dimensions. This demonstrates the roles and usages of the offset in UA for significantly reducing the complexity in large *n*-D array manipulations.

4.3. The Behavioral Model of the UA Update Process

The *UA element update* process, Update**PC**, is formally modeled as shown in Figure 7, which writes new data into the target element in the UA allocated by a set of *n* indexes where *n* is determined by the number of dimensions. The input arguments of the process are the given name of the UA, the number of dimensions, the indexes of each dimensions, and the data for updating. The output result of the process is the status of the update operation. Update**PC** checks if the target array exists before the following operations: a) Set initial values of Offset**N**:= 0 and assume all indexes corresponding to each dimension is valid; b) Iteratively check the validity of each index and calculate the offset address of the target element for updating. If any index for a certain dimension is out of bound as constrained by the size of the dimension, an exception condition IndexOutOfBound**BL**:= **T** is set, and the update process will be terminated; c) When the offset is successfully obtained, the given element value is written into the target array ele-

Figure 6. The UPM model of the UA initialization process

```
                                          #DimensionsN-1
InitializePC (<I: UArrayIDS, #DimensionsN,       R        SizeOfDimension(iN)N, InitValueRT>;
                                                iN=0
          <O:: UArrayIDST.ⓢInitializedBL>; <UDM:: UArrayST>) ≙
{
 → ( ◆ UArrayIDST.ⓢCreatedBL = T
                            #DimensionsN-1
        → #ElementsN :=           ∏         SizeOfDimension(iN)N
                                 iN=0
            #ElementsN-1
        →        R         (UArrayID(OffsetN)ST.ElementRT := InitValueRT)
            OffsetN=0
        → UArrayIDST.ⓢInitializedBL := T
   | ◆ ~
        → UArrayIDST.ⓢInitializedBL := F
        → ! ('UArrayIDST did not exist.')
   )
}
```

Box 5.

$$\underset{\text{Offset}\mathbf{N}=0}{\overset{\#\text{Element}\mathbf{N}-1}{R}} (\text{UArrayID}(\text{Offset}\mathbf{N})\mathbf{ST}.\text{Element}\mathbf{RT}:=\text{InitValue}\mathbf{RT})$$

$$= \underset{i\mathbf{N}=0}{\overset{\#\text{Dimensions}\mathbf{N}-1}{R}} \underset{\text{Index}(i\mathbf{N})\mathbf{P}=0}{\overset{\text{SizeofDimensions}(i\mathbf{N})\mathbf{N}-1}{R}} (\text{UArrayID}(\underset{i\mathbf{N}=0}{\overset{\#\text{Dimensions}\mathbf{N}-1}{R}} \text{Index}(i\mathbf{N})\mathbf{P})\mathbf{ST}.\text{Element}\mathbf{RT}:=\text{InitValue}\mathbf{RT})$$

$$= \underset{\text{Index}(0)\mathbf{P}=0}{\overset{\text{SizeofDimensions}(0)\mathbf{N}-1}{R}} \underset{\text{Index}(1)\mathbf{P}=0}{\overset{\text{SizeofDimensions}(i\mathbf{N})\mathbf{N}-1}{R}} \cdots \underset{\text{Index}(\#\text{Dimensions}\mathbf{N}-1)\mathbf{P}=0}{\overset{\text{SizeofDimension}(\#\text{Dimensions}\mathbf{N}-1)\mathbf{N}-1}{R}}$$

$$\text{UArrayID}(\text{Index}(0)\mathbf{P}, \text{Index }(1)\mathbf{P}, ...,\text{Index}(\#\text{Dimensions}\mathbf{N}-1)\mathbf{P})\mathbf{ST}.\text{Element}\mathbf{RT}$$

$$:=\text{InitValue}\mathbf{RT}$$

(13)

ment as located by the offset, and the status is set as UArrayID**ST**.&Updated**BL**:= **T**; c) Otherwise, report an error status UArrayID**ST**.&Updated**BL**:= F with an exception warning that an index was invalid. In case the given UArrayID**ST** did not

exist, Update**PC** results in a specific error message UArrayID**ST**.&Updated**BL**:= **F**.

It is noteworthy in the above UPM of UA updating that, according to Corollary 2, the fol-

Figure 7. The UPM model of the UA update process

Box 6.

$$UArrayID(Offset\textbf{N})\textbf{ST}.Element\textbf{RT} = ElementValue\textbf{RT}$$

$$= UArrayID(\mathop{R}_{i\textbf{N}=0}^{\#Dimensions\textbf{N}-1} Index(i\textbf{N})\textbf{P})\textbf{ST}.Element\textbf{RT} := ElementValue\textbf{RT} \tag{14}$$

lowing update operations are equivalent as presented in Box 6.

4.4. The Behavioral Model of the UA Retrieve Process

The *UA element retrieval* process, Retrieve**PC**, is formally modeled as shown in Figure 8, which reads and shows the contents of a target element in the UA allocated by a set of *n* given indexes. This process is a read-only operation. Hence, it is an inverse operation of element update. The input arguments of the process are the given name of the UA, the number of dimensions, and a set of indexes for each dimension. The output results of the process are the retrieved target element and the status of the retrieve operation. Retrieve**PC** checks if the target array exists before the following operations: a) Set initial values of Offset**N**:= 0 and assume all indexes corresponding to each dimension is valid; b) Iteratively check the validity of each index and calculate the offset address of the target element for retrieving. If any index for a certain dimension is out of bound as constrained by the size of the dimension, an exception condition IndexOutOfBound**BL**:=**T** is set, and the update process will be terminated; c) When the offset is successfully obtained, the target element as located by the offset is obtained, and the status is set as UArrayID**ST**.&Retrieved**BL**:=**T**; c) Otherwise, report an error status UArrayID**ST**.&Retrieved**BL**:= **F** with an exception warning that an index was invalidate. In case the given UArrayID**ST** did not exist, Retrieve**PC** results in a specific error message UArrayID**ST**.&Retrieved**BL**:= **F**.

According to Corollary 2, it is noteworthy that in the above UPM of UA retrieval as shown in Figure 8, the following retrieve operations are equivalent as presented in Box 7.

4.5. The Behavioral Model of the UA Release Process

The *UA release* process, Release**PC**, is formally modeled as shown in Figure 9, which physically removes the given UA and releases the memory occupied. The input argument of the process is the specific ID of the UA. Its output is the status of the release operation. Release**PC** frees and returns the memory block allocated by Create**PC** to the system by calling a system support process, ReleaseObject**PC** (Wang, 2007), for dynamic memory manipulation. It then disconnects the physical UA in memory and its logical name. If the target UA has not been created, Release**PC** produces a specific error message UArrayID**ST**.&Released**BL** = **F**.

5. THE DYNAMIC BEHAVIORAL MODEL OF THE UA

Dynamic behaviors of a system are run-time process dispatching mechanisms based on the static behaviors modeled in UPMs. The dynamic behaviors of UArray**§** integrate and dispatch the static behavioral processes of UA as modeled in UArray**§**.StaticBehaviors**PC**. Based on the UPMs developed in the preceding sections, this section models the dynamic behaviors of UArray**§** at runtime elaborated by the event-driven mechanisms of the system.

The dynamic behaviors of the UA, UArray**§**.DynamicBehaviors**PC**, are shown in Figure 10, which serve as an interface of the system to external users who can invoke any pre-defined

Figure 8. The UPM model of the UA retrieve process

Retrieve**PC** (<**I**:: UArrayID**S**, #Dimensions**N**, $\mathop{R}\limits_{i\mathbf{N}=0}^{\#Dimensions\mathbf{N}-1}$ Index(i**N**)**P**>;
    <**O**:: UArrayID**ST**.ⓢRetrieved**BL**, ElementValue**RT**>; <**UDM**:: UArray**ST**>) ≙
{
 → (◆ UArrayID**ST**.ⓢCreated**BL** = **T**
    → Offset**N** := 0
    → IndexOutOfBound**BL** := **F**
    → $\mathop{R}\limits_{i\mathbf{N}=0}^{\#Dimensions\mathbf{N}-1}$ (◆ 0 ≤ Index(i**N**)**P** ≤ UArrayID**ST**.SizeOfDimension(i**N**)**N** – 1
        → Offset**N** := Offset**N** * SizeOfDimension(i**N**)**N** + Index(i**N**)**P**
      | ◆ ~
        → IndexOutOfBound**BL** := **T**
        → ∅
)
    → (◆ IndexOutOfBound**BL** = **F**
      → ElementValue**RT** := UArrayID(Offset**N**)**ST**.Element**RT**
      → UArrayID**S**.ⓢRetrieved**BL** := **T**
     | ◆ ~
      → UArrayID**ST**.ⓢRetrieved**BL** := **F**
      → ! ('Index i**N** was out of bound.')
)
  | ◆ ~
    → UArrayID**ST**.ⓢRetrieved**BL** := **F**
    → ! ('UArrayID**ST** did not exist.')
)
}

process in UArray**§**. The dynamic behaviors of UArray**§**.DynamicBehaviors**PC** as given in Figure 10 establishes a set of top-level run-time relations between the 5 pairs of events and processes such as (@CreateArray**S** ↳ Create**PC**), (@ArrayInitial**S** ↳ Initialize**PC**), (@ArrayUpdate**S** ↳ Update**PC**),

Box 7.

ElementValue**RT**=UArrayID(Offset**N**)**ST**.Element**RT**

$$=UArrayID(\mathop{R}\limits_{i\mathbf{N}=0}^{\#Dimensions\mathbf{N}-1} Index(i\mathbf{N})\mathbf{P})\mathbf{ST}.Element\mathbf{RT} \quad (15)$$

Figure 9. The UPM model of the UA release process

(@ArrayRetrieve**S** ↪ Retrieve**PC**), and (@Release-Array**S** ↪ Release**PC**). Any exceptional event that is not specified as a valid one in the system will be ignored by the skip operator (→ ∅). The event-driven dispatching mechanism also enables UArray**S** as a prebuilt reusable component for any other real-world application.

6. IMPLEMENTATION OF THE UA MODELS IN JAVA

Based on the RTPA methodology and models (Wang, 2008a), software code can be seamlessly

generated in an automatic or manual implementation as shown in Figure 11 (Wang, Tan, & Ngolah, 2010). According to the scheme of RTPA-based code generation, the RTPA architectural model for a system, i.e., UA, is used to generate the structural framework and global/local variables of classes or objects; while the RTPA behavioral model is then transferred into object methods in a target programming language.

A case study on RTPA-based code generation in Java for UA is presented in the following subsection, as shown in Figures 12 and 13, based on manual transformations between the RTPA models of UA and the corresponding Java program.

Figure 10. The dynamic behavioral model of UA

Figure 11. Program code generation based on RTPA

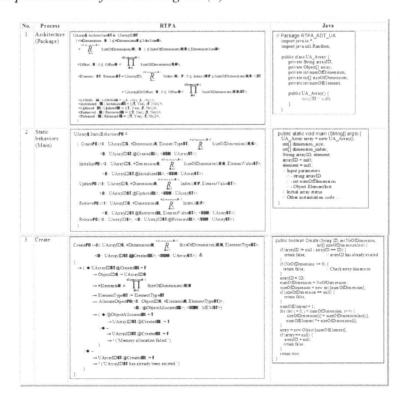

In the implementation of UA specifications as developed in preceding sections, the architectural model of UA is implemented by the code of the UA package as shown in Item 1 of Figure 12. The behavioural models of UA are implemented by the classes of create, initialization, update, retrieve, and release as shown in Figures 12 and 13 with Items 3 through 7. The program is integrated in the main class (Item 2) as shown in Figure 12 where some of the run-time initializa-

Figure 12. The Implementation of the UA Program (A)

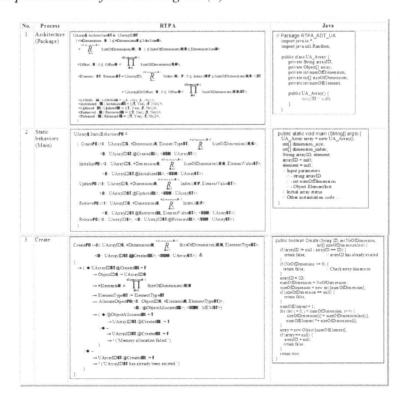

Figure 13. The Implementation of the UA Program (B)

No.	Process	RTPA	Java
4	Initialization	InitializePC (<I:: UArrayIDS, =DimensionsN, R SizeOfDimension(iN)N, InitValueRT>; <O:: UArrayIDST.@InitializedBL>; <UDM:: UArrayST>) ≙ ((◆ UArrayIDST.@CreatedBL = T → =ElementsN := ∏ SizeOfDimension(iN)N → R (UArrayID(OffsetN)ST.ElementRT := InitValueRT) → UArrayIDST.@InitializedBL := T	◆ ~ → UArrayIDST.@InitializedBL := F → ! ('UArrayIDST did not exist.')))	`public boolean Initialize (String ID, Object ElementInst) throws Exception { if (arrayID != ID		ID == null) { throw new Exception ("No such ArrayID!" + ID + "!"); return false; } for (int i = 0; i < numOfElement; i++) { array[i] = ElementInst; } return true; }`
5	Update	UpdatePC (<I:: UArrayIDS, =DimensionsN, R Index(iN)P, ElementValueRT>; <O:: UArrayIDST.@UpdatedBL>; <UDM:: UArrayST>) ≙ (→ (◆ UArrayIDS.@CreatedBL = T → OffsetN := 0 → IndexOutOfBoundBL := F → R (0 ≤ Index(iN)P ≤ UArrayIDST.SizeOfDimension(iN)N – 1 → OffsetN := OffsetN * SizeOfDimension(iN)N + Index(iN)P	◆ ~ → IndexOutOfBoundBL := T → ∅) → (◆ IndexOutOfBoundBL = F → UArrayID(OffsetN)ST.ElementRT := ElementValueRT → UArrayIDS.@UpdatedBL := T	◆ ~ → UArrayIDS.@UpdatedBL := F → ! ('Index iN was out of bound.'))	◆ ~ → UArrayIDS.@UpdatedBL := F → ! ('UArrayIDST did not exist.')))	`public boolean Update (String ID, int[] arrayIndex, Object ElementInst) throws Exception { if (arrayID != ID || ID == null) { throw new Exception ("No such ArrayID!" + ID + "!"); return false; } try array [Offset(arrayIndex)] = ElementInst; catch (Exception e) { System.out.println (e.getMessage()); return false; } return true; } private int Offset (int[] arrayIndex) throws Exception { int offset = 0; for (int i = 0; i < numOfDimension; i++) { if (sizeOfDimension[i] <= arrayIndex[i]) || (arrayIndex[i]) < 0 { throw new Exception ("Index out of bound!"); } offset = offset * sizeOfDimension[i] + arrayIndex[i]; } return offset; }`
6	Retrieve	RetrievePC (<I:: UArrayIDS, =DimensionsN, R Index(iN)P>; <O:: UArrayIDST.@RetrievedBL, ElementValueRT>; <UDM:: UArrayST>) ≙ (→ (◆ UArrayIDST.@CreatedBL = T → OffsetN := 0 → IndexOutOfBoundBL := F → R (0 ≤ Index(iN)P ≤ UArrayIDST.SizeOfDimension(iN)N – 1 → OffsetN := OffsetN * SizeOfDimension(iN)N + Index(iN)P	◆ ~ → IndexOutOfBoundBL := T → ∅) → (◆ IndexOutOfBoundBL = F → ElementValueRT := UArrayID(OffsetN)ST.ElementRT → UArrayIDS.@RetrievedBL := T	◆ ~ → UArrayIDST.@RetrievedBL := F → ! ('Index iN was out of bound.'))	◆ ~ → UArrayIDST.@RetrievedBL := F → ! ('UArrayIDST did not exist.')))	`public Object Retrieve (String ID, int[] arrayIndex) throws Exception { Object Element; if (arrayID != ID || ID == null) { throw new Exception("No such ArrayID!" + ID + "!"); } try { Element = array [Offset(arrayIndex)]; } catch (Exception e) { System.out.println (e.getMessage()); return null; } return Element; }`
7	Release	ReleasePC (<I:: UArrayIDS>; <O:: UArrayIDST.@ReleasedBL>; <UDM:: UArrayST>) ≙ (→ (◆ @UArrayIDST.CreatedBL = T → ObjectIDS := UArrayIDS → ReleaseObjectPC(<I:: ObjectIDP>; <O:: @ObjectReleasedBL>; <UDM:: MEMST) → (◆ @ObjectReleasedBL = T → UArrayIDS ↞ MEM[UArrayIDS]ST → UArrayIDST.@CreatedBL := F → UArrayIDST.@ReleasedBL := T	◆ ~ → UArrayIDST.@ReleasedBL := F → ! ('Memory release was failed.'))	◆ ~ → @ArrayID.ReleasedBL := F → ! ('UArrayIDST did not exist.')))	`public boolean Release (String ID) throws Exception { if (arrayID != ID || ID == null) { throw new Exception("No such ArrayID!" + ID + "!"); return false; } array = null; arrayID = null; sizeOfDimension = null; System.gc(); return true; }`

tion operations and test cases on deriving specific instance arrays are omitted. The program in Java demonstrates that the formal models of UA in RTPA can be implemented to flexibly derive any *n*-D array in real-world applications.

The practical formal engineering methodology of RTPA for system modeling and specification provides a coherent notation system and systematical approach for large-scale software and hybrid system design and implementation. A series of formal design models of real-world and real-time applications in RTPA have been developed using RTPA notations and methodologies (Wang, 2002, 2007, 2008a, 2008b, 2008c, 2008d, 2009a; Wang & Huang, 2008; Wang, Tan, & Ngolah, 2010) in the formal design-engineering approach, such as the telephone switching system (TSS) (Wang, 2009b), the lift dispatching system (LDS) (Wang et al., 2009), the automated teller machine (ATM) (Wang, Zhang, Sheu, Li, & Guo, 2010), the real-time operating system (RTOS+) (Wang et al., 2010a, 2010b), the autonomic code generator (RTPA-CG) (Wang, Tan, & Ngolah, 2010), the ADTs (Wang, Ngolah, Tan, Tian, & Sheu, 2010), the file management system (FMS) (Wang, Ngolah, Tan, Tian, & Sheu, 2011), the doubly-linked-circular list (DLC-List) (Wang, Ngolah, Tan, & Sheu, 2011), and the air traffic control system (to be reported). Further studies have demonstrated that RTPA is not only useful as a generic notation and methodology for software engineering, but also good at modeling human cognitive processes in cognitive informatics and computational intelligence as reported (Wang, 2008d, 2009a, 2010a, 2010b, 2011; Wang & Ruhe, 2007; Wang & Chiew, 2010).

6. CONCLUSION

Arrays have been recognized as one of the most fundamental and widely applied data structures, which are useful for modeling both logical designs and physical implementations of multi-dimensional data objects sharing the same type of homogeneous elements. This paper has presented a comprehensive design pattern of the universal array (UA) using a 4-tuple model. The conceptual, mathematical, logical, architectural, and static/dynamic behavioral models of UA have been systematically presented. It has been found that the general mathematical model of UA was extremely complicated than that of a specific array in applications because the requirements for the 4-degree design freedoms for the UA known as the number of dimensions, sizes of each dimension, type of data elements, and type of indexes. The generic UDM and the 6 UPMs of UA have provided a set of rigorous architectural and behavioral models of formal arrays based on them any concrete array can be derived and implemented. An expressive denotational mathematics, Real-Time Process Algebra (RTPA), has been adopted to rigorously design and refine both architectural and behavioral models of UA and their manipulations in a top-down approach. A case study on implementation of the UA in Java has been demonstrated. This work has been applied in a number of real-time and nonreal-time systems such as compilers and file management systems.

ACKNOWLEDGMENT

The authors would like to acknowledge the Natural Science and Engineering Council of Canada (NSERC) for its partial support to this work. We would like to thank the anonymous reviewers for their valuable comments and suggestions. We would also thank Philip Choy for providing an improved code implementation of the formal UA models.

REFERENCES

Becker, K., Becker, M., & Schwarz, J. H. (2007). *String theory and m-theory: A modern introduction*. Cambridge, UK: Cambridge University Press.

Broy, M., Pair, C., & Wirsing, M. (1984). A systematic study of models of abstract data types. *Theoretical Computer Science, 33*, 139–1274. doi:10.1016/0304-3975(84)90086-0

Cardelli, L., & Wegner, P. (1985). On understanding types, data abstraction and polymorphism. *ACM Computing Surveys, 17*(4), 471–522. doi:10.1145/6041.6042

Chapra, S. C., & Ganale, R. P. (2002). *Numerical methods for engineers* (4th ed.). New York, NY: McGraw-Hill.

Guttag, J. V. (1977). Abstract data types and the development of data structures. *Communications of the ACM, 20*(6), 396–404. doi:10.1145/359605.359618

Lipschutz, S., & Lipson, M. (1997). *Schaum's outline of theories and problems of discrete mathematics* (2nd ed.). New York: McGraw-Hill.

Matlab. (2010). *Matlab functional reference*. Natick, MA: The MathWorks.

McDermid, J. (Ed.). (1991). *Software engineer's reference book*. Oxford, UK: Butterworth Heinemann.

Mitchell, J. C. (1990). Type systems for programming languages. In van Leeuwen, J. (Ed.), *Handbook of theoretical computer science* (pp. 365–458). Amsterdam, The Netherlands: North-Holland.

Russel, B. (1903). *The principles of mathematics*. London, UK: George Allen & Unwin.

Stubbs, D. F., & Webre, N. W. (1985). *Data structures with abstract data types and Pascal*. Monterey, CA: Brooks/Cole.

Wang, Y. (2002). The real-time process algebra (RTPA). *Annals of Software Engineering: An International Journal, 14*, 235–274. doi:10.1023/A:1020561826073

Wang, Y. (2007). *Software engineering foundations: A software science perspective* (CRC Series in Software Engineering, Vol. II). New York, NY: Auerbach.

Wang, Y. (2008a). RTPA: A denotational mathematics for manipulating intelligent and computational behaviors. *International Journal of Cognitive Informatics and Natural Intelligence, 2*(2), 44–62. doi:10.4018/jcini.2008040103

Wang, Y. (2008b). Mathematical laws of software. *Transactions of Computational Science, 2*, 46–83. doi:10.1007/978-3-540-87563-5_4

Wang, Y. (2008c). Deductive semantics of RTPA. *International Journal of Cognitive Informatics and Natural Intelligence, 2*(2), 95–121. doi:10.4018/jcini.2008040106

Wang, Y. (2008d). On contemporary denotational mathematics for computational intelligence. *Transactions of Computational Science, 2*, 6–29. doi:10.1007/978-3-540-87563-5_2

Wang, Y. (2009a). Paradigms of denotational mathematics for cognitive informatics and cognitive computing. *Fundamenta Informaticae, 90*(3), 282–303.

Wang, Y. (2009b). The formal design model of a telephone switching system (TSS). *International Journal of Software Science and Computational Intelligence, 1*(3), 92–116. doi:10.4018/jssci.2009070107

Wang, Y. (2009c). A formal syntax of natural languages and the deductive grammar. *Fundamenta Informaticae, 90*(4), 353–368.

Wang, Y. (2010a). Cognitive robots: A reference model towards intelligent authentication. *IEEE Robotics and Automation, 17*(4), 54–62. doi:10.1109/MRA.2010.938842

Wang, Y. (2010b). On formal and cognitive semantics for semantic computing. *International Journal of Semantic Computing, 4*(2), 203–237. doi:10.1142/S1793351X10000833

Wang, Y. (2011). On concept algebra for computing with words (CWW). *International Journal of Semantic Computing, 4*(3), 331–356. doi:10.1142/S1793351X10001061

Wang, Y., & Chiew, V. (2010). On the cognitive process of human problem solving. *Cognitive Systems Research: An International Journal, 11*(1), 81–92. doi:10.1016/j.cogsys.2008.08.003

Wang, Y., & Huang, J. (2008). Formal modeling and specification of design patterns using RTPA. *International Journal of Cognitive Informatics and Natural Intelligence, 2*(1), 100–111. doi:10.4018/jcini.2008010108

Wang, Y., Ngolah, C. F., Ahmadi, H., Sheu, P. C.-Y., & Ying, S. (2009). The formal design model of a lift dispatching system (LDS). *International Journal of Software Science and Computational Intelligence, 1*(4), 98–122. doi:10.4018/jssci.2009062506

Wang, Y., Ngolah, C. F., Tan, X., & Sheu, P. C.-Y. (2011). The formal design models of a doubly-linked-circular list (DLC-List). *International Journal of Software Science and Computational Intelligence, 3*(2), 81–100.

Wang, Y., Ngolah, C. F., Tan, X., Tian, Y., & Sheu, P. C.-Y. (2010). The formal design models of a set of abstract data models (ADTs). *International Journal of Software Science and Computational Intelligence, 2*(4), 72–104. doi:10.4018/jssci.2010100106

Wang, Y., Ngolah, C. F., Tan, X., Tian, Y., & Sheu, P. C.-Y. (2011). The formal design models of a file management systems (FMS). *International Journal of Software Science and Computational Intelligence, 3*(1), 90–113.

Wang, Y., Ngolah, C. F., Zeng, G., Sheu, P. C.-Y., Choy, C. P., & Tian, Y. (2010a). The formal design models of a real-time operating system (RTOS+): Conceptual and architectural frameworks. *International Journal of Software Science and Computational Intelligence, 2*(2), 105–122. doi:10.4018/jssci.2010040106

Wang, Y., Ngolah, C. F., Zeng, G., Sheu, P. C.-Y., Choy, C. P., & Tian, Y. (2010b). The formal design models of a real-time operating system (RTOS+): Static and dynamic behavior models. *International Journal of Software Science and Computational Intelligence, 2*(3), 79–105. doi:10.4018/jssci.2010070106

Wang, Y., & Ruhe, G. (2007). The cognitive process of decision making. *International Journal of Cognitive Informatics and Natural Intelligence, 1*(2), 73–85. doi:10.4018/jcini.2007040105

Wang, Y., Tan, X., & Ngolah, C. F. (2010). Design and implementation of an autonomic code generator based on RTPA (RTPA-CG). *International Journal of Software Science and Computational Intelligence, 2*(2), 44–67. doi:10.4018/jssci.2010040103

Wang, Y., Zhang, Y., Sheu, P. C. Y., Li, X., & Guo, H. (2010). The formal design models of an automatic teller machine (ATM). *International Journal of Software Science and Computational Intelligence, 2*(1), 102–131. doi:10.4018/jssci.2010101907

Wiener, R., & Pinson, L. J. (2000). *Fundamentals of OOP and data structures in java.* Cambridge, UK: Cambridge University Press.

This work was previously published in the International Journal of Software Science and Computational Intelligence, Volume 3, Issue 3, edited by Yingxu Wang, pp. 69-89, copyright 2011 by IGI Publishing (an imprint of IGI Global).

Chapter 18
The Formal Design Models of Tree Architectures and Behaviors

Yingxu Wang
University of Calgary, Canada

Xinming Tan
Wuhan University of Technology, China

ABSTRACT

Trees are one of the most fundamental and widely used non-linear hierarchical structures of linked nodes. A binary tree (B-Tree) is a typical balanced tree where the fan-out of each node is at most two known as the left and right children. This paper develops a comprehensive design pattern of formal trees using the B-Tree architecture. A rigorous denotational mathematics, Real-Time Process Algebra (RTPA), is adopted, which allows both architectural and behavioral models of B-Trees to be rigorously designed and implemented in a top-down approach. The architectural models of B-Trees are created using RTPA architectural modeling methodologies known as the Unified Data Models (UDMs). The physical model of B-Trees is implemented using the left and right child nodes dynamically created in memory. The behavioral models of B-Trees are specified and refined by a set of Unified Process Models (UPMs) in three categories namely the management operations, traversal operations, and node I/O operations. This work has been applied in a number of real-time and nonreal-time system designs such as a real-time operating system (RTOS+), a general system organization model, and the ADT library for an RTPA-based automatic code generator.

DOI: 10.4018/978-1-4666-2651-5.ch018

1. INTRODUCTION

Data structure modeling is a process to creatively extract and abstractly represent a real-world problem by data models based on constraints of given computing resources. Abstract Data Types (ADTs) are a set of highly generic and rigorously modeled data structures in type theory (Guttag, 1977; Broy et al., 1984; Cardelli & Wegner, 1985; Stubbs & Webre, 1985), which is an abstract logical model of a complex data structure with a set of predefined operations. A number of ADTs have been identified in computing and system modeling such as *stack, queue, sequence, record, array, list, tree, file,* and *graph* (Broy et al., 1984; Mitchell, 1990; McDermid, 1991; Wang, 2007; Wang, Ngolah, Tan, Tian, & Sheu, 2010). ADTs possess the following properties: (i) An extension of type constructions by integrating both data structures and functional behaviors; (ii) A hybrid data object modeling technique that *encapsulates* both user defined data structures and allowable operations on them; (iii) The interface and implementation of an ADT are separated where detailed implementation of the ADT is hidden to applications that invoke the ADT and its predefined operations.

A tree is a non-linear hierarchical structure of linked nodes (Stubbs & Webre, 1985; McDermid, 1991; Gosling, Bollella, Dibble, Furr, & Turnbull, 2002), which can be formally modeled by an ADT. Trees can be classified, according to their topology, into the categories of *oriented* trees (in which the finite nodes except the root node are partitioned into k, $k \geq 0$, disjoint sub-oriented trees), *ordered* trees (an oriented tree where the subtrees are ordered by their subscripts), *binary* trees (in which the finite nodes except the root are partitioned into n, $0 \leq k \leq 2$, disjoint sub-binary trees), *n-nary* trees (in which the finite nodes except the root are partitioned into n, $0 \leq k \leq n$, disjoint sub-n-nary trees), *complete* trees (in which the subnodes of all nodes except the leave nodes are complete) (Stubbs & Webre, 1985; Wiener & Pinson, 2000). Trees may also be classified according to their types of applications such as

search trees (an ordered binary tree where for a certain node, all keys of nodes in the left and right subtrees are less or greater, respectively, than the key of the given node), *parse* trees (an oriented tree for syntax structures of compilers), *organization* trees (a complete *n*-nary tree for system organization and management), and *decision* trees (an ordered tree with nodes as value/alternatives and links as choices) (Stubbs & Webre, 1985; Wang, 2007; Wang & Ruhe, 2007). Various important data objects and system architectures can be modeled and implemented by trees such as a set of data with keys, a syntactic parse tree, and an expression tree (McDermid, 1991).

In order to formally model the tree ADT, an expressive denotational mathematics, Real-Time Process Algebra (RTPA) (Wang, 2002, 2007, 2008a, 2008b, 2008c, 2008d; Wang, Tan, & Ngolah, 2010), is adopted, which allows both architectural and behavioral models of lists to be rigorously designed and implemented in a top-down approach. According to the RTPA methodology for system modeling and refinement, a formal list can be rigorously modeled using two fundamental techniques known as the unified data model and the unified process model (Wang, 2007).

Definition 1: A *Unified Data Model* (UDM) is a generic architectural model for a software system as well as its internal control structures and its interfaces with hardware components, which can be rigorously modeled and refined as an *n*-tuple, i.e.:

$$UDM \triangleq \mathop{R}_{i=1}^{n} (S_i \mid \forall e \in S_i, p_i(e)) \tag{1}$$

where $\mathop{R}_{i=1}^{n}$ is the big-R notation of RTPA that denotes a repetitive or recursive structure or operation; S_i, $1 \leq i \leq n$, is a set that is equivalent to a type in computing for elements e, in which all e share the property $p_i(e)$.

Definition 2: The *Unified Process Model* (UPM) of a *program* ℘ is a composition of a finite set of *m* processes according to the event-based process dispatching rules, $@ e_k \mathbf{S} \hookrightarrow P_k \mathbf{PC}$, i.e.:

$$UPM \triangleq \wp$$

$$= \overset{m}{\underset{k=1}{R}} (@ e_k \mathbf{S} \hookrightarrow P_k \mathbf{PC})$$

$$= \overset{m}{\underset{k=1}{R}} [@ e_k \mathbf{S} \hookrightarrow \overset{n-1}{\underset{i=1}{R}} (s_i(k) \; r_{ij}(k) \; s_j(k))], j = i+1$$

$$(2)$$

where s_i and s_j are one of the 17 RTPA meta-processes, r_{ij} is one of the 17 RTPA algebraic process operators, and e_k is an event.

This paper develops a comprehensive design pattern of formal trees using the binary tree (B-Tree) model. In the remainder of this paper, the conceptual models of B-trees are described in Section 2. The architectural model of B-trees is created as a UDM in Section 3 using double links between nodes dynamically created in the memory. The static behaviors of B-trees are modeled and refined by a set of 12 UPMs in three categories namely the management operations, traversal operations, and node I/O operations in Section 4. The dynamic behaviors of B-trees are formally specified and refined by process scheduling and system dispatching models with UPMs in Section 5.

2. THE CONCEPTUAL MODEL OF B-TREES

A *tree* is a typical ADT with an organized hierarchy of nodes where there is no direct link between those belong to different subtrees except via their common parent. The most common node shared by all subtrees is called the *root*. A binary tree is a special tree where the fan-out of each node is at most two except the nodes at the leave level. The conceptual model of binary trees and their properties are introduced in this section. Based on it, formal models of the binary tree ADT in terms of its architectural and static/dynamic behavioral models will be rigorously developed in RTPA.

2.1. The Conceptual Structure of B-Trees

Definition 3: A *binary tree* (B-tree) is a hierarchical data structure where the fan-out of each node, except the leave nodes, is at most two known as the left and right children, and there is no interlinks (overlaps) between different subtrees.

It is noteworthy that there are two different but interactive facets in the models of B-trees known as its architectures and behaviors. The conceptual model of B-trees is depicted as shown in Figure 1. In the hierarchical structure of B-trees, each

Figure 1. The conceptual model of a B-tree

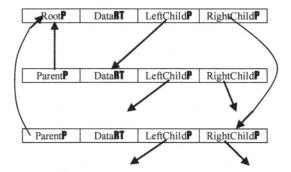

node is connected by a pair of edges linked to its left-child and right child. A B-tree may grow symmetrically from its root and a certain node may only belong to a single subtree.

In the conceptual model of B-trees, a root node is the first node when a B-tree is created with the root pointer Root$^\textbf{P}$ in the pointer type ($\textbf{P}$) links to nowhere, i.e., Root$^\textbf{P}$ = $\perp$.. However, the pointers of its left and right children link to corresponding child nodes, respectively. All children nodes are represented as a set of records, each of which consists of a set of attributes such as the Data$^\textbf{RT}$ in run-time type for implementation flexibility and the structural pointers of Parent$^\textbf{P}$, LeftChild$^\textbf{P}$, and RightChild$^\textbf{P}$. For a leaf node, LeftChild$^\textbf{P}$ and RightChild$^\textbf{P}$ will be left open, i.e., LeftChild$^\textbf{P}$ = RightChild$^\textbf{P}$ = $\perp$.

Definition 4: A *recursively* definition of a *B-tree* is a root node and two B-trees called the left and right subtrees that are disjoint from each other.

Based on the architectural model, the behavioral models of B-trees can be designed as shown in Figure 2. The typical functional behaviors of B-trees are identified in three categories known as the management behaviors such as create B-tree, create node, empty test, full test, clear, and release; the traversal behaviors such as find node, traverse, insert node, and delete subtree; and the node I/O behaviors such as retrieve node and update node.

Both the architectural and behavioral models of B-trees will be refined in the following sections.

2.2. The Algebraic Model of B-Trees

There are a number of approaches to specifying ADTs such as those of logic and algebra, as well as their combinations. Although each of these approaches has its advantages, there are gaps when applying them to solve real-world problems. An ADT interface of B-trees can be abstracted in an algebraic model as shown in Figure 3 (Stubbs & Webre, 1985; McDermid, 1991), where types and operations of the B-tree are described. The former specify the structure of the B-tree as a set of types such as $\mathbb{BT}$ – the B-tree, $\mathbb{E}$ – Elements, $\mathbb{BOOL}$ – Boolean values, N – Natural numbers, O - Traversal orders where $\mathbb{O}$ = {Preorder, Inorder, Postorder}, and $\mathbb{L}$ - Relative locations where $\mathbb{L}$ = {Root, Parent, Leftchild, Rightchild}. The latter models a set of eight operations defined onto the types of the B-tree as follows:

- **Traverse (bt, o, f):** Traverse the B-tree *bt* in the given order *o* performing function *f* on each element in *bt*;
- **Insert (bt, l, e):** Insert element *e* into B-tree *bt* at location *l*;
- **DeleteSub (bt, l):** Delete the subtree indicated by location *l* as its root in B-tree *bt*;
- **Update(bt, l, e):** Update the element *e* indicated by location *l* in B-tree *bt*;

Figure 2. The conceptual model of behaviors of B-trees

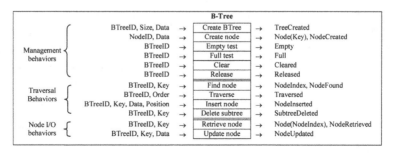

Figure 3. An algebraic model of a B-tree

ADT B-Tree

Types :
  BT, E, BOOL, N, O, L.

Operations :
  Traverse : $BT \times O \times (E \to E) \to BT$;
  Insert : $BT \times L \times E \to BT$;
  DeleteSub : $BT \times L \to BT$;
  Update : $BT \times L \times E \to BT$;
  Retrieve : $BT \times L \to E$;
  GetSize : $BT \to N$;
  EmptyTest : $BT \to BOOL$;
  Clear : $BT \to BT$.

- **Retrieve(bt, l):** Retrieve the element *e* indicated by location *l* in B-tree *bt*;
- **GetSize(bt):** Get the number of elements of B-tree *bt*;
- **EmptyTest(bt):** Test whether B-tree *bt* is an empty tree or not; and
- **Clear(bt):** Set B-tree *bt* as an empty tree.

It is noteworthy that the above algebraic ADT model of B-trees (Stubbs & Webre, 1985) only presents a schematic layout of the B-tree behaviors and the types of operated data objects. It is not detailed and rigorous enough for enabling machines to seamlessly transform the algebraic model into code, because there are too many gaps between the specification and implementation of the behavioural processes. In order to rigorously specify and refine the architectures and behaviors of B-trees, the RTPA methodology (Wang, 2002, 2007, 2008b) will be adopted throughout this paper.

2.3. Properties of Complete Trees

Binary and *n*-nary trees possess a number of predicative topological properties, particularly when they are complete trees.

Definition 5: A *complete n-nary tree* $T_c(n, N)$ is a normalized tree in which each node of T_c can have at most *n* children, each level *k* of T_c from top-down can have at most n^k nodes, and all levels have allocated the maximum number of possible nodes, except on the rightmost subtrees and at the leave level where there are *N* nodes, $N \leq n^k$.

It is noteworthy in Definition 5, a tree said to be *complete* means that all levels of the tree must possess the maximum number of possible nodes *n*, except two exceptions at the leave level and the rightmost subtrees. The advantage of complete trees is that the configuration of any complete *n*-nary tree $T_c(n, N)$ is uniquely determined by only two attributes: the unified fan-out *n* and the number of leave nodes *N* at the bottom level. For

Figure 4. Growth of complete B-Trees

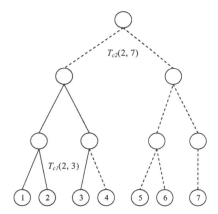

instance, two complete trees $T_{c1}(n_1, N_1) = T_{c1}(2, 3)$ and $T_{c2}(n_2, N_2) = T_{c1}(2, 7)$ are illustrated in Figure 4.

Complete trees are applied in a wide range of computing and system applications. One of the important applications is the modeling of normalized system architectures and topology.

Definition 6: A *normalized system* is a hierarchically structured system where no direct interconnections between nodes belong to different subtrees, and communications between such nodes should be coordinated through a common higher-level parent node.

Theorem 1: *The advantages of the complete tree* architecture of normalized systems are as follows:

1. **Equilibrium:** Looking down from any node at a level of the system tree, except at the leave level, the structural property of fan-out or the number of coordinated components are always the same and evenly distributed.
2. **Evolvablility:** A normalized system does not change the existing structure for future growth needs.
3. **Optimal Predictability:** There is an optimal approach to create a unique system structure $T_c(n, N)$ determined by the attributes of the unified fan-out n and the number of leave nodes N at the bottom level.

Therefore, the generic topology of systems tends to be normalized into a hierarchical structure in the form of a complete *n*-nary tree. Based on complete trees, the topology of normalized systems can be implemented by a system organization tree.

Definition 7: A *System Organization Tree* (SOT) is an *n*-nary complete tree in which all leave nodes represent a *component* and the remainder, all nodes beyond the leave level, represent a *subsystem*.

For instance, a ternary SOT, $SOT(n, N) = SOT(3, 24)$, is shown in Figure 5. Because an SOT is a complete tree, when the leaves (components) do not reach the maximum possible numbers, the right most subtree and related leaves of the SOT may left open according to the definition of complete trees.

SOT is an ideal model for implementing the topology of a normalized system where: a) No direct interconnection between nodes of different subtrees is allowed; and b) The communication needs between those nodes belong to different subtrees may go through a common higher-level parent node known as the *manager node*. A set of useful topological properties of SOT is identified as formally described in Theorem 2 (Wang, 2007).

Figure 5. A ternary system organization tree SOT(3, 24)

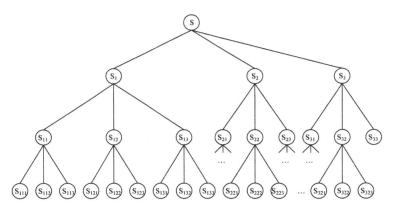

Theorem 2: An *n*-nary *system organization tree SOT(n, N)* with *N* leave nodes and *n* fan-out possesses the following topological properties:

1. The depth of the *SOT, d*:

$$d = \left\lceil \frac{\log N}{\log n} \right\rceil \quad (3)$$

2. The maximum number of nodes at a given level *k*, n_k, $2 \le k \le d$:

$$n_k = n^k \quad (4)$$

3. The maximum number of nodes in the *SOT*, N_{SOT}:

$$N_{SOT} = \sum_{k=0}^{d} n^k \quad (5)$$

4. The maximum number of *components* (on all leaves) in the *SOT, N*:

$$N = n^d \quad (6)$$

5. The maximum number of *subsystems* (nodes except all leaves) in the *SOT*, N_m:

$$N_m = N_{SOT} \text{-} N \text{-} 1 = \sum_{k=1}^{d-1} n^k \quad (7)$$

The following sections present a set of architectural and behavioral models of binary trees in order to explain how B-Trees may be rigorously modeled, implemented, and applied in software systems.

3. THE ARCHITECTURAL MODELS OF B-TREES

On the basis of the conceptual model developed in the preceding section, the top-level ADT model of B-trees as a system (**§**), BTree**§**, can be specified in Equation 8 in RTPA. The architectural model specifies that a B-tree encompasses three parallel subsystems known as its architecture, static behaviors, and dynamic behaviors. According to the RTPA methodology for system modeling, specification, and refinement (Wang, 2007, 2008a), the following subsections will refine the top level framework of BTree**§** into detailed UDMs, which serves as a generic architectural model of a software system as well as its hardware components, interfaces, and internal control structures. Then, the static and dynamic behavioral models, BTree**§**.StaticBehaviors**PC** and BTree**§**.

Figure 6. The UDM model of the B-tree ADT

```
BTree§.ArchitectureST ≙ BTreeIDST ::
  (<BTreeID : S | 1 = BTreeIDS = 255>,
   <Size : N | 0 = SizeN = MaxSizeN>,
   <#Nodes : N | 0 = #NodesN = SizeN>,
   <MemSize : N | 0 = MemSizeN = MaxMemN>,
        #NodesN
     <  R      Node(iN)ST :: (<Key : N | 0 = KeyN = SizeN>,
       iN=0
                              <Data : RT | DataRT ∈ {S, N, R, ST, ...}>,
                              <Parent : P | 0 = ParentP = MemSizeN>,
                              <LeftChild : P | 0 = LeftChildP = MemSizeN>,
                              <RightChild : P | 0 = RightChildP = MemSizeN>,
                              <Location : P | 0 = LocationP = MemSizeN>
                              )
   <Root : P | RootP = 0>,
   <NodeIndex : N | 0 = NodeIndexN = SizeN>,
   <Position . N | PositionN = {(1, Parent), (2, LeftChild), (3, RightChild)}>,
   <Order : N | OrderN = {(1, Preorder), (2, Inorder), (3, Postorder)}>,
   <ⓢTreeCreated : BL | ⓢTreeCreatedBL = {(T, Yes), (F, No)}>,
   <ⓢNodeCreated : BL | ⓢNodeCreatedBL = {(T, Yes), (F, No)}>,
   <ⓢNodeFound : BL | ⓢNodeFoundBL = {(T, Yes), (F, No)}>,
   <ⓢNodeRetrieved : BL | ⓢNodeRetrievedBL = {(T, Yes), (F, No)}>,
   <ⓢNodeUpdated : BL | ⓢNodeUpdatedBL = {(T, Yes), (F, No)}>,
   <ⓢTraversed : BL | ⓢTraversedBL = {(T, Yes), (F, No)}>,
   <ⓢNodeInserted : BL | ⓢNodeInsertedBL = {(T, Yes), (F, No)}>,
   <ⓢSubtreeDeleted : BL | ⓢSubtreeDeletedBL = {(T, Yes), (F, No)}>,
   <ⓢEmpty : BL | ⓢEmptyBL = {(T, Yes), (F, No)}>,
   <ⓢFull : BL | ⓢFulBL = {(T, Yes), (F, No)}>,
   <ⓢCleared : BL | ⓢClearedBL = {(T, Yes), (F, No)}>,
   <ⓢReleased : BL | ⓢReleasedBL = {(T, Yes), (F, No)}>
  )
```

DynamicBehaviors**PC**, will be developed and refined in Sections 4 and 5.

$$BTree§ ≙ BTree§.ArchitectureST$$
$$\| \ BTree§.StaticBehaviorsPC$$
$$\| \ BTree§.DynamicBehaviorsPC$$

(8)

The UDM model of BTrees, BTree**§**.Architecture**ST**, as shown in Figure 6 provides a generic architectural model for any concrete B-tree in applications with three categories of design attributes known as follows:

1. The *architectural* attributes determine the configuration of the B-tree such as its logical size (Size**N**), physical size (MemSize**N**), current number of nodes (#Nodes**N**), the root pointer (Root**P**), the index number of a node (NodeIndex**N**), the order for traverse (Order**N**) such as the preorder, inorder, and postorder, as well as the position for node insertion (Position**N**) such as a position at the current pointer as well as the parent, left child, or right child;

2. The *node* attributes model a logically sorted sequence of *n* nodes constrained by #Nodes**N** indexed by i**N** equivalent to its Key**N**. There are six fields for each node in the B-tree model: Key**N**, Data**RT**, Parent**P**, LeftChild**P**, RightChild**P**, and Location**P** (the physical location of the node);

3. The *status* attributes are a set of indicators of operational results in Boolean type with

a status prefix Ⓢ such as ⓈTreeCreated**BL**, ⓈNodeCreated**BL**, ⓈNodeFound**BL**, ⓈNodeRetrieved**BL**, ⓈNodeUpdated**BL**, ⓈTraversed**BL**, ⓈNodeInserted**BL**, ⓈSubtreeDeleted**BL**, ⓈEmpty**BL**, &Full**BL**, ⓈCleared**BL**, and ⓈReleased**BL**.

Each filed of attributes in the UDM of B-tree is modeled by a primitive type of RTPA (Wang, 2007) and constrained by a certain scope or initial value given in the right-hand side of the vertical bar. It is noteworthy that the type of the data elements in a node is specified in the run-time type **RT**, i.e., **RT** ∈ {**S**, **N**, **R**, **ST**, ...}, for design flexibility. However, the data elements of concrete nodes must be instantiated once it is chosen at run-time for a specific implementation of a concrete B-tree.

The architectural model, BTree**ST**, can be accessed or invoked in two ways as expressed in Equations 9 and 10. The random access in Equation 9 allows a node of the B-tree to be located by a pointer NodePtr**P**; While the sequential access in Equation 10 provides an additional approach to enable a node of the B-tree to be located by its index number NodeIndex**N** or the key.

TargetNode**P**:= BTree**ID**(NodePtr**P**)
ST.Location**P** (9)

TargetNode**P**:= BTreeID**ST**.Node(NodeIndex**N**)
ST.Location**P** (10)

4. THE BEHAVIORAL PROCESS MODELS OF B-TREES

The static behaviors of the B-tree ADT, BTree**S**.StaticBehaviorsPC, can be specified by a set of functional operations on its architectural model (UDM), i.e., BTree**S**.Architecture**PC**. On the basis of the UDM models of BTree**ST** developed in the preceding subsection, the behaviors of B-trees can be modeled as a set of UPMs operating on the UDMs of BTree**ST** and related input variables. The high-level behavioral model of the B-Tree ADT is specified by BTree**S**.StaticBehaviors**PC** as shown in Figure 7. The schemas of the UPMs in Figure 7 model the input data objects <**I**:: (...)>, output data objects <**O**:: (...)>, and operated UDMs <**UDM**:: (...)> for each specific process of BTree**S**. The UDMs play an important role in system architectural design as global and permanent I/O structures, which usually have a longer life-span than those of the process(es) that created and/or invoked them, particularly in real-time and embedded systems.

As informally modeled in Figure 2, the behavioral models of B-trees are specified by a set of 12 UPMs in three categories known as the management operations (such as CreateBTree**PC**, CreateNode**PC**, EmptyTest**PC**, FullTest**PC**, Clear**PC**, and Release**PC**), traversal operations (such as FindNode**PC**, Traverse**PC**, InsertNode**PC**, and DeleteSubTree**PC**), and node I/O operations (such as RetrieveNode**PC** and UpdateNode**PC**). In the following subsections, each of the static behaviors of the B-tree, BTree**S**.StaticBehaviors**PC**, as given in Figure 7 will be further refined by a set of UPMs using the denotational mathematical notations and methodologies of RTPA.

4.1. The Behavioral Model of the B-Tree Creation Process

The *B-Tree creation* process, CreateBTree**PC**, is formally modeled as shown in Figure 8, which establishes a new B-tree in system memory or on a disk and links it to a specified logical ID of the B-tree, BTreeID**S**. The input arguments of the process are the given name of the B-tree as well as its size (or maximum capacity of nodes) and the type of data in each node. The output result of the process is the status of the B-tree creation operation @ListCreated**BL**. The UDM operated by this process is BTree**ST**.

CreateBTree**PC** calls a system support process, AllocateObject**PC** (Wang, Ngolah, Tan, Tian, &

Figure 7. The high-level UPM model of B-tree behaviors

```
BTree§.StaticBehaviorsPC ≙
  ( CreateBTreePC(<I:: BTreeIDS, SizeN, DataRT>; <O:: ⓈTreeCreatedBL>; <UDM:: BTreeST>)
  | CreateNodePC(<I:: NodeIDS, DataRT>; <O:: Node(KeyN)ST, ⓈNodeCreatedBL>; <UDM:: BTreeST>)
  | FindNodePC(<I:: BTreeIDST, KeyN>; <O:: NodeIndexN, ⓈNodeFoundBL>; <UDM:: BTreeST>)
  | RetrieveNodePC(<I:: BTreeIDST, KeyN>; <O:: Node(NodeIndexN)ST, ⓈNodeRetrievedBL>; <UDM:: BTreeST>)
  | UpdateNodePC(<I:: BTreeIDST, KeyN, DataRT>; <O:: ⓈNodeUpdatedBL>; <UDM:: BTreeST>)
  | TraversePC(<I:: BTreeIDS, OrderN, ActionPC>; <O:: ⓈTraversedBL>; <UDM:: BTreeST>)
  | InsertNodePC(<I:: BTreeIDST, KeyN, DataST, PositionN>; <O:: ⓈNodeInsertedBL>; <UDM:: BTreeST>)
  | DeleteSubTreePC(<I:: BTreeIDST, KeyN>; <O:: ⓈSubTreeDeletedBL>; <UDM:: BTreeST>)
  | EmptyTestPC(<I:: BTreeIDS>; <O:: ⓈEmptyBL>; <UDM:: BTreeST>)
  | FullTestPC(<I:: BTreeIDS>; <O:: ⓈFullBL>; <UDM:: BTreeST>)
  | ClearPC(<I:: BTreeIDS>; <O:: ⓈClearedBL>; <UDM:: BTreeST>)
  | ReleasePC(<I:: BTreeIDS>; <O:: ⓈReleasedBL>; <UDM:: BTreeST>)
  )
```

Sheu, 2010), to physical set up the root node of the B-tree using dynamic memory allocation technology. If a memory block is successfully obtained for the root node of the B-tree, CreateBTree**PC** initializes the BTreeID**ST** by the following operations: a) *B-tree initialization* connects the root pointer to the allocated memory block, and assigns its expected size; b) *Root node initialization* sets the values of key and location of the root node, and leaves the data and both left/right child pointers undefined until the node insertion process is invoked; and c) *Status initialization* sets the initial values of statuses of the B-tree as modeled in BTree**ST**. Otherwise, it reports an error BTreeID**ST**.&Created**BL**:= **F** with an exception warning of memory allocation failed. In case the

Figure 8. The UPM model of B-tree creation process

```
CreateBTree PC(<I:: BTree ID S, SizeN, DataRT>; <O:: ⓈTreeCreatedBL>; <UDM:: BTree ST>) ≙
{
 → ( ◆ BTreeIDST.ⓈTreeCreatedBL = F
       → ObjectIDS := BTreeIDS
       → #ElementsN := 1
       → ElementTypeRT := DataRT
       ↣ AllocateObjectPC(<I:: ObjectIDS, #ElementsN, ElementTypeRT)>;
                       <O:: ⓈObjectAllocatedBL>; <UDM:: MEMST>)
       → ( ◆ ⓈObjectAllocatedBL = T
             → BTreeS := BTreeIDS
             → BTreeIDST.RootP ⇐ MEM(ObjectIDS)ST   // BTree initialization
             → BTreeIDST.SizeN := SizeN
             → BTreeIDST.#NodesN := 1
             → BTreeIDST.Nodes(0)ST.KeyN := 0                // Root node initialization
             → BTreeIDST.Nodes(0)ST.DataRT := ⊥
             → BTreeIDST.Nodes(0)ST.ParentP := ⊥
             → BTreeIDST.Nodes(0)ST.LeftChildP := ⊥
             → BTreeIDST.Nodes(0)ST.RightChildP := ⊥
             → BTreeIDST.Nodes(0)ST.LocationP ⇐ MEM(ObjectIDS)ST
             → BTreeIDST.ⓈEmptyBL := T                       // Status initialization
             → BTreeIDST.ⓈFullBL := F
             → BTreeIDST.ⓈCreatedBL := T
           | ◆ ~
             → BTreeIDST.ⓈTreeCreatedBL := F
             → ! 'BTreeIDST memory allocation is failed.')
         )
   | ◆ ~
       → BTreeIDST.ⓈTreeCreatedBL := F
       → ! ('BTreeIDST has already been existed.')
   )
}
```

Figure 9. The UPM model of the node creation process

```
CreateNodePC(<I:: NodeIDS, DataRT>; <O:: Node(KeyN)ST, ⓢNodeCreatedBL>; <UDM:: BTreeST>) ≜
{
  → <QbjectIDS, NofElementsN, ElementTypeRT> := <NodeIDS, 1, DataRT>
  ↣ AllocateObjectPC(<I:: ObjectIDS, #ElementsN, ElementTypeRT)>; <O:: ⓢObjectAllocatedBL>; <UDM:: MEMST>)
  → ( ◆ ⓢObjectAllocatedBL = T
        → ↑ (BTreeIDST.#NodesN)
        → iN := BTreeIDST.#NodesN - 1
        → BTreeIDST.Node(iN)ST.KeyN := iN
        → BTreeIDST.Node(iN)ST.DataRT := ⊥
        → BTreeIDST.Node(iN)ST.ParentP := ⊥
        → BTreeIDST.Node(iN)ST.LeftChildP := ⊥
        → BTreeIDST.Node(iN)ST.RightChildP := ⊥
        → BTreeIDST.Node(iN)ST.LocationP ⇐ MEM(ObjectIDS)ST
        → BTreeIDST.ⓢNodeCreatedBL := T
     | ◆ ~
        → BTreeIDST.ⓢNodeCreatedBL := F
        → ! ('Node memory allocation is failed.')
    )
}
```

given BTreeID**ST** has already existed, CreateBTree**PC** results in a specific error message BTreeID**ST**.ⓢCreated**BL**:= **F**.

4.2. The Behavioral Model of the Node Creation Process

The *node creation* process, CreateNode**PC**, is formally modeled as shown in Figure 9, which establishes a new node in system memory or on a disk and links it to a specified logical node, NodeID**S** of the B-tree. The input arguments of the process are the given name of the node and the type of data for dynamic memory allocation. The output results of the process are the node as identified by its key and the status of the node creation operation. CreateNode**PC** calls the system support process, AllocateObject**PC**, to physical set up the node in memory. If a memory block is successfully obtained for the node of the B-tree, CreateNode**PC** links the node to the allocated memory block and initializes the node's physical location and key, while leaves the data and other pointers undefined until the node insertion process is invoked; Otherwise, it reports an error BTreeID**ST**.&NodeCreated**BL**:= **F** with an exceptional warning of memory allocation failed.

4.3. The Behavioral Model of the Node Finding Process

The *node finding* process, FindNode**PC**, is formally modeled as shown in Figure 10, which searches for a specific node based on its given key. The input arguments of the process are the given name of the B-tree and the key of the node. The output results of the process are the index of the node and the status of the node searching operation. FindNode**PC** initializes the search result as false before checking if the size of the B-tree is empty. If not, FindNode**PC** iteratively compares the key of each node in the B-tree and the given key in order to find the target node. If it is found, FindNode**PC** returns the NodeIndex**N**, sets the search result as true, and exits the loop. Otherwise, the search result remains false. The result of FindNode**PC** will be used by other B-tree operation processes such as RetrieveNode**PC**, UpdateNode**PC**, and DeleteSubtree**PC** for identifying the target node.

4.4. The Behavioral Model of the Node Retrieval Process

The *node retrieval* process, RetrieveNode**PC**, is formally modeled as shown in Figure 11, which reads and shows the contents of a target node in the B-tree identified by the key. The input arguments of the process are the given name of the B-tree and the key of the target node. The output

Figure 10. The UPM model of the node finding process

```
FindNodePC(<I:: BTreeIDST, KeyN>; <O:: NodeIndexN, ⊙NodeFoundBL>; <UDM:: BTreeST>) ≙
{
  → BTreeIDST.⊙NodeFoundBL := F
  →( ◆ BTreeIDST.#NodesN ≠ 0
              BTreeST.#NodesN
     →           R            ◆ BTreeIDST.Node(iN)ST.KeyN = KeyN
                iN=0
                                  → NodeIndexN := iN
                                  → BTreeIDST.⊙NodeFoundBL := T
                                  → ⊘
    )
}
```

results of the process are the node as identified by its index and the status of the node retrieval operation. RetrieveNode**PC** checks if the target B-tree exists and is not empty before the following operations: a) Search the target node with Key**N** by calling FindNode**PC**; b) If the target node is found, display each field of the target node on the standard monitor, CRTST, of the system supported by the process ShowNode**PC**, and set BTreeID**ST**.&NodeRetrieved**BL**:= **T**; c) Otherwise, report an error BTreeID**ST**.&NodeRetrieved**BL**:= **F** with an exception warning of "node was not found." In case the given BTreeID**ST** did not exist or was empty, RetrieveNode**PC** results in a specific error message BTreeID**ST**.&Retrieved**BL**:= **F**.

4.5. The Behavioral Model of the Node Update Process

The *node update* process, UpdateNode**PC**, is formally modeled as shown in Figure 12, which puts new data into the target node in a B-tree identified by the key. The input arguments of the process are the given name of the B-tree, the key of the target node, and the data for updating. The output result of the process is the status of the node update operation. UpdateNode**PC** checks if the target B-tree exists and is not empty before the following operations: a) Search the target node with Key**N** by calling FindNode**PC**; b) If the target node is found, replace the data field of the target node with given Data**RT**, and set

Figure 11. The UPM model of the node retrieval process

```
RetrieveNodePC(<I:: BTreeID ST, KeyN>; <O:: BTreeID ST.Node(NodeIndexN)ST, ⊙NodeRetrievedBL>; <UDM:: BTree ST>) ≙
{
  → ( ◆ BTreeIDST.⊙TreeCreatedBL = T ∧ BTreeIDST.⊙EmptyBL ≠ T
        ↣ FindNodePC(<I:: BTreeIDST, KeyN>; <O:: NodeIndexN, ⊙NodeFoundBL>; <UDM:: BTreeST>)
        → ( ◆ BTreeIDST.⊙NodeFoundBL = T
              ↣ ShowNodePC(<I:: BTreeIDST, NodeIndexN>; <O:: BTreeIDST.Node(NodeIndexN)ST>;
                           <UDM:: BTreeST, CRTST>)
              → BTreeIDST.⊙NodeRetrievedBL:= T
           | ◆ ~
              → BTreeIDST.⊙NodeRetrievedBL:= F
              → ! ('The node was not found in BTreeIDST.')
          )
     | ◆ ~
        → BTreeIDST.⊙NodeRetrievedBL:= F
        → ! ('BTreeIDST did not exist or was empty.')
     )
}

ShowNodePC(<I:: BTreeIDST, iN>; <O:: BTreeIDST.Node(NodeIndexN)ST>; <UDM:: BTreeST, CRTST>) ≙
{
 → BTreeIDST.Node(iN)ST.KeyN |⋖ CRTST
 → BTreeIDST.Node(iN)ST.DataRT |⋖ CRTST
 → BTreeIDST.Node(iN)ST.ParentP |⋖ CRTST
 → BTreeIDST.Node(iN)ST.LeftChildP |⋖ CRTST
 → BTreeIDST.Node(iN)ST.RightChildP |⋖ CRTST
 → BTreeIDST.Node(iN)ST.LocationP |⋖ CRTST
}
```

Figure 12. The UPM model of the node update process

```
UpdateNodePC(<I:: BTreeIDST, KeyN, DataRT>; <O:: ⓢNodeUpdatedBL>; <UDM:: BTreeST>) ≜
{
    → ( ◆ BTreeIDST.ⓢTreeCreatedBL = T ∧ BTreeIDST.ⓢEmptyBL ≠ T
        → FindNodePC(<I:: BTreeIDST, KeyN>; <O:: NodeIndexN, ⓢNodeFoundBL>; <UDM:: BTreeST>)
        → ( ◆ BTreeIDST.ⓢNodeFoundBL = T
            → BTreeIDST.Node(NodeIndexN)ST.DataRT := DataRT
            → BTreeIDST.ⓢNodeUpdatedBL := T
          | ◆ ~
            → BTreeIDST.ⓢNodeUpdatedBL := F
            → ! ('The node was nor found in BTreeIDST,')
          )
      | ◆ ~
        → BTreeIDST.ⓢNodeUpdatedBL := F
        → ! ('BTreeIDST did not exist or was empty.')
      )
}
```

BTreeIDST.&NodeUpdatedBL:= T; c) Otherwise, report an error BTreeIDST.&NodeUpdatedBL:= F with an exception warning of "node was not found." In case the given BTreeIDST did not exist or was empty, UpdateNodePC results in a specific error message BTreeIDST.&NodeUpdatedBL:= F.

4.6. The Behavioral Model of the B-Tree Traversal Process

The traversal process provides a means to search through a B-tree in preorder, inorder, and postorder in which each node may only be process once. The process on a node in a B-tree is specific action such as to read the contents of the node, to update its contents, and to delete the node as well as its subnodes in its subtree.

Definition 8: A *preorder traversal* of a B-tree is a thorough search process in which each node is found and processed once before the child nodes in either of its subtrees.

Definition 9: An *inorder traversal* of a B-tree is a thorough search process in which each node is found and processed once after the child nodes in its left subtree but before those in the right subtree.

Definition 10: A *postorder traversal* of a B-tree is a thorough search process in which each node is found and processed once after the child nodes in both of its subtrees.

The main *traversal* process, TraversePC, is formally modeled as shown in Figures 13 and 14, which goes through all nodes of a B-tree in one of the desigbneated order, i.e., PreOrderTraversePC, InOrderTraversePC, and PostOrderTraversePC. The input arguments of the process are the given B-tree ID, the specified order of traverse, and the expected action on each node during traversal, i.e., ShowNodePC. The output results of the process are the embodiment of predefined action on all nodes as well as the status of the traversal operation. TraversePC checks if the target B-tree exists and is not empty before the following operations: a) Select one of the traversal method according to the given OrderN; and b) Call the corresponding traversal process or do nothing but exit when the given order is out of range. In case the given BTreeIDST did not exist or was empty, TraversePC results in an exceptional error BTreeIDST.&TraversedBL:= F.

The technologies for the three orders of sub-traversal processes on B-trees, PreOrderTraversePC, InOrderTraversePC, and PostOrderTraversePC, are formally modeled as shown in Figure 14. The functions of different traversal methods are designed according to Definitions 4 through 6. They are implemented as recursive processes, within each recursion one node will be processed by the given function, ActionPC, in each side of the subtrees. It is noteworthy that ActionPC during tree traversal is predefined by an external function

Figure 13. The UPM model of the main traversal process

```
TraversePC(<I:: BTreeIDS, OrderN, ActionPC>; <O:: ⓢTraversedBL>; <UDM:: BTreeST>) ≙
{
 → ( ◆ BTreeIDST.ⓢTreeCreatedBL = T ∧ BTreeIDST.ⓢEmptyBL ≠ T
     → ( ◆ OrderN =
           1: → PreOrderTraversePC(<I:: BTreeIDST, RootP, ActionPC >; <O:: NodeST, BTreeIDST.ⓢTraversedBL>;
                                   <UDM:: BTreeST>)
          | 2: → InOrderTraversePC(<I:: BTreeIDST, RootP, ActionPC >; <O:: NodeST, BTreeIDST.ⓢTraversedBL>;
                                   <UDM:: BTreeST>)
          | 3: → PostOrderTraversePC(<I:: BTreeIDST, RootP, ActionPC >; <O:: NodeST, BTreeIDST.ⓢTraversedBL>;
                                   <UDM:: BTreeST>)
          | ~: → ( → BTreeIDST.ⓢTraversedBL := F
                   → ! (@'Traverse order is invalid.')
                   → ∅
                 )
       )
   | ◆ ~
     → BTreeIDST.ⓢTraversedBL := F
     → ! ('BTreeIDS did not exist or was empty.')
   )
}
```

such as to retrieve or update nodes in the given order of traversal. Applications of B-tree traversal for node retrieve and update are described in Sections 4.4 and 4.5, respectively.

4.7. The Behavioral Model of the Node Insertion Process

The *node insertion* process, InsertNode**PC**, is formally modeled as shown in Figure 15, which inserts a newly created node at a specific position identified by the given key as a parent, left child, or right child in the B-tree. The input arguments

Figure 14. The UPM models of the sub-traversal processes

```
PreOrderTraversePC(<I:: BTreeIDST, CurrentNodeP, ActionPC>; <O:: ⓢTraversedBL>; <UDM:: BTreeST>) ≙
{
  → TempNodeP := CurrentNodeP
  → ActionPC(<I:: BTreeIDST, CurrentNodeP>; <O:: Node(NodeIndexN)ST>;
            <UDM:: BTreeST, MEMST, CRTST >)
  → CurrentNodeP := BTree(TempNodeP)ST.LeftChildP
  → PreOrderTraversePC(<I:: BTreeIDST, CurrentNodeP, ActionPC>, <O:: ⓢTraversedBL>; <UDM:: BTreeST>)
  → CurrentNodeP := TempNodeP
  → CurrentNodeP := BTree(CurrentNodeP)ST.RightChildP
  → PreOrderTraversePC(<I:: BTreeIDST, CurrentNodeP, ActionPC>, <O:: ⓢTraversedBL>; <UDM:: BTreeST>)
  → BTreeIDST.ⓢTraversedBL:= T
}

InOrderTraversePC(<I:: BTreeIDS, CurrentNodeP, ActionPC>; <O:: ⓢTraversedBL>; <UDM:: BTreeST>) ≙
{
  → TempNodeP := CurrentNodeP
  → CurrentNodeP := BTree(CurrentNodeP)ST.LeftChildP
  → InOrderTraversePC(<I:: BTreeIDST, CurrentNodeP, ActionPC >; <O:: ⓢTraversedBL>; <UDM:: BTreeST>)
  → CurrentNodeP := TempNodeP
  → ActionPC(<I:: BTreeIDST, CurrentNodeP>; <O:: Node(NodeIndexN)ST>;
            <UDM:: BTreeST, MEMST, CRTST >)
  → CurrentNodeP := BTree(TempNodeP)ST.RightChildP
  → InOrderTraversePC(<I:: BTreeIDST, CurrentNodeP, ActionPC >; <O:: ⓢTraversedBL>; <UDM:: BTreeST>)
  → BTreeIDST.TraversedBL:= T
}

PostOrderTraversePC(<I:: BTreeIDS, CurrentNodeP, ActionPC>; <O:: ⓢTraversedBL>; <UDM:: BTreeST>) ≙
{
  → TempNodeP := CurrentNodeP
  → CurrentNodeP := BTree(CurrentNodeP)ST.LeftChildP
  → PostOrderTraversePC(<I:: BTreeIDST, CurrentNodeP, ActionPC>; <O:: ⓢTraversedBL>; <UDM:: BTreeST>)
  → CurrentNodeP := BTree(TempNodeP)ST.RightChildP
  → PostOrderTraversePC(<I:: BTreeIDST, CurrentNodeP, ActionPC>; <O:: ⓢTraversedBL>; <UDM:: BTreeST>)
  → CurrentNodeP := TempNodeP
  → ActionPC(<I:: BTreeIDST, CurrentNodeP>; <O:: Node(NodeIndexN)ST>;
            <UDM:: BTreeST, MEMST, CRTST >)
  → BTreeIDST.ⓢTraversedBL:= T
}
```

Figure 15. The UPM model of the node insertion process

of the process are the B-tree ID, the key of target node, the data, and the position for node insertion. Its output is the status of the insert operation. InsertNode**PC** checks if the target B-tree exists and is not full before the following operations: a) Create the new node to be inserted by calling CreateNode**PC**; b) Save the target node's position and related pointers, increase the number of nodes of the B-tree by one, set BTreeID**ST**.&NodeInserted**BL**:= **T**, and check the full condition for the B-tree; c) Depending on the given insertion position, do the following: (i) If Position**N** = 1, insert the new node as a parent of the target node, link the target node as its left child, keep its right child as dummy, update other pointers of the new node, the target

node, and the original parent of the target node; (ii) If Position**N** = 2, insert the new node as the left child of the target node, keep its right child as dummy, update other pointers of the new node, the target node, and the original left child of the target node; (iii) If Position**N** = 3, insert the new node as the right child of the target node, keep its left child as dummy, update other pointers of the new node, the target node, and the original right child of the target node; and d) In cases the target node could not be found, the given node could not be created, or the B-tree did not exist or was full, an exception condition will be set by BTreeID**ST**.&NodeInserted**BL**:= **F**.

Figure 16. The UPM model of the subtree deletion process

```
DeleteSubTreePC(<I:: BTreeIDST, KeyN>; <O:: ⓢSubTreeDeletedBL>; <UDM:: BTreeST>) ≙
{
  → ( ◆ BTreeIDST.ⓢCreatedBL = T ∧ ◆ BTreeIDST.EmptyBL ≠ T
        → FindNodePC(<I:: BTreeIDST, KeyN>; <O:: NodeIndexN, ⓢNodeFoundBL>; <UDM:: BTreeST>)
        → ( ◆ ⓢNodeFoundBL = T
              → CurrentNodeP := BTreeIDST.Node(NodeIndexN)ST.LocationP
              → ParentNodeP := BTreeID(CurrentNodeP)ST.ParentP  // Update parent node of the deleted subtree
              → ( ◆ BTreeID(ParentNodeP)ST.LeftChildP = CurrentNodeP
                    → BTreeID(ParentNodeP)ST.LeftChildP := ⊥
                | ◆ ~
                    → BTreeID(ParentNodeP)ST.RightChildP := ⊥
                )
              → PostOrderTraversePC(<I:: BTreeIDS, CurrentNodeP, DeleteNodePC>; <O:: ⓢTraversedBL>;
                                    <UDM:: BTreeST>)
              → BTreeIDST.ⓢSubTreeDeletedBL := T
          | ◆ ~
              → BTreeIDST.ⓢSubTreeDeletedBL := F
              → ! ('The target node was not found.')
          )
    | ◆ ~
        → BTreeIDST.ⓢSubTreeDeletedBL := F
        → ! ('The tree did not exist or was empty.')
    )
}

DeleteNodePC(<I:: BTreeIDST, CurrentNodeP>; <O:: >; <UDM:: BTreeST>) ≙
{
  → ObjectIDP := CurrentNodeP
  → ReleaseObjectPC(<I:: ObjectIDP>; <O:: ⓢObjectReleasedBL>; <UDM:: MEMST>)
  → CurrentNodeP ⇍ MEM(ObjectIDP)ST
  → ↓ (BTreeIDST.#NodesN)
}
```

4.8. The Behavioral Model of the Subtree Deletion Process

The *subtree deletion* process, DeleteSubTree**PC**, is formally modeled as shown in Figure 16, which removes a specific node and its subtree in the B-tree. The input arguments of the process are the B-tree ID and the key of the target node. Its output is the status of the deletion operation. DeleteSubTree**PC** checks if the target B-tree exists and is not empty before the following operations: a) Find the target node to be deleted by calling FindNode**PC**; b) If the target node is allocated with the return of its NodeIndex**N**, do the following: (i) Determine the pointer of the target node and find its parent; (ii) Check if the target node is a left or right child of the parent node, and then, mark the corresponding left or right child and the subtree beneath it as dummy for deletion; (iii) Delete each node in the identified subtree by calling PostOrderTravrse**PC** with the support of DeleteNode**PC** in order to remove the subtree; and (iv) Each time when a node is deleted in the subtree, the number of nodes of the B-tree is decreased by one. In cases the target node could not be found and the B-tree did not exist or was empty, an exception condition will be set by BTreeID**ST**.&SunTreeDeleted**BL**:= **F**.

4.9. The Behavioral Model of the B-Tree Empty Test Process

The *empty test* process, EmptyTest**PC**, is formally modeled as shown in Figure 17, which detects whether a given B-tree is empty. The input argument of the process is the target B-tree ID. Its output is the status of the B-tree as being empty or not. The status of an empty B-tree is characterized by BTreeID**ST**.#Nodes**N** = 1 where only the root node exists. Therefore, EmptyTest**PC** verifies if the number of nodes in the B-tree is one in order to determine whether it is empty. When the given B-tree did not exist, EmptyTest**PC** generates a specific error message BTreID**ST**.&Empty**BL**:= **F**.

Figure 17. The UPM model of the B-Tree empty test process

```
EmptyTestPC(<I:: BTreeIDS>; <O:: ⓈEmptyBL>; <UDM:: BTreeST>) ≙
{
  → ( ◆ BTreeIDST.ⓈCreatedBL = T
        → (  ◆ BTreeIDST.#NodesP = 1
                → BTreeIDST.ⓈEmptyBL := T
                → BTreeIDST.ⓈFullBL := F
           | ◆ ~
                → BTreeIDST.ⓈEmptyBL := F
           )
     | ◆ ~
        → ! ('BTreeIDST did not exist.')
     )
}
```

4.10. The Behavioral Model of the B-Tree Full Test Process

The *full test* process, FullTest**PC**, is formally modeled as shown in Figure 18, which detects whether a given B-tree is full. The input argument of the process is the target B-tree ID. Its output is the status of the B-tree as being full or not. The status of a full B-tree is characterized by BTreeID**ST**.#Nodes**N** = BTreeID**ST**.Size**N**. Therefore, FullTest**PC** verifies if the number of nodes has reached the defined capacity of the B-tree in order to determine whether it is full. When the given B-tree did not exist, FullTest**PC** generates a specific error message BTreeID**ST**.&Full**BL**:= **F**.

4.11. The Behavioral Model of the B-Tree Clear Process

The *B-Tree clear* process, Clear**PC**, is formally modeled as shown in Figure 19, which not only logically sets the given B-tree as empty, but also physically releases all existing nodes in memory. The input argument of the process is the given B-tree ID. Its output is the status of the clear operation. Clear**PC** is equivalent to the sequential operations to first release the given B-tree and then to re-create an empty B-tree by calling Release**PC** and CreateBTree**PC**, respectively. In case the given B-tree did not exist, Clear**PC** generates a specific error message BTreeID**ST**.&Cleared**BL** = **F**.

4.12. The Behavioral Model of the B-Tree Release Process

The *B-Tree release* process, Release**PC**, is formally modeled as shown in Figure 20, which physically removes a given B-tree and releases the memory occupied. The input argument of the process is the given B-tree ID. Its output is the status of the release operation. Release**PC** frees and returns the memory block of each node to the system by calling a system support process, ReleaseObject**PC** (Wang, 2007) for dynamic memory manipulation. It then disconnects the logical name of the B-tree and its physical entity in memory. If the given B-tree has not been created, Release**PC** produces a specific error message BTreeID**ST**.&Released**BL** = **F**.

5. THE DYNAMIC BEHAVIOR MODELS OF B-TREES

According to the RTPA methodology, dynamic behaviors of a system are run-time process deployment and dispatching mechanisms based on the static behaviors modeled in UPMs, which is particularly useful when the BTree**§** is a compo-

Figure 18. The UPM model of the B-Ttree full test process

```
FullTestPC(<I:: BTreeIDS>; <O:: ⓈFullBL>; <UDM:: BTreeST>) ≙
{
  → ( ◆ BTreeIDST.ⓈCreatedBL = T
        → ( ◆ BTreeIDST.#NodesP = BTreeIDST.SizeN
                → BTreeIDST.ⓈFullBL := T
                → BTreeIDST.ⓈEmptyBL := F
            | ◆ ~
                → BTreeIDST.ⓈFullBL := F
          )
    | ◆ ~
        → ! ('BTreeIDST did not exist.')
    )
}
```

Figure 19. The UPM model of the B-tree clear process

```
ClearPC(<I:: BTreeIDS>; <O:: ⓈClearedBL>; <UDM:: BTreeST>) ≙
{
  → ( ◆ BTreeIDST.ⓈCreatedBL = T
        → SizeN := BTreeIDST.SizeN
        → DataRT := BTreeIDST.Node(0)RT.DataRT
        → ReleasePC(<I:: BTreeIDS>; <O:: ⓈReleasedBL>; <UDM:: BTreeST>)
        → CreateBTreePC(<I:: BTreeIDS, SizeN, DataRT>; <O:: ⓈTreeCreatedBL>; <UDM:: BTreeST>)
        → BTreeIDST.ⓈClearedBL := T
        → BTreeIDST.ⓈEmptyBL := T
    | ◆ ~
        → BTreeIDST.ⓈClearedBL := F
        → ! ('BTreeIDST did not exist.')
    )
}
```

Figure 20. The UPM model of the B-tree release process

```
ReleasePC(<I:: BTreeIDS>; <O:: ⓈReleasedBL>; <UDM:: BTreeST>) ≙
{
  → ( ◆ BTreeIDST.ⓈCreatedBL = T
              BTreeIDST.#NodesN
        →          R              ( → ObjectIDP := BTreeIDST.Node(iN)ST.LocationP
                 iN = 0
                                    → ReleaseObjectPC(<I:: ObjectIDP>; <O:: ⓈObjectReleasedBL>;
                                                      <UDM:: MEMST>)
                                    → BTreeIDST.Node(iN)ST.LocationP ⇍ MEM(ObjectIDP)ST
                                  )
        → BTreeIDS ⇍ MEM(BTreeIDP)ST
        → BTreeIDST.ⓈReleasedBL := T
        → BTreeIDST.ⓈCreatedBL := F
    | ◆ ~
        → BTreeIDST.Ⓢ ReleasedBL := F
        → ! ('BTreeIDST did not exist.')
    )
}
```

Figure 21. The dynamic behavioral model of the B-trees

```
BTree§.DynamicBehaviorsPC ≙
{ § →
  ( @CreateTreeS      ↳ CreateBTreePC(<I:: BTreeIDS, SizeN, DataRT>; <O:: ⓈTreeCreatedBL>; <UDM:: BTreeST>)
  | @CreateNodeS      ↳ CreateNodePC(<I:: NodeIDS, DataRT>; <O:: Node(KeyN)ST, ⓈNodeCreatedBL>;
                                      <UDM:: BTreeST>)
  | @FindNodeS        ↳ FindNodePC(<I:: BTreeIDST, KeyN>; <O:: NodeIndexN, ⓈNodeFoundBL>; <UDM:: BTreeST>)
  | @RetrieveNodeS    ↳ RetrieveNodePC(<I:: BTreeIDST, KeyN>; <O:: Node(NodeIndexN)ST,
                                       ⓈNodeRetrievedBL>; <UDM:: BTreeST>)
  | @UpdateNodeS      ↳ UpdateNodePC(<I:: BTreeIDST, KeyN, DataRT>; <O:: ⓈNodeUpdatedBL>; <UDM:: BTreeST>)
  | @TraverseS        ↳ TraversePC(<I:: BTreeIDS, OrderN, ActionPC>; <O:: ⓈTraversedBL>; <UDM:: BTreeST>)
  | @InsertNodeS      ↳ InsertNodePC(<I:: BTreeIDST, KeyN, DataST, PositionN>; <O:: ⓈNodeInsertedBL>;
                                      <UDM:: BTreeST>)
  | @DeleteSubtreeS   ↳ DeleteSubTreePC(<I:: BTreeIDST, KeyN>; <O:: ⓈSubTreeDeletedBL>; <UDM:: BTreeST>)
  | @EmptyTestS       ↳ EmptyTestPC(<I:: BTreeIDS>; <O:: ⓈEmptyBL>; <UDM:: BTreeST>)
  | @FullTestS        ↳ FullTestPC(<I:: BTreeIDS>; <O:: ⓈFullBL>; <UDM:: BTreeST>)
  | @ClearS           ↳ ClearPC(<I:: BTreeIDS>; <O:: ⓈClearedBL>; <UDM:: BTreeST>)
  | @ReleaseS         ↳ ReleasePC(<I:: BTreeIDS>; <O:: ⓈReleasedBL>; <UDM:: BTreeST>)
  | ~                              → ∅
  ) → §
}
```

nent or embedded part of a large software system. The dynamic behaviors of BTree§ integrate and dispatch the static behavioral processes of B-trees as modeled in BTree§.StaticBehaviorsPC. Based on the UPMs developed in the preceding sections, this section models the dynamic behaviors of the B-tree at run-time via the dynamic processes of system dispatching elaborated by the event-driven mechanisms of the system.

The dynamic behaviors of B-trees, BTree§. DynamicBehaviorsPC, are shown in Figure 21, which serve as an interface of the system to external users who can invoke any pre-defined process in the B-tree ADT. The dynamic behaviors of BTree§ at run-time can be formally specified using the RTPA process dispatching methodology. BTree§.DynamicBehaviorsPC as given in Figure 21 establishes a set of top-level run-time relations between the 12 pairs of events and processes such as (@CreateTreeS ↳ CreateTreePC), (@ CreateNodeS ↳CreateNodePC), (@FindNodeS ↳ FindNodePC), (@RetrieveNodeS ↳RetrieveNodePC), (@UpdateNodeS ↳UpdateNodePC), (@ TraverseS ↳ TraversePC), (@InsertNodeS ↳ InsertNodePC), (@DeleteSubTreeS ↳DeleteSubTreePC), (@ClearS ↳ClearPC), (@EmptyTestS ↳ EmptyTestPC), (@FullTestS ↳FullTestPC), and (@ReleaseS ↳ReleasePC). Any exceptional event that is not specified as a valid one in the system will be ignored by the skip operator (→ ∅). The event-driven dispatching mechanism also puts BTree§ into the context of a specific application.

The practical formal engineering methodology of RTPA for system modeling and specification provides a coherent notation system and a systematical approach for large-scale software and hybrid system design and implementation. A series of formal design models and frameworks of real-world and real-time applications in RTPA have been developed using RTPA notations and methodologies (Wang, 2002, 2007, 2008a, 2008b, 2008c, 2008d, 2009a; Wang & Huang, 2008; Wang, Zhang, Sheu, Li, & Guo, 2010) in the formal design engineering approach, such as the telephone switching system (TSS) (Wang, 2009b), the lift dispatching system (LDS) (Wang et al., 2009), the automated teller machine (ATM) (Wang, Zhang et al., 2010), the real-time operating system (RTOS+) (Wang, Tan, & Ngolah, 2010, 2010d), the autonomic code generator (RTPA-CG) (Wang, Zhang et al., 2010), the ADTs (Wang, Ngolah, Tan, Tian, & Sheu, 2010), the file management system (FMS) (Wang et al., 2011), and the air traffic control system (to be reported). Further studies have demonstrated that RTPA is not only elegant and practically useful as a generic notation and hierarchical methodology for software engineering, but also good at modeling human cognitive processes in cognitive informatics and computational intelligence as reported in Wang (2008d, 2009a, 2010a, 2010b, 2010c), Wang and Ruhe (2007), and Wang and Chiew (2010).

6. CONCLUSION

Trees are one of the most fundamental and widely used ADTs in data structure and system modeling. However, there was a lack of a formal and complete model for trees. This paper has develops a comprehensive design pattern of formal trees using the binary tree (B-tree) model. The conceptual model, architectural model, and static/dynamic behavioral models of B-trees have been systematically presented. The generic UDM and the 12 UPMs of B-trees have provided a set of rigorous architectural and behavioral models for formal trees based on them any concrete B-tree can be derived and implemented. An expressive denotational mathematics, Real-Time Process Algebra (RTPA), has been adopted to rigorously design and refine both architectural and behavioral models of B-trees and their manipulations in a top-down approach. This work has been applied in a number of real-time and nonreal-time system designs such as a real-time operating system (RTOS+), the air traffic control system (ATCS), and the ADT library for an RTPA-based automatic code generation tool.

ACKNOWLEDGMENT

The authors would like to acknowledge the Natural Science and Engineering Council of Canada (NSERC) for its partial support to this work. We would like to thank the anonymous reviewers for their valuable comments and suggestions.

REFERENCES

Broy, M., Pair, C., & Wirsing, M. (1984). A systematic study of models of abstract data types. *Theoretical Computer Science*, *33*, 139–1274. doi:10.1016/0304-3975(84)90086-0

Cardelli, L., & Wegner, P. (1985). On understanding types, data abstraction and polymorphism. *ACM Computing Surveys*, *17*(4), 471–522. doi:10.1145/6041.6042

Gosling, J., Bollella, G., Dibble, P., Furr, S., & Turnbull, M. (2002). *The real-time specification for Java*. Reading, MA: Addison-Wesley.

Guttag, J. V. (1977). Abstract data types and the development of data structures. *Communications of the ACM*, *20*(6), 396–404. doi:10.1145/359605.359618

Lipschutz, S., & Lipson, M. (1997). *Schaum's outline of theories and problems of discrete mathematics* (2nd ed.). New York, NY: McGraw-Hill.

McDermid, J. (Ed.). (1991). *Software engineer's reference book*. Oxford, UK: Butterworth Heinemann.

Mitchell, J. C. (1990). Type systems for programming languages. In van Leeuwen, J. (Ed.), *Handbook of theoretical computer science* (pp. 365–458). Amsterdam, The Netherlands: North-Holland.

Russel, B. (1903). *The principles of mathematics*. London, UK: George Allen & Unwin.

Stubbs, D. F., & Webre, N. W. (1985). *Data structures with abstract data types and Pascal*. Monterey, CA: Brooks/Cole.

Wang, Y. (2002). The Real-Time Process Algebra (RTPA). *Annals of Software Engineering: An International Journal*, *14*, 235–274. doi:10.1023/A:1020561826073

Wang, Y. (2007). *Software engineering foundations: A software science perspective (Vol. 2)*. Boca Raton, FL: Auerbach. doi:10.1201/9780203496091

Wang, Y. (2008a). RTPA: A denotational mathematics for manipulating intelligent and computational behaviors. *International Journal of Cognitive Informatics and Natural Intelligence, 2*(2), 44–62. doi:10.4018/jcini.2008040103

Wang, Y. (2008b). Mathematical laws of software. *Transactions of Computational Science, 2*, 46–83. doi:10.1007/978-3-540-87563-5_4

Wang, Y. (2008c). Deductive semantics of RTPA. *International Journal of Cognitive Informatics and Natural Intelligence, 2*(2), 95–121. doi:10.4018/jcini.2008040106

Wang, Y. (2008d). On contemporary denotational mathematics for computational intelligence. *Transactions of Computational Science, 2*, 6–29. doi:10.1007/978-3-540-87563-5_2

Wang, Y. (2009a). Paradigms of denotational mathematics for cognitive informatics and cognitive computing. *Fundamenta Informaticae, 90*(3), 282–303.

Wang, Y. (2009b). The formal design model of a Telephone Switching System (TSS). *International Journal of Software Science and Computational Intelligence, 1*(3), 92–116. doi:10.4018/jssci.2009070107

Wang, Y. (2010a). Cognitive robots: A reference model towards intelligent authentication. *IEEE Robotics and Automation, 17*(4), 54–62. doi:10.1109/MRA.2010.938842

Wang, Y. (2010b). On formal and cognitive semantics for semantic computing. *International Journal of Semantic Computing, 4*(2), 203–237. doi:10.1142/S1793351X10000833

Wang, Y. (2011). On concept algebra for Computing With Words (CWW). *International Journal of Semantic Computing, 4*(3), 331–356. doi:10.1142/S1793351X10001061

Wang, Y., & Chiew, V. (2010). On the cognitive process of human problem solving. *Cognitive Systems Research: An International Journal, 11*(1), 81–92. doi:10.1016/j.cogsys.2008.08.003

Wang, Y., & Huang, J. (2008). Formal modeling and specification of design patterns using RTPA. *International Journal of Cognitive Informatics and Natural Intelligence, 2*(1), 100–111. doi:10.4018/jcini.2008010108

Wang, Y., Huang, J., & Lei, J. (2011). The formal design models of the Universal Array (UA) and its implementations. *International Journal of Software Science and Computational Intelligence, 3*(3), 69–89. doi:10.4018/IJSSCI.2011070106

Wang, Y., Ngolah, C. F., Ahmadi, H., Sheu, P. C.-Y., & Ying, S. (2009). The formal design model of a Lift Dispatching System (LDS). *International Journal of Software Science and Computational Intelligence, 1*(4), 98–122. doi:10.4018/jssci.2009062506

Wang, Y., Ngolah, C. F., Tan, X., & Sheu, P. C.-Y. (2011). The formal design models of a Doubly-Linked-Circular List (DLC-List). *International Journal of Software Science and Computational Intelligence, 3*(2), 80–100. doi:10.4018/jssci.2011040106

Wang, Y., Ngolah, C. F., Tan, X., Tian, Y., & Sheu, P. C.-Y. (2010). The formal design models of a set of Abstract Data Models (ADTs). *International Journal of Software Science and Computational Intelligence, 2*(4), 72–104. doi:10.4018/jssci.2010100106

Wang, Y., Ngolah, C. F., Tan, X., Tian, Y., & Sheu, P. C.-Y. (2011). The formal design models of a File Management Systems (FMS). *International Journal of Software Science and Computational Intelligence, 3*(1), 90–113. doi:10.4018/jssci.2011010107

Wang, Y., Ngolah, C. F., Zeng, G., Sheu, P. C.-Y., Choy, C. P., & Tian, Y. (2010a). The formal design models of a Real-Time Operating System (RTOS+): Conceptual and architectural frameworks. *International Journal of Software Science and Computational Intelligence*, *2*(2), 105–122. doi:10.4018/jssci.2010040106

Wang, Y., Ngolah, C. F., Zeng, G., Sheu, P. C.-Y., Choy, C. P., & Tian, Y. (2010b). The formal design models of a Real-Time Operating System (RTOS+): Static and dynamic behavior models. *International Journal of Software Science and Computational Intelligence*, *2*(3), 79–105. doi:10.4018/jssci.2010070106

Wang, Y., & Ruhe, G. (2007). The cognitive process of decision making. *International Journal of Cognitive Informatics and Natural Intelligence*, *1*(2), 73–85. doi:10.4018/jcini.2007040105

Wang, Y., Tan, X., & Ngolah, C. F. (2010). Design and implementation of an autonomic code generator based on RTPA (RTPA-CG). *International Journal of Software Science and Computational Intelligence*, *2*(2), 44–67. doi:10.4018/jssci.2010040103

Wang, Y., Zhang, Y., Sheu, P. C.-Y., Li, X., & Guo, H. (2010). The formal design models of an Automatic Teller Machine (ATM). *International Journal of Software Science and Computational Intelligence*, *2*(1), 102–131. doi:10.4018/jssci.2010101907

Wiener, R., & Pinson, L. J. (2000). *Fundamentals of OOP and data structures in Java*. Cambridge, UK: Cambridge University Press. doi:10.1017/CBO9780511807176

This work was previously published in the International Journal of Software Science and Computational Intelligence, Volume 3, Issue 4, edited by Yingxu Wang, pp. 84-108, copyright 2011 by IGI Publishing (an imprint of IGI Global).

Section 4
Applications of Computational Intelligence and Cognitive Computing

Chapter 19
Four–Channel Control Architectures for Bilateral and Multilateral Teleoperation

Yuji Wang
Tsinghua University, China

Fuchun Sun
Tsinghua University, China

Huaping Liu
Tsinghua University, China

ABSTRACT

The four-channel architecture in teleoperation with force feedback has been studied in various existing literature. However, most of them focused on Lawrence architecture and did not research other cases. This paper proposes two other four-channel architectures: passive four-channel architecture and passive four-channel architecture with operator force. Furthermore, two types of multilateral shared control architecture based on passive four-channel architecture, which exists in space teleoperation, are put forward. One is dual-master multilateral shared control architecture, and the other is dual-slave multilateral shared control architecture. Simulations show that these four architectures can maintain stability in the presence of large time delay.

1. INTRODUCTION

Teleoperation has significant application in space (Sheridan, 1993; Nohmi, 2003), undersea (Jordán & Bustamante, 2007), toxic waste cleanup (Manocha, Pernalete, & Dubey, 2001), and telesurgery (Tavakoli, Patel, & Moallem,

2006; Tobergte, Konietschke, & Hirzinger, 2009) projects. A human operator conducts a remote task via the master and slave manipulators, and the contact force information is reflected to the human operator in bilateral teleoperation. The force-reflecting bilateral control can distinctly improve the performance in teleoperation, which enables the operator to feel present at the remote

DOI: 10.4018/978-1-4666-2651-5.ch019

location even though not really there. It is well known that the time delay is an intractable problem in bilateral teleoperation, especially in the space operations, the delay time sometimes will reach several seconds; this can easily destabilize the bilateral control system.

Up to now, the stability of a bilateral teleoperation system had been studied in various existing literature, and the most important method among them was passivity theory, which was introduced to the bilateral control to stabilize the system under random delay times. At first, Hannaford (1989) proposed a 2-port network mode, and took a hybrid matrix as bilateral representation, and then Anderson and Spong (1989) presented a control law for teleoperators by using passivity and scattering theory, which overcame the instability caused by time delay. Thereafter, Niemeyer and Slotine (1991) proposed a notion of wave variable to characterize time delay systems and got a new configuration for force-reflecting teleoperation. Kawashima et al. (2009) presented a controller for bilateral teleoperation based on the modified wave variable control method which provided superior position and force tracking performance compared to the traditional wave-variable-based method. Recently, Lee and Spong (2006) proposed a control framework for bilateral teleoperation of a pair of multi-degree-of-freedom nonlinear robotic systems under constant communication delays. Chopra et al. (2006) then improved the traditional passivity-based configuration by using additional position control on both the master and slave robots, to solve the steady-state position and force-tracking problem. Furthermore, Shahdi and Sirouspour (2009) proposed a systematic design procedure for improving teleoperation fidelity while maintaining its stability in the presence of dynamic uncertainty and a constant time delay.

With the development of the bilateral control strategy, Lawrence (1993) defined the performance of transparence and presented a general four-channel bilateral control mode. Since he proposed the four-channel control architecture, many researchers had amended and improved his works. For example, Hashtrudi-Zaad and Salcudean (2002) improved the Lawrence architecture and used master and slave local force feedback to improve the system performance and stability. Sumiyoshi and Ohnishi (2004) introduced the transformation of the Hashtrudi-Zaad architecture to clarify the meaning of the local force feedback. Guiatni et al. (2005) then utilized sliding-mode control in four-channel architecture. Naerum and Hannaford (2009) furthermore stated and proved necessary and sufficient conditions for transparency of the Lawrence architecture.

Although the Lawrence architecture has been studied by many researchers, it has many limitations which will be analyzed in detail in Section 2. In this paper, we propose a passive four-channel architecture, which maintains stability in the presence of arbitrary time delay. Furthermore, this mode is extended and passive four-channel architecture with operator force is put forward. In addition, Khademian and Hashtrudi-Zaad (2007) introduced four-channel multilateral shared control architecture for dual-user teleoperation system. By analyzing teleoperation tasks, we can find that not only dual-master mode is appeared, but also dual-slave mode is needed. Therefore, we introduce two types of multilateral shared control architecture based on passive four-channel architecture; one is dual-master multilateral shared control architecture, and the other is dual-slave multilateral shared control architecture. The simulations based on single degree-of-freedom (DOF) linear time-invariant (LTI) system will validate the performance of the bilateral and multilateral architectures. Finally, it is necessary to illuminate that part works in this paper has been reported in an international conference (Wang, Sun, Liu, & Li, 2010).

This paper is organized as follows: a description of passive four-channel architecture and passive four-channel architecture with operator force is given in Section 2. Dual-master multilateral shared control architecture is described in Section 3, and dual-slave multilateral shared control architecture is introduced in Section 4. Simulations are shown in Section 5. Finally, conclusions are drawn in Section 6.

2. PASSIVE FOUR-CHANNEL ARCHITECTURE

2.1. Lawrence Architecture

Lawrence (1993) proposed firstly the single axis four-channel bilateral control architecture shown in Figure 1, where F_h denotes the force applied by the human operator on the master, and F_e denotes the force exerted by the slave on the remote environment. The master sends F_h and V_h to the slave; and the slave sends F_e and V_e to the master.

This architecture has several disadvantages in actual projects:

1. The exact impedances of the operator and the environment, i.e., Z_h and Z_e, are difficult to obtain. Moreover, there exist very big differences between different operators and environments.
2. The force F_e is difficult to measure in practice. If the system is limited to single axis, and the force exerted on the slave by the remote environment is within a certain range, several force sensors may be used to measure it. However, if there are many axes in teleoperation, and crash zone is unlimited; then a large amount of force sensors may be needed for measuring F_e.
3. The Lawrence architecture had local position controllers, and Hashtrudi-Zaad and Salcudean (2002) added local force con-

Figure 1. Lawrence four-channel control block diagram

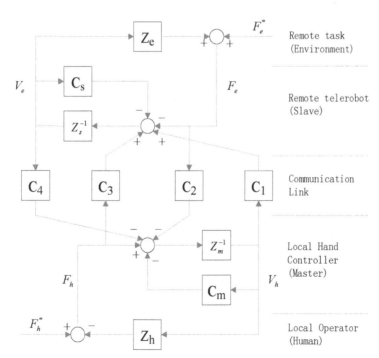

trollers. The application of this architecture became very complex.

To solve these problems, we propose a passive architecture based on Anderson solution in the presence of time delay. The details are shown in the next section.

2.2. Passive Four-Channel Architecture

Dealing with a one DOF LTI modeling, a bilateral 2-port network can be represented as (the variables are the styles of Laplace transform, and the operator s is dropped for clarity) (Hannaford, 1989):

$$\begin{bmatrix} F_m \\ -V_c \end{bmatrix} = H \begin{bmatrix} V_m \\ F_s \end{bmatrix} = \begin{bmatrix} h_{11} & h_{12} \\ h_{21} & h_{22} \end{bmatrix} \begin{bmatrix} V_m \\ F_s \end{bmatrix} \quad (1)$$

where F_m and F_s is the master and slave control force, respectively. V_m is the master velocity; V_c is the slave control velocity.

The dynamics of the master is modeled as (Anderson & Spong, 1989):

$$Z_m V_m = F_h - F_m \quad (2)$$

and the dynamics of the slave is modeled as

$$Z_s V_s = F_s - F_e \quad (3)$$

$$F_s = C_s (V_c - V_s) \quad (4)$$

According to scattering theory, we take S as the scattering operator and get

$$F - V = S(F + V) \quad (5)$$

In order to maintain system stability, we use the linear two-port lossless transmission line equation to represent the communication block.

$$S = \begin{bmatrix} 0 & e^{-Ts} \\ e^{-Ts} & 0 \end{bmatrix} \quad (6)$$

Using (6), we rewrite (5) as

$$\begin{bmatrix} F_m - V_m \\ F_s + V_c \end{bmatrix} = \begin{bmatrix} (F_s - V_c)e^{-Ts} \\ (F_m + V_m)e^{-Ts} \end{bmatrix} \quad (7)$$

In the time domain, the control law is derived as

$$F_m(t) = F_s(t - T) - V_c(t - T) + V_m(t) \quad (8)$$

$$V_c(t) = F_m(t - T) + V_m(t - T) - F_s(t) \quad (9)$$

According to these equations, we design the passive four-channel architecture as shown in Figure 2. In Figure 2, if four communication paths C1, C2, C3, C4 are set as

$$\begin{cases} C_1 = 1 \\ C_2 = 1 \\ C_3 = -1 \\ C_4 = 1 \end{cases} \quad (10)$$

Then the architecture just satisfies (2), (3), (4), (8) and (9). We call it passive four-channel architecture since the control system is passive.

We can see from Figure 2, the master sends the signals V_m and F_m to the slave through communication paths C_1 and C_2, and the slave produces control velocity V_c according to F_s and delayed V_m and F_m, while V_c and V_s flow into the slave controller C_s, and produce the slave

Figure 2. Passive four-channel control block diagram

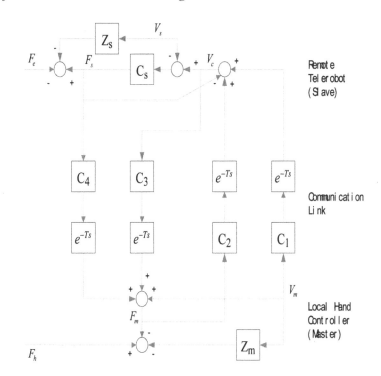

control force F_s.. The slave sends the signals V_c and F_s to the master through communication paths C_3 and C_4; and the master produces the master control force F_m according to velocity V_m and delayed V_c, F_s.

This architecture has following advantages:

1. The control system is passive, so it can maintain stability even in the presence of large time delay.
2. It is no need to measure the forces F_h and F_e, and the control forces F_m and F_s driving the master and slave are easy to measure, so this architecture is easier to realize.
3. There is only one controller C_s need to be designed, and therefore the architecture is simple.

2.3. Passive Four-Channel Architecture with Operator Force

In this section we consider another architecture in which the operator force F_h but not the master control force F_m is sent to the slave. The changed control block diagram is shown in Figure 3. Here the bilateral 2-port network can be represented as

$$\begin{bmatrix} F_h \\ -V_s \end{bmatrix} = H \begin{bmatrix} V_m \\ F_s \end{bmatrix} = \begin{bmatrix} h_{11} & h_{12} \\ h_{21} & h_{22} \end{bmatrix} \begin{bmatrix} V_m \\ F_s \end{bmatrix} \tag{11}$$

If we take out the controllers C_5 and C_6 which are linked with dotted line in Figure 3, the dynamics of the master and slave can be modeled as

$$Z_m V_m = F_h - C_2 e^{-Ts} F_s - C_4 e^{-Ts} V_s \tag{12}$$

$$Z_s V_s = C_3 e^{-Ts} F_h + C_1 e^{-Ts} V_m - F_e \tag{13}$$

Figure 3. Passive four-channel architecture with operator force

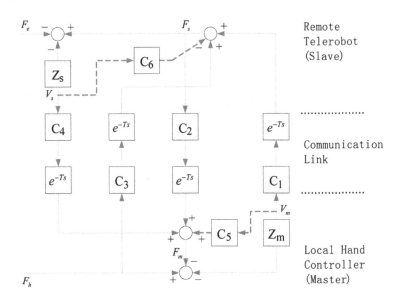

Since the matrix H in (11) is the inherent property of the 2-port network in Figure 3, we can only consider the case in which the environmental force $F_e = 0$. From (11), (12) and (13), we can see that the elements become

$$h_{11} = \left.\frac{F_h}{V_m}\right|_{F_s=0} = \frac{Z_m Z_s + C_1 C_4 e^{-2Ts}}{Z_s - C_3 C_4 e^{-2Ts}} \tag{14}$$

$$h_{12} = \left.\frac{F_h}{F_s}\right|_{V_m=0} = \frac{C_2 Z_s e^{-Ts}}{Z_s - C_3 C_4 e^{-2Ts}} \tag{15}$$

$$h_{21} = -\left.\frac{V_s}{V_m}\right|_{F_s=0} = -\frac{(C_3 Z_m + C_1)e^{-Ts}}{Z_s - C_3 C_4 e^{-2Ts}} \tag{16}$$

$$h_{22} = -\left.\frac{V_s}{F_s}\right|_{V_m=0} = -\frac{C_2 C_3 e^{-2Ts}}{Z_s - C_3 C_4 e^{-2Ts}} \tag{17}$$

According to the scattering theory, the relationship between the scattering operator S and the matrix H can be denoted as

$$S = \begin{pmatrix} 1 & 0 \\ 0 & -1 \end{pmatrix}(H - I)(H + I)^{-1} \tag{18}$$

If we use passive transmission line, i.e., (6) holds, then the matrix H should be

$$H = \begin{bmatrix} \dfrac{1 - e^{-2Ts}}{1 + e^{-2Ts}} & \dfrac{2e^{-Ts}}{1 + e^{-2Ts}} \\ \dfrac{-2e^{-Ts}}{1 + e^{-2Ts}} & \dfrac{1 - e^{-2Ts}}{1 + e^{-2Ts}} \end{bmatrix} \tag{19}$$

It is obviously that (14), (15), (16) and (17) can not satisfy (19) however we select the control parameters; therefore this architecture should be not passive. Yet, the case that the operator force information is sent to the slave directly will be more practical in some bilateral teleoperations. In order to sending the operator force directly as well as keeping a passive transmission line, we add the controllers C_5 and C_6 to the architecture show in Figure 3, and select the parameters as

$$\begin{cases} C_1 = 1 \\ C_2 = 1 \\ C_3 = 1 \\ C_4 = -1 \\ C_5 = 1 \\ C_6 = 1 \end{cases} \tag{20}$$

Then we have

$$F_m(t) = F_s(t-T) - (V_s(t-T) - V_m(t)) \tag{21}$$

$$F_s(t) = F_h(t-T) + (V_m(t-T) - V_s(t)) \tag{22}$$

(21) and (22) can ensure the passivity of the communication line, and we can see that the system is stable in the following simulations in Section 5.

3. DUAL-MASTER MULTILATERAL SHARED CONTROL ARCHITECTURE

Dual-master multilateral shared control system means two masters controlling one slave, and two masters influence each other. This mode appears in a lot of teleoperations, we take a case in space teleoperation as an example. The astronauts in space and the scientists on the ground jointly control the outer space manipulator. Some tasks can be accomplished by the astronauts in space independently; this control mode has small time delay, and thus has good performance. Some tasks can be accomplished by the scientists on the ground independently; this control mode has large time delay, but can finish the works which demand advanced technology and complicated knowledge, or the works which need a very long time (sometimes several months or several years). Other tasks need shared control by the astronauts and the scientists by using a factor to allocate the control power, and various results can be obtained

by changing the value of the factor. The mode of two masters controlling one slave is used in other applications, for instance, the shared control between the trainer and trainee are described (Khademian, 2007).

According to the work (Khademian, 2007), we propose dual-master multilateral shared control architecture based on passive four-channel architecture described in Section 2. The block diagram is shown in Figure 4, where F_{m1},, F_{m2} and F_s are the control forces of master 1, master 2 and the slave, respectively. V_{m1},, V_{m2} and V_s are the velocities of master 1, master 2 and the slave, respectively. V_c is the control velocity of the slave, and C_s is the slave controller. F_{h1} and F_{h2} are the forces applied by operator 1 and operator 2, respectively. F_s is the force exerted by the slave on the environment. Note that the delayed communication paths are omitted for simplicity.

In Figure 4, α is the influence factor, which satisfies

$$0 \le \alpha \le 1 \tag{23}$$

When α is set to 1, master 1 controls the slave independently, master 2 follows master 1 to move, and the slave only feeds back information to master 1. When α is set to 0, master 2 controls the slave independently, master 1 follows master 2 to move, and the slave only feeds back information to master 2. When α is between 0 and 1, master1 and master 2 jointly control the slave, two masters influence each other, and the slave feedback information to both masters.

Just like above methods in Section 2.2, the dynamics of master 1 is modeled as

$$Z_{m1}V_{m1} = F_{h1} - F_{m1} \tag{24}$$

and the dynamics of master 2 is modeled as

$$Z_{m2}V_{m2} = F_{h2} - F_{m2} \tag{25}$$

Figure 4. Dual-master multilateral shared control system block diagram

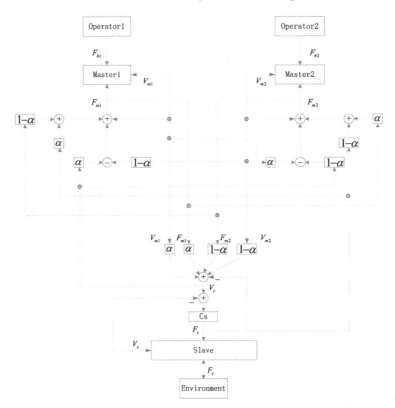

and the dynamics of the slave is modeled as

$$Z_s V_s = F_s - F_e \tag{26}$$

$$F_s = C_s(V_c - V_s) \tag{27}$$

where Z_{m1},, Z_{m2} and Z_s are the impedances of master 1, master 2 and the slave, respectively. In order to guarantee stability, we use the multilateral shared control law based on passive four-channel architecture.

$$F_{m1}(t) = \alpha F_s(t - T_1) - \alpha V_c(t - T_1) + V_{m1}(t) + (1 - \alpha)F_{m2}(t - T_3) - (1 - \alpha)V_{m2}(t - T_3) \tag{28}$$

$$F_{m2}(t) = (1 - \alpha)F_s(t - T_2) - (1 - \alpha)V_c(t - T_2) + \alpha F_{m1}(t - T_3) - \alpha V_{m1}(t - T_3) + V_{m2}(t) \tag{29}$$

$$V_c(t) = \alpha F_{m1}(t - T_1) + \alpha V_{m1}(t - T_1) - F_s(t) + (1 - \alpha)F_{m2}(t - T_2) + (1 - \alpha)V_{m2}(t - T_2) \tag{30}$$

where T_1 is the time delay between master 1 and the slave, T_2 is the time delay between master 2 and the slave, T_3 is the time delay between master 1 and master 2.

4. DUAL-SLAVE MULTILATERAL SHARED CONTROL ARCHITECTURE

Dual-slave multilateral shared control system means one master controlling two slaves, and two slaves influence each other. We take another case in space teleoperation as an example. In order to control accurately a space probe, another identical probe may be placed in the laboratory on the ground to simulate the space activities; the operator on the ground jointly controls the manipulator on the space probe and the other manipulator on the probe in the laboratory. Since the time delay between the operator and the manipulator on the ground is small, it can quickly feedback the results of the commands. Therefore, by using this mode, the operator can quickly obtain the movement result of a command, and avoid obstacle successfully. Of course, the probe in the laboratory can be replaced by virtual reality, but the real object can more accurately reflect the movement status. The system use a factor to allocate the control power, and various results can be obtained by changing the value of the factor.

We propose dual-slave multilateral shared control architecture based on passive four-channel architecture described in Section 2.2. The block diagram is shown in Figure 5, where F_m, F_{s1} and F_{s2} are the control forces of the master, slave 1 and slave 2, respectively. V_m, V_{s1} and V_{s2} are the velocities of the master, slave 1 and slave 2, respectively. V_{c1} and V_{c2} are the control velocities of slave 1 and slave 2, respectively. C_{s1} and C_{s2} are the controllers of slave 1 and slave 2, respectively. F_h is the force applied by the operator on the master. F_{s1} and F_{s2} are the slave environmental forces, respectively. Note that the delayed communication paths are omitted for simplicity, and α is the influence factor whose definition is the same as (23).

When α is set to 1, the master controls slave 1 independently, slave 2 follows slave 1 to move,

and only slave 1 feeds back information to the master. When α is set to 0, the master controls slave 2 independently, slave 1 follows slave 2 to move, and only slave 2 feeds back information to the master. When α is between 0 and 1, the master controls slave 1 and slave 2 together, two slaves influence each other, and both slaves feedback information to the master.

Just like above methods, the dynamics of the master is modeled as

$$Z_m V_m = F_h - F_m \tag{31}$$

The dynamics of slave 1 is modeled as

$$Z_{s1} V_{s1} = F_{s1} - F_{e1} \tag{32}$$

$$F_{s1} = C_{s1}(V_{c1} - V_{s1}) \tag{33}$$

and the dynamics of slave 2 is modeled as

$$Z_{s2} V_{s2} = F_{s2} - F_{e2} \tag{34}$$

$$F_{s2} = C_{s2}(V_{c2} - V_{s2}) \tag{35}$$

where Z_m, Z_{s1} and Z_{s2} are the impedances of the master, slave 1 and slave 2.

In order to guarantee stability, we use the multilateral shared control law based on passive four-channel architecture.

$$\begin{aligned} F_m(t) &= \alpha F_{s1}(t - T_1) - \alpha V_{c1}(t - T_1) + V_m(t) \\ &+ (1 - \alpha)F_{s2}(t - T_2) - (1 - \alpha)V_{c2}(t - T_2) \end{aligned} \tag{36}$$

$$\begin{aligned} V_{c1}(t) &= \alpha F_m(t - T_1) + \alpha V_m(t - T_1) - F_{s1}(t) \\ &+ (1 - \alpha)F_{s2}(t - T_3) + (1 - \alpha)V_{c2}(t - T_3) \end{aligned} \tag{37}$$

Figure 5. Dual-slave multilateral shared control system block diagram

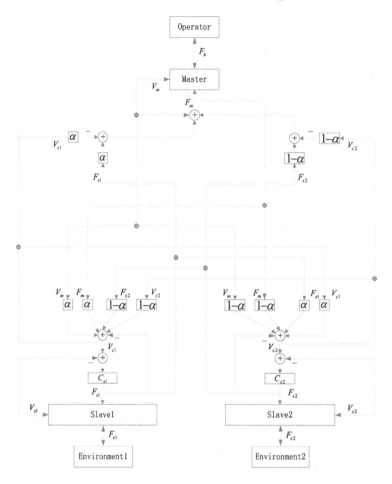

$$V_{c2}(t) = (1-\alpha)F_m(t-T_2) + (1-\alpha)V_m(t-T_2)$$
$$+ \alpha F_{s1}(t-T_3) + \alpha V_{c1}(t-T_3) - F_{s2}(t)$$

$$(38)$$

where T_1 is the time delay between the master and slave 1, T_2 is the time delay between the master and slave 2, and T_3 is the time delay between slave 1 and slave 2.

5. SIMULATIONS

In this section, several simulations are introduced to validate the control strategies of passive four-channel architecture, passive four-channel archi-

tecture with operator force, dual-master multilateral shared control architecture and dual-slave multilateral shared control architecture. In the actual project, generally, the master is a joystick or hand controller, and the slave is a robot manipulator. Therefore, the slave impedance is set to be much larger than the master impedance in simulations, here the master impedance is set to be $s+1$, and the slave is set to be $10s+10.$. Noted that the impedances are modeled by linear mass-damper for simplicity. In order to analyze the fidelity of the system, two different cases including free motion and hard contact are attempted in each simulation.

5.1. Passive Four-Channel Architecture

The channel controllers C_1, C_2, C_3 and C_4 are set to be the same as (10), and C_s is set to be $5/s+1$. In addition, the time delay is set to be 5 seconds to simulate the large delay. In the free motion case, ideally, the master can swing freely, and the slave can track the master position without going unstable. Therefore, the operator force is simulated with a simple sinusoidal function. In the contact case, we assume that the slave is commanded forward on a hard surface, and set the contact force to be $10/s$, which is proportional to the distance that the slave enters the surface. The operator force is simulated with a positive square function to simulate the repetitive contact. Figure 6 shows the velocity and force response in free motion and hard contact. We can find that the system is stable in the presence of large time delay. V_s can track V_m, and F_m can track F_s

after 5 seconds. Note that the amplitude difference in Figure 6 is caused by different properties of the master and slave.

5.2. Passive Four-Channel Architecture with Operator Force

The channel controllers C_1, C_2, C_3, C_4, C_5 and C_6 are set to be the same as (20), and the time delay is also set to be 5 seconds. Just like the simulation of passive four-channel architecture, the operator forces are simulated with a simple sinusoidal function in free motion and a positive square function in the contact case, and the contact force is also set to be $10/s$. Figure 7 shows the velocity and force response in free motion and hard contact. We can find that the system is stable in the presence of large time delay. V_s can track V_m, and F_h can track F_s in free motion.

Figure 6. Tracking performance of passive four-channel architecture

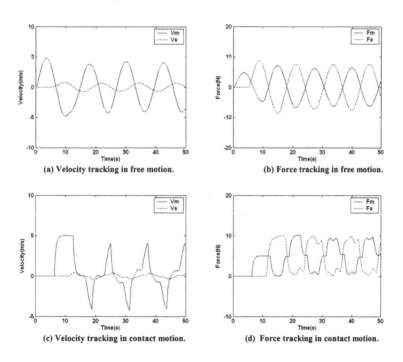

(a) Velocity tracking in free motion.

(b) Force tracking in free motion.

(c) Velocity tracking in contact motion.

(d) Force tracking in contact motion.

Figure 7. Tracking performance of passive four-channel architecture with operator force

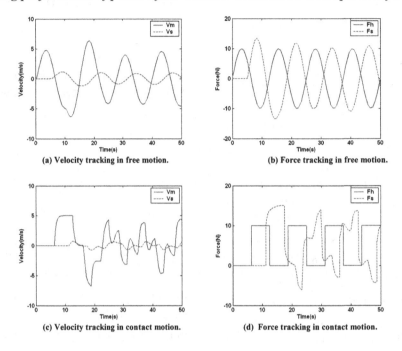

Figure 8. Tracking performance of dual-master multilateral shared control architecture

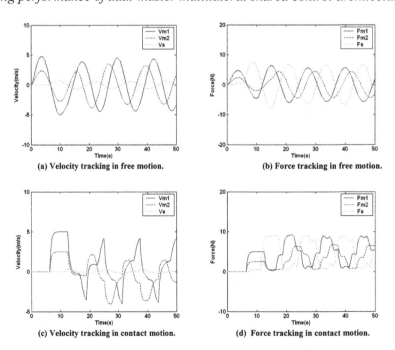

Figure 9. Tracking performance of dual-slave multilateral shared control architecture

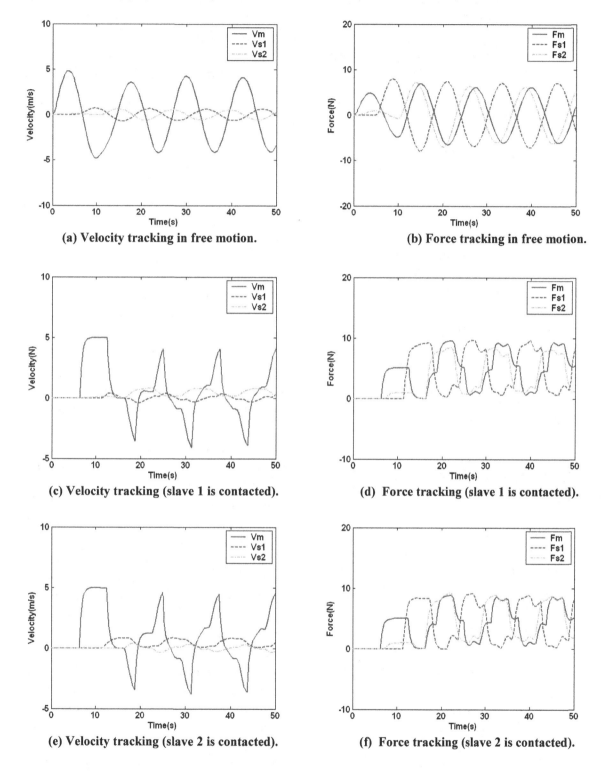

(a) Velocity tracking in free motion.

(b) Force tracking in free motion.

(c) Velocity tracking (slave 1 is contacted).

(d) Force tracking (slave 1 is contacted).

(e) Velocity tracking (slave 2 is contacted).

(f) Force tracking (slave 2 is contacted).

5.3. Dual-Master Multilateral Shared Control Architecture

Considering the characteristics of dual master multilateral shared control architecture and the actual projects, both master impedances are set to be uniform. Assuming that the scene is the space teleoperation described in Section 3, master 2 and the slave are in space, and master 1 is on the ground. Therefore T_1 is much larger than T_2 and T_1 is equal to T_3. We set $T_1 = T_3 = 5$ s, $T_2 = 1$ s. According to the definition of α, it can be set an arbitrary value between 0 and 1; we have many simulations with different values, all results are stable. Here as a sample, α is set to 0.9, means that master 1 mainly controls the slave, and master 2 provides aid. The controller values of four communication paths are the same as those in the system with passive four channel architecture. In order to analyze the fidelity of the responses are shown in Figure 8. The results prive that dual master multilateral shared control architecture can maintain stability in the prescence of large time delay.

5.4. Dual-Slave Multilateral Shared Control Architecture

In the simulation of dual-slave multilateral shared control architecture, both slave impedances are also set to be uniform. Assuming that the scene is the space teleoperation described in Section 4, the master and slave 2 are on the ground, and slave 1 is in space. Therefore, T_1 is much larger than T_2, and T_1 is equal to T_3. We also set $T_1 = T_3 = 5$ s, $T_2 = 1$ s. It is similar to the system of dual-master multilateral shared control architecture, α can be set to an arbitrary value between 0 and 1; here as a sample, α is also set to 0.9, means that the master mainly controls slave 1, and slave 2 is used to assist the operator. The controller values of four communication paths

are the same as those in the system with passive four-channel architecture. The velocity and force tracking responses in free motion and hard contact are shown in Figure 9. The results prove that dual-slave multilateral shared control architecture also can maintain stability in the presence of large time delay.

6. CONCLUSION

This paper has introduced four passive four-channel architectures. Two are bilateral system, and the other two are multilateral systems based on the bilateral system. The main contributions of this paper are twofold:

Firstly, we propose passive four-channel architecture. The performance of passivity ensures that it can maintain stability independently of time delay. In addition, it is simple to realize in actual projects. Furthermore, we send the operator force information to the slave side and develop another passive four-channel architecture with operator force.

Secondly, we propose two multilateral architectures owing to the space teleoperation demands: dual-master multilateral shared control architecture, and dual-slave multilateral shared control architecture. Since they are derived from passive four-channel architecture, dual-master and dual-slave systems are passive and therefore stable independently of time delay. Moreover, they are flexible to deal with various situations by changing the factor α; its application is convenient.

In the end, let me see the application of these four architectures proposed in this paper. Passive four-channel architecture do not need measuring the operator force and environmental force, therefore it is suitable for the systems in which the force sensors cannot be installed or too much force sensors are demanded so that the cost cannot be afforded. Of course, the operator force is correspondingly easy to measure sometimes since the grasping range of the operator on the master side can be limited to a small area; hence passive four-channel architecture with operator force can be used in this case. On the other hand, there are two masters in some system, and they want to control one slave together, here dual-master multilateral shared control architecture is just designed for this case. In addition, two slaves maybe appear in space mission or other remote tasks, our proposed dual-slave multilateral shared control architecture will be useful in their systems.

REFERENCES

Anderson, R. J., & Spong, M. W. (1989). Bilateral control of teleoperators with time delay. *IEEE Transactions on Automatic Control, 34*(5), 494–501. doi:10.1109/9.24201

Chopra, N., Spong, M. W., Ortega, R., & Barabanov, N. E. (2006). On tracking performance in bilateral teleoperation. *IEEE Transactions on Robotics, 22*(4), 861–866. doi:10.1109/TRO.2006.878942

Guiatni, M., Kheddar, A., & Melouah, H. (2005). Sliding mode bilateral control and four channels scheme control of a force reflecting master/slave teleoperator. In *Proceedings of the IEEE International Conference on Robotics and Automation* (pp. 1660-1665). Washington, DC: IEEE Computer Society.

Hannaford, B. (1989). A design framework for teleoperators with kinesthetic feedback. *IEEE Transactions on Robotics and Automation, 5*(4), 426–434. doi:10.1109/70.88057

Hashtrudi-Zaad, K. (2002). Transparency in time-delayed systems and the effect of local force feedback for transparent teleoperation. *IEEE Transactions on Robotics and Automation, 18*(1), 108–114. doi:10.1109/70.988981

Jordán, M. A., & Bustamante, J. L. (2007). On the presence of nonlinear oscillations in the teleoperation of underwater vehicles under the influence of sea wave and current. In *Proceedings of the American Control Conference* (pp. 894-899). Washington, DC: IEEE Computer Society.

Kawashima, K., Tadano, K., Wang, C., Sankaranarayanan, G., & Hannaford, B. (2009). Bilateral teleoperation with time delay using modified wave variable based controller. In *Proceedings of the IEEE International Conference on Robotics and Automation* (pp. 4326-4331). Washington, DC: IEEE Computer Society.

Khademian, B., & Hashtrudi-Zaad, K. (2007). A four-channel multilateral shared control architecture for dual-user teleoperation systems. In *Proceedings of the IEEE International Conference on Intelligent Robots and Systems* (pp. 2660-2666). Washington, DC: IEEE Computer Society.

Lawrence, D. A. (1993). Stability and transparency in bilateral teleoperation. *IEEE Transactions on Robotics and Automation, 9*(5), 624–637. doi:10.1109/70.258054

Lee, D., & Spong, M. W. (2006). Passive bilateral teleoperation with constant time delay. *IEEE Transactions on Robotics, 22*(2), 269–281. doi:10.1109/TRO.2005.862037

Manocha, K. A., Pernalete, N., & Dubey, R. V. (2001). Variable position mapping based assistance in teleoperation for nuclear cleanup. In *Proceedings of the IEEE International Conference on Robotics and Automation* (pp. 374-379). Washington, DC: IEEE Computer Society.

Naerum, E., & Hannaford, B. (2009). Transparency analysis of the Lawrence teleoperator architecture. In *Proceedings of the IEEE International Conference on Robotics and Automation* (pp. 4344-4349). Washington, DC: IEEE Computer Society.

Niemeyer, G., & Slotine, J. E. (1991). Stable adaptive teleoperation. *IEEE Journal of Oceanic Engineering, 16*(1), 152–162. doi:10.1109/48.64895

Nohmi, M. (2003). Space teleoperation using force reflection of communication time delay. In *Proceedings of the IEEE International Conference on Intelligent Robots and Systems* (pp. 2809-2814). Washington, DC: IEEE Computer Society.

Shahdi, A., & Sirouspour, S. (2009). Adaptive/robust control for time-delay teleoperation. *IEEE Transactions on Robotics, 25*(1), 196–205. doi:10.1109/TRO.2008.2010963

Sheridan, T. B. (1993). Space teleoperation through time delay: Review and prognosis. *IEEE Transactions on Robotics and Automation, 9*(5), 592–606. doi:10.1109/70.258052

Sumiyoshi, Y., & Ohnishi, K. (2004). The transformation of modified 4-channel architecture. In *Proceedings of the IEEE International Workshop Advanced Motion Control* (pp. 211-216). Washington, DC: IEEE Computer Society.

Tavakoli, M., Patel, R. V., & Moallem, M. (2006). Bilateral control of a teleoperator for soft tissue palpation: design and experiments. In *Proceedings of the IEEE International Conference on Robotics and Automation* (pp. 3280-3285). Washington, DC: IEEE Computer Society.

Tobergte, A., Konietschke, R., & Hirzinger, G. (2009). Planning and control of a teleoperation system for research in minimally invasive robotic surgery. In *Proceedings of the IEEE International Conference on Robotics and Automation* (pp. 4225-4232). Washington, DC: IEEE Computer Society.

Wang, Y., Sun, F., Liu, H., & Li, Z. (2010). Passive four-channel multilateral shared control architecture in teleoperation. In *Proceedings of the IEEE International Conference on Cognitive Informatics* (pp. 851-858). Washington, DC: IEEE Computer Society.

This work was previously published in the International Journal of Software Science and Computational Intelligence, Volume 3, Issue 2, edited by Yingxu Wang, pp. 1-18, copyright 2011 by IGI Publishing (an imprint of IGI Global).

Chapter 20
Entropy Quad–Trees for High Complexity Regions Detection

Rosanne Vetro
University of Massachusetts Boston, USA

Dan A. Simovici
University of Massachusetts Boston, USA

Wei Ding
University of Massachusetts Boston, USA

ABSTRACT

This paper introduces entropy quad-trees, which are structures derived from quad-trees by allowing nodes to split only when those correspond to sufficiently complex sub-domains of a data domain. Complexity is evaluated using an information-theoretic measure based on the analysis of the entropy associated to sets of objects designated by nodes. An alternative measure related to the concept of box-counting dimension is also explored. Experimental results demonstrate the efficiency of entropy quad-trees to mine complex regions. As an application, the proposed technique is used in the initial stage of a crater detection algorithm using digital images taken from the surface of Mars. Additional experimental results are provided that demonstrate the crater detection performance and analyze the effectiveness of entropy quad-trees for high-complexity regions detection in the pixel space with significant presence of noise. This work focuses on 2-dimensional image domains, but can be generalized to higher dimensional data.

INTRODUCTION

The concept of complexity relates to the presence of variation. In science there are many approaches that characterize complexity. A variety of scientific fields have dealt with complex mechanisms, simulations, systems, behavior and data complexity

DOI: 10.4018/978-1-4666-2651-5.ch020

as those have always been a part of our environment. In this work, we focus on the topic of data complexity which is studied in information theory. While randomness is not considered complexity in certain areas such as those related to the study of complex systems, information theory tends to assign high values of complexity to random noise. Many fields benefit from the identification of content or noise related complex areas. In data hiding, adaptive steganography takes advantage of high concentration of self-information on high complexity areas originated from both content and noise to embed data. Solanki, Dabeer, Madhow, Manjunath, and Chandrasekaran (2003) describe the benefits of selective embedding related to the reduction of perceptual degradation for transform domain steganographic techniques. Bio diversity is another area where complexity can be used for identification and localization of different species. In this case, the complexity originated from content is more important than the one originated from noise.

Our goal in this paper is to introduce a variant of quad-trees for mining high complexity sub-domains of a data domain. A *quad-tree* is a tree structure defined on a finite set of nodes that either contains no nodes or is comprised of a root node and 4 quad-subtrees. In a full quad-tree, each node is either a leaf or has degree exactly 4. Our variant of quad-trees requires that each node that has descendants corresponds to a region that has a sufficient level of diversity as assessed by the value of an information-theoretical measure. We also present an alternative measure that has its roots in fractal geometry where the so called box-counting dimension (BCD) is used to determine the fractal dimension of a set S in a Euclidean space R^n. We then provide an algorithm to capture high complexity areas of 2 dimensional images domains and observe that diversity originated from both data content and noise are mined.

As an application, we used our proposed data structure in the initial stage of a crater detection algorithm. The algorithm is composed by two methods. The first method uses an information-theoretical approach with entropy quad-trees to create an edge filter that generates a binary image from complex areas which may contain edges. The second method applies a Circle Hough Transform (CHT) with modified threshold to detect the presence of circular shapes in complex areas. The new threshold is imposed to increase the quality of the results given the lack of prior knowledge about the

number of craters in an image and the difficulty to estimate a good threshold for the minimum number of votes required in the parameter space to indicate true center points. Efficient methods for crater detection have been proposed (Bue & Stepinksi, 2007; Urbach & Stepinksi, 2009; Salamuniccar & Loncaric, 2008). We provide a distinct approach where no external pre-processing of the original image other than conversion to the JPEG format and resizing is needed. Likewise, no external image filters are used.

In the next section we introduce a framework for the rest of the paper. The notion of entropy associated to a partition is presented as well as its usefulness in measuring diversity. In section 2 we introduce the proposed data structures, an algorithm for high complexity detection and explain the searching process. In subsection 2.1 we describe the information-theoretic method used for mining complex sub-domains. An alternative method uses the concept of box-counting dimension and is introduced in subsection 2.2. We provide a brief description about implementation details in subsection 2.3. In subsection 2.4 we discuss the experiments and compare the results generated by both methods. In Section 3 we introduce the crater detection algorithm. In subsection 3.1 we describe the information theoretic method used for mining complex subareas that may contain edges. The CHT method with modified threshold is described in subsection 3.2. Subsection 3.3 contains a description of the experiments and major challenges we faced. Finally, Section 4 contains our conclusions and ideas for future work.

1. PARTITIONS, ENTROPY, AND TREES

The notion of entropy quantifies the uncertainty associated with probability distributions. Let S be a finite set. A *partition* on S is a non-empty collection of non-empty subsets of S, $\pi = \{B_1,...,B_n\}$ such that

1. $B_i \cap B_j = \varnothing$ for $1 \leq i, j \leq n$ and $i \neq j$;
2.   (ii) $\cup \{B_i \mid 1 \leq i \leq n\} = S$.

The sets $B_1,...,B_n$ are referred to as the *blocks* of π.

We denote by Part(S) the set of partitions of S. For $\pi, \sigma \in$ Part(S) define $\pi \geq \sigma$ if each block B of π is a union of blocks of σ. It is well-known that the relation "$\geq$" is a partial order on Part(S). The largest partition on S is the single-block partition $\omega_S = \{S\}$, while the smallest partition on S is $\iota_S = \{\{x\} \mid x \in S\}$.

We now define a partial order relation $\geq_k$ on Part(S) as follows. If $\pi = \{B_1,...,B_n\}$ and $\sigma = \{C_1,...,C_m\}$, then $\pi \geq_k \sigma$ if the following conditions are satisfied:

1.   There exists a sub-collection of σ that consists of k blocks $\{C_{j_1},...,C_{j_k}\}$ such that $\cup \{C_j \ell \mid 1 \leq \ell \leq k\}$ is a block B_h of π;
2.   For $1 \leq i \leq n$ and $i \neq h$, B_i is a block of σ.

For k=2 the relation $\geq_2$ is the direct coverage relation, where the larger partition π is obtained by fusing two blocks of σ.

If $\pi \in$ Part(S) and $\pi = \{B_1,...,B_n\}$, its entropy is the number

$$H(\pi) = -\sum_{i=1}^{n} \frac{|B_i|}{|S|} \log_2 \frac{|B_i|}{|S|}$$

which is actually the entropy of the discrete probability distribution

$$p = \left(\frac{|B_1|}{|S|},...,\frac{|B_n|}{|S|} \right)$$

Defining the entropy for partitions rather than for probability distributions has the advantage of linking the entropy properties to the partially ordered set of partitions. An important fact is that

the entropy is anti-monotonic relative to the partial order defined on partitions. In other words, for π, $\sigma \in$ Part(S), $\pi \leq \sigma$ implies $H(\pi) \geq H(\sigma)$. It is easy to verify that $H(\omega_S)=0$ and that $H(\iota_S) = \log_2 |S|$. This shows that the entropy can be used to evaluate the uniformity of the elements of S in the blocks of π since the entropy value increases with the uniformity of the distribution of the elements of S. Note that as the uniformity increases, so does the associated uncertainty.

If C is a non-empty subset of S, and $\pi \in$ Part(S), the *trace* of π on C is the partition

$$\pi_C = \{B \cap C \mid B \in \pi \text{ and } B \cap C \neq \varnothing\}.$$

The trace of a partition allows us to define the conditional entropy of two partitions. Namely, if π, $\sigma \in$ Part(S) and $\sigma = \{C_1,...,C_m\}$, then the *entropy of π conditioned by* σ is the number

$$H(\pi \mid \sigma) = \sum_{j=1}^{m} \frac{|C_j|}{|S|} H(\pi_{C_j})$$

It can be shown that the conditional entropy is an anti-monotonic function of the first argument and a monotonic function of the second (Simovici & Jaroszewicz, 2002, 2003). In other words, $\pi_1 \leq \pi_2$ implies $H(\pi_1 \mid \sigma) \geq H(\pi_2 \mid \sigma)$ and $\sigma_1 \leq \sigma_2$ implies $H(\pi \mid \sigma_1) \leq H(\pi \mid \sigma_2)$.

A *measure* on S is a function m: $P(S) \rightarrow R_{\geq 0}$ such that $m(U \cup V) = m(U) + m(V)$ for every disjoint subsets U and V of S. For example, if S is the set of pixels of a gray image S, m(U) can be defined as the number of pixels having a certain degree of grayness contained by the subset U.

Let D be a finite set. A D-feature function on S is a function f: $S \rightarrow D$. Each feature function f: $S \rightarrow D$ defines a partition ker f on S defined by

ker f = $\{f^{-1}(d) \mid d \in D, f^{-1}(d) \neq \varnothing\}$.

We refer to ker f as the *kernel partition* of f.

For example, if S is the set of pixels of an image, we could define f(p) as the degree of grayness of the pixel p ∈ S. Another example that is relevant in the study of biodiversity is to consider a set S of observation points in a territory, and define f(p) as the number of species of birds sighted in a certain day in p.

If C ⊆ S, then the characteristics of the trace partition $(\ker f)_C$ define the concentration of the values that f takes on the set C. If D = {$d_1,...,d_k$}, the blocks of the partition $(\ker f)_C$ have the relative sizes

$$\frac{\left|f^{-1}(d_1) \cap C\right|}{|C|}, ..., \frac{\left|f^{-1}(d_k) \cap C\right|}{|C|}$$

and the distribution of these sizes can be conveniently represented using a histogram.

Definition 1: *Let* $\Pi = (\pi_1, \pi_2, ..., \pi_n)$ *be a descending chain of partitions on* S *such that* $\pi_1 = \omega_S$, f: S → D *be a feature function,* m: P(S) → $R_{\geq 0}$ *be a measure defined on* S *and let* θ,μ > 0 *be two positive numbers referred to as the* entropy threshold *and the* measure threshold, *respectively.*

The entropy tree *defined by* Π, f, m, θ *and* μ *is a tree* $\tau(\Pi, f, m, \theta, \mu)$ *whose set of nodes consists of blocks of the partitions* π_i *such that the following conditions are satisfied:*

1. *The root of the tree is the set* S, *the unique block of* ω_S;
2. *An edge* (B, C) *exists in the tree only if* B ∈ π_i, C ∈ π_i+1, *and* C ⊆ B;
3. *If* B *is a block of the partition* π_i, *then* $\tau(\Pi, f, m, \theta, \mu)$ *contains the set of edges* {(B, C) | B ∈ π_i *and* C ∈ π_i+1, C ⊆ B} *if and only if* $H((\ker f)_B) \geq \theta$ *and* m(B) ≥ μ.

If $\tau(\Pi, f, m, \theta, \mu)$ contains the set of edges {(B, C) | B ∈ π_i and C ∈ π_i+1} we say that the node B is *split* in the tree $\tau(\Pi, f, m, \theta, \mu)$. Since splitting involves a sufficiently large value of the entropy and a node of sufficiently large measure, longer paths in the tree point towards subsets of S that contain a large diversity of values of the feature function f.

An entropy quad-tree is an entropy tree $\tau(\Pi, f, m, \theta, \mu)$ such that $\Pi = (\pi_1, ..., \pi_n)$ is a descending chain of partitions on S, $\pi_1 \geq_4 \pi_2 \geq_4 \cdots \geq_4 \pi_n$. The entire image area S corresponds to the root of the quad-tree.

The expansion of a node B is based on its entropy value and the predetermined threshold used for the splitting condition, as well as the size of the corresponding subarea. Only nodes with area greater or equal to the defined minimum window size are expanded. The complex areas correspond to leaves at the highest level on the quad-tree.

2. AN ALGORITHM FOR DETECTION OF HIGH COMPLEXITY REGIONS

The algorithm proposed constructs a full quad-tree related to the image entropy or box-counting dimension concentration to find high complexity areas.

The construction of the quad-tree is based on the measurements of the feature in image sub-areas, which can also be regarded as tree nodes. The algorithm receives as input the gray scale version of an image, a minimum area size for analysis and arguments relevant to the node splitting condition. For the entropy based method described in subsection 2.1, we use a predetermined threshold for the entropy in order to decide whether or not to split a node. For the box-counting dimension method, two distinct arguments are used in the splitting condition: a predefined threshold for the fraction of intercepting boxes or rectangles at any image sub-area and a predefined threshold for the number of gray shades to be considered at the intercepting analysis. The entire image area corresponds to the root of the quad-tree. The expansion of each node is based on its feature value and the predetermined threshold(s) used for the splitting condition, as well as the size of the corresponding sub-area. Only nodes with area greater or equal to the defined minimum area size are expanded.

Our algorithm corresponding to Table 1 outputs a quad-tree showing the feature concentration along the whole image area. In this representation, leaves are assigned with a shade of gray, depending on their location on the tree level. Leaves located closer to the root correspond to areas of the image assigned with darker shades of gray whereas leaves located further from the root correspond to areas of the image assigned with lighter shades of gray. The algorithm also highlights the leaves at the highest tree level with highest feature value. In most cases, those leaves correspond to high complexity regions of the image.

The function *ComputeFeature* evaluates the feature associated with the histogram of the pixels in the node's area. We present two versions for this function in subsection 2.1 and subsection 2.2 as it differs according to the measure used. The recursive method *Split* introduced in Table 2 expands a node if its feature satisfies the method related splitting condition and if its area is greater or equal to the defined minimum area size. A gray shade corresponding to a level in the final tree is assigned to every leaf node by the method *Draw*. The higher the level value, the lighter is the shade of gray assigned to the leaf. Information about each leaf such as its id, feature value and level is saved in a text file by the method *SaveNodeInfo*. The method *Release* frees the memory space previously allocated to a node. Finally, the method *HighlightHighFeatureLeaves* highlights in pink or white the leaves at the highest tree level with highest feature values, corresponding in most cases to high complexity regions. The white color leaves are the ones with the highest feature value among all pink leaves.

2.1 Information-Theoretical Method

Our method evaluates the entropy of the local histograms of image sub-areas to find high complexity regions. The partition blocks of a node, used for the entropy analysis, consist of pixels with the same shade of gray.

Table 3 presents an algorithm for the information-theoretic method proposed. It computes the entropy associated with the histogram of the pixels in a node's area. This histogram is created by the method *InsertGrayShade*. The result generated by *ComputeFeature* is successively used by the recursive method *Split* shown in Table 2. Only the nodes corresponding to sub-areas of the image where the entropy is above the predefined entropy threshold and have area greater or equal to the pre-defined minimum area size are expanded. We observed that leaves at the highest level in the resultant quad-tree may naturally have different associated entropy values.

Table 1. Algorithm 1: ComputeHCRegions(image, minArea, thr1, thr2)

Input: Gray scale image, minimum area size for the analysis, feature threshold, threshold corresponding to the number of shades of gray (used only by the BCD method)
Output: Quad-tree showing the feature concentration along the whole image area
nId ←ROOT
nLevel ← 0
root ← newNode(nId, nLevel, image.width, image.height)
ComputeFeature(root)
Split(root)
HighlightHighFeatureLeaves()

Table 2. Algorithm 2: Split(n)

Input: A node *n* from a quad-tree
Output: Expands the node creating four children, if node satisfies the necessary requirements
  if (n.feature > method lower bound) and (n.area > minArea) **then**
  nLevel ← n.level +1
  nId ← n.id + A
  topLeft ← newNode(nId, nLevel, n.rect.x, n.rect.y, n.rect.width/2, n.rect.height/2)
  ComputeFeature(topLeft)
  nId ← n.id + B
  topRight ← newNode(nId, nLevel, n.rect.x + n.rect.width/2, n.rect.y, n.rect.width/2,
  n.rect.height/2)
  ComputeFeature(topRight)
  nId ← n.id + C
  bottonLeft ←newNode(nId, nLevel, n.rect.x, n.rect.y + n.rect.height/2, n.rect.width/2,
  n.rect.height/2)
  ComputeFeature(bottonLeft)
  nId ← n.id + D
  bottonRight ← newNode(nId, nLevel, n.rect.x + n.rect.width/2, n.rect.y+ n.rect.height/2,
  n.rect.width/2, n.rect.height/2)
  ComputeFeature(bottonRight)
  Release(n)
  Split(topLeft)
  Split(topRight)
  Split(bottonLeft)
  Split(bottonRight)
  else
    SaveNodeInfo(n)
    Draw(n)
    Release(n)
  end if

2.2 Box-Counting Dimension Method

The box-counting dimension is a measure used to determine the fractal dimension of a set S in a metric space. It reflects the variation of the results of measuring a set at a diminishing scale, which allows the observation of progressively smaller details.

Let (S, O_d) be a topological metric space and let *T* be a precompact set. For every positive *r*,

Table 3. Algorithm 3: ComputeFeature(n)

Input: A node *n* from a quad-tree
Output: The node entropy related to the histogram of the pixels in the area.
  entropy ← 0
  for all pixel in n.area **do**
  InsertGrayShade(histogram,pixel.shade)
  end for
  for all shade in histogram **do**
  p ← number of pixels with shade
  s ← total number of pixels in the node
  g ← (p / s)
  entropy− =(g) × (lg$_2$(g))
  end for
  return entropy

there exists a *r*-net for *T*; that is a finite subset N_r of *S* such that $T \subseteq \{\cup C(x, r | x \in N_r\}$ for every *r* > 0. Denote by $n_T(r)$ the smallest size of an *r*-net of *T*. It is clear that $r < r'$ implies $n_T(r) \geq n_T(r')$. The box-counting dimension is introduced next (Leavers, 1993).

Definition 2: *Let* (S, O_d) *be a topological metric space and let T be a precompact set. The* upper box-counting dimension *of T is the* number

$$ubd(T) = \lim_{r \to 0} \sup \frac{n_T(r)}{\log \frac{1}{r}}$$

The lower box-counting dimension *of T is the number*

$$lbd(T) = \lim_{r \to 0} \inf \frac{n_T(r)}{\log \frac{1}{r}}$$

If ubd(T) = lbd(T), we refer to their common values as the box-counting dimension of T, denoted by bd(T).

We use the box-counting dimension of the local histograms of image sub-areas to find high complexity regions. The box-counting dimension of a sub-area is based on to the number of intercepting boxes in the sub-area.

Definition 3: *A box is a sub-area of the image with size equal to the predefined minimum area size. An intercepting box corresponds to a box where the number of different shades of gray is greater or equal to a predefined threshold.*

The version of the function *ComputeFeature* presented in Table 4 corresponds to the box-counting dimension method. It computes the

box-counting dimension associated with the histogram of the boxes in a node's area. As in the Information-theoretic version, the method *InsertGrayShade* constructs a histogram of each box in the node or image sub-area. If the area corresponding to the node is equal to a box area, the number of intercepting boxes is the same as the number of different shades of gray in its histogram. Otherwise, the number of intercepting boxes is equal to the number of boxes with histogram containing a number of shades of gray greater or equal to a predefined threshold. When the box-counting dimension method is used, the recursive method *Split* shown in Table 2 expands a node according to a threshold related to the fraction of intercepting boxes found. For instance, a fraction threshold=0.1 represents a node having 10% of intercepting boxes among all its boxes. So in this case, the algorithm expands a node if its box-counting dimension corresponds to a fraction greater than 10% of intercepting boxes. The area corresponding to the node should also be greater or equal to the predefined minimum area size in order to promote expansion. As in the Information-theoretic method, we also observed that leaves at the highest level in the resultant quad-tree may

Table 4. Algorithm 4: ComputeFeature(n)

```
Input: A node n from a quad-tree
Output: Box-counting dimension associated to the node's
area.
  boxesIntercepting ← 0
  bcd ← 0
  for all box in n.area do
for all pixel in box do
InsertGrayShade(box.histogram,pixel.shade)
    end for
    if n.area = box.area then
    boxesIntercepting ← box.histogram.size
    else if box.histogram.size ≥ threshold then
    boxesIntercepting ← boxesIntercepting +1
  end if
  Release(box.histogram)
  end for
  if boxesIntercepting > 0 then
  bcd− = boxesIntercepting / lg₁₀(1 / (n.area))
end if
return bcd
```

naturally have different BCD values associated. We show in subsection 2.4 that the leaves with highest BCD value among the ones at highest level can better represent high complexity areas of the image.

2.3 System Description

The algorithm was implemented in Java (JDK 6 Update 7) and the program is composed by 8 classes: Main, Image, Tree, EntropyTree, Box-CountingTree, Node, EntropyNode and Box-CountingNode. The class Tree is a super class for the classes EntropyTree and BoxCountingTree and the class Node is a super class for the classes EntropyNode and BoxCountingNode. The class Main instantiates an Image object. The class Image implements the methods for encoding and decoding images, as well as for treating the image prior to the generation of the quad-tree. Image treatment may involve resizing and conversion to gray scale. The class Tree is a super class with attributes and methods shared by both classes EntropyTree and BoxCountingTree. Those two classes, together with the classes EntropyNode and BoxCountingNode contain the implementation of the methods presented in 2.1 and in 2.2. The class Node is a super class with attributes and methods shared by both classes EntropyNode and BoxCountingNode.

2.4 Experimental Results

Experiments were performed over decompressed gray scale version of JPEG images. The use of gray scale images allowed the methods to be applied over a reduced color space. The resultant image files were again compressed and presented as JPEG files. The values chosen for all the thresholds promote a good capture of the complexity. The resultant images and statistics show that the quad-trees generated by both methods are quite similar. Figure 1(a) and Figure 1(b) present the relation between the values chosen as threshold for

both methods and the percentage of the number of pixels located in high complexity areas relative to the total number of pixels in each sample image. One can notice that the percentages of pixels in high complexity areas generated for each image file are very close in value for both methods. The files corresponding to the quad-trees generated for the first four sample images are presented in Figure 2. As mentioned in section 2, a gray shade corresponding to a level in the final tree, is assigned to every leaf node. The leaves at the highest tree level with highest feature values, corresponding in most cases to high complexity regions, are highlights in pink or white. The white color leaves are the ones with the highest feature value among all pink leaves. Results for both methods also show the relation between the characteristics of the images and the values used for the node splitting condition. Images corresponding to natural scenes or objects and faces with a textured background require a higher value for the entropy threshold, as well as for the threshold used for the box-counting dimension evaluation in order to capture well the complex regions. Those images present a higher number of pixels located in high complexity areas. Images with objects and faces exposed over a more uniform background require lower values for those parameters. Those images present a lower number of pixels located in high complexity areas.

Although only JPEG files were used in the experiments here presented, the algorithm and methods described in this paper are independent of image type. So in order to compare the results between different formats, we also performed experiments with BMP image files. In this case, each JPEG file was created from an original Bmp image. Results for both formats regarding both methods were also quite similar and demonstrate that our algorithm can capture high complexity domains independent of an image format. We also observed that as we lowered the compression quality of JPEG images, there was a decrease on the number of pixels located in high complexity

Figure 1(a). Fraction of pixels in high complexity areas of the image given the corresponding lower bound used for the entropy **(b).** *Fraction of pixels in high complexity areas of the image given the corresponding lower bound used for the BCD threshold.*

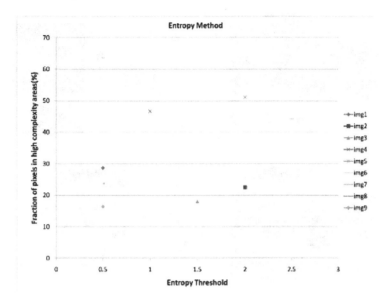

A.

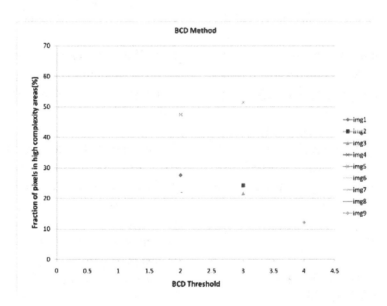

B.

Figure 2. Sample simulation results for original images comparing the corresponding Entropy Tree tTop right in each subfigure) and the corresponding BCD Tree (bottom right in each subfigure)

sub-domains. JPEG compression removes high frequency details from images as considered by Pevny and Fridrich (2008). Furthermore, the number of image artifacts increases as we lower the compression quality. Uncompressed formats (BMP, PCX) or lossless compression formats (PGM, TIFF) usually carry a higher degree of noise and less artifacts. As a consequence of the high frequency removal and addition of more artifacts, JPEG files with low quality usually have less high complexity areas when compared to the correspondent JPEG image files compressed with higher quality and Bmp images.

3. AN ALGORITHM FOR CRATER DETECTION USING ENTROPY QUAD-TREES

We applied entropy quad-trees to the first stage of an algorithm for crater detection. The proposed algorithm locates craters on the surface of Mars, represented by circles in digital images. The algorithm proposed constructs a full entropy quad-tree related to the image entropy concentration to find high complexity areas that can also contain edges. Later, a slightly modified CHT is used to detect the presence of circles in the complex areas found during the entropy analysis. The algorithm receives as input the 8 bits gray scale version of an image, a minimum window size for analysis, a threshold relevant to the node splitting condition, the minimum and maximum radius values for the searched craters and a threshold for the CHT. Its output lists the detected craters as well as their estimated center points highlighted and superimposed over the original image. A text file with data indicating the center points, radius and Hough Space bin points of each detected crater is also generated.

The construction of the entropy quad-tree is based on an information-theoretical method similar to the one described in subsection 2.1. The most significant difference between both versions is that the one used for crater detection also classifies complex areas corresponding to leaves at the highest level on the quad-tree according to the possibility of presence of an edge. Our new method is presented in subsection 3.1.

First, the algorithm determines the average gray intensity of the original image, as well as the low intensity average (average of gray shades below average intensity) and high intensity average (average of gray shades above average intensity). Then, the pixels in each area with minimum size for analysis are mapped to two different sets according to the thresholds corresponding to the average of low intensity shades or the average of high intensity shades of the original image. Crater edges can be found in areas that contain only dark shades of gray or areas containing light shades of gray.

The classification considers the number of pixels in a minimum size window that are above the high intensity average threshold if at least one pixel in the area has gray shade above the average intensity. Otherwise, if all the pixels in the area have low intensity, the classification considers the number of pixels in the minimum size window that have shade below the low intensity average threshold.

Let n be the number of pixels satisfying one of those conditions and h the height of our minimum window. Also, suppose we have a square window. When $h-2 < n < h^2-1$, the entropy value remains considerably high and the area is classified as a leaf that possibly contains an edge. Only those leaves are relevant to our algorithm.

After the high complexity regions that may contain edges are found, the algorithm determines another threshold corresponding to a high intensity shade which is higher than the high intensity average shade, lower than the maximum intensity found in the image and has the highest histogram value among the shades satisfying the couple previous conditions. This last threshold which we will call "near maximum intensity" threshold is used to highlight high intensity pixels corresponding to edges. Pixels with light shades of gray (higher than average intensity) that form edges usually

have intensity greater than the "near maximum intensity" threshold.

Finally, the entropy analysis generates a binary image where pixels with shades of gray below the low intensity threshold and pixels with shades of gray above the near maximum intensity threshold are mapped to white. All the other pixels are mapped to black. The resultant binary image corresponds to the output of the entropy analysis and input of the Circle Hough Transform method. As previously mentioned, the original image does not need any pre-processing. The entropy analysis works as an information theoretic edge filter that generates a binary image from complex areas which may contain edges.

Our next step is to apply the CHT to detect circles in the binary image. The CHT method maintains an accumulator array to find triplets (a, b, r) that describe circles where (a, b) is the center of a circle with radius r. Each point (a, b) in the image receives a score value referred to as the *number of votes* equal to the number of points (x, y) fall on the perimeter of the circle (a, b, r). This score is stored in an accumulator array. The detected center points have the highest numbers of votes.

Two stopping conditions are commonly used by the CHT algorithm: the maximum number of circles to be found and a threshold for the minimum number of votes related to a point in the parameter space. In our application, there is no systematic way to reasonably predict both values. Furthermore, it was observed that for any set of radius where the difference between the minimum and maximum radius is relatively small, the chances of a point to represent a real circle center decreases as the number of votes related to the point gets further from the peak value found in the accumulator array. Points with a number of votes relatively far from the peak value usually correspond to near true center points, near center points of poorly delimited circles or points that received votes in the parameter space simply due to noisy pixels that are not part of any circle edge. To alleviate this problem, we created a new threshold for the number of votes corresponding to the maximum distance from the peak value in the accumulator array as our stopping condition for the CHT method. We also restricted each search to small sets of contiguous radii. Details are provided in subsection 3.2.

The algorithm for crater detection corresponds to Table 5. The recursive method *Split* shown in Table 2 was introduced in section 2. Our method *ComputeFeature* corresponds to a slightly modified version of the one presented in Table 3 and described in section 2, since it also classifies each leaf according to the presence of an edge. Only leaves which may contain an edge are considered by the method *ProcessImageEntropy*. This method generates a binary image representing the entropy analysis to find complex areas that may contain edges. Pixels with shades of gray below the low intensity threshold and pixels with shades of gray above the near maximum intensity threshold are highlighting in white. All remaining pixels are mapped to black.

The method *ComputeCHT* detects circles in the binary image with radii between the minimum and maximum values given as arguments. It also highlights the detected craters as well as their estimated center points over the original image and generates a text file with data related to the craters found such as radius, center points and number of points in the bins associated with each center point.

3.1 Information-Theoretical Method

Table 6 presents an algorithm for the information-theoretic method similar to the one presented in Table 3. It computes the entropy associated with the histogram of the pixels in the area corresponding to a node. This histogram is created by the method *InsertGrayShade*. *ClassifyLeaf* classifies a minimum area node according to the possible presence of an edge. As previously mentioned, only leaves that may contain edges are relevant to our algorithm. The result generated by *ComputeFeature* is successively used by the recursive method *Split* shown in Table 2.

3.2 Circular Hough Transform Method

The Hough Transform is a standard method for shape recognition in digital images. It was first applied to the recognition of straight lines (Leavers, 1993; Illingworth & Kittler, 1988) and later extended to circles (Duda & Hart, 1972; Davis, 1987), ellipses (Yip, Tam, & Leung, 1992), and arbitrary shaped objects (Pao, Li, & Jayakumar, 1992). The Circular Hough Transform (CHT) can be used to determine the parameters of a circle when a number of points that fall on the perimeter are known. A circle with radius r and center (a, b) can be described with the parametric equations:

Table 5. Algorithm 5: ComputeCraters(image, minArea, thrEntropy, minRadius, maxRadius, thrCHT)

Input: 8 bits gray scale version of an image, a minimum area size, entropy threshold, the minimum and maximum radius, CHT threshold
Output: Detected craters as well as their estimated center points highlighted and superimposed over the original image; a text file with data indicating the center points, radius and Hough Space bin points of each detected crater
nId ← ROOT
nLevel ← 0
root ← newNode(nId, nLevel, image.width, image.height)
ConputeFeature(root)
Split(root)
entropyImg ← ProcessImageEntropy()
ComputeCHT (entropyImg, minRadius, maxRadius, thrCHT)

Table 6. Algorithm 6: ComputeFeature(n)

```
Input: A node n from a quad-tree
Output: The node entropy related to the histogram of the pixels in the area.
  entropy ← 0
  for all pixel in n.area do
  InsertGrayShade(histogram,pixel.shade)
  end for
  for all shade in histogram do
  p ← number of pixels with shade
  s ← total number of pixels in the node
  g ← (p / s)
  entropy− =(g) × (lg₂(g))
  end for
  if (n.area == minArea) then
  relevantLeaf ← ClassifyLeaf(histogram)
  if (!relevantLeaf) then
     return 0
  end if
  end if
  return entropy
```

$x = a + r \cos \alpha$ and $y = b + r \sin \alpha$, where $0 \leq \alpha \leq 2\pi$

The locus of (x, y) points in the Hough or parameter space falls on a circle of radius r centered at (a, b). The true center point will be common to all parameter circles, and can be found with an accumulator array that stores the number of votes for each point in the parameter space. Multiple circles with the same radius can be found with the same technique.

The main disadvantage of the transform is the fact that the parameter space corresponds to a 3-dimensional space, which makes the computational complexity and storage requirements $O(n^3)$. If the circles in an image are of known radius r, the search can be reduced to a 2-dimensional space.

The method used in our algorithm searches for all circles with radius between two values given as arguments. It differs from other version of CHT methods because of its stopping condition. For reasons previously mentioned, our method does not use the maximum number of circles or the minimum threshold for the number of votes in order to end the search. Instead, it uses a threshold corresponding to the maximum allowed difference between the peak value in the accumulator array of votes and any other number of votes related to a point in the parameter space.

Let $A_{[W][H][R]}$ denote the accumulator array of votes where W is the image width, H is the image height and R depends on the size of the radius set with minimum element rmin and maximum element rmax, and on the value for the chosen radius increment i. Let t denote the introduced threshold and v be the greatest value stored in the accumulator array A corresponding to a point (w, h, r) where $0 \leq w \leq W-1$, $0 \leq h \leq H-1$ and $0 \leq r <= (rmax - rmin) / i$. Then an arbitrary point (w',h',r') where $0 \leq w' \leq W-1$, $0 \leq h' \leq H-1$ and $0 \leq r' <= (rmax - rmin) / i$ having v' votes in A is detected as a circle center iff $v - v' \leq t$. We observed that our threshold works well for small groups of contiguous radii. Since the size of the group is small, all the radii are close in value and points corresponding to the center of a circle with one of those radii also have a relatively close number of votes in the parameter space. Therefore, the difference between the number of votes corresponding to centers of true circles that are reasonably well delimited cannot be large when the search is performed for a small group of contiguous radii.

Table 7 presents an algorithm for the CHT proposed. *HoughTransform* computes the Hough Transform of the binary image generated during the entropy analysis and *ComputeHS* generates an image corresponding to the Hough Space. *ComputeCenterPoints* finds circles and their center points by checking the accumulator array containing votes for each pixel in the image. *DrawCircles* highlights the detected craters as well as their estimated center points over the original image. *PrintCirclesData* generates a text file with data related to the craters found such as radius, center points and number of points in the bins associated with each center point.

3.3 Experimental Results

Experiments were performed over the decompressed 768x768, 8 bits gray scale version of a JPEG digital image corresponding to a picture of Mars surface presented in Figure 3(a). This image was obtained from the original 24 bits/pixel PGM digital image labeled 3_24 used as training site by Urbach and Stepinski (2009). 3_24 corresponds to one section of a footprint image (h0905 0000) from the High Resolution Stereo Camera (HRSC) instrument of the MarsExpress orbiter. This footprint is about 8248 x 65448 pixels in size and was split into 264 (6 x 44) sections of 1700 x 1700 pixels each. Image 3_24 corresponds to one of those sections.

The use of gray scale images allowed the methods to be applied over a reduced color space. We used a 3×3 minimum area for the entropy analysis and a high entropy threshold equal to 3 due to the heavy presence of texture in the original image. Images corresponding to natural scenes, objects and faces with a textured background or images with a high level of noise contain a large amount of information. It is natural that those images contain more areas with high entropy than images with less textured background. Figure 4(a) shows the binary image generated during the entropy analysis.

We chose a threshold equal to 30 for the CHT method and divided the search into runs containing 15 contiguous values of the radius. We focused on searching for craters with radii varying from 5 to 52 pixels. It was also observed that the choice regarding the search for only 15 radii at a time, combined with a threshold equals to 30 provided reasonably good results. Since the values of the radius in each run are close, the difference between the number of votes for the points corresponding to centers of well delimited circles is usually not greater than 30. Our algorithm was able to detect 50 craters with radii varying between 5 and 20 pixels, 2 craters with radii varying from 20 to 36 pixels and one crater with radius equal to 45 pixels.

Figure 3(b) shows the final image generated by the algorithm. The detected craters and estimated center points are highlighted over the original image. Notice that for some craters, the center points are slightly shifted to the left or right of the true

Table 7. Algorithm 7: ComputeCHT(entropyImg, minRadius, maxRadius, thrCHT)

Input: image generated by the entropy analysis, minimum and maximum radius, new threshold for stop condition **Output:** Detected circles, their estimated center points and radius HoughTransform(entropyImg,minRadius,maxRadius) ComputeHS() ComputeCenterPoints(thrCHT) DrawCircles() PrintCirclesData()

Figure 3. (a) Original image from Mars surface(768x768, 24 bits per pixel), (b) Final image generated by the algorithm where detected craters and their estimated centers are highlighted in pink or white

(a)

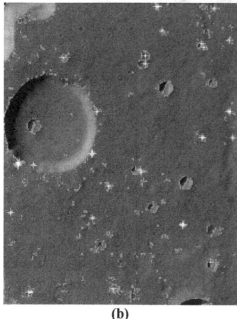

(b)

center point because the characteristic shadow inside the crater is also detected as an edge by the entropy analysis. As presented in Figures 4(b) through 4(d), the algorithm cleans the areas of the entropy analysis image corresponding to the craters found (by mapping their pixels to black) after each CHT run. This cleaning process helps to decrease the amount of noise and therefore undesirable circles overlapping for subsequent runs.

The heavy presence of texture in the image can highly impact the quality of the intermediate image generated by the entropy analysis, which works also as a edge detector tool based on entropy. As the level of texture or noise increases, so does the entropy of regions in the picture. As consequence, the distinction between high entropy nodes that may contain edges becomes harder. On the other hand, the quality of the results generated by the CHT method highly depends on the quality of the entropy analysis image taken as input. Specially, as the detected edges get more and more similar to the real crater edges, it becomes easier for the CHT method to accurately recognize those circles corresponding to craters. We noticed that the image generated by the entropy analysis does not show all the possible true edges corresponding to crater borders. In order to avoid the capturing of heavy noise, we use a high entropy threshold. By using such high threshold, the algorithm cannot capture true crater borders in areas where the variance among the pixels is not high. As a consequence, those craters cannot be detected by the CHT method. Therefore, improving the detection of edges for heavily noisy or textured images during the entropy analysis can directly impact the quality of the final results. Results also show that the algorithm may detect a larger number of false positives craters as the radius increases. Remains of smaller circles that were not completely cleaned from the binary image due to the imperfection of circle edges, may contribute for undesirable circle overlapping in the Hough Space.

Figure 4. (a) Intermediate result of crater detection, (b) Binary image generated after detection of craters with radius between 5 and 20. The pixels corresponding to the circles detected by the CHT are mapped to black, (c) Intermediate result of crater detection. Binary image generated after detection of craters with radius between 21 and 36. The pixels corresponding to the circles detected by the CHT are mapped to black, (d) Intermediate result of crater detection. Binary image generated after detection of craters with radius between 37 and 52. The pixels corresponding to the circles detected by the CHT are mapped to black

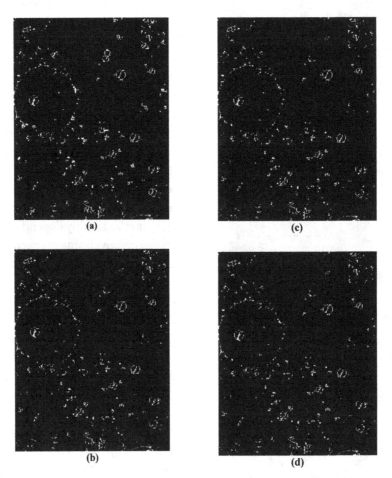

4. CONCLUSION

In this paper we introduced entropy quad-trees and demonstrate that those structures successfully capture high complexity sub-domains of a data domain. The analysis of 2-dimensional image domains showed that similar results are obtained by quad-trees generated with the BCD measure. Quad-trees created for different image formats – medium/high quality JPEG and BMP – are also similar for both measures. We observed that besides capturing image regions corresponding to content related complex areas, entropy and BCD quad-trees also mine other regions with high variance of shades among pixels caused by external factors such as light reflection originated from a camera flash. Nevertheless, the identification of any kind of high complexity region plays an important role for a variety of applications such as data hiding and bio-diversity systems.

As an application of our proposed technique, an algorithm using entropy quad-trees to detect circles that can possibly correspond to craters in images was introduced. The algorithm performs an information-theoretic analysis of the histogram of sub regions of the image in order to find complex areas that may contain edges. A modified CHT detects circles in those complex areas and provides information about center points and radius of the circles found. A threshold corresponding to the maximum distance from the peak value in the accumulator array is used as stopping condition for the method. There is no external pre-processing of the original PGM image 3_24 other than conversion to JPEG format and resizing. No external edge filter is used to process the original image prior to the CHT method. The entropy analysis works as an edge filter that generates the binary image given as input to the CHT method. The heavy presence of noise and texture may compromise the quality of the complex areas found during the entropy analysis and impact the quality of the final results. Therefore, by improving the robustness of the entropy analysis against heavy noise and texture, more craters will accurately be detected.

We intend to extend the application of information-theoretical techniques to other structures associated with spatial data sets such as grid-files, KD-trees, and R-trees. Another area of great potential is the application of entropy quad-trees to the identification of terrain areas that contain a high level of biodiversity.

REFERENCES

Bue, B. D., & Stepinski, T. F. (2007). Machine detection of martian impact craters from digital topography data. *IEEE Transactions on Geoscience and Remote Sensing, 45*(1), 265–274. doi:10.1109/TGRS.2006.885402

Davis, E. R. (1987). A modified hough scheme for general circle location. *Pattern Recognition Letters, 7*, 37–43. doi:10.1016/0167-8655(88)90042-6

Duda, R. O., & Hart, P. E. (1972). Use of the hough transformation to detect lines and curves in pictures. *Communications of the ACM, 15*(1), 11–15. doi:10.1145/361237.361242

Illingworth, J., & Kittler, J. (1988). Survey: A survey of the hough transform? *Computervision. Graphics and Image Processing: Image Understanding, 44*(1), 87–116.

Leavers, V. F. (1993). Survey: Which hough transform? *Computervision, Graphics, and Image Processing. Image Understanding, 58*(2), 250–264. doi:10.1006/ciun.1993.1041

Pao, D. C. W., Li, H. F., & Jayakumar, R. (1992). Shape recognition using the straight line hough transform: Theory and generalization. *IEEE Transactions on Pattern Analysis and Machine Intelligence, 14*(11), 1076–1089. doi:10.1109/34.166622

Pevny, T., & Fridrich, J. (2008). Benchmarking for steganography. In K. Solanki, K. Sullivan, & U. Madow (Eds.), *Proceedings of the 10th International Workshop on Information Hiding* (LNCS 5284, pp. 251-267).

Salamuniccar, G., & Loncaric, S. (2008). Gt-57633 catalouge of martian impact craters developed for evaluation of crater detection algorithms. *Planetary and Space Science, 56*.

Simovici, D. A., & Djeraba, C. (2008). *Mathematical tools for data mining: Set theory, partial orders, combinatorics*. London, UK: Springer-Verlag.

Simovici, D. A., & Jaroszewicz, S. (2003). Generalized conditional entropy and decision trees. *Extraction et la Gestion des Connaissances, 17*(1-3), 552.

Simovici, D. A., & Jaroszewicz, S. (2008). An axiomatization of partition entropy. *IEEE Transactions on Information Theory*, *48*, 2138–2142. doi:10.1109/TIT.2002.1013159

Solanki, K., Dabeer, O., Madhow, U., Manjunath, B. S., & Chandrasekaran, S. (2003). Robust image-adaptive data hiding: Modeling, source coding, and channel coding. In. *Proceedings of the Annual Allerton Conference on Communication Control and Computing*, *41*, 829–838.

Urbach, E. R., & Stepinski, T. F. (2009). Automatic detection of sub-kilometer craters in high resolution planetary images. *Planetary and Space Science*, *57*, 880–887. doi:10.1016/j.pss.2009.03.009

Yip, R. K. K., Tam, P. K. S., & Leung, D. N. K. (1992). Modification of hough transform for circles and ellipses detection using a 2-dimensional array. *Pattern Recognition*, *25*, 1007–1022. doi:10.1016/0031-3203(92)90064-P

This work was previously published in the International Journal of Software Science and Computational Intelligence, Volume 3, Issue 1, edited by Yingxu Wang, pp. 16-33, copyright 2011 by IGI Publishing (an imprint of IGI Global).

Chapter 21
Sitting Posture Recognition and Location Estimation for Human–Aware Environment

Yusuke Manabe
Chiba Institute of Technology, Japan

Kenji Sugawara
Chiba Institute of Technology, Japan

ABSTRACT

Realization of human-computer symbiosis is an important idea in the context of ubiquitous computing. Symbiotic Computing is a concept that bridges the gap between situations in Real Space (RS) and data in Digital Space (DS). The main purpose is to develop an intelligent software application as well as establish the next generation information platform to develop the symbiotic system. In this paper, the authors argue that it is necessary to build 'Mutual Cognition' between human and system. Mutual cognition consists of two functions: 'RS Cognition' and 'DS Cognition'. This paper examines RS Cognition, which consists of many software functions for perceiving various situations like events or humans' activities in RS. The authors develop two perceptual functions, sitting posture recognition and human's location estimation for a person, as RS perception tasks. In the resulting experiments, developed functions are quite competent to recognize a human's activities.

INTRODUCTION

Recently there are a lot of efforts to develop an innovative and intelligent space, room or environment relating data stored in Digital Space (DS) to situations in Real Space (RS) in the context of ubiquitous computing (Weiser, 1991). For example, Robotic Room (Sato, Nishida, & Mizoguchi, 1996), Intelligent Room (Coen, 1998), Easy Living (Shafer et al., 1998; Brumitt et al., 2000), Intelligent Space (Lee, Appenzeller, & Hashimoto, 1998; Lee & Hashimoto, 2002), Aware Home (Kidd et al., 1999), SELF (Nishida et

DOI: 10.4018/978-1-4666-2651-5.ch021

al., 2000), Smart Room (Pentland, 2000), Project Oxygen (Rudolph, 2001) and Robot Town Project (Hasegawa & Murakami, 2006; Murakami et al., 2008) have been proposed. Final goal of them will be to realize a secure society and community based on supporting daily life through recognizing situations in RS from various physical data that are obtained by ubiquitous and embedded sensors. Moreover, their projects will aspire to build new man-machine (human-computer) relationships.

In the above context, we have also proposed a concept of Symbiotic Computing since 1994 (Symbiotic Computing, 2010). The notion of human-computer symbiosis is the first used in 1960 (Licklider, 1960). About half a century has passed, however, people cannot receive satisfactory and suitable services without their proactive actions because systems cannot perceive dynamic situation in Real Space (RS). In other words, a lot of current computer service has been realized based on static information only in Digital Space (DS).

The purpose of Symbiotic Computing is mainly to develop flexible information service or application as well as to establish the next generation information platform based on multi-agent framework (Suganuma et al., 2009; Sugawara et al., 2008). In addition, a specific characteristic of Symbiotic Computing is to aim at establishment of 'Mutual Cognition' between RS and DS. Mutual cognition is a cognitive process defined by the relation between a personal feeling that "I know what you know about me" and a machine's activity as if "I know what you know about me."

Figure 1 shows a model of mutual cognition process which consists of four steps. The first step is to recognize actions of a person or a community. The next step is to infer a request from the recognized actions and send it to DS. The third step is to give valid information or services provided by DS to RS according to situation. The last step is to check feeling of contentment of the human to evaluate the process of the mutual cognition. The realization of mutual cognition can provide suitable and secure services based on a situation in RS to people. We aspire to build new man-machine (human-computer) relationships.

In other words, mutual cognition model is one of the specific models of context-awareness computing (Poslad, 2009). According to Poslad (2009), the term context-aware was first used by Schilit and Theimer (1994) in the context of mobile computing. Until now there were a lot of similar definitions of context or context-awareness (Dey & Abowd, 2000). In order to clear our purpose, we follow the definition of context and context-aware in reference (Dey & Aboed, 2000). Definition 2 is almost equivalent to the idea that symbiotic computing is trying to realize.

Definition 1: Context is any information that can be used to characterize the situation of an entity. An entity is a person, place, or object that is considered relevant to the interaction between a user and an application, including the user and applications themselves.

Figure 1. Mutual cognition process

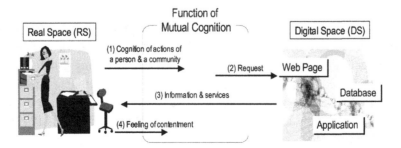

Definition 2: A system is context-aware if it uses context to provide relevant information and/or service to the user, where relevancy depends on the user's task.

This paper especially focuses on the first step in the mutual cognition processing, that is, to recognize human's activities. This is called 'RS cognition', which is perceptual function of software system for some events or human's activities. Perceptual function should be implemented in a context-awareness system. As information in RS are usually obtained as multi-variable and multi-dimensional time series measured by various sensors such as camera, microphone, thermometer, acceleration sensor and so on, it is important to build intelligent algorithms to segment and cluster complicated time series data as well as to associate clustered data with semantic representations of some kind.

In this study, we postulate personal office room/space as environment and we develop two perceptual functions, which can recognize sitting posture on the chair and location point in the room for an office worker in the context of telework application (Sugawara, Fujita, & Hara, 2007; Konno et al., 2008). We utilizes optical fiber pressure sensor mattress and acceleration sensor for sitting posture recognition and two USB cameras for location point recognition. Two experiments have been done to evaluate the developed functions. As the results, we find that the developed functions are quite competent to recognize human's activities.

HUMAN-AWARE ENVIRONMENT AND TWO PROPOSED PERCEPTUAL FUNCTIONS

This section explains about the proposed perceptual functions; sitting posture recognition and location recognition.

Environment: Personal Office Room/Space

In this study, we address a personal office room/space as environment although it is impossible to adapt for all of human's activities and environments. Figure 2 illustrates a personal office room/space as environment. We postulate that the area of personal space is around from 20 m2 to 30 m2. Pressure sensor mattress is put on the seat of an office chair and acceleration sensor is attached to the chair back because an office chair is a best tool of context-awareness when a person works at the desk. Moreover, two USB cameras are set up the high position and the angle between them is around 90 degree in order to estimate human's location point. This assumes that a worker may walk out and go to bookshelf for taking documents, books or something. Under the postulated environment we mentioned here, we develop the perceptual functions for recognizing a worker's activities.

Function 1: Sitting Posture Recognition

The first function is to recognize sitting posture on the chair with sensors. Figure 3 shows recognition process. This process is divided into two flows; registration process and perception process.

Registration process is to create symbols for perception process. Symbols denote a set of cluster vectors obtained from sensor data and linguistic labels (semantics) based on image data. The detail of this process is shown as follows.

1. Image data, pressure data and acceleration data are observed by respective devices, USB camera, pressure sensor mattress and acceleration sensor. USB camera is not used in perception process because it is used for confirming the actual sitting posture in registration process.

Figure 2. An example of human-aware environment

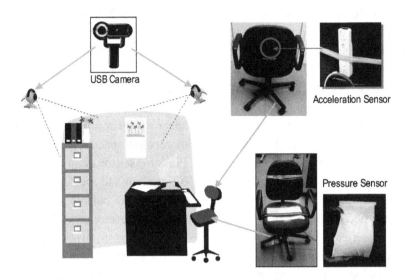

2. We used *k*-means algorithm to cluster each time series data set of pressure data and acceleration data respectively. Pressure data (54 dimensional vector) are clustered into 10 clusters. Acceleration data (3 dimensional vector) are clustered into 5 clusters. However, raw clustering result may be noisy because of sensing error and human's activity. Thus, clustering result is smoothened with respect to time based on the following equation;

$$L(t) = Mode(l(t-5), l(t-4), ..., l(t), ... l(t+4), l(t+5)), \quad (1)$$

where *t* denotes time, $L(t)$ denotes smoothened cluster label and $l(t)$ denotes raw cluster label at time *t*.

3. The continuous segments, which are clustered as the same cluster over 120 seconds,

Figure 3. Function 1: sitting posture recognition

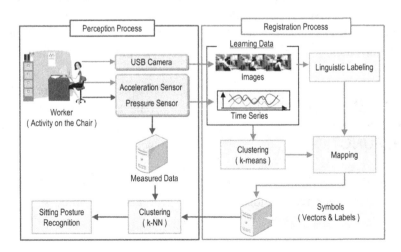

are extracted as the stable intervals which human keeps sitting posture. Then the extracted intervals are elected as candidates of symbol.

4. Image sequences corresponding to the extracted intervals are checked by manual, linguistic labels are created to each interval based on actual sitting posture estimated from image.

5. Finally, some pairs of cluster vector for the stable interval and linguistic label are registered as symbols.

Meanwhile, in perception process, the created symbols are used as knowledge to recognize sitting posture based on observed data. The detail of perception process is shown as follows.

1. Pressure data and acceleration data are observed by respective devices and stored in database.

2. Next, respective sensor data are clustered by *k*-NN algorithm using the cluster vectors, which is created in registration process.

3. Clustering result is smoothened based on Equation (1).

4. A specific linguistic label is assigned for the intervals being stabilized over 120 seconds.

Function 2: Location Point Estimation

The second function is to estimate human's location point in the small room/space by using two USB cameras. Figure 4 shows process flow. This process is also divided into two processes.

Registration process is shown as follows.

1. Two USB cameras, which are called camera A and B respectively, captured background image sequences. Needless to say, background images do not include human.

2. Next, image data of landmark object is prepared. Landmark object is located in the room/space in order to estimate human's precise location. Thus it is better that shape of landmark object is tetragon with the top and the bottom as well as with the left and the right.

3. From the several background image sequences, the matrix of mean and standard deviation of luminance are calculated for 100 image frames. The pixel (i,j) is identified as background when it satisfies the following equation;

Figure 4. Human's location point estimation

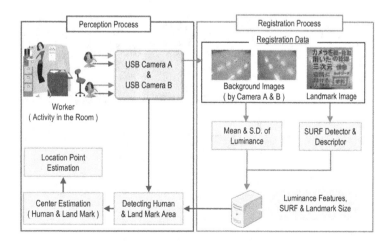

$$\overline{I} - \sigma \leq I(i, j) \leq \overline{I} + \sigma, \qquad (2)$$

where I denotes luminance value, $\overline{I}$ denotes mean of luminance and σ denotes standard deviation of luminance.

4. From landmark image, Speeded Up Robust Feature (SURF) (Bay et al., 2008) is extracted. SURF is a robust image detector and descriptor, first proposed by Herbert Bay et al. in 2006. SURF is a scale- and rotation-invariant feature as well as it can detect the target object area speedily.
5. Finally, SURF and luminance matrix are registered in order to detect landmark and human.

In perception process, extracted features are used for detecting human area and landmark area respectively. The detail is shown as follows.

1. Human detection is rather detection of area excepting background. Figure 5(a) shows an example of human area detection based on our algorithms. This algorithm provides human's location point in broad terms.

2. SURF detector and descriptor can find the landmark area. Figure 5(b) shows an example of landmark area detection. If once landmark is detected, it can be removed from the location.

3. From landmark area, length of four edges of landmark l_1, l_2, l_3 and l_4 are calculated. Then mapping ratio M_r is calculated as following equation;

$$M_r = \frac{4L_R}{l_1 + l_2 + l_3 + l_4} \text{[cm/pixel]} \qquad (3)$$

where L_R denotes actual length of an edge of landmarks.

4. In order to estimate precise location point of human, center point is calculated for each detection area.
5. Finally, precise human's location point is estimated by distance D between human's center and land mark's center and angle Θ between two vectors which are from land mark's center to top-right corner of landmark and human's center.

Figure 5. Detecting human and landmark area

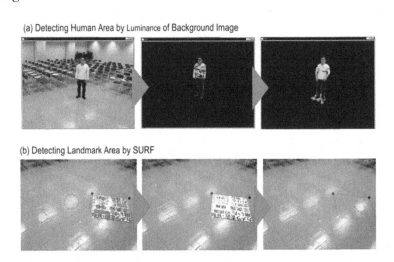

322

EXPERIMENT I

Experiment I is to evaluate the function of sitting posture recognition.

Experimental Environment

Figure 6 shows experimental environment. A subject sits on the chair in front of desk and works. The contents of work are "using PC", "reading the book", "writing", "watching online videos" and so on.

Pressure sensor mattress is KINOTEX sensor and acceleration sensor is WiiRemote controller. Specification of each sensor device is shown as Table 1. WiiRemote controller is attached as the coordination system shown in Figure 6.

Development environments are as follows;

- **PC:** AMD Athlon Dual CoreProcessor 5000B 2.6GHz 4GB memory,
- **OS:** Windows XP Professional,
- **Programming Language:** C#, Visual C++ (MFC)
- **IDE:** Visual Studio 2008 Express Edition (for Wii Remote Controller), Visual Studio 2005 Professional Edition (for KINOTEX)
- **Libraries:** Wiimote Lib v1.7 ("Nintendo's Wiimote", 2010)

Detail of Experiment

In this experiment, we measured pressure sensor data, acceleration data and image data in twice (which are called data set 1 and 2 respectively). Sampling rate is 1 Hz for all of data. Measurement time are 3680 seconds (data set 1) and 3755 seconds (data set 2) and we extracted only 3600 seconds from each data. We used data set 1 as learning data and used data set 2 as test data. Image data size is 320x240 and format is PNG (Portable Network Graphics).

Data clustering algorithms (*k*-means and *k*-NN) are achieved by *kmeans* function and *knn1* function in statistical package R ("R", 2010). Maximum iteration times of *k*-means is 1000000, the algorithm is Hartigan-Wong method.

Results

Figure 7 shows the result of clustering pressure sensor data by *k*-means algorithm for data set 1. Unfortunately, acceleration data could not be clustered successfully because of less of variant and lack of a part of data. Thus in this paper we mainly address the result of pressure sensor data and complementally address the result of acceleration data. From Figure 7, we can find that eight stable intervals are segmented by seven clusters. Each image means that a subject mainly keeps the posture in each interval. From these images, we create four linguistic labels on sitting postures as follows;

1. **Leaning Against The Backrest:** This posture means that a subject is leaning against a backrest of a chair.
2. **Leaning Against the Desk:** This posture means that a subject is leaning against a top of a desk. For example, he puts his elbow or arm on the desk.

Table 1. Specification of each sensor device

(A) KINOTEX Pressure Sensor Mattress	
Sensing Area Size (mm)	W200 x D270
Number of sensing points	54 (9 rows x 6 cols)
Pitch of sensing points (mm)	Rows=30, Cols=30
Measurable size (kPa)	about 0 - 10
Sampling rate (Hz)	about 40
(B) WiiRemote Controller	
Size (mm)	H148 x W36.2 x D30
Measurement Axis	3-axis (X, Y, Z)
Wireless Communication	& Bluetooth(Broadcom)

Figure 6. Experimental environment to evaluate function 1

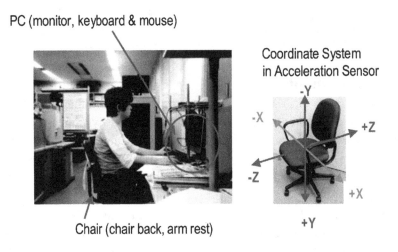

3. **Proper Sitting:** This posture means that a subject sits on the chair and mainly use keyboard while keeping proper sitting posture.
4. **Nobody:** This posture means that nobody else sit on the chair.

Finally, we can create six symbols from data set 1 in Figure 8 Symbol #1, #2, #4, #5 and #6 are corresponding to cluster #1, #2, #7, #9 and #10 respectively. Symbol #7 is created by the mean of cluster #3 and #5 because their cluster vectors are very strong correlation (correlation coefficient is 0.95) as well as their images of sitting posture are very similar condition.

Figure 9 shows clustering and recognition result for data set 2. Cluster number in *k*-NN al-gorithm is corresponding to symbol number created from data set 1. From this figure, six clusters segmented nine stable intervals (from 'A' to 'I'). For example, interval 'D' is recognized as *lean the desk* because it is labeled by symbol #4.

In order to evaluate the clustering and recognition accuracy, we checked movie files, which are created by combining image sequence in each interval. Figure 10 shows correspondence between human's clustering and *k*-NN clustering. The left bar graph denotes clustering result by humans and the right bar graph denotes clustering result by *k*-NN corresponding to Figure 9. As the result, we can find system's clustering results are not perfectly matched to human's clustering results in the interval 'A', 'F', 'G' and 'H' but the other

Figure 7. Clustering result by k-means (data set 1)

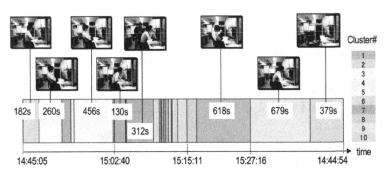

Figure 8. Acquired symbols (data set 1)

Symbol #1 leaning against the backrest 1		Symbol #4	
Symbol #2 nobody		leaning against the desk 1	
Symbol #3		Symbol #5 leaning against the desk 2	
leaning against the backrest 2		Symbol #6 proper sitting (use Keyboard)	

intervals are good accuracy. Figure 11 shows the typical sitting posture images in the interval 'A', 'F', 'G' and 'H'. From these images it seems that machine's clustering results are good performance in the interval 'F', 'G' and 'H'. These results can be caused by human's subjective aspect. On the other hand, we can find that the interval 'A' is not good performance because Figure 11(a) can not look like '*leaning against the desk*'. The failure of the interval 'A' means that sitting posture is not one-to-one correspondence to seat pressure pattern, that is, a sitting posture can include some seat pressure patterns.

Figure 12 (a) and (b) show variance of acceleration data of Z-axis, scaling data and low-pass filtering data respectively. Low-pass filtering is based on Fourier Transform. Alphabets 'D', 'E',

'H' and 'I' correspond to the stable intervals in Figure 9. We can find that a worker is not using chair back when variance is small, because 'D', 'E' and 'H' intervals denote '*leaning against the desk*' and 'I' interval denotes *nobody*. Especially, Figure 12 (b) shows that we can judge whether a chair back is used or not if the variance is under the threshold value 0.5. Although acceleration data is three-dimensional data (X, Y and Z), X-axis data hardly change because the backrest with acceleration sensor does not axially change with respect to X-axis. We checked that Y-axis data changes but it does not relate to sitting posture patterns.

Figure 9. Clustering results by k-NN (data set 2)

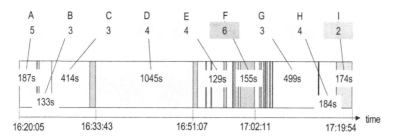

Figure 10. Correspondence between human's clustering and k-NN clustering

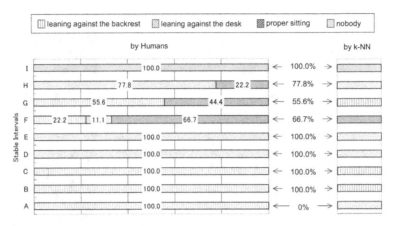

Figure 11. Typical sitting posture images for each interval

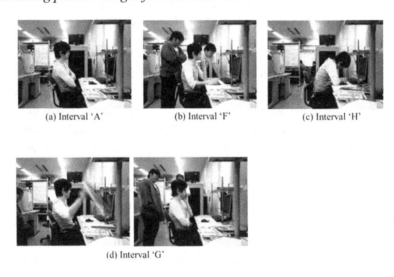

Figure 12. Acceleration data of Z-axis (data set 2)

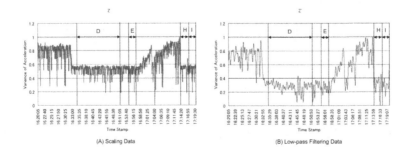

EXPERIMENT II

Experiment II is to evaluate the function of human's location point recognition.

Experimental Environment

Figure 13 shows experimental environment to evaluate function 2. The model of two USB cameras is Logicool Webcam Pro 9000, whose specification is shown as Table 2. The area of space is around 25 m² (5 meters by 5 meters). Human's move area is within a circle, whose size is around 3 meters in diameter. A subject walks within the circle area. Recognition accuracy is evaluated for each detection location point; 'A' to 'F', distance D and angle Θ are defined in Figure 13. Landmark is square and its edge length is 1 meter.

Development environments are as follows;

- **PC:** AMD Athlon Dual CoreProcessor 5000B 2.6GHz 4GB memory,
- **OS:** Windows XP Professional,
- **Programming Language:** C,
- **IDE:** Visual Studio 2008 Express Edition,
- **Libraries:** Open CV 2.0.0 α ("Open CV", 2010), Video Input 0.1995.

Results

Figures 14 and 15 show the results of detecting human's center position for each recognition point by camera A and B respectively. Small green-painted circle denotes center position. We can find that each human's location point can be detected successfully in camera A. On the other hand, in case of camera B, we can find that some location points such as A, E and F are not detected successfully.

Figure 16 shows distance error of actual value and estimated value between human's center point and landmark's center point for each location. The vertical axis denotes estimation error for distance. The average of error in camera A and camera B are 50.16cm, 83.75cm respectively. Figure 17 shows angle error of actual value and estimated value. The average of error in camera A and camera B are 21.75 degrees and 13.71 degrees respectively. From these graphs, we can find that in distance estimation camera A is better than camera B and in angle estimation camera B is better than camera A.

The reason is mainly due to no depth and height correction. In Figure 14 and 15, the upper part of each image is far from the lower part due to perspective. Moreover, these from figures human's center points are up and down based on whether human's upper-body is captured or not. Actually, in case of good estimation points such as the position 'C' and 'D' in camera A, human's center point is near the detection point in the floor because human's upper-body is not captured. The position 'B' is a fewer gap for depth direction although human's upper-body is captured. In case of bad estimation point such as the position 'F', it is located on the upper area of image although human's upper-body is not captured.

CONCLUSION

Symbiotic Computing is a post ubiquitous computing model to bring mutual cognition between Real Space and Digital Space. In this study, we

Table 2. Specification of Logicool Webcam Pro 9000

Size (mm)	W89.9 x D117.9 x H39.8
Focus	10 cm - ∞ (Auto Focus)
Angle of View	76 degrees
Video Capture	2 mega pixels (1600x1200) (MAX)
Frame Rate	30 frames / second (MAX)

Figure 13. Experimental environment to evaluate function 2

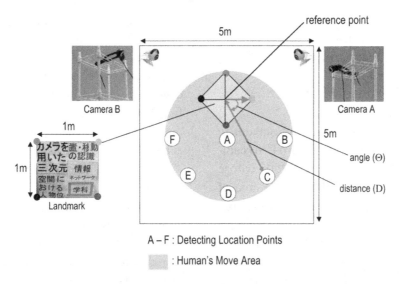

Figure 14. Detecting human's center position (camera a)

Figure 15. Detecting human's center position (camera b)

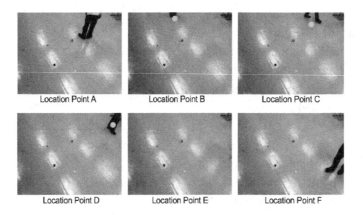

Figure 16. Error between actual and estimated distance for each location point

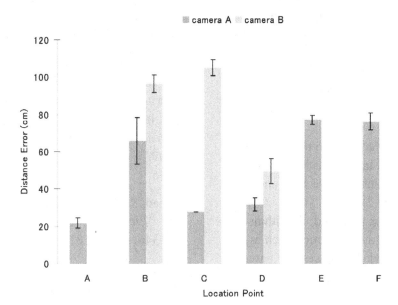

focused on 'RS Cognition' which is a perceptual function of software system and developed the two perceptual functions; sitting posture recognition (function 1) and human's location point recognition (function 2). In function 1, we found that our proposed algorithm can create the useful symbols and recognize sitting postures based on pressure sensor time series data. In function 2, our proposed algorithm can estimate the human's location point. Thus our developed functions are quite competent to recognize human's activities. Currently the following problems are remaining:

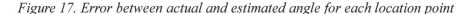

Figure 17. Error between actual and estimated angle for each location point

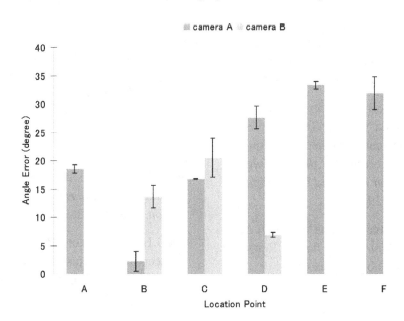

1. To create various symbols to recognize a lot of sitting posture pattern (function 1).

2. To solve depth correction problem in order to estimate human's location point in higher performance (function 2).

3. To use another sensor device such as laser range finder to estimate location point (function 2).

4. To apply our algorithm to the actual environment where includes chair and desk as well as drawer, chest, bookshelf and so on (function 1 and 2).

5. To integrate our proposed algorithms and high-order cognition function such as reasoning or knowledge processing based on multi-agent framework (function 1 and 2).

Perceptual function is a kind of symbol grounding mechanism proposed by Harnad (1991). We are trying to argue the realization of perceptual functions from the viewpoint of it (Manabe et al., 2010). In the next future, we are going to solve the above problems and realize the real context-aware system based on symbol grounding mechanism.

REFERENCES

Bay, H., Ess, A., Tuytelaars, T., & Gool, L. V. (2008). SURF: Speeded Up Robust Features. *Computer Vision and Image Understanding*, *110*(3), 346–359. doi:10.1016/j.cviu.2007.09.014

Brumitt, B., Meyers, B., & Krumm, J. Kern, A., & Shafer, S. (2000). EasyLiving: Technologies for intelligent environments, handheld and ubiquitous computing. In *Proceedings of the 2nd International Symposium on Handheld and Ubiquitous Computing* (pp. 12-29).

CodePlex Open Source Community. (2010). *Managed library for Nintendo's wiimote*. Retrieved from http://wiimotelib.codeplex.com/

Coen, M. H. (1998). Design principles for intelligent environments. In *Proceedings of the Fifteenth National Conference on Artificial Intelligence* (pp. 547-554).

Dey, A. K., & Abowd, G. D. (2000). Towards a better understanding of context and context-awareness. In []. Berlin, Germany: Springer-Verlag.]. *Proceedings of the Workshop on the What, Who, Where, When, and How of Context-Awareness, 4*, 1–6.

Harnad, S. (1990). The symbol grounding problem. *Physica D. Nonlinear Phenomena, 42*, 335–346. doi:10.1016/0167-2789(90)90087-6

Hasegawa, T., & Murakami, K. (2006). Robot town project: Supporting robots in an environment with its structured information. In *Proceedings of the 3rd International Conference on Ubiquitous Robots and Ambient Intelligence* (pp. 119-123).

Kidd, C. D., Orr, R., Abowd, G. D., Atkeson, C. G., Essa, I. A., MacIntyre, B., et al. (1999). The aware home: A living laboratory for ubiquitous computing research. In *Proceedings of the Second International Workshop on Cooperative Buildings, Integrating Information, Organization, and Architecture* (LNCS 1670, pp. 191-198).

Konno, S., Manabe, Y., Fujita, S., Sugawra, K., Kinoshita, T., & Shiratori, N. (2008). A framework for perceptual functions of symbiotic computing. In *Proceedings of the IEEE International Conference on Web Intelligence and Intelligent Agent Technology* (pp. 501-504).

Lee, J. H., Appenzeller, G., & Hashimoto, H. (1998). Physical agent for sensored, networked and thinking space. In. *Proceedings of the IEEE International Conference on Robotics and Automation, 1*, 838–843.

Lee, J. H., & Hashimoto, H. (2002). Intelligent space - concept and contents. *Advanced Robotics, 16*(3), 265–280. doi:10.1163/156855302760121936

Licklider, J. C. R. (1960). Man-computer symbiosis. *IRE Transactions on Human Factors in Electronics, 1*, 4–11. doi:10.1109/THFE2.1960.4503259

Manabe, Y., Fujita, S., Konno, S., Hara, H., & Sugawara, K. (2010). A concept of context-aware computing based on symbol grounding perspective. In *Proceedings of the International Symposium on Aware Computing* (pp. 86-91).

Murakami, K., Hasegawa, T., Kurazume, R., & Kimuro, Y. (2008). A structured environment with sensor networks for intelligent robots. In *Proceedings of the IEEE International Conference on Sensors* (pp. 705-708).

Nishida, Y., Hori, T., Suehiro, T., & Hirai, S. (2000). Sensorized environment for self-communication based on observation of daily human behavior. In *Proceedings of the IEEE/RSJ International Conference on Intelligent Robots and Systems* (pp. 1364-1372).

Pentland, A. (1996). Smart rooms, smart clothes. *Scientific American*, 68–76. doi:10.1038/scientificamerican0496-68

Poslad, S. (2009). *Ubiquitous computing: Smart devices, environments and interactions.* Chichester, UK: John Wiley & Sons.

Rudolph, L. (2001, June). Project oxygen: Pervasive, human-centric computing – an initial experience. In K. Dittrich, A. Geppert, & M. Norrie (Eds.), *Proceedings of the 13th International Conference on Advanced Information Systems Engineering,* Interlaken, Switzerland (LNCS 2068, pp. 1-12).

Sato, T., Nishida, Y., & Mizoguchi, H. (1996). Robotic room: Symbiosis with human through behavior media. *Robotics and Autonomous Systems, 18*(1-2), 185–194. doi:10.1016/0921-8890(96)00004-8

Schilit, B. N., & Theimer, M. M. (1994). Disseminating active map information to mobile hosts. *IEEE Network, 8*(5), 22–32. doi:10.1109/65.313011

Shafer, S., Krumm, J., Brumitt, B., Meyers, B., Czerwinski, M., & Robbins, D. (1998, July). The new EasyLiving project at Microsoft Research. In *Proceedings of the Joint DARPA/NIST Smart Spaces Workshop* (pp. 127-130).

Suganuma, T., Sugawara, K., Kinoshita, T., Hattori, F., & Shiratori, N. (2009). Concept of symbiotic computing and its agent-based Application to a ubiquitous care-support service. *International Journal of Cognitive Informatics and Natural Intelligence, 3*(1), 34–56. doi:10.4018/jcini.2009010103

Sugawara, K., Fujita, S., & Hara, H. (2007). A concept of symbiotic computing and its application to telework. In *Proceedings of the 6th IEEE Internatinal Conference on Cognitive Informatics,* Lake Tahoe, CA (pp. 302-311).

Sugawara, K., Fujita, S., Kinoshita, T., & Shiratori, N. (2008). A design of cognitive agents for recognizing real space –towards symbiotic computing. In *Proceedings of the 7th IEEE Internatinal Conference on Cognitive Informatics,* Stanford, CA (pp. 277-285).

Weiser, M. (1991). The computer for the twenty-first century. *Scientific American, 265*(3), 94–104. doi:10.1038/scientificamerican0991-94

This work was previously published in the International Journal of Software Science and Computational Intelligence, Volume 3, Issue 1, edited by Yingxu Wang, pp. 34-49, copyright 2011 by IGI Publishing (an imprint of IGI Global).

Chapter 22
Generic Cabling of Intelligent Buildings Based on Ant Colony Algorithm

Yunlong Wang
Tsinghua University, China

Kueiming Lo
Tsinghua University, China

ABSTRACT

Generic cabling is a key component for multiplex cable wiring. It is one of the basic foundations of intelligent buildings. Using operation flow in generic cabling, the index constraints affecting generic cabling have been evolved in this paper. A mathematical model is built based on the ant colony algorithm with multiple constraints, and improvements were made on the original basis to extend the ant colony algorithm from the regular simple ant colony and structure to a multi-ant colony and structure. The equilibrium settlement of multiplex wiring is realized according to the introduction of the multi-ant colony model. The ant cycle model is combined to extend the optimization target from the local wiring path to the entire wiring path, and to solve the drawbacks existing in the regular ant colony algorithm and other search algorithms that take the local wiring path as the optimization target. The introduced retrospective algorithm make the ants avoid the path marked "invalid" in the subsequent search process and improves the search performance and convergence speed of the ant colony algorithm.

INTRODUCTION

Intelligent buildings use computer technology and communication technology to monitor and control the equipment used in the buildings automatically, to manage information resources and to provide information services for users. Intelligent buildings are an important symbol of the information age; they are part of the international information superhighway and the intelligent urban network node. They play an important role because of their special function and efficiency.

DOI: 10.4018/978-1-4666-2651-5.ch022

Generic cabling is the physical basis of the high-speed information network in intelligent buildings and it is also the key component of intelligent building construction. Generic cabling is an information transmission media system that is made up of cable, optical fiber, various types of soft cable and related link hardware. Generic cabling can put the transmission medium and equipment into a certain order as an organic whole and support the transmission of voice, data, image and monitoring information (Xue, 2002). In the process of cabling, this paper will discuss how to meet the customers multiple constraints and reduce costs by using ant colony algorithm.

Djikstra's algorithm solves the single-source shortest-path problem when all edges have non-negative weights. It is usually used in the generic cabling system of intelligent buildings because it meets the users' simple and basic requirements. However, because intelligent buildings are becoming more intelligent, the traditional algorithm no longer meets the current complex needs.

The ant colony algorithm is a probabilistic technique for solving computational problems which can be reduced to finding good paths through graphs (Colorni, Dorigo, & Vaniezzo, 1991; Dorigo, 1992). The first algorithm was aiming to search for an optimal path in a graph; based on the behavior of ants seeking a path between their colony and a source of food. Investigation has revealed that the ant colony algorithm is a better algorithm with robustness; it provides a new way to solve complex combinatorial optimization problems (Ma & Xiang, 2001; Wang & See, 2009). It has been applied to many combinatorial optimization problems (Xing *et al.*, 2009; Garcia *et al.*, 2009), ranging from the multi-objective flexible job shop scheduling to the path planning for mobile robots and a lot of derived methods have been adapted to dynamic problems in real variables, stochastic problems, multi-targets and parallel implementations.

According to the users' requirements, we used the ant colony algorithm to solve the generic ca-

bling problem of intelligent buildings. The results prove that generic cabling with restriction based on the ant colony algorithm can meet the complex requirements and has better solution results, at the same time it can save much time for designers and workers and reduce the costs. Therefore, generic cabling with restriction based on the ant colony algorithm is very important, but also further enhances the level of intelligent buildings.

GENERIC CABLING SYSTEM

1. According to the description of generic cabling, before a generic cabling project is started, it is necessary to clear the known conditions; in other words, these conditions are the input of the problem. And the following describes the analysis of the known conditions:

    a. **Bridge:** It is also known as cable track or cable ladder used to place cables. Before the generic cabling of a building, engineers can discover the situation of the bridges laid from the drawings of civil work; therefore, the spatial position of the bridge is one of the known conditions.

    b. **Device:** Before the generic cabling, the location of every subsystem has been preassigned, and the position of each device that belongs to the subsystem has been preassigned, too. Therefore, the spatial position of the device is another known condition.

    c. **Connection Group:** Before the generic cabling, customers need to specify a number of connection groups (Flax, 1991), since different subsystems should be installed into different installations; this guarantees that there will be no interference between different subsystems. We can deal with a connection group as a device or a subsystem which will be presented as a node in the spatial net.

Based on the three known conditions above, we can generate a group of topology graphs, in which the bridge represents the edge, and the device represents the node in the graph. And now, the input of the problem in this paper is an undirected graph. The basic architecture is shown in Figure 1.

2. Additionally, before the generic cabling, customers will specify some other constraints; in this paper, the constraints are divided into two groups: mandatory and non-mandatory. The following are the mandatory constraints.

    a. **Fill Factor of the Bridge:** The bridge has its own attributes. One of the attributes is the cross-sectional area, and in the same way, the cable has its own cross-sectional area, too. Obviously, during the generic cabling, the sum of the cables' cross-sectional area should be less than a certain percentage of the bridge's cross-sectional area. This percentage is the fill factor, and it is specified by the customer. Generally, the value of the fill factor is from 60% to 70%, and the purpose of the fill factor is for expansion and contraction, extension, and so on (Ma & Xiang, 2001).

    b. **Matching between Cable and Bridge:** There are also some other attributes for the bridge, such as the voltage range, temperature range, acid and alkali resistance and diamagnetism (Han, 2004). The cable has related attributes. In this way, each cable going through the bridge must match the bridge according to these attributes.

    c. **Force Connection:** Before generic cabling, each device is numbered, for example, 01, 02, 03…, 09, and some customers may want some of the devices to be connected directly. It implies that the devices set to force-connected by specified bridge have to be connected at first. Naturally, the connections have the highest priority.

The following are the non-mandatory constraints:

Figure 1. Bridge topology architecture

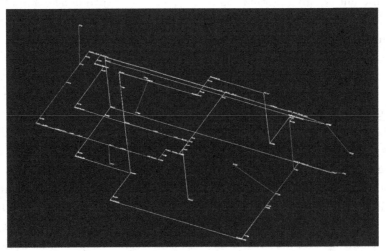

1. **Matching Level between Cable and Bridge:** During the generic cabling, according to the parameters of the cable and bridge, the cable can go through the bridge, and furthermore, we will compare the matching level, because we hope that the higher the matching level is, the more possible it will be to let the cable go through the bridge. In other words, to cable and cable, we try to make sure that every cable going through the bridge can stay more stable and won't be affected by each other in the process of working; to cable and bridge, we try to make sure cable is more suitable for the bridge, based on cable's attributes and bridge's attributes.

2. **Cost:** The cost is one of the problems customers care about most, since the cost of cable varies depending on the material, thickness, quality, and so on. Obviously, reducing the cost as much as possible is a goal.

In short, the problem is based on the premise of a given undirected topology graph and the need to meet the requirements of the mandatory constraints, and then, to find a solution that fits the non-mandatory constraints as closely as possible.

SYSTEM ANALYSIS

There are several restrictions during generic cabling in industry: restrictions of the bridge's cross-sectional area to the interior of the cables; restrictions of the maximum weight capacity of the bridge to the inside of the cables; restrictions in the compatibility and repellency between cable and bridge; restrictions in the compatibility and repellency between cable and cable; and restrictions to reduce costs. The former two are mandatory restrictions, they must be satisfied, and the other three are flexible; they should to be satisfied as much as possible. Related to these restrictions,

the problem can be abstracted by the following mathematical problems.

1. It can be abstracted with an undirected simple graph, which is composed of the bridges' finite set E and the devices' finite set V, named

$$G=(V, E, g, g_s, g_w, g_l, g_n).$$

And g is the injection from E to $V \times V$, g_s, g_w, and g_l are the mapping from E to the set of all non-negative real numbers i^+. $\forall e \in E$, $g_s(e)$ and $g_w(e)$ and $g_l(e)$ represent the cross-sectional area, maximum weight capacity and length. $\forall v \in V$, g_n is the mapping from v to the set of its adjacent edges, and the definition for the set of its adjacent edges as follows:

$$E_v = \{e \mid \text{if } \exists v' \neq v, \text{ satisfies } g(e) \rightarrow (v, v') \text{ or } g(e) \rightarrow (v', v)\}.$$

2. It can be abstracted by defining the set of all dimensionality vectors that are composed of elements in V, named Ω. If $\forall o \in \Omega$, set the dimensionality of o to dim(o), and set the i_{th} component to $o[i]$.

It can be abstracted with the set

$$H=(C, h_s, h_w, h_u), C \subset \Omega, \forall c \in C.$$

Its dimensionality satisfies: $0 < \dim(c) < +\infty$. h_s, h_w and h_u are the mapping from C to the set of all non-negative real numbers i^+. To any connection group $c \in C$, $h_s(c)$, $h_w(c)$, and $h_u(c)$ represent the cross-sectional area, the weight of the unit length and the price of the unit length of the cable which are related to the connection group.

It can be abstracted by defining the mapping

$$\psi : C \times C \rightarrow [-1, 1]$$

to represent the compatibility and repellency between cable and cable. Stipulate $\forall c \in C$, $\psi(c,c) \equiv 1$. $\forall c_i, c_j \in C$; if the value of $\psi(c_i,c_j)$ is larger, then the matching level is higher; if the value is lower, the matching level is lower.

Definite the mapping:

$$\phi : E \times C \to [-1, 1]$$

It represents the compatibility and repellency between cable and bridge. $\forall e \in E$, $\forall c \in C$, if the value of $\phi(e,c)$ is larger, then the matching level is higher, conversely, lower.

To resolve the problem of cabling means to generate the set of cabling paths $W \subset \Omega$ and mapping:

$$f : C \to W, \text{ such that } \forall c \in C, \ w = f(c),$$

1. $\forall w[k], w[k+1](k = 1,2,\ldots \dim(w)-1)$,
   $\exists e \in E$ satisfy $g(e) \to (w[k], w[k+1])$ or
   $g(e) \to (w[k+1], w[k])$.
   This represents that cabling path w must be continuous;

2. $\forall c[i] (i = 1,2,\ldots m)$, satisfy
   $c[i] \in \{w[k] \mid k = 1,2,3,\ldots \dim[w]\}$;
   This represents that cabling path w must pass through all the nodes that belong to the connection group c;

3. $\dim(w) < +\infty$; this represents that the length of cabling path w cannot be infinite;

4. $\forall e \in E$,
   $$\lambda_s(e) = \frac{\sum\limits_{c \in C} \delta(e, f(c)) h_s(c)}{g_s(e)} \leq 1$$

This represents that the sum of the cross-sectional area of cables that pass through the bridge must be less than the bridge's cross-sectional area;

5. $\forall e \in E$,
   $$\lambda_w(e) = \frac{\sum\limits_{c \in C} \delta(e, f(c)) h_w(c) g_l(e)}{g_w(e)} \leq 1$$

This represents that the sum of the weight of cables that pass through the bridge must be less than the bridge's maximum weight capacity;

6. $\forall e \in E$, let
   $$\overline{\psi}(e) = \frac{\sum\limits_{c_i,c_j \in C} \delta(e, f(c_i))\delta(e, f(c_j))\psi(c_i,c_j)}{\sum\limits_{c_i,c_j \in C} \delta(e, f(c_i))\delta(e, f(c_j))}$$
   approaches to 1

It can be certified that: $-1 \leq \overline{\psi}(e) \leq 1$; this represents that make the cables with a higher matching level with each other pass through the same bridge as much as possible;

7. $\forall e \in E$, let
   $$\overline{\varphi}(e) = \frac{\sum\limits_{c \in C} \delta(e, f(c))\varphi(e,c)}{\sum\limits_{c \in C} \delta(e, f(c))} \text{ approaches to 1}$$

It can be certified that: $-1 \leq \overline{\phi}(e) \leq 1$; this represents that make the cables with a higher matching level to bridge e pass through the bridge;

8. The definition of the whole cost is:
   $$\mu = \sum_{e \in E} \sum_{c \in C} \delta(e, f(c)) h_u(c) g_l(e)$$

It can be certified that: $\mu \geq 0$, and needs to be reduced as much as possible. $\forall e \in E$, and $\forall w \in W$, function $\delta(e,w)$ represents the times which cabling path w passed through the bridge e.

$$\delta(e, w) = \sum_{k=1}^{\dim[w]-1} \sigma(e, w[k], w[k+1])$$

is its definition. $\forall e \in E$, $\forall v_i, v_j \in V$, function $\sigma(e, v_i, v_j)$ represent that if the nodes v_i and v_j are the endpoints of the bridge e, the following is the definition:

$$\sigma(e, v_i, v_j) = \begin{cases} 1, & \text{if } g(e) \to (v_i, v_j) \text{ or } g(e) \to (v_j, v_i) \\ 0, & \text{other} \end{cases}$$

To evaluate and compare the result of cabling, it is necessary to converts multiple optimized targets to a single target. With regards to this, Ψ is defined, and represents the average of all bridges' $\bar{\psi}(e)$, and Φ is also defined, representing the average of all bridges' $\bar{\varphi}(e)$. In order to compare them with the cost μ, Ψ and Φ have been normalized to the interval $[0,1]$.

$$\Psi = \frac{1}{2}\left(\frac{\sum\limits_{e \in E} \bar{\psi}(e)}{\dim(E)} + 1\right), \Phi = \frac{1}{2}\left(\frac{\sum\limits_{e \in E} \bar{\varphi}(e)}{\dim(E)} + 1\right)$$

Additionally, the whole cost μ needs to be normalized to interval $[0,1]$. Assume that the maximum and minimum of the cost are μ_{max} and μ_{min}; then there are two methods for normalization:

$$1 - \frac{\mu}{\mu_{max}} \text{ and } \frac{\mu_{min}}{\mu}.$$

Although it is difficult to define and calculate μ_{max}, even though it is hard to calculate μ_{min}, but we can choose the minimum μ^*_{min} from the multiple results to obtain it. As a result, we adopt μ^*_{min}/μ as the normalized result of μ. The following is the definition:

$$M = \frac{\mu^*_{min}}{\mu}$$

And now, we have converted the evaluating indicator from multiple to single, and the goal is to make the values of Ψ and Φ and M as large as possible at the same time. In this case, define the comprehensive evaluating indicator η_x:

$$\eta_x = \Psi^{\alpha}\Phi^{\beta}M^{(1-\alpha-\beta)}$$

α and β in the formula above are the undetermined constants; they represent the weight factor of related indicators, and they are specified by the customer. They satisfy: $\alpha \geq 0$, $\beta \geq 0$, $\alpha + \beta \leq 1$.. In this case, the range of η_x is $[0,1]$. So far, we can take the cabling problem as solving the maximum of η_x with the restrictions from 1) to 8).

MATHEMATICAL MODELING

In order to construct the set of cabling path $W \subset \Omega$ (Ω is the set of all vectors which consists of all the nodes in the bridge net) and mapping

$f: C \to W$

An ant ac is needed to assign for each connection group $c \in C$ (Dorigo & Luca, 1996), and all of these ants construct a set of the ant colony AC, and the bijection from C to AC is

$\zeta : C \to AC$

Since the cabling path is implemented by an ant colony, we can converting the problem of constructing f into the problem of constructing the mapping from AC to W. Assume the mapping

$\xi : AC \to W$, then, $f = \xi \bullet \zeta$.

Construct the mapping

$f_k: AC \times E \to Pher.\ Pher \subset i^+$

is the set for the pheromone concentration (Wang & Wu, 2003). $\forall ac \in AC$, $\forall e \in E$, $f_\kappa(ac, e)$ represents the distributed pheromone concentration on bridge e by the ant ac. In the initial moments, assume $\forall pher \in Pher$, $pher = \kappa$ ($\kappa \geq 0$).

At the beginning of each cycle, the ant $ac \in AC$ chooses a random node from the connection group $c = \zeta^{-1}(ac)$ as the start node, and then all the ants enter into the path finding a status, until all the ants finish work or one of the ants fails (Duan, Wang, & Yu, 2006). $\forall ac \in AC$; assume that the ant is located in node $v \in V$ at a certain moment, and then, define the probability of selecting the bridge $e \in g_n(v)$ as the next step, as follows (Sheng, 2005):

$$p(v, e, ac) = \frac{\chi(v, e, ac)}{\sum_{e \in f_n(v)} \chi(v, e, ac)}.$$

Definite the utility function of selecting the bridge e when the ant ac is located in node v as follows in Box 1.

In the formula above, the meanings of constants α and β are same as they are in η_x, and the constants $\theta, \vartheta > 0$. $\forall v \in V$, $\forall ac \in AC$, $\forall e \in E$, and the definition of the functions $\rho(v, e, ac)$, $\omega(e, ac)$, $\varphi(e, ac)$, $\gamma(v, e, ac)$, $s(e, ac)$ and $w(e, ac)$ are as follows:

$$\rho(v, e, ac) = \frac{f_\kappa(ac, e)}{\sum_{\tau \in f_n(v)} f_\kappa(ac, \tau)}.$$

Function $\rho(v, e, ac)$ represents the pheromone concentration, and it is normalized to $[0, 1]$:

$$w(e, ac) = \frac{1}{2} \left(\frac{\sum_{\varepsilon_1 \in AC} \delta(e, \xi(\varepsilon_1)) \psi(\zeta^{-1}(ac), \zeta^{-1}(\varepsilon_1))}{\sum_{\varepsilon_2 \in AC} \delta(e, \xi(\varepsilon_2))} + 1 \right)$$

Function $w(e, ac)$ represents the compatibility and repellency between the cable related to the ant ac and the cables located in the bridge e, and it is normalized to $[0, 1]$:

$$\phi(e, ac) = \frac{1}{2} \left(\varphi(e, \zeta^{-1}(ac)) + 1 \right) \cdot$$

Function $\varphi(e, ac)$ represents the compatibility and repellency between the cable related to the ant ac and the bridge e. It is normalized to $[0, 1]$:

$$\gamma(v, e, ac) = 1 - \frac{h_u\left(\zeta^{-1}(ac)\right) g_l(e)}{\sum_{\tau \in g_n(v)} h_u\left(\zeta^{-1}(ac)\right) g_l(\tau)}$$

Function $\gamma(v, e, ac)$ represents the cost to pay if the ant ac which is in node v chooses the bridge e as the next path, and it is normalized to $[0, 1]$.

$$s(e, ac) = \max \left\{ \frac{g_s(e) - h_s(\zeta^{-1}(ac)) - \sum_{\varepsilon \in C} \delta(e, \xi(\varepsilon)) h_s(\zeta^{-1}(\varepsilon))}{g_s(e)}, 0 \right\}$$

Function $s(e, ac)$ represents the percentage of the bridge's residual cross-sectional area to the bridge's total cross-sectional area if the cable related to the ant ac passes through the bridge e, and it is normalized to $[0, 1]$.

Box 1.

$$\chi(v, e, ac) = s(e, ac) w(e, ac) \rho^\theta(v, e, ac) \left(w^\alpha(e, ac) \phi^\beta(e, ac) \gamma^{(1-\alpha-\beta)}(v, e, ac) \right)^\vartheta$$

$$w(e, ac) =$$

$$\max \left\{ \frac{g_w(e) - h_w(\zeta^{-1}(ac)) - \sum_{\varepsilon \in C} \delta(e, \xi(\varepsilon)) h_w(\zeta^{-1}(\varepsilon))}{g_w(e)}, 0 \right\}$$

Function $w(e, ac)$ represents the percentage of the bridge's residual weight capacity to the bridge's total weight capacity if the cable related to the ant ac pass through the bridge e, and it is normalized to $[0, 1]$. According to the formulas above, the range of $\chi(v, e, ac)$ is $[0, 1]$.

It should be noted that, since the bridge network G is not always a complete connected graph, and each bridge has its restrictions, such as weight capacity and the compatibility and repellency with the cable, as a result, some of the ants may fail to find the path. Therefore, we introduced backtracking (Gambardella & Dorigo, 1995). In this case, the ant returns back along the original path when it meets a dead end, until it returns back to a node that exists or until other adjacent bridges can be chosen, and it will mark the path as invalid. In this case, it prevents other ants from interring into the dead ends again.

On the operation of pheromone's volatilization and updating, the method introduced in this paper uses the idea from the model of the Ant-Cycle, which is from Dorigo and Stutzle (2004). In this model, the pheromone will be volatilized and updated after a successful cycle, and the volatilization will be taken on all edges. $\forall pher \in Pher$; the following is the definition of the pheromone volatilization function (Dorigo & Stutzle, 2004; Stutzle & Hoos, 2000):

$$pher \leftarrow pher \bullet (1 - q)$$

Constant q is the rate of the pheromone volatilization, and $0 < q < 1$.

The operation of the pheromone updating will be carried out on the path that is found by any ant in the current cycle. $\forall ac \in AC$; the cabling path

is $w = \xi(ac)$. The following is the pheromone updating formula on edge (Thomas *et al.*, 2001)

$$e = g^{-1}((w[i], w[i+1]))\ (i = 1, 2, \dots \dim(w) - 1)$$

$$pher \leftarrow pher + \Delta \kappa \eta_x, \text{ and constant } \Delta \kappa > 0.$$

Experiments

With respect to the mathematical model described above, in this paper, we tested it with four sets of data, as listed in Table 1.

Each set of data was calculated ten times, and there are 500 cycles each time. The parameters were set as follows: set $\alpha = 0.33333$, $\beta = 0.33333$, $\Delta \kappa = 0.1$ and $q = 0.05$. Figure 2 shows the average curve of η_x. The chart demonstrates satisfactory astringency of the model. The slope was larger at the early time, which reflects the diversity of the solutions, and then converges to a better solution.

Table 2 shows the average and standard deviation. From the last field in the table, the solutions are better except for the last set. Referring to the input data of the last set, there are more nodes and edges. This meant that it took longer to calculate η_x, but it can be improve by expanding the time.

Table 1. Simulated data

	Bridge net		Connection group	
	Count of nodes	Count of edges	Count	Average count of nodes
First set	110	117	2	14.5
Second set	110	118	5	30.8
Third set	95	123	5	33.2
Fourth set	252	297	3	20

Table 2. Average and standard deviation of η_x

	Average	**Standard deviation**	**Standard deviation / Average**
First set	0.941072	0.0453249	0.0481631
Second set	0.909570	0.0417983	0.0459539
Third set	0.969426	0.0203151	0.0209558
Fourth set	0.856579	0.1007400	0.1176080

CONCLUSION

With the increasingly complex needs of generic cabling, the principle of generic cabling has been concerned in this paper. It is translated generic cabling into an NP-complete problem. Then for the complex requirements of modern generic cabling a mathematical model based on the ant colony algorithm has been established. At the same time the basic ant colony algorithm is modified to include a number of ants cabling. A parallel processing generic cabling problem is added and expanded the optimization objectives. Finally, the experimental data showed that this algorithm had better convergence and effective solution.

This paper discussed application of the ant colony algorithm in the generic cabling of intelligent buildings. Actually, it can be applied to the projects outside of intelligent buildings, such as mining projects.

Mining project has cabling work as well. Different motors have to be connected to Busbar (power supply) and PLC (motor control) by cables. These cables have to go through cable ladders which are similar as the bridge mentioned above. One more constraint for generic cabling in mining project is to try reducing the number of bend of each cable. This is because it will be hard for workers to pull and install in the site if the cable has too many bends. And a cable with many bends is easier to be broken in the process of pulling.

The difference of mining projects from intelligent buildings is that the cable ladder is position-changeable before generic cabling. In other words, both the cable ladder position and the cable position are variables going to be calculated. However, how to cabling depends on the position

Figure 2. Average curve of η_x

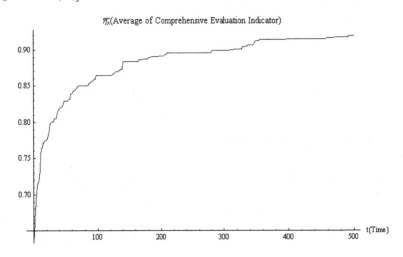

of the cable ladder. Meanwhile, what kind of cable ladder could be used depends on how many cables going through the ladder.

So, two groups of ants can be released to seek the path for both ladder and cable at the same time. This is a parallel calculation.

ACKNOWLEDGMENT

This work is funded by NSFC 60973049, 60635020 and TNList cross-discipline foundations.

REFERENCES

Colorni, A., Dorigo, M., & Maniezzo, V. (1991). Distributed optimization by ant colonies. In *Proceedings of the Actes de la Première Conférence Européenne sur la Vie Artificielle*, Paris, France (pp. 134-142).

Dorigo, M. (1992). *Optimization, learning and natural algorithms.* Unpublished doctoral dissertation, Politecnico di Milano, Milan, Italy.

Dorigo, M., & Gambardella, L. M. (1996). *Study of some properties of ants* (Tech. Rep. No. TR/IRIDIA/1996-4). Brussels, Belgium: University Librede Bruxelles.

Dorigo, M., & Stützle, T. (2004). *Ant colony optimization.* Cambridge, MA: MIT Press. doi:10.1007/b99492

Duan, H. B., Wang, D. B., & Yu, X. F. (2006). Novel approach to nonlinear PID parameter optimization using ant colony optimization algorithm. *Journal of Bionics Engineering, 3*(2), 73–78. doi:10.1016/S1672-6529(06)60010-3

Flax, B. M. (1991). Intelligent buildings. *IEEE Communications Magazine, 4*(1), 24–27. doi:10.1109/35.76555

Gambardella, L. M., & Dorigo, M. (1995). Ant-Q: A reinforcement learning approach to the traveling salesman problem. In *Proceedings of the 12th International Conference on Machine Learning,* Tahoe City, CA (pp. 252-260).

Garcia, M. A. P., Montiel, O., Castillo, O., Sepúlveda, R., & Melin, P. (2009). Path planning for autonomous mobile robot navigation with ant colony optimization and fuzzy cost function evaluation. *Applied Soft Computing, 9*(3), 1102–1110. doi:10.1016/j.asoc.2009.02.014

Han, C. M. (2004). *Academic analysis and software realization of generic cabling* (pp. 35–87). Beijing, China: Southeast University.

Ma, L., & Xiang, P. J. (2001). Application of ant algorithm in combinatorial optimization. *Journal of Management Sciences in China, 4*(2), 32–37.

Sheng, Z. H. (2005). *Probability theory and mathematical statistics* (3rd ed.). Beijing, China: Higher Education Press.

Stutzle, T., & Hoos, H. H. (2000). MAX-MIN ant system. *Future Generation Computer Systems, 16*(9), 889–914. doi:doi:10.1016/S0167-739X(00)00043-1

Thomas, H. C., Charles, E. L., Ronald, L. R., & Clifford, S. (2001). *Introduction to algorithms* (2nd ed.). Cambridge, MA: MIT Press.

Wang, L., & Wu, Q. D. (2003). Application of ant colony algorithm in solving optimization problems in continuous space. *Control and Decision, 18*(1), 45–48.

Wong, K. Y., & See, P. C. (2009). A new minimum pheromone threshold strategy (MPTS) for max-min ant system. *Applied Soft Computing, 9*(3), 882–888. doi:10.1016/j.asoc.2008.11.011

Xing, L. N., Chen, Y. W., & Yang, K. W. (2009). Multi-objective flexible job shop schedule: Design and evaluation by simulation modeling. *Applied Soft Computing*, *9*(1), 362–376. doi:10.1016/j. asoc.2008.04.013

Xue, S. S. (2002). *Intelligent building and generic cabling system*. Beijing, China: Posts and Telecom Press.

Chapter 23
Potentials of Quadratic Neural Unit for Applications

Ricardo Rodriguez
Czech Technical University in Prague, Czech Republic, & Technological University of Ciudad Juarez, Mexico

Ivo Bukovsky
Czech Technical University in Prague, Czech Republic, & Tohoku University, Japan

Noriyasu Homma
Tohoku University, Japan

ABSTRACT

The paper discusses the quadratic neural unit (QNU) and highlights its attractiveness for industrial applications such as for plant modeling, control, and time series prediction. Linear systems are still often preferred in industrial control applications for their solvable and single solution nature and for the clarity to the most application engineers. Artificial neural networks are powerful cognitive nonlinear tools, but their nonlinear strength is naturally repaid with the local minima problem, overfitting, and high demands for application-correct neural architecture and optimization technique that often require skilled users. The QNU is the important midpoint between linear systems and highly nonlinear neural networks because the QNU is relatively very strong in nonlinear approximation; however, its optimization and performance have fast and convex-like nature, and its mathematical structure and the derivation of the learning rules is very comprehensible and efficient for implementation. These advantages of QNU are demonstrated by using real and theoretical examples.

INTRODUCTION

During last ten years of our research, we investigated nonconventional neural architectures and their applications to modeling of dynamical systems, control, prediction, and novel evaluation of dynamic systems. In this paper, we review

some achievements with quadratic neural unit (QNU) (Gupta et al., 2003; Bukovsky et al., 2009) in order to highlight its aspects for real applications. Generally from nowadays point of view, QNU can be considered a special class of polynomial neural network or as a special unit of higher order neural networks that are getting very

DOI: 10.4018/978-1-4666-2651-5.ch023

popular today (Ivakhnenko, 1971; Zhang, 2010). The important aspects of QNU discussed in this paper are not unknown, but they are unnecessarily shadowed by focusing on many various too nonlinear neural networks (NN). Today, we can notice enthusiasm about theoretical validations for stability and convergence of powerful cognitive systems such as NN, fuzzy systems, to name but a few in real applications. The theoretical achievements can be difficult to understand and can be costly, at least timely to be applied without thorough mathematical background and without rich experiences in the relevant fields. For example, multilayer perceptron NN (MLP) are very often called universal function approximators; however, it is not usually considered (stated) that it is valid rather from the theoretical point of view; the local minima problem and the related overfitting can disqualify a trained neural model for its real application with new testing data. Thus, managers and process engineers still may not always have full trust or interest in applying the relatively complicated theoretical NN, especially in contrast to the uniqueness of the solution of linear systems and their solvability. Nevertheless, we do not have to use always complicated and too nonlinear NN to achieve superior results with real applications for many (industrial) processes.

Studies of nonconventional neural units have been running on investigation of QNU and Cubic Neural Unit (CNU), mainly, denoted also by higher order (nonlinear) neural units (HONU) (Gupta et al., 2003; Bukovsky et al., 2009). In Ivakhnenko (1971) author deals with polynomial networks. In Gupta et al. (2003) one of the first notations of higher order neural units was introduced. In Bukovsky et al. (2003), Quadratic Neural Unit and Cubic Neural Unit were presented for fast state feedback control of nonlinear systems; for unstable and unknown nonlinear dynamic systems, indicating the capability of the neural units for faster response than a liner state feedback controllers. Also, the stability criteria of a non-linear control loop that include QNU and CNU were analyzed.

Later, a new classification of nonconventional neural units was proposed by Bukovsky et al. (2007) where a very comprehensible mathematical structure was remained. These neural architectures were settled to an understandable description with respect to conventional neural networks that usually are seen as black box or gray box. However, not only the last advantages were obtained, also a minimum number of neural elements were needed for maximum approximation capabilities. In Bukovsky et al. (2008), it was shown that a low dimensional quadratic neural unit can be used for adaptive evaluation of higher dimensional chaotic systems. Here, static and dynamic neural units were applied by the gradient descent based on back-propagation learning rule. Recently, in Bukovsky et al. (2010a), it was presented a Discrete Dynamic QNU applied to predict lung respiration dynamics using the real time recurrent learning for dynamic QNU. The prediction time considered was long term and the results obtained were very promising comparing with the recent literature. In Bukovsky et al. (2010b) a novel Quadratic Neural Network (QNN) based on the Quadratic Neural Unit to model measured data in energetic processes was presented. The authors used a sequential learning to reduce computational time with the large number of inputs and show nonlinear approximation for the real process. A comparison between QNU, QNN and Multilayer Perceptron trained by Levenberg-Marquard algorithm was also presented.

In the next section we recall mathematical simplicity of static QNU and dynamic QNU and also the easiness of their fundamental supervised learning techniques. Then we review some most important results from our applications and we highlight most significant attributes of QNU in discussion, where we conclude why QNU is the important and promising compromise between limited linear models and highly nonlinear neural networks for real applications, especially, for technical systems.

STRUCTURE AND LEARNING OF QNU

It can be basically distinguished between static and dynamic (recurrent) version of QNU and the dynamic version can be implemented in a discrete time or a continuous time version (e.g., Bukovsky et al., 2009). The most comprehensible and very useful supervised learning rules are the famous Levenberg-Marquardt (L-M) (batch adaptation) rule and the gradient descent (sample by sample) rule, which is also known as real time recurrent learning (RTRL) for dynamic neural networks (Williams & Zipser, 1989). The notation, is the learning rate $\mu > 0$ the error e between the reference y_r and the neural output y_n, $e = y_r - y_n$, the column vector j_{ij} that is a column vector of the Jacobian matrix whose definition varies according to the type of QNU and according to the definition of neural input vector **x**, w_{ij} denotes neural weights, n_s is the prediction time for discrete dynamic QNU, and m is the number of external inputs. The next two sections show fundamental mathematical structures of QNUs and present the sample by sample and batch adaptation rules.

Static Quadratic Neural Unit

QNU may be considered as a case of polynomial neural network architecture or as special case of higher order neural unit. The aim with polynomial curve fitting is to fit a polynomial to a set of n data points by minimizing an error function. The static QNU is sketched in Figure 1.

The elements of the static quadratic neural unit are given in Equation (1). Where yn is the neural output $x_1, x_2, \ldots, x_n$ are external neural inputs, and W stands for upper triangular weight matrix (Gupta et al. 2003).

$$y_n = \sum_{i=0}^{n} \sum_{j=i}^{n} x_i x_j w_{ij} = x^T W x \qquad (1)$$

According to the above, x denotes $(1+n) \times 1$ vector with bias $x_0 = 1$ and W is the above mentioned $(1+n) \times (1+n)$ upper triangular weight matrix shown in Equation (2).

$$x = \begin{bmatrix} 1 \\ x_1 \\ \vdots \\ x_n \end{bmatrix} \qquad W = \begin{bmatrix} w_{00} & w_{01} & \cdots & w_{0n} \\ 0 & w_{11} & \cdots & w_{1n} \\ \vdots & \ddots & \ddots & \vdots \\ 0 & \cdots & 0 & w_{nn} \end{bmatrix} \qquad (2)$$

Using gradient descent learning rule to minimize the square error at each time k, the adaptation of the static QNU can be written for each single neural weight and for each k sample number by means of sample by sample adaptation as in Equation (3).

$$w_{ij}(k+1) = w_{ij}(k) + \Delta w_{ij}(k)$$

$$\Delta w_{ij}(k) = \frac{1}{2}\mu e(k)^2 = \mu e(k) x_i(k) x_j(k) \qquad (3)$$

Figure 1. Static QNU architecture

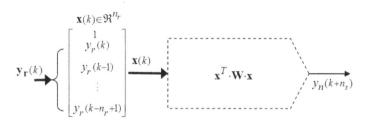

In the Levenberg Marquard optimization, sometimes called batch optimization the whole training set is presented for every weight update (epoch). The common formula for calculation of weight increments is presented in Equation (4). Where N denotes the number of samples (data length).

$$\triangle w_{ij} = -(j_{ij}^T \cdot j_{ij} + \frac{1}{\mu})^{-1} \cdot j_{ij}^T \cdot e$$

$$j_{ij} = \frac{\partial y_n}{\partial w_{ij}} = \begin{bmatrix} x_i(1)x_j(1) \\ x_i(2)x_j(2) \\ \vdots \\ x_i(N)x_j(N) \end{bmatrix} \tag{4}$$

where $\triangle w_{ij}$ stands for the incremental change for the weight updating e is the vector of errors, ^{T} stands for transposition and j_{ij} contains the first derivatives of the network errors with respect to weights and biases in all patterns.

Discrete Dynamic QNU

The architecture of dynamic QNU is shown in Figure 2, where $y_n(k+ns)=x^TWx$ and y_r stands for the real value. Typically for time series prediction: $x_1(k)=y_r(k)$ and $x_m(k)=y_r(k-m+1)$.

The derivation of the implemented supervised adaptation learning for sample by sample adaptation using RTRL is presented in Equation (5). We use gradient descent to minimize the square of the error at each prediction time k, j_{ij} is a vector of Jacobian matrix of neural inputs starting from zero initial conditions.

$$\triangle w_{ij}(k) = \mu e(k)\frac{\partial y_n(k+n_s)}{\partial w_{ij}}$$

$$\frac{\partial y_n(k+n_s)}{\partial w_{ij}} = \frac{\partial(x^TWx)}{\partial w_{ij}} = j_{ij}^TWx + x_ix_j + x^TWj_{ij}$$

$$j_{ij} = \frac{\partial x}{\partial w_{ij}} =$$
$$\begin{bmatrix} 0 & \frac{\partial y_n(k+n_s-1)}{\partial w_{ij}} & \frac{\partial y_n(k+n_s-2)}{\partial w_{ij}} & \cdots & \frac{\partial y_n(k+1)}{\partial w_{ij}} & 0\cdots0 \end{bmatrix}^T \tag{5}$$

The vector of Jacobian matrix is recurrent evolved during adaptation, where $j_{ij}(k+1)$ is shifted $j_{ij}(k)$ with the value as on the second row.

Continuous Dynamic QNU (Example of 2nd Order Dynamics)

The neural weights are adapted by RTRL sample by sample learning rule. The dynamics order is referred as the number of integrations of neural aggregated variable, i.e., the dynamic order is the number of time derivatives of internal neural state variable. In the Equation (6) the sample by sample adaptation for continuous Dynamic QNU is presented using RTRL learning rule.

$$\triangle w_{ij}(k) = \mu e(t)\frac{\partial y_n(t)}{\partial w_{ij}}$$

$$\frac{\partial y_n(t)}{\partial w_{ij}} =$$
$$\frac{\partial}{\partial w_{ij}} \int\int(x^TWx)dt^2 = \int\int(j_{ij}^TWx + x_ix_j + x^TWj_{ij})dt^2$$

$$j_{ij} =$$
$$\begin{bmatrix} 0 & \frac{\partial y_n(t)}{\partial w_{ij}} & \frac{\partial y_n'(t)}{\partial w_{ij}} & 0\cdots0 \end{bmatrix}^T, \frac{\partial y_n''(t)}{\partial w_{ij}} = \tag{6}$$
$$j_{ij}^TWx + x_ix_j + x^TWj_{ij}$$

Figure 2. Dynamic QNU architecture

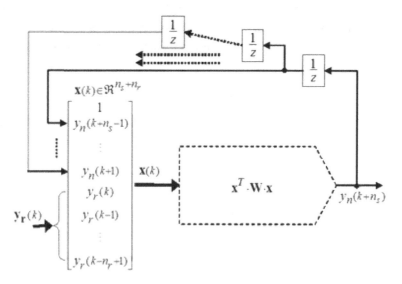

The goal of this section was to highlight the simplicity of mathematical notation of static and dynamic QNUs and clarity of their supervised learning rules. QNU and its learning rules can be very efficiently realized in software environments that work with matrix operations such as Matlab, Python, Scilab, and so on.

In the next section, we review and discuss some important results of QNU implementations to real systems and to real data and we highlight important aspects of QNUs that are important for practical applications.

APPLICATIONS AND ASPECTS OF QNUS

In this section, we review some of our recent results and highlight important aspects that emerge from results of applications of QNU to real processes (Bukovsky & Bila, 2007, 2008a, 2008b, 2010; Smetana, 2008) supported with some theoretical results (Bukovsky et al., 2003, 2008; Bukovsky & Bila, 2008a, 2010).

The first remarkable attribute of global-solution-like nature of QNU is demonstrated in Figure

3 with the application of static QNU to redundant modeling (and data validation) of measured data of energetic processes (Bukovsky & Bila, 2007, 2008b); QNUs and MLP NN were trained by L-M algorithm to model individual process variables (17 input variables - single output). The MLP neural networks and QNUs were trained from various initial conditions and we can clearly see in Figure 3 that outputs of QNU have smaller variance compared to MLP NN.

In other words, all the QNUs that were trained from various initial conditions were converged to much more similar results contrary to the outputs of MLP NN that had much larger variance. To demonstrate the universality of QNU, Figure 4 shows the superior results of control of real laboratory system bathyscaph (Hofreiter, 2010; Klan et al., 2005) where QNU was used as the internal adaptive model and also as an adaptive state feedback controller (Smetana, 2008). We have also confirmed the similar results theoretically (Bukovsky et al., 2003).

In Figure 5, we demonstrate the approximation strength of dynamic QNU on the prediction of time series generated by MacKey–Glass equation in chaotic regime that was obtained with sampling

Figure 3. The picture compares the variance of outputs of all static 10xQNU and 20xMLP neural networks for redundant modeling of real turbine hot steam flow (trained networks tested on a new data) (Bukovsky & Bila, 2007; Bukovsky & Bila, 2008b; Bukovsky et al., 2010b); the solid lines are the measured process variable (blue) and the vertically averaged value (green); the lighter dots (cyan, yellow) are redundant values by MLP networks that have much larger variance than outputs of QNU; sampling interval is 5 minutes

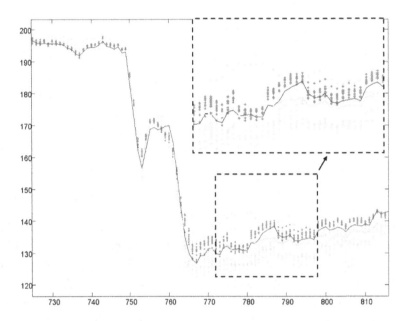

interval of 1 second. The green color in Figure 5 shows testing of the trained QNU for prediction 11 samples ahead (11 seconds). The middle red curve shows the error between the predicted and the original value. The dynamic QNU was adapted (RTRL) in epochs on 1000 training samples as shown in Figure 6 and the testing is performed as a pure prediction (without adaptation) on new following 1000 samples.

In the next section, we discuss the important aspects of the above reviewed results that signify the attractive properties of QNU for real and reliable applications.

DISCUSSION

Figure 6 compares learning performance of dynamic QNU with recurrent linear predictor (dynamic linear neural unit –DLNU) and with a conventional recurrent neural network (RNN). The architecture of the DLNU used for time series prediction is shown in the Equation (7).

$$y_n(k + n_s) =$$
$$\sum_{i=1}^{n_s-1} w_i \cdot y_n(k + n_s - i) + \sum_{i=0}^{m-1} w_{n_s} + i \cdot y_r(k - i)$$
(7)

Where, similarly to the notation, y_n denotes the neural output (i.e., the predicted values), y_r stands for real (measured) values, w_i are neural weights, n_s is prediction time, and m is the number of measured values. The RNN architecture consists of the recurrent hidden layer of (ten) neurons with linear aggregation function and sigmoid output function and with a linear static output neuron (Bukovsky & Homma, 2010).

Figure 4. Comparison of the state feedback QNU control (magenta) with classical PID control (green) of a real dynamic system bathyscaph (Smetana,2008; Hofreiter, 2010; Klan et al., 2005)

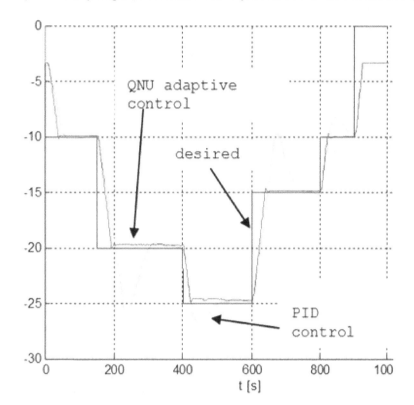

We have found that the situation shown in Figure 6 is the typical situation for learning performance of QNU, either static or dynamic for either RTRL adaptation or L-M training.

We can observe in Figure 6 that the dynamic QNU adapts faster and much precisely than the DLNU, and also that QNU tends to be similarly accurate as RNN; however, RNN displays temporary getting stacked in a poor local minima while QNU almost always does not get stacked.

As an attempt to investigate and visualize the issue of local minima during learning of QNU, we present Figure 7; the figure shows how 20xDLNU, 20xDQNU, and 20xRNN were trained to the chaotic MacKey-Glass time series (Figure 5 and Figure 6) from various initial conditions.

Figure 5. Prediction of chaotic MacKey-Glass equation (normalized data) by the discrete dynamic QNU (Tab. 1); the 11 seconds ahead prediction is superimposed on original data and the middle line is the error between original and predicted values (Bukovsky & Homma, 2010; Bukovsky et al., 2010a); dynamic QNU has surprising prediction accuracy

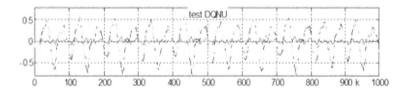

Figure 6. The typical situation when QNU is almost always trained to the minimum of high accuracy and without getting stacked in some less accurate local minima (SSE...sum of square errors)

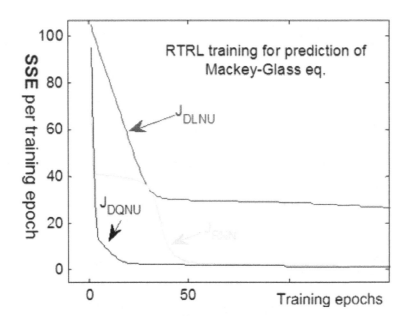

The vertical axis represents the prediction performance ($J(\mathbf{W})$...SSE=sum of square errors) tested on non-training data after each epoch of training. Then, the upper part of the figure locates the sum of square errors after first epoch of training and the markers fall down as the prediction accuracy improves with each epoch of training. The value on the horizontal axis is the absolute Euclidean distance of the neural weight configuration measured from the corresponding best trained neural architecture. Thus, the best trained DLNU, RNN, and DQNU converge (fall down) into the origin and the neural architectures that get stack in worse local minima converges toward the bottom–right part of the chart.

The summary of QNU aspects resulting from this section is as follows:

- QNU has smaller variance of neural outputs when trained from various initial conditions than the common MLP NN (Figure 3), (Bukovsky & Bila, 2007, 2008b; Bukovsky et al., 2010b),

- QNU has attractive quality of nonlinear approximation (Figure 3, Figure 4, Figure 5), (Bukovsky & Bila, 2007, 2008b, 2010; Smetana, 2008),

- QNU does not suffer from the existence of multiple local minima such as conventional neural networks do when common and simple learning algorithms are used (Figure 6, Figure 7).

The above aspects were observed in many experimental analyses that involved also real data case–studies. From the fundamental point of view, of course, all these conclusions are natural to the quadratic system, i.e., to QNU, and relate to its convex character and non–multiple solution nature such as when the linear equation has only one solution and quadratic equation can have two solutions.

Therefore, we summarize this section by Figure 8 that conceptually sketches error surfaces of linear models, the common MLP neural networks, and QNUs. We can see that linear models can be trained to the worse accuracy because linear

Figure 7. DQNUs trained form various initial conditions (IC) usually behave very similar and also the weight configurations of trained DQNUs is close to the best one of them (all DQNUs fall close to the origin); all DLNUs arrive to the same global minima but with poor accuracy; RNN trained from various IC converge (fall) into various local minima; (Figure 5, Figure 6)

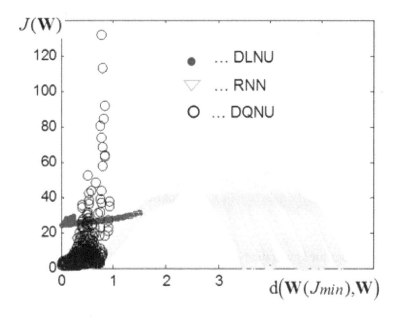

Figure 8. QNU can be trained fast, significantly more precisely than linear models, and does not suffer from local minima issue as nonlinear neural networks do when simple and feasible learning algorithms are used

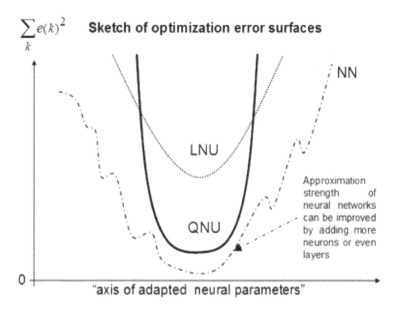

models are unable to learn nonlinearity; however, linear models have only single solution and do not suffer from local minima. The common (highly nonlinear) neural networks can be trained most precisely but they suffer from local minima and overfitting. QNU is steep (can be trained fast) and much more accurate than linear models, and do not suffer so much from local minima compared to common and highly nonlinear neural networks; the bottom of the QNU surface is sketched flat as some local minima of QNU can be encountered, however, always within the close vicinity of the global minima.

PAPER SUMMARY

According to our study cases the Quadratic Neural Unit allows getting higher order correlations between the input vector coming from the time series or from the neural model, according to the application. It can be seen that it is possible to capture the nonlinear properties of such input vector. According to this, the quadratic nonlinear approximator is able to capture the linear correlation existing in the input vector and also the higher-order correlation existing between its elements (Gupta et al., 2003).

In this paper we have reviewed recent results on application of a special class of polynomial neural networks or a higher order neural unit called the Quadratic Neural Unit; we highlight the attractive features of QNU that are promising for real industrial or technical applications, where the most nonlinear and too complicated neural networks or other approaches are not necessary to be used in order to achieve superior results.

ACKNOWLEDGMENT

This work was supported by the grant No. SGS10/252/OHK2/3T/12, and in part by Japanese grant # 19500413. Authors thank to Dr. Madan M. Gupta from the University of Saskatchewan and to Dr. Zeng–Guang Hou from the Chinese Academy of Science for their inspiration and valuable suggestions during research and applications of nonconventional neural units. We are also very grateful to the Matsumae International Foundation that partially supported our biomedical–engineering–oriented research of nonconventional neural architectures in 2009 and that also enforced our international cooperation.

REFERENCES

Bukovsky, I., Anderle, F., & Smetana, L. (2008). Quadratic neural unit for adaptive prediction of transitions among local attractors of lorenz system. In *Proceedings of the IEEE International Conference on Automation and Logistics*, Qingdao, China (pp. 147-152).

Bukovsky, I., & Bila, J. (2007). *Analysis of methods for evaluation of data uncertainty for control of energetic systems (report for I&C Energo, a.s. U12110)*. Prague, Czech Republic: Czech Technical University in Prague.

Bukovsky, I., & Bila, J. (2008a). Adaptive evaluation of complex time series using nonconventional neural units. In *Proceedings of the 7th IEEE International Conference on Cognitive Informatics* (pp. 128-137).

Bukovsky, I., & Bila, J. (2008b). *Program system for advanced reconciliation of process data: Program System I&C NEURECON (Final report for I&C Energo, a.s. U12110)*. Prague, Czech Republic: Czech Technical University in Prague.

Bukovsky, I., & Bila, J. (2010). Adaptive evaluation of complex dynamic systems using low-dimensional neural architectures. In Wang, Y., Zhang, D., & Kinsner, W. (Eds.), *Advances in cognitive informatics and cognitive computing* (pp. 33–57). Berlin, Germany: Springer-Verlag. doi:10.1007/978-3-642-16083-7_3

Bukovsky, I., Bila, J., Gupta, M. M., Hou, Z.-G., & Homma, N. (2009). Foundation and classification of nonconventional neural units and paradigm of nonsynaptic neural interaction. In Wang, Y. (Ed.), *Discoveries and breakthroughs in cognitive informatics and natural intelligence* (pp. 508–523). Hershey, PA: IGI Global. doi:10.4018/978-1-60566-902-1.ch027

Bukovsky, I., & Homma, N. (2010). Dynamic backpropagation and prediction [in Czech]. *Automatizace*, *53*(1-2), 61–66.

Bukovsky, I., Hou, Z.-G., Gupta, M. M., & Bila, J. (2007). Foundation of notation and classification of nonconventional static and dynamic neural units. In *Proceedings of the 6th IEEE International Conference on Cognitive Informatics* (pp. 401-407).

Bukovsky, I., Ichiji, K., Homma, N., Yoshizawa, M., & Rodriguez, R. (2010a). Testing potentials of dynamic quadratic neural unit for prediction of lung motion during respiration for tracking radiation therapy. In *Proceedings of the IEEE International Joint Conference on Neural Networks*, Barcelona, Spain (pp. 1-6).

Bukovsky, I., Lepold, M., & Bila, J. (2010b). Quadratic neural unit and its network in validation of process data of steam turbine loop and energetic boiler. In *Proceedings of the IEEE International Joint Conference on Neural Networks*, Barcelona, Spain (pp. 1-7).

Bukovsky, I., Redlapalli, S., & Gupta, M. M. (2003). Quadratic and cubic neural units for identification and fast state feedback control of unknown non-linear dynamic systems. In *Proceedings of the Fourth International Symposium on Uncertainty Modeling and Analysis* (pp. 330-334).

Gupta, M. M., Liang, J., & Homma, N. (2003). *Static and dynamic neural networks: From fundamentals to advanced theory*. Hoboken, NJ: John Wiley & Sons. doi:10.1002/0471427950

Hofreiter, M. (2010). *Laboratory system batyscaphe*. Prague, Czech Republic: Czech Technical University in Prague. Retrieved from http://vlab.fsid.cvut.cz/en/ulohy/batyskaf.php

Ivakhnenko, A. G. (1971). Polynomial theory of complex systems. *IEEE Transactions on Systems, Man, and Cybernetics*, *1*(4), 364–378. doi:10.1109/TSMC.1971.4308320

Klan, P., Hofreiter, M., Machacek, J., Modrlak, O., Smutny, L., & Vasek, V. (2005). Process models for a new control education laboratory. In *Proceedings of the 16th World Congress of the International Federation of Automatic Control*, Prague, Czech Republic (CD-ROM).

Kosmatopoulos, E., Polycarpou, M., Christodoulou, M., & Ioannou, P. (1995). High-order neural network structures for identification of dynamical systems. *IEEE Transactions on Neural Networks*, *6*(2), 422–431. doi:10.1109/72.363477

Nikolaev, N. Y., & Iba, H. (2006). *Adaptive learning of polynomial networks: Genetic programming, backpropagation and Bayesian methods: Genetic and evolutionary computation*. New York, NY: Springer.

Shin, Y., & Ghosh, J. (1991). The Pi-sigma network: An efficient higher-order neural network for pattern classification and function approximation. In *Proceedings of the Joint International Conference on Neural Networks*, Seattle, WA (pp. 13-18).

Smetana, L. (2008). *Nonlinear neuro-controller for automatic control laboratory system*. Unpublished master's thesis, Czech Technical University in Prague, Prague, Czech Republic.

Softky, R. W., & Kammen, D. M. (1991). Correlations in high dimensional or asymmetrical data sets: Hebbian neuronal processing. *Neural Networks*, *4*(3), 337–347. doi:10.1016/0893-6080(91)90070-L

Taylor, J. G., & Commbes, S. (1993). Learning higher order correlations. *Neural Networks*, *6*(3), 423–428. doi:10.1016/0893-6080(93)90009-L

Werbos, P. J. (1990). Backpropagation through time: What it is and how to do it. *Proceedings of the IEEE, 78*(10), 1550–1560. doi:10.1109/5.58337

Williams, R. J., & Zipser, D. (1989). A learning algorithm for continually running fully recurrent neural networks. *Neural Computation, 1*(2), 270–280. doi:10.1162/neco.1989.1.2.270

Zhang, M. (Ed.). (2008). *Artificial higher order neural networks for economics and business.* Hershey, PA: IGI Global. doi:10.4018/978-1-59904-897-0

Zhang, M. (Ed.). (2010). *Artificial higher order neural networks for computer science and engineering: Trends for emerging applications.* Hershey, PA: IGI Global. doi:10.4018/978-1-61520-711-4

This work was previously published in the International Journal of Software Science and Computational Intelligence, Volume 3, Issue 3, edited by Yingxu Wang, pp. 1-12, copyright 2011 by IGI Publishing (an imprint of IGI Global).

Chapter 24
A Value–Based Framework for Software Evolutionary Testing

Du Zhang
California State University, USA

ABSTRACT

The fundamental objective in value-based software engineering is to integrate consistent stakeholder value propositions into the full extent of software engineering principles and practices so as to increase the value for software assets. In such a value-based setting, artifacts in software development such as requirement specifications, use cases, test cases, or defects, are not treated as equally important during the development process. Instead, they will be differentiated according to how much they are contributing, directly or indirectly, to the stakeholder value propositions. The higher the contributions, the more important the artifacts become. In turn, development activities involving more important artifacts should be given higher priorities and greater considerations in the development process. In this paper, a value-based framework is proposed for carrying out software evolutionary testing with a focus on test data generation through genetic algorithms. The proposed framework incorporates general principles in value-based software testing and makes it possible to prioritize testing decisions that are rooted in the stakeholder value propositions. It allows for a cost-effective way to fulfill most valuable testing objectives first and a graceful degradation when planned testing process has to be shortened.

1. INTRODUCTION

The fundamental objective in value-based software engineering is to integrate consistent stakeholder value propositions into the full extent of software engineering principles and practices so as to increase the value for software assets (Biffl et al., 2006; Boehm, 2006). In such a value-based setting, artifacts in software development such as requirement specifications, use cases, test cases, or defects, are not treated as equally important during the development process. Instead, they

DOI: 10.4018/978-1-4666-2651-5.ch024

will be differentiated according to how much they are contributing, directly or indirectly, to the stakeholder value propositions. The higher the contributions, the more important the artifacts become. In turn, development activities involving more important artifacts should be given higher priorities and greater considerations in the development process. In the value-neutral setting of software engineering practices, the focus is primarily on technical issues and activities, and there is generally a lack of economic driving force behind the technical activities. The value-based approach broadens this narrow view and brings new perspectives into software engineering theory and practice. Developing successful software systems hinges not only on the body of software engineering knowledge, but also on knowledge from economics, management sciences, cognitive sciences, and humanities (Biffl et al., 2006). The value-based approach also makes it explicit that the ultimate goal for software systems to satisfy and conform to evolving human and organizational needs is to create value (Biffl et al., 2006).

Another emerging trend over the last two decades has been the application of machine learning to the development and maintenance of large and complex software systems. Though the types of machine learning applications to software engineering issues and tasks thus far are primarily restricted to the value-neutral setting (Zhang, 2000; Zhang & Tsai, 2003, 2005, 2007; Zhang, 2009), there does not exist any fundamental obstacle that would prevent machine learning applications from outgrowing into value-based setting. The objective in value-based software engineering is to make software development decisions that are better for value creation. The hallmark of machine learning is that it results in an improved ability to make better decisions. Therefore, we think machine learning has an active and important role to play with regard to the agenda items in value-based software engineering. In this paper, our focus is on the interplay of machine learning methods in value-based software engineering (Figure 1).

One of the machine learning methods is genetic algorithms. Genetic algorithms have been used in what is referred to as *evolutionary testing* for generating test data (McMinn, 2004). However, the state-of the-practice in evolutionary testing has been largely confined to the value-neutral setting. In this paper, we propose a value-based framework for carrying out software evolutionary testing with a focus on test data generation through genetic algorithms. The proposed framework, which falls into the area of value-based verification and validation, incorporates general principles in value-based software testing and aligns stakeholder value propositions with the technical activities in the test data generation process. The framework also makes it possible to prioritize decisions in the testing process. It allows for a cost-effective way to fulfill most valuable testing objectives first and a graceful degradation when planned testing process has to be shortened.

The rest of the paper is organized as follows. Section 2 summarizes the state-of-the-practice of machine learning applications to software test data generation in a value-neutral setting. In Section 3, we provide definitions for several concepts that will be utilized in the framework. Section 4 describes the proposed value-based framework for software evolutionary testing. An illustrative example is given in Section 5 of how the proposed framework can be put to work. Finally in Section 6 we conclude the paper with remark on future work.

Figure 1. Machine learning applications to value-based software engineering

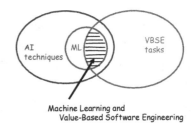

2. MACHINE LEARNING APPLICATION TO VALUE-NEUTRAL SOFTWARE TEST DATA GENERATION

Software testing has been a task of pivotal importance in developing quality software (Beizer, 1990; Wang & King, 2000; Wang, 2007). How to generate test data to ensure test coverage and adequacy is a challenging issue (Zhu et al., 1997). The state-of-the-practice in machine learning based test data generation has been so far confined to the value neutral setting and can be summarized in Table 1.

Given a program P to be tested, a test set T, and a set E(P, T) = {<i, o>| i ∈ T ∧ P(i) = o}, the inductive logic programming is used in (Bergadano & Gunetti, 1996) to infer P_1 from E(P, T) where $P \equiv P_1$. According to the program adequacy concept (Weyuker, 1983), T is likely to be useful for testing P.

In Emer and Vergilio (2003), genetic programming is used to support fault-based testing through deriving mutant programs for the original program P to be tested. A mutant can differ from P by more than simple modifications. An accompanying tool includes two GP-procedures that allow for both

the selection of test cases and the evaluation of a test set.

Genetic algorithms have been applied to test data generation for the following types of testing.

- **Structure-Based Testing or Coverage Analysis:** Test data are generated via genetic algorithms to cover structural constructs in a given source code such as statements, branches, paths, or multi-condition (Bueno & Jino, 2002; Michael et al., 2001; Wegener & Baresel, 2001). The following URL contains additional references: http://www.systematic-testing.com/evolutionary_testing/structural_testing.php

- **Temporal Testing:** Genetic algorithms are used to generate inputs that result in the longest or shortest execution time for real-time programs for temporal correctness assessment (Wegener et al., 1997) (see also the URL: http://www.systematic-testing.com/evolutionary_testing/temporal_testing.php).

- **Functional Testing:** This is a specification based approach to testing. Genetic algorithms are used in generating test data for the black-box test (http://www.systematic-testing.com/evolutionary_testing/functional_testing.php).

- **Safety Testing:** Safety critical systems often have safety constraints that cannot be violated under any circumstances. Genetic algorithms are used to generate test data that are geared toward violating those constraints as an attempt to prove exception freeness (Tracey et al., 2000; Tracey, 2000).

A rule-based active learning framework is proposed in (Xiao et al., 2005) for black-box testing of game software.

Though there have been many tools and methodologies developed for automated test data generation, their value-neutral nature results in

Table 1. Machine learning applications in test data generation

Machine Learning Methods	Test Data Generation
Inductive logic programming	Generating test data based on program adequacy concept
Genetic programming	Fault-based testing (mutation analysis)
Genetic algorithms (evolutionary testing)	- Structural testing (coverage of statements, branches, paths, multi-condition) - Temporal behavior testing - Functional testing (specification-based, boundary value analysis) - Safety testing
Rule-based active learning	Black-box software testing

each test specification, test case, and defect being treated as equally important. This practice creates a discrepancy from the software project reality where a typical situation can be more succinctly described as a Pareto distribution in which 80% of the mission value stems from 20% of the software components (Boehm, 2006) (Figure 2).

The dotted line in Figure 2 reflects the value-neutral practice in which an automated test data generation tool assumes that all tests have the same value. On the other hand, the Pareto curve for the empirical data in (Bullock, 2000) displays the actual business value (each customer billing type tested resulted in ameliorated initial billing revenues from 75% to 90% and significantly reduced customer complaint rates, and one of the fifteen customer types accounted for 50% of all billing revenues). We refer to modules that have such a higher positive impact on return-on-investment (ROI) as *Pareto modules* (see Section 3 for detail). A case analysis in (Boehm, 2006) indicates that although the value-neutral testing approach arrives at a higher ROI of 1.22 at the 100% tested level, the value-based Pareto testing approach accomplishes an even higher ROI of 1.74 when finishing only about 40% of the most valuable tests.

This discrepancy between the existing value-neutral testing practice and the value-sensitive software project reality has led to the following startling conclusion: one of the consequences of the value-neutral software engineering methods is that substantial amounts of scarce resources are spent on activities with negative ROI (Boehm, 2006). In the area of software testing alone, this translates into squandered resources that are measured at $300 billion a year worldwide (Boehm, 2006).

3. SOME DEFINITIONS

Our proposed framework hinges critically on several important concepts (Pareto modules as the most valuable modules, modules with varying defect densities, and impact/nonimpact defects). In this section, we define those concepts in terms of some established software engineering principles and models.

The first concept is about the Pareto modules, the most important modules of a software system with regard to its product value[1]. For a given software system Ω, we can define a set $\mathbf{M}_\Omega$ of modules, a valuation function υ, and a value set V as follows:

$$\mathbf{M}_\Omega = \{m_i \mid m_i \in \Omega\}; \tag{1}$$

$$\upsilon: \mathbf{M}_\Omega \to [0, 1]; \tag{2}$$

$$V = \{\upsilon(m_i) \mid m_i \in \mathbf{M}_\Omega\} \tag{3}$$

The valuation function υ can be defined by stakeholder value propositions (SVPs) and has the following properties:

- $0 < \upsilon(m_i) \leq 1$, for all i; (4)

$$\sum_{i=1}^{n}(mi) = 1. \tag{5}$$

We define a partially ordered set $(V, \leq)$ where $\leq$ is a binary order relation on V and satisfies reflexivity, anti-symmetry and transitivity for all

Figure 2. Pareto distribution for varying test case value

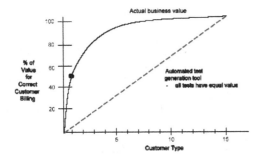

358

elements in V. We say that $\upsilon(m_p)$ is a *principal element* for $(V, \leq)$ if we have the following:

$$\forall \upsilon(m_j) \in V \, [\upsilon(m_j) \leq \upsilon(m_p)]^2 \quad (6)$$

We use ρ to denote the *principal module* as specified by $\upsilon(m_p)$. We define a *principal-element-ordered subset* $V_{[mi, \rho]}$ of V and its cumulative value $\mu_{[mi, \rho]}$ as follows:

$$V_{[mi, \rho]} = V - \{\upsilon(m_k) \mid \upsilon(m_k) < \upsilon(m_i)\} \quad (7)$$

$$\mu_{[mi, \rho]} = \sum \left(mj\right) \in V\left[mi,\right] \quad (8)$$

Now we are in a position to formally define the concept of Pareto modules.

Definition 1: Given a threshold value $\tau \in (0, 1]$, we identify a principal-element-ordered subset $V_{[mi, \rho]}$ such that $\tau = \mu_{[mi,}\rho_]$. Modules in $V_{[mi,}\rho_]$ are referred to as Pareto modules with regard to τ.

If $\tau < \mu_{[mi, \rho]}$ but removing any m_j from $\mu_{[mi, \rho]}$ would result in $\tau > \mu_{[mi, \rho]}$, then the condition of $\tau = \mu_{[mi, \rho]}$ is relaxed to that of $\tau \leq \mu_{[mi, \rho]}$.

In practice, to identify the Pareto modules, we can apply the Pareto principle as follows: (1) arrange modules according to the descending order of their value contributions to the total product value; (2) calculate cumulative percentages of contribution with regard to all the modules; (3) draw a line graph based on the cumulative percentages and modules involved; and (4) identify the most valuable modules with regard to an established threshold value. Table 2 contains a hypothetical example of six modules and their respective contributions to the overall product value in both the percentages and dollar amounts. Figure 3 depicts the Pareto application process. If the given threshold value τ for determining the Pareto modules is 0.8, then modules to the left of the vertical dotted line (modules A, B and C) will be identified as such.

The next set of concepts is about modules with varying defect densities. Item four on the software defect reduction top ten list in (Boehm & Basili, 2001) indicates that "*About 80% of the defects come from 20% of the modules, and about half the modules are defect free.*" Clearly, there are three types of modules here in terms of defect density measure: *defect-intensive modules* that refer to those 20% of the modules causing the bulk (80%) of defects, *defect-prone modules* that are the next 30% of modules containing the remaining 20% of defects, and *defect-free* modules that include the remaining 50% of modules. Figure 4 is a schematic view of those three types of modules.

In practice, there are different ways to specify the criteria for defect-intensive and defect-prone modules. The criteria we use in this paper are based on the software Constructive Quality Model (COQUALMO). In COQUALMO (Steece et al., 2002; Huang & Boehm, 2006), there are two components: a defect introduction sub-model that estimates the rates at which software requirements, design and code defects are introduced, and a defect removal sub-model. Let KSLOC stand for thousand source line of code. The calibrated baseline (nominal) defect introduction rates DIR_{nom} in COQUALMO are given in Table 3 (Boehm et al., 2000; Steece et al., 2002; Huang & Boehm, 2006):

Table 2. An example for Pareto modules

Modules	% of Contribution (Dollar Amount)	Cumulative %
Module A	45% (247.5K)	45%
Module B	20% (110.0K)	65%
Module C	15% (82.5K)	80%
Module D	10% (55.0K)	90%
Module E	8% (44.0K)	98%
Module F	2% (11.0K)	100% (550.0K)

Figure 3. Identification of Pareto modules

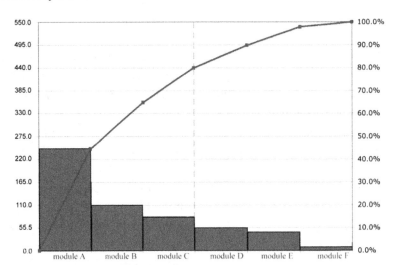

Thus the total of the nominal defect introduction rate for a software system is 60 defects/KSLOC. Multiplying the baseline rates with the size of a software system provides the total number of defects introduced in each of the three categories (requirements, design, and coding) and summing them up returns the total number of nominal defects introduced into a software system. We use $\mathbf{NDI}_\Omega$ to denote it[3]. Scaling $\mathbf{NDI}_\Omega$ down to the module level (e.g., if a module m has a size of 100 SLOC, then its nominal coding defects are scaled down to 3 accordingly), let $\mathbf{NDI}_m$ denote the nominal defects introduced into a module m

and $\mathbf{TDI}_m$ the actual total number of defects in m. we can define defect-intensive and defect-prone modules using $\mathbf{NDI}_m$ as follows.

Definition 2: A module m is defect-intensive if its defect introduction rates (in some or all three categories) are higher than the nominal rates DIR_{nom}. Therefore, we have $\mathbf{TDI}_m > \mathbf{NDI}_m$.

Definition 3: A module m is defect-prone if its defect introduction rates (in some or all three categories) are lower than the nominal rates DIR_{nom}. Therefore, we have $\mathbf{TDI}_m \leq \mathbf{NDI}_m$.

Figure 4. Types of modules in terms of defect density

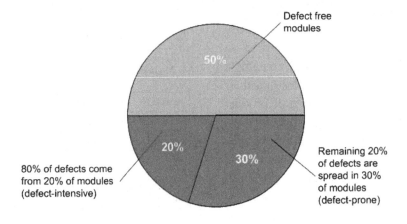

Table 3. Nominal defect introduction rates

Type of Defects	DIR_{nom}
Requirements defects	$DIR_{nom}(req) = 10/KSLOC$
Design defects	$DIR_{nom}(des) = 20/KSLOC$
Coding defects	$DIR_{nom}(cod) = 30/KSLOC$

The last concept to be defined is about the nature of defects. Item five on the software defect reduction top ten list in (Boehm & Basili, 2001) states that "*About 90% of the downtime comes from, at most, 10% of the defects.*" We refer to those 10% of the defects as *impact defects*. Figure 5 is a schematic view of such defects.

Definition 4: Impact defects (or high risk defects) are those defects that result in loss of human life or high financial loss. This translates into the Required Reliability (RELY) ratings of *Extra High*, *Very High* and *High* according to the Constructive Cost Model (CO-COMO) II (Boehm et al., 2000), and rough Mean Time Between Failures (MTBF) of one million hours, 300K hours and 10K hours, respectively (Boehm et al., 2004; Huang & Boehm, 2006).

Definition 5: Non-impact defects are those defects that result in moderate recoverable loss, easily recoverable loss or slight inconvenience. They have the RELY ratings of *Nominal*, *Low* and *Very Low*, and the MTBF of 300 hours, 10 hours and 1 hour, respectively (Huang & Boehm, 2006).

4. A VALUE-BASED FRAMEWORK

In this section, we describe a value-based framework for test data generation through genetic algorithms (Figure 6). The framework hinges on three cornerstones for testing a given software system: (1) identifying Pareto modules, defect-intensive and defect-prone modules, and delineating impact and non-impact defects based on SVPs; (2) setting up testing priorities with regard to the types of modules identified in (1); and (3) translating SVPs from the business value level to the technical level in test construction and execution.

The framework has the following features:

- It promotes the stakeholder value propositions to be aligned and utilized in identifying Pareto modules, defect-intensive and defect-prone modules, and impact and non-impact defects, and in prioritizing testing objectives.
- It accommodates staged test data generations with the most valuable testing objectives (the ones that yield the highest ROI) being fulfilled first.
- It permits value propositions to be factored into the fitness definitions in genetic algorithms within each test data generation cycle.
- It allows hints and clues learned in a previous cycle to be used to devise a more cost-effective way for the next cycle of test data generation.
- It makes it possible for a graceful degradation when the testing budget (or resource constraints, or scheduled deadlines) is scaled back (objectives with the highest ROI would have been finished earlier).

In the remainder of this section, we describe the proposed framework from the following perspectives: contribution chain and costs of testing, identification of critical, lesser critical and non-critical components, setting up priorities for the test data generation cycles, considerations in each test cycle for translating stakeholder value propositions from the business value level to the technical level in test construction and execution, the issue of feedbacks and adjustments between test cycles, and the costs and the benefits.

Figure 5. Impact vs. non-impact defects

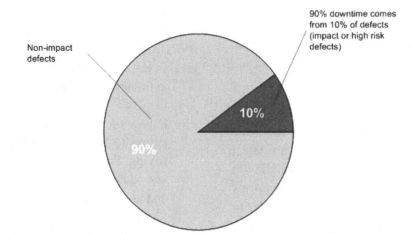

4.1. Contribution Chain and Costs of Testing

Though it does not yield direct and immediate product value, testing supports other value generating tasks in software development through a contribution chain, which forges the link from testing to the final product that eventually adds value for the stakeholders (Ramler et al., 2006). This contribution chain of testing includes the following clients: customers and users, project managers, quality managers, marketing and product managers, requirement engineers, and developers (Ramler et al., 2006).

The cost of quality model (Slaughter et al., 1998) establishes the basis for testing costs. It separates the cost in obtaining quality into two categories: costs of conformance and costs of nonconformance. Costs of conformance have two components: *prevention costs* as a result of preventing errors, and *appraisal costs* for evaluating properties of a product through activities such as test planning and setup, test data generation, test execution, results analysis and reporting. Costs of nonconformance are composed of two components: *internal failure costs* as a consequence of

defects found prior to release, and *external failure costs* due to defects found after a product's release.

The costs of testing consist of appraisal costs and internal failure costs (Ramler et al., 2006).

4.2. Identifying Critical Components

We use the following to denote the attributes for modules:

- **P:** Pareto modules.
- **DI:** Defect-intensive modules.
- **DP:** Defect-prone modules.
- **DF:** Defect-free modules.
- **ID:** Impact defect.
- **NID:** Non-impact defect.

Thus, we can have a conjunction of symbols to denote all the attributes a module possesses. For instance, a Pareto module that is defect-intensive with non-impact defects can be annotated with P $\wedge$ DI $\wedge$ NID (heavy lines in Figure 7).

From a value-based standpoint, to improve the return on investment, we want to make sure to maximize the success rate of Pareto modules and to minimize the risk of having impact defects in the system. Therefore, in the proposed framework,

Figure 6. Value-based software test data generation process through genetic algorithms

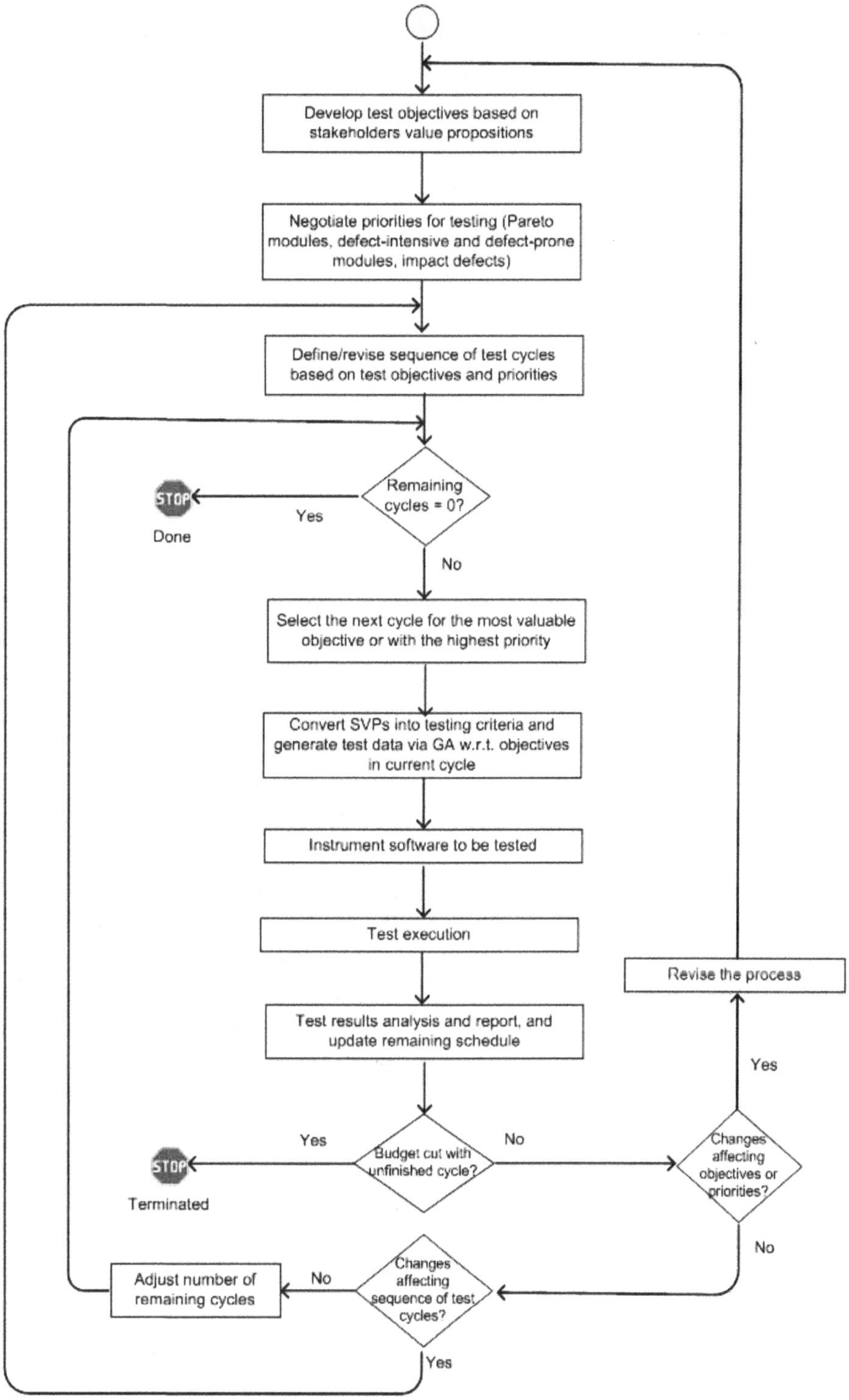

Figure 7. Possible module attributes

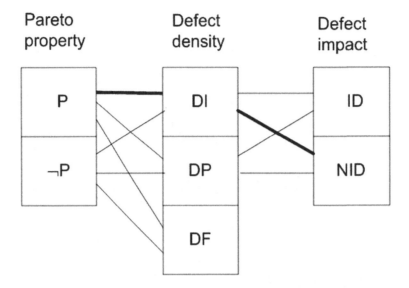

we consider modules with the following attributes as *critical components*:

P ∧ DI ∧ ID

P ∧ DP ∧ ID

DI ∧ ID

DP ∧ ID

The next level of critical components includes:

P ∧ DI ∧ NID

P ∧ DP ∧ NID

P ∧ DF

DI ∧ NID

DP ∧ NID

The non-critical components are non-Pareto DF modules in the systems.

There are a number of issues in this identification process. The first issue is to bring together the stakeholders to consolidate SVPs, reconcile differences in value models and analyses (Grunbacher et al., 2006), and obtain a set of common test objectives. In addition, there are context-dependent and context-independent issues. Context-dependent factors include: platform and personnel related issues, system's operation profiles, and high-risk scenarios. Context-independent causes are: (1) product characteristics such as size, complexity, the amount of change to reused code, and the level of data coupling and cohesion (Boehm & Basili, 2001); and (2) product historical data such as number of defects found in the previous version or release, number of modifications made thus far, the amount of verification and validation.

The outcome of this process should yield sets of modules with distinct characterization and sets of delineated impact and non-impact defects.

4.3. Setting Priorities

In the framework, we decompose the overall test data generation process for a given software system into a sequence of test data generation cycles with each focusing on some specific testing objective(s). Based on the types of modules and the types of defects, we have a landscape of possible testing scenarios as shown in Figure 8. The dotted area indicates Pareto modules that can also be defect-intensive, defect-prone, or defect-free modules, and that can intersect with impact or non-impact defects. There are three issues here: how many cycles are needed, what goes to each cycle, and how cycles are prioritized.

From a value-based standpoint, to improve the return on investment, we want to make sure to first maximize the success rate of Pareto modules and to minimize the chance of having impact defects that devastate the value contribution. Afterwards, attention can be focused on non-impact defects and non-Pareto modules. As a result, the general approach would be to have the following priority groups: (1) the top priority is to thoroughly test Pareto modules with impact defects; (2) the next priority is to devote attention to modules with impact defects; (3) the third priority group is to deal with Pareto modules with non-impact defects or defect-free Pareto modules; and (4) the last priority group consists of modules with non-impact defects or defect-free modules[4].

There are specific cases in each priority group. Table 4 lists a possible prioritized list of all the cases in the aforementioned four priority groups. A sequence of test cycles can be prioritized based on the guideline in Table 4 where the case 1.1 is the highest priority class and the case 4.3 is the lowest priority class.

Each test cycle may correspond to a particular priority class. Alternatively, several priority classes may be included in a single cycle or several cycles are devoted to a single priority class.

4.4. Translating SVPs to Testing Activities

Within a test cycle, a specific type of modules (e.g., modules with $P \wedge DI \wedge ID$) is considered. Based on the circumstance, any combination of structural, functional, non-functional, temporal, safety and mutation testing can be carried out. To convert SVPs from the business value level to the technical level details of test data generation, we

need to identify code blocks and execution paths that are critical to sustain SVPs, and scrutinize factors such as untested new capabilities, fixes that have to be re-tested, or existing capabilities that have to be regression tested to expose possible side effects (Ramler et al., 2006), safety constraints or boundary conditions the violation of which will result in impact defects, temporal properties that have significant impact on system performance, or the robustness properties (e.g., the minimum number of faults causing certain failure, or the maximum number of faults with the system still maintaining successful operation).

For the test data generation, we adopt a genetic algorithm system with the features as shown in Table 5.

An objective function can be used to guide the search process on how close or fit it is to select the test data that will fulfill the given testing objective (e.g., exercising a desired code block or traversing a particular path). Its definition is given in Table 6 (Tracey, 2000). Depending on the SVPs involved and the testing objectives, the fitness functions can be defined differently within each cycle.

The results analysis will focus on whether adequate test data have been generated for all modules belonging to the current priority class and whether all conditions specifying impact defects or circumstances leading up to impact defects have been considered.

4.5. Feedbacks Between Test Cycles

The framework allows feedbacks between test cycles, and accommodates rearrangement to the sequence of cycles and adjustment to priorities and objectives.

When the testing budget (or resource constraints, or scheduled deadlines) gets scaled back to the point that no further testing activities can be supported, the framework achieves a graceful degradation in the system quality because prior to the cutback point, test objectives with the highest ROI would have been done by then.

Figure 8. Possible testing scenarios

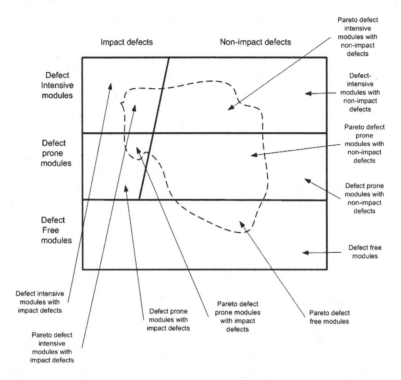

4.6. Costs and Benefits

The additional costs the proposed framework incurs are in the appraisal costs category in the form of stakeholders' deliberation on identifying various types of modules and defects in terms of SVPs, and the feedback loop's necessary adjustment to the remaining test cycles. However, the framework enjoys the benefits of having a better chance to accomplish the system's business goals, and reduced external failure costs.

5. AN ILLUSTRATIVE EXAMPLE

In this section, we use an online banking system as an example to demonstrate how the proposed framework can be adopted to help align the value propositions with activities in the testing process which in turn improves return on investment for the business.

Table 4. Priority classes

Priority Group and Case	Module Type
1.1	Pareto modules that are defect-intensive with impact defects
1.2	Pareto modules that are defect-prone with impact defects
2.1	Defect-intensive modules with impact defects
2.2	Defect-prone modules with impact defects
3.1	Pareto modules that are defect-intensive with non-impact defects
3.2	Pareto modules that are defect-prone with non-impact defects
3.3	Pareto modules that are defect-free
4.1	Defect-intensive modules with non-impact defects
4.2	Defect-prone modules with non-impact defects
4.3	Defect-free modules

Table 5. A genetic algorithm system for test data generation

Genetic Algorithm component	Implementation
Solution encoding	Non-binary
Crossover operator	Simple, uniform, weighted, averaging (Tracey, 2000)
Mutation operator	Simple, random, neighborhood (Tracey, 2000)
Rates of crossover and mutation operations	Tunable
Selection strategy	Tournament, rank, elitism, random (McMinn, 2004; Tracey, 2000)
Population size	tunable
Fraction of population to be replaced at each generation	tunable
Population survival strategy	Fittest, best of old and new, all offspring, random (Tracey, 2000)

The online banking system provides an increasingly popular array of online services by a major commercial bank in the U.S. The entire system offers online services and products covering a wide range of banking business, from personal, small business, merchant services, to corporate and institutional. For the purpose of this paper, we only focus our attention on the main components of its personal online banking subsystem (POBS). The main modules of POBS are summarized as follows (the module numbers are in parentheses for easy reference).

- **Authentication (M_1):** This module prompts for online ID, personalized Site-Key security questions, and pass-code to identify and accept a legitimate bank client.
- **Account Overview (M_2):** It provides an overview of account names and their balances.
- **Account Details (M_3):** The module offers, for each account, (1) transaction activities organized according to each statement period; (2) statements that can be viewed

and printed out, or downloaded; (3) search function for transactions containing specific information between a time period; and (4) additional account-specific services (e.g., rewards for credit cards).

- **Bill Pay (M_4):** It allows a client to pay either a company or an individual. The module includes the following functions: (1) make payment (payee name, amount, deliver-by, and pay from); (2) add a payee; (3) request and manage e-Bills; and (4) monitor outgoing payments.
- **Transfers (M_5):** It enables funds to be transferred either between intra-bank accounts or between inter-bank accounts (from, to, amount, and frequency).
- **Checking and Saving Customer Service (M_6):** The module includes the following services: (1) dispute ATM/Check card transaction; (2) order check copy; (3) reorder checks and/or deposit slips; (4) setup a payroll direct deposit; (5) stop check payment; (6) view rates and fees; (7) change delivery method of your statements and canceled checks; (8)

Table 6. Objective function for guiding the search process

Element	Value for the objective function z()
Boolean	If TRUE then 0 else K^5
a = b	If $abs(a - b) = 0$, then 0 else $abs(a - b)$ K
a ≠ b	If $abs(a - b) \neq 0$, then 0 else K
a < b	If $a - b < 0$, then 0 else $(a - b) + K$
a ≤ b	If $a - b \leq 0$, then 0 else $(a - b) + K$
a > b	If $b - a < 0$, then 0 else $(b - a) + K$
a ≥ b	If $b - a \leq 0$, then 0 else $(b - a) + K$
¬a	Negation is moved right in front of a
a ∧ b	$z(a) + z(b)$
a ∨ b	$min(z(a), z(b))$
a ⇒ b	$min(z(\neg a), z(b))$
a ⇔ b	$min((z(a) + z(b)), (z(\neg a) + z(\neg b)))$
a xor b	$min((z(a) + z(\neg b)), (z(\neg a) + z(b)))$

view or print statements; and (9) check card settings.

- **Credit Card Customer Service (M$_7$):** This customer service module contains the functions below: (1) request a credit line increase; (2) request a replacement card; (3) add an authorized user; (4) manage alerts; (5) order payment check copies; (6) order access check copies; (7) request credit reference letter; (8) stop or start receiving your paper statements; (9) view or print statements; (10) request a balance transfer; (11) request a PIN; (12) request access checks; (13) monitor your credit report; and (14) payments.

- **Personal Information Customer Service (M$_8$):** This module supports the following services: (1) profile management (update e-mail address, update street address or phone number, change online ID or pass-code or Site-Key and its challenge questions and answers, and language preference); (2) preferences (add or change account nicknames, select default accounts, and select default file format for downloads); and (3) get assisted (chat with an online banking professional, email communication with customer service, ask a technical question, fees and processes explained, online banking FAQs, and customer service phone numbers).

- **Mobile Banking (M$_9$):** This module enables clients to, through mobile devices, access banking information, pay bills, transfer funds, and locate banking centers or ATMs along with maps and directions.

- **Investments (M$_{10}$):** It offers a way to integrate online banking with online investing (equity trades). The investment choices include mutual funds, stocks, bonds, and exchange traded funds.

- **Special-Offer (M$_{11}$):** Special offers of banking products and services (e.g., savings and CDs, credit cards, mortgage, insurance, auto loans, home equity lines of credit and loans,

retirement and education) are made through this module.

- **Announcements (M$_{12}$):** New services and technical supports are being put out by this module.

- **InfoCenter (M$_{13}$):** It presents various types of tutorials on the products and services the system supports.

- **My-Portfolio (M$_{14}$):** This module provides a tool for the bank client to track spending by category, use the real estate center to add home to the profile of personal assets and net worth, add an outside account, create groups of related accounts, and choose a personalized portfolio home page.

- **Locations (M$_{15}$):** It helps locate the bank's ATMs and banking centers throughout the U.S.

- **Feedback (M$_{16}$):** This gives an online banking client the opportunity to express the level of satisfaction and specific comments about the services and personal experience.

- **Alerts (M$_{17}$):** It provides a whole host of alerts (e.g., balances, payments, transactions) about the products and services that are part of the personal banking services or of interest to bank clients.

- **Search (M$_{18}$):** This is a tool that helps a client track down a particular banking item.

- **Sign-Off (M$_{19}$):** It allows a client to appropriately terminate an online banking session.

The overriding SVPs for POBS include: secured access to personal financial data, reliability, robustness, trustworthiness, promptness, and capabilities that allow clients to tailor online services to their individual financial circumstances and preferences.

Based on the extent to which module functionalities provide direct (or indirect) support to the SVPs of POBS, a mapping can be defined that allows us to establish the percentage of contributions modules make to POBS' SVPs. Table 7 describes the outcome of one possible mapping.

Table 7. Contributions of modules to SVPs

Module	% Contribution	Cumulative %
M_4	10%	10%
M_5	9%	19%
M_7	9%	28%
M_1	8%	36%
M_3	8%	44%
M_6	8%	52%
M_{14}	8%	60%
M_2	4%	64%
M_8	4%	68%
M_9	4%	72%
M_{10}	4%	76%
M_{11}	3%	79%
M_{12}	3%	82%
M_{13}	3%	85%
M_{15}	3%	88%
M_{16}	3%	91%
M_{17}	3%	94%
M_{18}	3%	97%
M_{19}	3%	100%

Let $\wp_\tau(\Omega)$ denote the set of Pareto modules for a software system Ω with regard to a given threshold τ. Let $\tau = 0.6$, then we have the following for POBS:

$$V_{[M1, M4]} = \{\upsilon(M_1), \upsilon(M_3), \upsilon(M_4), \upsilon(M_5), \upsilon(M_6), \upsilon(M_7), \upsilon(M_{14})\} \quad (9)$$

$$\wp_\tau(POBS) = \{M_1, M_3, M_4, M_5, M_6, M_7, M_{14}\} \quad (10)$$

There are context-dependent and context-independent factors in identifying defect density attributes for modules. Based on the SVPs and POBS specific empirical data, a possible scenario could be that M_4, M_9, M_{10}, are identified as defect-intensive modules and $M_1, M_6, M_7, M_8, M_{14}, M_{15}$ as defect-prone modules.

The impact defects for POBS could include security breach (M_1), late payment (M_4, as a result,

the bank has to pay late penalty on behalf of the client), and unable to connect in mobile banking scenario (M_9). Non-impact defects may include a range of anomalies from tardiness in updating banking information (e.g., a charge to an account) to inaccurate or inconsistent information (e.g., address of a banking center).

Based on the aforementioned analysis, the landscape for modules in POBS can be depicted in Figure 9. Thus the testing priorities (for unit, integration and system tests) can be set according to the guideline in Table 4. For instance, since M_4 has the following attributes $P \wedge DI \wedge ID$, it should be scrutinized early and most closely.

To incorporate the SVPs into the testing activities of, say, structural or white-box testing, we identify code blocks and branch conditions that are critical to sustain SVPs, and make sure that priority is given to test data generations that result in those critical control paths traversed and critical code blocks exercised. For instance, suppose we have the following control flow graph (Figure 10) in a module of POBS for the current testing cycle, and code block C is identified as critical in supporting some SVP.

To generate test data to exercise code block C, both Branch 1 and Branch 2 are critical. For a possible test case of $<P = 12, Q = 7>$, we are searching for test data that will satisfy the constraint of $\neg(12 \geq 8)$ at Branch 1. In other words, if the test data enables the execution to go through code block C, the objective function $z(\neg(12 \geq 8))$ has to return a zero at Branch 1. However, the objective function of $z(\neg(12 \geq 8))$ yields the following result:

$$z(\neg(12 \geq 8)) = z(12 < 8) = 12 - 8 + K = 4 + K \quad (11)$$

Since the objective function returns a non-zero value, the test case of $<P = 12, Q = 7>$ would not result in code block C being executed because it will commit the execution to a different path.

Figure 9. A possible landscape for POBS modules

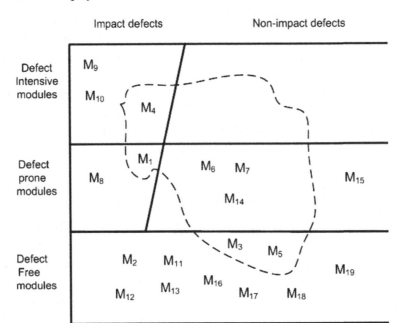

Figure 10. Control flow graph for module under test

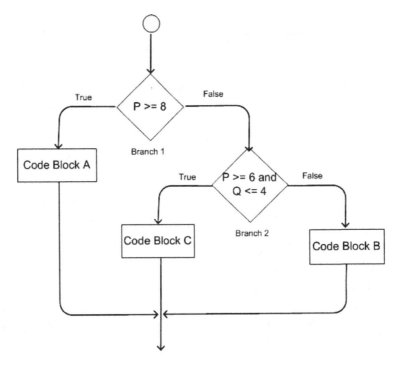

If we have another test case of <P = 7, Q = 4>, then the objective function will return a zero at Branch 1. The evaluation of the objective function at Branch 2 produces:

$$z(7 \geq 6) + z(4 \leq 4) = 0 + 0 = 0 \qquad (12)$$

This result indicates that a desirable test case has been found that will result in code block C being executed.

6. CONCLUSION

In this paper, we recognize the importance of value consideration in developing software systems and discuss the issue of machine learning applications to value-based software engineering. We propose a framework for value-based software test data generation through genetic algorithms. The framework has the following features: (1) prioritizing testing decisions that are rooted in the stakeholder value propositions, (2) electing to fulfill the most valuable testing objectives (the ones that yield the highest ROI) first, (3) devising a more cost-effective way (based on lessons learned in achieving the most valuable objectives) to carry out the remaining testing objectives, and (4) obtaining a graceful degradation when the testing budget is cut back (objectives with the highest ROI would have been finished earlier). The moral of the work is two-fold: value-based software engineering offers a ROI-conscious approach to software development, and machine learning has an active and important role to play in various agenda items in value-based software engineering.

Top on the agenda of our future work is some empirical study. This is a very important step, the results of which can further substantiate the viability of the proposed framework. How to solidify SVPs and map them into decisions on genetic algorithms related parameters and choices is another topic in our agenda. Yet another direction in future work is to explore augmented genetic algorithms with ant colony optimization for test data generation.

ACKNOWLEDGMENT

We would like to express our sincere appreciation to the anonymous reviewers for their comments which help improve the technical contents and the presentation of this paper.

REFERENCES

Beizer, B. (1990). *Software testing techniques*. New York, NY: Van Nostrand Reinhold.

Bergadano, F., & Gunetti, D. (1996). Testing by means of inductive program learning. *ACM Transactions on Software Engineering and Methodology, 5*(2), 119–145. doi:10.1145/227607.227611

Biffl, S., Aurum, A., Boehm, B., Erdogmus, H., & Grunbacher, P. (Eds.). (2006). *Value-based software engineering*. Berlin, Germany: Springer-Verlag. doi:10.1007/3-540-29263-2

Boehm, B. (2006). Overview and agenda. In Biffl, S., Aurum, A., Boehm, B., Erdogmus, H., & Grünbacher, P. (Eds.), *Value-based software engineering*. Berlin, Germany: Springer-Verlag. doi:10.1007/3-540-29263-2_1

Boehm, B., Abts, C., Brown, A. W., Chulani, S., Clark, B. K., & Horowitz, E. (2000). *Software cost estimation with COCOMO II*. Upper Saddle River, NJ: Prentice Hall.

Boehm, B., & Basili, V. R. (2001). Software defect reduction top 10 list. *IEEE Computer, 34*(1), 135–137. doi:10.1109/2.962984

Boehm, B., Huang, L., Jain, A., & Madachy, R. (2004). The ROI of software dependability: The iDAVE model. *IEEE Software, 21*(3), 54–61. doi:10.1109/MS.2004.1293073

Bueno, P. M. S., & Jino, M. (2002). Automatic test data generation for program paths using genetic algorithms. *International Journal of Software Engineering and Knowledge Engineering, 12*(6), 691–709. doi:10.1142/S0218194002001074

Bullock, J. (2000). Calculating the value of testing. *Software Testing and Quality Engineering,* 56-62.

Emer, M. C. F. P., & Vergilio, S. R. (2003). Selection and evaluation of test data based on genetic programming. *Software Quality Journal, 11*(2), 167–186. doi:10.1023/A:1023772729494

Grunbacher, P., Koszegi, S., & Biffl, S. (2006). Stakeholder value proposition elicitation and reconciliation. In Biffl, S., Aurum, A., Boehm, B., Erdogmus, H., & Grünbacher, P. (Eds.), *Value-based software engineering.* Berlin, Germany: Springer-Verlag. doi:10.1007/3-540-29263-2_7

Huang, L., & Boehm, B. (2006). How much software investment is enough: A value-based approach. *IEEE Software, 23*(2), 88–95. doi:10.1109/MS.2006.127

McMinn, P. (2004). Search-based software test data generation: A survey. *Software: Testing. Verification and Reliability, 14*(2), 105–156. doi:10.1002/stvr.294

Michael, C. C., McGraw, G., & Schatz, M. A. (2001). Generating software test data by evolution. *IEEE Transactions on Software Engineering, 27*(12), 1085–1109. doi:10.1109/32.988709

Ramler, R., Biffl, S., & Grunbacher, P. (2006). Value-based management of software testing. In Biffl, S., Aurum, A., Boehm, B., Erdogmus, H., & Grünbacher, P. (Eds.), *Value-based software engineering.* Berlin, Germany: Springer-Verlag. doi:10.1007/3-540-29263-2_11

Slaughter, S. A., Harter, D. E., & Krishnan, M. S. (1998). Evaluating the cost of software quality. *Communications of the ACM, 41*(8), 67–73. doi:10.1145/280324.280335

Steece, B., Chulani, S., & Boehm, B. (2002). Determining software quality using COQUALMO. In Blischke, W., & Murphy, D. (Eds.), *Case studies in reliability and maintenance.* Hoboken, NJ: John Wiley & Sons.

Tracey, N. (2000). *A search-based automated test data generation framework for safety critical software.* Unpublished doctoral dissertation, University of York, York, UK.

Tracey, N., Clark, J., Mander, K., & McDermid, J. (2000). Automated test data generation for exception conditions. *Software, Practice & Experience, 30*(1), 61–79. doi:10.1002/(SICI)1097-024X(200001)30:1<61::AID-SPE292>3.0.CO;2-9

Wang, Y. (2007). *Software engineering foundations: A software science perspective (Vol. 2).* Boca Raton, FL: Auerbach Publications. doi:10.1201/9780203496091

Wang, Y., & King, G. (2000). *Software engineering processes: Principles and applications (Vol. 1).* Boca Raton, FL: CRC Press.

Wegener, J., Baresel, A., & Sthamer, H. (2001). Evolutionary test environment for automatic structural testing. *Information and Software Technology, 43*(14), 841–854. doi:10.1016/S0950-5849(01)00190-2

Wegener, J., Sthamer, H., Jones, B., & Eyres, D. (1997). Testing real-time systems using genetic algorithms. *Software Quality Journal, 6*(2), 127–135. doi:10.1023/A:1018551716639

Weyuker, E. J. (1983). Assessing test data adequacy through program inference. *ACM Transactions on Programming Languages and Systems, 5*(4), 641–655. doi:10.1145/69575.357231

Xiao, G., Southey, F., Holte, R. C., & Wilkinson, D. (2005). Software testing by active learning for commercial games. In *Proceedings of the 20th AAAI Conference,* Pittsburgh, PA (pp. 898-903).

Zhang, D. (2000). Applying machine learning algorithms in software development. In *Proceedings of the Monterey Workshop on Modeling Software System Structures*, Santa Margherita Ligure, Italy (pp. 275-285).

Zhang, D. (2009). Machine learning and value-based software engineering. *International Journal of Software Science and Computational Intelligence*, 1(1), 112–125. doi:10.4018/jssci.2009010108

Zhang, D., & Tsai, J. J. P. (2003). Machine learning and software engineering. *Software Quality Journal*, 11(2), 87–119. doi:10.1023/A:1023760326768

Zhang, D., & Tsai, J. J. P. (Eds.). (2005). *Machine learning applications in software engineering*. Singapore: World Scientific. doi:10.1142/5700

Zhang, D., & Tsai, J. J. P. (Eds.). (2007). *Advances in machine learning applications in software engineering*. Hershey, PA: IGI Global. doi:10.4018/978-1-59140-941-0

Zhu, H., Hall, P. A. V., & May, J. H. R. (1997). Software unit test coverage and adequacy. *ACM Computing Surveys*, 29(4), 366–427. doi:10.1145/267580.267590

ENDNOTES

[1] A module refers to a discrete, well-defined, small component of a software system.

[2] If there are several principal elements in V, we can use other criteria to designate one for the discussion.

[3] Even though a better estimate calls for adjusting the total defect number in each category with a different calibration constant and a different quality adjustment factor (an aggregate of 22 defect introduction drivers about the characteristics of platform, product, personnel and project) (Boehm et al., 2000), for our purpose in identifying modules with different defect density, we simply use nominal defect introduction estimate as the measure.

[4] The reason to include defect-free modules (Pareto or non-Pareto) is because of the need to test for other performance related criteria.

[5] K is a positive constant value that serves to "punish" the current selection of the test data because they do not satisfy all the constraints. The objective function z() will return a zero when all the constraints are satisfied.

This work was previously published in the International Journal of Software Science and Computational Intelligence, Volume 3, Issue 2, edited by Yingxu Wang, pp. 62-82, copyright 2011 by IGI Publishing (an imprint of IGI Global).

Chapter 25
Comparison of Promoter Sequences Based on Inter Motif Distance

A. Meera
BMS College of Engineering, India

Lalitha Rangarajan
University of Mysore, India

ABSTRACT

Understanding how the regulation of gene networks is orchestrated is an important challenge for characterizing complex biological processes. The DNA sequences that comprise promoters do not provide much direct information about regulation. A substantial part of the regulation results from the interaction of transcription factors (TFs) with specific cis regulatory DNA sequences. These regulatory sequences are organized in a modular fashion, with each module (enhancer) containing one or more binding sites for a specific combination of TFs. In the present work, the authors have proposed to investigate the inter motif distance between the important motifs in the promoter sequences of citrate synthase of different mammals. The authors have used a new distance measure to compare the promoter sequences. Results reveal that there exists more similarity between organisms in the same chromosome.

1. INTRODUCTION

Common activities in bioinformatics/cognitive informatics include developing a unified analysis of pattern and organization of biological structures. Developing computational techniques that give insight into these areas is of utmost importance.

The hereditary information for organisms is carried in its genes. Genes are sequences of the polymer DNA which, for our purposes, can be viewed as strings over the alphabet {A,C,G,T}, where each of the four characters corresponds to one of the nucleotide bases that makes up DNA. Individual genes are subsequences of the much larger strings of DNA that comprise the chromosomes of an organism. In addition to specifying

DOI: 10.4018/978-1-4666-2651-5.ch025

the structural information for proteins, genes must be turned on and off at precisely the right time and in the correct tissue in the developing and mature organism. This process is termed as gene regulation and is one of the central problems in modern biology.

The first step in gene regulation is transcription, where the information in a gene is amplified by copying it into RNA, a polymer similar to DNA. Short DNA sequences termed transcription elements, typically of the order of 6-10 base pairs in length, are recognized and bound by sequence-specific binding proteins termed transcription factors to form transcription complexes through protein-protein as well as DNA-protein interactions. Important transcription elements are located immediately preceding the start of genes. More surprisingly, transcription elements are also found thousands of bases upstream, downstream and even within the boundaries of a gene. The transcriptional state of a gene (i.e., its time, tissue and rate of expression) is determined through formation of a "transcription complex" composed of multiple, interacting transcription factors bound to their respective transcription elements. The information needed to specify a transcription factor binding site is not all local to an individual transcription element, but requires interactions with other binding sites through protein-protein interactions to stabilize the complex.

In this paper, we propose to compare promoter sequences by considering the important motifs that are responsible for expression of that particular gene. Some of the available tools that compare promoter sequences are ConReal (Berezikov, Guryev, & Cuppen, 2005) MUMmer (Kurtz, Phillippy, Delcher, Smoot, Shumway, Antonescu, & Salzberg, 2004). Pair wise comparison is possible with these tools and also they do not provide a similarity score. Another class of methods uses prior knowledge of TFBSs to construct the alignments. While ConReal focuses on generating an ordered chain of conserved TFBSs, thus not aligning regions that do not contain them, Site-

blast is a BLAST (Michael, Dieterich, & Vingron, 2005)-like heuristic where the TFBS hits are used as seeds. The method of Hallikas et al. (2006) also falls in this category. Here, the sequence of hit pairs is aligned using a scoring scheme that considers clustering of sites, binding affinity and conservation, though the underlying sequences themselves are not aligned. Other approaches like Monkey (Moses, Chiang, Pollard, Iyer, & Eisen, 2004) explicitly take into account evolutionary properties of the TFBSs, but still perform the alignment independent of the annotation step.

The focus of bioinformatics has begun to extend from the identification of genes toward understanding how the expression and regulation of genes is orchestrated in a genomic level. Genes expressed within the same biological context often share promoter modules/frameworks (Fessele, Maier, Zischek, Nelson, & Werner, 2002; Werner, 1999, 2001).

Understanding how the regulation of gene networks is orchestrated is an important challenge for characterizing complex biological processes. Gene transcription is regulated in part by nuclear factors that recognize short DNA sequence motifs, called transcription factor binding sites, in most cases located upstream of the gene coding sequence in promoter and enhancer regions. Genes expressed in the same tissue under similar conditions often share a common organization of at least some of these regulatory binding elements. In this way the organization of promoter motifs represents a "footprint" of the transcriptional regulatory mechanisms in a specific biologic context and thus provides information about signal and tissue specific control of expression. Promoters are the central processors of transcriptional control, as the regulatory information contributed by the other elements must be integrated within the context of a promoter in order to influence gene expression (Werner, 1999). Understanding how networks of promoters are organized provides insight into when and how the expression of specific genes is controlled.

The DNA sequences that comprise promoters do not provide much direct information about regulation. Promoter function is not coupled to fixed stretches of sequence homology, but rather to highly variable elements representing individual transcription factor binding sites that act as a binding site for their cognate protein. The sites are generally composed of 6 to 18 nucleotides, often separated by non conserved sequences. Although binding site detection is important in higher organisms, it is generally not sufficient to elucidate promoter function. In more complex systems the functional transcription factor binding sites within promoters are organized hierarchically (Klingenhoff, Frech, Quandt, & Werner, 1999; Klingenhoff, Frech, & Werner, 2002). Combinatorial biology appears to be the key to understanding regulation in higher organisms where promoter function is determined more by the functional context within which the binding sites are located (Werner, 2001). The regulation of gene transcription is mainly based on the interaction between transcription factors and the genomic regulatory regions of genes within the genome. A given transcription factor can have different effects on different promoters. Tightly orchestrated spatial and temporal regulation of gene transcription is critical to the proper development of all metazoans. A substantial part of the regulation results from the interaction of transcription factors (TFs) with specific cis regulatory DNA sequences. These regulatory sequences are organized in a modular fashion, with each module (enhancer) containing one or more binding sites for a specific combination of TFs (Davidson, 2001). The tissue-restricted and signal-activated TFs then bind to specific sites within the enhancers of particular genes, defining a combinatorial transcriptional code that facilitates the expression of those genes in a particular developmental context. This type of regulation system is called a cis regulatory module (CRM). Such a module consists of (1) specific sequences of DNA called motifs to which transcription factors bind, (2) logical relationships between these sites and (3) spatial relationships between these sites (Noto & Craven, 2006).

Promoter modules represent the next level of functional organization after individual transcription factor binding sites. Promoter modules are defined as two or more individual elements that act in a coordinated way (either synergistically or antagonistically) with the contributing elements arranged within a defined distance and sequential order (Firulli & Olson, 1997; Klingenhoff, Frech, & Werner, 2002). Here, the locations of individual motifs are irrelevant and only the distance between them is of concern. A given promoter module may show a robust stimulus specific response in one tissue but in a second cell type may not be functional. This can result, for example, from a different complement or concentration of specific transcription factors or from selective signaling events further upstream in an activation pathway. Promoter modules can also exhibit cooperative protein binding and often include one binding element that represents a "poor" binding site for a specific transcription factor (Boehlk et al., 2000). Through cooperative effects, the stronger binding protein partner can stabilize the binding of the weaker partner, but the loss of either binding site abolishes function. This highlights an important aspect of transcriptional regulation, namely, that a weak binding site embedded in the correct context can be functionally as important as a strong binding site. Changing the order or spacing of important transcription factor binding sites can change the overall structure of the promoter and thus has great effect on transcription. Promoter modules and frameworks are important in mediating tissue and signal-specific transcriptional responses (Werner, Fessele, Maier, & Nelson, 2003).

The information governing how transcription factors influence gene expression is laid down in the regulatory genomic sequences, not in the proteins themselves, and thus a tremendous amount of information can be mined from regulatory regions. Computer modeling of promoter organization is an important new tool in the study of transcriptional regulation and promoter regulatory network by quickly identifying potential regulatory regions and providing information about the functional context in gene expression (Werner, Fessele, Maier, & Nelson, 2003). Linking the results of functional analysis of gene regulation can allow rapid identification of a series of potential co-regulated genes and thus facilitate target gene characterization and identification. The target genes that have position-specific motifs or the distance-specific motif-pairs tend to be co-expressed and have similar functions (Halfon, Grad, Church, & Michelson, 2002).

Eukaryotic transcriptional regulation is complex. Typically, it takes place by cooperative regulation. The regulation of gene transcription depends on interactions among transcription factors and the polymerase. This imposes location constraints on the corresponding DNA elements. For example, several cis elements occur at a specific distance relative to the transcription start site (TSS) (Lim, Santoso, Boulay, Dong, Ohler, & Kadonaga, 2004). Also, several cis elements occur in the same promoter with restricted spacing between them. Several previous works have shown positional constraint of cis-regulatory motifs to. Xie et al. (2005) have reported such a large number of motifs in the human genome based on multiple genome comparison . In this work, we have proposed to investigate the inter motif distance between the important motifs in the promoter sequences of citrate synthase of different mammals using a distance measure proposed by Meera, Rangarajan, and Bhat (2009).

2. METHODOLOGY

The promoter sequences are extracted from NCBI database upstream of the coding region of citrate synthase gene of different mammals. It has been reported (Kraft, LeMoine, Lyons, Michaud, Mueller, & Moyes, 2005) that the citrate gene is mainly regulated by four transcription factors

namely sp1, CBP, MyoD and NF1. Also, we have extracted the consensus sequences of these motifs from available literature.

We have developed a string matching method (Table 1) to identify the given set of motifs (TFBS) in a given promoter sequence along with the positions of occurrences of motifs in the promoter. Then the results are tabulated from the following algorithm and analysis is done regarding the distance between these motifs (inter motif distance).

2A. MOTIF IDENTIFICATION

The idea behind the proposed algorithm is to find sum of absolute difference values.

The proposed algorithm has two phases:

1. **Preprocessing Phase:** In this, periodic of pattern is obtained so that pattern length i.e., window size is equal to text size.
2. **Searching Phase:** In this phase, absolute difference of ASCII value of each alphabet of text and pattern is obtained and stored in the array, then the summing absolute difference (for the length of pattern) and comparing

Table 1. Comparison of different string matching algorithms

Algorithm	Time Complexity for Pre-Phase	Time Complexity for Searching Phase
Proposed algorithm	$O(n/m)$	$O(mn)$
Brute- force	-	$O(mn)$
Boyer-Moore	$O(m+\sigma)$	$O(mn)$
Quick search	$O(m+\sigma)$	$O(mn)$
Horspool	$O(m+\sigma)$	$O(mn)$
Raita	$O(m+\sigma)$	$O(mn)$
Berry-Ravindran	$O(m+\sigma^2)$	$O(mn)$
K.M.P.	$O(m)$	$O(m+n)$

with zero. Wherever sum is zero, pattern is detected and noting down the position at which pattern is present in the text. This is repeated till the end of array. Then the window is shifted by one and procedure is repeated. The number of shifts required is equal to the length of pattern sequence (Box 1).

Working Example

```
Y= ATCTAACATCATAACCCTAATTG (Text)
X=TAATT (Pattern)
N=23=Length of text
M=5 = Length of pattern
```

Box 1.

Step1: Read the text [DNA sequence]
Step2: Read pattern list [motifs list] to be detected in text.
{Total number of patterns $P_1 \ldots\ldots\ldots. P_n$
Where $P_1=p_{11}, \; p_{12}\ldots\ldots\ldots.$
$P_2= p_{21}, \; p_{22} \ldots\ldots\ldots.$
•
•
$P_n=p_{n1}, \; p_{n2}\ldots\ldots\ldots$
}
Step3: For n=1 to total_num_pattern sequence (motif sequence)
{
For m=1 to total_num_elements for n_{th} pattern sequence
}

$$\text{Number of cycles} = \frac{\left[length\ of\ text\right]}{\left[length\ of\ element\ of\ n_{th}\,pattern\ sequence\right]}$$

a) Generate a periodic of element of n_{th} pattern sequence
Pattern_length = (Number of cycles) * (Length of element of n_{th} Pattern sequence)
b) Find [store in an array] the absolute value of difference between each alphabet of text sequence and periodic pattern of an element of n_{th} pattern sequence.
c) Calculate the sum of the elements in the array sequentially for every N elements.
Where N= Length of element in the pattern sequence.
If (sum==0) then note the position of first element of p_{th} cycle corresponding to the zero sum.
d) Repeat the above step till the end of an array.
e) Repeat the steps from (c) with a relative position between periodic pattern and the text   increased by one till the relative position value is equal to the length of element.

(a) Preprocessing Phase

Number of cycles =23/5=4

Therefore, Periodic of pattern generated are= TAATT TAATT TAATT TAATT

(b) Searching Phase

Since SUM≠0, pattern is not detected in first attempt (See Figure 1).

Since SUM≠0, pattern is not detected in second attempt (See Figure 2).

Since SUM=0, pattern is detected in third attempt (See Figure 3).

Since SUM≠0, pattern is not detected in forth attempt (See Figure 4).

Since SUM≠0, pattern is not detected in fifth attempt (See Figure 5).

Main Features of Proposed Algorithm

- Easy to implement;
- Searching phase in O(mn) time complexity;
- Preprocessing phase in O(n/m) time complexity;
- Always shifts the window by exactly 1 position;

- Shifts required are equals to length of pattern.

The important motifs and their inter motif distance is found out and tabulated using the string matching method. A new distance measure has been derived for finding the similarity between sequences of different mammals.

2B. DISTANCE MEASURE

Let M_x and M_y be two motif sequences of length i and j respectively. Tx and Ty are the TFs of the sequences M_x and M_y. i.e.,

$M_x=T_{x1},T_{x2},T_{x3}\ldots\ldots T_{xi}$ &
$M_y=T_{y1},T_{y2},T_{y3}\ldots\ldots\ldots T_{yj}$, are the two motif sequences. Let S(x,y) be the score between a pair of TF-mapped sequences.

We have developed an algorithm,' Similarity measure' to compute the score $\sum$ between two motif sequences M_x & M_y. This algorithm finds matches between sites in the motif sequences. For each match of a TF in both the sequences, a similarity measure score α is used. So for computing similarity with respect to the presence of motifs in the given two sequences;

Figure 1. Attempt-1

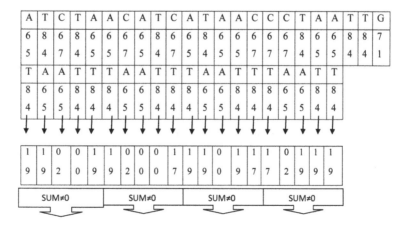

Figure 2. Attempt-2

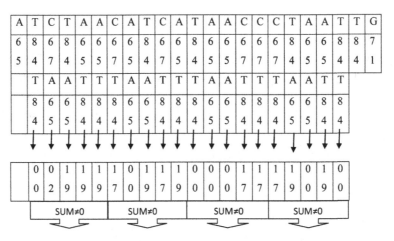

Figure 3. Attempt-3

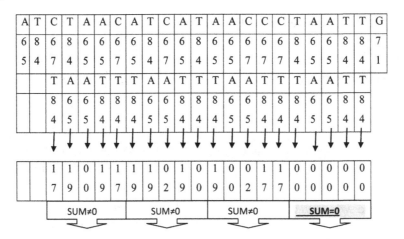

Figure 4. Attempt-4

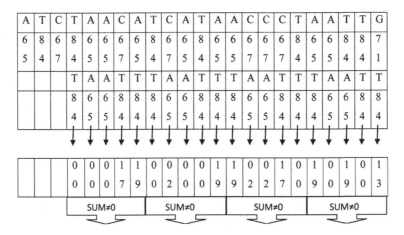

Figure 5. Attempt-5

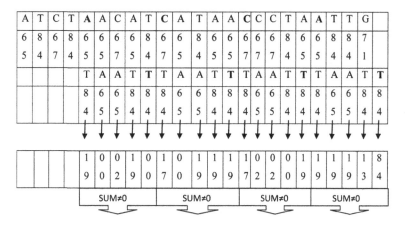

$$\alpha \sum\nolimits_{Tx=1}^{i} \sum\nolimits_{Ty=1}^{j} T_{x,y}. \qquad (1)$$

Function 'Difference' computes a score regarding the order of the motifs in the promoter sequences. For each motif in sequence 'M$_x$', a corresponding motif in sequence 'M$_y$' is searched and differences in their positions $|\, p_x - p_y \,|$ where p_x and p_y are positions of motif 'm' in sequences 'M$_x$' and 'M$_y$' respectively, is calculated. Let μ be dissimilarity score;

$$\mu = (1/i+j).\text{Then the score of the comparison}$$
when order of motifs is considered is

$$\mu \sum\nolimits_{Tx=1}^{i} (p_x - p_y) \qquad (2)$$

Combining Equation (1) and Equation (2), the total similarity score between the two sequences;

$$S_{x,y} = \alpha \sum\nolimits_{Tx=1}^{i} \sum\nolimits_{Ty=1}^{j} T_{x,y} - \mu \sum\nolimits_{Tx=1}^{i} (p_x - p_y) \qquad (3)$$

3. RESULTS

See Table 2, Table 3, and Table 4.

Table 2. The presence or absence of the four important motifs of citrate synthase in different mammals

\Motif Organism\	Sp1	CBP	MyoD	NF1
Homosapien Chromosome 19	yes	yes	yes	no
Pan trygolodytes Chromosome 19	yes	yes	yes	no
Homosapien Chromosome 12	yes	yes	yes	no
Pan trygolodytes Chromosome 12	yes	yes	yes	no
Bos taurus Chromosome 5	no	yes	yes	yes
Sus scrofa Chromosome 5	yes	yes	yes	no
Bos taurus Chromosome 10	yes	yes	yes	no
Cannis felis Chromosome 10	yes	yes	yes	no
Rattus Chromosome 7	no	yes	yes	no
Homosapien Chromosome 6	no	yes	yes	yes
Pan trygolodytes Chromosome 3	yes	yes	yes	no
Mcaca Mullata Chromosome 11	yes	yes	yes	yes

Table 3. Motifs exhibiting constraint inter-motif distance in citrate synthase

	MyoD	CBP	Sp1
Homosapien Chromosome 19	-523 -216	-1810	-93
Pan trygolodytes Chromosome 19	-518 -214	-1812	-88
Homosapien Chromosome 12	-664 -289 -616	-2679 -2549 -146	-184 -312 -210 -186
Pan trygolodytes Chromosome 12	-666 -289 -618	-2676 -2542 -146	-184 -312 -210 -186
Bos taurus Chromosome 5	-544 -133	-795	
Sus scrofa Chromosome 5	-537 -170	-605	
Bos taurus Chromosome 10	-535 -422		-542
Cannis felis Chromosome 10	-505 -448		-746

4. DISCUSSION AND CONCLUSION

In this work, we have made an attempt to investigate the inter motif distance between the important motifs in the promoter sequences of citrate synthase of different mammals. Promoter sequences are extracted from NCBI database. Important motifs for citrate synthase (Table 2) are obtained from available literature. Using a new string matching method, the important motifs are

Table 4. The similarity score between different mammals of the enzyme citrate synthase using the new distance measure

	Bos-5	Bos-10	Can-10	Hs-6	Hs-12	Hs-19	Pan-3	Pan-12	Pan-19	Rat-7	mac-11	Sus-5
Bos-5	8.1	6.9	7.8	7.8	7.0	8.1	9.2	7.2	7.3	6.7	7.8	8.0
Bos-10	6.9	8.1	7.4	6.8	7.7	9.1	9.9	7.7	8.2	5.1	7.4	7.1
Can-10	7.8	7.4	6.8	4.8	6.4	9.1	10.5	6.2	8.3	7.2	5.6	4.8
Hs-6	7.8	6.8	4.8	5.7	5.4	8.5	9.7	5.5	7.6	7.0	5.6	5.2
Hs-12	7.0	7.7	6.4	5.4	12.2	9.6	11.5	11.8	8.7	7.2	11.3	6.6
Hs-19	8.1	9.1	9.1	8.5	9.6	9.7	9.5	9.8	9.6	8.7	9.4	8.0
Pan-3	9.2	9.9	10.5	9.7	11.5	9.5	11.6	11.4	9.5	9.9	10.4	9.2
Pan-12	7.2	7.7	6.2	5.5	11.8	8.9	8.5	10.0	8.8	7.2	9.6	5.5
Pan-19	7.3	8.2	8.3	7.6	8.7	8.8	8.7	8.8	8.8	8.0	8.6	7.2
Rat-7	6.7	5.1	7.2	7.0	7.2	5.2	7.4	7.2	5.2	7.3	7.1	6.7
Mc-11	7.8	7.4	5.6	5.6	11.3	8.8	8.5	9.6	6.9	5.5	6.6	5.1
Sus-5	8.0	7.1	4.8	5.2	6.6	7.2	7.8	5.5	6.4	4.9	5.1	7.2

extracted from the promoter sequences along with their positions in the sequences and tabulated. Using the distance measure described in Section 2B, distance between the promoter sequences of different mammals is calculated and tabulated.

It has been reported that the citrate synthase gene is mainly regulated by four transcription factors namely sp1,CBP,MyoD, NF1 (Kraft, LeMoine, Lyons, Michaud, Mueller, & Moyes, 2005). Also Klingenhoff, Frech, and Werner (2000) have reported that some transcription factors interact cooperatively with RNA polymerase to bind to motifs upstream of coding region to initiate transcription. Interacting TF pairs may satisfy certain spatial requirements to have a functional interaction – their corresponding binding motifs may demonstrate characteristic distance relationships in promoter sequences (Noto & Craven, 2006).

It has been observed that sp1 and CBP are present in all the promoter sequences considered and also a significant observation has been made regarding inter-motif distance between MyoD, sp1 and CBP in the same chromosome of different mammals. Genome wide sequence comparisons and studies of individual genes have confirmed that regulatory elements are indeed conserved between related species (Zhang & Gerstein, 2003).The results show the inter motif distance constraint between these three motifs (Table 3). However regarding the transcription factor NF1, its presence is not uniform in all the mammals.

GATA-1 is a hematopoietic transcription factor that is essential for the terminal maturation of proerythroblasts, megakaryocytic cells and mast cells. Loss of GATA-1 leads to erythroid maturation arrest. GATA and AP1 interact co operatively.

Table 4 reveals that when chromosome wise comparison is made, Homoosapien chromosome 12 and Pantrygolodytes chromosome 12 and Homoosapien chromosome19 and Pantrygolodytes chromosome 19 and canis felis chromosome 10

and Bos Taurus chromosome 10 show similar scores with the remaining organisms.

The analysis of promoters for organizational features provides a link between the genomic nucleotide sequence and important aspects of gene regulation and expression. In this work we have attempted to find the positional constraint of some motifs and also inter-motif distance constraint between few motifs of citrate synthase which is present in the citric acid cycle (Krebs cycle) of Central metabolic pathway since this pathway is present in almost all organisms of prokaryotes and eukaryotes Also, we have proposed to find the distance between promoter sequences of different mammals based on cis regulatory module using a distance measure (Meera, Rangarajan, & Bhat, 2009).

REFERENCES

Berezikov, E., Guryev, V., & Cuppen, E. (2005). CONREAL web server: identification and visualization of conserved transcription factor binding sites. *Nucleic Acids Research, 33.*

Berry, T., & Ravindran, S. (1977). A fast string matching algorithm and experimental. *Communications of the ACM, 20*(10), 762–772. doi:10.1145/359842.359859

Boehlk, S., Fessele, S., Mojaat, A., Miyamoto, N. G., Werner, T., & Nelson, E. L. (2000). ATF and Jun transcription factors, acting through an Ets/CRE promoter module, mediate lipopolysaccharide inducibility of the chemokine RANTES in monocytic Mono Mac 6 cells. *European Journal of Immunology, 30*, 1102–1112. doi:10.1002/(SICI)1521-4141(200004)30:4<1102::AID-IMMU1102>3.0.CO;2-X

Boyer, R. S., & Moore, J. S. (1999). A fast string searching algorithm. *Communications of the ACM, 20*(10).

Burke, S. A., Lo, S. L., & Krzycki, J. A. (1998). *Clustered genes encoding the methyltransferases of methanogenesis from monomethylamine*. Columbus, OH: Ohio State University.

Davidson, E. H. (2001). *Genomic regulatory systems*. San Diego, CA: Academic Press.

Fessele, S., Maier, H., Zischek, C., Nelson, P. J., & Werner, T. (2002). Regulatory context is a crucial part of gene function. *Trends in Genetics*, *18*, 60–63. doi:10.1016/S0168-9525(02)02591-X

Firulli, A. B., & Olson, E. N. (1997). Modular regulation of muscle gene transcription: a mechanism for muscle cell diversity. *Trends in Genetics*, *13*, 364–336. doi:10.1016/S0168-9525(97)01171-2

Frech, K., & Werner, T. (1997). Specific modelling of regulatory units in DNA sequences. In *Proceedings of the Pacific Symposium on Biocomputing* (pp. 151-162).

Halfon, M. S., Grad, Y., Church, G. M., & Michelson, A. M. (2002). Computation-based discovery of related transcriptional regulatory modules and motifs using an experimentally validated combinatorial model. *Genome Research*, *12*, 1019–1028.

Hallikas, O., Palin, K., Sinjushina, N., Rautiainen, R., Partanen, J., Ukkonen, E., & Taipale, J. (2006). Genome-wide prediction of mammalian enhancers based on analysis of transcription-factor binding affinity. *Cell*, *124*(1), 47–59. doi:10.1016/j.cell.2005.10.042

Horspool, R. N. (1980). Practical fast searching in strings. *Software, Practice & Experience*, *10*(6), 501–506. doi:10.1002/spe.4380100608

Klingenhoff, A., Frech, K., Quandt, K., & Werner, T. (1999). Functional promoter modules can be detected by formal models independent of overall nucleotide sequence similarity. *Bioinformatics (Oxford, England)*, *15*, 180–186. doi:10.1093/bioinformatics/15.3.180

Klingenhoff, A., Frech, K., & Werner, T. (2000). Regulatory modules shared within gene classes as well as across gene classes can be detected by the same in silico approach. *In Silico Biology*, *2*, 17–26.

Knuth, D. E., Morris, J. H., & Pratt, V. R. (1977). Fast pattern matching in strings. *SIAM Journal on Computing*, *6*(1), 323–350. doi:10.1137/0206024

Kraft, C. S., LeMoine, C. M. R., Lyons, C. N., Michaud, D., Mueller, C. R., & Moyes, C. D. (2005). Control of mitochondrial biogenesis during myogenesis. *The American Journal of Physiology*, *290*, 1119–1127. doi:10.1152/ajpcell.00463.2005

Kurtz, S., Phillippy, A., Delcher, A. L., Smoot, M., Shumway, M., Antonescu, C., & Salzberg, S. L. (2004). Versatile and open software for comparing large genomes. *Genome Biology*, *5*(2), R12. doi:10.1186/gb-2004-5-2-r12

Lim, C. Y., Santoso, B., Boulay, T., Dong, E., Ohler, U., & Kadonaga, J. T. (2004). The MTE, a new core promoter element for transcription by RNA polymerase II. *Genes & Development*, *18*(13), 1606–1617. doi:10.1101/gad.1193404

Meera, A., Rangarajan, L., & Bhat, S. (2009). Computational approach towards promoter sequence comparison via TF mapping using a new distance measure *Interdisciplinary Sciences: Computational. Life Sciences*, *3*(1), 43–49.

Michael, M., Dieterich, C., & Vingron, M. (2005). SITEBLAST—rapid and sensitive local alignment of genomic sequences employing motif anchors. *Bioinformatics (Oxford, England)*, *21*(9), 2093–2094. doi:10.1093/bioinformatics/bti224

Moses, A. M., Chiang, D. Y., Pollard, D. A., Iyer, V. N., & Eisen, M. B. (2004). MONKEY: Identifying conserved transcription factor binding sites in multiple alignments using a binding site-specific evolutionary model. *Genome Biology*, *5*(2), 98. doi:10.1186/gb-2004-5-12-r98

Noto, K., & Craven, M. (2006). Learning probabilistic models of cis-regulatory modules that represent logical and spatial aspects. *Bioinformatics (Oxford, England), 23*, 156–162. doi:10.1093/bioinformatics/btl319

Werner, T. (1999). Models for prediction and recognition of eukaryotic promoters. *Mammalian Genome, 10*, 168–175. doi:10.1007/s003359900963

Werner, T. (2001). The promoter connection. *Nature Genetics, 29*, 105–106. doi:10.1038/ng1001-105

Werner, T., Fessele, S., Maier, H., & Nelson, P. J. (2003). Computer modeling of promoter organization as a tool to study transcriptional coregulation. *The FASEB Journal, 17*, 1228–1237. doi:10.1096/fj.02-0955rev

Xie, X., Lu, J., Kulbokas, E. J., Golub, T. R., Mootha, V., & Lindblad-Toh, K. (2005). Systematic discovery of regulatory motifs in human promoters and 3' UTRs by comparison of several mammals. *Nature, 434*, 338–345. doi:10.1038/nature03441

Zhang, Z., & Gerstein, M. (2003). Of mice and men: phylogenetic footprinting aids the discovery of regulatory elements. *Journal of Biology, 2*(2), 11. doi:10.1186/1475-4924-2-11

This work was previously published in the International Journal of Software Science and Computational Intelligence, Volume 3, Issue 2, edited by Yingxu Wang, pp. 57-68, copyright 2011 by IGI Publishing (an imprint of IGI Global).

Compilation of References

Abbott, K. W. (1988). Robust operative diagnosis as problem solving in a hypothesis space. In *Proceedings of the AAAI Conference on Artificial Intelligence* (pp. 369-374).

Agrawal, R., Mannila, H., Srikant, R., Toivonen, H., & Verkamo, A. I. (1996). Fast discovery of association rules. In Fayyad, U. M., Piatetsky-Shapiro, G., Smyth, P., & Uthurusamy, R. (Eds.), *Advances in knowledge discovery and data mining*. Menlo Park, CA: AAAI Press.

Albrecht, A. J. (1979, October). Measuring application development productivity. In *Proceedings of the IBM Applications Development Joint SHARE/GUIDE Symposium* (pp. 83-92).

Albrecht, A. J., & Gaffney, J. E. (1983). Software function, source lines of code, and development effort prediction: A software science validation. *IEEE Transactions on Software Engineering*, 9(6), 639–648. doi:10.1109/TSE.1983.235271

Anderson, R. J., & Spong, M. W. (1989). Bilateral control of teleoperators with time delay. *IEEE Transactions on Automatic Control*, 34(5), 494–501. doi:10.1109/9.24201

Aravindh, K. B., Saranya, G., Selvakumar, R., Swetha, S. R., Saranya, M., & Sumesh, E. P. (2010). Fault detection in induction motor using WPT and multiple SVM. *International Journal of Control and Automation*, 3(2).

Arrowsmith, D. K., & Place, C. M. (1990). *An introduction to dynamical systems*. Cambridge, UK: Cambridge University Press.

Baker, J. W., & Vink, E. P. (1996). A metric approach to control flow semantics. *Annals of the New York Academy of Sciences*, 806, 11–27. doi:10.1111/j.1749-6632.1996.tb49156.x

Baker, J. W., & Vink, E. P. (1998). Denotational models for programming languages: Applications of Banach's fixed point theorem. *Topology Applications*, 85, 35–52. doi:10.1016/S0166-8641(97)00140-5

Balakrishnan, K., & Honavar, V. (1995). *Evolutionary design of neural architecture – A preliminary taxonomy and guide to literature* (Tech. Rep. No. 95-01). Ames, IA: Artificial Intelligence Research Group, Iowa State University.

Ball, M. O., Barnhart, C., Nemhauser, G., & Odoni, A. (2007). Air transportation: Irregular operations and control. In Barnhart, C., & Laporte, G. (Eds.), *Handbook in operations research and management science* (Vol. 14, pp. 1–73). Oxford, UK: Elsevier.

Banko, M., & Etzioni, O. (2007, October). Strategies for lifelong knowledge extraction from the web. In *Proceedings of the Fourth International Conference on Knowledge Capture*, Whistler, BC, Canada (pp. 95-102).

Barquilla, N. L., Nuñez, M., & Pelayo, F. L. (2008). A comparative study of STOPA and RTPA. *Transactions on Computational Science*, 2, 224–245.

Basili, V. R. (1980). *Qualitative software complexity models: A summary in tutorial on models and methods for software management and engineering*. Los Alamitos, CA: IEEE Press.

Bass, L., Clements, P., & Kazman, R. (1998). *Software architecture in practice*. Reading, MA: Addison-Wesley.

Bay, H., Ess, A., Tuytelaars, T., & Gool, L. V. (2008). SURF: Speeded Up Robust Features. *Computer Vision and Image Understanding*, 110(3), 346–359. doi:10.1016/j.cviu.2007.09.014

Becker, K., Becker, M., & Schwarz, J. H. (2007). *String theory and m-theory: A modern introduction.* Cambridge, UK: Cambridge University Press.

Begg, R. K., Palaniswami, & Owen, M., B. (2005). Support vector machines for automated gait classification. *IEEE Transactions on Bio-Medical Engineering, 52*(5), 828–838. doi:10.1109/TBME.2005.845241

Beizer, B. (1990). *Software testing techniques.* New York, NY: Van Nostrand Reinhold.

Belnap, N. D. (1977). A useful four-valued logic. In Epstein, G., & Dunn, J. (Eds.), *Modern uses of multiple-valued logic* (pp. 8–37). Dordrecht, The Netherlands: D. Reidel. doi:10.1007/978-94-010-1161-7_2

Bender, E. A. (1996). *Mathematical methods in artificial intelligence.* Los Alamitos, CA: IEEE Press.

Berezikov, E., Guryev, V., & Cuppen, E. (2005). CON-REAL web server: identification and visualization of conserved transcription factor binding sites. *Nucleic Acids Research, 33.*

Berg, E., & Friedlander, M. (2007). *SPGL1: A solver for large-scale sparse reconstruction.* Retrieved from http://www.cs.ubc.ca/labs/scl/spgl1/

Bergadano, F., & Gunetti, D. (1996). Testing by means of inductive program learning. *ACM Transactions on Software Engineering and Methodology, 5*(2), 119–145. doi:10.1145/227607.227611

Berger, A., Caruana, R., Cohn, D., Freitag, D., & Mittal, V. (2000). Bridging the lexical chasm: Statistical approaches to answer-finding. In *Proceedings of the 23rd Annual International ACM SIGIR Conference on Research and Development in Information Retrieval* (pp. 192-199).

Berry, T., & Ravindran, S. (1977). A fast string matching algorithm and experimental. *Communications of the ACM, 20*(10), 762–772. doi:10.1145/359842.359859

Bertossi, L., & Chomicki, J. (2003). Query answering in inconsistent databases. In Chomicki, J., Meyden, R., & Saake, G. (Eds.), *Logics for emerging applications of databases* (pp. 43–83). Berlin, Germany: Springer-Verlag.

Besnard, P., & Hunter, A. (2008). *Elements of argumentation.* Cambridge, MA: MIT Press.

Bhattacharya, P., & Gavrilova, M. L. (2008). Roadmap-based path planning - Using the Voronoi diagram for a clearance-based shortest path. *IEEE Robotics & Automation Magazine, 15*(2), 58–66. doi:10.1109/MRA.2008.921540

Biffl, S., Aurum, A., Boehm, B., Erdogmus, H., & Grunbacher, P. (Eds.). (2006). *Value-based software engineering.* Berlin, Germany: Springer-Verlag. doi:10.1007/3-540-29263-2

Blankertz, B., Sannelli, C., Halder, S., Hammer, E. M., Kübler, A., & Müller, K. R. (2010). Neurophysiological predictor of SMR-based BCI performances. *NeuroImage, 51*(4), 3–9. doi:10.1016/j.neuroimage.2010.03.022

Boehlk, S., Fessele, S., Mojaat, A., Miyamoto, N. G., Werner, T., & Nelson, E. L. (2000). ATF and Jun transcription factors, acting through an Ets/CRE promoter module, mediate lipopolysaccharide inducibility of the chemokine RANTES in monocytic Mono Mac 6 cells. *European Journal of Immunology, 30,* 1102–1112. doi:10.1002/(SICI)1521-4141(200004)30:4<1102::AID-IMMU1102>3.0.CO;2-X

Boehm, B. (2006). Overview and agenda. In Biffl, S., Aurum, A., Boehm, B., Erdogmus, H., & Grünbacher, P. (Eds.), *Value-based software engineering.* Berlin, Germany: Springer-Verlag. doi:10.1007/3-540-29263-2_1

Boehm, B., Abts, C., Brown, A. W., Chulani, S., Clark, B. K., & Horowitz, E. (2000). *Software cost estimation with COCOMO II.* Upper Saddle River, NJ: Prentice Hall.

Boehm, B., & Basili, V. R. (2001). Software defect reduction top 10 list. *IEEE Computer, 34*(1), 135–137. doi:10.1109/2.962984

Boehm, B., Huang, L., Jain, A., & Madachy, R. (2004). The ROI of software dependability: The iDAVE model. *IEEE Software, 21*(3), 54–61. doi:10.1109/MS.2004.1293073

Bollella, G. (2002). *The real-time specification for java.* Reading, MA: Addison-Wesley.

Bollella, G., Brosgol, B., Furr, S., Hardin, D., Dibble, P., Gosling, J., & Turnbull, M. (2002). *The real-time specification for java.* Reading, MA: Addison-Wesley.

Boyer, R. S., & Moore, J. S. (1999). A fast string searching algorithm. *Communications of the ACM, 20*(10).

Bracewell, R. N. (1986). *The Fourier transform and its applications* (2nd rev. ed.). New York, NY: McGraw-Hill.

Brachman, R. J., & Levesque, H. J. (2004). *Knowledge representation and reasoning.* San Francisco, CA: Morgan Kaufmann.

Bratton, D., & Kennedy, J. (2007). Defining a standard for particle swarm optimization. In *Proceedings of the IEEE Swarm Intelligence Symposium* (pp. 120-127). Washington, DC: IEEE Computer Society.

Braun, E. L., & Gianoplus, A. S. (2009). A digital computer system for terminal-area air traffic control. *IRE Transactions on Space Electronics and Telemetry, 5*(2), 66–72.

Brewster, C., O'Hara, K., Fuller, S., Wilks, Y., Franconi, E., & Musen, M. A. (2004). Knowledge representation with ontologies: The present and future. *IEEE Intelligent Systems, 19*(1), 72–81. doi:10.1109/MIS.2004.1265889

Broy, M., Pair, C., & Wirsing, M. (1984). A systematic study of models of abstract data types. *Theoretical Computer Science, 33*, 139–1274. doi:10.1016/0304-3975(84)90086-0

Brumitt, B., Meyers, B., & Krumm, J. Kern, A., & Shafer, S. (2000). EasyLiving: Technologies for intelligent environments, handheld and ubiquitous computing. In *Proceedings of the 2nd International Symposium on Handheld and Ubiquitous Computing* (pp. 12-29).

Bue, B. D., & Stepinski, T. F. (2007). Machine detection of martian impact craters from digital topography data. *IEEE Transactions on Geoscience and Remote Sensing, 45*(1), 265–274. doi:10.1109/TGRS.2006.885402

Bueno, P. M. S., & Jino, M. (2002). Automatic test data generation for program paths using genetic algorithms. *International Journal of Software Engineering and Knowledge Engineering, 12*(6), 691–709. doi:10.1142/S0218194002001074

Bukovsky, I., & Bila, J. (2008a). Adaptive evaluation of complex time series using nonconventional neural units. In *Proceedings of the 7th IEEE International Conference on Cognitive Informatics* (pp. 128-137).

Bukovsky, I., Anderle, F., & Smetana, L. (2008). Quadratic neural unit for adaptive prediction of transitions among local attractors of lorenz system. In *Proceedings of the IEEE International Conference on Automation and Logistics*, Qingdao, China (pp. 147-152).

Bukovsky, I., Hou, Z.-G., Gupta, M. M., & Bila, J. (2007). Foundation of notation and classification of nonconventional static and dynamic neural units. In *Proceedings of the 6th IEEE International Conference on Cognitive Informatics* (pp. 401-407).

Bukovsky, I., Ichiji, K., Homma, N., Yoshizawa, M., & Rodriguez, R. (2010a). Testing potentials of dynamic quadratic neural unit for prediction of lung motion during respiration for tracking radiation therapy. In *Proceedings of the IEEE International Joint Conference on Neural Networks*, Barcelona, Spain (pp. 1-6).

Bukovsky, I., Lepold, M., & Bila, J. (2010b). Quadratic neural unit and its network in validation of process data of steam turbine loop and energetic boiler. In *Proceedings of the IEEE International Joint Conference on Neural Networks*, Barcelona, Spain (pp. 1-7).

Bukovsky, I., Redlapalli, S., & Gupta, M. M. (2003). Quadratic and cubic neural units for identification and fast state feedback control of unknown non-linear dynamic systems. In *Proceedings of the Fourth International Symposium on Uncertainty Modeling and Analysis* (pp. 330-334).

Bukovsky, I., & Bila, J. (2007). *Analysis of methods for evaluation of data uncertainty for control of energetic systems (report for I&C Energo, a.s. U12110).* Prague, Czech Republic: Czech Technical University in Prague.

Bukovsky, I., & Bila, J. (2008b). *Program system for advanced reconciliation of process data: Program System I&C NEURECON (Final report for I&C Energo, a.s. U12110).* Prague, Czech Republic: Czech Technical University in Prague.

Bukovsky, I., & Bila, J. (2010). Adaptive evaluation of complex dynamic systems using low-dimensional neural architectures. In Wang, Y., Zhang, D., & Kinsner, W. (Eds.), *Advances in cognitive informatics and cognitive computing* (pp. 33–57). Berlin, Germany: Springer-Verlag. doi:10.1007/978-3-642-16083-7_3

Bukovsky, I., Bila, J., Gupta, M. M., Hou, Z.-G., & Homma, N. (2009). Foundation and classification of nonconventional neural units and paradigm of nonsynaptic neural interaction. In Wang, Y. (Ed.), *Discoveries and breakthroughs in cognitive informatics and natural intelligence* (pp. 508–523). Hershey, PA: IGI Global. doi:10.4018/978-1-60566-902-1.ch027

Bukovsky, I., & Homma, N. (2010). Dynamic back-propagation and prediction [in Czech]. *Automatizace, 53*(1-2), 61–66.

Bullock, J. (2000). Calculating the value of testing. *Software Testing and Quality Engineering*, 56-62.

Burke, R. D., Hammond, K., Kulyukin, V., Lytinen, S. L., Tomuro, N., & Schoenberg, S. (1997). *Question answering from frequently-asked-question files: experiences with the FAQ finder system* (Tech. Rep. No. TR-97-05). Chicago, IL: University of Chicago.

Burke, S. A., Lo, S. L., & Krzycki, J. A. (1998). *Clustered genes encoding the methyltransferases of methanogenesis from monomethylamine*. Columbus, OH: Ohio State University.

Burton, R. R. (1976). *Semantic grammar: A technique for efficient language understanding in limited domains* (Unpublished doctoral dissertation). University of California, Irvine, CA.

Buy Answers Consultation Ltd. (2008). *BuyAns*. Retrieved from http://www.BuyAns.com/

Calvanese, D., De Giacomo, G., Lembo, D., Lenzerini, M., & Rosati, R. (2008). Inconsistency tolerance in P2P data integration: An epistemic logic approach. *Information Sciences, 33*, 360–384.

Candes, E., Romberg, J., & Tao, T. (2006). Stable signal recovery from incomplete and inaccurate measurements. *Communications on Pure and Applied Mathematics, 59*(8), 1207–1223. doi:10.1002/cpa.20124

Candes, E., & Tao, T. (2006). Near-optimal signal recovery from random projections: Universal encoding strategies? *IEEE Transactions on Information Theory, 52*(12), 5406–5425. doi:10.1109/TIT.2006.885507

Cardelli, L., & Wegner, P. (1985). On understanding types, data abstraction and polymorphism. *ACM Computing Surveys, 17*(4), 471–522. doi:10.1145/6041.6042

Carlson, A., Betteridge, J., Kisiel, B., Settles, B., Hruschka, E. R., Jr., & Mitchell, T. M. (2010, July). Toward an architecture for never-ending language learning. In *Proceedings of the AAAI Conference on Artificial Intelligence*, Atlanta, GA.

Chandola, V., Banerjee, A., & Kumar, V. (2009). Anomaly detection: A survey. *ACM Computing Surveys, 41*(3). doi:10.1145/1541880.1541882

Chang, C., & Lin, C. (2001). *LIBSVM: A library for support vector machines*. Retrieved from http://www.csie.ntu.edu.tw/~cjlin/libsvm/

Chang, C.-H., Kayed, M., Girgis, M. R., & Shaalan, K. (2006). A survey of web information extraction system. *IEEE Transactions on Knowledge and Data Engineering, 18*(10), 1411–1428. doi:10.1109/TKDE.2006.152

Chaplot, S., Patnaik, L. M., & Jagannathan, N. R. (2006). Classification of magnetic resonance brain images using wavelets as input to support vector machine and neural network. *Journal of Biomedical Signal Processing, 1*(2), 86–92. doi:10.1016/j.bspc.2006.05.002

Chapra, S. C., & Ganale, R. P. (2002). *Numerical methods for engineers* (4th ed.). New York, NY: McGraw-Hill.

Chen, P., & Garcia, W. (2010, July 7-9). Hypothesis generation and data quality assessment through association mining. In *Proceedings of the 9th IEEE International Conference on Cognitive Informatics*, Beijing, China.

Chen, P., Verma, R., Meininger, J. C., & Chan, W. (2008). Semantic analysis of association rules. In *Proceedings of the International FLAIRS Conference* (pp. 270-275).

Chen, J., Xin, B., & Peng, Z. (2009). Statistical learning makes the hybridization of particle swarm and differential evolution more efficient--a novel hybrid optimizer. *Science in China Series F: Information Sciences, 52*(7), 1278–1282. doi:10.1007/s11432-009-0119-4

Chen, S., Donoho, D., & Saunders, M. (2001). Atomic decomposition by basis pursuit. *Society for Industrial and Applied Mathematics Review, 43*(1), 129–159.

Chiew, V., & Wang, Y. (2006, May 8-10). Design of a cognitive complexities measurement and analysis tool (CCMAT). In *Proceedings of the 19th Canadian Conference on Electrical and Computer Engineering*, Ottawa, ON, Canada.

Chomsky, N. (1957). *Syntactic structures*. The Hague, The Netherlands: Mouton.

Chopra, N., Spong, M. W., Ortega, R., & Barabanov, N. E. (2006). On tracking performance in bilateral teleoperation. *IEEE Transactions on Robotics, 22*(4), 861–866. doi:10.1109/TRO.2006.878942

Clancey, W. J. (1997). *Situated cognition: On human knowledge and computer representations.* Cambridge, UK: Cambridge University Press.

Cocchiarella, N. (1996). Conceptual realism as a formal ontology. In Poli, R., & Simons, P. (Eds.), *Formal ontology* (pp. 27–60). London, UK: Kluwer Academic.

CodePlex Open Source Community. (2010). *Managed library for Nintendo's wiimote.* Retrieved from http://wiimotelib.codeplex.com/

Coen, M. H. (1998). Design principles for intelligent environments. In *Proceedings of the Fifteenth National Conference on Artificial Intelligence* (pp. 547-554).

Colorni, A., Dorigo, M., & Maniezzo, V. (1991). Distributed optimization by ant colonies. In *Proceedings of the Actes de la Première Conférence Européenne sur la Vie Artificielle,* Paris, France (pp. 134-142).

Crystal, D. (1987). *The Cambridge encyclopedia of language.* Cambridge, UK: Cambridge University Press.

Csurka, G., Dance, C., Fan, L., Willamowski, J., & Bray, C. (2004). Visual categorization with bags of keypoints. In *Proceedings of the International Workshop on Statistical Learning of the European Conference on Computer Vision* (pp. 1-22).

Dague, P., Raiman, O., & Devès, P. (1987). Troubleshooting: When modeling is the trouble. In *Proceedings of the AAAI Conference on Artificial Intelligence* (pp. 590-595).

Dalal, N., & Triggs, B. (2005). Histograms of oriented gradients for human detection. In. *Proceedings of the IEEE Conference on Computer Vision and Pattern Recognition, 1,* 886–893.

David, R. (1991). Modeling of dynamics systems by Petri Nets. In *Proceedings of the 1st European Control Conference* (pp. 136-147).

David, R., & Alla, H. (1994). Petri nets for modeling of dynamics systems. *Automatica, 30,* 136–147. doi:10.1016/0005-1098(94)90024-8

Davidson, E. H. (2001). *Genomic regulatory systems.* San Diego, CA: Academic Press.

Davis, E. R. (1987). A modified hough scheme for general circle location. *Pattern Recognition Letters, 7,* 37–43. doi:10.1016/0167-8655(88)90042-6

De Kleer, J., & Brown, J. S. (1984). A qualitative physics based on confluences. *Artificial Intelligence, 24*(1-3), 7–83. doi:10.1016/0004-3702(84)90037-7

de Neufville, R., & Odoni, A. (2003). *Airport systems: Planning, design and management.* New York, NY: McGraw-Hill.

Debelack, A. S., Dehn, J. D., Muchinsky, L. L., & Smith, D. M. (2010). Next generation air traffic control automation. *IBM Systems Journal, 34*(1), 63–77. doi:10.1147/sj.341.0063

Debenham, J. K. (1989). *Knowledge systems design.* Upper Saddle River, NJ: Prentice Hall.

Deepak, R., & Eduard, H. (2002). Learning surface text patterns for a question answering system. In *Proceedings of the 40th Annual Meeting on Association for Computational Linguistics,* Philadelphia, PA.

Denning, P. J. (2006). The locality principle. In Barria, J. (Ed.), *Communication Networks and Computer Systems* (pp. 43–67). London, UK: Imperial College Press.

Dey, A. K., & Abowd, G. D. (2000). Towards a better understanding of context and context-awareness. In []. Berlin, Germany: Springer-Verlag.]. *Proceedings of the Workshop on the What, Who, Where, When, and How of Context-Awareness, 4,* 1–6.

Dhawale, C. A., & Sanjeev, J. (2007). Comparison of statistical methods for texture analysis. In *Proceedings of the International Conference Advances in Computer Vision and Information Technology* (pp. 686-698).

Donoho, D. (2006). For most large underdetermined systems of linear equations the minimal l_1-norm solution is also the sparest solution. *Communications on Pure and Applied Mathematics, 59*(6), 797–829. doi:10.1002/cpa.20132

Dorigo, M. (1992). *Optimization, learning and natural algorithms.* Unpublished doctoral dissertation, Politecnico di Milano, Milan, Italy.

Dorigo, M., & Gambardella, L. M. (1996). *Study of some properties of ants* (Tech. Rep. No. TR/IRIDIA/1996-4). Brussels, Belgium: University Librede Bruxelles.

Dorigo, M., & Stützle, T. (2004). *Ant colony optimization*. Cambridge, MA: MIT Press. doi:10.1007/b99492

Duan, H. B., Wang, D. B., & Yu, X. F. (2006). Novel approach to nonlinear PID parameter optimization using ant colony optimization algorithm. *Journal of Bionics Engineering, 3*(2), 73–78. doi:10.1016/S1672-6529(06)60010-3

Dubois, D., Lang, J., & Prade, H. (1994). Possibilistic logic. In Hogger, C., Gabbay, D., & Robinson, J. (Eds.), *Handbook of logic in artificial intelligence and logic programming* (*Vol. 3*, pp. 439–513). Oxford, UK: Oxford University Press.

Duda, R. O., & Hart, P. E. (1972). Use of the hough transformation to detect lines and curves in pictures. *Communications of the ACM, 15*(1), 11–15. doi:10.1145/361237.361242

Eberhart, R. C., & Shi, Y. H. (2001). Particle swarm optimization: Developments, applications, and resources. In *Proceedings of the IEEE International Conference on Evolutionary Computation 1*, (Vol. 1, pp. 81-86). Washington, DC: IEEE Computer Society.

Egyed, A. (2011). Automatically detecting and tracking inconsistencies in software design models. *IEEE Transactions on Software Engineering, 37*(2), 188–204. doi:10.1109/TSE.2010.38

Eissa, M., Meininger, J. C., Nguyen, T., & Chan, W. (2001). The relationship of ambulatory blood pressure to physical activity in a tri-ethnic population of obese and nonobese adolescents. *American Journal of Hypertension, 20*(2), 140–147. doi:10.1016/j.amjhyper.2006.07.008

El-Dahshan, E. A., Salem, A. B. M., & Younis, T. H. (2009). A hybrid technique for automatic MRI brain images classification. *Informatica, 54*(1), 55–67.

Emer, M. C. F. P., & Vergilio, S. R. (2003). Selection and evaluation of test data based on genetic programming. *Software Quality Journal, 11*(2), 167–186. doi:10.1023/A:1023772729494

Fan, W., Geerts, F., Lakshmanan, L., & Xiong, M. (2009). Discovering conditional functional dependencies. In *Proceedings of the International Conference on Data Engineering* (pp. 1231-1234).

Fan, Y., Shen, D., & Davatzikos, C. (2005). Classification of structural images via high-dimensional image warping, robust feature extraction, and SVM. In J. S. Duncan & G. Gerig (Eds.), *Proceedings of the 8th International Conference on Medical Image Computing and Computer Assisted Intervention* (LNCS 3749, pp. 1-8).

Fellbaum, C. (1998). *WordNet: An electronic lexical database*. Cambridge, MA: MIT Press.

Fenton, N. E., & Pfleeger, S. L. (1997). *Software metrics: A rigorous & practical approach*. Boston, MA: PWS.

Fenton, N. E., & Pfleeger, S. L. (1998). *Software metrics: A rigorous and practical approach* (2nd ed.). Pacific Grove, CA: Brooks/Cole Wadsworth.

Fergus, R., Perona, P., & Zisserman, A. (2003). Object class recognition by unsupervised scale-invariant learning. In *Proceedings of the IEEE Conference on Computer Vision and Pattern Recognition* (pp. 264-271).

Fessele, S., Maier, H., Zischek, C., Nelson, P. J., & Werner, T. (2002). Regulatory context is a crucial part of gene function. *Trends in Genetics, 18*, 60–63. doi:10.1016/S0168-9525(02)02591-X

Findlay, J. M., & Gilchrist, I. D. (2003). *Active vision*. Oxford, UK: Oxford University Press. doi:10.1093/acprof:oso/9780198524793.001.0001

Firulli, A. B., & Olson, E. N. (1997). Modular regulation of muscle gene transcription: a mechanism for muscle cell diversity. *Trends in Genetics, 13*, 364–336. doi:10.1016/S0168-9525(97)01171-2

Fitting, M. (1991). Bilattices and the semantics of logic programming. *The Journal of Logic Programming, 11*, 91–116. doi:10.1016/0743-1066(91)90014-G

Fitting, M. (2002). Fixpoint semantics for logic programming: A survey. *Theoretical Computer Science, 278*(1-2), 25–51. doi:10.1016/S0304-3975(00)00330-3

Flax, B. M. (1991). Intelligent buildings. *IEEE Communications Magazine, 4*(1), 24–27. doi:10.1109/35.76555

Forbus, K. D., & Whalley, P. B. (1994). Using qualitative physics to build articulate software for thermodynamics education. In *Proceedings of the AAAI Conference on Artificial Intelligence* (pp. 1175-1182).

Foursov, M. V., & Hespel, C. (2006). Weighted petri nets and polynomial dynamical systems. In *Proceedings of the 17th International Symposium on Mathematical Theory of Networks and Systems* (pp. 1539-1546).

Frech, K., & Werner, T. (1997). Specific modelling of regulatory units in DNA sequences. In *Proceedings of the Pacific Symposium on Biocomputing* (pp. 151-162).

Gade, S., Herlufsen, H., Konstantin-Hensen, H., & Wismer, N. J. (1995). *Order tracking analysis (Tech. Review Note No. 2)*. Naerum, Denmark: Bruel & Kjaer.

Gambardella, L. M., & Dorigo, M. (1995). Ant-Q: A reinforcement learning approach to the traveling salesman problem. In *Proceedings of the 12th International Conference on Machine Learning*, Tahoe City, CA (pp. 252-260).

Ganter, B., Stumme, G., & Wille, R. (Eds.). (2005). *Formal concept analysis: Foundations and applications (LNAI 3626)*. Berlin, Germany: Springer-Verlag.

Gao, S., Tsang, I., Chia, L., & Zhao, P. (2010). Local features are not lonely – Laplacian sparse coding for image classification. In *Proceedings of the IEEE Conference on Computer Vision and Pattern Recognition* (pp. 3555-3561).

Garcia, M. A. P., Montiel, O., Castillo, O., Sepúlveda, R., & Melin, P. (2009). Path planning for autonomous mobile robot navigation with ant colony optimization and fuzzy cost function evaluation. *Applied Soft Computing*, *9*(3), 1102–1110. doi:10.1016/j.asoc.2009.02.014

Garrett, D., David, A. P., Anderson, C. W., & Thaut, M. H. (2003). Comparison of linear, nonlinear, and feature selection methods for EEG signal classification. *IEEE Transactions on Neural Systems and Rehabilitation Engineering*, *11*(2), 141–144. doi:10.1109/TNSRE.2003.814441

Genesereth, M. R., & Nilsson, N. J. (1987). *Logical foundations of artificial intelligence*. San Francisco, CA: Morgan Kaufmann.

Gerald, M., & Javadpour, K. R. (2000). An ARTMAP neural network-based machine condition monitoring system. *Journal of Quality in Maintenance Engineering*, *6*(2), 86–105. doi:10.1108/13552510010328095

Gibbs, W. (1994). Software's chronic crisis. *Scientific American*, 86–95. doi:10.1038/scientificamerican0994-86

Ginsberg, M. L. (1988). Multivalued logics: A uniform approach to inference in artificial intelligence. *Computational Intelligence*, *4*(3), 265–316. doi:10.1111/j.1467-8640.1988.tb00280.x

Gosling, J., Bollella, G., Dibble, P., Furr, S., & Turnbull, M. (2002). *The real-time specification for Java*. Reading, MA: Addison-Wesley.

Gotesky, R. (1968). The uses of inconsistency. *Philosophy and Phenomenological Research*, *28*(4), 471–500. doi:10.2307/2105687

Gruber, T. (1993). A translation approach to portable ontology specifications. *Knowledge Acquisition*, *5*(2), 199–220. doi:10.1006/knac.1993.1008

Grunbacher, P., Koszegi, S., & Biffl, S. (2006). Stakeholder value proposition elicitation and reconciliation. In Biffl, S., Aurum, A., Boehm, B., Erdogmus, H., & Grünbacher, P. (Eds.), *Value-based software engineering*. Berlin, Germany: Springer-Verlag. doi:10.1007/3-540-29263-2_7

Guermeur, Y. (2007). *SVM multiclass: Théorie et applications*. Retrieved from http://www.loria.fr/~guermeur/HDR_YG.pdf

Guger, C., Daban, S., Sellers, E., Holzner, C., Krausz, G., & Carabalona, R. (2009). How many people are able to control a P300-based brain-computer interface (BCI)? *Neuroscience Letters*, *462*(1), 94–98. doi:10.1016/j.neulet.2009.06.045

Guger, C., Schlögl, A., Neuper, C., Walterspacher, D., Strein, T., & Pfurtscheller, G. (2001). Rapid prototyping of an EEG-based brain-computer interface (BCI). *IEEE Transactions on Neural Systems and Rehabilitation Engineering*, *9*(1), 49–58. doi:10.1109/7333.918276

Guiatni, M., Kheddar, A., & Melouah, H. (2005). Sliding mode bilateral control and four channels scheme control of a force reflecting master/slave teleoperator. In *Proceedings of the IEEE International Conference on Robotics and Automation* (pp. 1660-1665). Washington, DC: IEEE Computer Society.

Guirao, J. L. G., Pelayo, F. L., & Valverde, J. C. (2011). Modelling dynamics of concurrent computing systems. *Computers & Mathematics with Applications (Oxford, England)*, *61*, 1402–1406. doi:10.1016/j.camwa.2011.01.008

Gupta, M. M., Liang, J., & Homma, N. (2003). *Static and dynamic neural networks: From fundamentals to advanced theory*. Hoboken, NJ: John Wiley & Sons. doi:10.1002/0471427950

Gupta, N. K., Mueller, W. H., Chan, W., & Meininger, J. C. (2002). Is obesity associated with poor sleep quality in adolescents? *American Journal of Human Biology: The Official Journal of the Human Biology Council, 14*(6).

Guttag, J. V. (1977). Abstract data types and the development of data structures. *Communications of the ACM, 20*(6), 396–404. doi:10.1145/359605.359618

Guttag, J. V. (2002). Abstract data types, then and now. In Broy, M., & Denert, E. (Eds.), *Software pioneers* (pp. 443–452). Berlin, Germany: Springer-Verlag. doi:10.1007/978-3-642-59412-0_28

Gysels, E., Renevey, P., & Celka, P. (2005). SVM-based recursive feature elimination to compare phase synchronization computed from broadband and narrowband EEG signals in brain-computer interfaces. *Signal Processing, 85*(11), 2178–2189. doi:10.1016/j.sigpro.2005.07.008

Halfon, M. S., Grad, Y., Church, G. M., & Michelson, A. M. (2002). Computation-based discovery of related transcriptional regulatory modules and motifs using an experimentally validated combinatorial model. *Genome Research, 12*, 1019–1028.

Hallikas, O., Palin, K., Sinjushina, N., Rautiainen, R., Partanen, J., Ukkonen, E., & Taipale, J. (2006). Genome-wide prediction of mammalian enhancers based on analysis of transcription-factor binding affinity. *Cell, 124*(1), 47–59. doi:10.1016/j.cell.2005.10.042

Halstead, M. H. (1977). *Elements of software science*. New York, NY: Elsevier North-Holland.

Hammond, K., Bruke, R., Martin, C., & Lytinen, S. (1995). Faq-Finder: a case based approach to knowledge navigation. In *Proceedings of the Working Notes of the AAAI Spring Symposium on Information Gathering from Heterogeneous Distributed Environments*.

Han, J., Wang, J., Lu, Y., & Tzvetkov, P. (2002). Mining top-k frequent closed patterns without minimum support. In *Proceedings of the IEEE International Conference on Data Mining* (pp. 211-218).

Han, C. M. (2004). *Academic analysis and software realization of generic cabling* (pp. 35–87). Beijing, China: Southeast University.

Hannaford, B. (1989). A design framework for tele-operators with kinesthetic feedback. *IEEE Transactions on Robotics and Automation, 5*(4), 426–434. doi:10.1109/70.88057

Hansman, R. J., & Odoni, A. (2009). Air traffic control. In Belobaba, P., Odoni, A., & Barnhart, C. (Eds.), *The global airline industry*. New York, NY: John Wiley & Sons. doi:10.1002/9780470744734.ch13

Hao, T. Y., Song, W. P., & Liu, W. Y. (2008, January 16-18). Automatic generation of semantic patterns for user-interactive question answering. In *Proceedings of the Asia Information Retrieval Symposium*, Harbin, China.

Hao, L. (2010). Ontology based automatic attributes extracting and queries translating for deep web. *Journal of Software, 5*, 713–720.

Hao, T. Y., Hu, D. W., Liu, W. Y., & Zeng, Q. T. (2007). Semantic patterns for user-interactive question answering. *Journal of Concurrency and Computation-practice & Experience, 20*, 1–17.

Hao, T. Y., Ni, X. L., Quan, X. J., & Liu, W. Y. (2009). Automatic construction of semantic dictionary for question categorization. *Journal of Systemics. Cybernetics and Informatics, 7*(6), 86–90.

Haralick, R., Shanmugam, K., & Dinstein, I. (1973). Textural features for image classification. *IEEE Transactions on Systems, Man, and Cybernetics*, 610–621. doi:10.1109/TSMC.1973.4309314

Harnad, S. (1990). The symbol grounding problem. *Physica D. Nonlinear Phenomena, 42*, 335–346. doi:10.1016/0167-2789(90)90087-6

Hartmanis, J., & Stearns, R. E. (1965). On the computational complexity of algorithms. *Transactions of the AMS, 117*, 258–306. doi:10.1090/S0002-9947-1965-0170805-7

Hartmanis, J. (1994). On computational complexity and the nature of computer science, 1994 Turing award lecture. *Communications of the ACM, 37*(10), 37–43. doi:10.1145/194313.214781

Hasegawa, T., & Murakami, K. (2006). Robot town project: Supporting robots in an environment with its structured information. In *Proceedings of the 3rd International Conference on Ubiquitous Robots and Ambient Intelligence* (pp. 119-123).

Hashtrudi-Zaad, K. (2002). Transparency in time-delayed systems and the effect of local force feedback for transparent teleoperation. *IEEE Transactions on Robotics and Automation, 18*(1), 108–114. doi:10.1109/70.988981

Heaton, J. (2008). *Introduction to neural networks in C* (2nd ed.). Chesterfield, MO: Heaton Research.

Helwig, S., & Wanka, R. (2008). Theoretical analysis of initial particle swarm behavior. In G. Rudolph, T. Jansen, S. Lucas, C. Poloni, & N. Beume (Eds.), *Proceedings of the 10th International Conference on Parallel Problem Solving from Nature* (LNCS 5199, pp. 889-898).

Hoffmann, U., Vesin, J. M., Ebrahimi, T., & Diserens, K. (2008). An efficient P300-based brain-computer interface for disabled subjects. *Journal of Neuroscience Methods, 167*(1), 15–25. doi:10.1016/j.jneumeth.2007.03.005

Hofreiter, M. (2010). *Laboratory system batyscaphe.* Prague, Czech Republic: Czech Technical University in Prague. Retrieved from http://vlab.fsid.cvut.cz/en/ulohy/batyskaf.php

Höllinger, P., Beisteiner, R., Lang, W., Lindinger, G., & Berthoz, A. (1999). Mental representations of movements. Brain potentials associated with imagination of eye movements. *Clinical Neurophysiology, 110*(5), 790–805. doi:10.1016/S1388-2457(98)00042-X

Horspool, R. N. (1980). Practical fast searching in strings. *Software, Practice & Experience, 10*(6), 501–506. doi:10.1002/spe.4380100608

Horty, J. (1994). Some direct theories of nonmonotonic inheritance. In D. Gabbay, C. Hogger, & J. Robinson (Eds.), *Handbook of logic in artificial intelligence and logic programming. Volume 3: Nonmonotonic reasoning and uncertain reasoning* (pp. 111-187). Oxford, UK: Oxford University Press.

Hsiao, D., & Harary, F. (1970). A formal system for information retrieval from files. *Communications of the ACM, 13*, 67–73. doi:10.1145/362007.362015

Huang, Z., van Harmelen, F., & ten Teije, A. (2005). Reasoning with inconsistent ontologies. In *Proceedings of the 19ᵗʰ International Joint Conference on Artificial Intelligence*, Edinburgh, Scotland (pp. 454-459).

Huang, C. L., & Wang, C. J. (2006). A GA-based feature selection and parameters optimization for support vector machine. *Journal of Expert Systems with Application, 31*(2), 231–240. doi:10.1016/j.eswa.2005.09.024

Huang, L., & Boehm, B. (2006). How much software investment is enough: A value-based approach. *IEEE Software, 23*(2), 88–95. doi:10.1109/MS.2006.127

Huang, T., & Mohan, A. S. (2005). A hybrid boundary condition for robust particle swarm optimization. *IEEE Antennas and Wireless Propagation Letters, 4*, 112–117. doi:10.1109/LAWP.2005.846166

Hu, K., Wang, Y., & Tian, Y. (2010). A web knowledge discovery engine based on concept algebra. *International Journal of Cognitive Informatics and Natural Intelligence, 4*(1), 80–97. doi:10.4018/jcini.2010010105

Hurley, P. J. (1997). *A concise introduction to logic* (6th ed.). Belmont, CA: Wadsworth Publishing.

Hwang, H. J., Kwon, K., & Im, C. H. (2009). Neurofeedback-based motor imagery training for brain-computer interface (BCI). *Journal of Neuroscience Methods, 179*(1), 50–56. doi:10.1016/j.jneumeth.2009.01.015

Illingworth, J., & Kittler, J. (1988). Survey: A survey of the hough transform? *Computervision. Graphics and Image Processing: Image Understanding, 44*(1), 87–116.

Ince, N. F., Arica, S., & Tewfik, A. (2006). Classification of single trial motor imagery EEG recordings with subject adapted non-dyadic arbitrary time-frequency tilings. *Journal of Neural Engineering, 3*(3), 235–244. doi:10.1088/1741-2560/3/3/006

Ion, M. (1999). Extraction patterns for information extraction tasks: a survey. In *Proceedings of the Workshop on Machine Learning for Information Extraction*, Orlando, FL.

Ivakhnenko, A. G. (1971). Polynomial theory of complex systems. *IEEE Transactions on Systems, Man, and Cybernetics, 1*(4), 364–378. doi:10.1109/TSMC.1971.4308320

Iversen, I. H., Ghanayim, N., Kübler, A., Neumann, N., Birbaumer, N., & Kaiser, J. (2008). A brain-computer interface tool to assess cognitive functions in completely paralyzed patients with amyotrophic lateral sclerosis. *Clinical Neurophysiology, 119*(10), 14–23. doi:10.1016/j.clinph.2008.07.001

Jeannerod, M., & Frak, V. (1999). Mental imaging of motor activity in humans. *Current Opinion in Neurobiology, 9*(6), 35–39. doi:10.1016/S0959-4388(99)00038-0

Jeon, J., Croft, W. B., & Lee, J. H. (2005). Finding similar questions in large question and answer archives. In *Proceedings of the 14th ACM International Conference on Information and Knowledge Management*, Bremen, Germany.

Jing, F., Li, M., Zhang, H., & Zhang, B. (2004). An efficient and effective region-based image retrieval framework. *IEEE Transactions on Image Processing, 13*(5), 699–709. doi:10.1109/TIP.2004.826125

Jin, Y., Joshua, K., & Lu, H. (2008). The landscape adaptive particle swarm optimizer. *Application Soft Computing, 8*(1), 295–304. doi:10.1016/j.asoc.2007.01.009

Johnson-Laird, P. N., Legrenzi, P., & Girotto, V. (2004). Reasoning from inconsistency to consistency. *Psychological Review, 111*(3), 640–661. doi:10.1037/0033-295X.111.3.640

Jordán, M. A., & Bustamante, J. L. (2007). On the presence of nonlinear oscillations in the teleoperation of underwater vehicles under the influence of sea wave and current. In *Proceedings of the American Control Conference* (pp. 894-899). Washington, DC: IEEE Computer Society.

Jury, E. I. (1964). *Theory and application of the z-transform method*. New York, NY: John Wiley & Sons.

Kadir, T., Zisserman, A., & Brady, M. (2004). An affine invariant salient region detector. In T. Pajdla & J. Matas (Eds.), *Proceedings of the 8th European Conference on Computer Vision* (LNCS 3021, pp. 228-242).

Kalpalatha, R. T., & Kumaravel, N. (2009). Texture analysis of bone CT images for classification and characterization of bone quality. *International Journal of Soft Computing, 4*(5), 223–228.

Kamousi, B., Amini, A. N., & He, B. (2007). Classification of motro imagery by means of cortical current density estimation and Von Neumann entropy. *Journal of Neural Engineering, 4*, 17–25. doi:10.1088/1741-2560/4/2/002

Kaplan, R. M., & Bresnan, J. (1982). Lexical functional grammar: A formal system for grammatical representation. In Bresnan, J. (Ed.), *The mental representation of grammatical relations* (pp. 173–281). Cambridge, MA: MIT Press.

Kawashima, K., Tadano, K., Wang, C., Sankaranarayanan, G., & Hannaford, B. (2009). Bilateral teleoperation with time delay using modified wave variable based controller. In *Proceedings of the IEEE International Conference on Robotics and Automation* (pp. 4326-4331). Washington, DC: IEEE Computer Society.

Kayikcioglu, T., & Aydemir, O. (2010). A polynomial fitting and k-NN based approach for improving classification of motor imagery BCI data. *Pattern Recognition Letters, 31*(11), 1207–1215. doi:10.1016/j.patrec.2010.04.009

Kearney, J. K., Sedlmeyer, R. L., Thompson, W. B., Gray, M. A., & Adler, M. A. (1986). Software complexity measurement. *Communications of the ACM, 29*(11), 1044–1050. doi:10.1145/7538.7540

Keith, A. J., & Alex, J. B. (1999). *The whole brain atlas*. Boston, MA: Harvard Medical School.

Kennedy, J. (2005). Why does it need velocity? In *Proceedings of the IEEE Swarm Intelligence Symposium* (pp 38-44). Washington, DC: IEEE Computer Society.

Kennedy, J., & Eberhart, R. C. (1995). Particle swarm optimization. In []. Washington, DC: IEEE Computer Society.]. *Proceedings of the IEEE International Conference on Neural Networks, 4*, 1942–1948. doi:10.1109/ICNN.1995.488968

Kennedy, J. (2008). How it works: Collaborative trial and error. *International Journal of Computational Intelligence Research, 4*(2), 71–78. doi:10.5019/j.ijcir.2008.127

Khademian, B., & Hashtrudi-Zaad, K. (2007). A four-channel multilateral shared control architecture for dual-user teleoperation systems. In *Proceedings of the IEEE International Conference on Intelligent Robots and Systems* (pp. 2660-2666). Washington, DC: IEEE Computer Society.

Kharrat, A., BenMessaoud, M., Benamrane, N., & Abid, M. (2009). Detection of brain tumor in medical images. In *Proceedings of the 3rd IEEE International Conference on Signals, Circuits & Systems*, Tunisia (pp. 1-6).

Kharrat, A., BenMessaoud, M., Benamrane, N., & Abid, M. (2010). Genetic algorithm for feature selection of MR brain images using wavelet co-occurrence. In *Proceedings of the IEEE International Conference on Signals and Information Processing, Changsha, China* (pp. 606-610).

Kidd, C. D., Orr, R., Abowd, G. D., Atkeson, C. G., Essa, I. A., MacIntyre, B., et al. (1999). The aware home: A living laboratory for ubiquitous computing research. In *Proceedings of the Second International Workshop on Cooperative Buildings, Integrating Information, Organization, and Architecture* (LNCS 1670, pp. 191-198).

Kittler, J. (1978). Feature set search algorithms. *Pattern Recognition and Signal Processing*, 41-60.

Klan, P., Hofreiter, M., Machacek, J., Modrlak, O., Smutny, L., & Vasek, V. (2005). Process models for a new control education laboratory. In *Proceedings of the 16th World Congress of the International Federation of Automatic Control*, Prague, Czech Republic (CD-ROM).

Klaus, J. (1984). *Topology*. New York, NY: Springer.

Klingenhoff, A., Frech, K., Quandt, K., & Werner, T. (1999). Functional promoter modules can be detected by formal models independent of overall nucleotide sequence similarity. *Bioinformatics (Oxford, England)*, *15*, 180–186. doi:10.1093/bioinformatics/15.3.180

Klingenhoff, A., Frech, K., & Werner, T. (2000). Regulatory modules shared within gene classes as well as across gene classes can be detected by the same in silico approach. *In Silico Biology*, *2*, 17–26.

Knuth, D. E., Morris, J. H., & Pratt, V. R. (1977). Fast pattern matching in strings. *SIAM Journal on Computing*, *6*(1), 323–350. doi:10.1137/0206024

Kohavi, R., & George, H. J. (1997). Wrappers for feature subset selection. *Artificial Intelligence*, *1*(2), 273–324. doi:10.1016/S0004-3702(97)00043-X

Konno, S., Manabe, Y., Fujita, S., Sugawra, K., Kinoshita, T., & Shiratori, N. (2008). A framework for perceptual functions of symbiotic computing. In *Proceedings of the IEEE International Conference on Web Intelligence and Intelligent Agent Technology* (pp. 501-504).

Kontogiannis, T., & Malakis, S. (2009). A proactive approach to human error detection and identification in aviation and air traffic control. *Safety Science*, *47*(5), 693–706. doi:10.1016/j.ssci.2008.09.007

Kosmatopoulos, E., Polycarpou, M., Christodoulou, M., & Ioannou, P. (1995). High-order neural network structures for identification of dynamical systems. *IEEE Transactions on Neural Networks*, *6*(2), 422–431. doi:10.1109/72.363477

Kraft, C. S., LeMoine, C. M. R., Lyons, C. N., Michaud, D., Mueller, C. R., & Moyes, C. D. (2005). Control of mitochondrial biogenesis during myogenesis. *The American Journal of Physiology*, *290*, 1119–1127. doi:10.1152/ajpcell.00463.2005

Kuipers, B. (1994). *Qualitative reasoning*. Cambridge, MA: MIT Press.

Kumaraswamy, S., Rakesh, J., & Nalavade, A. K. (2002). Standardization of absolute vibration level and damage factors for machinery health monitoring. In *Proceedings of the Second International Conference on Vibration Engineering and Technology of Machinery* (pp. 16-18).

Kurtz, S., Phillippy, A., Delcher, A. L., Smoot, M., Shumway, M., Antonescu, C., & Salzberg, S. L. (2004). Versatile and open software for comparing large genomes. *Genome Biology*, *5*(2), R12. doi:10.1186/gb-2004-5-2-r12

Lavrač, N., & Džeroski, S. (1994). *Inductive logic programming: Techniques and applications*. New York, NY: Ellis Horwood.

Lawrence, D. A. (1993). Stability and transparency in bilateral teleoperation. *IEEE Transactions on Robotics and Automation*, *9*(5), 624–637. doi:10.1109/70.258054

Lawry, J. (2001). An alternative to computing with words. *International Journal of Uncertainty. Fuzziness and Knowledge-Based Systems*, *9*, 3–16. doi:10.1142/S0218488501000958

Lawry, J., Shanahan, J., & Ralescu, A. (Eds.). (2003). *Modeling with words (LNAI 2873)*. New York, NY: Springer.

Lazebnik, S., Schmid, C., & Ponce, J. (2006). Beyond bags of features: Spatial pyramid matching for recognizing natural scene categories. In *Proceedings of the IEEE Conference on Computer Vision and Pattern Recognition* (pp. 2169-2178).

Leavers, V. F. (1993). Survey: Which hough transform? *Computervision, Graphics, and Image Processing. Image Understanding, 58*(2), 250–264. doi:10.1006/ciun.1993.1041

Lee, J. H., Appenzeller, G., & Hashimoto, H. (1998). Physical agent for sensored, networked and thinking space. In. *Proceedings of the IEEE International Conference on Robotics and Automation, 1*, 838–843.

Lee, D., & Spong, M. W. (2006). Passive bilateral teleoperation with constant time delay. *IEEE Transactions on Robotics, 22*(2), 269–281. doi:10.1109/TRO.2005.862037

Lee, J. H., & Hashimoto, H. (2002). Intelligent space - concept and contents. *Advanced Robotics, 16*(3), 265–280. doi:10.1163/156855302760121936

Lee, J. H., Ryu, J., Jolesz, F. A., Cho, Z. H., & Yoo, S. S. (2009). Brain-machine interface via real-time fMRI: Preliminary study on thought-controlled robotic arm. *Neuroscience Letters, 450*(1), 1–6. doi:10.1016/j.neulet.2008.11.024

Lenz, M., Hbner, A., & Kunze, M. (1998). Question answering with textual CBR. In *Proceedings of the International Conference on Flexible Query Answering Systems*, Denmark (pp. 236-247).

Leone, N., Pfeifer, G., Faber, W., Eiter, T., Gottlob, G., Perri, S., & Scarcello, F. (2006). The DLV system for knowledge representation and reasoning. *ACM Transactions on Computational Logic, 7*(3), 499–562. doi:10.1145/1149114.1149117

Lewis, H. R., & Papadimitriou, C. H. (1998). *Elements of the theory of computation* (2nd ed.). Upper Saddle River, NJ: Prentice Hall.

Lewis, W. D. (2001). Measuring conceptual distance using WordNet: The design of a metric for measuring semantic similarity. *Coyote Papers, 12*, 9–16.

Li, F., & Perona, P. (2005). A Bayesian hierarchical model for learning natural scene categories. In *Proceedings of the IEEE Conference on Computer Vision and Pattern Recognition* (pp. 524-531).

Li, J., Ren, B., & Wang, C. (2007). A random velocity boundary condition for robust particle swarm optimization. In K. Li, G. W. Irwin, M. Fei, & S. Ma (Eds.), *Proceedings of the Life System Modeling and Simulation International Conference on Bio-Inspired Computational Intelligence and Applications* (LNCS 4688, pp. 92-99).

Liang, J., Qin, A., & Baskar, S. (2006). Comprehensive learning Particle swarm optimizer for global optimization of multimodal functions. *IEEE Transactions on Evolutionary Computation, 10*(3), 81–295. doi:10.1109/TEVC.2005.857610

Licklider, J. C. R. (1960). Man-computer symbiosis. *IRE Transactions on Human Factors in Electronics, 1*, 4–11. doi:10.1109/THFE2.1960.4503259

Liddy, E. D. (2001). Natural language processing. In Drake, M. (Ed.), *Encyclopedia of library and information science* (2nd ed.). New York, NY: Marcel Decker.

Lim, C. Y., Santoso, B., Boulay, T., Dong, E., Ohler, U., & Kadonaga, J. T. (2004). The MTE, a new core promoter element for transcription by RNA polymerase II. *Genes & Development, 18*(13), 1606–1617. doi:10.1101/gad.1193404

Lin, H. J., & Yeh, J. P. (2009). Optimal reduction of solutions for support vector machines. *Applied Mathematics and Computation, 214*(2), 329–335. doi:10.1016/j.amc.2009.04.010

Lipschutz, S., & Lipson, M. (1997). *Schaum's outline of theories and problems of discrete mathematics* (2nd ed.). New York: McGraw-Hill.

Liu, B., Zhao, K., Benkler, J., & Xiao, W. (2006). Rule interestingness analysis using OLAP operations. In *Proceedings of the 12th ACM SIGKDD International Conference on Knowledge Discovery and Data Mining*, Philadelphia, PA (pp. 297-306).

Liu, H., & Singh, P. (2004). ConceptNet - A practical commonsense reasoning toolkit. *BT Technology Journal, 22*(4), 211–225. doi:10.1023/B:BTTJ.0000047600.45421.6d

Liu, W., Hao, T., Chen, W., & Feng, M. (2009). A Web-based platform for user-interactive question-answering. *World Wide Web: Internet and Web Information Systems, 12*(2), 107–124.

Liu, Y., Jiao, L., Bai, G., & Feng, B. (2010). Feature based rule learner in noisy environment using neighbourhood rough set model. *International Journal of Software Science and Computational Intelligence, 2*(2), 66–85. doi:10.4018/jssci.2010040104

Li, Y. Q., Long, J. Y., Yu, T. Y., Yu, Z. L., Wang, C. C., Zhang, H. H., & Guan, C. T. (2010). An EEG based BCI system for 2-D cursor control by combining Mu/Beta rhythm and P300 potential. *IEEE Transactions on Bio-Medical Engineering, 57*(10), 495–505.

Lloyd, R. (1999). *Metric mishap caused loss of NASA orbiter.* Retrieved from http://www.cnn.com/TECH/space/9909/30/mars.metric.02/

Lowe, D. (2004). Distinctive image features from scale-invariant keypoints. *International Journal of Computer Vision, 60*(2), 91–110. doi:10.1023/B:VISI.0000029664.99615.94

Magnin, B., Mesrob, L., Kinkingnéhun, S., Pélégrini, I. M., Colliot, O., & Sarazin, M. (2009). Support-vector-machine based classification of Alzheimer's disease from whole brain anatomical MRI. *Journal of Neuroradiology, 51*(2), 73–83. doi:10.1007/s00234-008-0463-x

Ma, L., & Xiang, P. J. (2001). Application of ant algorithm in combinatorial optimization. *Journal of Management Sciences in China, 4*(2), 32–37.

Mallat, S. G. (1989). A theory of multiresolution signal decomposition: The wavelet representation. *IEEE Transactions on Pattern Analysis and Machine Intelligence,* 674–693. doi:10.1109/34.192463

Manabe, Y., Fujita, S., Konno, S., Hara, H., & Sugawara, K. (2010). A concept of context-aware computing based on symbol grounding perspective. In *Proceedings of the International Symposium on Aware Computing* (pp. 86-91).

Manocha, K. A., Pernalete, N., & Dubey, R. V. (2001). Variable position mapping based assistance in teleoperation for nuclear cleanup. In *Proceedings of the IEEE International Conference on Robotics and Automation* (pp. 374-379). Washington, DC: IEEE Computer Society.

Martinez, M. V., Pugliese, A., Simari, G. I., Subrahmanian, V. S., & Prade, H. (2007). How dirty is your relational database? An axiomatic approach. In K. Mellouli (Ed.), *Proceedings of the 9th European Conference on Symbolic and Quantitative Approaches to Reasoning with Uncertainty,* Hammamet, Tunisia (LNCS 4724, pp. 103-114).

Matlab. (2010). *Matlab functional reference.* Natick, MA: The MathWorks.

Maximiliano, S. N., Armando, S., & Manuel, P. (2001). Semantic pattern learning through maximum entropy-based wsd technique. In *Proceedings of the 5th Workshop on Computational Language Learning,* Toulouse, France.

McCabe, T. H. (1976). A complexity measure. *IEEE Transactions on Software Engineering, 2*(6), 308–320. doi:10.1109/TSE.1976.233837

McCormick, A. C., & Nandi, A. K. (1996). A comparison of artificial neural networks and other statistical methods for rotating machine condition classification. In *Proceedings of the IEEE Colloquium on Modeling and Signal Processing for Fault Diagnosis,* Leicester, UK (pp. 2/1-2/6).

McDaniel, E., & Lawrence, C. (1990). *Levels of cognitive complexity: An approach to the measurement of thinking* (pp. 1–49). New York, NY: Springer. doi:10.1007/978-1-4612-3420-3_1

McDermid, J. (1991). *Software engineer's reference book.* Boca Raton, FL: CRC Press.

McDermid, J. (Ed.). (1991). *Software engineer's reference book.* Oxford, UK: Butterworth Heinemann.

McFarland, D. J., & Wolpaw, J. R. (2005). Sensorimotor rhythm-based brain-computer interface (BCI): feature selection by regression improves performance. *IEEE Transactions on Neural Systems and Rehabilitation, 13*(3), 372–379. doi:10.1109/TNSRE.2005.848627

McMinn, P. (2004). Search-based software test data generation: A survey. *Software: Testing. Verification and Reliability, 14*(2), 105–156. doi:10.1002/stvr.294

Meera, A., Rangarajan, L., & Bhat, S. (2009). Computational approach towards promoter sequence comparison via TF mapping using a new distance measure *Interdisciplinary Sciences: Computational. Life Sciences, 3*(1), 43–49.

Meininger, J. C., Liehr, P., Chan, W., Smith, G., & Mueller, W. H. (2001). Developmental, gender, and ethnic group differences in moods and ambulatory blood pressure in adolescents. *Annals of Behavioral Medicine: A Publication of the Society of Behavioral Medicine, 28*(1), 10-19.

Meininger, J. C., Liehr, P., Mueller, W. H., Chan, W., Smith, G. L., & Portman, R. J. (1999). Stress-induced alterations of blood pressure and 24h ambulatory blood pressure in adolescents. *Blood Pressure Monitoring, 4*(3-4).

Melton, A. (Ed.). (1996). *Software measurement*. International Thomson Computer Press.

Mendel, J. M. (1999, June). Computing with words, when words can mean different things to different people. In *Proceedings of the Third International ICSC Symposium on Fuzzy Logic and Applications*, Rochester, NY.

Mendel, J. M. (2003). Fuzzy sets for words: A new beginning. In *Proceedings of the 12th IEEE International Conference on Fuzzy Systems*, St. Louis, MO (pp. 37-42).

Mendel, J. M., & John, R. I. (2002, July). Footprint of uncertainty and its importance to type-2 fuzzy sets. In *Proceedings of the 6th IASTED International Conference on Artificial Intelligence and Soft Computing*, Banff, AB, Canada (pp. 587-592).

Mendel, J. M. (2001). *Uncertain rule-based fuzzy logic systems: Introduction and new directions*. Upper Saddle River, NJ: Prentice Hall.

Mendel, J. M. (2002). An architecture for making judgments using computing with words. *International Journal of Applied Mathematics and Computer Science, 12*(3), 325–335.

Mendel, J. M. (2007). Computing with words and its relationships with fuzzistics. *Information Sciences, 177*, 988–1006. doi:10.1016/j.ins.2006.06.008

Michael, J. C. (1994). *The effect of variation in illuminant direction on texture classification*. Unpublished doctoral dissertation Heriot-Watt University. Edinburgh, Scotland.

Michael, C. C., McGraw, G., & Schatz, M. A. (2001). Generating software test data by evolution. *IEEE Transactions on Software Engineering, 27*(12), 1085–1109. doi:10.1109/32.988709

Michael, M., Dieterich, C., & Vingron, M. (2005). SITEBLAST—rapid and sensitive local alignment of genomic sequences employing motif anchors. *Bioinformatics (Oxford, England), 21*(9), 2093–2094. doi:10.1093/bioinformatics/bti224

Mikolajczyk, K., & Schmid, C. (2005). A Performance evaluation of local descriptors. *IEEE Transactions on Pattern Analysis and Machine Intelligence, 27*(10), 1615–1630. doi:10.1109/TPAMI.2005.188

Mikolajczyk, K., Tuytelaars, T., Schmid, C., Zisserman, A., Matas, J., & Schaffalitzky, F. (2005). A comparison of affine region detectors. *International Journal of Computer Vision, 65*(1-2), 43–72. doi:10.1007/s11263-005-3848-x

Mitchell, T. (2006). *The discipline of machine learning* (Tech. Rep. No. CMU-ML-06-108). Pittsburgh, PA: Carnegie Mellon University.

Mitchell, J. C. (1990). Type systems for programming languages. In van Leeuwen, J. (Ed.), *Handbook of Theoretical Computer Science* (pp. 365–458). Cambridge, MA: MIT Press.

Mitchell, T. (1997). *Machine learning*. New York, NY: McGraw-Hill.

Mizoguchi, F., Nishiyama, H., Ohwada, H., & Hiraishi, H. (1999). Smart office robot collaboration based on multi-agent programming. *Artificial Intelligence, 114*(1-2), 57–94. doi:10.1016/S0004-3702(99)00068-5

Moritz, C. H., Haughton, V. M., Cordes, D., Quigley, M., & Meyerand, M. E. (2000). Whole-brain functional MR imaging activation from finger tapping task examined with independent component analysis. *AJNR. American Journal of Neuroradiology, 21*(9), 1629–1635.

Moses, A. M., Chiang, D. Y., Pollard, D. A., Iyer, V. N., & Eisen, M. B. (2004). MONKEY: Identifying conserved transcription factor binding sites in multiple alignments using a binding site-specific evolutionary model. *Genome Biology, 5*(2), 98. doi:10.1186/gb-2004-5-12-r98

Müller-Putz, G. R., Scherer, R., Pfurtscheller, G., & Rupp, R. (2005). EEG-based neuroprosthesis control: A step towards clinical practice. *Neuroscience Letters, 382*(1-2), 69–74.

Murakami, K., Hasegawa, T., Kurazume, R., & Kimuro, Y. (2008). A structured environment with sensor networks for intelligent robots. In *Proceedings of the IEEE International Conference on Sensors* (pp. 705-708).

Naerum, E., & Hannaford, B. (2009). Transparency analysis of the Lawrence teleoperator architecture. In *Proceedings of the IEEE International Conference on Robotics and Automation* (pp. 4344-4349). Washington, DC: IEEE Computer Society.

Narendra, P. M., & Fukunaga, K. (1977). A branch and bound algorithm for feature subset selection. *IEEE Transactions on Computers*, *26*(9), 917–922. doi:10.1109/TC.1977.1674939

Neagoe, V., & Bishop, M. (2006, September 19-22). Inconsistency in deception for defense. In *Proceedings of the Workshop on New Security Paradigms*, Schloss Dagstuhl, Germany (pp. 31-38).

Neeraj, S., & Lalit, M. A. (2010). Automated medical image segmentation techniques. *Journal of Medical Physics*, *35*(1), 3–14. doi:10.4103/0971-6203.58777

Ngolah, C. F., Morden, E., & Wang, Y. (2011). An intelligent fault recognizer for rotating machinery via remote characteristic vibration signal detection. In *Proceedings of the 10th IEEE International Conference on Cognitive Informatics & Cognitive Computing* (pp. 135-143).

Niemeyer, G., & Slotine, J. E. (1991). Stable adaptive teleoperation. *IEEE Journal of Oceanic Engineering*, *16*(1), 152–162. doi:10.1109/48.64895

Nikolaev, N. Y., & Iba, H. (2006). *Adaptive learning of polynomial networks: Genetic programming, backpropagation and Bayesian methods: Genetic and evolutionary computation*. New York, NY: Springer.

Nishida, Y., Hori, T., Suehiro, T., & Hirai, S. (2000). Sensorized environment for self-communication based on observation of daily human behavior. In *Proceedings of the IEEE/RSJ International Conference on Intelligent Robots and Systems* (pp. 1364-1372).

Nohmi, M. (2003). Space teleoperation using force reflection of communication time delay. In *Proceedings of the IEEE International Conference on Intelligent Robots and Systems* (pp. 2809-2814). Washington, DC: IEEE Computer Society.

Nolan, M. (1999). *Fundamentals of air traffic control* (3rd ed.). Pacific Grove, CA: Brooks/Cole Wadsworth.

Norman, D. A., & Bobrow, D. G. (1975). On data-limited and resource-limited processes. *Cognitive Psychology*, *7*, 44–64. doi:10.1016/0010-0285(75)90004-3

Noto, K., & Craven, M. (2006). Learning probabilistic models of cis-regulatory modules that represent logical and spatial aspects. *Bioinformatics (Oxford, England)*, *23*, 156–162. doi:10.1093/bioinformatics/btl319

Ohwada, H., & Mizoguchi, F. (1988). An examination for applicability of FGHC: The experience of designing qualitative reasoning system. In *Proceedings of the International Conference on Fifth Generation Computer Systems* (pp. 1193-1200).

Ozcan, E., & Mohan, C. (1999). Particle swarm optimization: Surfing the waves. In *Proceedings of the IEEE International Congress on Evolutionary Computation* (pp. 1939-1944). Washington, DC: IEEE Computer Society.

Padmanabhan, B., & Tuzhilin, A. (1998). A belief-driven method for discovering unexpected patterns. In *Proceedings of the 4th ACM SIGKDD International Conference on Knowledge Discovery and Data Mining*.

Padmanabhan, B., & Tuzhilin, A. (2000). Small is beautiful: Discovering the minimal set of unexpected patterns. In *Proceedings of the 6th ACM SIGKDD International Conference on Knowledge Discovery and Data Mining*, Boston, MA (pp. 54-63).

Pao, D. C. W., Li, H. F., & Jayakumar, R. (1992). Shape recognition using the straight line hough transform: Theory and generalization. *IEEE Transactions on Pattern Analysis and Machine Intelligence*, *14*(11), 1076–1089. doi:10.1109/34.166622

Payne, D. G., & Wenger, M. J. (1998). *Cognitive psychology*. Geneva, IL: Houghton Mifflin.

Pelayo, F. L., Cuartero, F., Valero, V., Pelayo, M. L., & Merayo, M. G. (2005). How does memory work? By timed-arc petri nets. In *Proceedings of the 4th IEEE International Conference on Cognitive Informatics* (pp. 128-135).

Peng, Y. (2004). Intelligent condition monitoring using fuzzy inductive learning. *Journal of Intelligent Manufacturing*, *15*, 373–380. doi:10.1023/B:JIMS.0000026574.95637.36

Pentland, A. (1996). Smart rooms, smart clothes. *Scientific American*, 68–76. doi:10.1038/scientificamerican0496-68

Perry, T. S. (1997). In search of the future of air traffic control. *IEEE Spectrum*, *34*(8), 18–35. doi:10.1109/6.609472

Peters, J. F., & Pedrycz, W. (2000). *Software engineering: An engineering approach*. New York, NY: John Wiley & Sons.

Petri, C. A. (1966). *Communications with automata* (Tech. Rep. No. RADC-TR-65-377). New York, NY: New York University Press.

Pevny, T., & Fridrich, J. (2008). Benchmarking for steganography. In K. Solanki, K. Sullivan, & U. Madow (Eds.), *Proceedings of the 10th International Workshop on Information Hiding* (LNCS 5284, pp. 251-267).

Pfurtscheller, H., & Schlögl, A. (2002). *BCI competition II: Data set III (motor imagery)*. Retrieved May 18, 2009, from http://www.bbci.de/competition/ii/

Pfurtscheller, G., & Neuper, C. (2001). Motor imagery and direct brain-computer communication. *Proceedings of the IEEE*, *89*, 23–34. doi:10.1109/5.939829

Pfurtscheller, G., Solis-Escalante, T., Ortner, R., Linortner, P., & Muller-Putz, G. R. (2010). Self-paced operation of an SSVEP-based orthosis with and without an imagery-based "brain switch:" A feasibility study towards a hybrid BCI. *IEEE Transactions on Neural Systems and Rehabilitation Engineering*, *18*(4), 9–14. doi:10.1109/TNSRE.2010.2040837

Pipino, L., Lee, Y., & Wang, R. (2002). Data quality assessment. *Communications of the ACM*, *45*(4). doi:10.1145/505248.506010

Poesio, M., & Almuhareb, A. (2008). Extracting concept descriptions from the web: the importance of attributes and values. In *Proceedings of the Conference on Ontology Learning and Population: Bridging the Gap between Text and Knowledge* (pp. 29-44).

Pojman, L. P. (2003). *The theory of knowledge: Classical and contemporary readings*. Belmont, CA: Wadsworth/Thomson Learning.

Polikar, R., Topalis, A., Green, D., Kounios, J., & Clark, C. M. (2007). Comparative multiresolution wavelet analysis of ERP spectral bands using an ensemble of classifiers approach for early diagnosis of Alzheimer's disease. *Computers in Biology and Medicine*, *37*, 542–556. doi:10.1016/j.compbiomed.2006.08.012

Poslad, S. (2009). *Ubiquitous computing: Smart devices, environments and interactions*. Chichester, UK: John Wiley & Sons.

Princeton University. (2007). *WordNet: A lexical database for English*. Retrieved from http://wordnet.princeton.edu/

Pudil, P., Novovicova, J., & Kittler, J. (1994). Floating search methods in feature selection. *Pattern Recognition Letters*, *15*(11), 1119–1125. doi:10.1016/0167-8655(94)90127-9

Pullman, S. (1997). *Computational linguistics*. Cambridge, UK: Cambridge University Press.

Pylyshyn, Z. (1989). Computing in cognitive science. In Posner, M. I. (Ed.), *Foundations of cognitive science* (pp. 49–92). Cambridge, MA: MIT Press.

Pylyshyn, Z. (1999). Is vision continuous with cognition? The case for cognitive impenetrability of visual perception. *The Behavioral and Brain Sciences*, *22*, 341–423. doi:10.1017/S0140525X99002022

Quillian, M. R. (1998). Semantic memory. In Minsky, M. (Ed.), *Semantic information processing*. Cambridge, MA: MIT Press.

Quinlan, J. R., & Cameron-Jones, R. M. (1993, April 5-7). FOIL: A midterm report. In *Proceedings of the European Conference on Machine Learning*, Vienna, Austria (Vol. 667, pp. 3-20).

Ramirez, C., & Valdes, B. (2010). A general knowledge representation model for the acquisition of skills and concepts. *International Journal of Software Science and Computational Intelligence*, *2*(3), 1–20. doi:10.4018/jssci.2010070101

Ramler, R., Biffl, S., & Grunbacher, P. (2006). Value-based management of software testing. In Biffl, S., Aurum, A., Boehm, B., Erdogmus, H., & Grünbacher, P. (Eds.), *Value-based software engineering*. Berlin, Germany: Springer-Verlag. doi:10.1007/3-540-29263-2_11

Ramsey, N. F., van de Heuvel, M. P., Kho, K. H., & Leijten, F. S. S. (2006). Towards human BCI applications based on cognitive brain systems: an investigation of neural signals recorder from the dorsolateral prefrontal cortex. *IEEE Transactions on Neural Systems and Rehabilitation, 14*(2), 14–17.

Reisinger, J., & Pasca, M. (2009). Low-cost supervision for multiple-source attribute extraction. In *Proceedings of the 10th International Conference on Intelligent Text Processing and Computational Linguistics* (pp. 382-393).

Ring, M. B. (1997). CHILD: A first step towards continual learning. *Machine Learning, 28*, 77–105. doi:10.1023/A:1007331723572

Roberts, D. C. (1972). File organization techniques. *Advances in Computers, 12*, 115–174. doi:10.1016/S0065-2458(08)60509-4

Robinson, J., & Yahya, R. (2004). Particle swarm optimization in electromagnetic. *IEEE Transactions on Antennas and Propagation, 52*(2), 397–407. doi:10.1109/TAP.2004.823969

Rodriguez, A. (2004). Inconsistency issues in spatial databases. In L. Bertossi, A. Hunter, & T. Schaub (Eds.), *Inconsistency Tolerance* (LNCS 3300, pp. 237-269).

Rodriguez-Lopez, J., Romaguera, S., & Valero, O. (2008). Denotational semantics for programming languages, balanced quasi-metrics and fixed points. *International Journal of Computer Mathematics, 85*(3), 623–630. doi:10.1080/00207160701210653

Romaguera, S., & Sanchis, M. (2003). Applications of utility functions defined on quasi-metric spaces. *Journal of Mathematical Analysis and Applications, 283*, 219–235. doi:10.1016/S0022-247X(03)00285-3

Ross, N. (1986). Air traffic control systems. In Bonsall, P., & Bell, M. (Eds.), *Information technology applications in transport* (pp. 165–189). Leiden, The Netherlands: VNU Science.

Ross, T. J. (1995). *Fuzzy logic with engineering applications*. New York, NY: McGraw-Hill.

Rudolph, L. (2001, June). Project oxygen: Pervasive, human-centric computing – an initial experience. In K. Dittrich, A. Geppert, & M. Norrie (Eds.), *Proceedings of the 13th International Conference on Advanced Information Systems Engineering,* Interlaken, Switzerland (LNCS 2068, pp. 1-12).

Ruhe, G., Eberlein, A., & Pfahl, D. (2003). Trade-off analysis for requirements selection. *International Journal of Software Engineering and Knowledge Engineering, 13*, 345–366. doi:10.1142/S0218194003001378

Ruhe, G., & Ngo-The, A. (2004). Hybrid intelligence in software release planning. *International Journal of Hybrid Intelligent Systems, 1*, 99–110.

Rumelhat, D. E., Durbin, R., Golden, R., & Chauvin, Y. (1995). *Backpropagation: Theory, architectures, and applications* (pp. 1–33). Mahwah, NJ: Lawrence Erlbaum.

Russel, B. (1903). *The principles of mathematics*. London, UK: George Allen & Unwin.

Sahar, S. (2002). On incorporating subjective interestingness into the mining process. In *Proceedings of the IEEE International Conference on Data Mining* (p. 681).

Salamuniccar, G., & Loncaric, S. (2008). Gt-57633 catalougue of martian impact craters developed for evaluation of crater detection algorithms. *Planetary and Space Science, 56*.

Samhouri, M., Al-Ghandoor, A., Ali, S. A., Hinti, I., & Massad, W. (2009). An intelligent machine condition monitoring system using time-based analysis: Neuro-fuzzy versus neural network. *Jordan Journal of Mechanical and Industrial Engineering, 3*(4), 294–305.

Sanchez, D. (2010). A methodology to learn ontological attributes from the web. *Data & Knowledge Engineering, 69*(6), 573–597. doi:10.1016/j.datak.2010.01.006

Sato, T., Nishida, Y., & Mizoguchi, H. (1996). Robotic room: Symbiosis with human through behavior media. *Robotics and Autonomous Systems, 18*(1-2), 185–194. doi:10.1016/0921-8890(96)00004-8

Saxena, A., & Saad, A. (2004). Fault diagnosis in rotating mechanical systems using self-organizing maps. In *Proceedings of the Conference on Artificial Neural Networks in Engineering*, St. Louis, MO.

Schalk, G., Bruuner, P., Gerhardt, L. A., Bischof, H., & Wolpaw, J. R. (2008). Brain-computer interfaces (BCIs): Detection instead of classification. *Journal of Neuroscience Methods*, *167*(1), 51–62. doi:10.1016/j.jneumeth.2007.08.010

Schilit, B. N., & Theimer, M. M. (1994). Disseminating active map information to mobile hosts. *IEEE Network*, *8*(5), 22–32. doi:10.1109/65.313011

Scholkopf, B. (1999). *Advances in kernel methods: Support vector learning*. Cambridge, MA: MIT Press.

Scholkopf, B., & Smola, A. J. (2001). *Learning with kernels support vector machines, regularization, optimization and beyond*. Cambridge, MA: MIT Press.

Schoning, U. (1989). *Logic for computer scientists*. New York, NY: Birkhauser Boston.

Sellers, E. W., & Donchin, E. (2006). A P300-based brain-computer interface: initial tests by ALS patients. *Clinical Neurophysiology*, *117*(3), 38–48. doi:10.1016/j.clinph.2005.06.027

Shafer, S., Krumm, J., Brumitt, B., Meyers, B., Czerwinski, M., & Robbins, D. (1998, July). The new EasyLiving project at Microsoft Research. In *Proceedings of the Joint DARPA/NIST Smart Spaces Workshop* (pp. 127-130).

Shahdi, A., & Sirouspour, S. (2009). Adaptive/robust control for time-delay teleoperation. *IEEE Transactions on Robotics*, *25*(1), 196–205. doi:10.1109/TRO.2008.2010963

Sha, L., Rajkumar, R., & Lehoczky, J. P. (1990). Priority inheritance protocols: An approach to real-time synchronization. *IEEE Transactions on Computers*, *1175*. doi:doi:10.1109/12.57058

Shao, J., & Wang, Y. (2003). A new measure of software complexity based on cognitive weights. *IEEE Canadian Journal of Electrical and Computer Engineering*, *28*(2), 69–74. doi:10.1109/CJECE.2003.1532511

Shastri, L., & Grannes, D. J. (1996). A connectionist treatment of negation and inconsistency. In *Proceedings of the 18th Conference of the Cognitive Science Society*, San Diego, CA (pp. 142-147).

Sheng, Z. H. (2005). *Probability theory and mathematical statistics* (3rd ed.). Beijing, China: Higher Education Press.

Sheridan, T. B. (1993). Space teleoperation through time delay: Review and prognosis. *IEEE Transactions on Robotics and Automation*, *9*(5), 592–606. doi:10.1109/70.258052

Sheu, P., Yu, H., Ramamoorthy, C. V., Joshi, A., & Zadeh, L. A. (2010). *Semantic computing*. New York, NY: John Wiley & Sons.

Shi, Y. H., & Eberhart, R. C. (1998). A modified particle swarm optimizer. In *Proceedings of the IEEE International Congress on Evolutionary Computation* (pp. 69-73). Washington, DC: IEEE Computer Society.

Shin, Y., & Ghosh, J. (1991). The Pi-sigma network: An efficient higher-order neural network for pattern classification and function approximation. In *Proceedings of the Joint International Conference on Neural Networks*, Seattle, WA (pp. 13-18).

Shiroishi, J., Li, Y., Liang, S., Kurfess, T., & Danyluk, S. (1997). Bearing condition diagnostics via vibration & acoustic emission measurements. *Mechanical Systems and Signal Processing*, *11*(5), 693–705. doi:10.1006/mssp.1997.0113

Siedlecki, W., & Sklanky, J. (1989). A note on genetic algorithms for large-scale feature selection. *Journal of Pattern Recognition Letters*, *10*(5), 335–347. doi:10.1016/0167-8655(89)90037-8

Silberschatz, A., Galvin, P., & Gagne, G. (2003). *Applied operating system concepts* (1st ed.). New York, NY: John Wiley & Sons.

Silva, M., & Valette, R. (1990). *Petri nets and flexible manufacturing*. Retrieved from http://homepages.laas.fr/robert/papers.pri/design.pri/maphiro89.pdf

Simovici, D. A., & Djeraba, C. (2008). *Mathematical tools for data mining: Set theory, partial orders, combinatorics*. London, UK: Springer-Verlag.

Simovici, D. A., & Jaroszewicz, S. (2003). Generalized conditional entropy and decision trees. *Extraction et la Gestion des Connaissances*, *17*(1-3), 552.

Simovici, D. A., & Jaroszewicz, S. (2008). An axiomatization of partition entropy. *IEEE Transactions on Information Theory*, *48*, 2138–2142. doi:10.1109/TIT.2002.1013159

Simpson, T., & Dao, T. (2011). *WordNet-based semantic similarity measurement*. Retrieved from http://www.codeproject.com/KB/string/semanticsimilaritywordnet.aspx

Sitaram, R., Zhang, H. H., Guan, C. T., Thulasidas, M., Hoshi, Y., & Ishikawa, A. (2007). Temporal classification of multichannel near-infrared spectroscopy signals of motor imagery for developing a brain-computer interface. *NeuroImage, 34*(4), 16–27. doi:10.1016/j.neuroimage.2006.11.005

Sivic, J., & Zisserman, A. (2003). Video Google: A text retrieval approach to object matching in videos. In *Proceedings of the IEEE International Conference on Computer Vision* (pp. 1470-1477).

Slaughter, S. A., Harter, D. E., & Krishnan, M. S. (1998). Evaluating the cost of software quality. *Communications of the ACM, 41*(8), 67–73. doi:10.1145/280324.280335

Smetana, L. (2008). *Nonlinear neuro-controller for automatic control laboratory system*. Unpublished master's thesis, Czech Technical University in Prague, Prague, Czech Republic.

Smith, K. J. (2001). *The nature of mathematics* (9th ed.). Belmont, CA: Brooks Cole Publishing.

Smith, R. E. (1993). *Psychology*. Eagan, MN: West.

Sneiders, E. (2002). Automated question answering using question templates that cover the conceptual model of the database, natural language processing and information systems. In *Proceedings of the 6th International Conference on Applications of Natural Language to Information Systems-Revised Papers*, Sweden.

Softky, R. W., & Kammen, D. M. (1991). Correlations in high dimensional or asymmetrical data sets: Hebbian neuronal processing. *Neural Networks, 4*(3), 337–347. doi:10.1016/0893-6080(91)90070-L

Solanki, K., Dabeer, O., Madhow, U., Manjunath, B. S., & Chandrasekaran, S. (2003). Robust image-adaptive data hiding: Modeling, source coding, and channel coding. In. *Proceedings of the Annual Allerton Conference on Communication Control and Computing, 41*, 829–838.

Sperschneider, V., & Antoniou, G. (1991). *Logic: A foundation for computer science*. Reading, MA: Addison-Wesley.

Srinivasan, K. S. (2003). *Fault diagnosis in rotating machines using vibration monitoring and artificial neural network* (Unpublished doctoral dissertation). Indian Institute of Technology, Delhi, India.

Steece, B., Chulani, S., & Boehm, B. (2002). Determining software quality using COQUALMO. In Blischke, W., & Murphy, D. (Eds.), *Case studies in reliability and maintenance*. Hoboken, NJ: John Wiley & Sons.

Sternberg, R. J. (1998). *In search of the human mind* (2nd ed.). New York, NY: Harcourt Brace.

Stubbs, D. F., & Webre, N. W. (1985). *Data structures with abstract data types and Pascal*. Monterey, CA: Brooks/Cole.

Stutzle, T., & Hoos, H. H. (2000). MAX-MIN ant system. *Future Generation Computer Systems, 16*(9), 889–914. doi:doi:10.1016/S0167-739X(00)00043-1

Šuc, D., Vladusic, D., & Bratko, I. (2004). Qualitatively faithful quantitative prediction. *Artificial Intelligence, 158*(2), 189–214. doi:10.1016/j.artint.2004.05.002

Suchanek, F. M., Kasneci, G., & Weikum, G. (2007). YAGO: A core of semantic knowledge unifying WordNet and Wikipedia. In *Proceedings of the International World Wide Web Conference* (pp. 697-706).

Suganuma, T., Sugawara, K., Kinoshita, T., Hattori, F., & Shiratori, N. (2009). Concept of symbiotic computing and its agent-based Application to a ubiquitous care-support service. *International Journal of Cognitive Informatics and Natural Intelligence, 3*(1), 34–56. doi:10.4018/jcini.2009010103

Sugawara, K., Fujita, S., & Hara, H. (2007). A concept of symbiotic computing and its application to telework. In *Proceedings of the 6th IEEE Internatinal Conference on Cognitive Informatics,* Lake Tahoe, CA (pp. 302-311).

Sugawara, K., Fujita, S., Kinoshita, T., & Shiratori, N. (2008). A design of cognitive agents for recognizing real space –towards symbiotic computing. In *Proceedings of the 7th IEEE Internatinal Conference on Cognitive Informatics,* Stanford, CA (pp. 277-285).

Sumiyoshi, Y., & Ohnishi, K. (2004). The transformation of modified 4-channel architecture. In *Proceedings of the IEEE International Workshop Advanced Motion Control* (pp. 211-216). Washington, DC: IEEE Computer Society.

Surmann, H. (2000). Learning a fuzzy rule based knowledge representation. In *Proceedings of the ICSC Symposium on Neural Computation*, Berlin, Germany (pp. 349-355).

Tan, P. N., Kumar, V., & Srivastava, J. (2002, July). Selecting the right interestingness measure for association patterns. In *Proceedings of the 8th ACM SIGKDD International Conference on Knowledge Discovery and Data Mining* (pp. 32-41).

Tanenbaum, A. S. (1994). *Distributed operating systems.* Upper Saddle River, NJ: Prentice Hall.

Tang, K., Yao, X., Suganthan, P. N., MacNish, C., Chen, Y. P., Chen, C. M., et al. (2007). *Benchmark functions for the CEC'2008 special session and competition on large scale global optimization* (Tech. Rep. No. NCL-TR-2007012). Hefei, China: University of Science and Technology of China.

Tavakoli, M., Patel, R. V., & Moallem, M. (2006). Bilateral control of a teleoperator for soft tissue palpation: design and experiments. In *Proceedings of the IEEE International Conference on Robotics and Automation* (pp. 3280-3285). Washington, DC: IEEE Computer Society.

Taylor, J. G., & Commbes, S. (1993). Learning higher order correlations. *Neural Networks, 6*(3), 423–428. doi:10.1016/0893-6080(93)90009-L

Tetsuro, M. H., & Wang, P. C. (2008). Fault diagnosis and condition surveillance for plant rotating machinery using partially-linearized neural network. *Computers & Industrial Engineering, 55*(4), 783–794. doi:10.1016/j.cie.2008.03.002

Thomas, E. A. C., & Weavery, W. B. (1975). Cognitive processing and time perception. *Perception & Psychophysics, 17*(4), 363–367. doi:10.3758/BF03199347

Thomas, H. C., Charles, E. L., Ronald, L. R., & Clifford, S. (2001). *Introduction to algorithms* (2nd ed.). Cambridge, MA: MIT Press.

Thrun, S. (1995). *Lifelong learning: A case study* (Tech. Rep. No. CMU-CS-95-208). Pittsburgh, PA: Carnegie Mellon University.

Thrun, S. (1998). Lifelong learning algorithms. In Thrun, S., & Pratt, L. (Eds.), *Learning to learn.* Boston, MA: Kluwer Academic. doi:10.1007/978-1-4615-5529-2_8

Thrun, S., & Mitchell, T. (1995). Lifelong robot learning. *Robotics and Autonomous Systems, 15*, 25–46. doi:10.1016/0921-8890(95)00004-Y

Tian, Y., Wang, Y., & Hu, K. (2009). A knowledge representation tool for autonomous machine learning based on concept algebra. *Transactions of Computational Science, 5*, 143–160.

Tiberino, A., Embley, D., Lonsdale, D., Ding, Y., & Nagy, G. (2005). Towards ontology generation from tables. *WWW: Internet and Information Systems, 8*(3), 261–285.

Tobergte, A., Konietschke, R., & Hirzinger, G. (2009). Planning and control of a teleoperation system for research in minimally invasive robotic surgery. In *Proceedings of the IEEE International Conference on Robotics and Automation* (pp. 4225-4232). Washington, DC: IEEE Computer Society.

Tomassi, P. (1999). *Logic.* London, UK: Routledge. doi:10.4324/9780203197035

Tomuro, N. (2002). Question terminology and representation for question type classification. In *Proceedings of the 2nd International Workshop on Computational Terminology*, Taipei, Taiwan.

Touretzky, D., Horty, J., & Thomason, R. (1987). A clash of intuitions: the current state of monmonotonic multiple inheritance systems. In *Proceedings of the Tenth International Joint Conference on Artificial Intelligence* (pp. 476-482).

Tracey, N. (2000). *A search-based automated test data generation framework for safety critical software.* Unpublished doctoral dissertation, University of York, York, UK.

Tracey, N., Clark, J., Mander, K., & McDermid, J. (2000). Automated test data generation for exception conditions. *Software, Practice & Experience, 30*(1), 61–79. doi:10.1002/(SICI)1097-024X(200001)30:1<61::AID-SPE292>3.0.CO;2-9

Tsumoto, S., & Hirano, S. (2011, August). Fuzziness from attribute generalization in information table. In *Proceedings of the 7ᵗʰ IEEE International Conference on Cognitive Informatics*, Stanford, CA (pp. 455-461).

Tucker, A. B. Jr. (1997). *The computer science and engineering handbook.* Boca Raton, FL: CRC Press.

U. S. National Library of Medicine. (2007). *Unified medical language system.* Retrieved from http://www.nlm.nih.gov/research/umls/

Umesh, K. N., & Srinivasan, K. S. (2005). Study of effects of misalignment on vibration signatures of rotating machinery. In *Proceedings of the National Conference Mechanical Engineering*, Mangalore, India.

Urbach, E. R., & Stepinski, T. F. (2009). Automatic detection of sub-kilometer craters in high resolution planetary images. *Planetary and Space Science, 57*, 880–887. doi:10.1016/j.pss.2009.03.009

van Heijenoort, J. (1997). *From Frege to Godel, a source book in mathematical logic 1879-1931.* Cambridge, MA: Harvard University Press.

Voorhees, E. (1999). The TREC-8 question answering track report. In *Proceedings of the Eighth National Institute of Standards and Technology Text REtrieval Conference* (pp. 743-751).

Vuckovic, A. (2009). Non-invasive BCI: how far can we get with motor imagination? *Clinical Neurophysiology, 120*(8), 22–23. doi:10.1016/j.clinph.2009.06.007

Waldert, S., Pistohl, T., Braun, C., Ball, T., Aertsen, A., & Mehring, C. (2009). A review on directional in neural signals for brain-machine interfaces. *The Journal of Physiology, 103*(3-5), 44–54.

Wang, K., Jiang, Y., & Lakshmanan, L. V. S. (2003, August). Mining unexpected rules by pushing user dynamics. In *Proceedings of the 9th ACM SIGKDD International Conference on Knowledge Discovery and Data Mining*, Washington, DC (pp. 246-255).

Wang, Y. (2002). Cognitive models of the brain. In *Proceedings of the 1st IEEE International Conference on Cognitive Informatics* (pp. 259-269).

Wang, Y. (2002b, August). Keynote: On cognitive informatics. In *Proceedings of the First IEEE International Conference on Cognitive Informatics*, Calgary, AB, Canada (pp. 34-42). Washington, DC: IEEE Computer Society.

Wang, Y. (2003). On cognitive informatics. *Brain and Mind: A Transdisciplinary Journal of Neuroscience and Neurophilosophy, 4*(2), 151-167.

Wang, Y. (2003b, May). The measurement theory for software engineering. In *Proceedings of the Canadian Conference on Electrical and Computer Engineering*, Montreal, QC, Canada (pp. 1321-1324). Washington, DC: IEEE Computer Society.

Wang, Y. (2005, August). Keynote: Psychological experiments on the cognitive complexities of fundamental control structures of software systems. In *Proceedings of the 4th IEEE International Conference on Cognitive Informatics* (pp. 4-5). Washington, DC: IEEE Computer Society.

Wang, Y. (2007). *Software engineering foundations: A software science perspective* (CRC Series in Software Engineering, Vol. II). New York, NY: Auerbach.

Wang, Y. (2008). On contemporary denotational mathematics for computational intelligence. In M. L. Gavrilova et al. (Eds.), *Transactions on Computational Science 2* (LNCS 5150, pp. 6-29).

Wang, Y. (2009a). Fuzzy inferences methodologies for cognitive informatics and computational intelligence. In *Proceedings of the IEEE 8th International Conference on Cognitive Informatics* (pp. 241-248). Washington, DC: IEEE Computer Society.

Wang, Y., Sun, F., Liu, H., & Li, Z. (2010). Passive four-channel multilateral shared control architecture in teleoperation. In *Proceedings of the IEEE International Conference on Cognitive Informatics* (pp. 851-858). Washington, DC: IEEE Computer Society.

Wang, L., & Wu, Q. D. (2003). Application of ant colony algorithm in solving optimization problems in continuous space. *Control and Decision, 18*(1), 45–48.

Wang, Y. (2002a). The real-time process algebra (RTPA). *Annals of Software Engineering: An International Journal, 14*, 235–274. doi:10.1023/A:1020561826073

Wang, Y. (2004). Operating systems. In Dorf, R. (Ed.), *The engineering handbook* (2nd ed.). Boca Raton, FL: CRC Press.

Wang, Y. (2006). On the informatics laws and deductive semantics of software. *IEEE Transactions on Systems, Man and Cybernetics. Part C, Applications and Reviews, 36*(2), 161–171. doi:10.1109/TSMCC.2006.871138

Wang, Y. (2007). *Software engineering foundations: A software science perspective* (*Vol. 2*). Boca Raton, FL: Auerbach Publications.

Wang, Y. (2007a). The OAR model of neural informatics for internal knowledge representation in the brain. *International Journal of Cognitive Informatics and Natural Intelligence*, *1*(3), 66–77. doi:10.4018/jcini.2007070105

Wang, Y. (2007b). *Software engineering foundations: A software science perspective*. Boca Raton, FL: Auerbach.

Wang, Y. (2007b). The cognitive processes of formal inferences. *International Journal of Cognitive Informatics and Natural Intelligence*, *1*(4), 75–86. doi:10.4018/jcini.2007100106

Wang, Y. (2007c). The theoretical framework of cognitive informatics. *International Journal of Cognitive Informatics and Natural Intelligence*, *1*(1), 1–27. doi:10.4018/jcini.2007010101

Wang, Y. (2007c). Towards theoretical foundations of autonomic computing. *International Journal of Cognitive Informatics and Natural Intelligence*, *1*(3), 1–21. doi:10.4018/jcini.2007070101

Wang, Y. (2008a). On contemporary denotational mathematics for computational intelligence. *Transactions of Computational Science*, *2*, 6–29. doi:10.1007/978-3-540-87563-5_2

Wang, Y. (2008a). RTPA: A denotational mathematics for manipulating intelligent and computational behaviors. *International Journal of Cognitive Informatics and Natural Intelligence*, *2*(2), 44–62. doi:10.4018/jcini.2008040103

Wang, Y. (2008b). Mathematical Laws of Software. *Transactions on Computational Science*, *2*, 46–83. doi:10.1007/978-3-540-87563-5_4

Wang, Y. (2008b). On concept algebra: A denotational mathematical structure for knowledge and software modeling. *International Journal of Cognitive Informatics and Natural Intelligence*, *2*(2), 1–19. doi:10.4018/jcini.2008040101

Wang, Y. (2008b). On the Big-R notation for describing iterative and recursive behaviors. *International Journal of Cognitive Informatics and Natural Intelligence*, *2*(1), 17–28. doi:10.4018/jcini.2008010102

Wang, Y. (2008c). Deductive Semantics of RTPA. *International Journal of Cognitive Informatics and Natural Intelligence*, *2*(2), 95–121. doi:10.4018/jcini.2008040106

Wang, Y. (2008c). RTPA: A denotational mathematics for manipulating intelligent and computational behaviors. *International Journal of Cognitive Informatics and Natural Intelligence*, *2*(2), 44–62. doi:10.4018/jcini.2008040103

Wang, Y. (2008d). Mathematical laws of software. *Transactions of Computational Science*, *2*, 46–83. doi:10.1007/978-3-540-87563-5_4

Wang, Y. (2008d). On contemporary denotational mathematics for computational intelligence. *Transactions of Computational Science*, *2*, 6–29. doi:10.1007/978-3-540-87563-5_2

Wang, Y. (2008e). Deductive semantics of RTPA. *International Journal of Cognitive Informatics and Natural Intelligence*, *2*(2), 95–121. doi:10.4018/jcini.2008040106

Wang, Y. (2009). On cognitive computing. *International Journal of Software Science and Computational Intelligence*, *1*(3), 1–15. doi:10.4018/jssci.2009070101

Wang, Y. (2009). On the cognitive complexity of software and its quantification and formal measurement. *International Journal of Software Science and Computational Intelligence*, *1*(2), 31–53. doi:10.4018/jssci.2009040103

Wang, Y. (2009a). A formal syntax of natural languages and the deductive grammar. *Fundamenta Informaticae*, *90*(4), 353–368.

Wang, Y. (2009a). Paradigms of denotational mathematics for cognitive informatics and cognitive computing. *Fundamenta Informaticae*, *90*(3), 282–303.

Wang, Y. (2009b). On abstract intelligence: Toward a unified theory of natural, artificial, machinable, and computational intelligence. *International Journal of Software Science and Computational Intelligence*, *1*(1), 1–17. doi:10.4018/jssci.2009010101

Wang, Y. (2009b). The formal design model of a Telephone Switching System (TSS). *International Journal of Software Science and Computational Intelligence*, *1*(3), 92–116. doi:10.4018/jssci.2009070107

Wang, Y. (2009b). Toward a formal knowledge system theory and its cognitive informatics foundations. *Transactions of Computational Science, 5*, 1–19.

Wang, Y. (2009c). A formal syntax of natural languages and the deductive grammar. *Fundamenta Informaticae, 90*(4), 353–368.

Wang, Y. (2009c). On cognitive computing. *International Journal of Software Science and Computational Intelligence, 1*(3), 1–15. doi:10.4018/jssci.2009070101

Wang, Y. (2010). On formal and cognitive semantics for semantic computing. *International Journal of Semantic Computing, 4*(2), 203–237. doi:10.1142/S1793351X10000833

Wang, Y. (2010a). Cognitive robots: A reference model towards intelligent authentication. *IEEE Robotics and Automation, 17*(4), 54–62. doi:10.1109/MRA.2010.938842

Wang, Y. (2010a). Cognitive robots: A reference model towards intelligent authentication. *IEEE Robotics and Automation, 17*(4), 54–62. doi:10.1109/MRA.2010.938842

Wang, Y. (2010b). On formal and cognitive semantics for semantic computing. *International Journal of Semantic Computing, 4*(2), 203–237. doi:10.1142/S1793351X10000833

Wang, Y. (2010c). On concept algebra for computing with words (CWW). *International Journal of Semantic Computing, 4*(3), 331–356. doi:10.1142/S1793351X10001061

Wang, Y. (2011). On cognitive models of causal inferences and causation networks. *International Journal of Software Science and Computational Intelligence, 3*(1), 50–60.

Wang, Y., & Chiew, V. (2010). On the cognitive process of human problem solving. *Cognitive Systems Research, 11*(1), 81–92. doi:10.1016/j.cogsys.2008.08.003

Wang, Y., & Huang, J. (2008). Formal modeling and specification of design patterns using RTPA. *International Journal of Cognitive Informatics and Natural Intelligence, 2*(1), 100–111. doi:10.4018/jcini.2008010108

Wang, Y., Huang, J., & Lei, J. (2011). The formal design models of the Universal Array (UA) and its implementations. *International Journal of Software Science and Computational Intelligence, 3*(3), 69–89. doi:10.4018/IJSSCI.2011070106

Wang, Y., & King, G. (2000). *Software engineering processes: Principles and applications* (*Vol. 1*). Boca Raton, FL: CRC Press.

Wang, Y., Kinsner, W., Anderson, J., Zhang, D., Yao, Y., & Sheu, P. (2009). A doctrine of cognitive informatics. *Fundamenta Informaticae-Cognitive Informatics, Cognitive Computing, and Their Denotational Mathematical Foundations, 90*(3), 203–228.

Wang, Y., Ngolah, C. F., Ahmadi, H., Sheu, P. C.-Y., & Ying, S. (2009). The formal design model of a Lift Dispatching System (LDS). *International Journal of Software Science and Computational Intelligence, 1*(4), 98–122. doi:10.4018/jssci.2009062506

Wang, Y., & Ruhe, G. (2007). The cognitive process of decision making. *International Journal of Cognitive Informatics and Natural Intelligence, 1*(2), 73–85. doi:10.4018/jcini.2007040105

Wang, Y., Tan, X., & Ngolah, C. F. (2010). Design and implementation of an autonomic code generator based on RTPA (RTPA-CG). *International Journal of Software Science and Computational Intelligence, 2*(2), 44–67. doi:10.4018/jssci.2010040103

Wang, Y., Tian, Y., & Hu, K. (2011). Semantic manipulations and formal ontology for machine learning based on concept algebra. *International Journal of Cognitive Informatics and Natural Intelligence, 5*(3), 1–29. doi:10.4018/IJCINI.2011070101

Wang, Y., Wang, Y., Patel, S., & Patel, D. (2006). A layered reference model of the brain (LRMB). [C]. *IEEE Transactions on Systems, Man, and Cybernetics, 36*(2), 124–133. doi:10.1109/TSMCC.2006.871126

Wang, Y., Zeng, G., Ngolah, C. F., Sheu, P. C.-Y., Choy, C. P., & Tian, Y. (2010). The formal design models of a real-time operating system (RTOS+): Static and dynamic behavior models. *International Journal of Software Science and Computational Intelligence, 2*(3), 79–105. doi:10.4018/jssci.2010070106

Wang, Y., Zhang, Y., Sheu, P. C.-Y., Li, X., & Guo, H. (2010). The formal design models of an Automatic Teller Machine (ATM). *International Journal of Software Science and Computational Intelligence, 2*(1), 102–131. doi:10.4018/jssci.2010101907

Weaver, W. (1949). Translation. In Locke, W. N., & Booth, A. D. (Eds.), *Machine translation of languages: Fourteen essays* (pp. 15–23). Cambridge, MA: MIT Press.

Webb, G. I. (2006). Discovering significant rules. In *Proceedings of the 12th ACM SIGKDD International Conference on Knowledge Discovery and Data Mining*, Philadelphia, PA (pp. 434-443).

Wegener, J., Baresel, A., & Sthamer, H. (2001). Evolutionary test environment for automatic structural testing. *Information and Software Technology, 43*(14), 841–854. doi:10.1016/S0950-5849(01)00190-2

Wegener, J., Sthamer, H., Jones, B., & Eyres, D. (1997). Testing real-time systems using genetic algorithms. *Software Quality Journal, 6*(2), 127–135. doi:10.1023/A:1018551716639

Weiser, M. (1991). The computer for the twenty-first century. *Scientific American, 265*(3), 94–104. doi:10.1038/scientificamerican0991-94

Werbos, P. J. (1990). Backpropagation through time: What it is and how to do it. *Proceedings of the IEEE, 78*(10), 1550–1560. doi:10.1109/5.58337

Werner, T. (1999). Models for prediction and recognition of eukaryotic promoters. *Mammalian Genome, 10*, 168–175. doi:10.1007/s003359900963

Werner, T. (2001). The promoter connection. *Nature Genetics, 29*, 105–106. doi:10.1038/ng1001-105

Werner, T., Fessele, S., Maier, H., & Nelson, P. J. (2003). Computer modeling of promoter organization as a tool to study transcriptional coregulation. *The FASEB Journal, 17*, 1228–1237. doi:10.1096/fj.02-0955rev

Weyuker, E. J. (1983). Assessing test data adequacy through program inference. *ACM Transactions on Programming Languages and Systems, 5*(4), 641–655. doi:10.1145/69575.357231

Whitehead, S. D. (1995). Auto-FAQ: An experiment in cyberspace leveraging. *Journal of Computer Networks and ISDN Systems, 28*, 137–146. doi:10.1016/0169-7552(95)00101-2

Widrow, B. C., & Aragon, J. (2010). Cognitive memory: Human like memory. *International Journal of Software Science and Computational Intelligence, 2*(4), 1–15. doi:10.4018/jssci.2010100101

Wiener, R., & Pinson, L. J. (2000). *Fundamentals of OOP and data structures in Java*. Cambridge, UK: Cambridge University Press. doi:10.1017/CBO9780511807176

Williams, R. J., & Zipser, D. (1989). A learning algorithm for continually running fully recurrent neural networks. *Neural Computation, 1*(2), 270–280. doi:10.1162/neco.1989.1.2.270

Wilson, R. A., & Keil, F. C. (2001). *The MIT encyclopedia of the cognitive sciences*. Cambridge, MA: MIT Press.

Witten, I. H., & Frank, E. (2005). *Data mining: Practical machine learning tools and techniques* (2nd ed.). San Francisco, CA: Morgan Kaufmann.

Wolpaw, J. R., Birbaumer, N., McFarland, D. J., Pfurtscheller, G., & Vaughan, T. M. (2002). Brain-computer interfaces for communication and control. *Clinical Neurophysiology, 113*(6), 67–91. doi:10.1016/S1388-2457(02)00057-3

Wong, K. Y., & See, P. C. (2009). A new minimum pheromone threshold strategy (MPTS) for max-min ant system. *Applied Soft Computing, 9*(3), 882–888. doi:10.1016/j.asoc.2008.11.011

Wright, J., Yang, A., Ganesh, A., Sastry, S., & Ma, Y. (2009). Robust face recognition via sparse representation. *IEEE Transactions on Pattern Analysis and Machine Intelligence, 31*(2), 210–227. doi:10.1109/TPAMI.2008.79

Wu, C. H., Yeh, J. F., & Chen, M. J. (2005). Domain-specific FAQ retrieval using independent aspects. *ACM Transactions on Asian Language Information Processing, 4*(1), 1–17. doi:10.1145/1066078.1066079

Xiao, G., Southey, F., Holte, R. C., & Wilkinson, D. (2005). Software testing by active learning for commercial games. In *Proceedings of the 20th AAAI Conference*, Pittsburgh, PA (pp. 898-903).

Xie, X., Lu, J., Kulbokas, E. J., Golub, T. R., Mootha, V., & Lindblad-Toh, K. (2005). Systematic discovery of regulatory motifs in human promoters and 3' UTRs by comparison of several mammals. *Nature, 434*, 338–345. doi:10.1038/nature03441

Xin, D., Cheng, H., Yan, X., & Han, J. (2006). Extracting redundancy-aware top-k patterns. In *Proceedings of the 12th ACM SIGKDD International Conference on Knowledge Discovery and Data Mining*, Philadelphia, PA (pp. 444-453).

Xing, L. N., Chen, Y. W., & Yang, K. W. (2009). Multi-objective flexible job shop schedule: Design and evaluation by simulation modeling. *Applied Soft Computing*, *9*(1), 362–376. doi:10.1016/j.asoc.2008.04.013

Xue, S. S. (2002). *Intelligent building and generic cabling system*. Beijing, China: Posts and Telecom Press.

Xu, S., & Yahya, R. (2007). Boundary conditions in particle swarm optimization revisited. *IEEE Transactions on Antennas and Propagation*, *55*(3), 760–765. doi:10.1109/TAP.2007.891562

Yamawaki, N., Wilke, C., Liu, Z. M., & He, B. (2006). An enhanced time-frequency-spatial approach for motor imagery classification. *IEEE Transactions on Neural Systems and Rehabilitation Engineering*, *14*(2), 50–54. doi:10.1109/TNSRE.2006.875567

Yang, J., Jiang, Y., Hauptmann, A., & Ngo, C.-W. (2007). Evaluating bag-of-visual-words representations in scene classification. In *Proceedings of the International Workshop on Multimedia Information Retrieval* (pp. 197-206).

Yang, J., Yu, K., Gong, Y., & Huang, T. (2009). Linear spatial pyramid matching using sparse coding for image classification. In *Proceedings of the IEEE Conference on Computer Vision and Pattern Recognition* (pp. 1794-1801).

Yan, H. S. (2006). A new complicated-knowledge representation approach based on knowledge meshes. *IEEE Transactions on Knowledge and Data Engineering*, *18*(1), 47–62. doi:10.1109/TKDE.2006.2

Yeh, P., & Puri, C. (2010, October). An efficient and robust approach for discovering data quality rules. In *Proceedings of the 22nd IEEE International Conference on Tools with Artificial Intelligence*, Arras, France (pp. 248-255).

Yip, R. K. K., Tam, P. K. S., & Leung, D. N. K. (1992). Modification of hough transform for circles and ellipses detection using a 2-dimensional array. *Pattern Recognition*, *25*, 1007–1022. doi:10.1016/0031-3203(92)90064-P

Yu, B., & Yuan, B. (1993). A more efficient branch and bound algorithm for feature selection. *Pattern Recognition*, *26*(6), 883–889. doi:10.1016/0031-3203(93)90054-Z

Zacharaki, E., Wang, S., Chawla, S., Soo, Y. D., Wolf, R., Melhem, E., & Davatzikos, C. (2009). Classification of brain tumor type and grade using MRI texture and shape in a machine learning scheme. *Magnetic Resonance in Medicine*, *62*(6), 1609–1618. doi:10.1002/mrm.22147

Zadeh, L. A. (1965). Fuzzy sets. *Information and Control*, *8*, 338–353. doi:10.1016/S0019-9958(65)90241-X

Zadeh, L. A. (1975). Fuzzy logic and approximate reasoning. *Syntheses*, *30*, 407–428. doi:10.1007/BF00485052

Zadeh, L. A. (1996). Fuzzy logic = computing with words. *IEEE Transactions on Fuzzy Systems*, *4*, 103–111. doi:10.1109/91.493904

Zadeh, L. A. (2004). Precisiated Natural Language (PNL). *AI Magazine*, *25*(3), 74–91.

Zadeh, L. A. (2006). Generalized theory of uncertainty (GTU) – principal concepts and ideas. *Computational Statistics & Data Analysis*, *51*, 15–46. doi:10.1016/j.csda.2006.04.029

Zhang, D. (2000). Applying machine learning algorithms in software development. In *Proceedings of the Monterey Workshop on Modeling Software System Structures*, Santa Margherita Ligure, Italy (pp. 275-285).

Zhang, D. (2005). Fixpoint semantics for rule base anomalies. In *Proceedings of the 4th IEEE International Conference on Cognitive Informatics*, Irvine, CA (pp. 10-17). Washington, DC: IEEE Computer Society.

Zhang, D. (2009). Taming inconsistency in value-based software development. In *Proceedings of the 21st International Conference on Software Engineering and Knowledge Engineering*, Boston, MA (pp. 450-455).

Zhang, D. (2009a). On temporal properties of knowledge base inconsistency. In M. L. Gavrilova, C. J. K. Tan, Y. Wang, & K. C. C. Chan (Eds.), *Transactions on Computational Science V* (LNCS 5540, pp. 20-37).

Zhang, D. (2009b, July). Taming inconsistency in value-based software development. In *Proceedings of the Twenty First International Conference on Software Engineering and Knowledge Engineering*, Boston, MA (pp. 450-455).

Zhang, D. (2010a). Harnessing locality for knowledge inconsistency management. In *Proceedings of the 9th IEEE International Conference on Cognitive Informatics*, Beijing, China (pp. 325-332).

Zhang, D. (2010b). Toward A classification of antagonistic manifestations of knowledge. In *Proceedings of the 22th IEEE International Conference on Tools with Artificial Intelligence*, Arras, France (pp. 375-382).

Zhang, D. (2010b). Toward a classification of antagonistic manifestations of knowledge. In *Proceedings of the Twenty Second International Conference on Tools with Artificial Intelligence*, Arras, France (pp. 375-382).

Zhang, H., Berg, A., Maire, M., & Malik, J. (2006). SVM-KNN: Discriminative nearest neighbor classification for visual category recognition. In *Proceedings of the IEEE Conference on Computer Vision and Pattern Recognition* (pp. 2126-2136).

Zhang, W. J., Xie, X. F., & Bi, D. C. (2004). Handling boundary constraints for numerical optimization by particle swarm flying in periodic search space. In []. Washington, DC: IEEE Computer Society.]. *Proceedings of the IEEE International Congress on Evolutionary Computation, 2*, 2307–2311.

Zhang, D. (2007). Fixpoint semantics for rule base anomalies. *International Journal of Cognitive Informatics and Natural Intelligence, 1*(4), 4–25. doi:10.4018/jcini.2007100102

Zhang, D. (2008). Quantifying knowledge base inconsistency via fixpoint semantics. *Transactions on Computational Science 2. LNCS, 5150*, 145–160.

Zhang, D. (2009). Machine learning and value-based software engineering. *International Journal of Software Science and Computational Intelligence, 1*(1), 112–125. doi:10.4018/jssci.2009010108

Zhang, D. (2010a). Inconsistency: The good, the bad, and the ugly. *International Transactions on Systems Science and Applications, 6*(2-3), 131–145.

Zhang, D. (2011a). On localities of knowledge inconsistency. *International Journal of Software Science and Computational Intelligence, 3*(1), 61–77. doi:10.4018/jssci.2011010105

Zhang, D. (2011b). The utility of inconsistencies in information security and digital forensics. In Özyer, T., Kianmehr, K., & Tan, M. (Eds.), *Recent trends in information reuse and integration* (pp. 381–397). Berlin, Germany: Springer-Verlag. doi:10.1007/978-3-7091-0738-6_19

Zhang, D., & Grégoire, É. (2011). The landscape of inconsistency, a perspective. *International Journal of Semantic Computing, 5*(3), 1–22. doi:10.1142/S1793351X11001237

Zhang, D., & Tsai, J. J. P. (2003). Machine learning and software engineering. *Software Quality Journal, 11*(2), 87–119. doi:10.1023/A:1023760326768

Zhang, D., & Tsai, J. J. P. (Eds.). (2005). *Machine learning applications in software engineering*. Singapore: World Scientific. doi:10.1142/5700

Zhang, D., & Tsai, J. J. P. (Eds.). (2007). *Advances in machine learning applications in software engineering*. Hershey, PA: IGI Global. doi:10.4018/978-1-59140-941-0

Zhang, J., Marszalek, M., Lazebnik, S., & Schmid, C. (2007). Local features and kernels for classification of texture and object categories: A comprehensive study. *International Journal of Computer Vision, 73*(2), 213–238. doi:10.1007/s11263-006-9794-4

Zhang, M. (Ed.). (2008). *Artificial higher order neural networks for economics and business*. Hershey, PA: IGI Global. doi:10.4018/978-1-59904-897-0

Zhang, M. (Ed.). (2010). *Artificial higher order neural networks for computer science and engineering: Trends for emerging applications*. Hershey, PA: IGI Global. doi:10.4018/978-1-61520-711-4

Zhang, Z., & Gerstein, M. (2003). Of mice and men: phylogenetic footprinting aids the discovery of regulatory elements. *Journal of Biology, 2*(2), 11. doi:10.1186/1475-4924-2-11

Zhao, Q., & Sui, Z. (2008). To extract ontology attribute value automatically based on WWW. In *Proceedings of the International Conference on Natural Language Processing and Knowledge Engineering* (pp. 1-7).

Zhou, Z. H., & Li, M. (2010). Semi-supervised learning by disagreement. *Knowledge and Information Systems, 24*(3), 415–439. doi:10.1007/s10115-009-0209-z

Zhu, H., & Shan, L. (2006). Well-formedness, consistency and completeness of graphic models. In *Proceedings of the 9th International Conference on Computer Modeling and Simulation* (pp. 47-53).

Zhu, H., Hall, P. A. V., & May, J. H. R. (1997). Software unit test coverage and adequacy. *ACM Computing Surveys, 29*(4), 366–427. doi:10.1145/267580.267590

Zuse, H. (1997). *A framework of software measurement*. Berlin, Germany: Walter de Gruyter.

About the Contributors

Yingxu Wang is Professor of Cognitive Informatics and Software Science, President of International Institute of Cognitive Informatics and Cognitive Computing (ICIC), Director of Laboratory for Cognitive Informatics and Cognitive Computing, and Director of Laboratory for Denotational Mathematics and Software Science at the University of Calgary. He is a Fellow of WIF (UK), a Fellow of ICIC, a P.Eng of Canada, a Senior Member of IEEE and ACM. He received a PhD in Software Engineering from the Nottingham Trent University, UK, and a BSc in Electrical Engineering from Shanghai Tiedao University. He has industrial experience since 1972 and has been a full professor since 1994. He was a visiting Professor on sabbatical leaves in the Computing Laboratory at Oxford University in 1995, Dept. of Computer Science at Stanford University in 2008, the Berkeley Initiative in Soft Computing (BISC) Lab at University of California, Berkeley in 2008, and MIT (2012), respectively. He is the founder and steering committee chair of the annual IEEE International Conference on Cognitive Informatics and Cognitive Computing (ICCI*CC). He is founding Editor-in-Chief of *International Journal of Cognitive Informatics and Natural Intelligence* (IJCINI), founding Editor-in-Chief of *International Journal of Software Science and Computational Intelligence* (IJSSCI), Associate Editor of *IEEE Trans on System, Man, and Cybernetics* (Part A), and Editor-in-Chief of *Journal of Advanced Mathematics and Applications* (JAMA). Dr. Wang is the initiator of a few cutting-edge research fields or subject areas such as Cognitive Informatics (CI, the theoretical framework of CI, neuroinformatics, the logical model of the brain (LMB), the layered reference model of the brain (LRMB), the cognitive model of brain informatics (CMBI), the mathematical model of consciousness, and the cognitive learning engine); Abstract Intelligence (αI); Cognitive Computing (such as cognitive computers, cognitive robots, cognitive agents, and cognitive Internet); Denotational Mathematics (i.e., concept algebra, inference algebra, semantic algebra, real-time process algebra, system algebra, granular algebra, and visual semantic algebra); Software Science (on unified mathematical models and laws of software, cognitive complexity of software, and automatic code generators, the coordinative work organization theory, and built-in tests (BITs)); basic studies in Cognitive Linguistics (such as the cognitive linguistic framework, the deductive semantics of languages, deductive grammar of English, and the cognitive complexity of online text comprehension). He has published over 130 peer reviewed journal papers, 220+ peer reviewed conference papers, and 27 books in cognitive informatics, cognitive computing, software science, denotational mathematics, and computational intelligence. He is the recipient of dozens international awards on academic leadership, outstanding contributions, research achievement, best papers, and teaching in the last three decades.

* * *

Mohamed Abid is currently Professor at Sfax University in Tunisia. He obtained a Diploma in Electrical Engineering in 1986 from the University of Sfax in Tunisia and received his Ph.D. degree in Computer Engineering in 1989 from the University of Toulouse in France. His current research interests are Automatic Processing of Signals and Images.

Nacéra Benamrane, Ph.d Assistant Professor Department of Computer Science University of Science and Technology "Mohamed Boudiaf" Oran –Algérie. Her current research interests are Information Technologies for the Management and use of Brain Data and Cognitive Informatics.

Ping Chen is an Associate Professor of Computer Science and the Director of Artificial Intelligence Lab at the University of Houston-Downtown. His research interests include Bioinformatics, Data Mining, and Computational Semantics. Dr. Chen has published over 40 papers in major Data Mining, Artificial Intelligence, and Bioinformatics conferences and journals, and his current research is supported by NSF and DHS. Dr. Ping Chen received his BS degree on Information Science and Technology from Xi'an Jiao Tong University, MS degree on Computer Science from Chinese Academy of Sciences, and Ph.D degree on Information Technology at George Mason University.

Vincent Chiew is a PhD candidate in cognitive computing and software engineering with the Cognitive Informatics and Cognitive Computing Lab and the Theoretical and Empirical Software Engineering Center (TESERC) in dept. of electrical and computer engineering at the University of Calgary, Canada. He received an MS degree in software engineering from University of Calgary in 2003. He is senior member of IEEE and has more than 20 years experience in the software industry. His research interests are in software engineering, cognitive informatics, cognitive computing, and industrial applications.

Wei Ding has been an Assistant Professor of Computer Science in the University of Massachusetts Boston since 2008. She received her Ph.D. degree in Computer Science from the University of Houston in 2008. Her main research interests include Data Mining, Machine Learning, Artificial Intelligence, Computational Semantics, and with applications to astronomy, geosciences, and environmental sciences. She has published more than 30 referred research papers, 1 book, and has 1 patent. She is the recipient of an excellence service award at ACM SIGSPATIAL GIS 2010, a Best Paper Award at IEEE ICCI 2010, a Best Poster Presentation award at ACM SIGSPAITAL GIS 2008, and a Best PhD Work Award between 2007 and 2010 from the University of Houston. Her research projects are currently sponsored by NASA and DOE.

Walter Garcia graduated from Computer Science program in the University of Houston-Downtown in 2010. He worked as a research assistant in the Artificial Intelligence lab in the University of Houston-Downtown from 2008 to 2010. He currently works as a software Engineer at Houston area.

Karim Gasmi received the MS Degree in Computer Science (2010) from the National Engineering School of Sfax (Tunisia). Currently, he is a PhD student at National Engineering School of Sfax (Tunisia). Her main research interests include Signal and Image Processing.

Marina L. Gavrilova is an Associate Professor and associate head of the Department of Computer Science, University of Calgary. Dr. Gavrilova's research interests include computational geometry, image processing, optimization, exact computation and computer modeling. Dr. Gavrilova is a founder of two innovative research labs, the SPARCS Laboratory for Spatial Analysis in Computational Sciences and the Biometric Technologies Laboratory. Her publication list includes over 80 research papers, books and book chapters. Dr. Gavrilova is an Editor-in-Chief of Transactions on Computational Science, Springer and serves on the Editorial Board for International Journal of Computational Sciences and Engineering and Computer Graphics and CAD/CAM Journal. She is an ACM, IEEE and Computer Society member.

Juan L. G. Guirao is full professor of applied mathematics at Universidad Politécnica de Cartagena in Spain. His fields of interested are dynamical systems in general and applications of them in particular. Currently, he has three active research lines: topological dynamics of low dimensional systems, analysis of the periodic structure of differentiable systems defined on compact manifolds and roto-traslational dynamics of Hamiltonian systems coming from the celestial mechanic. He has supervised several PhD's and a big number of master thesis and has more than 50 research papers published.

Tianyong Hao received his Ph.D. degree in computer science from the City University of Hong Kong, Hong Kong, in 2010. He is currently a research fellow in the department of Chinese, Translation and Linguistics, City University of Hong Kong. Before he joined CTL department in 2010, he has visited the Mathematics & Computer Science Department, Emory University, USA, as a researcher from 2009 to 2010. His research interest includes question answering, information retrieval, data mining, knowledge acquisition, domain ontology design and construction. Dr. Hao has published more than 30 articles in refereed journals and conference proceedings, and is PC member in more three conferences currently.

Hironori Hiraishi received BS degree in 1993, his MS degree in 1996, and a PhD in 1999 in information technology from Tokyo University of Science. He was a research associate of Information Media Center in Tokyo University of Science from 2000 to 2005 and chief technological officer of WisdomTex, Inc. from 2001 to 2009. He is an associate professor of department of electrical and computer engineering in Akita National College of Technology from 2010. He received the winning award on the Innovative Application conference (IAAI2003). His recent research interests have focused on the real world applications integrating AI and embedded computing technology.

Hirotoshi Iwasaki received the BS and MS degrees in Electrical Engineering from Nagoya University in 1988 and 1990, respectively. PhD from 1990 to 2000, he worked for DENSO COOPORATION. Since 2000, he has been on loan to DENSO IT LABORATORY, Inc. He received the best paper award on the international symposium on Web & Wireless Geographical Information Systems (W2GIS2011). His research interests include in-vehicle information systems and intelligent interface, and recommender systems.

Ahmed Kharrat received the MS Degree in Computer Science (2007) from the National Engineering School of Sfax (Tunisia). Currently, he is a PhD student at National Engineering School of Sfax (Tunisia). Her main research interests include Cognitive Informatics and Image Processing.

Jingsheng Lei is currently a professor with the School of Computer and Information Engineering, Shanghai University of Electronic Power. His research interests include Web information retrieval, Machine learning, Data mining, and Cloud computing. He received his B.S. in Mathematics from Shanxi Normal University in 1987, and MS and Ph.D in Computer Science from Xinjiang University in 2000 and 2003 respectively. Currently, he is leading a group of research students doing research on Cloud computing.

Qing Li is a professor at the City University of Hong Kong. His research interests include multimedia database and web mining, question answering, graphics recognition, and performance evaluation. He has a BEng in computer science from Hunan University, Changsha and a DSc from University of Southern California, Los Angles. He is a Fellow of IET and a senior member of IEEE.

Huaping Liu is currently an associate professor in the Department of Computer Science and Technology at Tsinghua University, Beijing, China. He received the Ph.D. degree from the Department of Computer Science and Technology at Tsinghua University in 2004. His research interests include intelligent control and robotics.

Kueiming Lo (Guiming Luo), received his PhD. in system control from the Institute of Systems Science, Chinese Academy of Sciences in 1992, and then joined in Tsinghua University, Beijing, China. He is currently a full professor in the School of Software at Tsinghua University. From September 2000 to September 2001, he held a visiting Professor position at Seoul National University. From October 2001 to March 2003, he was with the University of Tokyo, Tokyo, Japan as a PSJS Fellow. From January 2008 to November 2008, he was with the Kyoto University as a PSJS Fellow. His research interests include system identification, adaptive control, artificial intelligent, software modeling, and model checking.

Meiliu Lu received her Ph.D. degree in Computer Science from the University of Illinois. She is a Professor of the Computer Science Department at California State University, Sacramento. Her current research interests include: data warehousing, data mining, machine learning, bioinformatics, and interactive media for user-paced learning. She has authored or coauthored publications in journals, conference proceedings, and book chapters, in these and other areas. She is a member of ACM since 1980's.

Zhenghua Ma is currently a professor and postgraduate supervisor in Information College of Changzhou University. His main research interest is embedded system and its application. He is the correspondent author.

Yusuke Manabe is an assistant professor of the Department of Information and Network Science, Chiba Institute of Technology, Chiba, Japan. He received a Ph. D. in software and information science (2008) from Iwate Prefectural University, Japan. His research interests include Intelligent Informatics, Cognitive Science, Chaotic Time Series Analysis and Soft Computing. Especially, he interests human skill analysis, context-aware computing and symbol-grounding mechanism. He is a member of JSAI, JCSS, SOFT and IEICE in Japan.

Mohamed Ben Messaoud joined ENIS's Department of Electrical Engineering in University of Sfax from 1983. He received his Engineer degree from the University of Sfax (Tunisia) in 1981 and his Ph.D. from Paul Sabatier University (France) in 1983, and HDR degree in 2008. He is currently a Professor in the Electrical Engineering. His research interests Automatic Control and Signal processing.

Fumio Mizoguchi was born in Tokyo, Japan on July 15, 1941. He received the BS and MS from Science University of Tokyo in industrial Chemistry in 1966 and 1968 respectively and PH.D in electrical engineering from Tokyo University in 1978. He is an Emeritus Professor and a Researcher of Next Generation of Data Mining Division at Science University of Tokyo. He is also a senior research associate at the Center for the Study on Language and Information of the Stanford University. He has served as a member of the editorial boards of Artificial Intelligence Journal, New Generation Computing Journal, and the Journal of Logic Programming. Also, He has worked as 10 years for a member of the review committee of the research found of Ministry of Education, Culture, Sports, Science and Technology in Japan. He has published more than 150 papers and thirty books in computer science. 2001, he has started up his venture company based upon the best paper on the innovative Application conference, and he is the chief executive officer of WisdomTex, Inc. He is the member of the IEEE, American Association of Artificial Intelligence.

Cyprian F. Ngolah received a PhD in Software Engineering from the University of Calgary, Canada in 2006, an MSc in Control Engineering from the University of Bradford, England in 1989, and a BSc in Mathematics and Computer Science from the University of Essex, England in 1988. He taught several computer science and software engineering courses at both the graduate and undergraduate levels for thirteen years at University of Buea, Cameroon. He is currently a senior software engineer in the Research and Development Department of Sentinel Trending & Diagnostics Ltd, Calgary, carrying out research on the development of a neural network for machine condition monitoring and predictive maintenance using vibration analysis. His main research interests are in real-time process algebra and its applications, tool support for formal specification languages, real-time operating systems, formal methods in software engineering and real-time software systems, and artificial neural networks.

Fernando L. Pelayo is professor of Computer Science at Universidad de Castilla La Mancha in Spain. His fields of interested are formal models of concurrency, discrete dynamical systems and cognitive informatics. Currently, he has two active works running on verification and automatic analysis of Complex Computing Systems. He has more than 50 research papers published.

Guenther Ruhe received a doctorate rer. nat degree in Mathematics with emphasis on Operations Research from Freiberg University, Germany and a doctorate habil. nat. degree from both the Technical University of Leipzig and University of Kaiserslautern, Germany. He holds an Industrial Research Chair in Software Engineering at University of Calgary. His main expertise and research interests are in Software Engineering Project Management, Decision Support, Product Release Planning, Empirical Software Engineering, Software Measurement, Modeling and Simulation, Combinatorial Optimization. Dr. Ruhe has published more than 170 reviewed research papers at journals, workshops and conferences. He is a member of the ACM, the IEEE Computer Society, and the Informatics Society German GI. Ruhe received an iCORE Research ward for the period from 2001 to 2007 and an IBM Faculty award in 2008.

Shinichiro Sega received his BS degree from the University of Tokyo in 1994. He is a chief engineer of DENSO IT LABORATORY, Inc., a subsidiary of the automotive appliance company DENSO COOPORATION in Japan. He is engaged in research and development of the next-generation car system. His current major research is to study a driver's actions and to work out the in-car device controls that fit the sense or intention of the driver. He received the best paper award on the 10th IEEE International Conference on COGNITIVE INFORMATICS & COGNITIVE COMPUTING (ICCI*CC2011).

Phillip C-Y. Sheu is currently a professor of Computer Engineering, Information and Computer Science, and Biomedical Engineering at the University of California, Irvine. He received his Ph.D. and M.S. degrees from the University of California at Berkeley in Electrical Engineering and Computer Science in 1986 and 1982, respectively, and his B.S. degree from National Taiwan University in Electrical Engineering in 1978. Between 1982 and 1986, he also worked as a computer scientist at Systems Control Technology, Inc., Palo Alto, CA., where he designed and implemented aircraft expert control systems, and he worked as a product planning engineer at Advanced Micro Devices Inc., Sunnyvale, CA, where he designed and integrated CAD systems. From 1986 to 1988, he was an assistant professor at School of Electrical Engineering, Purdue University. From 1989 to 1993, he was an associate professor of Electrical and Computer Engineering at Rutgers University. He has published two books: (1) Intelligent Robotic Planning Systems and (2) Software Engineering and Environment - An Object-Oriented Perspective, and more than 100 papers in object-relational data and knowledge engineering and their applications, and biomedical computations. He is currently active in research related to complex biological systems, knowledge-based medicine, semantic software engineering, proactive web technologies, and large real-time knowledge systems for defense and homeland security. His current research projects are sponsored by the National Science Foundation, National Institute of Health, and Department of Defense. Dr. Sheu is a Fellow of IEEE.

Dan A. Simovici is a Professor of Computer Science and Graduate Program Director at the University of Massachusetts Boston. He obtained his Ph.D. from the University of Bucharest and is the author of several books and of more than 150 research papers. His most recent book "Mathematical Tools for Data Mining" was published by Springer-Verlag in 2008. His main research interests are in Data Mining (clustering, genetic algorithms in data mining, graph mining, classification) and in algebraic and information-theoretical methods in Multiple-Valued logic. He is a managing editor of the "Journal for Multiple-Valued Logic and Soft Computing".

Kenji Sugawara is a professor of the Department of Information and Network Science, and a dean of Faculty of Information and Computer Science, Chiba Institute of Technology, Chiba, Japan. He received a doctoral degree in engineering (1983) from Tohoku University, Japan. His research interests include Multi-agent System, Artificial Intelligence, Ubiquitous Computing and Symbiotic Computing. He is a fellow of IEICE Japan and a member of IEEE, ACM and IPSJ.

Fuchun Sun is a professor in the Department of Computer Science and Technology at Tsinghua University, Beijing, China. He received the B.S. and M.S. degrees from Naval Aeronautical Engineering Academy, Yantai, China, in 1986 and 1989, respectively, and Ph.D degree from the Department of Computer Science and Technology, Tsinghua University, Beijing, China, in 1998. He worked over four years for the Department of Automatic Control at Naval Aeronautical Engineering Academy. From 1998 to 2000 he was a Postdoctoral Fellow of the Department of Automation at Tsinghua University, Beijing, China. His research interests include intelligent control, networked control system and management, neural networks, fuzzy systems, nonlinear systems and robotics. He has authored or coauthored two books and over 150 papers which have appeared in various journals and conference proceedings. Dr. Sun is the recipient of the excellent Doctoral Dissertation Prize of China in 2000 and the Choon-Gang Academic Award by Kerea in 2003, and was recognized as a Distinguished Young Scholar in 2006 by

National Science Foundation of China. He has been a member of the Technical Committee on Intelligent Control of the IEEE Control System Society since 2006. Now, he serves as an associate editor of IEEE Trans. on Fuzzy Systems.

Xinming Tan is a professor in the School of Computer Science and Technology at Wuhan University of Technology, China. He is the head of the Department of Computer Science. He received a BSc and an MSc in Computer Science at Wuhan University of Technology, and a PhD in Software Engineering at University of Calgary, Canada in 2007. His major research interests are in formal methods, real-time systems, and cognitive informatics.

Yousheng Tian is a PhD candidate in cognitive computing and software engineering with the International Center for Cognitive Informatics and Cognitive Computing (ICCICC) as well as Theoretical and Empirical Software Engineering Center (TESERC) in Dept. of Electrical and Computer Engineering at the University of Calgary, Canada. He received a PhD from Xian Jiantong University, China, in Computer Science in 2002 and was a Post Doctoral Fellow at ICCICC during 2006 to 2007. His research interests are in cognitive informatics, cognitive computing, software engineering, machine learning, and denotational mathematics.

Rosanne Vetro received the B.S. degree in Computer Science from the Federal University of Rio de Janeiro, Brazil. After graduation, she worked for 3 years as a team leader in the Research and Development Engineering Department of TV Globo, a Brazilian broadcast company. In recognition of her work on television broadcast systems, she received an Outstanding Engineer Award. She also held a visiting researcher position at the Tokyo Science & Technology Research Labs of NHK, a Japanese broadcast company, where she contributed to the development of the ISO/IEC MPEG-7 International Standard. Since 2008, she has been pursuing a Ph.D. degree in Computer Science of the University of Massachusetts Boston. Her research interests are in the area of data mining with application to multimedia content, clustering, security and data hiding. In 2010, she received a best paper award for her work on mining high complexity regions.

Xinguang Wang received the MS degree in computer science from the Changzhou University in 2010. His research interests are neural networks and biomedical signal processing.

Yuji Wang is a Ph.D student in the Department of Computer Science and Technology at Tsinghua University, Beijing, China. His major research interests are in teleoperation, bilateral control, and robotics.

Yunlong Wang received his Msc. degree in Software Engineering from Tsinghua University in 2008. From 2003 to 2010 he was an electrical software engineer in Bentley Systems Pty. Ltd. He is working at Ausenco Pty. Ltd. in Brisbane Queensland, Australia recently. His research interest is development of graphics software.

Liu Wenyin is an assistant professor at the City University of Hong Kong. He was a full time researcher at Microsoft Research China/Asia. His research interests include anti-phishing, question answering, graphics recognition, and performance evaluation. He has a BEng and MEng in computer science from Tsinghua University, Beijing and a DSc from the Technion, Israel Institute of Technology, Haifa. In 2003, he was awarded the International Conference on Document Analysis and Recognition Outstanding Young Researcher Award by the International Association for Pattern Recognition (IAPR). He had been TC10 chair of IAPR for 2006-2010. He had been on the editorial board of the International Journal of Document Analysis and Recognition (IJDAR) from 2006-2011. He is a Fellow of IAPR and a senior member of IEEE.

Feifei Xu received her Ph.D. degree in Pattern Recognition and Artificial Intelligence from Tongji University, Shanghai, in 2009. Currently, she is a lecturer in the School of Computer and Information Engineering, Shanghai University of Electronic Power. She visited the Department of Computer Science, University of Regina, Canada, from 2007 to 2008 as a visiting student. Her research interest includes granular computing, fuzzy rough sets, knowledge spaces, data mining, and knowledge acquisition. Dr. Xu has published more than 20 articles in refereed journals and conference proceedings.

Bo Zhang is now a professor in the Department of Computer Science and Technology, Tsinghua University and a Fellow of Chinese Academy of Sciences, Beijing, China. He graduated from the Tsinghua University, Beijing, China, in 1958. His main research interests include artificial intelligence, neural networks and pattern recognition. He has published about 150 papers and three books in these fields.

Du Zhang received his Ph.D. degree in Computer Science from the University of Illinois. He is a Professor of the Computer Science Department at California State University, Sacramento. His current research interests include: knowledge inconsistency, machine learning in software engineering, knowledge-based systems and multi-agent systems. He has authored or coauthored over 150 publications in journals, conference proceedings, and book chapters, in these and other areas. In addition, he has edited or co-edited eleven books and conference proceedings. He has served as the conference general chair, the program committee chair, a program committee co-chair, or a program vice chair/area chair for 24 international conferences, most of which are IEEE sponsored international conferences. Currently, he is an Associate Editor for International Journal on Artificial Intelligence Tools, an Area Editor for International Journal of Software Engineering and Knowledge Engineering, a member of editorial board for International Journal of Cognitive Informatics and Natural Intelligence, a member of editorial board for International Journal of Software Science and Computational Intelligence, and a member of editorial board of the Open Software Engineering Journal. In addition, he has served as a guest editor for special issues of International Journal of Software Engineering and Knowledge Engineering, International Journal on Artificial Intelligence Tools, Software Quality Journal, IEEE Transactions on SMC-Part B, EATCS Fundamenta Informaticae, International Journal of Semantic Computing, International Journal of Cognitive Informatics and Natural Intelligence, and International Journal of Computer Applications in Technology. Du Zhang is a senior member of IEEE and a senior member of ACM.

Ling Zou is an associate professor in the faculty of information science and engineering, Changzhou University, China. Dr. Zou served as the review editor of *Journal of Clinical Rehabilitative Tissue Engineering Research* and *Neural Regeneration Research.* She is the senior member of Chinese Institute of Electronics. Her research interests are neural networks, pattern recognition and biomedical signal processing.

Yuanyuan Zuo is currently pursuing the Ph.D. degree in Department of Computer Science and Technology, Tsinghua University, Beijing, China. She received the B.S. degree and M.S. degree from Xidian University, Xi'an, China, both in electronic engineering, in 1996 and 1999, respectively. Her research interests include content based image retrieval, pattern recognition and statistical learning.

Index